# Time Out

# New York Guide

Penguin Books

PENGUIN BOOKS

Published by the Penguin Group
Penguin Books Ltd, 27 Wrights Lane, London W8 5TZ, England
Penguin Books USA Inc., 375 Hudson Street, New York, New York 10014, USA
Penguin Books Australia Ltd, Ringwood, Victoria, Australia
Penguin Books Canada Ltd, 10 Alcorn Avenue, Toronto, Ontario, Canada M4V 3B2
Penguin Books (NZ) Ltd, 182–190 Wairau Road, Auckland 10, New Zealand

Penguin Books Ltd, Registered Offices: Harmondsworth, Middlesex, England

First published 1990
Second edition 1992
Third edition 1994
Fourth edition 1996
10 9 8 7 6 5 4 3 2 1



Colour reprographics by Precise Litho, 34–35 Great Sutton Street, London EC1
Mono reprographics, printed and bound by William Clowes Ltd, Beccles, Suffolk NR34 9QE

**Edited and designed by**
Time Out Magazine Limited
Universal House
251 Tottenham Court Road
London W1P 0AB
Tel: 0171 813 3000
Fax: 0171 813 6001

**Editorial**
**Managing Editor** Peter Fiennes
**Editor** Frank Broughton
**Deputy Editor** Ruth Jarvis
**Researchers** Tony Karon, Jann Cheifitz
**Indexer** Jacqueline Brind

**Design**
**Art Director** Warren Beeby
**Art Editor** John Oakey
**Designers** Paul Tansley, James Pretty
**Picture Editor** Catherine Hardcastle
**Ad make-up** Carrie Lambe

**Advertising**
**Group Advertisement Director** Lesley Gill
**Sales Director** Mark Phillips
**Advertisement Sales (New York)** Jonah Communications International, Inc (JCI)

**Administration**
**Publisher** Tony Elliott
**Managing Director** Mike Hardwick
**Financial Director** Kevin Ellis
**Marketing Director** Gillian Auld
**Production Manager** Mark Lamond

**Features in this Guide were written and researched by:**
**Introduction** Frank Broughton. **Essential Information** Frank Broughton, Gerda-Marie McDonough. **Getting Around** Frank Broughton. **Accommodation** Sue Nelson. **New York by Season** Gerda-Marie McDonough, Frank Broughton, Sue Stemp. **Architecture** Frank Broughton. **History** Frank Broughton, Mary Trewby, Robert W Snyder. **New York Today** Frank Broughton, Tony Karon. **New York by Neighbourhood** Frank Broughton, Mary Trewby. **Eating & Drinking** Frank Broughton, Gerda-Marie McDonough, Russell Cronin, Kathy McFarland, Albertus Swanepoel. **Art Galleries** Heather Waddell, Frank Broughton. **Museums** Sue Nelson. **Media** Frank Broughton. **Cabaret** Jill Pearlman, Frank Broughton. **Clubs** Frank Broughton. **Dance** Maitland McDonough, Frank Broughton. **Film** Frank Broughton, Gerda-Marie McDonough, Mary Trewby. **Music: Classical & Opera** Maitland McDonough, Frank Broughton. **Music: Rock, Blues & Jazz** Frank Broughton, John Platt. **Sport & Fitness** Frank Broughton. **Theatre** Murray Nossel, Beth Lawrence, Frank Broughton. **Business** Frank Broughton, Kathy MacFarland, Gerda-Marie McDonough. **Children** Frank Broughton, Mary Trewby, Gerda-Marie McDonough. **Gay New York** Frank Broughton, Murray Nossel. **Lesbian New York** Nora Burns. **Students** Frank Broughton, Kathy McFarland. **Trips out of Town** Frank Broughton, Kathy McFarland. **Survival** Mary Trewby, Frank Broughton, Gerda Marie McDonough.

**The Editors would like to thank the following for help and information:**
Thom Storr, Bill Brewster, Aner Candelario, Jim Clarke, Adam Goldstone, New York Transit Authority, New York Convention & Visitors' Bureau, Ravi Mirchandani, Jeffrey Rouault, Tracy Thompson, Vanessa Valle, Steve Wier, Mamie Healey and the staff of *Time Out New York*.


**Photography** by Arnhel de Serra except for: pages 61, 62, 63, 64, 68, 70, 71, 78 **Range/ Bettmann/ UPI**; page 77 **Ernst Haas/ Magnum Photos**; page 79 **Bruce Davison/ Magnum Photos**; page 84 **Thomas Hoepker/ Magnum Photos**; page 102 **Richard Reyes**; page 112 **Frank Broughton**; pages 131, 133, 139, 178, 257, 273 **Isa Brito**; page 189 **Ruth Orkin/ Witkin gallery**; pages 206, 216 **Michael Ackermann**; page 229 **Lois Greenfield**; page 230 **Johan Elbers**; page 234 **Bob Zucker**; page 239 **Winnie Klotz**; page 241 **Peter Schaaf**; page 263 **William Rivelli**; pages 293, 295, 296, 297, 299, 302, 304 NYS **Economic Development**; pages 294,307**Audience Planners/USTTA**.
Pictures on pages 143, 193, 198, 199, 200, 201, 209 were supplied by the featured establishments.

# Contents

# About the Guide

The *Time Out New York Guide* is one of an expanding series of city guides that also includes London, Paris, Berlin, Rome, Prague, Madrid, Budapest, Amsterdam and San Francisco. They're published by the company responsible for *Time Out*, London's definitive arts and entertainment magazine. In 1995, the new weekly *Time Out New York* was launched, covering the city's life with the same authority and wit as its London counterpart. If you want to know what's going on in New York, buy it the minute you step off the plane.

If *Time Out New York* is your weekly events bible, then our *New York Guide* will convert you into an instant New Yorker. We provide you with all the information you'll need to take on the world's most exciting city and win, researched afresh for this new edition. Many chapters have been rewritten from scratch, all have been thoroughly revised and new features have been added, including a fully indexed street map of the whole of Manhattan.

## CHECKED & CORRECT

We give you as much relevant listings information as we can – nearest transport, fax numbers, details of credit cards and any special facilities are included along with the name and address. We have also tried to include information on facilities for the disabled, especially in the major chapters such as **Sightseeing**, **Restaurants** and **Accommodation**. All these details were checked and correct as we went to press, but inevitably things change, and we urge you to call before you set out for any of the places listed, not only to check that they're still in business but to confirm any other details that attracted you to visit in the first place.

The prices we've given should be treated as guidelines, not gospel. Fluctuating exchange rates and inflation can cause prices, in shops and restaurants especially, to change rapidly. If, however, you find things have changed beyond recognition, ask why – and then write to let us know. We aim to give the best and most up-to-date advice so we always appreciate feedback.

## CREDIT CARDS

The following abbreviations have been used for credit cards: **AmEx**: American Express; **DC**: Diners' Club; **Discover**: Discover; **JCB**: Japanese credit cards; **MC**: Mastercard (Access); **V**: Visa (Barclaycard). Virtually all shops, restaurants and attractions will accept dollar travellers' cheques issued by a major financial institution (such as American Express).

## TELEPHONE NUMBERS

All telephone numbers given are as dialled from Manhattan. If you are calling a location off the island you need to prefix the seven-figure number with a '1' followed by a three-figure dialling code: 718 for Brooklyn, Queens, Staten Island and the Bronx; 516 for Long Island and 201 or 908 for New Jersey. We have given the full codes for all non-Manhattan numbers. If you're calling into Manhattan, prefix the number listed with 1-212. Numbers preceded by 1-800 are free of charge, but can only be dialled from within the States.

## BOLD

When we mention people or places or events that are listed more fully elsewhere in the guide, we have put them in **bold**. Use the index at the back to locate the full listing.

## TELL US ABOUT IT

In all cases the information we give is impartial. No organisation has been included because its owner or manager has advertised in our publications. We hope you enjoy the *New York Guide*, but equally we'd like you to let us know if you don't. We welcome tips for places that you think we should include and also take notice of criticism of our choices. There's a reader's reply card in the back of the book.

> There's an on-line version of this guide, as well as weekly events listings for New York and other international cities, at: http//:www.timeout.co.uk

# Introduction

Anyone can be a New Yorker. The budget-busting sets are already in place, the millions of extras have been costumed and a multitude of bizarre cameo actors are rehearsing their lines. The city is just waiting for a cast of unknowns to take centre stage. And gradually, relentlessly, they arrive – the energetic imports destined to pedal the city's dynamo.

Three boys from Leeds, full of free airline Budweiser, bounce from the airport in a yellow cab over potholes big enough to hide a body in; a Kentucky prom queen steps gingerly off the bus at the Port Authority in a silky dress that already feels a little less exotic than when she put it on in Louisville; a Kiwi couple drive through the night from Canada in a Chevy Impala they're going to sell for the first month's rent of a cramped railroad apartment.

There are few qualifications required to merge into the life of this daunting and majestic place: a fever for achieving something; a vision of success perhaps; a one-way ticket and a little 'just-off-the-boat' immigrant spirit. That's how it was built after all – by countless millions of newcomers, armed with New Yorkers' favourite things: a dollar and a dream....

You've seen their city in a thousand movies: an island of concrete canyons, rivers of Detroit steel driving through them, and swarms of buzzing helicopters flying overhead. The night is pierced by sirens, gunshots and arguments, all ignored by a population which has evolved beyond sleep. It's a warning from the future, a neurotoxic place dedicated to Art, Information, Commerce and Power.

In fact, New York is one of the most human cities in the world. Its arrogant aspirations are written large in skyscrapers and six-lane avenues, but New Yorkers treat these like cosy cottages and winding lanes. It tries hard to be cold and intimidating, but it ends up as an inefficient tangle, populated with extreme characters brimming with the friendliness of adversity. It's driven by money – by gold and greed and inequality – but these abstractions are brought down to size by the human pressure of ten million loud, witty, romantic, ugly, dangerous, beautiful people.

The melting pot, of course, is a myth. People arrived here from all corners of the earth, but they stuck together in villages of common custom, preserving their language and their memories of the old country. And that's what makes New York so intriguing. It's a patchwork of neighbourhoods which are each an intense representation of somewhere else. So strangers and foreigners are thrown together in the streets and subways, running in parallel narratives, holding onto their unique stake in New York City.

The worst thing about living here is that you are obliged to show it off regularly to visitors. But travellers' reactions are telling. Some crawl back to the airport clutching their passports, exhausted from a pace they could never sustain for more than a few days. Others, only hours after arriving, will recognise their future home and wonder how they ever lived anywhere else.

While LA is the ultimate American city, New York is the capital of the world. Anything feels possible here, even today, and there are plenty of believers busily pursuing their fates. From the suburban truant teens rollerblading down stone stairs in Central Park to the Black Muslims in Times Square haranguing passers-by; from the jeep-driven hip-hop kids hanging out in the Village to the rich old maids walking their dogs down Museum Mile; the Senegalese traders selling carvings to middle-class Harlem to the punks drinking malt liquor from the store opposite CBGBs; and the stocky Italians parading their families through Little Italy to the Wall Street suits grabbing a burger in between selling the earth...

Anyone can be a New Yorker. You've just got to get here.

*Frank Broughton*

# Essential Information

***You'll need to know a thing or two about tipping and telephones before you can develop a real New York attitude.***

For more detailed advice on coping with emergencies and staying sane and healthy, *see chapter* **Survival**; for details of the abbreviations used within this Guide, *see page vi* **About the Guide**.

## Visas

Most airlines and shipping companies have an arrangement with US Immigration whereby citizens of the UK, Japan, New Zealand and all West European countries (except for Ireland, Portugal, Greece and the Vatican City) do not need a visa for stays of less than 90 days (business or pleasure), as long as they have a passport that is valid for the full 90-day period and a return or onwards ticket. An open standby ticket is acceptable.

Canadians and Mexicans do not need visas but must present proof of their Canadian or Mexican citizenship. Travellers from American Samoa, Guam, Puerto Rico and the US Virgin Islands are US citizens and do not require visas. All other travellers must have visas. Full information and visa application forms can be obtained from your nearest US embassy or consulate. In general, send in your application at least three or four weeks before you plan to travel. Visas required urgently should be applied for via the travel agent booking your ticket.

If you're visiting on business or pleasure no inoculations are necessary.

Signs of the times in the Plant District.

## Immigration & Customs

Your flight crew will give you two forms to fill out: one each for immigration and customs. On arrival you hand these to officials in person. There may be a long wait (sometimes up to an hour) at immigration. You may be expected to explain your visit, so be polite and be prepared. The officials work on the assumption that everyone wants to come and live in America, and the onus is on you to prove otherwise (with visas, return tickets etc). Expect close questioning if you are planning a long visit or don't have a return ticket or any money. You will usually be granted an entry permit to cover the length of your stay. Work permits are hard to get, and you are not permitted to work without one. *See also chapters* **Business** and **Students**.

Customs allow foreigners to bring in $100 worth of gifts ($400 for returning Americans) before paying duty. One carton of 200 cigarettes (or 100 cigars) and one litre of liquor (spirits) are allowed. No plants, fruit, meat or fresh produce can be taken through customs. (For more detailed information, contact your nearest US embassy or consulate.) A customs official will take your declaration card as you leave the baggage claim area.

## Insurance

It's best to take out medical and baggage insurance before you leave; it's almost impossible to arrange in the US. Make sure that you have adequate medical cover; medical expenses can be very high.

## Banks & Foreign Exchange

Banks are open 9am to 3pm Monday to Friday. You need photo identification, such as a passport, to change travellers' cheques. Many banks do not exchange foreign currency, and

the bureau de changes, limited to tourist-trap areas, close at around 6pm or 7pm. It's best to arrive with some dollars in cash and use travellers' cheques like cash (possible in most restaurants and larger stores – but ask first and be prepared to show ID). In an emergency, most big hotels offer 24-hour change facilities but charge extortionate commission and give atrocious rates.

### Currency

A dollar ($) is 100 cents (¢). A cent is copper and more likely to be called a 'penny'. Then there are nickels (5¢), dimes (10¢) and quarters (25¢), which are all silver. Paper money is all the same size and colour so make sure you dispense the right denomination. Occasionally you might get a silver dollar or a two-dollar note in change. These are quite unusual and worth keeping.

### Credit Cards

Bring plastic if you have it, because that's the American way. It's essential for things like car hire and booking hotels in advance and handy for buying tickets over the phone. Get a personal identification number (PIN) from your credit company before you travel and you can use Access or Visa to draw cash from all of the city's cashpoints ('ATMs') labelled with the appropriate symbol.

**American Express Travel Service**
*65 Broadway, between Rector Street & Exchange Place (493 6500).* **Train** 1, N or R to Rector Street. **Open** 8.30am-5.30pm Mon-Fri.
Will change money and travellers' cheques and offer other services such as poste restante. Call for other branches.

**Chequepoint USA**
*22 Central Park South (750 2400).* **Train** N or R to 59th Street. **Open** 8am-8pm Mon-Fri; 10am-8pm Sat; 10am-7pm Sun.
Foreign currency, travellers' cheques and bank drafts are handled.
**Branches**: 609 Madison Avenue, at 58th Street (750 2255); 1568 Broadway, at 47th Street (869 6281); 708 Seventh Avenue, at 47th Street (262 1030).

**People's Foreign Exchange**
*19 West 44th Street, Suite 306 (944 6780).* **Train** B, D, F or Q to 42nd Street. **Open** 9am-6pm Mon-Fri; 10am-3pm Sat, Sun.
Free foreign exchange on banknotes and travellers cheques.

**Thomas Cook Currency Services**
*29 Broadway, at Morris Street (757 6915).* **Train** 4 or 5 to Bowling Green. **Open** 9am-5pm Mon-Fri.
A complete foreign exchange service is offered. There are seven other branches in JFK Airport, all open 8am-9pm daily (718 656 8444), in addition to those listed below.
**Branches**: 41 East 42nd Street; 1590 Broadway; 511 Madison Avenue (all branches 757 6915).

## Disabled Access

New York is one of the most challenging cities for a disabled visitor, but there is support and guidance close by. The Society for the Advancement of Travel for the Handicapped, which promotes travel for the disabled worldwide, is based in New York City. The non-profitmaking group was founded in 1976 for the exchange of information and to educate people about travel facilities for the disabled. Membership is $45 a year, $25 for students and senior citizens, and includes access to an information service and a quarterly newsletter. Write or call: SATH, 347 Fifth Avenue, Suite 610, New York, NY 10016 (447 7284/fax 725 8253).

Another useful resource is Hospital Audiences Inc's (HAI) guide to New York's cultural institutions, *Access For All*. The book points out that very few institutions are completely accessible, but lets you know just how accessible each is, and includes information on the height of telephones and water fountains, hearing and visual aids, passenger loading zones and alternative entrances.

HAI also offers audio description services for theatre performances for the blind and visually impaired. The program, called Describe!, features pre-recorded audio cassettes with a description of the theatre, the sets, characters, costumes and special effects. It also offers a live service where

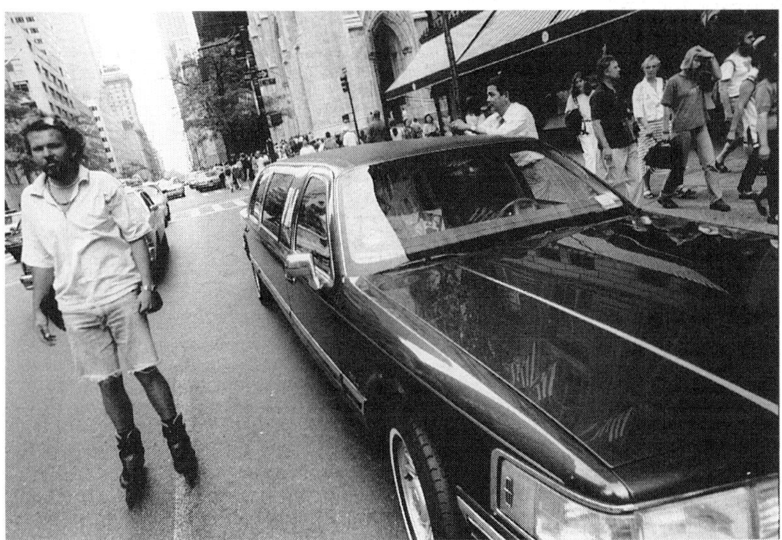

*When bladers overtake limos you know you're in a city with attitude. See page 8.*

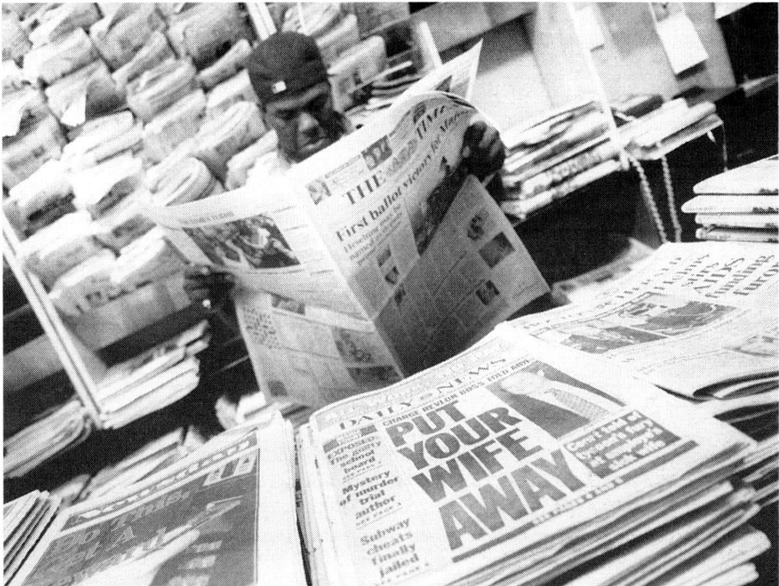


*Get down to your nearest newsstand to get the scoop on what's on.*

volunteers seated in the audience transmit descriptions of the action taking place on stage during pauses in dialogue through a small receiver with an earpiece. Call 575 7660 for more information.

The Theater Development Fund's Theater Access Program (TAP) arranges sign language interpretation for Broadway shows. Call 221 1103 (voice) or 719 4537 (TDD). Hands On does the same for Off-Broadway performances. Call 627 4898 (voice/TDD).

For more information on facilities for the disabled, *see chapter* **Survival**.

## Time & Dates

New York is on Eastern Standard Time, which extends from the Atlantic coast across to the eastern side of Lake Michigan south to the Georgia coast: this is five hours behind Britain, six behind France, 17 behind New Zealand. Clocks are put forward one hour at the start of summer and back one hour at the end of October.

Going from east coast to west, Eastern Standard Time is one hour ahead of Central Time (from Manitoba to Texas), two hours ahead of Mountain Time (Alberta to Arizona and New Mexico) and three hours ahead of Pacific Time (California).

Americans write dates in the order month, day, year, so 2.5.96 is the fifth of February, not the second of May.

## Electricity

Throughout the USA electricity voltage is 110 or 120 with two-pronged plugs. If you want to use electrical appliances with different voltages use a transformer or travel plug adaptor (available from pharmacies, department stores and airport stores).

## Safety

New York has a frightening crime rate, but this shouldn't worry you because most of it is generated late at night in poor outlying 'ghetto' neighbourhoods. It's one of the world's busiest cities and you should act accordingly, of course, but don't arrive thinking you need an armed guard to accompany you wherever you go. It really is highly unlikely that you will ever be troubled.

Use common sense about flashing your money and valuables, and avoid lonely and poorly lit streets. Walk in the opposite direction to the traffic so no-one can kerb-crawl you at night. Another trick is to walk down the centre of the street: muggers prefer to hang back in doorways and shadows. If the worst happens and you find yourself threatened by someone with a weapon, hand over your wallet or camera at once (your attacker will be as anxious to get it over with as you are) and then call the police as soon as you can (dial 911 from any pay phone).

Beware of pickpockets and street hustlers, especially in busy tourist areas like Times Square, and don't be seduced by any card sharps or other tricksters you may come across. You will see a lot of homeless people on the streets, some of whom may be quite aggressive when asking for money. Politely refuse them or carefully give them change (but don't get your wallet or purse out). Don't buy anything off the street unless it's obvious what you're getting. A shrink-wrapped camcorder for fifty bucks will look very much like a brick when you open the box.

As a rule, if you look comfortable rather than lost you should deter wrongdoers. Make sure you know exactly where are and where you're going when you're in any of the following areas: anywhere west of Eighth Avenue; anywhere east of Avenue A; anywhere above 96th Street; anywhere off the island of Manhattan. That's not to say that these are dangerous areas, just that everywhere else should be wholly unproblematic.

## Telephones

Public payphones are easy to find. Most of them work, but the Nynex ones are best: those from other phone companies tend to be poorly maintained and more likely to do something to annoy. If someone's left the handset dangling down it's a helpful sign that something's wrong. Phones take any combination of silver coinage; local calls usually cost 25¢ for about four minutes. The ringing tone is long; the engaged tone is short and higher pitched.

The Manhattan code is 212, but you don't need to dial it unless you're off the island (eg at the airport). In this guide, all seven-figure numbers are Manhattan numbers. Other numbers include their area code and the 1 you have to put in front of it.

To call a number made up of letters (eg 1-800 CALL ATT) you simply press the phone key marked with that letter. A, B and C are on key 2, DEF on key 3 and so on.

If you want to call long distance/international, you need to go via one of the long-distance companies. In New York, most payphones automatically link you up with AT&T. Make the call either by dialling 0 for an operator or dialling direct (cheaper). To find out how much a call will cost, dial the number first and a voice will tell you how much to deposit. For long-distance calls you will need to dial 1 followed by the three-digit area code, followed by the number; for international calls, dial 011 followed by the country code. You can pay for operator calls with your credit card. There's a different access number for each phone company: look in the *Yellow Pages* under Telephone Companies. AT&T's is 1-800 CALL ATT. A recorded message will give you the choice of going through an operator or punching your card number and expiry date in yourself (cheaper). This is a convenient but somewhat insecure system – if you can make expensive calls using your credit card number, so can anyone else. Keep your receipt slips carefully.

If you don't have a credit card, the best way to make international or long-distance calls without feeding endless quarters into a payphone is to buy a phone card. These are available from large stores such as 7-11 and Payless Drug. They aren't swipe cards – you call a toll-free number and key in the code on the card.

**Operator assistance** dial 0.
**Emergency** (police, ambulance, fire) dial 911.
**Directory enquiries** (local) dial 411 (free from payphones).
**Long-distance directory enquiries** dial 1 + area code + 555 1212 (long-distance charges apply).
**Collect calls** (reverse charges) dial 0 followed by the area code and number, or dial 1-800 COLLECT, or for calls to the UK 1-800 445 5667.

## Tipping

You'll be hard pressed to find anything more expensive in New York than in Europe, but you will have to account for a few extras. Sales tax (8.25 per cent) is added to the price of most purchases, but is absent from price tags. In addition, there's a lot of tipping to do. Waiting staff get 15-20 per cent (as a rough guide, double the sales tax on your bill) and cabbies 15 per cent. But don't forget to tip bartenders ($1 a round), hairdressers (10-15 per cent), hotel doormen ($1 for hailing a cab) and porters ($1 per 1 or 2 bags), and remember that the person who delivers your Chinese food probably receives no wage at all ($2 is considered a good tip).

## Tourist Information

Hotels are usually full of maps, leaflets and free tourist magazines, including *Where* magazine (monthly) and *City Guide* (weekly), which give good comprehensive advice about entertainment and events. Be aware that advice from hotels is not always impartial. Plenty of other magazines (including the new weekly *Time Out New York*) offer entertainment information (*see chapter* **Media**).

### New York Convention and Visitors Bureau

*2 Columbus Circle, at West 59th Street & Broadway (397 8222).* **Train** 1, 9, A, B, C or D to Columbus Circle/M6, M10 or M104 bus. **Open** 9am-6pm Mon-Fri; 10am-6pm Sat, Sun, public holidays.

A barrage of leaflets on all manner of things; free, helpful advice on accommodation and entertainment; coupons for discounts; and free maps. The phone number gives you access to either a multilingual human or a huge menu of recorded information. In addition to the main office there are booths at 2 World Trade Center, JFK Airport International Arrivals Building, Grand Central Station and Penn Station.

## Attitude

New Yorkers pride themselves on their psychoses. Argument and insult are basic life-skills here. The meek might inherit the earth, but they won't get what they want in New York City. You are not only welcome to be as obnoxious as you please, it's expected of you. Try it. You may even find you like it.

Be specific and demanding. Forget phrases like 'Would you mind/If it's not too much trouble' and replace them with 'I need/I want...'. And always be decisive. Indecision is something you sort out with your shrink; New Yorkers are too busy to tolerate it. When asked 'Whaddya want?' avoid replying with the standard British courtesy of 'Hmmm, well, what do you have?' Instead, announce aggressively 'I'll have a sardine and Swiss cheese with lettuce and onion, on rye (lightly toasted) with a pickle on the side', and that's exactly what you'll get. Manhattanites are direct and assertive but they are also always polite. Listen and you will hear them address waiters, taxi drivers and total strangers as sir or madam.

## When to Visit

The climate is at its sublime best in spring and early summer (April-June), when the Atlantic sea breezes are still fighting off the inevitable humidity that can make July and August insufferably hot; and in autumn or 'fall' (September-November), when the heat subsides in readiness for the extremely cold winter round the corner.

Summer temperatures will often reach the 90s (31°C), but even below this the humidity makes it feel much hotter. At the same time, air-conditioned buildings are cool to the point of cold, so wear layers. The converse problem occurs in winter, when outside may be well below freezing and inside has the dry burnt air of some far-off central furnace.

In terms of things to do, New York is alive throughout the year, but during the summer the parks and plazas and other public places are especially busy with free entertainment. At the same time, indoor diversions take a break and the museum, gallery and concert calendar slows to a halt. The American summer officially lasts from Memorial Day (end of May) to Labor Day (beginning of September), and most New Yorkers will try to leave the heat of the city as often as possible, those with money making regular weekend trips to their summer houses.

Springtime has the most parades and is when the stores are full of the newest bargains (though the traditional sale season is getting earlier and earlier and now seems to precede Christmas), while late summer and fall have the most festivals. Winter can be bitterly cold, but is the busiest time for cultural activities. Christmas is a very special time in the city, with street decorations, ice-skating, roaming Santas and a wonderland in every shop window.

# Getting Around

***Trains, planes and automobiles: we tell you where to go, where to get off and how to buy a ticket.***

New York is a collection of boroughs, but for most visitors New York means Manhattan, an island only 13.4 miles (22km) long and 2.3 miles (4km) at its widest. The roads above 14th Street are laid out in a grid pattern, which makes finding your way around relatively simple. The avenues run north/south and are numbered from east to west (with Lexington, Park and Madison – in that order – between Third and Fifth). Sixth Avenue is also known as the Avenue of the Americas. There are four short avenues around the East Village that are lettered: A to D.

The cross streets run east/west (Fifth Avenue marks the dividing line between east and west; the lower the building number the closer it is to Fifth Avenue) and are numbered from the south. Most streets are one-way: traffic flow on even-number streets tends to be eastwards; on odd-number streets it's usually westwards.

The major exception to the grid rule is Broadway, an old Indian trail that was well established when the grid was laid down in around 1811. It runs north/south, then cuts diagonally downtown from the west to the East Side.

Downtown streets, below 14th Street, are more confusing, since they were built on before the grid pattern was established; here you will need a map.

## Information

Information on subways and buses is available on 1-718 330 1234 (or 1-718 330 4847 for non English speakers). The phone line is staffed from 6am to 9pm daily and offers recorded information at other times. Alternatively, you can phone the New York Convention and Visitors Bureau Information Center (397 8222; 9am-6pm Mon-Fri; 10am-6pm Sat, Sun) for instructions on the best way to get between any two places in the city.

## The Subway

Much maligned, but actually clean, efficient, heated, air-conditioned and far safer than most people will tell you, the subway is easily the fastest way to get around during daylight hours. It runs all night, but with sparse service and fewer riders it's advisable (and usually quicker) to take a cab after seven or eight in the evening. Entry to the system is with a token costing $1.50 (use them on buses as well). You buy these, in any quantity, from a booth inside the entrance to a station. Staff won't accept notes bigger than $20. The token lets you through a turnstile, after which you can travel anywhere on the network (a 'Metrocard' magnetic card system is being introduced, which will simplify things, but as yet not all stations have the necessary hardware). Trains are known by letters and numbers and are colour-coded according to which line they run on. 'Express' trains run between major stops (passing through the stations in between), 'local' trains stop at every station. Check on the map (available free at all stations from the token booth) before you board. A subway map of Manhattan is reproduced in our **Maps** section at the back of the book. Stations are usually named after the street they're on, so they're easy to find. Entrances are marked with a green globe (a red globe marks an entrance that is not always open). The other key thing is to know which way you're going. Some stations don't have connecting walkways so there are separate entrances to the uptown and downtown platforms. Feel free to ask advice: New York subway etiquette assumes that no-one has a clue where they're going or even which train they're on, and directions will be gladly given.

To ensure safety, don't wear flashy jewellery, keep your bag with the opening facing you and board the train from the off-peak waiting area marked at the centre of every platform. This is monitored by video and is where the conductor's car will stop. Call 1-718 330 1234 (6am-9pm daily; recorded information at other times) for advice on any aspect of the system.

### PATH Trains

The PATH (Port Authority Trans Hudson) trains run from six stations in Manhattan to various places across the river in New Jersey (including Hoboken, Jersey City and Newark). The system is fully automated and costs $1 for each journey. You need change or a crisp dollar bill to put in the machines. Trains run 24 hours, but you can face a very long wait outside commuter hours. Manhattan PATH stations are marked on the MTA subway map. For more information call 1-800 234 PATH.

## Buses

Buses are fine if you aren't in a hurry. If your feet hurt from walking around, a bus is a good way of continuing your street-level sightseeing. They're white and blue with a route number and a digital destination sign. The fare is $1.50, either with a token (the same one that you buy for the subway) or in change (no notes accepted). Express buses operate on some routes; these cost $4 (coins and tokens; no notes). If you're travelling on a bus going up or downtown and want to continue your journey crosstown (or vice versa) ask the driver for a 'transfer' when you get on – you'll be given a ticket for use on the second stage. Again, you can rely on other passengers for advice, but bus maps are available from all subway stations. Almost all buses are now equipped with wheelchair lifts and many are 'kneeling buses', which lower themselves hydraulically so the less firm of foot can climb aboard. Call 1-718 330 1234 (6am-9pm daily; recorded information at other times) for information.

## Taxis

Once you start using cabs in New York you begin to wish they were this cheap everywhere in the world. Yellow cabs are hardly ever in short supply, except in the rain and at around 4 or 5pm, when rush hour gets going and when many cabbies – inexplicably – change shifts. They have a light on to show they're available, and will stop if you stick your arm out. The practice is to jump

# Getting from the airport

'If the Martians landed they'd better not use JFK or they'd be two hours late getting into the city'. The same joke could be applied to Newark and LaGuardia, New York's other two airports.

Though using public transport is the cheapest method, the links are poor and frustrating to use (*see below*). The private bus services are usually the best budget option. Grayline runs a minibus service from each of the three airports to any address in midtown (between 23rd and 63rd Streets) from 7am to 11pm. On the outward journey, it picks up at several hotels. Call 757 6840 or 1-800 451 0455 for details. Or take a Carey Bus, operating between 6am and midnight, with stops at Grand Central Station, the Port Authority terminal (both on 42nd Street) and a host of midtown hotels. Call 1-718 632 0500 for recorded details. For a full list of these and other transport services between New York City and its three airports call 1-800 AIR RIDE, a touch-tone menu of recorded information provided by the Port Authority.

A yellow cab is the most effortless method to get from plane to hotel, but unless you can find some similarly-destined travellers to share with, a trip to Manhattan can easily cost you as much as $40. It's actually cheaper to book a 'private hire' taxi or limousine to meet you (arrange it before you fly or call from the airport). This will cost around $25 plus tolls and tip. Tel Aviv (777 7777) aims to pick you up from any airport three minutes after you call. For a little more you can order a 'stretch' limo and arrive in true style. Finally, for big spenders, a helicopter into Manhattan costs $299 for up to five people. Call Island Helicopters (925 8807/toll-free 1-800 645 3494).

**LaGuardia Airport.**

### John F Kennedy Airport

*(244 4444).*

There's a subway link from JFK (extremely cheap at $1.50 ), but this involves waiting for a shuttle bus to Howard Beach station and then more than an hour's ride into Manhattan. Gray Line minibus $16; Carey Bus $13; yellow cab $30-$40.

### LaGuardia Airport

*(1-718 476 5000).*

Seasoned New Yorkers take a 20-minute ride on the M60 bus ($1.50) to 125th Street in Harlem (not a good place to be at night), where you can get off at Lexington Avenue subway station for the 4, 5 and 6 trains or Lenox Avenue for the 2 and 3. Otherwise Gray Line $13; Carey Bus $10; yellow cab $25-$35.

### Newark Airport

The New Jersey Transit bus company goes to the Port Authority bus terminal (41st Street and Eighth Avenue). The fare is $7 and buses leave every 10-15 minutes (information on 629 8767). Olympia Trails Coach Service buses go to the World Trade Center and Grand Central Station. The fare is $7. Various hotels also offer a minibus shuttle. Yellow cab $35.

RIHGA ROYAL HOTEL
151 WEST 54TH STREET
NEW YORK, NY 10019
RIHGA ROYAL HOTEL®
NEW YORK
Location, Suites, Service.
Spectacular Views, Multilingual Staff, State-of-the-art Security.
800-937-5454
Halcyon
Breakfast, Lunch, Dinner.
Pre/Post Theatre, Piano Lounge, Catering.
4 Hours Free Parking.
212-468-8888

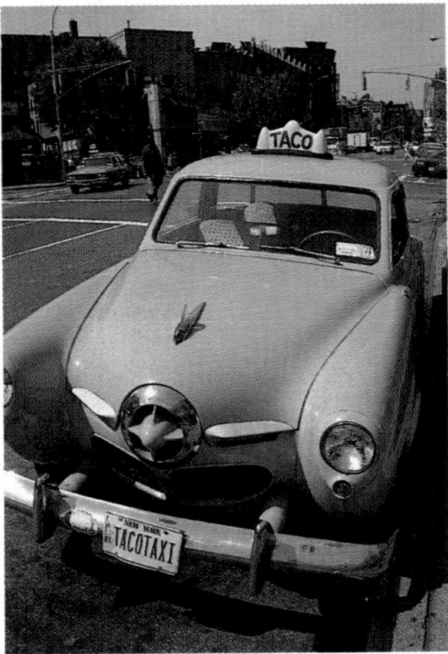


*Grab it while you can.*

right in and then tell the driver where you're going. Cabs carry up to four people for the same price: $1.50 plus 25¢ per fifth of a mile, with an extra 50¢ charge after 8pm. This makes an average fare for a three-mile (4.5km) ride about $5 to $7, depending on the traffic and time of day. Unfortunately, some cabbies will know the city as poorly as you do (though they do now have to pass an English test), so it helps if you know precisely where you're going. Tip 10-15 per cent or round the fare up to the nearest dollar plus one. The cab number and driver's number are on a little sign on the dashboard if you have a problem. There's also a meter number on the receipt. If you wish to complain or trace lost property, call the Taxi and Limousine Commission on 302 8294 (9am-5pm Mon-Fri).

Late at night, cabbies stick to fast-flowing routes and reliably lucrative areas. Try the Avenues and the key east/west streets (Canal, Houston, 14th, 23rd, 42nd, 59th, 86th). Bridge and tunnel exits are also good for a steady flow from the airports, and passengerless cabbies will usually head for nightclubs and big hotels. Here are some other late night taxi tips.

### Chinatown

Chatham Square, where Mott Street meets the Bowery, is an unofficial taxi stand, or try the Bowery at Canal Street, where you can hail one coming off the Manhattan Bridge.

### Financial District

Not the most nocturnal of neighbourhoods; try the Vista Hotel or 1 World Trade Center. There may be a queue but there'll certainly be a cab.

### Lincoln Center

The crowd will head towards Columbus Circle for a cab. Those in the know go west to Amsterdam Avenue.

### Lower East Side

Katz's Deli (corner of Houston & Ludlow Streets) is a cabbies' hangout; otherwise try Delancey Street, where cabs come in over the Williamsburg Bridge.

### Midtown

Penn Station and Grand Central attract cabs through the night, as does the Port Authority building (42nd & 8th) and Times Square.

### SoHo

If you're west, try Sixth Avenue; east, the gas station on Houston Street at Broadway.

### TriBeCa

Cabs here (many arriving from the Holland Tunnel) head up Hudson Street. Canal Street is also a good bet.

### Car Service Companies

The following companies will pick you up anywhere in the city, at any time of day or night.: All City Taxis (718 402 2323), Bell Radio Taxi (691 9191), Communicar (718 457 7777), Sabra (777 7171), Tel Aviv (777 7777).

## Driving

Like good manners, a car, though essential everywhere else, is useless in New York. Drivers here are among the worst in the world and taking to the streets, not to mention finding a place to park, is not for the faint-hearted. It's not worth the hassle of hiring a car unless you are planning a trip out of town. Car hire is much cheaper on the city's outskirts and in neighbouring states such as New Jersey and Connecticut. Book ahead for weekends, and note that street parking is very restricted, especially in the summer. Don't ever park within 15 feet (5m) of a fire hydrant and make sure you read the parking signs. Unless there are meters, most streets have 'alternate side parking', ie one side is out of bounds for certain hours on alternate

## 'You can't get there from here'

The trick to asking directions in New York is to deliver your question within earshot of at least two people. One of them will be completely wrong, but the inevitable debate (sometimes involving the entire bus, subway carriage or street-corner) will ensure that the issue is hammered out sufficiently for you to know where to head. The arguments sparked by your innocent enquiry may well continue long after you have left.

*Go on, get on board. It's perfectly safe.*

days. The New York City Department of Transportation (442 7080) provides information on daily changes to parking regulations.

Most New York authorities will be happy for you to drive on a UK licence for a limited time, though an international one (available in the UK from the AA or RAC) is better.

All car hire companies listed below add relevant sales tax (13.25 per cent in Manhattan). They also offer a 'loss damage waiver' (LDW). This is expensive – almost as much as the rental itself – but without it you are responsible for the cost of repairing even the slightest damage. If you pay with an AmEx card or a gold Visa or Mastercard the LDW may well be covered by them. Personal liability insurance is optional but recommended (but check whether your holiday or home insurance covers it already). You will invariably need a credit card to rent a car and usually have to be over 25.

If you know you want to rent a car before you travel, ask your travel agents if they, or any of the airlines, can offer any good deals

### Avis

*(1-800 331 1212)*. **Open** 24 hours daily. **Rates** from $55 a day unlimited mileage; special weekend rates. **Credit** AmEx, DC, Discover, MC, V.

### Budget Rent-a-Car

*(807 8700)*. **Open** *city* 7am-12am; *airport* 5am-2am daily. **Rates** from $60 a day unlimited mileage; special weekend rates. **Credit** AmEx, DC, Discover, JCB, MC, V.

### Enterprise

*(1-800 325 8007)*. **Open** 8am-9pm Mon-Sat; 9am-9pm Sun. **Rates** from $35 a day off Manhattan; around $60 a day on the island; unlimited mileage restricted to New York, New Jersey and Connecticut.
**Credit** AmEx, DC, Discover, MC, V.
We highly recommend this cheap and extremely reliable service. The most accessible branches off Manhattan are Hoboken (PATH train to 34th Street) and Greenwich (Metro North to Grand Central). Agents will collect you from the station.

## Long Distance

Don't ask for single or return tickets, but for one-way and round-trip. All long-distance trains now depart from Penn Station.

### Penn Station

*West 34th Street, between Seventh & Eighth Avenues (582 6875)*. **Train** A, C or E to Penn Station. **Open** 24 hours daily. **Credit** AmEx, Discover, DC, MC, V.

### Greyhound Trailways

*(1-800 231 2222)*. **Open** 24 hours daily. **Credit** AmEx, Discover, MC, V.
Long-distance bus travel.

### Port Authority Bus Terminal

*Eighth Avenue & West 41st Street (564 8484)*. **Train** A, C, E or K to 42nd Street. **Open** 24 hours daily.
The information number listed above gives information and times on almost all bus transport out of New York. But be careful: the area around the Port Authority is a notoriously nasty place.

# Accommodation

***There are some fantastic hotels in New York – and some fantastic prices, too. Here's how to get the best deal.***

The best way to stay in New York is to rummage through your address book and exhaust all possible contacts. Seriously. Hotels are notoriously expensive and even the nationwide budget chains hoik their prices up once they cross the Hudson. But this is New York, so there's always a deal. Business rates, weekend specials, discounts for AA members, family promotions, holiday discounts, you name it, you might just get it. Even New York's Visitors Bureau recommends hustling for a deal, asking for an upgrade or using a reservation agency (*see box*) to save money. Larger parties and families can also save by taking just one room – extra beds are extremely economical (just $10 a night). If this is more than just a flying visit, it's worth comparing weekly rates – they're often considerably better value.

Even the cheaper hotels will offer in-room phones (but check the rates) and cable TV. Few places, on the other hand, include breakfast in the deal. In-house parking is also rare but the larger hotels can usually get you a reduced rate with a nearby public car park. Most hotels accept American Express, Diners Club, MasterCard and Visa but some may specify AmEx as a guarantee of payment. The clean-air lobby has been heeded at most hotels: virtually all have no-smoking rooms; some entire no-smoking floors.

Hotel taxes are not included in rates quoted and they push up the price of a room considerably. A week's worth of taxes on a $100 room, for example, add up to nearly $130. The system was recently simplified, with a standard 16.25 per cent tax total replacing a sliding scale. This includes sales tax and a state sales tax but, as if that weren't enough, there's also a $2 a night occupancy tax.

Whether it's a luxury hotel or a youth hostel, try to sort out your accommodation as early as possible. After a brief slump in the early 1990s, the hotel industry has picked up again and occupancy levels have been at record highs, making package flight and room deals well worth considering. If you do find yourself stuck, go to one of the reservations agencies listed, notably Hotel Reservations Network, which promises to find you a room even if the city is 'sold out'.

*Snuggle up in the lap of luxury at the* **Pierre**. *See page 20.*

*The baronial lobby of the* **Radisson Empire**. *See page 25.*

For more information contact the Hotel Association of New York City, 437 Madison Avenue, NY 10022 (754 6700), or write to the New York Convention and Visitors Bureau at 2 Columbus Circle, NY 10019, to ask for a copy of its accommodation booklet.

## Only The Best Will Do

### Four Seasons

*57 East 57th St, NY 10022, between Park & Madison Avenues (758 5700/fax 758 5711).* **Train** 4, 5, 6 to 59th Street; N or R to Lexington Avenue. **Rates** *single* $420-$560; *double* $470-$610; *suites* $795-$6000. **Credit** AmEx, DC, JCB, MC, V.

Two years after it opened in 1993, the Four Seasons was voted best hotel in New York by Condé Nast's *Traveller* magazine. The art deco style rooms are the largest in the city, bathrooms are made from Florentine marble and the tub fills in just 60 seconds. This honey coloured limestone building is also the tallest hotel in town so views over Manhattan are superb. The lobby, with its 33ft-high onyx ceiling, is where *Absolutely Fabulous* filmed Edina's search for the perfect doorknob – fans have even asked where it is. Since it's now back in the BBC props department from whence it came, they'll just have to console themselves by getting suitably wasted on one of the 14 different types of martini served in the Fifty Seven Fifty Seven bar.

**Hotel services** *Air-conditioning. Babysitting. Bar. Car park. Conference facilities. Currency exchange. Disabled: access, rooms. Fax. Laundry. Multi-lingual staff. Restaurants. Spa & fitness rooms.*
**Room services** *Cable TV. Fax. Hair dryer. Mini-bar. Radio. Refrigerator. Room service. Safe. VCR.*

### Hotel Carlyle

*35 East 76th Street, NY 10021, between Park & Madison Avenues (7441600/1-800 227 5737/fax 717 4682).* **Train** 6 to 77th Street. **Rates** *single* $285-$395; *double* $310-$440; *suite* $500-$1600. **Credit** AmEx, DC, MC, V.

The sumptuous Carlyle is New York's only five-star hotel,

with whirlpools in every bathroom and a private entrance foyer for each of the apartment-style rooms. Since it opened, in 1930, the hotel has attracted numerous famous guests – especially those who desire privacy. In fact, service is so discreet that two members of the Beatles stayed here separately after the group split without either of them knowing the other was there. Cabaret entertainers perform in the Café Carlyle and there's the enduring appeal of Ludwig Bemelmans' murals in his namesake bar.
**Hotel services** *Air-conditioning. Babysitting. Bar. Beauty salon. Cable TV. Conference facilities. Currency exchange. Fax. Fitness centre. Laundry. Multi-lingual staff. Restaurant. Reduced rate parking.*
**Room services** *Cable TV. CD/tape player (some rooms). Hair dryer. Mini-bar. Radio. Refrigerator. Room service. Safe. VCR. Fax. Whirlpool.*

### Lowell Hotel

*28 East 63rd Street, NY 10021, between Park & Madison Avenues (838 1400/fax 319 4230).* **Train** 4, 5 or 6 to 59th Street. **Rates** *single* $295-$365; *double* from $365; *suite* from $475. **Credit** AmEx, DC, Discover, MC, V, En Route, JCB
Lowell's is a small, charming hotel in a landmark art deco building. Its rooms are delightfully old fashioned with Scandinavian comforters, Chinese porcelains and marble baths – there are even wood-burning fireplaces in the suites. It's perennially popular with the entertainment industry, with the gym suite particularly in demand by well-known keep-fit fans such as Madonna, Arnold Schwarzenegger and Michelle Pfeiffer.
**Hotel services** *Air-conditioning. Babysitting. Bar. Cable TV. Currency exchange. Fax. Fitness centre. Laundry. Multi-lingual staff. Restaurant.*
**Room services** *Fax. Hair dryer. Mini-bar. PC ports. Radio. Refrigerator. Room service. VCR.*

### Mayfair Hotel

*610 Park Avenue, NY 10021, at 65th Street, (288 0800/fax 737 0538).* **Train** 6 to 68th Street. **Rates** *single* from $275; *double* from $295; *suite* from $440. **Credit** AmEx, DC, CB, MC, V.
The Mayfair is an elegant, intimate hotel whose exclusive, luxurious rooms appeal to exclusive, luxurious clients such as Issey Miyake, Barbra Streisand and the King of Spain. French cuisine is served at Le Cirque restaurant and the service is gracious.
**Hotel services** *Air-conditioning. Babysitting. Bar. Conference facilities. Currency exchange. Disabled: access. Fax. Laundry. Multi-lingual staff. Fitness centre & putting green. Restaurant.*
**Room services** *Cable TV. Fax on request. Hair dryer. Radio. Refrigerator. Room service. VCR.*

### Millenium Hilton

*55 Church Street, at Fulton and Dey Streets (693 2001/1-800 835 2220/fax 571 2316).* **Train** 1 or 9 to Wall Street; N or R to Courtland Street. **Rates** *single* $195-$245; *double* $220-$270; *junior suite* from $295; *suite* from $425. **Credit**: AmEx, DC, Discover, JCB, MC, V.
This 58-storey black skyscraper next to the World Trade Center is solidly aimed at the corporate client. Each room has a fax and facilities are high-tech – including a glass-enclosed swimming pool to relax in after a hard day at the office. The upper floors have superb views of New York Harbour and Brooklyn Bridge.
**Hotel services** *Air-conditioning. Bar. Car park. Conference facilities. Currency exchange. Disabled: access, rooms. Fax. Laundry. Multi-lingual staff. Fitness centre. Restaurant.*
**Room services** *Cable TV. Fax. Hair dryer. Mini-bar. Radio. Refrigerator. Room service. Safe. VCR.*

## The best hotels for...

### Celebrity spotting

The **Lowell**, where gym users can compare biceps with Madonna and Arnie (*listed under* **Only The Best Will Do**), or the **Mayflower**, whose regulars include Pavarotti and Jack Nicholson.

### Business travellers

The **New York Helmsley**, whose every room has a phone by the bath, for executives who really know how to relax (*listed under* **First Class**).

### Drop-dead views

**The Metro**, whose roof terrace underlooks the Empire State (*listed under* **Comfortable**).

### Illicit liaisons

**The Carlyle**, where staff are so discreet that two of the Beatles stayed here separately after the group split, with neither knowing the other was in residence (*listed under* **Only The Best Will Do**).

### Parents

The **Howard Johnson**, where children under 18 stay free with a parent and there's a babysitting service (*listed under* **Under $100**).

### Senseless spending

The **Plaza**, whose penthouse suite costs a mere $15,000. To rent, that is, not buy. *Listed under* **Only The Best Will Do**.

### Architecture

The **Lowell**, a landmark art deco building (*listed under* **Only The Best Will Do**).

### Killing your partner

The **Chelsea**, where Sid Vicious dispatched his girlfriend, Nancy Spungeon (*see box* **Dive Hotels**).

### Afternoon tea

The **Pierre**, the closest New York gets to London's Ritz (*listed under* **Only The Best Will Do**).

### Food trivia buffs

The **Waldorf-Astoria**, home of the famous if somewhat over-rated salad (*listed under* **Only The Best Will Do**).

### Style seekers

The chicer-than-thou **Paramount**, where lifts issue a weather report on each floor (*listed under* **Sleek & Chic**).

### Budget travellers (who like Warhol)

The **Gershwin**, where rates are great and the pop art furnishings include a Campbell's soup can autographed by the man himself (*listed under* **Budget**).

### Fashion victims

**Hotel 17**, second home of clubbers, fashion tramps and drag queens, where makeovers are all just part of the service (*see box* **Dive Hotels**).

### New York Palace

*455 Madison Avenue, NY 10022, at 50th Street (888 7000/1-800 697 2522/fax 303 6000).* **Train** E or F to Fifth Avenue/53rd Street. **Rates** *single/double* from $275; *tower room* from $325; *suite* $450-$1200. **Credit** AmEx, DC, Discover, JCB, MC, V.

Look out from the central lobby and it's hard to believe you're in New York. There's a leafy courtyard and a view of St Patrick's cathedral across the street. Things look just as good inside – the Palace was once the Villard Houses, a cluster of mansion town homes designed by Stanford White. Rooms are elegant and luxurious but the hotel's real attractions are its Gold Room and the nineenth-century Madison Room. There's a wonderful club-like feel to the place – it's well worth popping in if only to appreciate the interior.

**Hotel services** *Air-conditioning. Babysitting. Bar. Car park. Conference facilities. Disabled: access, rooms. Fax. Laundry. Multi-lingual staff. Restaurant.*

**Room services** *Cable TV. Hair dryer. Mini-bar. Radio. Refrigerator. Room service. VCR.*

### Pierre

*795 Fifth Avenue, NY 10021, at 61st Street (838 8000 1-800 332 3442/fax 940 8109).* **Train** N or R to Fifth Avenue. **Rates** *single* from $285; *double* from $325. **Credit** AmEx, DC, En Route, JCB, MC, V.

Once Salvador Dali's favourite hotel, the Pierre has been seducing guests since 1929 with its superb service and discreet, elegant atmosphere. Even if a room here is out of your price range, try and take afternoon tea in the magnificently opulent Rotunda – its setting is on a par with the Ritz in London. Rooms at the front overlook Central Park and it's just one block away from some of the most famous designer stores on Fifth Avenue – naturally.

**Hotel services** *Air-conditioning. Babysitting. Bar. Beauty salon. Car park. Conference facilities. Currency exchange. Disabled: access, rooms. Fax. Fitness centre. Laundry. Multi-lingual staff. Restaurant. Theatre desk. Valet packing/unpacking.*

**Room services** *Cable TV. Hair dryer. Mini-bar. Radio. Refrigerator on request. Room service. Safe. VCR & fax on request.*

### Plaza Hotel

*768 Fifth Avenue, NY 10019, at 59th Street (759 3000/1-800 228 3000/fax 759 3167).* **Train** N or R to Fifth Avenue/59th Street. **Rates** *single/double* $235-505; *suite* $395-$15,000. **Credit** AmEx, Discover, DC, JCB, MC, V.

Ivana Trump may no longer run the Plaza, smack in the middle of Fifth Avenue's most expensive stores, but it still bears her inimitable stamp of style. Apart from the delightful Tiffany ceiling in the famous Palm Court, there's the 1500sq ft Frank Lloyd Wright Suite, where the architect stayed while designing the Guggenheim. The furniture is a mixture of reproduction designs and originals, commissioned by the Trumps after researching the Wright archives. On a less historic note, scenes from *Crocodile Dundee* were filmed here.

**Hotel services** *Air-conditioning. Bar. Beauty salon. Car park. Conference facilities. Fax. Fitness centre. Laundry. Multi-lingual staff. Restaurant. Wheelchair access.*

**Room services** *Cable TV. Dual-line phones. Hair dryer. Mini-bar. Radio. Room service. Safe. VCR on request. Voice mail.*

### UN Plaza – Park Hyatt

*One United Nations Plaza, NY 10017, at East 44th Street (758 1234/1-800 228 9000/fax 702 5051).* **Train** 4, 5, 6 or 7 to Grand Central. **Rates** *single/double* $210-$270; *suite* $375-$700. **Credit** AmEx, Discover, DC, JCB, MC, V.

The lobby may be on the ground floor but the rooms go from the 28th floor upwards. As the name suggests, the hotel is a revenue-earning enterprise for the United Nations and is an interesting glass curtain-wall building.

**Hotel services** *Air-conditioning. Babysitting. Bar. Car park. Conference facilities. Currency exchange. Disabled: access, rooms. Fax. Fitness centre & indoor pool. Laundry. Multi-lingual staff. Restaurant.*

**Room services** *Cable TV. Fax on request. Hair dryer. Mini-bar. Radio. Refrigerator. Room service. Safe. VCR in suites.*

### Waldorf-Astoria

*301 Park Avenue, NY 10022, at 50th Street (355 3000/1-800 924 3673/fax 872 7272).* **Train** 6 to 51st Street. **Rates** *single* $221-$304; *double* $251-$344. **Tower rates** *single* $255-$375; *double* $335-$425; *suite* from $550. **Credit**: AmEx, DC, Discover, JCB, MC, V.

The famous Waldorf salad made its debut at the hotel's opening in 1931. At the time, this was the world's largest hotel and it has been associated with New York's high society ever since. Several years later, the Astoria Hotel was built and later connected to the Waldorf by a walkway which became known as Peacock's Alley, such was the posturing and promenading. There's a magnificent 148,000-piece art deco mosaic in the lobby that was hidden for more than 30 years, while the four-storey Grand Ballroom houses numerous charity balls and political bashes. Incidentally, the Presidential Suite is so named because of its guests. Get the picture?

**Hotel services** *Air-conditioning. Babysitting. Bar. Beauty salon. Car park. Conference facilities. Fax. Laundry. Multi-lingual staff. Fitness centre with steam rooms. Restaurant. Wheelchair access.*

**Room services** *Cable TV. Fax in tower rooms. Hair dryer, mini-bar, refrigerator in some rooms. Radio. Room service. Safe in tower rooms on request.*

## Sleek & Chic

### Morgans

*237 Madison Avenue, NY 10016, between 37th & 38th Streets (686 0300/1-800 334 3408/fax 779 8352).* **Train** 4, 5, 6 or 7 to Grand Central. **Rates** *single* $195-$350; *double* $220-$350; *suite* from $325. **Credit** AmEx, Discover, DC, JCB, MC, V.

*The reassuringly old-fashioned* **Algonquin**.

Morgans is an understated hotel, designed by Schrager and Rubell and named in honour of JP Morgan, whose nearby home now serves as the Pierpont Morgan Library. The Andre Putnam interior has been recently renovated and lightened at a cost of $2 million. All in all, there's a residential feel to this 1929 building, once described by *Vanity Fair* as the 'handsomest hotel in New York'.
**Hotel services** *Air-conditioning. Babysitting. Bar & café. Conference facilities. Disabled: access. Fax. Laundry. Multi-lingual staff. Fitness centre & spa due to open early 96. Restaurant.*
**Room services** *Cable TV. Hair dryer. Mini-bar. Refrigerator. Room service. VCR on request.*

### Paramount

*235 West 46th Street, NY 10036, between Broadway & Eighth Avenue (764 5500/1-800 225 7474/fax 575 4892).* **Train** N or R to 49th Street. **Rates** *single* $99-$195; *double* $165-$215; *suite* $360-$460. **Credit** AmEx, DC, Discover, JCB, MC, V.
The Phillipe Starck-designed Paramount, like the Royalton, is chic almost beyond belief. It's an astoundingly modern and stylish hotel, with a lobby inspired by the great transatlantic liners and multi-coloured lifts that give a weather report on each floor. Rooms verge on the small side but beds sport Vermeer's *Lacemaker* silkscreen headboards and the stainless steel bathrooms are a pristine delight. Terribly in with the in crowd and there's a Dean & Deluca shop and espresso bar off the lobby.
**Hotel services** *Air-conditioning. Bar. Business centre. Conference facilities. Currency exchange. Disabled: access, rooms on request. Fax. Fitness centre. Laundry. Multi-lingual staff. Non-smoking floors. Restaurants.*
**Room services** *Cable TV. Room service. VCR.*

### Royalton

*44 West 44th Street, NY 10036, between Fifth & Sixth Avenues (869 4400/1-800 635 9013/fax 869 8965).* **Train** 4, 5, 6 or 7 to Grand Central. **Rates** *single* from $245; *double* from $275; *suite* from $375. **Credit** AmEx, DC, JCB, MC, V.
Like Morgan's, this is a Rubell-Scrager production, but the Starck interiors are more likely to remind visitors of the Paramount. Waitresses in satin mini-dresses serve fashionable young things in the lobby and the restaurant has some of the most sought-after tables in town. So many of the regulars work for nearby Condé Nast, it's sometimes referred to as Club Condé. The rooms are gorgeous with sleek slate fireplaces and marvellous round Starck bathtubs.
**Hotel services** *Air-conditioning. Bar. Car park. Conference facilities. Currency exchange. Fax. Fitness centre. Laundry. Multi-lingual staff. Restaurant.*
**Room services** *Cable TV. Mini-bar. Radio. Room service. VCR.*

## First Class

### Doral Tuscany

*120 East 39th Street, NY 10016, between Lexington & Park Avenues (686 1600/1-800 223 6725/fax 779 7833 or 779 0148 for reservations).* **Train** 4, 5, 6 or 7 to Grand Central. **Rates** *single* $194-$249; *double* $194-$249; *suite* from $350. **Credit** AmEx, DC, Discover, MC, V.
Hard to believe Grand Central Station is just around the corner: the Doral Tuscany is nestled among brownstones in the historic Murray Hill district. Standard rooms are absolutely enormous: there's an entrance hallway with separate dressing room, vanity mirror and Italian marble baths. Suites go one step further with a tiny portable TV in the bathrooms. The Time and Again restaurant reopens in 1996 but try the charming rustic Adirondack grill instead.
**Hotel services** *Air-conditioning. Bar. Conference facilities. Disabled: access, rooms. Fax. Fitness centre one block away. Laundry. Multi-lingual staff. Restaurant.*
**Room services** *Cable TV. Hair dryer. Mini-bar. Radio. Refrigerator. Room service. VCR on request.*

### Helmsley Windsor Hotel

*100 West 58th Street, NY 10019, at Sixth Avenue (265 2100/1-800 221 4982/fax 315 0371).* **Train** Q, N or R to West 58th Street/Sixth Avenue. **Rates** *single* $145; *double* $155; *suite* from $215. **Credit** AmEx, DC, Discover, MC, V.
Rooms don't quite live up to the wonderfully old-fashioned panelled lobby but Central Park is close by and the hotel is both comfortable and charming.
**Hotel services** *Air-conditioning. Babysitting. Disabled: access, rooms. Fax. Laundry. Meeting room for 10 people. Multi-lingual staff.*
**Room services** *Cable TV. Hair dryer on request. Radio. Refrigerator on request and in suites. Safe. VCR.*

### New York Helmsley

*212 East 42nd Street, NY 10017, between Second & Third Avenues (490 8900/1-800 221 4982/fax 682 6299).* **Train** 4, 5, 6 or 7 to Grand Central. **Rates** *single* $190-$240; *double* $215-$265; *suite* from $400. **Credit** AmEx, MC, V.
It may have the same owners as the Helmsley Windsor, but this is primarily a business hotel, with full business centre and telephones by the bath. All rooms are the same size – so there are no worries about getting a rough deal – and facilities are sleek, modern and stylish.
**Hotel services** *Air-conditioning. Babysitting. Bar. Car park. Conference facilities. Disabled: access, rooms. Fax. Laundry. Multi-lingual staff. Restaurant.*
**Room services** *TV. Hair dryer. Radio. Room service. VCR on request.*

### Roger Smith

*501 Lexington Avenue, NY 10017, between 47th & 48th Streets (755 1400/1-800 445 0277/fax 319 9130).* **Train** 4, 5, 6 or 7 to Grand Central. **Rates** *single* from $180; *double* from $190. **Credit** AmEx, DC, JCB, MC, V.
The hotel is owned by sculptor and painter James Knowles and consequently some of his work can be found decorating the lobby. The large rooms are individually furnished, the staff are friendly and there's a well stocked VCR library for those who want to spend the night in. It's popular with bands and there's often live jazz in the restaurant.
**Hotel services** *Air-conditioning. Babysitting. Bar. Conference facilities. Disabled: access, rooms. Fax. Laundry. Multi-lingual staff. Restaurant. Valet parking.*
**Room services** *Cable TV. Hair dryer on request. Radio. Refrigerator. Room service. VCR.*

### Sheraton Park Avenue Hotel

*45 Park Avenue, NY 10016, at 37th Street (685 7676/1-800 537 0075/fax 889 3193).* **Train** 4, 5, 6 or 7 to Grand Central. **Rates** *single/double* $245-$700; *suite* from $375. **Credit** AmEx, DC, Discover, JCB, MC, V.
A mellow old hotel with an oak-panelled lobby and handsomely furnished bedrooms, some with fireplaces. Russell's restaurant is often the venue for live jazz and the bar was seen in the Paul Newman film *The Verdict*.
**Hotel services** *Air-conditioning. Babysitting. Bar. Conference facilities. Exchange. Disabled: access, rooms. Fax. Laundry. Fitness centre. Restaurant. Valet parking.*
**Room services** *Cable TV. Hair dryer. Radio. Refrigerator on request. Room service. Safe. VCR*

## Comfortable

### Algonquin

*59 West 44th Street, NY 10036, between Fifth & Sixth Avenues (840 6800/1-800 548 0345/fax 944 1419).* **Train** B, D, F or Q to 42nd Street. **Rates** *single* from

*Opulence unlimited at the* **Four Seasons**. *See page 17.*

$220; *double* from $240; *suite* from $400. **Credit** AmEx, DC, Discover, JCB, MC, V.
A reassuringly old-fashioned hotel, built at the turn of the century and opulently historic. Each floor has a different colour scheme and rooms are instantly appealing. Suites pay tribute to Dorothy Parker, whose literary circle exchanged witticisms here, the *New Yorker* and *Vanity Fair*, while the lobby honours Matilda, the hotel cat, with her own miniature suite and four-poster bed in a hidden recess in the panelling. Renovations continue but the Oak Room retains its attractive Round Table mystique and the lobby remains the best place to meet and sip tea – even if it does come as a plastic pot of hot water with teabags on the side. Shame!
**Hotel services** *Air-conditioning. Babysitting. Bar. Conference facilities. Currency exchange. Disabled: access, rooms. Fax. Laundry. Multi-lingual staff. Non-smoking floors. Restaurant.*
**Room services** *Cable TV. Hair dryer. Radio. Refrigerator in suites and on request. Room service. Safe. VCR on request. Voice mail.*

## Ameritania

*1701 Broadway, NY 10019, at 54th Street (247 5000/1-800 922 0330/fax 247 3316).* **Train** N or R to 49th Street. **Rates** *single* $119-$129; *double* $129-$139; *suites* $149-$179. **Credit** AmEx, DC, Discover, JCB, MC, V.
The futuristic 'A' logo of the Ameritania resembles the *Star Trek Next Generation* emblem, which may explain why the lobby is so broodingly futuristic. Rooms are more traditionally decorated. The hotel is next door to the Ed Sullivan Theatre, home of the David Letterman Show, hence the occasional appearance of cameras – Dave likes to pop in unannounced. Location-wise, it's perfect for theatres but there are also numerous sex clubs nearby.
**Hotel services** *Air-conditioning. Bar. Fax. Fitness centre. Laundry. Multi-lingual staff. Restaurant. Theatre/excursion desk. 24-hour bagel shop.*
**Room services** *Cable TV. Hair dryer in suites and on request in rooms. Radio. Refrigerator on request. Room service.*

## Barbizon

*140 East 63rd Street, NY 10021, at Lexington Avenue (838 5700/1-800 223 1020/fax 888 4271).* **Train** B or Q to Lexington Avenue. **Rates** *single* $105-$170; *double* $105-$190; *suite* $295-$650. Children under 12 free if sharing with parents. **Credit** AmEx, DC, MC, V.
The Barbizon was originally a hotel for emancipated women, whose parents could feel confident that their daughters were safe in its care. During its 50 years as a women-only residence, guests including Grace Kelly, Ali McGraw and Candice Bergen abided by rules such as only entertaining men in the music room and lounge. Today, a $40 million renovation is due to be completed by autumn 1996.
**Hotel services** *Air-conditioning. Currency exchange. Disabled: access, rooms. Fax. Laundry. Multi-lingual staff.*
**Room services** *Cable TV. Hair dryer on request. Refrigerator.*

## Days Hotel

*790 Eighth Avenue, NY 10019, between 48th & 49th Streets (581 7000/1-800 572 6232/fax 974 0291).* **Train** C or E to 50th Street. **Rates** *single* $110-$130; *double* $122-$142. **Credit** AmEx, DC, Discover, MC, V.
This is a dependable hotel, decorated as you'd expect from a chain and reasonably priced. It's in a good Midtown location and, 15 floors up, there's a rooftop swimming pool and cocktail lounge.
**Hotel services** *Air-conditioning. Babysitting on request. Bar. Car park. Conference facilities. Disabled: access, rooms. Fax. Outdoor pool open in summer. Restaurant.*
**Room services** *Cable TV. Hair dryer on request. Radio. Room service. Safe.*

## Dorset

*30 West 54th Street, NY 10019, between Fifth & Sixth Avenues (247 7300/fax 581 0153).* **Train** B or Q to 57th Street/Sixth Avenue. **Rates** *single* $175; *double* $185; *one-bedroom suite* $250; *two-bedroom suite* $325. Children under 14 free if sharing with parents. **Credit** AmEx, DC, MC, V.

The Dorset attracts a mostly business clientèle. All rooms and hallways have been renovated and suites are larger than the average New York apartment. Some rooms have views of the MoMA sculpture park and the café-bistro has good-value snacks.
**Hotel services** *Air-conditioning. Babysitting. Bar/café. Beauty salon. Conference facilities. Disabled: access. Fax. Laundry. Multi-lingual staff. Fitness centre for corporate guests. Restaurant. Valet parking.*
**Room services** *Hair dryer on request. Radio. Refrigerator. Room service until 11pm. VCR on request.*

### Elysée

*60 East 54th Street, NY 10022, between Park & Madison Avenues (753 1066/fax 980 9278).* **Train** B or Q to 63rd Street. **Rates** *single/double* $225-$245; *suite* $325-$775. **Credit** AmEx, DC, JCB, MC, V.
A charming and discreet hotel with friendly service, antique furniture and Italian marble bathrooms. Some of the rooms also have coloured glass conservatories and roof terraces. It's popular with publishers so don't be surprised if you see a famous author enjoying the complimentary afternoon tea in the club room. Other eating options are the famous Monkey Bar and restaurant. Room prices include continental breakfast and, in the evening, wine and hors d'oeuvres. The Elysée has been restored to its original 1930s decor and displays photographs showing the likes of Joan Crawford and Marlene Dietrich gathered around the piano.
**Hotel services** *Air-conditioning. Babysitting. Bar. Conference facilities. Disabled: access, rooms. Fax. Laundry. Library. Multi-lingual staff. Health club two blocks away. Valet parking.*
**Room services** *Cable TV. Hair dryer. Microwaves in suites. Mini-bar. Radio. Refrigerator. Room service. TV. VCR. Voice mail.*

### Franklin

*164 East 87th Street, NY 10128, between Third & Lexington Avenues (369 1000/fax 369 8000).* **Train** 4, 5 or 6 to 86th Street. **Rates** *single* $135; *double* $145. **Credit** AmEx, MC, V.
A pleasant reasonably priced hotel frequented by models from the Ford and Elite agencies – maybe that's why there's so much closet space. Rooms are functional and modern with light canopies draped over the beds. Reasonably close to the major East Side museums and well located for eating out. Breakfast and parking are both free.
**Hotel services** *Air-conditioning. Car park. Fax. Laundry.Multi-lingual staff.*
**Room services** *Cable TV. Hair dryer. Refrigerator on request. VCR. Video library.*

### Gorham

*136 West 55th Street, NY 10019, between Sixth & Seventh Avenues (245 1800/1-800 735 0710/fax 582 8332).* **Train** N or R to 57th Street; B or Q to 57th Street. **Rates** *single/double* $170-$300; *suite* $195-$350. **Credit** AmEx, DC, JCB, MC, V.
The Gorham stands opposite the unusual domed City Center dance theatre. Unfortunately, the room furnishings look rather tacky after the stylish marble and maple in the lobby. However, there's a wet bar in each room and kitchen facilities in suites are particularly good. Espresso coffee machines are available on request.
**Hotel services** *Air-conditioning. Babysitting. Bar. Car park. Conference facilities. Fax. Disabled: access, rooms. Fitness centre. Laundry. Multi-lingual staff. Restaurant.*
**Room services** *Cable TV. Fax connection. Hair dryer. Microwave. Mini-bar. Radio. Refrigerator. Room service. Safe. Spa baths in suites. VCR on request.*

### Gramercy Park Hotel

*2 Lexington Avenue, NY 10010, at East 21st Street (475 4320/1-800 221 4083/fax 505 0535).* **Train** 6 to 23rd Street. **Rates** *single* $125-$135; *double* $135-$140; *suite* from $160. **Credit** AmEx, DC, Discover, JCB, MC, V.
The hotel is in a surprisingly quiet location for Midtown Manhattan, adjoining the small green oasis of Gramercy Park. Guests vary from business travellers to rock stars. Unusually, there are no non-smoking rooms.
**Hotel services** *Air-conditioning. Bar. Beauty salon. Car park. Conference facilities. Disabled: access, rooms Fax. Laundry. Multi-lingual staff. Newsstand/theatre ticket office. Restaurant.*
**Room services** *Cable TV. Radio. Fridge. Room service.*

### Lexington

*511 Lexington Avenue, NY 10017, at 48th Street (755 4400/fax 751 4091).* **Train** 6 to 51st Street. **Rates** *single/double* $110-$185; *suite* $250-$500. **Credit** AmEx, Discover, DC, MC, V.
The Lexington is particularly popular with business travellers and is close to both Grand Central Station and the United Nations. The lobby is marble-floored with rosewood pillars and 15 of the 27 floors have been renovated. There are two restaurants: La Piccola Fontana, serving north Italian dishes, and the Chinese J Sung Dynasty. Some of the suites have private terraces and the many services on the premises include a barber, tailor and haberdashery.
**Hotel services** *Air-conditioning. Babysitting on request. Bar. Coffee shop. Conference facilities. Currency exchange. Disabled: access, rooms. Exercise room. Fax. Laundry. Multi-lingual staff. Restaurants.*
**Room services** *Cable TV. Hair dryer. Radio on request. Refrigerator. Room service. Safe.*

### Metro

*45 West 35th Street, NY 10001, between Fifth & Sixth Avenues (947 2500/1-800 356 3870/fax 279 1310).* **Train** B, D, F, Q or R to 34th Street. **Rates** *single* $125-$140; *double* $125-$150. **Credit** AmEx, DC, MC, V.
This is New York's newest hotel and a fine addition it is, too, housed in a 1901 building that has been completely renovated and reconstructed in sleek art deco style. Rooms are modern in design, mostly black and taupe, complemented by chic black and white photographs from the 1930s. A free continental breakfast is served in the lounge and library and there's a spectacular unobscured view of the Empire State Building from the 14th-floor roof terrace.
**Hotel services** *Air-conditioning. Conference facilities planned. Disabled: access, rooms. Fax. Fitness centre. Laundry. Multi-lingual staff. Rooftop terrace.*
**Room services** *Cable TV. Hair dryer on request. Radio.*

### Mansfield Hotel

*12 West 44th Street, NY 10019, between Fifth & Sixth Avenues (944 6050/fax 764 4477).* **Train** 4, 5, 6 or 7 to Grand Central. **Rates** *single/double* $145-$245; *suite* $195. **Credit** AmEx, V, MC.
The Broadway actor John Mansfield once lived in this block, which became a hotel in the 1920s. Although there's no restaurant, dozens can be found within five blocks. Rooms are minimalist and starkly decorated in black and white – perhaps too minimalist for some guests, as rugs have been ordered to cover the stripped wooden floors.
**Hotel services** *Air-conditioning. Babysitting on request. Bar. Fax. Multi-lingual staff. Restaurant. VCR library.*
**Room services** *Cable TV. CD players. Hair dryer. Radio. VCR. Spa baths/saunas in some rooms.*

### Mayflower

*15 Central Park West, NY 10023, at 61st Street (265 0060/fax 265 5098).* **Train** 1, 9, A, B, C or D to Columbus Circle. **Rates** *single* $145-$160; *double* $160-$175; *suite* from $200, extra for park view. **Credit** AmEx, DC, Discover, MC, V.
This haven for entertainment types faces Central Park and is just around the corner from the Lincoln Centre. Pavarotti and

Domingo can sometimes be seen at the bar alongside members of visiting opera and ballet companies. Jane Fonda, Jack Nicholson and Alec Baldwin are among the hotel's numerous 'name' guests. The front rooms have spectacular views over the park. A plaque outside the Conservatory restaurant explains recounts that this was the birthplace of musical composer Vincent Youmans (*Tea for Two* and *I Want to be Happy*).
**Hotel services** *Air-conditioning. Babysitting. Bar. Car park. Conference facilities. Fax. Fitness centre. Laundry. Multi-lingual staff. Restaurant.*
**Room services** *Cable TV. Hair dryer on request. PC dataports. Radio. Refrigerator. Room service. VCR on request.*

### Radisson Empire

*44 West 63rd Street, NY 10023, at Broadway (265 7400/1-800 333 3333/fax 245 3382).* **Train** 1, 9, A, B, C or D to Columbus Circle. **Rates** *single/double* from $148; *suites* $250-$540. **Credit** AmEx, DC, Discover, JCB, MC, V.
This hotel is perfectly located opposite the Lincoln Centre and next door to the eccentrically stylish Iridium bar. The lobby is surprisingly baronial with wood panelling, velvet drapes, a tapestry and two oil paintings depicting Lady Macbeth and Laurence Olivier as Romeo. The rooms are small but tasteful with plenty of chintz and an adequate amount of closet space.
**Hotel services** *Air-conditioning. Bar. Conference facilities. Currency exchange. Disabled facilities: access, rooms. Fax. Self-service laundry. Multi-lingual reception staff. Restaurant. Theatre/tour ticket desk. Valet parking.*
**Room services** *Cable TV. Hair dryer. Mini-bar. Modems available. Radio. Refrigerator on request. Room service. VCR. CD & cassette player.*

### Shelburne Murray Hill

*303 Lexington Avenue, NY 10016, between 37th & 38th Streets (689 5200/fax 779 7068).* **Train** 4, 5, 6 or 7 to Grand Central. **Rates** *studio suite* from $135; *one-bedroom suite* $170-$270; *two-bedroom suite* $335-$435. **Credit** AmEx, MC, V.
An elegantly furnished all-suite hotel with an attractive lobby and pleasant rooms. Suites have a full kitchen with all the necessarly appliances: microwave, iron and filter coffee machine with constantly replenished coffee. It's good value for New York, considering its facilities, which include a restaurant and a sauna in the health club.
**Hotel services** *Air-conditioning. Bar. Car park. Conference facilities. Disabled: access, rooms. Fax. Fitness club. Laundry. Multi-lingual staff. Restaurant. Safe.*
**Room services** *Cable TV. Hair dryer on request. Microwave. Iron/ironing board. Radio. Refrigerator. Room service. VCR on request.*

### Shoreham

*33 West 55th Street, NY 10019, at Fifth Avenue (247 6700/fax 765 9741).* **Train** E or F to Fifth Avenue/33rd Street. **Rates** *single/double* $195; *suite* $245; *penthouse suite* $300-$675. **Credit** AmEx, DC, MC, V.
The Shoreham makes a refreshing change from the floral chintz of many hotels with its chic minimalist black and white lobby. The rooms are similarly modern, elegant and spacious and are furnished with gorgeous cedar closets. Japanese-style screens separate the sleeping area in suites. Complimentary continental breakfast comes with the papers – a rare treat here.
**Hotel services** *Air-conditioning. Babysitting. Disabled: access, rooms. Fax. Laundry. Multi-lingual staff. Video & CD library.*
**Room services** *Cable TV. CD player. Hair dryer. Radio. Refrigerator. VCR.*

### Southgate Tower

*371 Seventh Avenue, NY 10001, at 31st Street (563 1800/1-800 637 8483/fax 643 8028).* **Train** A, C or E to Penn Station. **Rates** *studio suite* $125-$180; *one-bedroom suite* $147-$250. **Credit** AmEx, DC, Discover, JCB, MC, V.
Popular with conference-goers headed for the Javits Convention Center nearby, the Southgate Tower has been completely renovated. It's an all-suite hotel so none of the rooms are boxy – in fact, some of the balcony suites are positively enormous. Kitchens contain toasters, filter coffee machines and microwaves but there's also room service until midnight.
**Hotel services** *Air-conditioning. Bar. Car park. Conference facilities. Currency exchange. Disabled: access, rooms. Drug store. Fax. Fitness centre. Laundry. Multi-lingual staff. Restaurants.*
**Room services** *Cable TV. Hair dryer on request. Microwave. Radio. Refrigerator. Room service. Toasters. VCR on request.*

### Wales

*1295 Madison Avenue, NY 10128, at East 92nd Street (876 6000/fax 860 7000).* **Train** 6 to 96th Street. **Rates** *single/double* from $155; *suite* from $215. **Credit** AmEx, MC, V.
The Wales is a charming, European-style turn-of-the-century hotel in the attractive Carnegie Hill historic district. There's complimentary afternoon tea served in the delightful Pied Piper Room, a Victorian-style parlour with palm plants, red roses and, occasionally, a harpist or pianist. Some of the higher corner suites overlook the Central Park reservoir. Quite an oasis.
**Hotel services** *Air-conditioning. Car park. Disabled: access, rooms. Fax. Laundry. Multi-lingual staff. Restaurant.*
**Room services** *Cable TV. Hair dryer. Radio. Refrigerator in some rooms. Room service. Safe. VCR. VCR library.*

### Warwick

*65 West 54th Street, NY 10019, at Sixth Avenue (247 2700/fax 957 8915).* **Train** B or Q to 57th Street/Sixth Avenue. **Rates** *single* $180; *double* $205. **Credit** AmEx, DC, JCB, MC, V.
Built by William Randolph Hearst and patronised by Elvis and the Beatles in the 1950s and 1960s, the Warwick is still polished and gleaming. It was once an apartment building, and the rooms are exceptionally large by Midtown standards. Ask for a view of Sixth Avenue (double glazing keeps out the noise). The top floor suite, once the home of Cary Grant, is bookable for wedding ceremonies.
**Hotel services** *Air-conditioning. Babysitting. Bar. Car park. Conference facilities. Currency exchange. Disabled: access, rooms. Drug store. Fax. Fitness centre. Laundry. Men's clothing store. Multi-lingual staff. Restaurant. Theatre desk.*
**Room services** *Cable TV. Hair dryer. Mini-bar. Radio. Refrigerator. Room service. Safe. VCR.*

### Wyndham Hotel

*42 West 58th Street, NY 10019, between Fifth & Sixth Avenues (753 3500/1-800 257 1111/fax 754 5638).* **Train** N or R to Fifth Avenue; B or Q to Sixth Avenue/57th Street. **Rates** *single* $115-$125; *double* $130-$140; *suite* $175-$205. **Credit** AmEx, DC, MC, V.
Popular with actors and directors, the Wyndham contains generous rooms and beautiful spacious suites (no cooking facilities) with walk-in closets. It's in a good location and keenly priced so book well ahead.
**Hotel services** *Air-conditioning. Bar. Disabled: access, rooms. Fax. Multi-lingual staff. Restaurant.*
**Room services** *Cable TV. Hair dryer on request. Radio. Refrigerator in suites only.*

## Under $100

### Comfort Inn Murray Hill

*42 West 35th Street, NY 10001, between Fifth & Sixth Avenues (947 0200/1-800 228 5150/fax 594 3047).* **Train** B, D, F, N, Q or R to 34th Street. **Rates** *single* $99-$109; *double* $114-$139. **Credit** AmEx, DC, CB, JCB, MC, V.

A small, family-oriented hotel around the corner from Macy's and the Empire State Building, which underwent a $4.5 million renovation several years ago. Guests get a free continental breakfast complete with *New York Times*. Alex at the front desk is a hoot. A hotel fixture for more than 13 years, he loves collecting bizarre English place names, so take along a Ramsbottom or a Puddletown.

**Hotel services** *Air-conditioning. Fax. Multi-lingual staff.*
**Room services** *Cable TV. Hair dryer on request. Radio.*

### Edison

*228 West 47th Street, NY 10036, near Broadway (840 5000/1-800 637 7070/fax 596 6850).* **Train** N or R to 49th Street. **Rates** *single* $95; *double* $105; *suite* $108-$145. **Credit** AmEx, DC, Discover, JCB, MC, V.

After its full renovation, the Edison looks decidedly spruced up. The colourful art deco lobby is particularly lovely and even the green marble-lined corridors look good. Rooms are standard. As wells as Sofia's Restaurant, there's a supper club, café and the English-style Rum House bar.

**Hotel services** *Air-conditioning. Babysitting. Bar. Beauty salon. Car park. Currency exchange. Disabled: access, rooms. Dry cleaning. Fax (guest fax 596 6868). Laundry. Multi-lingual staff. Restaurants. Travel/tour desk.*
**Room services** *Cable TV. Hair dryer on request. Radio.*

### Excelsior

*45 West 81st Street, NY 10024, between Columbus Avenue & Central Park West (362 9200/1-800 368 4575/fax 721 2994).* **Train** 1 or 9 to 79th Street; C or D to 81st Street. **Rates** *single* from $65; *double* from $75; *suite* from $99. **Credit** AmEx, MC, V.

A favourite with visiting lecturers at the American Museum of Natural History, this is a comfortable Midtown hotel close to Central Park.

**Hotel services** *Air-conditioning. Coffee shop. Fax.*
**Room services** *TV. Radio. Kitchenettes in suites. Refrigerator in suites. Room service from coffee shop.*

### Howard Johnson

*429 Park Avenue South, NY 10016, between 29th & 30th Streets (532 4860/1-800 258 4290/fax 545 9727).* **Train** N or R to 28th Street; 6 to 28th Street/Park. **Rates** *single* $89-$109; *double* $95-$145; *suite* $135-$215. Children under 18 free if with an adult. **Credit** AmEx, DC, Discover, JCB, MC, V.

Popular with Europeans, this recently renovated hotel offers particularly good value suites and friendly staff. There's a small breakfast bar which doubles as a cocktail lounge in the evenings. Enough to make you forget you're at the less fashionable end of Park Avenue.

**Hotel services** *Air-conditioning. Babysitting on request. Bar. Disabled: access, rooms. Fax. Laundry. Multi-lingual staff.*
**Room services** *Cable TV. Hair dryer. Mini-bar. Radio. Refrigerator in suites. Room service for breakfast only.*

### Iroquois

*49 West 44th Street, NY 10036, between Fifth & Sixth Avenues (840 3080/1-800 332 7220/fax 398 1754).* **Train** 4, 5, 6 or 7 to Grand Central. **Rates** *single* $75-$99; *double* $85-$125; *suite* $120-$200. **Credit** AmEx, DC, JCB, MC, V.

It's hard to imagine James Dean kickin' back in any of the Iroquois' dusky pink and blue rooms but he was a guest here in 1951, staying in room 82. These days the hotel is favoured by hard-up tourists.

**Hotel services** *Air-conditioning. Bars. Fax. Laundry. Multi-lingual staff. Two restaurants. Barber's.*
**Room services** *Cable TV. Hair dryer on request. Radio. Refrigerator. Room service. Computer & fax on request.*

### Manhattan

*17 West 32rd Street, NY 10001, between Broadway & Fifth Avenue (736 1600/800 551 2303 or 0800 964 002 from the UK/fax 563 4007).* **Train** N to 23rd Street. **Rates** *single* $85-$95; *doubles* from $95; *suites* from $130; *quads* $105-$115; *family suites* (three beds) $160. **Credit** AmEx, DC, Discover, JCB, MC, V.

A good-value hotel – particularly for two or more – with a swish monochrome lobby, reasonably sized rooms and funky Empire State Building and Statue of Liberty bedside lights. It was recently renovated and some rooms are themed for different areas so guests can choose between a sophisticated Fifth Avenue or a trendier SoHo decor.

**Hotel services** *Air-conditioning. Beauty salon. Disabled: access, rooms. Fax. Multi-lingual staff. Restaurant. Valet parking.*
**Room services** *Cable TV. Hair dryer & mini-bar in most rooms.*

### Olcott

*27 West 72nd Street, NY 10023, off Central Park West (877 4200/fax 580 0511).* **Train** 1, 2, 3, or 9 to 72nd Street. **Rates** *single* $85; *double* $95; *suite* $115. **Credit** MC, V.

Furnishings are basic but the Olcott is good value – suites especially – and it's right by Central Park. Try and get an upgrade.

**Hotel services** *Air-conditioning. Bar. Beauty salon. Disabled: access. Fax. Multi-lingual staff. Restaurant.*
**Room services** *Cable TV. Refrigerator.*

### Howard Johnson's on 34th Street

*215 West 34th Street, NY 10001, between Seventh & Eighth Avenues (947 5050/1-800 633 1911/fax 268 4829).* **Train** 1, 2, 3 or 9 to 34th Street/Penn Station. **Rates** *single* $77-$105; *double* $95-$120; *suite* from $150. **Credit** AmEx, DC, Discover, JCB, MC, V.

Although recently refurbished, the rooms are still basic (though clean and soundproofed) and the suites rather small. It's in a busy street, close to Macy's, the garment district, Penn Station and the Empire State Building. Prices include continental breakfast.

**Hotel services** *Air-conditioning. Disabled: access. Fax. Multi-lingual staff. Non-smoking floors. Snack bar.*
**Room services** *Hair dryer in suites. Radio. Refrigerator in suites. TV.*

### Pickwick Arms

*230 East 51st Street, NY 10022, between Second & Third Avenues (355 0300/fax 755 5029).* **Train** 6 to 51st Street. **Rates** *single* $45-$75; *double* $95-$105; *studio* $110. **Credit** AmEx, DC, MC, V.

This offers one of the best hotel rates for poorly served single customers and, although rooms are small, it's clean and in a reasonably quiet district. Handy for restaurants, cinemas, Radio City Music Hall and the United Nations. Most, but not all, rooms have private bathroom.

**Hotel services** *Air-conditioning. Coffee shop. Fax. Multi-lingual staff.*
**Room services** *Radio. Room service. TV. Voice mail.*

### Ramada Milford Plaza

*270 West 45th Street, NY 10036, at Eighth Avenue (869 3600/1-800 221 2690/fax 944 8357).* **Train** 1, 9, 7, A or C to 42nd Street/Port Authority. **Rates** *single* $95-$149; *double* $110-$164. **Credit** AmEx, Discover, JCB, CB, MC, V.

This enormous hotel has a hideous shopping mall lobby whose lighting makes guests resemble extras from *The Living Dead*. It was recently renovated but nothing can give

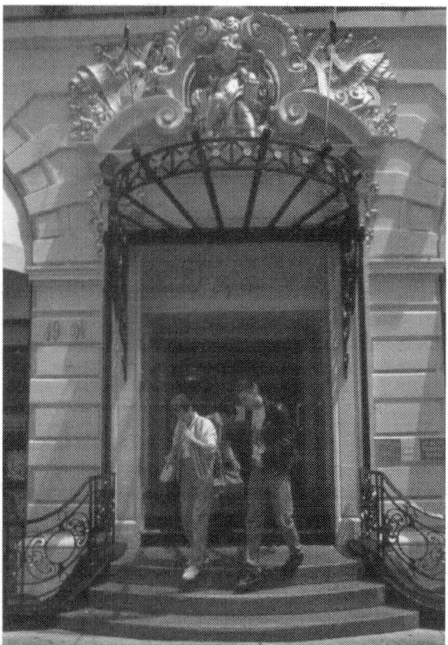

*Good value at the* **Herald Square**, *page 31.*

a place this big much in the way of character. Handy for Broadway shows and there's 24-hour security.
**Hotel services** *Air-conditioning. Bar. Beauty salon. Car park. Conference facilities. Disabled: access. Fax. Fitness centre. Laundry. Multi-lingual staff. Restaurant. Tour/transport desk.*
**Room services** *Cable TV. Radio.*

### Remington Hotel

*129 West 46th Street, NY 10036, between Sixth Avenue & Broadway (221 2600/fax 764 7481).* **Train** 1, 2, 3, 7, 9, N, R or S to Times Square/42nd Street. **Rates** *single/double* $70 with shared bathroom; *single* $85-$90 with bathroom; *double* $95 with bathroom; *triples/quads* $95-$100. **Credit** AmEx, DC, JCB, MC, V.
Another hotel in the Times Square district, this is cheap, clean and basic.
**Hotel services** *Air-conditioning. Fax. Lifts. Multi-lingual staff. Restaurant.*
**Room services** *Cable TV. Hair dryer on request. Radio.*

### Rosoff's Hotel

*147 West 43rd Street, NY 10036, between Sixth Avenue & Broadway (869 1212/fax 944 6223).* **Train** 1, 2, 3, 7, 9, N, R or S to Times Square/42nd Street. **Rates** *single* $79; *double* $89; *triple* $99; *quad* $109. **Credit** AmEx, MC, V.
This decent European-style hotel provides good access to the theatre district. There's a laundry and seating area on the second floor.
**Hotel services** *Air-conditioning. Conference facilities. Disabled: access, rooms. Fax. Laundry. Multi-lingual staff. Restaurant.*
**Room services** *Cable TV. Radio. Refrigerator at reception.*

### Washington Square Hotel

*103 Waverly Place, NY 10011, between Fifth & Sixth Avenues, corner of MacDougal Street (777 9515/1-800 222 0418/fax 979 8373).* **Train** A, B, C, D, E, F or Q to West 4th Street. **Rates** *single* $60-$70; *double* $89-$99; *quads* $128. **Credit** AmEx, JCB, MC, V.
In the heart of Greenwich Village, across from the Washington Arch, this hotel represents extremely good value given that it's in such a great location. All rooms have been refurbished and rates include continental breakfast. Look for the flamboyantly decorated tiles in the corridors and restaurant. They're by Rita Paul, the manager's wife, who has a kiln downstairs.
**Hotel services** *Air-conditioning. Babysitting. Bar. Conference facilities. Coffee shop. Fax. Fitness centre. Multi-lingual staff. Restaurant.*
**Room services** *Hair dryer on request.*

### Wellington

*871 Seventh Avenue, NY 10019, at 55th Street (247 3900/fax 581 1719).* **Train** N or R to 57th Street/Seventh Avenue. **Rates** *single/double* $120; *suite* from $145; *triple* $135. **Credit** AmEx, DC, Discover, JCB, MC, V.
A centrally located hotel, close to Central Park, Broadway and the Museum of Modern Art, with a diner and steakhouse. Popular with tour groups.
**Hotel services** *Air-conditioning. Bar. Beauty salon. Car park. Conference facilities. Disabled: access. Fax. Laundry. Multi-lingual staff. Restaurant. Ticket service.*
**Room services** *Cable TV. Refrigerator in some rooms. Room service.*

### Wentworth Hotel

*59 West 46th Street, NY 10036, between Fifth & Sixth Avenues (719 2300/toll-free 800 848 0020/fax 768 3477).* **Train** B, D, F or Q to Rockefeller Centre. **Rates** *single* $85; *double* $95; *two doubles* $105-$120; *suite* $130-150. **Credit** AmEx, CB, DC, MC, V.
Despite a recent renovation, the lobby is filled with tacky murals of New York City and the rooms with equally tasteless prints. Still, if you can cope with the decor, it's reasonably priced and well located for the theatre.
**Hotel services** *Air-conditioning. Beauty salon. Barber shop. Fax. Multi-lingual staff.*
**Room services** *Cable TV. Radio.*

### Westpark Hotel

*308 West 58th Street, NY 10019, between Eighth & Ninth Avenues (246 6440/1-800 248 6440/fax 246 3131).* **Train** 1, 9, A, B, C or D to Columbus Circle. **Rates** *single* $70-$100; *double* $80-$110. **Credit** AmEx, DC, Discover, JCB, MC, V.
This is quite a catch. The Westpark is cheap and rooms are small but it's around the corner from the Lincoln Center and Central Park. During the day the tiny Columbus Circle street market sets up stalls on the pavement opposite. Book well in advance. Park views cost more.
**Hotel services** *Air-conditioning. Fax. Multi-lingual staff.*
**Room services** *Hair dryer.*

## Budget

### Broadway American

*2178 Broadway, at 77th Street, NY 10024 (362 1100/fax 787 9521).* **Train** 1 or 9 to 79th Street. **Rates** *single* $45, *double* $65, with shared bathroom; *single* $79, *double* $89, with private bathroom. **Credit** AmEx, DC, MC, V.
Lots of hotel for your money, as the rooms are huge and decorated in a spruce, vaguely art deco style. There's a 24-hour restaurant on the premises and numerous places to eat on Amsterdam Avenue around the corner. The Natural History Museum is a couple of blocks away along with Central Park and the recently opened New York Historical Society.
**Hotel services** *Air-conditioning. Fax. Lifts. Mulit-lingual staff.*
**Room services** *Cable. Refrigerator. Safe.*

# Dive hotels

Some hotels simply transcend minor details such as whether there's a hair dryer in the room or a beauty salon on the premises. Atmosphere is all that counts, even if they are, to all intents and purposes, dives. The **Chelsea** reigns supreme as a shabby, slightly tacky place for lovers of art, music, adventure and history. It's part hotel, part landmark. For decades, famous writers ruined their livers here and, more recently and notoriously, Sid Vicious killed his girlfriend Nancy Spungeon behind one of its doors. Beyond spectacle and sleaze, Chelsea gains kudos by supporting the arts – and its own legend at the same time, of course. In this respect **Hotel 17** also holds its own, even though its rooms are laughable in both decor and facilities. Yet it could, in years to come, totally overshadow the Chelsea because of its chic crowd of fashion designers, fashion models and fashion victims. It's the place to stay if you're a frenetic clubber or drag queen – although manager Billy Candis can't understand why British transvestites, dressed to the nines and wearing high heels, always register under their own masculine names. Call me madam? The **Carlton Arms** can't compete against the two major leaguers' trendiness but what it lacks in street-life authenticity it makes up with colour. This budget hotel treats itself as an artist's canvas. Some rooms work brilliantly but others are so lurid they send people rushing into the kaleidoscopically mosaic bathroom. So naff and basic it's almost kitsch.

### Carlton Arms

*160 East 25th Street, NY 10010, near Third Avenue (679 0680/684 8337).* **Train** 6 to 23rd Street. **Rates** *single* $44-$53; *double* $57-$65; all rooms cheaper with shared bath. **Credit** MC, V.

A cheerful basic budget/dive hotel popular with Europeans. The corridors are brightly decorated with murals of New York City and each room has been painted by a different artist. Hit and miss, but fun – we like the astroturf in one of the bathrooms. Discounts for students and overseas guests.

**Hotel services** *Multi-lingual staff. Cafe. Telephone in lobby.*

**Room services** *Hair dryer on request.*

### Chelsea

222 West 23rd Street, NY 10011, between Seventh & Eighth Avenues (243 3700). **Train** 1, 2, 3 or 9 to West 23rd Street. **Rates** *single* $110; *double* $125-$300; *studio* $145; *suite* from $225. **Credit** AmEx, MC, V.

The Chelsea has a reputation to uphold. Plaques dedicated to former residents Mark Twain, Thomas Wolfe and Brendan Beehan set standards for aspiring writers, while the lobby doubles as an art gallery, showing work by past and present guests. No evidence remains of the hotel's infamous murder in room 100 – where Sid Vicious killed Nancy Spungeon – as the room was immediately destroyed to make a larger apartment. Although there's an air of seediness, the Chelsea has atmosphere. Stay if you want an adventure and can cope with the occasional cockroach. Most, but not all, rooms have a private bathroom.

**Hotel services** *Air-conditioning. Disabled: access, rooms. Fax. Multi-lingual staff. Valet parking.*

**Room services** *Kitchenettes & refrigerators in some rooms. Safe. TV.*

### Hotel 17

*225 East 17th Street, NY 10003, between Second & Third Avenues (475 2845/fax 677 8178).* **Train** 4, 5, 6, L, N or R to Union Square. **Rates** *single* $55; *double* $65-$90; *weekly rates from* £210. **No credit cards**.

The magazine ads say it all: no room service, no bright lights, no phony staff, no rip-off prices. Seventeen is the ultimate dive hotel and one of the hippest places to stay if you're an artist, clubber or drag queen. The rooms are basic beyond belief but that didn't stop Madonna showing her knickers for the front cover of *Details* magazine in room 114. Manager Billy Candis encourages his guests' talents and increases their contacts. Makeovers on request and leave anything of value in the safe. Think of it as an experience.

**Hotel services** *Air-conditioning in some rooms. Fax. Laundry. Roof terrace.*

**Room services** *Cable TV in some rooms. Hair dryer on request.*

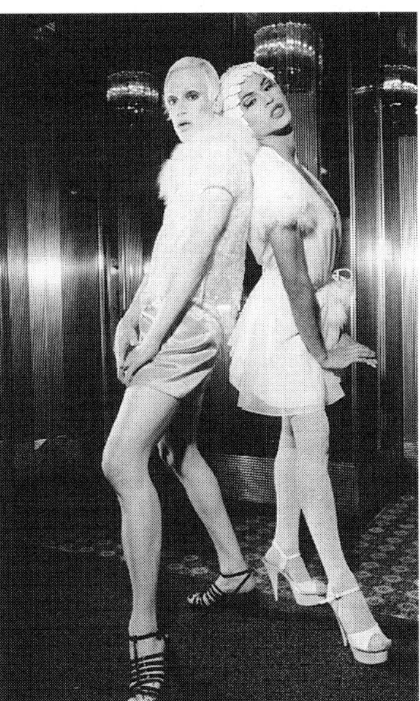

**Hotel 17** – *great for pose value.*

### Gershwin Hotel

*7 East 27th Street, NY 10016, between Fifth & Madison Avenues (545 8000/fax 684 5546).* **Train** N or R to 28th Street; 6 to 28th Street. **Rates** $20 per person in 4-8 bed dorms; $65-$82 for 1-3 people in private rooms. **Credit** MC, V.

The colourful, snazzy Gershwin, offering extremely good value accommodation just off Fifth Avenue, is a recent and welcome addition to New York's hotel scene. It's dedicated to pop art and there's a Campbell's soup can on display in the foyer, autographed by Warhol himself. British artist Lynne Packwood was given free rein with the decor and has clearly had a ball. The lobby is a homage to Roy Lichtenstein, the wine bar attractively umber and the TV room has a Statue of Liberty motif and an enormous carved wooden 1908 fireplace. The rooms are clean and bright, each with its own quirk of decor. There's even an astroturf roof terrace. The Gershwin is recommended both as a budget hotel and an upmarket hostel – there are 212 beds and 62 private rooms with en-suite bathroom.

**Hotel services** *Bars. Fax. Lockers. Multi-lingual staff. Non-smoking hotel. Public telephones. Restaurant. Roof garden. Transport desk.*
**Room services** *TV in private rooms.*

### Herald Square

*19 West 31st Street, NY 10001, between Fifth Avenue& Broadway (279 4017/1-800 727 1888/fax 643 9208).* **Train** 1, 2, 3 or 9 to 34th Street/Penn Station. **Rates** *single* $45-$75; *double* $60-$95. **Credit** AmEx, Discover, JCB, MC, V.

Herald Square was the original *Life* magazine building and retains its charming cherub-adorned entrance. All rooms were recently renovated and most have private bathrooms; corridors are filled with framed *Life* illustrations. Well located for Macy's and the Empire State Building at the edge of the garment district, it's a good deal, so book well in advance. Discounts for ISIC members and holders of an International Youth Travel Card.

**Hotel services** *Air-conditioning. Fax. Multi-lingual staff.*
**Room services** *Cable TV. Radio. Safe.*

### Malibu Studios Hotel

*2688 Broadway, NY 10025, at 103rd Street (222 2954/fax 678 6842).* **Train** 1 or 9 to 103rd Street. **Rates** *single* from $35; *double* from $50. **No credit cards.**

The kitsch canopy above the entrance prepares visitors for the stencilled palm trees on the blue lobby walls. This is basic, clean, no-frills accommodation: there are no room telephones but there is a messaging service. Only 40 of the 150 rooms have private bathrooms. Staff are friendly.

**Hotel services** *Air-conditioning in rooms with private bathrooms. Fax. Laundry. Multi-lingual staff.*
**Room services** *Refrigerator. TV in rooms with private bathrooms.*

### Off-Soho Suites

*11 Rivington Street, NY 10002, between Christie & the Bowery (979 9808/1-800 OFF SOHO or 800 633 7646/fax 979 9801).* **Train** F, B or D to Grand Street. **Rates** *suite for two* $79; *suite for four* $129. **Credit** AmEx, MC, V.

Excellent value for suite accommodation, but the Lower East Side location might not suit everyone. If you're into clubbing, bars and the SoHo scene, however, then it's perfectly placed – just off the Bowery near Little Italy. Take a cab back at night. All suites are well sized, spotlessly clean and bright, with a fully equipped kitchen and polished wooden floors. There's a new café on the ground floor by the lobby.

**Hotel services** *Air-conditioning. Car park. Café Disabled: access, rooms. Fax. Fitness room. Laundry. Multi-lingual staff.*
**Room services** *TV. Hair dryer. Microwave. Refrigerator. Room service.*

*The* **Vanderbilt YMCA**. *See page 32.*

### Park Savoy

*158 West 58th Street, NY 10019, between Sixth & Seventh Avenues (245 5755/fax 765 0668).* **Train** A, B, C, D, 1 or 9 to Columbus Circle. **Rates** *single* $39 with shared bathroom; *single/double* $59 with private bathroom; *suites* from $89. **Credit** AmEx, MC, V.

Basic, cheap newly decorated rooms and an Italian restaurant downstairs. Not much character but it's in a good Midtown location.

**Hotel services** *Air-conditioning. Disabled: access. Fax. Multi-lingual staff. Restaurant.*
**Room services** *Cable TV.*

### Portland Square Hotel

*132 West 47th Street, NY 10036, between Sixth & Seventh Avenues (382 0600/1-800 388 8988/fax 382 0684).* **Train** 1, 2, 3, 7, 9, N, R or S to Times Square/42nd Street. **Rates** *single* $45-$99; *double* $79-$99. **Credit** AmEx, JCB, MC, V.

Basic, recently renovated and good value, the Portland Square is one of the older hotels in the theatre district. James Cagney once stayed here but today it's popular with less theatrical Europeans. Discounts for ISIC card-carrying students.

**Hotel services** *Air-conditioning. Conference facilities. Fax. Fitness room. Laundry. Multi-lingual staff.*
**Room services** *Cable TV. Radio. Safe.*

### Riverside Towers Hotel

*80 Riverside Drive, NY 10024, at 80th Street (877 5200/1-800 724 3136/fax 873 1400).* **Train** 1 or 9 to 79th Street. **Rates** *single* $45-$50; *double* $55; *suite* $65-$85 **Credit** AmEx, MC, V.

A good price for the Upper West Side and the only hotel located on the Hudson River. This provides some good views but accommodation is basic and this is strictly a place to sleep. The wonderful Zabar's deli is around the corner on Broadway.

**Hotel Services** *Air-conditioning. Fax. Laundry. Multi-lingual staff.*
**Room services** *TV. Hair dryer on request. Refrigerator.*

### Wolcott

*4 West 31st Street, NY 10001, between Broadway & Fifth Avenues (268 2900/fax 563 0096).* **Train** 1, 2, 3 or 9 to 34th Street/Penn Station. **Rates** *single* $70; *double* $75; *suite* from $85. **Credit** AmEx, JCB, MC, V.

The ornate, gilded, mirror-lined lobby comes as a surprise in this garment district hotel. Rooms are small but inexpensive and air conditioned.

**Hotel services** *Air-conditioning. Bar. Fax. Laundry. Multi-lingual staff.*

**Room services** *Cable TV.*

## Hostels

### Banana Bungalow

*250 West 77th, NY 10024, at Broadway (769 2441/1-800 6HOSTEL/fax 877 5733).* **Train** 1 or 9 to 79th Street. **Rates** $15-$18 per person in 6-bed dorms including linen and lockers. **Credit** MC, V.

This is only a place to stay if you want to save money at all costs. It shares rooms with the rather seedy Hotel Belleclaire in the same block and only accepts international (non-American) travellers. There's a maximum stay of two weeks and the small rooms are crammed tight with three bunk beds, rather like a Chinese crash pad in south east Asia. As there's no air-conditioning, think twice during the summer. It's well located in the Upper West Side and, surprisingly, there's a roof garden with a good view over the Hudson River.

**Hotel services** *Fax. Multi-lingual staff. TV lounge/common room.*

**Room services** *Refrigerator in some rooms. Telephones (incoming calls only).*

### Chelsea Center

*313 West 29th Street, NY 10001, between Eighth & Ninth Avenues (643 0214/fax 473 3945).* **Train** A, C or E to 34th Street. **Rates** $18-$20 per person in dorm including linen. **No credit cards.**

A small, friendly hostel with clean bathrooms and a patio/garden at the back. It has the feel of a shared student house and, as there are a limited number of beds in each dorm, try to book at least a week in advance. No curfew. Price includes continental breakfast.

**Hotel services** *All rooms non-smoking. Fax. Multi-lingual staff. Patio. Kitchen facilities. TV room. Garden/patio.*

### International House of New York.

*500 Riverside Drive, NY 10027, at 122nd Street (316 6300/fax 316 8415).* **Train** 1 or 9 to 116th street. **Rates** *single* $25-$35; *double/suite* $85-$110. **Credit** MC, V.

This student-only hostel is in a peaceful location surrounded by college buildings and overlooking the small but well-tended Sakura park. There's a subsidised cafeteria with main dishes at around $3 and a delightful living room and terrace overlooking the park. Only the suites have private bathroom.

**Hotel services** *Air-conditioning in suites. Bar. Cafeteria. Conference facilities. Fax. Games room. Laundry. Multi-lingual staff. Gymnasium. TV room.*

### New York International American Youth Hostel

*891 Amsterdam Avenue, NY 10025, at 103rd Street (932 2300/fax 932 2574).* **Train** 1 or 9 to 103rd Street. **Rates** $22 for bed in dorm sleeping 10-12 people; $23 for bed in dorm sleeping 6-8; $25 in rooms sleeping 4; $3 extra for non-members; en-suite rooms sleeping 1-4 $75. **Credit** MC, V.

The hostel building, formerly a home for women, was designed by the man behind the Statue of Liberty, Richard Morris Hunt. With 500 beds, it's pretty large and was recently renovated to include a new coffee bar with CD juke box. Rooms sleep two, four, six or eight and are basic but clean. Staff are friendly and there's a pleasant garden at the back.

**Hotel services** *Air-conditioning. All rooms non-smoking. Café. Conference facilities. Disabled: access, rooms. Fax. Garden. Laundry. Lockers. Multi-lingual staff. Travel bureau. TV lounge & games room.*

### YMHA (de Hirsch Residence at the 92nd St Y)

*1395 Lexington Avenue, NY 10128, at 92nd Street (415 5650/1-800 858 4692/fax 415 5578).* **Train** 6 to 96th Street. **Rates** *for stays less than two months* $210 per week or $440-$525 per month in shared room; *for stays greater than two months* $294 per week or $650 per month in private rooms. **Credit** AmEx, MC, V.

The Young Men's Hebrew Association is rather like its Christian counterpart, the YMCA, in that to stay there you don't have to be young, male or – in this case – Jewish. All rooms are spacious and clean with two desks and plenty of closet space. There are kitchen and dining facilities on each floor. As well as its classy Upper East Side location, the YMHA is good for tours, lectures and classes.

**Hotel services** *Air-conditioning (extra charge). Disabled: access, rooms. Fitness centre with pool, steam room & sauna (free for weekly rates). Laundry. Library. Multi-lingual staff. Public telephones on each floor. TV lounge.*

**Room services** *Refrigerator on request.*

### YMCA (Vanderbilt)

*224 East 47th Street, NY 10017, between Second & Third Avenues (756 9600/fax 752 0210).* **Train** 4, 5, 6 or 7 to Grand Central. **Rates** *single* $46-$49; *double* $57-$72; *suites $95.* **Credit** MC, V.

A cheerful standard YMCA that was completely redone in 1992. There's a restaurant and two pools and while the more expensive rooms have sinks, they are not particularly large. Some rooms can barely fit the beds in. Try and book well in advance by writing to the Reservations Department and including a deposit for one night's rent. There are 377 rooms but only executive suites have private bath.

**Hotel services** *Air-conditioning. Conference facilities. Fax. Laundry. Multi-lingual staff. Restaurant. Disabled: access, rooms. Gift shop. Left luggage room. Sport & fitness facilities including two pools. Public telephones on each floor.*

**Room services** *All rooms non-smoking. Cable TV. Radio. Refrigerator on request. Room service.*

### YMCA (West Side)

*5 West 63rd Street, NY 10023, between Central Park West & Broadway (787 4400/fax 875 1334).* **Train** !, 9, A, B, C or D to Columbus Circle. **Rates** *single* $47-$75; *double* $57-$85. **Credit** MC, V.

A large, echoing building close to Central Park and the Lincoln Centre, whose rooms are simple and clean. Book well in advance. A deposit is required to hold a reservation. Most of the 540 rooms have shared bathrooms.

**Hotel services** *Air-conditioning. Cafeteria. Disabled: access, rooms. Fax. Laundry. Multi-lingual staff. Sport & fitness facilities including swimming pool.*

**Room services** *Cable TV.*

## Bed & Breakfast

New York's bed and breakfast scene is deceptively large. There are thousands of beds available but as there isn't a central B&B organisation rooms aren't publicised terribly well – and there are no boards up outside the houses, either. The term is used slightly differently: many of the rooms are unhosted and breakfast is usually continental (if it exists at all), so the main difference from a hotel is in the more personal ambiance. Prices are not necessarily extremely low – some hotels in the budget section are cheaper, for instance – but B&Bs are a good way of feeling less like a tourist and more like a New Yorker, especially if you go for a hosted room. Sales tax of 8.25% is applicable on hosted rooms but not on unhosted apartments if staying for more than seven days.

### At Home in New York Inc

*PO Box 407, NY 10185 (956 3125/1-800 692 4262/fax 247 3249. Private number so please call at reasonable hour).* **Rates** *hosted single* from $60; *hosted double* from $75; *unhosted studio* from $100. **Credit** AmEx, MC, V.
Reasonably priced accommodation in more than 300 properties, most of them in Manhattan, with a few in Brooklyn. There's a two-night minimum requirement.

### Bed & Breakfast (& Books)

*35 West 92nd Street, Apt 2C, NY 10025 (865 8740. Private number, please call between 10am-5pm Mon-Fri).* **Rates** *hosted single* $55-$70; *hosted double* $45-$90; *unhosted studio* from $100. **No credit cards.**
Several of the hosts in this organisation are literary types, hence the bookish title. Prices for the 40 hosted and unhosted rooms vary from $75 for a single/$85 double to up to $200 for two-bedroomed apartments.

### Bed & Breakfast in Manhattan

*PO Box 533, NY 10150 (472 2528/fax 988 9818).* **Rates** *hosted* $65-$95; *unhosted* from $100. **No credit cards.**
Each of the 100 or so properties have been personally vetted by the owner – who, as a woman, is particularly concerned about late-night safety for female travellers.

### Bed & Breakfast Network

*134 West 32nd Street, Suite 602, NY 10001 (645 8134/1-800 900 8134).* **Rates** *hosted single* $50-$70 or $300-$450 weekly; *hosted double* $80-$90 or $500-$600 weekly; *unhosted apartments* $90-$300 or $600-$2000 weekly. **No credit cards.**
The B&B Network has more than 200 properties, mainly in Manhattan. The best deals are for stays of a week or more; monthly rates are best, generally three times the weekly rate. A 25 per cent deposit is required in advance with the balance payable on arrival to the host by cash or travellers cheque.

### City Lights Bed & Breakfast

*PO Box 20355, NY 10021 (737 7049 9am-5pm Mon-Fri; 9am-noon Sat/24 hour fax 535 2755).* **Rates** *hosted single* private bathroom $75-$85, shared bath $60-$65; *hosted double* private bathroom $85-$97; *unhosted 1-4 bedroom apartments* $95-$250. **Credit** DC, MC, V.
A helpful agency requiring a minimum two-night stay and a 25 per cent deposit.

### Colby International

*139 Round Hey, Liverpool, L28 1RG, UK (0151 220 5848/fax 0151 228 5453).* **Open** 9am-5.30pm Mon-Fri. **Rates** *hosted single* $55-$75; *hosted double* $70-$85; *studio* from $90; *one-bedroom apartment* $110-$140; *two-bedroom apartments* from $170. **No credit cards.**
This British-based B&B organisation offers hundreds of places in Manhattan. Cheaper rates apply for stays longer than seven days (unhosted only) and a small deposit is required. Minimum stay three nights.

### New World Bed & Breakfast

*150 Fifth Avenue, Suite 711, NY 10011 (675 5600/fax 675 6366).* **Rates** *hosted single* $60-$70; *hosted double* $80-$90; *unhosted studio* $70-$120; *unhosted 1-bedroom apartment* $120-$135. Larger apartments also available. **Credit** AmEx, DC, MC, V.
Accommodation is most neighbourhoods of Manhattan. Hosted apartments include continental breakfast and there are reduced rates for monthly stays.

### Urban Ventures Inc

*38 West 32nd Street, Suite 1412, NY 10001 (594 5650/fax 947 9320).* **Open** 9am-5pm Mon-Fri. **Rates** *hosted single* from $65; *hosted double* from $80; *unhosted studios* $100-$120; *unhosted one-bedroom apartments* from $150; *unhosted two-bedroom apartments* from $280; *three-bedroom apartments* from $240.**Credit** AmEx, DC, Discover, MC, V.
One of the oldest and largest agencies in New York. There's a two-night minimum stay.

## Apartments

### Apartments International

*67 Chiltern Street, London, W1M 1HS, UK (0171 935 3551/fax 0171 935 5351).* **Open** 7am-10pm Mon-Fri. **Rates** from £450 per week. **No credit cards.**
A recent venture offering more than 150 unhosted apartments in Manhattan, mostly on the Upper East side. The one-bedroom apartments have two twin beds. A 20 per cent deposit is required, with the balance payable a full eight weeks before departure. There's a minimum three-night stay.

## Hotel reservation agencies

These companies block-book reservations in advance and can therefore offer reduced rates on hotel rooms. Discounts cover most price ranges from economy upwards and although some agencies claim savings of up to 65 per cent, around 20 per cent is more likely. If you already know where you'd like to stay it's worth calling-up a few agencies before booking directly in case the hotel is on their list. The following agencies work with selected hotels in New York and are free of charge.

### Central Reservation Service

*11420 North Kendall Drive, Miami, Florida 33176 (305 274 6832/1-800 950 0232).*

### Hotel Reservations Network

*8140 Walnut Hill Lane, Suite 1010, Dallas, Texas 75231 (1-800 964 6835/96 HOTEL).*
Operating in a number of cities and promises rooms even if a city is 'sold out', although the discount is then forfeited. Rates in New York: $69-$280.

### Express Hotel Reservations

*3800 Arapahoe, Boulder, Colorado 80303 (1-303 440 8481/1-800 440 8481).*

### The Room Exchange

*450 Seventh Avenue, NY 10123 (760 1000/1-800 846 7000/fax 760 1013).*

# New York by Season

***New Yorkers love a parade. And a circus; and fireworks; and baseball; and a carnival.... From the summer fun of Central Park's free concerts to the Christmas Spectacular at Radio City, the calendar is never empty.***

Each new season, New York undergoes a personality change. The romance of the winter – when the ice skaters whirl around the Rockefeller Center – is a sudden transformation from autumn's calming warmth, with its film festivals, and the beginning of the opera, dance and music seasons. Spring is a flower-filled wake-up call from the wrappings of winter. And summertime is hot and sweaty and lived outdoors, at cafés, street festivals, concerts and theatre in the parks and by the river.

The following parades and events are held regularly. For more information, including newer and smaller happenings which may not be included here, contact the New York Convention and Visitors Bureau (397 8200), open 9am-6pm Mon-Fri; 10am-6pm Sat, Sun, public holidays. For other sources of entertainment information, *see chapter* **Media**. Don't forget to confirm that an event is happening before you head off to attend it.

## Spring

### New York Flower Show

*(757 0915 information).* **Date** early Mar.

The Horticultural Society of New York always announces its annual show with a Peter Max poster. The usual location is the passenger-ship terminal at Pier 92, which is turned into a series of gardens for nine days. Blooms and marrows are judged and a series of lectures is held. Plants are for sale.

### Whitney Biennial

*Whitney Museum of American Art, 945 Madison Avenue, at 75th St (570 3600).* **Train** 6 to 77th Street. **Date** early Mar-mid June.

The Whitney showcases the most important American art each two years, generating much controversy in the process. The next show is in 1997.

### St Patrick's Day Parade

*Fifth Avenue, from 44th to 86th Streets (397 8222 information).* **Date** 17 Mar.

New York becomes a mass of green for the annual American-Irish day of days, starting at 11am with the parade up Fifth Avenue and ending in bars all over the city late into the night. The Avenue is decorated with a green stripe to guide the marchers, requiring 40gal (180l) of paint.

### Earth Day

**Date** spring equinox (March 20/21 depending on Mother Nature).

Celebrations include the ringing of the UN peace bell at the moment the sun crosses the equator, when there is singing, dancing and cries for people to take care of the earth. Various institutions organise their own events, including ecological street fairs.

### Ringling Brothers and Barnum & Bailey Circus

*Madison Square Garden, Seventh Avenue, between 31st & 33rd Streets (465 6741).* **Train** 1, 2, 3, 9, A, C or E to Penn Station. **Date** late Mar-early May.

One half of this famous three-ring circus – the Barnum & Bailey half – annexed the line 'The Greatest Show on Earth' back in its early days in New York City. There is usually a parade of animals through the streets to open the circus.

### Baseball season begins

**Date** Apr-Oct. *See chapter* **Sport & Fitness**.

### Easter Parade

*Fifth Avenue, from 44th to 59th Streets (397 8222).* **Date** Easter Sunday.

The annual Easter Sunday parade. Try and get a spot around St Patrick's Cathedral, which is the best viewing platform; but get there early.

*Don your glad rags for* **Lesbian & Gay Pride**. *See page 37.*

## Public holidays

**New Year's Day** 1 Jan
**Martin Luther King Day** third Mon in Jan
**President's Day** mid-Feb
**Memorial Day** end May
**Independence Day** 4 July
**Labor Day** 1st Mon in Sept
**Columbus Day** second Mon in Oct
**Election Day** first Tue in Nov
**Veteran's Day** Nov 11
**Thanksgiving** fourth Thur in Nov
**Christmas Day** 25 Dec

*New York's very own festival of kitsch. The* **Mermaid Parade**. *See page 39.*

### New York City Ballet Spring Season

*Lincoln Center, Broadway, at 64th Street (870 5570).* **Train** 1 or 9 to Lincoln Center. **Date** late Apr-June.
The NYCB's spring season usually features a new ballet by Jerome Robbins or Peter Martins, as well as at least one Balanchine classic.

### You Gotta Have Park

*(360 3456 information).* **Date** May.
An annual celebration of New York's public spaces, with free events in all the city's major parks. This is the signal for the start of a busy schedule of concerts and other events in green places throughout the five boroughs.

### Martin Luther King Jr Day Parade

*Fifth Avenue, from 44th to 86th Streets (information 397 8222).* **Date** 3rd Sun in May.
This annual event celebrates the life of the assassinated civil rights activist.

### Ninth Avenue International Food Festival

*Ninth Avenue, between 37-57th Streets (581 7029).* **Train** A, C or E to Penn station. **Date** mid-May.
A glorious 20 blocks full of hundreds of stalls serving every type of food. Fabulously fattening.

## Summer

### Toyota Comedy Festival

*(toll-free 1-800 79 TOYOTA).* **Date** early-mid June.
America's funniest men and women congregate in the city for some side-splitting events.

### Puerto Rico Day Parade

*Fifth Avenue, from 44th to 86th Streets (information 397 8222).* **Date** first Sun in June.
A colourful display of floats and marching bands participate in what is now one of the city's busiest street celebrations.

### Central Park Summerstage

*Rumsey Playfield, Central Park, at 72nd Street (360 CPSS).* **Train** 6 to 77th Street. **Date** June-Aug.
Free afternoon concerts featuring top international musicians and a wide variety of music. The schedule usually includes one or two paying gigs.

### Metropolitan Opera Parks Concerts

*(362 6000 information).* **Date** June.
The Metropolitan Opera Company presents two different operas at evening open-air concerts in Central Park and other parks throughout the five boroughs. They are free – tickets are available on a first-come, first-served basis, and you need to get here hours ahead to be sure of entry.

### Museum Mile Festival

*Fifth Avenue, between 82nd & 102nd Streets (535 7710 information).* **Date** second Tue in June.
Ten of New York's major museums hold an open-house festival. Crowds are attracted not only by the free admission (most of the museums are free on Tuesday evenings in any case) but by highbrow street entertainment.

### Lesbian & Gay Pride

*From Columbus Circle, downtown along Fifth Avenue to Christopher Street (807 7433 information).* **Date** late June.
Every year New York's gay community parades through the

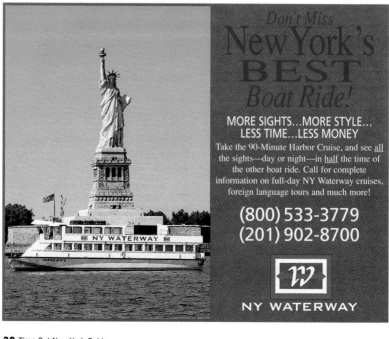

midtown streets to the Village, to commemorate the Stonewall Riots of 1968. The celebrations have expanded into a full week, and in addition to a packed clubs schedule, there is an open-air dance party on the westside piers.

### Buskers' Fare Festival

*Lower Manhattan (432 0900 information).* **Date** June-July.

A vast number of street entertainers appear in locations throughout lower Manhattan, including the Seaport and World Trade Center Plazas, in a free festival of busking. Some may decide now is the time to check out the Adirondacks.

### Shakespeare in the Park

*Delacorte Theatre, Central Park at 79th Street (598 7100).* **Train** B or C to 81st Street. **Date** late June-Sept.

The Shakespeare Festival is one of the highlights of a Manhattan summer, with big-name stars pulling on their tights for a bite of the bard. There are two plays each year and tickets are free, distributed first-come, first-served (two per person) from 1pm on the day of performance, at the Public Theater box office (not where the performances are). The queue starts early.

### JVC Jazz Festival

*(information 787 2020).* **Date** late June-early July.

Saxophonists and percussionists thrill and trill all over new York City for two weeks as some of the world's finest jazzeteers appear. Call the above number for information on programmes, venues and tickets.

### L'eggs Mini-Marathon

*starts at Central Park West at 66th Street; finishes at Tavern on the Green, Central Park West at 67th Street (860 4455).* **Date** late June.

Over 8,000 take part in the world's largest women-only road race. The course is 6.2 miles (10km).

### Bryant Park Free Festivals

*Sixth Ave, between West 40th & West 42nd Streets, behind the NY Public Library (983 4142).* **Train** B, D, F, Q or 7 to 42nd Street. **Date** June-Aug

This reclaimed park, a lunching oasis for midtown's office population, is the site of a packed season of free dance, comedy, food festivals and music. Best of all are the evening open air movies.

### Mermaid Parade

*From Steeplechase Park to Boardwalk at 8th Street, Coney Island, Brooklyn (718-372 5159).* **Train** B, D or F to Stillwell Avenue. **Date** first Sat after Memorial Day.

Floats, people dressed up as seafood, kiddie's beauty contests and other kitsch celebrations at Coney Island.

### Macy's Fireworks Display

*East River (494 4495).* **Date** 4 July, starts 9.15pm.

The Independence Day highlight is the spectacular 4th of July firework display. FDR Drive between 14th and 51st Streets is the best viewpoint; it's closed to traffic for a few hours as a million dollars of bangs and flashes light up the night. There's another display launched from the South Street Seaport.

### Mostly Mozart

*Avery Fisher Hall, Lincoln Center, Broadway & 65th Street (875 5135).* **Train** 1 or 9 to Lincoln Center. **Date** July-Aug.

For more than a quarter century, the Mostly Mozart festival has given New York an intensive four-week schedule of performances of Mozart's work. There are also lectures and other side attractions.

### Macintosh Music Festival

*(information 777 6800).* **Date** mid-late July.

In the gap left by the bankrupted New Music Festival is this new event, started in 1995, which links a great deal of con-

## The fashionable thing to do

Every April and October the international fashion circus finally winds up with Fashion Week in New York. Following Milan, Paris and London, the American designers' ready-to-wear womenswear collections are previewed – six months before they're available in the shops – to the world's buyers and the sensation-seeking press.

When fashion fever hits this city excitement soars, whether hemlines do or not. Even if you only have a passing interest in clothes, when the pack-in-black arrive for Fashion Week they cannot be ignored. Whether they shop at swanky Fifth Avenue stores or trendy downtown boutiques, New Yorkers take fashion very seriously, even if they are somewhat lacking in the style stakes.

The major names in the American industry – Calvin Klein, Donna Karan and Ralph Lauren – along with 30 or so other designers, show in the tents erected in Bryant Park, behind the New York Public Library. The tightly scheduled timetable of runway shows is dubbed 7th On Sixth (Seventh Avenue is 'Fashion Avenue', but the shows are on Sixth), and it entices over a handful of European designers, such as Ghost, Miu-Miu and Joop, who all now show their wares in New York. Some newer designers opt out of showing in the official tents and turn to alternative spaces, ranging from scuzzy vacant office buildings to the chi-chi Oyster Bar at Grand Central Station. The snag is that entrance to these trade shows is strictly invite only – unless you're carrying a de rigeur Prada nylon bag or are a ligger extraordinaire.

However, if you just want the glamour of hanging out with the Ab no-flab set of models and their inevitable entourage of A-list stylists, photographers, hairdressers et al, then going to some of the salubrious parties held during Fashion Week is the answer. Here you'll be able to watch Kate, Naomi and Linda devour a leaf of lollo rosso and a crate of Bolly between them, and catch the truly chic and the merely trying-to-be shake down on the dancefloor.

But again, if blagging's not your forte and you don't have a film/rock star hanging off your arm, then sweetie, you're not coming in.

certs in venues throughout downtown, as well as hosting some forums and industry get-togethers. The general theme, in keeping with its sponsor, is the latest communications technology. Whether it will become the sprawling music-biz freebie of its predecessor remains to be seen.

### New York Philharmonic Concerts

*(information 875 5709).* **Date** late July-early Aug.
Go early and take a picnic to these evening treats. The Philharmonic presents a varied programme, from Mozart to Weber, at eight of New York's larger parks – including Central, Prospect and Van Cortlandt.

### Summerpier

*Pier 16, South Street Seaport, South Street at Fulton Street (SEA PORT).* **Train** 2, 3, 4, 5, J, M or R to Fulton Street. **Date** July-Labor Day.
Free outdoor concerts – of all types of music – are held throughout the summer in the seaport.

### Summergarden

*Museum of Modern Art, 11 West 53rd Street, between Fifth & Sixth Avenues (708 9500).* **Train** B, D or F to Rockefeller Center; E or F to Fifth Avenue. **Date** July-Aug.
Free classical music concerts are organised with the Juillard School, in MOMA's sculpture garden.

### Washington Square Music Festival

*Washington Square Park, south end of Fifth Avenue (information 431 1088).* **Train** A, B, C, D, E, F or Q to West 4th Street. **Date** late July-early Aug.
This open-air concert season, mainly featuring chamber music recitals, has been running in Greenwich Village for years.

### Harlem Week

*(427 7200 information).* **Date** early-mid Aug.
The largest black and Hispanic festival in the world features celebrations of music, film, dance, fashion, exhibitions and sport. The highlight is the street festival between 125th and 135th Streets, which includes an international carnival of arts, jazz, gospel, R&B, entertainment and great food.

### Dragon Boat Races

*(information 265 8888 ).* **Date** mid Aug.
The traditional Chinese dragon boats are ornately carved masterpieces. They race each other, powered by highly competitive international teams, either in the Hudson River or in the East River at Flushing Meadows, Queens.

### US Open Tennis

*USTA Tennis Center, Flushing, Queens (760 6200).* **Train** 7 to Willets Point/Shea Stadium. **Date** late Aug-early Sept.
One of the most entertaining tournaments on the international circuit.

### Jazz at Lincoln Center

*Lincoln Center, Broadway, at 65th Street (875 5599).* **Train** 1 or 9 to Lincoln Center. **Date** Sept-May.
The season kicks off with a week of classical jazz followed by months of concerts by some of the best international musicians plus films, talks, seminars and more.

### Greenwich Village Jazz Festival

*(information 691 0045).* **Date** late Aug-early Sept.
This week-long festival brings together the Village jazz clubs and includes lectures and films, culminating with a free concert in Washington Square Park.

### West Indian Carnival

*(1-718 625 1515 information).* **Date** Labor Day weekend.
A loud and energetic festival of Caribbean culture, with a parade-full of flamboyant costumes, that takes place in Brooklyn, centred around the Museum.

*The Empire State Building, Independence Day.*

### Wigstock

*(213 2438 information).* **Date** Labor Day.
A celebration of drag, glamour and artificial hair, when anyone who can muster some foundation and lipstick dresses up as a woman. Real girls had better be extra fierce to cope with the competition. It has outgrown its origins in the East Village's Tompkins Square Park and may well be held in Central Park, though it may also be kept in place on the Christopher Street piers on the Hudson River. Phone for information.

### Richmond County Fair

*Historic Richmond Town, 441 Clarke Avenue, Staten Island (1-718 351 1611).* **Date** Labor Day.
An authentic country fair, with crafts and produce and strange agricultural competitions, just like in America but in New York instead.

### Football season starts

**Date** Sept-Dec. *See chapter* **Sport & Fitness**.

## Autumn

### Atlantic Avenue Street Festival (Brooklyn)

*(information 1-718 875 8993).* **Date** last Sun in Sept
A huge multicultural street fair in Brooklyn.

### Feast of San Gennaro

*Mulberry Street to Worth Street, Little Italy (information 226 9546).* **Train** 6, B, D, J, M, N or R to Canal Street. **Date** third week Sept.
Celebrations for the feast of the patron saint of Naples last a modest ten days, from noon to midnight daily, with fairground booths, stalls and lots of Italian food and wine.

### New York Film Festival
*Alice Tully Hall, Lincoln Center, Broadway at 66th Street (875 5050).* **Train** 1 or 9 to Lincoln Center. **Date** late Sept-early Oct.
Premieres of a number of American movies, plus art films from around the world. *See chapter* **Film**.

### Hockey season starts
**Date** Oct-Apr. *See chapter* **Sport & Fitness**.

### New York City Opera Season
*State Theater, Broadway, at 63rd Street (870 5570).* **Train** 1 or 9 to Lincoln Center. **Date** Sept-Nov; Feb-Apr.
Popular and classical operas, a more daring but lesser known work and the occasional musical comedy.

### Columbus Day Parade
*Fifth Avenue, between 44th & 86th Streets (397 8222).* **Date** second Mon in Oct.
To celebrate the first recorded sighting of America by Europeans the whole country gets a holiday with an Italian flavour, and the inevitable parade up Fifth Avenue.

### Big Apple Circus
*Damrosch Park, Lincoln Center, 65th Street & Amsterdam Avenue (268 0055).* **Train** 1 or 9 to Lincoln Center. **Date** Oct-Jan.
Performances are based around a theme – the Wild West one year, the monkey kingdom the next.

### Hallowe'en Parade
*from Spring Street & Broadway up Sixth Avenue to Union Square Park.* **Date** 31 Oct.
The parade started life as a small neighbourhood event, but now attracts some 50,000 revellers each year, culminating in a grand finale of ghouls, ghosts, witches and warlocks at around 10pm.

### Basketball season starts
**Date** Oct-June. *See chapter* **Sport & Fitness**.

### New York City Marathon
*starts at the Staten Island side of the Verrazano Narrows Bridge (860 4455).* **Date** last Sun in Oct or first Sun in Nov, starts 10.45am.
Over 20,000 runners cover all five boroughs over a 26 mile (42km) course. The race finishes at the Tavern on the Green, in Central Park at West 67th Street.

### Macy's Thanksgiving Day Parade
*Central Park West and 79th Street to Macy's at Broadway & 34th Street (494 4495).* **Date** Thanksgiving Day, starts 9am.
This is the one to take the kids to: it features enormous inflated cartoon characters, elaborate floats and Santa on his way to sit out December in Santaland at Macy's department store.

## Winter

### Christmas Tree Lighting Ceremony
*Rockefeller Center, Fifth Avenue between 49th & 50th Streets (397 8222 information).* **Train** B, D or F to Rockefeller Center. **Date** early Dec.
The giant tree, in front of the RCA Building, is festooned with five miles (7.4km) of lights. The tree, the skaters on the rink in the sunken plaza and the shimmering statue of Prometheus make this the most enchanting Christmas spot in New York.

### The Nutcracker Suite
*New York State Theater, Lincoln Center, Broadway at 65th Street (870 5570).* **Train** 1 or 9 to Lincoln Center. **Date** Nov-Dec.
The New York City Ballet performances of this famous work, assisted by students from the School of American Ballet, have become a much-loved Christmas tradition. *See also chapter* **Dance**.

### Messiah Sing-in
*Avery Fisher Hall, Lincoln Center, Broadway & West 65th Street (875 5000).* **Train** 1 or 9 to Lincoln Center. **Date** mid-Dec.
Usually one week before Christmas, 21 conductors lead the capacity audience of 3,000 in a rehearsal and then a performance of Handel's *Messiah.* You don't need any experience and can buy the score in the foyer.

### Christmas Spectacular
*Radio City Music Hall, 1260 Sixth Avenue, at 50th Street (212 632 4000).* **Date** Dec.
This is the long-running, famous show in which the fabulous high-kicking Rockettes top off an evening of tableaux and musical numbers exhausting the thematic possibilities of Christmas.

### New Year's Eve Fireworks
*Central Park (360 3456 information).* **Date** 31 Dec.
The best viewing points for a night of flash-banging are: the Bethsheda Fountain (Central Park at 72nd Street); Tavern on the Green (Central Park West at 67th Street); and Fifth Avenue at 90th Street. The fun and festivities start at 11.30pm and include hot cider and food.

### The Ball Drop
*Times Square (768 1560).* **Date** 31 Dec.
A traditional New York year begins and ends in Times Square, watching a light-bulb-encrusted ball get hoisted above the crowd and dropped at midnight. There are plenty of other diversions, but the overall theme is drunken overcrowding.

### Chinese New Year
*around Mott Street in Chinatown (information 397 8222).* **Train** 6, J, M, N or R to Canal Street.
**Date** first day of the full moon (between 21 Jan and 19 Feb).
The Chinese population of New York celebrates the New Year in style, with dragon parades, fireworks and delicious food on offer throughout Chinatown.

### National Boat Show
*Jacob K Javits Convention Center, Eleventh Avenue between 34th & 39th Streets (216 2000).* **Train** A, C or E train to Penn Station. **Date** mid-Jan.
Great displays of boats, yachts and pleasure cruisers. Don't take your chequebook.

### Winter Antiques Show
*7th Regiment Armory, Park Avenue, at East 66th Street (718-665 5250).* **Train** 6 to 68th Street.
**Date** mid-Jan.
The most prestigious of New York's antique fairs, with items from most of the great antiques shops on the Upper East Side, as well as from all over the country.

### Black History Month
**Date** Feb.
Events to celebrate African American history. They change each year and take place at venues around the city. Watch the press for details.

### Empire State Building Run-Up
*350 Fifth Avenue, at 34th Street (860 4455).* **Train** B, D, F, N or R to 34th Street. **Date** early Feb.
It starts in the lobby; runners speed up the 1,575 steps to the 86th floor; the average winning time is an astonishing – or suicidal – 12 minutes.

# Sightseeing

***See all the sights of New York in a mere 25 minutes, go rambling in Central Park or hook up with a local for a trip round the South Bronx.***

Asked to choose a new slogan for New York on the David Letterman show, Mayor Guiliani plumped for 'We can kick your city's ass'. In terms of things to see, the city has no equal. Most people's problem is just finding time for all the celebrated sights on their list. This is a guide to some of the essential and most famous ones, as well as recommendations for guided tours and hints about finding more unusual perspectives on the city. Many of the places listed here are also covered in other chapters, notably **New York by Neighbourhood**, **Architecture** and **History**.

## The Views

Flying in to New York on a clear day or night provides one of the world's most unforgettable views. It's impossible to be certain which landing route your plane will take, but the odds are best if you sit on the left side of the plane (for any of the three airports). Other jaw-dropping vistas are available at the Promenade in Brooklyn Heights (2 or 3 train to Clarke Street); from Liberty Park, New Jersey, and the nearby length of the New Jersey Turnpike; from the elevated sections of the Brooklyn Queens Expressway; from the many bridges and tall buildings; and from the Staten Island Ferry.

## The Statue

### The Statue of Liberty & Ellis Island Museum

*ferry from Battery Park to Liberty Island and then on to Ellis Island (363 3200/269 5755 ferry information).*
**Train** (to Battery Park) 4 or 5 to Bowling Green. **Ferries** every half hour 9.15am-4.30pm daily. **Fare** $7 adults; $5 senior citizens, $3 children 3-17, including admission. **Ticket sales** Castle Clinton, Battery Park. **Open** 8.30am-4.30pm daily. **No credit cards**.

'A big girl who is obviously going to have a baby. The Birth of a Nation, I suppose', wrote wartime wit James Agate about the Statue of Liberty. Get up close to this most symbolic New York structure by visiting the island it's on, along with one of the tackiest gift shops the city has to offer. Frederic Auguste Bartholdi's statue was a gift from the people of France (with a framework designed by Gustav Eiffel), but it took the Americans years to collect enough money to give Liberty the pedestal she now stands on. There's an excruciating wait to get to the top – we'd recommend that you don't

*Enjoy it while it lasts: the increasingly sanitised* **Times Square**. *See page 45.*

bother. It's claustrophobic, very rarely takes less than an hour or two and, since you can no longer get out into the torch, not such a big deal anyway. Much better to spend your time on Ellis Island, walking through the restored buildings dedicated to the millions of immigrants who passed through the quarantine station here and pondering the ghostly personal belongings that hundreds of people left behind in their hurry to become part of a new nation. It's an arresting and moving museum. If you're on a tight budget, the way to see Liberty is to buy a 50¢ round trip on the Staten Island ferry, which passes close to the statue (*see below* **Tours**).
*Disabled: access.*

## The Places

*See chapter* **New York by Neighbourhood** for more information on the areas listed below plus a round up of the city's other unmissable districts.

### Times Square

*Broadway & West 42nd Street.* **Train** 1, 2, 3, 7, N or R to Times Square.
Visit Times Square at night and you'll find yourself among floods of people weaving between hotels, restaurants and big Broadway shows. This is New York's tourist mecca, full of busloads of Iowans gasping at the glittering acres of overhead neon. Have a look at the city-sponsored art projects which fill the dead movie theatres along 42nd Street towards Eighth Avenue: bizarre window displays and epigrams in place of movie titles, and soak up the (relatively safe) sleaziness of the place, soon to be a thing of the past as new zoning laws threaten the many sex shops and peep-shows. Even squeaky-clean Disney is planning a development here. Originally called Longacre Square in the late nineteenth century, Times Square was renamed after the *New York Times* moved there in 1924, announcing its arrival with a spectacular New Year's Eve fireworks display. The *Times* erected the world's first moving sign, where it posted election returns in 1928. The paper has now moved a few blocks uptown but the New Year's celebrations and moving signs remain.

### South Street Seaport

*Water Street to the East River, between John Street and Peck Slip (SEA PORT for information about shops and events).* **Train** 2, 3, 4, 5, J, M or Z to Fulton Street. **Admission** free. **Seaport Museum** *(visitors' center) 12 Fulton Street, at Front Street (748 8600).* **Open** 10am-6pm daily. **Admission** $6 adults; $5 senior citizens; $4 students; $3 children.
Despite being over-prettified, the seaport is well worth a visit to get a feel for the maritime history of the city. As well as dining on some of the finest seafood in New York and imbibing rum alongside the dubious fellows who work at the fish-yard (currently in the news for its alleged mafia connections), you have the added pleasure of an all-American mall ambience. Admission to the Seaport Museum includes entry to the interesting galleries and tours around the historic vessels docked here. There are also several other boats on which you can take a quick cruise.
*Disabled: access to galleries.*

### Chinatown

**Train** 6, J, M, N, R or Z to Canal Street.
New York's Chinatown is the closest you'll get to Hong Kong without actually going there. It's a colourful, noisy and smelly marketplace where traders will sell you anything from fresh fish to a fake Rolex. Tables and hand carts jam the sidewalks and the shops are filled to overflowing with Chinese treasures and kitsch *objets*. It has hundreds of excellent and inexpensive restaurants (everyone in New York has their favourite, the location of which it is impossible to describe to others). Additional attractions include the Mott Street Buddhist Temple (64B Mott Street) and the statue of Confucius in Confucius Plaza. You may be in America, but few locals speak English here.

*The quintessential New York welcome: the **Statue of Liberty**. See page 43.*

*A child's eye view of that famous skyline.*

## The Buildings

*See also chapter* **Architecture**.

### Empire State Building

*350 Fifth Avenue, at 34th Street (736 3100).* **Train** B, D, F, N, Q or R to 34th Street. **Open** 9.30am-midnight daily. Last elevator up 11.30pm. **Admission** $4 adults; $2 children 5-11, senior citizens. **No credit cards**.
As well as some amazing photos of its construction (and of the time a plane crashed into it), the lobby has occasional displays of bizarre artwork and a collection of useless facts about this art deco pinnacle. (Did you know that in theory it's structurally strong enough to build on 13 more storeys, adding enough height to regain the tallest-in-the-world title?) The best time to visit is in time to watch the sun set over the New Jersey smog (angry reds and oranges merging into a green-black night), with the glittering lights of New York flickering on beneath you. It's impossibly romantic so don't forget to pack a loved one for the ascent. The biggest queue is on the second stage at the 86th floor, where you wait for an elevator to take you to the giddying heights of floor 102.
*Disabled: access.*

Express Navigation
Express Navigation, Inc
1(800) BOAT-RIDE

### World Trade Center

*between Church, Vesey, West & Liberty Streets (435 4170).* **Train** 1, 2, 3, 9, C or E to World Trade Center. **Open** *Oct-July* 9.30am-9.30pm daily; *Aug, Sept* 9.30am-11.30pm daily. **Admission** $6 adults; $3 children 6-12; $3.50 senior citizens. **No credit cards**.

With the stainless steel ribbing of these twin giants working to accentuate their size, the view, even from the bottom looking up, is enough to make your head spin. Zip up to the 110th floor, however, and you'll really feel the vertigo: the scariest thing is that there's another tower of equal size only a stone's throw away. Marvel at the city below and the view out to sea across the bay and enjoy the slight swaying as the building bends in the wind. Back on the ground, the lower concourse is a fast foodie's paradise and cheaper than the nastier offerings at observation-deck level. The Windows of the World restaurant on the 107th floor of Tower 1 is pricey, but recommended for the view alone. Security following the bombing is tight so leave your explosives at the hotel.

*Disabled: access.*

### Brooklyn Bridge

**Train** 4, 5 or 6 to Brooklyn Bridge (Manhattan side); A or C to Brooklyn Bridge (Brooklyn side).

New York has many bridges but none as beautiful or famous as the Brooklyn Bridge. The twin Gothic arches of its towers offered a grand entrance for each city, though this symbolism was lessened somewhat when Brooklyn (thanks largely to the bridge) became part of New York in 1898. The walkway, with its overhead network of supporting cables, is a great afternoon stroll (take the subway to Brooklyn and walk back into town for some incredible views). It took over 600 men some 16 years to build and when completed in 1883 was the world's largest suspension bridge – and the first to be constructed of steel. Engineer John A Roebling was one of 20 men who died on the project – before construction even started. His son continued the work until he was struck by caisson disease (the bends) and supervised construction, with the help of his wife, from the window of his Brooklyn apartment. 'All that trouble just to get to Brooklyn' was the Vaudevillian quip on the matter.

*Disabled: access.*

### Rockefeller Center

*between Fifth & Seventh Avenues and 47th & 51st Streets (637 3975).* **Train** B, D, F or Q to Rockefeller Center. **Admission** free.

Urban planners have been trying to emulate the Rockefeller Center ever since it was built in the 1930s, but no-one has come near it. The scale is extraordinary – it originally covered three large city blocks and now stretches even further across Sixth Avenue. People crowd the pedestrian spaces between the low-massed Maison Française and the British Empire Buildings, looking down on the ice-skating rink (a café in summer) and up at the slender apex of the RCA Building (now called the GE Building). If you go at sunset, the views accompanying the cocktails at the RCA's Rainbow Room can be spectacular. The famous art deco Radio City Music Hall is on the western side of the complex. An excellent finishing point for a Fifth Avenue shopping expedition.

*Disabled: access.*

## The Museums

*See also chapter* **Museums**.

### Metropolitan Museum of Art

*Fifth Avenue, at 82nd Street (535 7710).* **Train** 4, 5 or 6 to 86th Street. **Open** 9.30am-5.15pm Tue-Thur, Sun; 9.30am-8.45pm Fri, Sat. **Admission** suggested donation $7 adults; $3.50 students, senior citizens; free members and accompanied under-12s. **No credit cards**.

The city's attic, containing all manner of objects from modern art and sculpture to Native American antiquities. At 1.4 million square feet of floor space and 130 000 square feet of walls, don't even think about trying to 'do' the Met. Visit for one of its excellent themed exhibitions, where a particular corner of the vast treasure trove is highlighted, or lose yourself wandering through the centuries until it's time for tea in the fabulous roof garden overlooking Central Park.

*Disabled: access, toilets. No pushchairs in special exhibitions on Sundays.*

### Museum of Modern Art

*11 West 53rd Street, between Fifth & Sixth Avenues (708 9400/708 9480 recorded information).* **Train** E or F to Fifth Avenue; B or D to Rockefeller Center; 6 to Lexington Avenue; 1 or 9 to 50th Street. **Open** 11am-6pm Mon, Tue, Sat, Sun; noon-8.30pm Thur, Fri. **Admission** $8 adults; $5 students, senior citizens, under-16s (voluntary donation 5.30-8.30pm Thur). **No credit cards**.

Even the most clueless of visitors will recognise almost every work here. With room after room of twentieth-century genius, arranged more or less chronologically, it's an unforgettable experience. It's not physically that big but the strength of the collection will soon have you aesthetically exhausted. Avoid the astronomical prices in the cafeteria but do have a look at the gift shop across the street selling classic design objects.

*Disabled: access, toilets, touch tours.*

### Solomon R Guggenheim Museum

*1071 Fifth Avenue, at 88th Street (360 3500).* **Train** 4, 5 or 6 to 86th Street. **Open** 10am-6pm Mon-Wed, Sun; 10am-8pm Fri, Sat. **Admission** $7 adults; $4 students, senior citizens; free under-7s (volutary donation 6-8pm Fri). **Credit** AmEx, MC, Visa.

In 1943, when Frank Lloyd Wright drew a citrus press, labelled it Guggenheim and presented it to the New York building authorities, all hell broke loose. It was 16 years before the building, commissioned by Solomon R Guggenheim to house his remarkable collection of works by modern artists, was completed, six months after Wright died. It was his masterwork and his only New York building. There is a permanent collection of impressionist and post-impressionist works which are displayed in rotation; in the grand spiral walkway inside the shell are intriguing temporary exhibitions. The Guggenheim now has a downtown branch in SoHo that is well worth visiting and is open late. *See chapter* **Museums**.

*Disabled: access.*

## A Whole Day Out

### Bronx Zoo (International Wildlife Conservation Park)

*Bronx Park, corner of Fordham Road & Bronx River Parkway (718 367 1010).* **Train** 2 or 5 to East Tremont Avenue. **Open** 10am-5pm Mon-Fri; 10am-5.30pm Sat, Sun, public holidays. **Admission** $6.75 adults; $2 senior citizens; $3 under-12s; free under-2s; free on Wed; under-16s must be accompanied by an adult. **No credit cards**.

The pythons crawl around a lush, indoor tropical rain forest not far beneath your feet. The ponds are fat with crocodiles; the elusive snow leopard wanders around the mountain tops of the Himalayan Highlands; over 30 species of the Rodentia family co-exist in the Mouse House; birds, giraffes, lions and reptiles abound; and apes mercilessly mimic anyone who catches their eye. This is the largest urban zoo in America, home to over 4000 creatures. Although it covers 265 acres (107 hectares), it's not too hard on the feet: there's a choice of trams, monorails, express trains or camels. Nearby is the New York Botanical Garden, where you'll find a complex of grand glasshouses set

# Central Park

New Yorkers like their relaxation to be as intensive as possible, and for this there is Central Park: the condensed NYC version of the great outdoors. This vast (840 acre/340 hectare) expanse of greenery, set in the centre of Manhattan Island, is home to a huge array of activities and has scores of distinct areas, each with their own atmosphere and purpose.

In 1840 when the park was first planned, the area was little more than a swamp, with a garbage dump, abbatoirs and squatters' camp. Journalist and landscaper Frederick Law Olmstead and architect Calvert Vaux worked for the next 20 years to create their masterpiece: millions of tons of soil and rocks were moved, five million trees were planted, 58 miles (93km) of paths were laid, several lakes and a series of small ponds were dug out, along with a reservoir, and four sunken transverse roads were excavated to allow traffic to pass discreetly through. Another road loops around the perimeter, time-shared by traffic and the park's joggers, cyclists and rollerbladers.

**Bethesda fountain and terrace**, at the centre of the 72nd Street Transverse Road, is a formal Byzantine ornament, a focal point for the park and the most heavily populated meeting place. Just south is the **Mall**, a romantic promenade, used for volleyball at the weekends and a playground for countless careening rollerskaters and bladers. Pressure from rich, elderly upper Eastsiders brought about the removal of their famous disco-funk sound system, so they now synchronise radio stations on their Walkmans.

East of the Mall is a terrace centred around the derelict **Naumberg Bandshell**. On the rise behind is an area used for the **Central Park Summerstage** and its impressive series of free performances (June-Aug). To the west is the **Sheep Meadow**, the Manhattan equivalent of the beach. You may see some kites flying around the edges, as well as frisbee games and the odd small-scale soccer match, but the majority of people, at least in the summer months, are hard at work on their tans. You can buy cheap cold drinks here (illegally) from a costumed, bicycling superhero named Beer-man. If the day's lounging leaves you peckish, repair to the sheepfold-turned-restaurant **Tavern on the Green**, to the west, where there's a choice of expensive food in a picturesque setting (*see chapter* **Eating & Drinking**); or wolf down a hot dog from a nearby concession stand.

West of Bethesda Terrace, near the 72nd Street entrance, is **Strawberry Fields**, an area where games are outlawed in favour of contemplative quiet. This is where John Lennon, who lived and died nearby, is remembered.

*A dog-day afternoon in the park.*

Above Bethesda terrace is the **Lake**, crossed by the elegant **Bow Bridge**. You can hire a boat here, or even a gondola, and meander round the ornamental waters. East of the lake is the **Conservatory Water**, where model sailing boats are raced. North of the lake is the **Ramble**, a wild area known for birdwatching in the day and anonymous couplings in the night (Central Park after dark is not the safest place to be).

Above this is **Belvedere Castle**, with its children's centre, the **Delacorte Theater**, where the outdoor Shakespear Festival is performed, and the Great Lawn, where the classical concerts and large events are held.

North of this is the **Reservoir**, its perimeter a favourite jogging route, and then an area of sports fields and tennis courts. Above the Reservoir, the Park is mostly wild and wooded, with the recently restored **Harlem Meer** at the top eastern corner and the beautiful formal **Conservatory Garden** just below this.

### Department of Parks and Recreation

*(360 3456).*

24-hour recorded information on activities in all city parks.

### Urban Park Rangers

*(360 2774).* **Open** 9am-5pm daily.

The Rangers are a division of the Department of Parks and Recreation, and provide information and emergency services. Call for information about guided walks and other activities.

### Belvedere Castle

*Central Park, at West 79th Street (772 0210).* **Train** B or C to 81st Street. **Open** *15 Oct-15 Feb* 11am-4pm Wed-Sun; *16 Feb-14 Oct* 11am-5pm Wed-Sun. **Admission** free.

At the Discovery Chamber here kids can learn about the park through games and activities. Family workshops are held on Saturdays (1-2.30pm); children should be aged 5 to 11, should bring their parents and must book. Occasional dance concerts, magic shows and musicals are held.
*Disabled: limited access.*

### Central Park Zoo (Wildlife Conservation Center)

*Fifth Avenue, at 64th Street (861 6030).* **Train** B or Q to Lexington Avenue. **Open** *Apr-Oct* 10am-5pm Mon-Fri; 10.30am-5.30pm Sat, Sun; *Nov-Mar* 10am-4.30pm daily. **Admission** $2.50 adults; $1.25 seniors; 50¢ children 3-12.
This small but perfectly formed zoo is one of the highlights of the park. You can watch seals frolic both above and below the waterline, crocodiles snapping at monkeys swinging on branches of tropical forest and huge polar bears swimming underwater laps.
*Disabled: wheelchair access.*

### The Dairy

*Central Park, at 64th Street (794 6564).* **Open** *mid-April-mid-Oct* 11am-5pm Tue-Sun; *mid-Oct-mid-April* 11am-4pm Tue-Sun. **Admission** free.
At this information centre for Central Park there is an interactive exhibition and a six-minute video on the history of the park. The Dairy was built in 1870 to show city kids where their milk came from. Nearby is the beautiful antique carousel (90¢ a ride) and Herscksher Playground, which has handball courts, horseshoes, several softball diamonds, a puppet theatre, a wading pool and a crèche. Note that the centre is closed in winter.
*Disabled: access.*

### Hansom Cabs

*Fifth Avenue & Central Park South.* **Open** depending on weather daily.
Avoid these unless you really have to. It's a very tedious way of spending a lot of money and the poor horses suffer abysmally. If you're still keen the rates are rarely displayed so check before you get in.

### Loeb Boathouse

*Central Park, near Fifth Avenue & East 74th Street (517 4723).* **Train** 6 to 77th Street. **Open** *May-Sept* 11.30am-6pm daily; *spring & autumn* 10.30am-6pm weekends only.
**Rates** $10 per hour plus $20 refundable deposit; $30 per hour for chauffeured gondola. **No credit cards.**
Rowing boats can be hired on the Fifth Avenue side of the lake at the boathouse, which incorporates an Italian restaurant and café; picnic lunches are available.

### Wollman Memorial Rink

*Mid-Park, at 63rd Street (517 4800).* **Train** B, N, Q or R to 57th Street. **Open** *ice skating* Oct-Mar; *rollerskating and rollerblading* Apr-Sept 10am-5pm Mon; 10am-9.30pm Tue-Thur, Sun; 10am-11pm Fri, Sat. **Rates** $6 adults; $3 under-12s, senior citizens. Ice-skate/rollerskate hire $3.25; rollerblades $6.50. **Credit** MC, V.
Donald Trump scored major points when he took over the renovation of this long-derelict ice-rink. Quite the best open-air rink in Manhattan, and impossibly romantic at night, when the city lights tower over the park's leafy canopy. In summer months it's a roller disco.

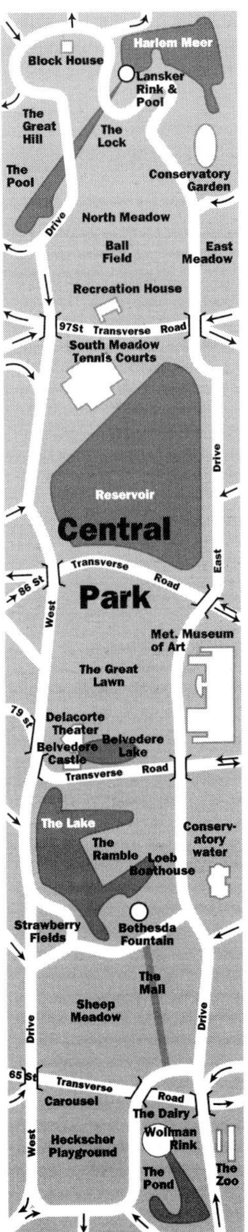

amongst 250 acres (101 hectares) of lush greenery, including a large area of virgin forest along the Bronx River.
*Disabled: access.*

### Coney Island

*Brooklyn.* **Train** B, D or F to Coney Island.
In the 1920s and 1930s a series of apocalyptic fires destroyed the original wooden structures of the various competing funfairs here. Nowadays, despite a thriving collection of rides, sideshows and other spangly things, the greatest attraction is the air of decayed grandeur. Grab a Nathans hot dog, take a look at the man-sized Vietnamese rats in the sideshows ('more feared than a sniper's bullet'), have a go on the new Cyclone at Astroland (718 372 0275) (the old Cyclone rots scenically next to the famous parachute jump, now restored), walk out to the beach and stroll along the boardwalk, perhaps as far as the Aquarium with its famous Beluga whales.

### Corona Park, Flushing Meadows & Shea Stadium

*Queens.* **Train** 7 to Shea Stadium.
If you've ever wondered what all those strange structures are on the way into the city from JFK, this is the answer. Corona Park contains the remnants of the 1939 and 1964 World's Fair, a series of bizarre buildings, including the New York Hall of Science (718 699 0005) with its children's workshops and exhibitions and delapidated space junk (actual retrieved rocket bits) outside. Then there's the Unisphere, a 100ft (31m) diameter stainless steel globe, backdrop for a hundred rap videos, and the Canadian Pavilion, a crown-of-thorns amphitheatre with a huge map of New York State inlaid in the floor. The park itself has a fierce local soccer league, where you can watch Puerto Rico take on Peru or Poland, and barbecue pits, a boating lake and wide expanses of quiet space. Come out here for a Mets baseball game at Shea Stadium or to the tennis centre (home of the US Open), and spend an afternoon wandering amongst the weirdness.

### Historic Richmond Town

*441 Clarke Avenue, Richmondtown, Staten Island (718 351 1611).* **Transport** Staten Island ferry from Battery Park, then S74 bus. **Open** *June-Sept* 10am-5pm Wed-Fri; 1-5pm Sat, Sun, public holidays; *Oct-May* 1-5pm Wed-Fri, Sun. **Admission** $4 adults; $2.50 under-18s, students, senior citizens. *No credit cards.*
This collection of 29 restored historic buildings is the best place to get an idea of the history of New York. Fourteen of them are open to the public, including Lake-Tysen House, a wooden farmhouse built in about 1740 in Dutch Colonial style for a French Huguenot, and Voorlezer's House, the oldest surviving elementary school in America. Many of the buildings, which include a courthouse, general store, baker's and butcher's as well as private homes, have been moved on site from elsewhere on the island. Actors in appropriate eighteenth-century clothing lurk in the doorways and crafts workshops are never far away. The overall feeling is as if you've left the city far behind for some historical excursion into upstate New York.
*Disabled: access to most areas.*

## Tours

## By Boat

### Circle Line

*Pier 83, West 42nd Street & Twelfth Avenue (563 3200).* **Train** A, C or E to 42nd Street. **Sailings** every 45 mins 9.15am-4pm; Harbor Light Cruise 7pm. **Tickets** $18 adults; $16 senior citizens; $9 under-12s. **Credit** AmEx, DC, JCB, MC, V.
From April to November Circle Line operates a three-hour 35 mile (56km) trip which circumnavigates Manhattan Island. From June to August there's also a two-hour Harbor Light Cruise in the evening, one of the cheapest and best ways to see the city.
*Disabled: access.*

### Petrel

*Battery Park (825 1976).* **Train** 1 or 9 to South Ferry. **Sailings** *May-Nov* 3-5 per day noon-10.30pm. **Tickets** $8-$26. **Credit** MC, V.
A 70ft (21m) yawl designed by Sparkman & Stephens, *Petrel* is built of teak and mahogany. It was launched in 1938 as a racing yacht, and the owners still pride themselves on using sail as much as possible. This is a New York favourite, so you need to book two weeks in advance.

### Seaport Liberty Cruises

*Pier 16 at the South Street Seaport (630 8888).* **Train** 2, 3, 4, 5, J, M or Z to Fulton Street. **Sailings** phone for details. **Tickets** $12 adults; $6 under-13s; $15-$25 music cruises. **Credit** AmEx, DC, JCB, MC, V.
One-hour cruises and two-hour evening music cruises in a large sightseeing boat.

### Staten Island Ferry

*Battery Park (806 6940).* **Train** 1 or 9 to South Ferry. **Open** 24 hours daily. **Tickets** 50¢.
A sightseeing bargain; the fare is only 50¢ for the round trip – you pay leaving from the Manhattan end. Boats depart the South Ferry at Battery Park every half hour and provide views of New York harbour and Manhattan.

## By Bus

### Gray Line

*900 Eighth Avenue, between 53rd & 54th Streets (397 2600).* **Train** C or E to 50th Street. **Open** 7.45am-8pm daily. **Tickets** $17-$49. **Credit** AmEx, Discover, JCB, MC, V.
Grayline offers 20 bus tours around New York City, from a basic two-hour ride to the monster nine-hour all-day

## New York in 25 minutes

If your intensive shopping schedule is cutting into your sightseeing, or if your three-clubs-a-day nightlife has destroyed your will to traipse, try the Skyride, a small slice of virtual reality designed especially for time-pressed New York visitors. Using the same technology as a military flight simulator, the Skyride takes you on a low-flying big-screen blast around all of the city's famous attractions in no more than 25 minutes.

### New York Skyride

*Second Floor, Empire State Building, 350 Fifth Avenue, at 34th Street (279 9777).* **Train** B, D, F, Q, N or R to 34th Street. **Open** 10am-10pm daily. **Admission** $7.95 adults; $5.95 under-13s, seniors; combination tickets including Empire State Building observatory are available. **Credit** AmEx, JCB, MC, V.
*Disabled: access.*

'Manhattan Comprehensive', which includes lunch. The company also runs Central Park trolley tours ($15) at 10.30am, 1pm and 3pm.
*Disabled: some access; call for details.*

### New York Doubledecker Tours

*Empire State Building, 350 Fifth Avenue, at 34th Street (967 6008).* **Open** 9am-5pm daily. **Tickets** $15-$25. **Credit** MC, V.
Take a two-hour guided tour either uptown or downtown, or combine the two for a four-hour ride around Manhattan in open-top, ex-London-Transport double-deckers. Once you have a ticket, you can get on and off at any point on the route (on the combined tour you can spread this over two days). Buses are frequent enough to make this practicable: they leave the Empire State Building every hour to go uptown, every half hour for downtown.

## By Helicopter

### Island Helicopters

*Heliport East River, at East 34th Street (564 9290/683 4575 recorded information).* **Train** 6 to 33rd Street.

*It may be touristy, but it's still the real thing:* **South Street Seaport**. *See page 45.*

**Open** 9am-9pm daily. **Tickets** $44-$129. **Credit** AmEx, DC, JCB, MC, V.
Tours include the Statue of Liberty and a circuit of Manhattan; reservations aren't necessary. The tours are best on clear days with little wind. Long trips are better; get a seat by the window.

### Liberty Helicopter Tours

*Corner of Twelfth Avenue & West 30th Street (967 6464/465 8905 recorded information).* **Train** A, C or E to 34th Street. **Open** 9am-8.45pm daily. **Tickets** $45-$129. **Credit** MC, V.
Several different tours are offered. The Liberty 'copters are larger than most, which apparently makes the ride smoother. There are between 10 and 40 rides a day, depending on the weather, and reservations are unnecessary. Even the shortest ride is long enough to get a good close-up view of the Statue of Liberty, Ellis Island and the Twin Towers.

## On Foot

### Urban Park Rangers

*1234 Fifth Avenue, at 104th Street (360 2774).* **Open** 9am-5pm daily. **Train** 6 to 103rd Street.
A service of the Parks Department, the Rangers' central office organises pleasant free walks and talks in all the city parks. Subjects and activities covered include fishing, wildlife, birdwatching and Native American history.

### Harlem Spirituals

*1697 Broadway, Suite 203, at 53rd Street (212 757 0425).* **Train** 1 or 9 to 50th Street; B, D or E to Seventh Avenue. **Open** 9am-6pm Mon-Sat. **Credit** AmEx, MC, V.
Sunday morning gospel tours (8.45am-12.45pm, $29) take in Sugar Hill, Hamilton Grange and Morris-Jumel Mansion as well as a service at a Baptist church. Wednesday morning gospel tours (9am-1pm, $32) include a visit to the Schomburg Institute for Research into Black Culture and a Baptist church choir. Visit cabarets on the evening 'soul food and jazz' tours (7pm-midnight Thur-Sat, $65). The historical tour (which includes lunch) costs $37 (9am-1.30pm Thur).

### Municipal Art Society Tours

*457 Madison Avenue, between East 50th & East 51st Streets (935 3960).* **Train** 6 to 51st Street. **Open** 11am-5pm Mon-Wed, Fri, Sat. **No credit cards**.
The Society organises some very informative tours, including hikes around Harlem, the Upper West Side, Greenwich Village, Grand Central Station and Brooklyn Heights. All tours cost $10.

### Tours with the 92nd Street Y

*1395 Lexington Avenue, at East 92nd Street (996 1100).* **Train** 4, 5 or 6 to 86th Street. **Open** *June-Aug* 10am-6pm Mon-Thur; 10am-4pm Fri, Sun; *Sept-May* 9am-9pm Mon-Thur; 9am-4pm Fri; noon-8pm Sun. **Credit** AmEx, MC, V.
Tours include Park Avenue, Irish New York and the Bowery. Most tours are on Sunday and prices vary. Advance booking is required.

### Heritage Trails New York

*Federal Hall National Memorial, 26 Wall Street (767 0637).* **Train** 4 or 5 to Wall Street. **Open** 9am-5pm daily.
Your guides are a booklet and a trail of coloured markers set in the sidewalk, along with panels of information and photographs at various sites. There are four trails, all taking you, at your own pace, through an area of interest in downtown Manhattan. The necessary guidebook costs $5 and is available from the office.

### Grand Central & 34th Street Partnerships

These neighbourhood organisations offer free tours of their districts, including a monthly tour of the remnants of the demolished Penn Station (868 0521 for information) and a grand tour of midtown, including Grand Central Station itself (986 9217 for information).

### Talk-A-Walk

*Waterside Plaza, NY 10010 (686 0356).* **No credit cards**.
This service offers by mail order a choice of five 85-minute tour cassettes to slot into your Walkman, each containing directions and commentary for a walk lasting two to four hours. Pop one into your Walkman and you can explore at your own pace. They're $9.95 each, and you can order by mail or phone. If you have a fax that can be set to call and receive, dial 632 7812 for a three-page catalogue.

## A Big Apple greeting

Go visit Vinny's mom in Bensonhurst, have Renata show you round the hidden treasures of Polish Greenpoint or let Carmine take you to the parks in the South Bronx where hip-hop was invented.

If you don't feel like letting one of the many tour companies herd you round the New-York-by-numbers trail, or if you would simply like to have a knowledgeable and enthusiastic friend to accompany you in discovering the city, put in a call to the Big Apple Greeter programme. This immensely successful scheme has been in operation since 1992, introducing visitors to one of 600 carefully chosen volunteer 'greeters' and giving them a chance to see New York beyond the well-trodden tourist traps.

Like a dating agency, the programme links visitors with greeters on a one-to-one basis. They might live in a particular neighbourhood that you have expressed an interest in or they may be knowledgeable about a particular subject or area. Greeters are also available for travellers with disabilities, for senior citizens, business travellers and the generally intimidated. Between the current greeters more than 40 foreign languages are spoken. The service is completely free, though donations are welcome. Write, phone or fax the office to find yourself a New York friend. Just don't let Milton leave you in East Harlem after dark.

### Big Apple Greeter

*1 Center Street NY 10007 (669 2896/fax 669 4900).* **Open** 9.30am-5pm Mon-Fri, recorded information at other times.

# Architecture

***From the clapboard houses of the first settlers to the glass canyons of its unfeasible skyscrapers, New York's architecture is nothing short of astounding.***

O Henry said of New York: 'It'll be a great place if they finish it' – and it is the constant construction of the city, layer on Troy-like layer, that has made it such an architectural wonderland. Its influx of European immigrants brought with them a wide range of architectural styles to be adopted, adapted or ignored, and the city's riches and arrogance encouraged nothing but the very finest, most impressive buildings.

Like few other cities, New York is truly three dimensional. A map is useless in conjuring it; better a model, or a helicopter ride. Space, rather than land, is what is valuable here, so a building plot is a mere footprint: its true worth can only be measured when multiplied by height. And apart from Inwood Hill Park at Manhattan's northernmost tip, hardly a square inch of the island has escaped the attention of planners, builders and architects. Even the seemingly haphazard geography of Central Park is a deliberate architectural feat.

These are some of the architectural highlights of New York, though there are hundreds of other notable buildings worth seeing. Most are accessible to the public in at least a limited way (especially the lobbies), and many of the more historic ones are now museums.

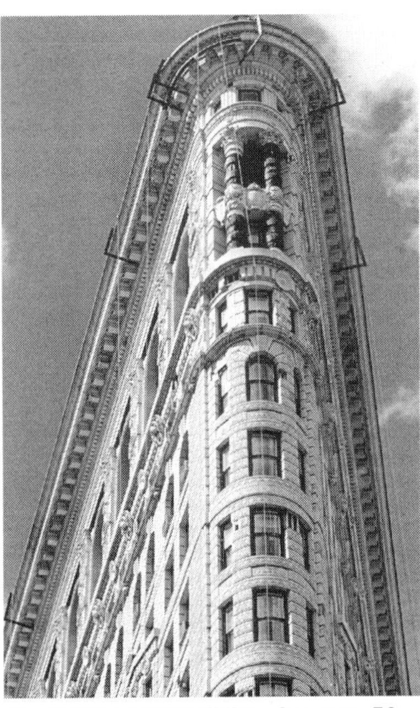

*The 1902* **Flatiron Building**. *See page 56.*

## Dutch Beginnings

Under Dutch rule (1626-1664) the city grew only as far north as Wall Street (the site of a defensive wall) and resembled a Dutch country town, even down to the odd windmill. The earliest buildings were built of fieldstone or were wooden-framed with brick facing, and had quirks brought from the Netherlands, such as tile roofs, stepped gables, decorative brickwork and stone stoops (from the Dutch 'stoep' for step), originally designed to elevate the entrance from the wet Dutch landscape.

None of the buildings on Manhattan have survived, but in Brooklyn you can see the **Pieter Claesen Wyckoff House**, built in 1652 and the oldest home in New York City. In Queens there is **Bowne House** (1661), built by John Bowne, a Quaker who secured the rights of religious freedom for the colony, as well as the Friends' Meeting House he built in 1694. **Dyckman House**, the only remaining Dutch farmhouse in Manhattan, wasn't built until 1785, though it retains the high-shouldered gambrel roof and flared eaves of the mature Dutch Colonial style. **Historic Richmond Town** on Staten Island (*see chapter* **Sightseeing**) contains several buildings in the Dutch manner.

### Pieter Claesen Wyckoff House Museum

*Clarendon Road, at Ralph Avenue, Brooklyn (1-718 629 5400).* **Bus** B7, B8 or B78. **Open** *Apr-Nov* noon-5pm Thur, Fri; *Dec-Mar* noon-4pm Thur, Fri. **Admission** $2 adults; $1 senior citizens, under-12s. **No credit cards.**

### Bowne House

*37-01 Bowne Street, between 37th & 38th Avenues, Flushing, Queens (1-718 359 0528).* **Train** 7 to Main Street, Flushing. **Open** 2.30-4.30pm Sat, Sun. **Admission** $2; $1 seniors, under-12s. **No credit cards.**

### Dyckman House

*4881 Broadway, at West 204th Street (304 9422).* **Train** A to Dyckman Street. **Open** 11am-4pm Tue-Sun. **Admission** free.

## The British

The arrival of the British was a spur to growth, and there was much building during the 100 years of their rule. Landfill projects extended the island's shoreline and commercial buildings were erected, driving the wealthier residents northwards. New York grew to become the second largest city in the British Empire and expanded as far as the site of City Hall. The British were eager to make their mark, and many of the new structures were built in the Georgian style of the new colonists.

The present **Trinity Church** is actually the third to stand on this site. The first was consecrated in 1698 but was destroyed by fire soon after the Revolution. The second was completed in 1790 but demolished due to structural problems and the present structure, a square-towered Episcopal church designed by Richard Upjohn, was built in 1846. Its elegant Gothic Revival spire was the tallest structure in Manhattan until the 1860s.

In fact very few buildings remain from the century of British rule. One exception is **St Paul's Chapel** (1766), on Broadway at Fulton Street, a beautiful example of the style of church popularised in London by Christopher Wren. It is modelled on St Martin-in-the-Fields, with an elegant temple portico and a steeple rising from the roof.

**Fraunces Tavern** is actually a twentieth-century reconstruction, but it gives a good idea of how the original structure, built in 1719 as a private residence, must have looked. This was where George Washington celebrated victory against the British in 1783. **Van Cortlandt Mansion** was built by Frederick Van Cortlandt in 1748, as the homestead for his wheat plantation in what is now the Bronx. Though simply constructed, with rugged fieldstone walls and hand-carved keystones, its traditional Georgian proportions are evident. The wooden **Morris-Jumel Mansion**, built in 1765, has the elegant low-pitched roof and colossal portico of the grand Georgian style. Apart from these selected buildings, the best place to see Colonial New York is at Historic Richmond Town, where many buildings of the period have been gathered and restored (*see chapter* **Sightseeing**).

### Trinity Church Museum

*Broadway, at Wall Street (602 0872).* **Train** 2 or 3 to Wall Street. **Open** 7am-4pm Sat, Sun; 7am-6pm Mon-Fri (closed during concerts). **Admission** free.

### Fraunces Tavern Museum

*54 Pearl Street, at Broad Street (425 1778).* **Train** 4 or 5 to Bowling Green; 1 or 9 to Wall Street. **Open** 10am-4.45pm Mon-Fri; noon-4pm Sat. **Admission** $2.50 adults; $1 children, seniors. **Credit** AmEx, MC, V.

The restored tavern contains exhibits telling the story of New York during the Revolutionary War and its brief life as the nation's capital.

### Van Cortlandt Mansion

*Van Cortlandt Park, Broadway, north of West 242nd Street, Riverdale, Bronx (1-718 543 3344).* **Train** 1 or 9 to 242nd Street/Van Cortlandt Park. **Open** 10am-3pm Tue-Fri; 11am-4pm Sat, Sun. **Admission** $2 adults; $1.50 senior citizens, students; free under-14s. **No credit cards.**

*1930's* **Chrysler Building**. *See page 56.*

### Morris-Jumel Mansion

*Roger Morris Park, Edgecombe Avenue, at 160th Street (923 8008).* **Train** A or B to 163rd Street. **Open** 10am-4pm Wed-Sun. **Admission** $3 adults; $2 senior citizens, students. **No credit cards.**

## A Proud City

After the Revolution, architecture was used to express the city's new independence and its brief role as capital of the fledgling United States. The favoured building style in the first half-century of the new republic was Federal, an Americanised version of English Georgian.

Pockets of Federal architecture can still be seen in lower Manhattan. The 1832 **Old Merchant's House** is a lonely survivor of the period when this area was fashionable. A row of nine red-brick houses dating from 1828 in **Harrison Street**,

TriBeCa, have recently been restored as private homes. The largest group of Federal-style houses in New York City is in the **Charlton-King-Vandam Historic District** (1820s) on the southern boundary of Greenwich Village.

Many grand civic buildings were also erected, in an area known as the Civic Center. The beautiful **City Hall** (1811) combined the Federal style with French Renaissance influences, with its delicate columns and domed rotunda.

The continuing vogue for neo-classicism led to an American version of Greek Revival architecture, exemplified by the massive colonnaded **Federal Hall** (1842) on Wall Street, which is in the form of a Greek temple. Another fine surviving example of this fashion is the 1832 **Colonnade Row** (Lafayette Street between 4th Street and Astor Place), which contained some of the most exclusive houses in the city. The less wealthy lived in brownstones: elegant middle-class row houses (terraces) which were built in their thousands through the nineteenth century. At the same time, vast overcrowded tenement buildings were built to house the poorest and most recent immigrants.

### Old Merchant's House

*29 East 4th Street, between Lafayette Street & the Bowery (777 1089).* **Train** 6 to Astor Place; N or R to 8th Street. **Open** 1-4pm Mon-Thur, Sun. **Admission** $3 adults; $2 senior citizens, students; free under-12s accompanied by adult. **No credit cards.**

### Charlton-King-Vandam Historic District

*9-43 & 20-42 Charlton Street, 11-49 & 16-54 King Street, 9-29 Vandam Street, 43-51 MacDougal Street.* **Train** 1 or 9 to Houston Street.

As well as the largest concentration of Federal-style houses in New York, the historic district includes fine examples of Greek Revival, Italianate and late nineteenth-century domestic architecture.

### City Hall

*City Hall Park, Broadway & Park Row (788 6870).* **Train** 4, 5 or 6 to Brooklyn Bridge; J, M or Z to Chambers Street. **Open** 10am-4pm Mon-Fri. **Admission** free.

### Federal Hall National Monument

*26 Wall Street, at Nassau Street (825 6888).* **Train** 2, 3, 4 or 5 to Wall Street. **Open** 9am-5pm daily. **Admission** free.

George Washington took the presidential oath in the Federal Hall that once stood on this site. The present building was erected from 1834-42 as a customs building. It is now a national monument and contains exhibits relating to the Constitution.

## Beaux Arts

Another period of proud expansion around the turn of the century saw further landmarks erected, the majority in the Beaux Arts style, a careful appropriation of European Renaissance forms. Richard Morris Hunt gave the city **The Metropolitan Museum** (1895; Fifth Avenue at 82nd Street. *See chapter* **Museums**), and, under Andrew Carnegie's patronage, **Carnegie Hall** (1891; Seventh Avenue & 57th Street. *See chapter* **Music: Classical & Opera**). Cass Gilbert, later to design the **Woolworth Building** (*see below*), created the **Custom House** (1907; Bowling Green), a beautiful tribute to the city's role as a seaport (now **The Museum of the American Indian**; *see chapter* **Museums**).

The firm of Carrere & Hastings provided a home for the **New York Public Library** (1911; Fifth Avenue at 42nd Street), a building which epitomises the city's Beaux Arts architecture. Warren & Wetmore built the majestic soaring spaces of **Grand Central Station** (1913), still New York's grandest port of entry, as well as the **Helmsley Building** (1929; 46th Street at Park Avenue).

The city's most important architectural firm, and easily the most famous, was that of McKim, Mead and White, which propounded the classical idioms of the Italian Renaissance. Its **Municipal Building** (1914; Centre Street) echoes the City Hall it faces with a grand colonnaded tower. Charles McKim's **University Club** (1899; Fifth Avenue at 54th Street) is an elegant Renaissance-style palazzo, and White's grand **Metropolitan Club** (1894; Fifth Avenue at 60th Street) is more French than Italian, with an inventive colonnaded gateway.

McKim was also responsible for the **Pierpont Morgan Library** (1917; Madison Avenue at 36th Street), one of New York's great buildings (*see chapter* **Museums**). It's a low classical temple, built of marble blocks carefully honed so they could be laid without mortar, in the Greek manner. His last work, Pennsylvania Station, is now, alas, destroyed, living on only in the firm's complementary design for the **United States General Post Office** (1913, Eighth Avenue at 34th Street), across the street. White is probably best remembered for his **Washington Arch** (1895), which enriches the southern end of Fifth Avenue.

### Grand Central Station

*42nd Street, at Park Avenue.* **Train** 4, 5, 6 or 7 to Grand Central. **Open** 24 hours daily. **Free tours** (935 3960) 12.30pm Wed; meet on Chemical Bank Concourse.

## Cast Iron

Coinciding with the massive waves of immigration which did so much to define New York, new building techniques were also being imported. Based on the British factories of the Industrial Revolution, structures made of prefabricated cast iron parts could be built large, fast and cheap. In fact, you could bolt together your building by ordering numbered parts from a foundry catalogue. The resulting buildings were made of layers of columns, their gridded skeletons clearly visible in their facades, which were often painted

*Echoing tradition: the* **Woolworth Building**.

to resemble stone. Architects made classical, Renaissance and Baroque forms with the cast iron building blocks – you can see examples of the evolving styles throughout mid- and downtown Manhattan, especially around SoHo, which has the highest concentration of cast iron architecture anywhere in the world.

Since the medium lent itself to repetitive use of a single element, it was the Palazzo style, often with successive rows of slender columns, which dominated. The first cast iron building to use this defining style was the **AT Stewart Dry Goods Store** (1846; 280 Broadway between Chambers and Reade Streets).

One of the finest examples is the **Haughwort Building** (1856; Broome Street and Broadway), which has been called 'the Parthenon of cast iron architecture' for its elegant proportions and beautiful detail. It is notable, too, as the site of the first Otis safety elevator, another development of this time which allowed buildings to grow ever taller.

Another early cast iron masterpiece is the **Carey Building** (1857; 105-107 Chambers Street), a five-storey Palazzo design of Corinthian columns topped with a triangular pediment.

Other fine examples include **72-76 Greene Street**, the 'King Of Greene Street', and **28-30 Greene Street**, known as 'The Queen', as well as a great many larger buildings in the district known as **Ladies' Mile** (Broadway between Union and Madison Squares).

#### Cast Iron Tours

*c/o The 92nd Street Y, 1395 Lexington Avenue, at 92nd Street (996 1100).* **Train** 6 to 96th Street.

Joyce Mendelsohn, an expert on New York's cast iron buildings, offers guided tours of SoHo's Cast Iron Historical District and Ladies' Mile.

## Touching the Sky

The architecture that is most closely associated with New York is the assertive verticality of its skyscrapers. With the development of steel-framed construction – an advancement of the techniques used for cast iron buildings – the restrictions on height imposed by the need for load-bearing walls were eliminated. The first skyscrapers, such as the **Flatiron Building** (1902; Fifth Avenue and 23rd Street) and the **Woolworth Building** (1913; Broadway at Park Place), echoed traditional construction in their facades – the former a restrained Renaissance palazzo and the latter a gothic cathedral complete with gargoyles – but by the 1920s and 1930s the curtain wall had an expressive life of its own and was used as a palette for many art deco designs.

The famous **Empire State Building** (1931; Fifth Avenue at 34th Street. *See chapter* **Sightseeing**), a perfectly massed 102-storey tower of limestone and granite with thin vertical strips of nickel that glint when they catch the sun, was the work of William F Lamb, who was given a brief to 'make it big'. It took only 18 months to build and quickly became the world's favourite building, as well as the tallest.

The **Chrysler Building** (1930; Lexington Avenue and 42nd Street) was William van Alen's homage to the automobile. Its glinting stainless steel spire with its illuminated 'sunrise' motif (an addition to the original plans to add prestigious height) is just one part of the design which conjures up the steel forms of its tenant's products. At the foot of the main tower are brickwork cars complete with chrome hubcaps, their radiator caps enlarged to vast proportions and projected out over the edge as gargoyles.

A lesser known but equally striking example of the art deco skyscraper is across the street: the **Chanin Building** (1929; Lexington Avenue and

# Build your own New York skyscraper

You will need: a plot of land, lots of money and plenty of spare time. The process begins with the intricately interwoven details of financing and site acquisition. An average skyscraper (say around 60 storeys or so) will cost you somewhere between $500 million and a cool billion. You'll probably need to borrow some money from the bank.

The other tricky thing is planning permission. Size, height, usage, social impact on the surrounding neighbourhood and a gazillion smaller factors will be subject to the regulations of the city and other important agencies. These people might get you to sign away rights to 'hostage space' in the building. This means, for example, that until you complete the bus station in the basement, the bus company owns three floors of your building and you are forbidden to rent these out.

Once the paperwork, the plans and the inevitable bribery and corruption are sorted out, you can get on with construction. You'll need a big hole that goes right down to the bedrock (Manhattan has great bedrock, but you'll need to start about 30 feet below street level). On this you can start to erect your steel framework (which you should have already fabricated somewhere out of town). The completed building will stand on big steel plates embedded in concrete and the underlying rock. These should each be strong enough to support four or five thousand tons. Any mistakes here could easily show up later, as your building will have a tendency to fall over.

The steel framework will bolt together fairly fast, and your skyscraper will grow at a surprising rate, the crane on the top being jacked up by hydraulics as every three or four floors are built. You will probably end up using American Indians as your steel erectors. Whether by racial characteristic (they have no fear of heights) or simple tradition, most skyscrapers have been built by Iroquois people, notably folk from the Montreal-based Mohawks.

While the framework is being erected, it's time to add the floors. High pressure concrete should be pumped up from ground level and smoothed out before it has time to set. Don't forget to leave holes for elevators, plumbing, sewage, electrical lines and air conditioning. The necessary equipment for these essential services can be added later.

Finally, to give your building that 'finished' look you should choose the material you want to clad it with. Obviously a lot of this (perhaps all of it) will be glass, but you might want something else as well. Popular 'curtain walls' are built from stainless steel, concrete or even good old bricks and stone. Be careful though, as these may fall off if their fixings aren't sufficiently flexible. Remember, even the best skyscrapers will sway up to three feet when the wind blows.

For more information on the astounding feats involved in making tall buildings, read Karl Sabbagh's enthralling book, *Skyscraper: The Making of a Building* (Penguin, 1990).

**World Trade Center** – *beat that. See p58.*

42nd Street). The Chanin housed a network of public passageways which connected it to the nearby subway station. This, along with its ground-level storefronts accessible from inside the complex, made it the first building to be a 'city-within-a-city'.

**Rockefeller Center** (1931; *see chapter* **Sightseeing**) was a far grander expression of this idea. Occupying three city blocks and comprising 21 buildings connected by open plazas and an extensive subterranean world of shops, restaurants and subway connections, it provides all the services its daytime occupants could ever need. Built by John D Rockefeller and designed by a committee of architects led by Raymond Hood, it is an urban complex much admired for its masterful coordination of public space. The centre was extended in the 1970s with the addition of four powerful towers on the west side of Sixth Avenue.

Other important art deco works include the monochrome tower of the **Fuller Building** (1929; 45 East 57th Street); the twin copper crowns of the **Waldorf Astoria Hotel** (1931; Park Avenue at 50th Street); Raymond Hood's **Daily News Building** (1930; 42nd Street at Second Avenue), a soaring skyscraper of white brick piers with black and reddish-brown spandrels (as seen in the *Superman* films); and the **McGraw Hill Building** (1931; 42nd Street and Eighth Avenue), with shimmering blue-green bricks and ribbons of double-hung windows, once described as 'proto jukebox modern'.

## Monuments of Glass & Steel

The Depression and World War II slowed New York's architectural pace but by the 1950s designers were once again experimenting with the daring forms made possible by steel-framed construction. The main building of the **UN Secretariat** (1950), a perfectly proportioned single rectangle (its face is designed to the 'Golden Ratio' of the Greeks), included New York's first entirely glass walls. It is attributed to Le Corbusier, but in fact he was just one of an international committee of architects and was said to be unhappy with the final result.

**Lever House** (1952; Park Avenue at 54th Street), took glass curtain walls to the staid respectability of Park Avenue. Mies van der Rohe's **Seagram Building** (1958; Park Avenue and 52nd Street) epitomised the new glass architecture, reflecting the world in its elegant bronze-framed surfaces. It was notable, too, for its pioneering atrium, a public space in a private building. The building laws were changed to encourage this concept. Frank Lloyd Wright's only New York building, the **Guggenheim Museum** (1959; Fifth Avenue at 88th Street. *See chapter* **Sightseeing**) caused a stir for its daring form. The upturned shell of its striking exterior contains a single spiral walkway.

The **Pan Am Building**, now the Met Life Building (1963; 45th Street at Park Avenue), towers behind Grand Central Station. Designed by Walter Gropius, it was the largest commercial building in the world and, with its famous (now closed) roof heliport, symbolised the modern jet-set life of the 1960s in countless movies.

With a daytime population of around 50,000, the **World Trade Center** (1970; Church Street and Liberty Street. *See chapter* **Sightseeing**) carries the 'city-within-a-city' concept to its modernist limits. The famous twin towers are just one element of a network of connected blocks, their colossal height further emphasised by the narrow stainless steel detailing rising vertically across their surface (actually a load-bearing structure rather than a decorative curtain wall). The Center's architecture has been widely criticised as banal but, especially since 1993's bomb attack, it is looked on with some affection – at least by New Yorkers.

Hugh Stubbins and Associates' **Citicorp Building** (1977; Lexington Avenue at 53rd Street) is instantly recognisable for its smooth aluminium skin and sloping 'sliced' roof. From street level you see the radical way the building's bulk is supported on huge stilts.

One of New York's most famous postmodernist buildings is Philip Johnson's **AT&T** (now **Sony**) **Building** (1983; Madison Avenue at 55th Street), with its grand six-storey entrance arch and instantly recognisable 'Chippendale' top. Cesar Pelli's **World Financial Center** (1988) is the focal point of the landfill development of Battery Park City on the tip of Manhattan. Its quirky yet elegant towers are topped by domes and pyramids with stepped cut-backs and walls whose proportion of reflective glass increases with their height.

### United Nations Headquarters

*First Avenue, at 46th Street (963 1234 recorded information).* **Train** 4, 5, 6 or 7 to Grand Central. **Open** 9.15am-4.45pm daily. **Admission** free. **Guided tours** (every half hour) $6.50 adults; $4.50 senior citizens, students; $3.50 children.

The Modernist headquarters of the United Nations is so very 1950s. You can visit the foyer and basement of the General Assembly Building, but to see any of the council rooms and the General Assembly itself, you must take a tour which lasts about an hour and is rather dull. Free tickets are available to General Assembly and council sessions on a first-come, first-served basis from the Information Desk (754 7539).

### World Financial Center

*West Street, at Liberty Street (945 0505).* **Train** 1, 2, 3, 9, A, C or E to Chambers Street.

The WFC is a sleek 1990s public space in the tradition of the Rockefeller Center, with restaurants and stores, great views of the Hudson River and a pretty new park. Its focal point is the Winter Garden, a frequent venue for concerts and recitals (*see chapter* **Music: Classical & Opera**).

# History

# Key Events

## The First New Yorkers

**1524** Giovanni da Verrazano is the first European to visit Manhattan.
**1570** Hiawatha's Five Nations alliance brings together the Iroquois tribes. They declare war on the Algonquin.
**1600** The Algonquin are all but defeated.
**1609** Henry Hudson sails into the bay.
**1613** Trading post established at Fort Nassau (now Albany).
**1624** The Colony of New Amsterdam is founded and settlers arrive.
**1626** Peter Minuit, the first governor, arrives and 'buys' Manhattan from the Indians. New Amsterdam has a population of 300.
**1637** William Kieft, the governor, antagonises the native population until war breaks out between the Dutch and the Indians.
**1643** Peter Stuyvesant is made governor.
**1644** Manuel de Gerrit is the first free black man to settle in New York, farming an area of what is now SoHo.
**1661** The Dutch colony is nearly bankrupt.
**1662** John Bowne's struggle wins New Amsterdam's people the rights of religious freedom.

## British Rule

**1664** The British Invasion. New Amsterdam becomes New York.
**1683** A 21-month rebellion is led by Jacob Leisler, in protest at British plans for the colony.
**1700** New York's population is around 20,000.
**1725** *The Gazette* is New York's first newspaper.
**1733** T*he New York Weekly Journal,* a more independent paper, establishes the right to free speech.
**1754** King's College (now Columbia University) founded.
**1774** Colonial delegates protest British rule with the Declaration of Independence, and urge revolution.
**1776** The War of Independence rages. The British send 200 ships to occupy New York.
**1789** George Washington is elected the United States' first President.
**1783** The defeated British army leaves New York.

## An American City

**1785-90** New York is made US capital.
**1811** The Randel Plan envisages the grid into which the city is to grow.
**1812-14** America fights a further war with Britain. New York is isolated from international trade.
**1837** Financial panic ruins all but three of the city's banks.
**1843** Waves of mass immigration flood into the city.
**1851** *New York Times* first published.
**1858** Central Park laid out.
**1859** The Cooper Union, the city's foremost political forum, is established.
**1860** Abraham Lincoln elected president.
**1861** Civil war over the issue of slavery.
**1863** Conscription causes riots in New York.
**1865** The Union (the North) wins and slavery is ended.
**1870** Metropolitan Museum of Art founded.

**1872** Organised labour strikes for an eight-hour day.
**1883** Brooklyn Bridge completed.
**1886** Statue of Liberty unveiled.
**1895** Photo-journalist Jacob Riis publishes *How The Other Half Lives*, encouraging new housing regulations. New York Public Library founded.
**1898** Brooklyn ceases to be a separate city, making New York the world's second-largest.

## Twentieth Century

**1902** The Flatiron, the world's first skyscraper, is built.
**1907** Metered taxicabs introduced.
**1911** Triangle Shirtwaist Fire encourages workplace safety regulations.
**1917** America enters WWI.
**1920** Women win the right to vote. Prohibition introduced.
**1929** Wall Street Crash brings massive hardship and unemployment.
**1930s** Roosevelt's New Deal funds massive public works schemes. Empire State Building, Chrysler Building and Rockefeller Center built.
**1939** Corona Park, Queens, hosts the World's Fair. America enters WWII.
**1946** United Nations established, based in New York.
**1947** Brooklyn Dodger Jackie Robinson breaks the colour bar in major league baseball.
**1959** Guggenheim Museum opens.
**1962** Lincoln Center opens
**1964** Race riots in Harlem and Brooklyn. Beatles play Shea Stadium.
**1968** Columbia University sit-in. Hippies camp in Central park.
**1970** World Trade Center built.
**1975** The city is bankrupt.
**1977** 25-hour city-wide power blackout.
**1978** Mayor Ed Koch presides over a shortlived economic turnaround.
**1986** The other Wall Street crash.
**1990** David Dinkins is the city's first black mayor.
**1991** The city's budget deficit hits a record high.
**1993** Terrorists attempt to blow up the World Trade Center. Rudolph Guiliani is the city's first Republican mayor for 28 years. Staten Islanders vote to secede from New York City.

# The First New Yorkers

***Genocide seals the fate of New York's indigenous peoples as they are evicted by the Dutch and the English.***

The story of New York as a settlement begins with the Algonquins and the Iroquois, two distinct groups of Native Americans – with different languages and cultures – who lived in the surrounding area. Their fate was decided swiftly by the genocidal attitudes and foreign diseases brought by European settlers and, apart from various Algonquin placenames – such as Weckquaesgeek, Canarsee and Mannahatta or Manhattan, their name for a certain 13-mile-long island – the white man left little trace of the original New Yorkers.

The Native Americans of the New York region lived in longhouses covered in bark. They cultivated fields of corn, squash, potatoes, beans and peas; grew tobacco; planted fruit orchards; and raised domesticated animals and livestock. In the winter, they supplemented their diet by hunting. Clothes were made of cured skins, often fringed and brilliantly decorated with complicated beadwork.

The women cooked and cleaned, grew crops and raised the children, while their men went out to fight and hunt. But the women were the centre of the community. The tribes were organised into matrilineal family units, called *owachira*, with the eldest woman at the head. Husbands lived with their wives' families, the women owned all the marriage property – land, house and chattels – and inheritance of name and property was through the female line.

Leisure time was spent playing games like lacrosse (played with a solid-headed curved bat, and balls made of deer hide), and a violent type of football, both played on large fields without boundaries and with any number of players. Teams would train hard before an important game, a considerable number of bets would be laid and the winners would be the heroes of the hour.

## HIAWATHA & THE FIVE NATIONS

The Iroquois enjoyed a powerful political structure based around the Five Nations alliance, a confederacy of the Mohawk, Seneca, Onondaga, Cayuga and Oneida tribes. This was created in around 1570, when Hiawatha, the warrior-turned-pacifist immortalised in verse by poet Henry Longfellow, united these previously feuding Iroquois tribes. The resulting confederacy controlled a huge swathe of the northern USA from the Mississippi River to New England.

*Early explorer* **Henry Hudson**.

Not long before the coming of the Europeans, the Iroquois engaged the Algonquin in a series of bloody wars. When the Dutch began trading firearms for fur, the Five Nations ensured their victory by arming themselves with guns.

The war was long and bloody, bringing great losses to both sides. This tragic conflict lasted until the mid-1600s, when the Native Americans found themselves confronting a powerful new enemy – the colonising Europeans.

*The 'purchase' of Manhattan.*

## MASSACRES AND LAND THEFT

The explorer Henry Hudson, in 1609, described how the Indians welcomed him and his crew in the waters off Manhattan – 'This day the people of the country came aboard of us, seeming very glad of our coming'. Little could the Native Americans have dreamed that these friendly intruders would be back to destroy their society and culture.

The treatment of the American Indian is a disgraceful blot on American history. It's a story of the misappropriation of native land by treachery and gunpowder, and the introduction of European diseases and alcohol that wiped out whole tribes.

The nineteenth century was probably the darkest period for the country as a whole, with massacres, forced relocations and the wholesale theft of Indian land. In New York the genocide was completed much earlier and few Indians remained alive after the eighteenth century.

It is often noted that, ironically, the US Constitution mirrors the unique political structure that Hiawatha created for the Five Nations confederacy – with states, like the Iroquois tribes, being both independent and interdependent. How tragic that the fundamental rights of liberty and property later enshrined in America's defining document were not accorded to the country's original inhabitants.

## THE 'DISCOVERERS'

Christopher Columbus never set eyes on what is now New York City. The first European to do so was Giovanni da Verrazano in 1524. A Florentine sailing under the French flag, searching for the fabled North-West Passage to Chin a, Verrazano took refuge from a storm in what is now the New York harbour, and later took a small boat into the Upper Bay, where he was greeted by the local Indians.

It was a full 85 years later – in 1609 – when the next European arrived. Henry Hudson was employed by the Dutch East India Company, a purely commercial concern, involved in the romance of discovery only in so far as it furthered the company's economic gains.

Hudson, too, was searching for the North-West Passage. He sailed his ship, the *Half-Moon*, up the river that now bears his name, as far as Fort Nassau (today the state capital Albany). According to the ship's log book, they found 'friendly and polite people who had an abundance of provisions, skins, and furs of martens and foxes, and many other commodities, such as birds and fruit, even white and red grapes, and they traded amicably with the peoples'.

## DUTCH RULE

In 1611, Adriaen Block, an Amsterdam lawyer, heard of the riches of the newly discovered land, and tried his hand at trading with the Indians for fur. His first ship, the Tiger, was burned to the waterline with a full cargo, but using Indian labour, he built a new vessel, *Onrust* ('Restless'), with which he charted much of the local coastline. In 1613 a trading post was established at Fort Nassau, the beginnings of the eventual Dutch settlement of the area.

In 1624, the Dutch West India Company was granted a long-term trade and governing monopoly by the Dutch government. It was authorised to make alliances with native rulers, to establish colonies, to appoint and discharge governors and other officers and to administer justice.

Following this, the first settlers arrived – 30 families, most of whom were Protestants fleeing a Belgian inquisition. Of these, eight families stayed on Nut Island (now Governor's Island), while the others sailed up the river to Fort Nassau.

The company imposed tough conditions on the colonists: they were to stay put for six years, worship only through the Reformed Protestant Church, buy all their supplies from company stores and provide community labour on forts and public buildings. Trading outside the limits of the colony was forbidden, as was the sale of home-made goods for profit.

## BUYING MANHATTAN FOR BEADS

By 1626, when the first governor, Peter Minuit, had arrived, there were 300 Europeans living on the tip of Manhattan in a settlement named New Amsterdam. In the honourable tradition of European colonisers, Minuit negotiated a land deal with the locals – that is, he gave an Indian chief a few trinkets and blankets, got him to sign an incomprehensible document and assumed that the Dutch had bought themselves all of Manhattan Island.

In fact, the Indians had very different ideas about the possession of property, and could not conceive of individuals – rather than groups – owning land, let alone in perpetuity; the trading goods that Minuit gave to the chief were probably considered to be no more than the traditional gifts exchanged between visitors and their hosts.

Once the Europeans had moved in they refused to budge. Later governors exercised a deliberate policy of harassing Indian hunters, even though they were the main source of fur supplies and therefore crucial to the company's financial success. Attempts were made to tax them, they were forbidden firearms and harsh reprisals for petty crimes were enforced. As a result, a bloody war between the Dutch and the Indians broke out in the 1640s, which lasted for two and a half years.

### 'PEG-LEG' PETE

The war drastically reduced the Dutch West India Company's profits. After a massacre of more than 100 Indians in 1643, the company decided its best interests would be served by trying to calm things down. Their solution was Peter Stuyvesant, an experienced colonialist and staunch authoritarian. Stuyvesant's right leg had been shattered by a cannonball, hence his nickname, 'Peg-leg' Pete. He was sent out with express orders to restore the peace and consolidate the company's investment in New Amsterdam.

*'Peg-leg' Pete surrenders to Britain.*

Stuyvesant saw how the strain of living under constant threat of attack had prevented the town's proper establishment. 'The people have grown very wild and loose in their morals,' he commented, and set about cleaning up the inhabitants, their town and their habits.

He ordered a fortified structure (a defensive ditch and wall) built along the northern end of New Amsterdam – today's Wall Street. The

## So good they named it twice

The Naked City', 'The City That Never Sleeps', 'Babylon on the Hudson' – New York, New York (for city and state) has been named many more times than twice.

The first name, **Mannahatta**, or Manhattan, was given to the sheltered island by its original tenants, the Algonquin Indians. Centuries later, Brooklyn-born poet Walt Whitman praised the name: "'Manahatta, the place encircled by many swift tides and sparkling waters.' How fit a name for America's great democratic island city!".

When the Dutch moved in it became **New Amsterdam**, the name gaining currency after about 1624 when the first settlers began arriving. The settlement wasn't called **New York** until August 1664, when four British warships were welcomed into town and Captain Richard Nicolls signified British rule by honouring the king's brother, the Duke of York.

Besides its official appellations, New York, in fact, fiction and fantasy, has had many names. **Gotham**, its comic-book alter-ego – the city Batman inhabits – is a name taken from a village near Nottingham famous for its insane residents (Gotham actually means 'goat town'). It was coined in 1807 in a satirical story by Washington Irving, who felt, as many have noticed since, that New Yorkers work hard to preserve an appropriately impressive level of madness. The satire is subtle as the original Gothamites were only feigning insanity, in order to avoid King John's taxation.

The **Big Apple** was a phrase popularised around the 1920s meaning 'the pinnacle'. It was used by actors and musicians (especially jazz folk) to signify that performing in New York represented the height of success. In 1971, the nickname was given a boost when the city began using it to market itself to tourists, replacing the less successful 1960s sloganeering campaign which had christened New York **Fun City** (the subject of much derision).

**Metropolis**, alluding to the city of the future, was the title of Fritz Lang's 1926 film in which a world of skyscrapers and flying cars is the background for a Fascistic society of exploited workers. The same name was used for Superman's home town, a thinly veiled version of New York.

In the real future, as satellite communities ooze over the naked countryside and the notion of a city centre dies – killed by the flight to the suburbs and an era of telecommuting – New Yorkers might find themselves living in a gigantic conurbation extending from Boston to Washington DC. William Gibson, who gave us the word 'cyberspace', has written about this scenario, giving New York surely the last name it will need – **The Sprawl**.

muddy streets were paved with cobblestones; houses were built in Dutch style, with gables, checkered brickwork and brass door knockers; gardens were planted. Most importantly, a commercial infrastructure was established – banks, brokers' offices, wharves – and the waterfront, experiencing a boom, was soon lined with chandlers and taverns.

Stuyvesant founded the first municipal assembly, where members represented New Amsterdam and towns in the outlying areas, and encouraged the education of the colony's children. In the 17 years that he was governor, trade prospered and the settlement doubled in size.

### STUYVESANT'S INTOLERANCE

As it grew, New Amsterdam attracted and accepted a number of religious refugees, a challenge to the dominance of the Dutch Reformed Church. When a group of Jews arrived in 1653, Stuyvesant wrote to the directors of the Dutch West India Company, complaining that such immigrants jeopardised the cohesion of the colony. He didn't want to see it, as he put it, 'populated by the scrapings of all sorts of nationalities'. However, Holland had a tradition of religious tolerance and, in any case, European Jews were important shareholders in the company. Stuyvesant was very firmly rebuked.

However, he persisted in his intolerance, sparking a rebellion by the people of Flushing, led by John Bowne, a merchant and landowner. Bowne stood firm and invited members of the Religious Society of Friends, known as the Quakers, to hold meetings of worship in his kitchen.

Bowne was arrested and banished in 1662, only to be vindicated by the directors of the Dutch West India Company, who once again scolded Governor Stuyvesant and allowed Bowne to return two years later, thus giving the official nod of approval to religious freedom in the colony.

### THE BRITISH ARRIVE

In the end, Stuyvesant was a little too authoritarian for his own good. And the Dutch West India Company was a little too eager to exploit the colony. By 1661 New Amsterdam was bankrupt.

When four British warships sailed into town one day in August 1664, the population abandoned the fortifications Stuyvesant had built and welcomed Captain Richard Nicolls and his crew. New Amsterdam was renamed after the British king's brother, the Duke of York. Apart from a brief period from 1673 to 1674 when the city fell into Dutch hands again, the British ruled uninterrupted until the American Revolution.

The British inherited a cosmopolitan settlement that was predominantly Dutch but included English, French, Portuguese, Scandinavians and the first African slaves among its inhabitants. Both English and Dutch were spoken. The administrative system that Stuyvesant had put in place was retained, and the Dutch were allowed to continue their way of life. The settlement continued growing.

Strategically, New York was important for the British. They had long claimed the entire east coast of America, from New England south to Virginia, and year by year their settlements crept towards New York. In British eyes, New York was first and foremost a port: the finest natural harbour in the eastern United States, well protected from the elements, and providing access along the Hudson to the agriculturally rich Midwest.

In 1683, while they squabbled with the Dutch in Europe, the British attempted to rationalise New York, New Jersey and New England into a single dominion to cut administrative costs. The colonies rebelled. Affluent German merchant Jacob Leisler led a militia to take control of New York City and Long Island for 21 turbulent months. The town was divided, and Leisler and his supporters – Dutch and German artisans, retailers and farmers who were known as 'the Black people', alienated the rich merchants and landowners, the 'Whites'. When the British regained New York, Leisler and nine supporters were hanged for treason.

### THE MELTING POT

By 1700, New York's population had reached about 20,000. It was, as it continues to be, a population of immigrants. Alongside the English and Dutch were sizeable groups from France and Germany; settlers from Ireland and Sweden and some from other American colonies. Perhaps as many as 15 per cent were Africans, almost all of them slaves.

The mix of religions was just as complex. In 1687 Governor Dongan reported that there were 'not many of the Church of England, few Roman Catholicks, but an abundance of Quakers, ranting Quakers, Sabbatarians, Anti-sabbatarians, some Anabaptists, some Independents, some Jews; in short, of all sorts of opinions there are some, and the most part of none at all'.

New York's first newspaper, the *New York Gazette*, was established in 1725, at which time it was not much more than a mouthpiece for the British. Eight years later John Peter Zenger founded a rival, the *New York Weekly Journal*. Zenger soon got himself into trouble when he attacked Governor Cosby and his corrupt administration. Zenger's trial on libel charges brought a landmark decision: the newspaper publisher was acquitted because, his lawyer argued, the truth cannot be libellous. The Zenger verdict sowed the seeds for the First Amendment to the Constitution, in which are enshrined the principles of freedom of the press and the public's right to know.

This was just the beginning of trouble for the British.

# Independence & Civil War

***Britain loses its American colony. Less than a century later the new nation fights a civil war over slavery.***

In eighteenth-century Europe, the Age of Reason had arrived and the monarchy was hanging on by its coat-tails. The radical European social philosophies were studied by such Americans as Benjamin Franklin, Thomas Jefferson and John Adams, who in turn spread the ideals of fair and democratic government. Meanwhile, the British were imposing more and more taxes on their colonial possessions in order to pay off debts accumulated in colonial wars against France. Bostonians rebelled by dumping British tea into Boston Harbour.

In 1774 the Americans set up the Continental Congress, made up of delegates from each of the colonies. One of its earliest and most far-reaching decisions was to accept the Declaration of Independence, drawn up principally by Thomas Jefferson. The Declaration was 'the greatest single effort of national deliberation that the world has ever seen', proclaimed John Adams.

And with the interests of the colonies growing ever further apart from those of the British government, the colonial delegates, meeting in Philadelphia in September 1774, urged the people to withold taxes and – more importantly – to arm themselves. Revolution had become inevitable.

## NEW YORK AT WAR

New York was in a key position during the revolutionary war because of its dominant position on the Hudson River, which divided the New England colonies from their southern counterparts. The British commander, Lord Howe, sailed 200 ships into New York Harbour in the summer of 1776 and occupied the town. New Yorkers vented their fury by tearing down a gilded equestrian statue of George III which stood on Bowling Green.

At the Battle of White Plains the American forces, led by George Washington, were initially defeated and forced to regroup away from New York, preparing for a long drawn-out war.

On 11 September 1776, there was a peace initiative. Three colonists, led by Benjamin Franklin, met Lord Howe in Staten Island's Billop-Manor House (now known as the **Conference House**) only to refuse his conciliatory offer of rights and treatment equal to all other British subjects. 'America cannot return to the domination of Great Britain', said Franklin, demanding independence.

Life in occupied New York was grim. The population swelled from 20,000 to 30,000 as the town was overrun with British soldiers and loyalists fleeing the American army. As war raged throughout the colonies, the besieged town succumbed to disease and lack of essential supplies. Fires destroyed much of the city and many of the inhabitants died slowly of starvation.

In 1783 the British surrendered; two years later they were driven out of the American colonies.

## THE NEW REPUBLIC

New York was relieved in November 1783. The last British act was to grease the flagpole in the hope of making it harder for the Revolutionaries to raise the flag of the new Republic.

But the war was won. On 4 December, Washington joined his officers for an emotional farewell dinner held at the **Fraunces Tavern** in Pearl Street, where the Virginian farmer and victorious general declared his retirement. However, he was not to fade from public life, and on 23 April 1789, in the Old Federal Hall (on the same site as the present one) took the oath of office as the first President of the United States of America. New York was the new nation's first capital.

Though the capital for barely a year, in this time the city's business boomed, merchants grew richer and the port was busy. However, the city streets were narrow and dirty, and hygiene wasn't helped by the pigs, goats and horses that roamed free. Rents were high and demand was great. At the turn of the century, over 60,000 people lived in what is now downtown New York. The City Fathers decided the city was getting most untidy and came up with the famous 'grid' plan.

In 1811, the commissioners presented their blueprint. It ignored all the existing roads – with the exception of Broadway, which ran the length of the island, following an old Indian trail – and organised New York into a rectangular grid with wide numbered avenues and streets river to river. Commenting on the vast area thus earmarked for the city, they observed: 'It may be a subject of merriment that the Commissioners have provided space for a greater population than is collected at any spot on this side of China'.

## FORTUNES & PHILANTHROPY

When the 362-mile (582-km) Erie Canal opened in 1825, New York was linked, via the Hudson and the Great Lakes, with the Midwest. Along with the new railroads this trade route facilitated the making of many fortunes, and New York's merchants and traders flourished. Summer estates and mansions were built and by 1830 new villas had sprung up along Fifth Avenue as far as Madison Square. When met with the democratic ideals of the Revolution, these new riches spawned a clutch of charitable organisations philanthropic institutions.

Education was highly valued and the New York Society Library, which was established in 1754, rebuilt its collection, which had been vandalised during the British occupation. The Astor Library, a mid-nineteenth-century building opposite Colonnade Row on Lafayette (now the **Public Theater**), was built as the city's first free library, and Peter Cooper made plans for his Cooper Union for the Advancement of Science and Art.

Raised by authority of the State, at the request of the Secretary of War and Major-General McCLELLAN.

ONLY FIRST-CLASS RECRUITS
WANTED FOR THE
FIRST REGIMENT NEW-YORK HEAVY ARTILLERY
FOR GARRISON DUTY.
Col. T. D. DOUBLEDAY,
Lieut. Col. S. GRAHAM,
First Major H. H. HALL,
Second Major THOS. ALLCOCK.

Companies to be ordered to proceed at once to Washington.
GOOD POSITIONS GIVEN TO SOLDIERS WHO HAVE SEEN SERVICE.
JAS. B. GRANT,
Recruiting Officer.

GEORGE F. NESBITT & CO., Printers and Stationers, corner of Pearl and Pine Streets, N. Y.

*When recruitment calls like this failed, conscription was brought in – and led to riots.*

## POPULATION BOOM

Up until the 1830s, most families lived in row (terrace) houses. But the city was too successful, and growing too fast. By 1840, 300,000 people lived here, and the flood of immigrants from Ireland and Europe had started. The first grim tenement buildings, where whole families rented a bare room or two and shared washing facilities, were built.

By 1850, the wealthy in their Fifth Avenue mansions were enjoying indoor plumbing and central heating, benefits of the reliable water supply that the city had secured with the building in 1842 of the Croton Reservoir system (where the 42nd St New York Public Library now stands). In addition, more than 100 miles (161km) of sewer pipes had been installed in the city streets.

Middle-class neighbourhoods were also establishing themselves. In Brooklyn Heights and Park Slope, you can still see the rows of houses built in various styles – including Federal and Greek Revival – but all in brownstone, creating a unified, elegant whole.

## CIVIL WAR

Throughout the first half of the nineteenth century a bitter division was deepening between the northern and the southern states of America. The issue was slavery. For the South, there seemed no other way; its agricultural prosperity was based on the possession of slaves. But the urbanised and increasingly egalitarian northerners found it impossible to continue to accept this inhuman practice. The numbers involved were staggering: in 1860, over four million black people were shackled to a white population numbering eight million.

Attempts by the northern states to legislate nationwide against slavery horrified the white southerners. They could not conceive of a peaceful end to slavery (as had happened in the North), believing that freed blacks would want revenge. And as new states were joining the Union, upsetting the balance of power in Congress, violent conflict between North and South grew inevitable.

## THE ABOLITIONISTS

'For revolting barbarity and shameless hypocrisy, America reigns without a rival', declared former slave Frederick Douglass, stoking the fires of the abolitionist cause.

In Boston William Lloyd Garrison had published an anti-slavery journal, *The Liberator*, since 1831. In New York, the cause was kept alive in the columns of Horace Greeley's *Tribune* newspaper and in the sermons of Henry Ward Beecher, pastor of the Plymouth Church of the Pilgrims in Orange Street, Brooklyn. The minister (the brother of Harriet Beecher Stowe, who wrote *Uncle Tom's Cabin*) once shocked his congregation by auctioning a slave from his pulpit and using the proceeds to buy her freedom.

## LINCOLN & WAR

Abraham Lincoln was known in the country as a vehement opponent of slavery. But in an attempt to preserve the Union, he proposed the return of runaway slaves to their 'owners', and supported the idea of returning the black population to Africa. This prompted abolitionist orator Wendell Phillips to call him 'that slavehound from Illinois'.

Despite his complex position, Lincoln took a firm abolitionist stance addressing a meeting in the Great Hall of the Cooper Union in New York (the first American school open to any race, religion, or sex). Here he declared: 'Neither let us be slandered from our duty by false accusations against us, nor frightened from it by menaces of destruction to the government nor of dungeons to ourselves. Let us have faith that right makes might, and in that faith, let us to the end, dare to do our duty as we understand it.'

Following this famous speech, the newly formed Republican Party – a liberal alliance with little in common with the party of today – took Lincoln up as a serious contender for their presidential candidacy. In 1860, with the announcement of his victory, the southern states seceded from the Union.

## WARTIME NEW YORK

Although New York sided with the Union against the Southern Confederacy, there was considerable sympathy for the South, particularly among poor Irish and German immigrants, who feared that freed slaves would compete with them for work.

When Lincoln introduced conscription in 1863, the streets of New York erupted in rioting. The rioters protested conscription and the fact that since the wealthy could buy out of the army it was the poor who'd have to fight – in a battle for the freedom of people they felt would take their jobs.

For three days New York raged. Blacks were attacked in the streets, the homes and offices of the abolitionists were gutted. The violence came to an end only when Union troops returning from victory at Gettysburg subdued the city. There were 100 fatalities and over a thousand people injured. It was the worst riot in American history.

## VICTORY

The inevitable northern victory was achieved in 1865, engineered by General Ulysses S Grant, who had been made supreme commander of the Union armies two years earlier. It was helped by General Sherman's infamous 'scorched earth' march through the South, during which the Union army burned mansions, wrecked railroads, freed slaves and gorged themselves on the crops and livestock they found en route. Robert E Lee's southern troops surrendered in April 1865.

For his efforts, Lincoln was assassinated a week after victory. After the disastrous presidency of Andrew Johnson, the country elected General Grant, who had ended the Civil War.

# The Making of the Metropolis

***New York becomes a vast, sprawling city of fantastic wealth and grotesque poverty, defined by waves of immigration.***

New York emerged from the Civil War virtually unscathed. It had not seen any actual fighting (only rioting) and instead had prospered as the financial centre of the North and the most convenient port of entry from Europe. But as the city thrived, rich and poor grew further apart and there was desperate economic competition between the immigrant groups.

## IMMIGRATION

'Give me your tired, your poor, your huddled masses yearning to breathe free,' entreats Frederic Auguste Bartholdi's 1886 **Statue of Liberty**, one of the first sights of America that ocean-borne arrivals would have seen.

The first great waves of immigration to America's twin ports of welcome – Boston and New York – started well before the Civil War. German liberals were fleeing their failed 1848 revolution and a huge influx of Irish had begun after the 1843 potato famine. In the 1880s large numbers of immigrants from the old Russian empire – Ukrainians, Poles, Romanians and Lithuanians, many of them Jews – arrived, along with southern Italians. Additionally, many of the Chinese labourers who had been brought to America to do the back-breaking work on the railroads in California moved east to New York.

From 1855 to 1890, the immigration centre at Castle Clinton in Battery Park processed eight million newcomers. The **Ellis Island** centre, built in 1892, served the same purpose for roughly the same length of time, and handled double that number. To the immigrants it was the 'Isle of Tears', where they were herded about like cattle, separated from loved ones, physically examined and sometimes – thoroughly isolated – sent back to their homelands. With the introduction of a quota system in 1921, the flood of newcomers slowed, and Ellis was closed in 1932.

The new arrivals stuck together in communities of common origin. While they preserved their religion, customs, cuisine and language, they also relentlessly pursued the dream of bettering themselves and their children. The Jews, in particular, opened schools and libraries, published newspapers and supported theatres and charitable institutions. By 1910, over 1.5 million Jews were living in New York City.

At the same time, a quarter of New York's population was Irish. Although they were stuck in poverty, the Irish experienced a freedom which they hadn't enjoyed in three centuries of British occupation: the right of political action. They entered city government wholeheartedly, and within a few decades controlled it.

## HOMES OF PAUPERS & KINGS

New immigrants usually ended up in the grim, crowded tenements of the Lower East Side, which in 1894 filled six blocks. Whole families lived in one or two dark rooms, with no hot water or heating, sharing toilets with neighbours.

When Jacob Riis published his *How the Other Half Lives*, an exposé of life in the ghetto, the city was horrified. The children working in the sweatshops of the Lower East Side, the squalid housing conditions and the struggle to retain human dignity were evident in Riis's harrowing story and in his photographs (now in the **Museum of the City of New York**).

Stirred into action, in 1879 the city passed the first of a series of housing laws which laid down minimum water and toilet requirements, allowed for airshafts between buildings to let in light and air and made fire escapes mandatory.

As the population of New York swelled, the established middle classes – the merchants and industrialists who were benefitting from the city's vigorous post-war economy – moved into brownstones like those on Park Slope in Brooklyn, or the row houses that sprang up in Midtown.

The very wealthy were drawn further north by the magnet of **Central Park**, the construction of which had started in 1857. The Fifth Avenue side became the playground of the rich, with enormous

*Italian immigrants at Ellis Island.*

mansions built for monied families such as the Vanderbilts, the Astors and the Whitneys.

On the Upper West Side street after street of row houses were built, attracting well-off European immigrants and intellectuals to the neighbourhood. Massive luxury apartment blocks, such as the stately Dakota on West 72nd Street and Central Park West, started to dominate the skyline and, after a slow start, the neighbourhood became very desirable.

## ESTABLISHING AN INFRASTRUCTURE

The city's infrastructure was gradually developed to sustain its crowded population. Supplies of clean water had been ensured by the Croton Reservoir, sewers built throughout the island, and electricity harnessed by New Yorker Thomas Edison (even today, New Yorkers' electricity is delivered by his company, Consolidated Edison).

Railroads already connected the city to the rest of the country: now elevated railways cast shadows over the avenues and subway lines were excavated under the streets. Trams, too, rattled their way through the city; the perilous, occasionally fatal, turn at Broadway and 14th Street was dubbed 'Dead Man's Curve' and drew crowds of morbidly curious onlookers.

All these great technological feats paled into insignificance beside the extraordinary achievement of the **Brooklyn Bridge** (1869-1883). At the time it was built, it was the longest suspension bridge in the world and the first to use steel cable. Designed by John A Roebling, who died in an accident on site before construction started, and completed by his son Washington, the bridge opened up the independent city of Brooklyn to Manhattan, and eventually led to its 'secession' to New York in 1898.

## THE SAD LOT OF LABOUR

The frenetic growth of the city's industrial strength created appalling health and safety conditions. Combined with low wages – some women workers would average only $2 or $3 for a 60-hour week – the squalid conditions forced labour to organise. In 1872, 100,000 workers went on strike for three months until they won the eight-hour day. Doubts about their 'Americanism' were raised.

A year later, the country was plunged into a serious depression, and many of New York's workforce were forced on to the streets: 90,000 hungry and unemployed people were homeless.

Enormous crowds overflowed from labour and political meetings at the Cooper Union. The whole country was in disarray for nearly five years: the railroad strikes, in particular, turned very bloody, with the companies hiring private security forces and enlisting the sympathetic and often brutal support of the police.

*Building the* **Brooklyn Bridge** *was a mammoth feat of engineering.*

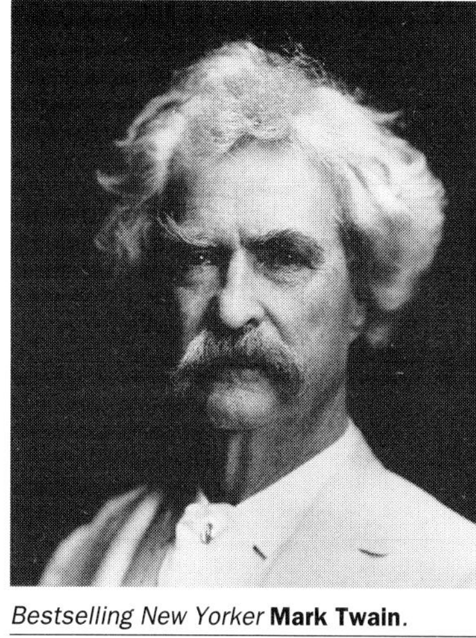

*Bestselling New Yorker* **Mark Twain**.

The workers' resistance was eventually broken when the bosses took to employing newly arrived immigrants, whom they could pay even less. In addition child labour was common. 'Nearly any hour on the East Side of New York City you can see them – pallid boy o r spindling girl – their faces dulled, their backs bent under a heavy load of garments piled on head and shoulders, the muscles of the whole frame in a long strain', wrote Edwin Markham in 1907.

It took the horror of the 1911 fire at the Triangle Shirtwaist Factory in Washington Place, Greenwich Village, in which 146 workers died, to stir politicians into action. Over 50 health and safety measures were passed by the state legislature within months of the fire.

## HIGH FINANCE

With the industrial revolution spurring the economy ever onwards, New York's financiers, dominated by the Dutch since the early days of European settlement, made sure to carve themselves a substantial piece of the pie.

Market activity was frenzied. Swindles, panics and collapses were frequent, but seemed to reach new heights in the late nineteenth century. Jay Gould made enormous profits during the Civil War by having the outcome of military engagements cabled to him secretly and trading on the results before they became public knowledge. Another master swindler was Jim Fisk, who, together with Gould, seduced Cornelius Vanderbilt into buying vast quantities of Erie Railroad bonds before the price dropped out of the market. Vanderbilt had the resources to sit out such a crisis, and the grace to call Gould 'the smartest man in America'. Vanderbilt, Andrew Carnegie and banker JP Morgan had consolidated their fortunes on the railroads. John D Rockefeller made his in oil, owning, by 1879, 95 per cent of the refineries in the United States. His company, Standard Oil, was finally broken up by an anti-monopoly case bought by Theodore Roosevelt, who insisted 'no amount of charities in spending such fortunes can compensate for the misconduct in acquiring them.'

## POLITICAL MACHINATIONS

Theodore Roosevelt became president in 1901 on the assassination of William McKinley, after having been Governor of New York State. He was an instinctive politician who was among the first world leaders to understand the importance of public image. Roosevelt was also an empire-builder. He took America into the Philippines, leased a coast-to-coast stretch of Panama and stationed US troops there, built up the navy fleet and increased the regulatory powers of his own federal government.

In New York, politics had become mired in corruption. William Marcy 'Boss' Tweed, the young leader of a Democratic Party faction called Tammany Hall (named after a famous Indian chief) had turned city government into a lucrative operation. As commissioner of public works he collected large payoffs from companies receiving city contracts. Tweed and his 'Ring' are estimated to have misappropriated $160 million, enough of which they distributed in political bribes to keep a lot of influential mouths shut.

But by 1871 Boss Tweed's number was up. A disgusted City Hall clerk passed damaging documents to *The New York Times*, whose publisher was reputed to have refused a half-million dollar bribe. The crusade against Tammany Hall corruption continued in cartoonist Thomas Nast's *Harper's Weekly*. Tweed said he didn't care what the newspapers wrote, because most of his supporters couldn't read, but they could understand 'them damn pictures'.

The most spectacular monument to Tweed's graft is the **New York County Courthouse**, known as the Tweed Courthouse. The city paid $14 million for it, $10 to $12 million more than its true cost. Consequently, some of the work was very fine indeed: 'if you pay a carpenter $360,747 for a month's work, they have to do something'. In recent years the Tweed Courthouse has been declared a landmark and restored for use as municipal offices.

## FURTHER PHILANTHROPY

As the wealth of the city grew, further gifts were made to the city as the millionaires of New York signalled their success in the form of concert halls, libraries and entire art collections complete with a building to put them in.

Steel baron Andrew Carnegie, who, they say, never forgot his penniless immigrant origins, gave

New York **Carnegie Hall**. And when **The New York Public Library** was established in 1895 he offered $52 million to establish branch libraries. The nucleus of the library is the combined collections of John Jacob Astor, Samuel Jones Tilden and James Lenox.

The **Metropolitan Museum of** was founded in 1870 by members of the Union League Club and opened two years later with a modest collection of 174 Dutch and Flemish paintings and some antiquities given by General di Cesnola, a former US consul to Cyprus. Now it is the largest art museum in the Western world.

### NEW YORK LITERATURE

The successful city developed further its own artistic and literary movements. Following on from the first figures of New York letters – people like satirist Washington Irving and gothic storyteller Edgar Allen Poe – were Brooklyn poet Walt Whitman and writers like Edith Wharton and Mark Twain. Wharton became one of the most astute critics of old New York society and her most memorable novels, such as *The Age of Innocence*, are detailed renderings of New York life at the turn of the century.

Mark Twain (real name Samuel Clemens), one of the most widely read writers in nineteenth-century America, moved from the West Coast to New York in 1870. *The Adventures of Tom Sawyer* was published six years later, followed by *Huckleberry Finn* in 1884. In addition to his humorous and optimistic tales, Twain was a gifted satirist and a robust political commentator, publishing pithy columns about government corruption and social conditions.

## The subway

New York's subway system, an unceasing network of civic arteries pumping a human fluid of 3.5 million passengers a day (a billion and a quarter a year), was this century's largest single factor in the growth of the city. By offering a fast and inexpensive method of travelling between home and work, it finally allowed working people to leave the polluted congestion of lower Manhattan while retaining their stake in the life of New York. Only once the tracks had been laid would the city extend northwards.

The subways hold a unique place in the city's imagination, offering the perfect metaphor for New Yorkers' fast, crowded lives lived among strangers. Most famously, Duke Ellington's song implored its listeners to 'Take the A-train', noting 'that's the quickest way to get to Harlem'. Tin Pan Alley's songwriters penned such popular ditties as 'Rapid Transit Gallop' and 'The Subway Glide', and new words and phrases like 'rush hour' entered the language. The most lyrical homage to the subway was New York wit O Henry's observations on the opening of the first underground line. Capturing the city's delirious affection for its new way of getting around, he wrote: 'The rapid transit is poetry and art; the moon but a tedious, dry body moving by rote.' In the 1980s the system was a gallery for the graffiti writers of Brooklyn and the Bronx, as hip-hop culture made the trains into giant canvases.

The ancestor of the subway system was an elevated 1868 line, which ran along Greenwich Street, powered by a steam-driven cable. By the turn of the century it had been electrified and was part of an aerial network which extended into the Bronx, Queens and Brooklyn, darkening the streets above which it clattered and encouraging hookers to rent third-floor rooms level with the trains where they could sit in the window to lure the punters in. Outside Manhattan much of the elevated track remains in use to this day, but on the island it was gradually dismantled and the routes sunk underground.

In 1900 building started on the first of three subterranean systems which were eventually united to make up today's subway. The first was the IRT (Interborough Rapid Transit), running from City Hall to Grand Central, to Times Square, and then following Broadway to 145th Street. After digging a ceremonial hole to inaugurate construction, the mayor was so moved that he took away some soil in his hat.

New lines followed – the BMT, the IND – their names preserved in old signs, and in the confusing alternatives many New Yorkers still use to describe various routes. By the 1940s the system was very much as it is today.

There are now 714 miles (1142km) of subway routes, with 469 stations. The trains are new, the graffiti is gone, crime in the subway is beaten back to a minimum and apart from the occasional flooding and derailment ('I DROVE TRAINS HIGH ON CRACK' is perhaps the best tabloid headline for many years), it is the most convenient daytime way to travel round the city. That doesn't mean it's perfect: sample the air in Union Square station and you'll see why the transit police call the subway 'The Electric Sewer'.

For more about the subway's history, visit the **Transit Museum**.

# The Twentieth Century

***New York grows up and endures Prohibition, Depression, World War, Cold War and a still-increasing population.***

*The jazz age roared through the twenties.*

World War I thrust America onto centre stage as a world power. Its pivotal role in the defeat of Germany had strengthened the nation's confidence. New York, particularly, had benefited from wartime trade and commerce. When Wall Street prospered, the nation prospered. As President Calvin Coolridge said in 1925: 'the business of America is business'.

## THE JAZZ AGE

The Roaring Twenties, perhaps the nation's adolescence, were ushered in with two important legislative changes. Firstly the 19th Amendment gave women the vote, giving them an independence also evident in fashions for shorter hair, shorter skirts and supposedly provocative dances like the Charleston. The other law passed in 1920 was Prohibition, which may not have been the cause of the Jazz Age but which certainly added to its wildness. The bootleg liquor that flowed at the speakeasies made many a gangster's fortune.

In Harlem's Cotton Club such musicians as Lena Horne, Josephine Baker and Duke Ellington played for an exclusively white audience, as New Yorkers enjoyed 'that Negro vogue', as poet Langston Hughes called it. On Broadway, the Barrymore family – Ethel, John and Lionel (Drew's forebears) – were treading the boards between movies. Over at the New Amsterdam Theater on West 42nd Street the high-kicking Ziegfeld Follies dancers were opening for such entertainers as WC Fields, Fanny Brice and Marion Davies. In 1926, hundreds of thousands of New Yorkers were on the streets mourning the death of matinee idol Rudolph Valentino. The same year the city elected Jimmy Walker, a party-loving ex-songwriter, as mayor.

## THE WALL STREET CRASH

On 29 October 1929 the party was over. New York was in panic as the stock market collapsed, destroying many small investors and leading to massive poverty and unemployment. Central Park filled with the shantytowns of the newly-homeless – known as Hoovervilles, after President Herbert Hoover. One in four New Yorkers were out of work by 1932. Banks were failing every day – 1,326 of them in 1930 alone – wiping out people's savings and making bankers one of the most hated groups in the country. The song of the day was Yip Harburg's 'Brother, Can You Spare a Dime?'

## LAGUARDIA AND THE NEW DEAL

With the country in turmoil, people searched for new political ideas. New York became a bastion of socialism, as Trotskyites, anarchists and communists gained influence. Against this background the city elected a young congressman, Fiorello LaGuardia, as mayor in 1932. LaGuardia, a stocky, short-tempered man, took over the crisis-strewn city and, surprisingly, his austerity programmes won wide support.

He was boosted by Franklin D Roosevelt's election as president. Roosevelt's New Deal restored public confidence by re-employing the jobless on public works programmes and allocating federal funds to roads, housing and parks. The Works

Progress Administration (WPA) also made money available to actors, writers, artists and musicians – the only time in American history that the arts have been adequately subsidised by federal government.

LaGuardia held mayoral office for 12 years, during which he reduced corruption within city government, waged war against organised crime and launched the most extensive public housing programme in the country. He is still regarded as the city's best-loved mayor.

## ART & ARCHITECTURE

Some of the great twentieth-century New York buildings went up in this period: the **Chrysler Building**, the **Empire State**, and the **Rockefeller Center** were all built in the 1930s. And as the Nazis terrorised the intelligentsia in Europe, New York became the favoured refuge for artists, architects and designers. Walter Gropius, the former director of the influential Bauhaus school of design, and architect Ludwig Mies van der Rohe moved to America from Germany.

When painters such as Arshile Gorky, Piet Mondrian, Hans Hofmann and Willem de Kooning shifted to New York, gradually the centre of the art world did too. The **Museum of Modern Art** was founded, the idea of three collectors – Abby Aldrich Rockefeller, Lillie P Bliss and Mrs Cornelius Sullivan – to document the Modern Movement and represent the most important contemporary artists, a daring concept in 1929.

## NEW YORK VOICES

The literary scene was dominated by Ernest Hemingway and his friend F Scott Fitzgerald, whose *The Great Gatsby* turned a dark gaze on the 1920s. They worked with the editor Maxwell Perkins at Scribner's publishing house, along with Thomas Wolfe, who constructed enormous semi-autobiographical mosaics of small-town life, and Erskine Caldwell, author of *Tobacco Road*, the Depression novel set in the rural deep South.

The city's two other great chroniclers of the time were Dorothy Parker and HL Mencken, the two caustic wits around whom the famous Round Table at the Algonquin Hotel was centred. Parker wrote articles, columns, poems and short stories for a select number of magazines, most notably *The New Yorker*, *The Nation* and *The New Republic*. Mencken remains the journalist's journalist, a brilliant and incisive essayist, who founded and edited *The American Mercury*.

## WORLD WAR II

America's involvement in World War II jolted it out of the Depression. Government spending for war production revived the economy and New York Harbor bustled with ships carrying soldiers, sailors and supplies to the battlefields of Europe.

After the victory began a long period of paranoia and distrust as the Cold War raged between the United States and the Soviet Union. New York, a city with a long tradition of radicalism in its politics, saw bitter disputes between communists, anti-communists and civil libertarians. The crusading political spirit of the 1930s and 1940s gave way to the enforced conformity and conservativeness of the 1950s.

The United Nations established its headquarters overlooking the East River in Manhattan, seeing New York as very much a world city. Artists venturing into the new world of abstract expressionism also made the city their own, and a new generation of Le Corbusier-inspired architects, transformed its skyline with new buildings that took the form of glass and steel boxes.

## POPULATION GROWTH

With increasing affluence, many families moved out to the suburbs. Towns sprang up around the new highways and about one million children and grandchildren of European immigrants – mostly Irish, Jewish and

– moved to live in them. Their places were taken by a new wave of immigrants, as one million Puerto Ricans and African-Americans from the South, moved to the city.

By the mid-1960s, New Yorkers could no longer ignore the large and growing non-white communities, largely excluded from the city's power structure and prosperity. Until then, the Democratic politicians who dominated the city had given little more than token recognition to the newcomers. Discrimination and the decline in the city's manufacturing base limited black and Latino prospects for economic success.

Despite some creative efforts to bring these newcomers into the city's mainstream – especially in the administration of Mayor John Lindsay – entrenched poverty and prejudice made for slow progress. Meanwhile, increases in street crime cast a shadow of fear across the entire city.

## 1960S COUNTER-CULTURE

New York remained a centre for radical politics and the avant-garde. The Beat movement of the 1950s evolved into the hippie counter-culture of the 1960s, and Manhattan provided the stage: from the folk music that floated from the coffee houses of Greenwich Village to the student protests against racism and the Vietnam war that boiled out of the campus of Columbia University.

Elsewhere in the city, in more conservative working- and middle-class neighbourhoods, many white New Yorkers grew disenchanted with liberalism, which seemed incapable of providing safe streets or effective schooling. To make matters

*New York remains a city of tensions – but the force is with it.*

8044
POLICE
POLICE
POLICE
POLICE
POLICE

*New York's jazz heritage strikes the right note in the city's street art.*

worse, by 1975 the city was all but bankrupt. With a growing population on welfare and a declining tax base caused by middle-class flight to the suburbs it had resorted to heavy municipal borrowing.

## BOOM & BUST

To the rescue rode Mayor Edward I Koch, a onetime liberal from Greenwich Village, who steered the city back to fiscal solvency with austerity measures and state and federal help. By shrewdly, if cynically, playing the city's racial and ethnic politics and riding the 1980s boom in construction and finance, Koch won three successive four-year terms.

But there would not be a fourth. Amid the greed and conspicuous consumption of the 1980s Koch was finally undone by a combination of corruption scandals, growing black political strength and an inability to defuse the city's racial hostilities.

He was succeeded by David N Dinkins, the city's first African-American mayor. Dinkins, an old-fashioned clubhouse politician with liberal instincts, took office in 1990, inheriting a multitude of problems left over from the ugly underside of the Koch years: racial conflicts, poverty and large numbers of homeless people. Soon afterwards, the city was battered by a deep economic recession. Dinkins excelled at grand symbolic gestures, such as handsomely welcoming Nelson Mandela to the city. He made important initiatives in the fight against crime by implementing new community policing strategies. But he could not overcome global economic trends that drew manufacturing jobs away from the city. And as a likeable, conciliatory man, many felt he lacked the sabre-toothed aggression necessary to run New York.

He was succeeded in 1994 by Rudolph Guiliani, a tough Italian-American lawyer, who had entered the political limelight as a fearless federal prosecutor. Though initially welcomed as the antidote to the equivocal, often bumbling Dinkins, Guiliani's dictatorial style and the social implications of his policies, quickly alienated him from many of his supporters.

## TOWARDS THE MILLENNIUM

The problems facing the mayor of New York are many, but they are simply those of any other city, magnified. Racial tension, a depleted tax base, increasingly polarised wealth and a concentration of AIDS, homelessness and crime are simply the sad signs of urban life in the 1990s. The city is a modern invention struggling to survive in these confused post-modern times. However, there are still plenty of people willing to stake their claim here. Recent arrivals – legal and otherwise – from Asia, Latin America, the Caribbean and the former Soviet Union make up a foreign-born population of more than two million.

As at any time throughout its history, New York remains a city of pioneers. It is the constant flow of humanity which gives the city its energy, and it is the hope of harnessing some of it which keeps people coming. After all, if you can make it here, you'll make it anywhere.

# New York Today

***Like a self-destructive superstar, New York in the 1990s is a city loved and loathed with equal passion.***

*'As the Mercedes ascended the bridge's great arc, he could see the island of Manhattan off to the left. The towers were jammed together so tightly, he could feel the mass and stupendous weight. Just think of the millions, from all over the globe, who yearned to be on that island, in those towers, in those narrow streets! There it was, the Rome, the Paris, the London of the twentieth century, the city of ambition, the dense magnetic rock, the irresistible destination of all those who insist on being where things are happening.'*

**Tom Wolfe**, *Bonfire of the Vanities.*

A grey-suited commuter rides the F train in from Queens. She hangs from a tubed steel handle, an ad for the Bronx Zoo behind her shoulder. Despite her smart office clothes, her feet are decked in comfy white Reeboks. It's only 7am and she's headed to the gym, where she will read some reports while pounding a Stairmaster machine. Then to work so as to be at her desk before her boss arrives. As the train barrels its way to Rockefeller Center, she battles the morning crush to drink her coffee (from a blue and white deli cup with a plastic top), and manages to read a folded paper held in the same hand. All along the carriage, the crackle of turning newsprint tells a familiar set of stories.

One of the city's sports teams came second in something big. The mayor managed to convince an important New York company (by offering some deft last-minute tax-breaks) not to move its

*John Gotti, the Dapper Don, looks sharp.*

headquarters to Colorado. A four-year-old child was caught in crossfire between duelling crack monsters out in some public housing project. A minor official in city government is under investigation for corruption. A Californian soap star has announced that she's divorcing her husband to pursue a career on Broadway. And a poll reveals that while 92 per cent of New Yorkers would love to leave the city and never come back, 93 per cent of them think there is no greater place to live.

This is the daily reality of New York. A city whose headlines are polarised into celebration or despair. It may be a town broken by the weight of its problems: by crime, homelessness, AIDS, and an annual three- or four-billion dollar budget deficit, but somehow New York manages to reconstruct itself each morning into the most exciting and seductive place on Earth.

## 'CAN I PUT YOU ON HOLD FOR A MINUTE?'

One of the first things you notice as a visitor is something often called the city's 'pace'. You are experiencing a combination of factors. Crammed within the shoreline of a small island, New York is undeniably overcrowded; it is a world capital for so many spheres of art and commerce; it is full of energetic, single-minded people; and, most importantly, these people are fully armed with the American Dream, paying devout homage to capitalism and the power of the individual.

For most people (excepting visitors, the rich and the well-supported), New York is not a place for hanging out. There's too much work to be done. People here work frighteningly hard. Unlike state-assisted Europeans, their jobs are lifelines to such essentials as pensions and medical treatment, and New Yorkers – ambitious and impatient – put their working lives a clear first, ruthlessly regimenting their personal time to fit. In corporate America, as little as two weeks vacation a year is standard. And self-employed people would consider themselves lucky to manage even that.

The flipside to this work-to-live/live-to-work mode of existence can be seen in New York's large and growing homeless population. When you live hand-to-mouth, as many hard-working New Yorkers do, there is not far to fall before an illness or an accident takes away your savings, your job, your home. With the bare minimum of medical services provided by the state, and a scary 17 per cent of Americans working without the protection of health insurance, the implications of falling off the tracks are clear. New York has no safety net.

## '...STRONG SUPPORT AMONG BLACK AND HISPANIC VOTERS....'

Another thing visitors notice is the obsession with race. This is a persistent theme of New York life. Neighbourhoods are characterised wholly by the complexion of their inhabitants; politicians divide their support up into precise ethnic groups; and mixed-race couples still act as if they are engaged in some rebellious deviance.

America's experience of slavery and segregation has left a society where the colour of your skin has serious implications. And even in cosmopolitan New York people have trouble conceiving of any end to these artificial divisions. There are so many cultures, nations and languages represented in the city that it would seem difficult for anyone here to be racist. And yet rather than see themselves as members of a vibrant culture with contributions from all over the planet, New Yorkers instead prefer to shrink back into their little ethnic groups and portray themselves as members of beleaguered minorities. Very rarely do they come out fighting as citizens of the same place.

Watch the TV news for the most amusing examples of this. Erroneously believing that race is 'controversial' per se, the news teams tread ludicrously carefully. If a cop shoots a kid in Harlem you'll see a black reporter gathering opinions from black people; for a story about a fire in a Puerto Rican neighbourhood, they'll send a Latin guy to talk to

*Another night, another bust: the NYPD gets through one of 267,000 arrests in 1995.*

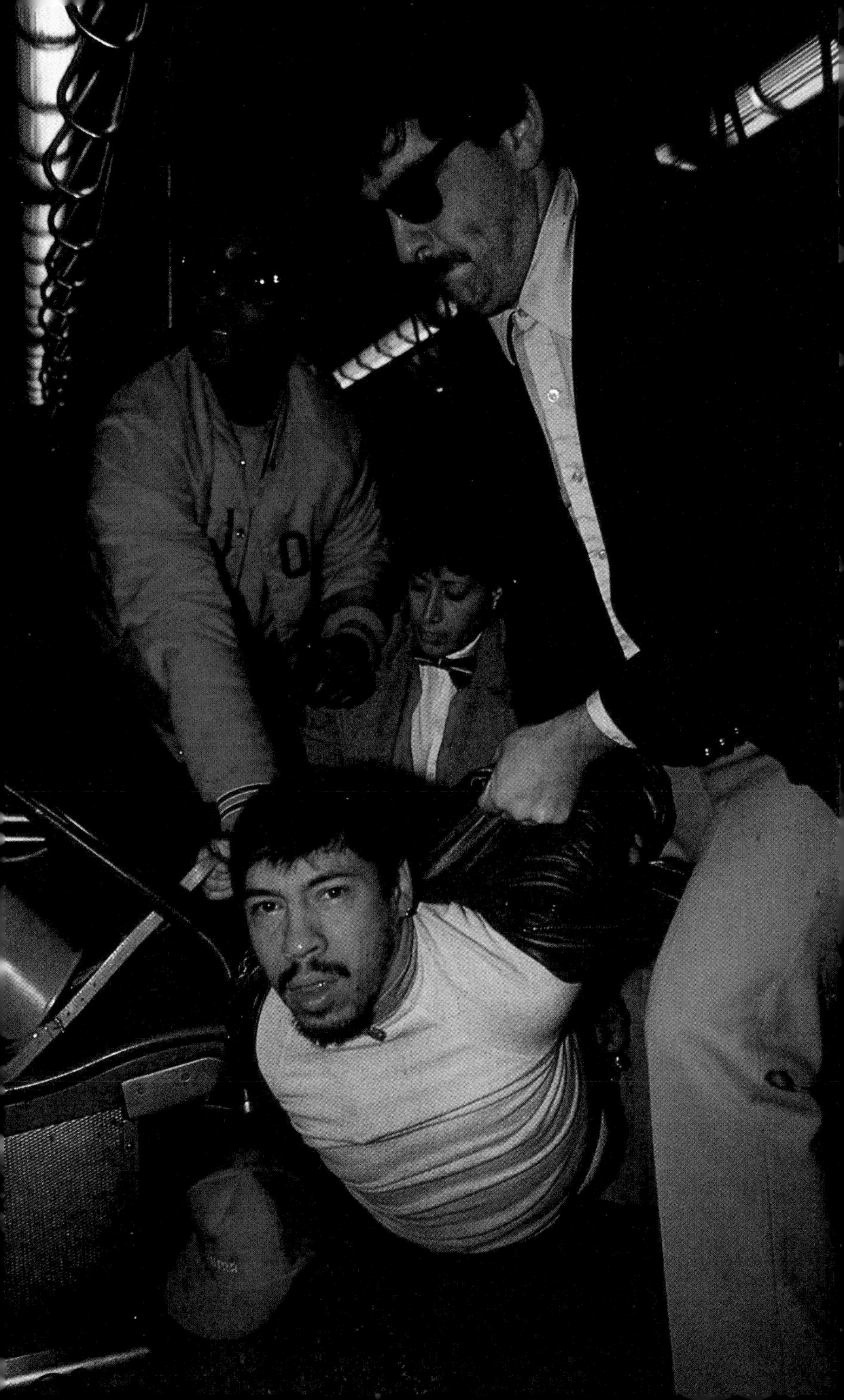

Latinos, and if the story's about Chinatown it'll be a Chinese face doing the reporting. New Yorkers fail to see the absurdity of this.

Still, when a black girl sitting in a diner tells you that because of segregation hers is the first generation able to eat there, you start to see things a little less clearly.

### 'PEOPLE CALLED IT THE SAINT'S DISEASE'

In August 1995 they demolished the brick shell that had housed the Saint nightclub. Throughout the 1980s it had been an incredible place containing a planetarium-sized aluminium dome: the site of unprecedented dancefloor freedom for the city's gay population. But it was at the Saint that a mysterious disease was first noticed; a sickness that claimed the lives of the club's partygoers.

Fifteen years later and although the Saint lives on with a new constituency in huge, explosive quarterly parties, almost all the people who originally danced there have died. AIDS has claimed the lives of tens of thousands of young, unique, loving people.

AIDS is now an equal opportunity disease. In fact it is one of the leading killers of young New Yorkers. It strains the city's public health resources, and continues to spread, aided by ignorance, apathy and despair.

As for the Saint, it's been suggested that there would be no more appropriate place to build a memorial commemorating the thousands of New Yorkers who are now dead from the disease. Instead the plot will house an apartment block.

### 'IT'S CALVIN KLEIN: COCAINE AND KETAMINE'

They say the drugs coming into a city control its mood. After the disco-opulent cocaine 1970s – when Studio 54's dancefloor displayed a man-in-the-moon with a coke-spoon up his nose – the 1980s brought New York crack, a downmarket version of the same chemical. The great unwashed embraced this super-capitalist drug, with its brand names and millionaire franchise distributors, in a spiralling craziness of bullets that made battlegrounds out of already forgotten neighbourhoods. Some residents call the South Bronx 'Vietnam'. Crack is still here, and even

## New York by numbers

| | |
|---|---|
| Official population (1990 census) | **7.3 million** |
| Unofficial population | **10 million** |
| Number of New Yorkers per square mile | **33,223** |
| Children in public (city-run) schools in 1995 | **1,036,000** |
| Visitors to New York in 1994 | **24.6 million** |
| Annual flights in and out of NYC's three airports | **1,116,000** |
| Average annual snowfall | **29.3 inches** |
| Annual economic impact of fashion industry in New York | **$14 billion** |
| Heroin confiscated in 1995 | **1,101lbs** |
| Cocaine confiscated in 1995 | **16,104lbs** |
| Marijuana confiscated in 1995 | **2,613lbs** |
| Number of eating establishments | **17,000** |
| Average traffic speed across town | **5.3mph** |
| Number of cars towed for parking violations in 1995 | **140,604** |
| Area of New York City | **301 square miles** |
| Miles of subway track | **722** |
| Average number of subway riders per day | **3.4 million** |
| Record for visiting all stations | **26hrs, 21mins, 8secs** |
| Average daily prison population | **18,736 (17,109 men; 1,635 women)** |

in parts of Central Park or the East Village you can see the tell-tale inch-long plastic vials and their colourful stoppers lying on the ground.

However, as the 1990s grow older the city has also seen heroin become ever cheaper. The police said you could feel the difference as the hopeless classes gave up the frenzy of crack for opium's deathly sedation. And as a result of changing smuggling routes, the drug is stronger than ever, and street heroin now averages 60 per cent purity. This makes it pure enough to be snorted, removing the nasty spectre of needles and AIDS, and making it a middle-class drug, popular amongst downtown's arty rebels and, worryingly, amongst a teenage population that seems ever more lifelessly nihilistic.

## 'THE CORRUPTION REACHES SENIOR MANAGEMENT'

The manner of New York politics is something which will certainly surprise an onlooker. Communities, corporations and individuals see elections not as an exercising of democracy but a chance to extort favours and favouritism. The scale of New York's corruption surprises many. But greed is built into the city's bureaucracy. Political positions here carry tremendous potential to enhance personal worth, not least through the hundreds of appointed positions. There are constant news stories announcing investigations into city officials big and small, and the tales of Tammany Hall's legendary nineteenth-century misappropriations seem strangely familiar.

Further indicating the crooked nature of much of New York, and also surprising many visitors, is the fact that the mafia, more often known as 'the Mob', is still very much in business. As well as its traditional holdings in gambling, drugs and extortion, New Yorkers know it as the force behind such unglamorous industries as garbage collection, concrete and road haulage, which are firmly controlled by a handful of 'families'. John Gotti, 'the Dapper Don' for his expensive courtroom clothes, or 'the Teflon Don' for the length of time it took before prosecutors could make charges stick, is in jail now, but his successors ensure it all continues.

There are always investigations under way to find mafia-led coercion at the bottom of protective employment practices. When such an inquiry was

| | |
|---|---|
| AIDS cases in NYC in 1995 | **66,906** |
| New AIDS cases in 1995 | **13,536** |
| Different languages spoken by New York cabbies | **60** |
| Position in FBI list of most crime-ridden US cities | **22nd** |
| Position in 1993 | **18th** |
| Annual free events sponsored by NYC parks dept | **325** |
| Reported crimes in 1995 | **558,198** |
| Murders and non-negligent manslaughters in 1995 | **1551** |
| Total NYPD arrests in 1995 | **267,000** |
| Average time for police to respond to a 911 emergency call | **7.9 minutes** |
| Complaints to the Civilian Complaint Review Board about police behaviour | **5,418** |
| Proportion of streets deemed 'filthy' | **3.9%** |

**Sources**

NY Convention and Visitors' Bureau; March 1995 edition of the Mayor's management Report. 1995 figures extrapolated from data for the first four months of 1995.

# African New York

New York is the secret capital of the African diaspora; a city seen by many emigrants and sojourners as more African than any on their mother continent for the diversity of experience gathered in one place.

There is an obvious outward Afrocentricity here, from the kente cloth uniforms worn in Harlem McDonald's, to the mass-produced African fabrics and sculptures (many of them made in Korea and the Phillipines) eagerly bought by middle-class black Americans from wily Senagalese traders. And there are clear African roots throughout much of the city. From jazz and rock to reggae, salsa and hip-hop, much of the music you'll hear owes a great debt to African rhythms; as does the ecstatic form of worship practised in the black churches. While the symbols may be Christian, the idea of the spirit entering the body through ecstatic physical acts of worship came from Africa with the congregants' slave ancestors.

However, the idea of New York as an African city goes far deeper than these obvious signs. For example, more than a million New Yorkers practise *Santeria*, a Caribbean-Latino religion brought from Cuba, Puerto Rico and the Dominican Republic, which blends African religious traditions with the Catholic symbols of the slavemasters.

A sight as banal as a pumpkin floating in the East river might be evidence of New York's African undercurrent. The pumpkin is the preferred food of Ochun, Santeria's river goddess, and her New York followers regularly make offerings. Similarly, the incessant drumming heard at weekends in Brooklyn's Prospect Park is often about *Santeros* or Haitian *Voudouisants* communing with the gods of the Yoruba and Bakongo.

Yoruba slaves in the Catholic New World were forced at gunpoint to adopt their masters' religion and forbidden from maintaining their own, which led them to mask their own sacred practices with the symbols of Catholicism. Each of the Yoruba deities was given a Catholic alter ego (Santa Barbara for Shango, for example) and the slaves convinced their captors that their all-night ecstatic drum- and dance-driven ceremonies were homage to the saints. Thus was born *Santeria*, a cultural and psychological triumph of the slaves and also the fastest-growing religion in the US.

For a taste of Santeria, visit a *botanica*. Two are listed below. These small religious stores dotted around Latino neighbourhoods sell what appear to be Catholic artefacts: figurines and candles, as well as mysterious totems and potions. Their true meaning is a little more complicated. If you're seriously interested, most storekeepers will offer advice; otherwise, they're generally happy to let you browse – but mind you don't step on the chickens which often walk freely around the store.

### Botanica San Miguel

*454 West 125th Street, between Broadway & Amsterdam Avenue (316 2181).* **Open** 9am-1am Mon-Sat. **Train** 1 or 9 to 125th Street. **No credit cards**.

### Botanica San Jose

*1810 Amsterdam Avenue, between 149 & 150th Streets (368 9190).* **Open** 11am-7.30pm Mon-Sat. **Train** 1 or 9 to 145th Street. **No credit cards**.

Santeria *meets Catholicism in a* botanica.

announced to examine the workings of the Fulton Fish Market, a mysterious fire destroyed much of the building, including any records. Most New York business people are resigned to paying strange prices for certain services. They see it as a kind of extra taxation.

## 'NEW YORK FUCKING CITY'

So this is New York today: a place busily conducting a battle with itself. The very modernity of the city – its density and velocity – is at odds with its survival. The description presented here may seem a little sobering, but this is far from a character assassination. It is these very things – these tragedies, confusions and intractable problems – that create the out-of-control intensity that attracts people to New York. It sounds dark, dangerous, hyperactive, and that's what we want it to be.

Furthermore, it's not the whole story. The city's crime figures are at their lowest for 20 years, and there are 21 cities in America where statistically you are in more danger of being a victim of crime than in New York. Success stories such as the rehabilitation of Bryant Park or the present Disney-led clean-up of Times Square undoubtedly 'improve' the city, but they also threaten to rob it of its hard-earned reputation for danger and excitement.

For the time being at least, New York continues to be a truly demanding place to live, heaving and palpitating its way towards the millennium. New Yorkers love to extract fun from this, knowing they're all caught up in an insane practical joke. As a visitor, they'll slap you on the back, welcome you to the madhouse and slyly query your reasons for venturing into bedlam, knowing full well that you are cruelly envious of their astonishing city.

And no-one is better than a New Yorker for pointing out the drab limitations of everywhere else. As Bette Midler pointed out: 'When it's three o'clock in New York, it's still 1938 in London.'

# New York by Neighbourhood

# Downtown

***Everyone heads downtown eventually. To the wealth of Wall Street, the art of SoHo or to the relaxed chat of the Village.***

New York City grew upwards from its southern tip, leaving the richest and most diverse concentration of places and people in the area below 14th Street. Here the streets are crooked, made for walking, and with names, not numbers. This is the place most visitors concentrate on, wandering from the architectural wonderland of the financial and civic centre, through the pretensions of SoHo and the vivid ethnicities of the Lower East Side, to the 'punk's-not-dead' spirit of the East Village and the café society of Greenwich Village.

## The Seaport

Though it now wears many faces, New York was always a port, its fortune built by the salt water that crashes around its natural harbour. It was perfectly placed for trade with Europe – with goods from middle America reaching the city via the Erie Canal and Hudson River. And as the open-handed point of entry for millions of immigrants, the city's character was formed primarily by the waves of humanity which arrived on its docks.

The **South Street Seaport**, an area of reclaimed and renovated buildings given over to shops, restaurants, bars and a museum, is where you'll best see this seafaring heritage. Though the shopping area of Pier 17 is not much more than a picturesque mall of gift shops by day and an after-office yuppie watering hole by night, the other piers are crowded with antique vessels and the **Seaport Museum** – detailing New York's maritime history – is fascinating and well presented. The Seaport's public spaces are a favourite with street performers and there's a season of outdoor concerts through the summer. The **Fulton Market** building, with gourmet food stalls and seafood restaurants that expand onto the cobbled streets in summer, is great for slurping oysters as you watch tourists scurry by.

There are fine views of the **Brooklyn Bridge** just to the north (*see chapter* **Sightseeing**) and plenty of restored nineteenth-century buildings, including Schermerhorn Row, constructed on landfill in 1812. **Fulton Fish Market**, America's largest, is here too, though the fish come in by road and the market lives under the constant threat of relocation. If you wish to continue with a salt-water theme to your day, Pier 16 is where you'll find the tour boats of **Seaport Liberty Cruises** (*see chapter* **Sightseeing**).

### South Street Seaport

*Water Street to the East River, between John Street & Peck Slip (for information about shops and special events call SEA PORT).* **Train** 2, 3, 4, 5, J, M or Z to Fulton Street.

### Seaport Museum

*Visitors' Center, 12 Fulton Street (748 8600).* **Open** 10am-6pm daily. **Admission** $6 adults; $3 children; $5 senior citizens; $4 students. **Credit** AmEx, MC, V.
Tickets for the museum may be purchased here or at the ticket booth on Pier 16. They allow admission to several galleries and exhibits throughout the Seaport area, as well as the *Peking*, the second largest sailing boat in existence; the *Ambrose*, a turn-of-the-century lightship; and the *Wavertree* tall ship. You'll have to pay extra to see the other vessels, including the 1885 schooner *Pioneer*, which makes regular two-hour tours around the harbour (669 9417 for reservations or private charter).

### Fulton Fish Market

*South Street, at Fulton Street (669 9416 tour information).* **Open** midnight-9am daily. **Tours** *Apr-Oct* 6am first and third Thur of the month. **Tour tickets** $10; reservations required. **Credit** AmEx, MC, V.

## Battery Park

The southern tip of Manhattan is where you are most conscious of being on an island. The Atlantic breeze blows in from the bay, taking the route of the millions who arrived here by sea: past the golden torch of the **Statue of Liberty** (*see chapter* **Sightseeing**), over the immigration and quarantine centre of **Ellis Island** (now a splendid museum) and onto the promenade of **Battery Park**, with its ranks of coin-operated telescopes and numerous monuments and statues. It's not unusual to see marquees and circus big tops here, as the park often plays host to international touring events such as Cirque du Soleil.

**Castle Clinton**, inside the park, was originally built during the Napoleonic wars when New York felt threatened by the British colonists it had just thrown out. It's been a theatre and an aquarium, and now it's a National Parks visitors' centre with historical displays. This where you buy your tickets for Liberty and Ellis Island.

Round the shore to the east is where you catch the famous **Staten Island Ferry**, the least expensive way to capture the wonder of arriving by sea (*see chapter* **Sightseeing**). The historic terminal was recently destroyed by fire, and a replacement is yet to be built, but next door is the beautiful

*Merchant Seamen's Memorial, Battery Park.*

Battery Maritime Building, a terminal for the many ferry services which sailed between Manhattan and Brooklyn in the years before the Brooklyn Bridge.

North of Battery Park is the triangle of **Bowling Green**, the city's first park and home to the beautiful Beaux Arts **US Custom House**, now the fascinating **Museum of the American Indian**. Near here is the dynamic bronze bull sculpture that represents the snorting power of Wall Street, as well as the **Shrine of Elizabeth Ann Seton** (1793; 7-8 State Street), a strange curved building in the Federal style, dedicated to the first American-born saint. Also nearby is the **Fraunces Tavern Museum**, a restoration of the alehouse where Washington celebrated his victory against the British, now a museum of revolutionary New York (*see chapter* **Architecture**).

## Civic Center

The business of running New York takes place among the many grand buildings of the **Civic Center**. Originally this was very much the city's focal point, and when **City Hall** was built in 1812, its architects were so confident that the city would grow no further north that they didn't bother to put any marble on its northern side. The building, a beautiful blend of Georgian formality, Federal detailing and French Renaissance influences, sits in its own area of green: **City Hall Park**. In 1776, this was where the Declaration of Independence was read to Washington's army. You are still likely to see city officials giving press interviews here.

The much larger **Municipal Building,** which faces City Hall and reflects it architecturally, is home to the overspill of civic offices, including the marriage bureau, which can churn out newlyweds with frightening speed. **Park Row**, east of the park and now home to an array of cafés and stereo shops, used to be known as 'Newspaper Row', and once held the offices of 19 daily papers. It was also the site of Phineas T Barnum's sensationalist American Museum, which burnt down in 1865.

Facing the park from the west is Cass Gilbert's famous **Woolworth Building** (1913; Broadway at Park Place), a vertically elongated gothic cathedral of an office building that has been called 'the Mozart of Skyscrapers'. Its beautifully detailed lobby is open to the public during working hours. Two blocks down Broadway is **St Paul's Chapel**, an oasis of peace, modelled after London's St Martin-in-the-Fields in 1766, and one of few buildings left from the century of British rule.

The Civic Center is also the focus of crime and punishment, with a concentration of various courts. Here you'll find the **New York County Courthouse** (1926; 60 Centre Street), a hexagonal building with a beautiful interior rotunda, and the **United States Courthouse** (1933; 40 Centre Street), a golden pyramid-topped tower above a Corinthian temple, both overlooking Foley Square.

Back next to City Hall, the Old New York County Courthouse, known more popularly as the **Tweed Courthouse**, was a symbol of the runaway corruption of mid-nineteenth-century city government, as Boss Tweed, leader of the political strong-arm faction Tammany Hall, pocketed $10 million of the building's soaring $14 million cost. But you can't spend that much and fail to get a beautiful building. Though symbolic of immense greed, its Italianate detailing is the very best.

The **Criminal Courts Building** (1939; 100 Centre Street) is by far the most intimidating of them all. Great Babylonian slabs of granite give it an awesome presence, emphasised by the huge judgemental towers guarding the entrance. This Kafka-esque home of justice has been known since its creation as 'the Tombs', a reference not only to its architecture but to the deathly conditions of the city jail it contains.

All of these courts are open to the public (9am-5pm Mon-Fri), though only some of the courtrooms will allow spectators. Your best bet for a little courtroom drama is the Criminal Courts, where if you can't slip into a trial you can at least observe the hallways full of seedy-looking lawyers and the criminals they are representing.

### City Hall

*City Hall Park, Broadway & Park Row.* **Train** 4, 5 or 6 to City Hall; J, M or Z to Chambers Street. **Open** 10am-2pm Mon-Fri. **Admission** free.

## Wall Street

From New York's earliest days as a fur trading post to its place today at the hub of international finance, commerce has always been the backbone of the city's prosperity. Wall Street is the thoroughfare synonymous with the world's greatest capitalist gambling den.

It took its name from a defensive wall the Dutch settlers built and which, for a long time, marked the city's northern limits. In the days before speedy telecommunications, financial institutions crowded their headquarters here to be near the action. This was where corporate America made its first architectural assertions – there are many great buildings built here by grand old banks and businesses. Some notable ones are the **Citibank Building** (1842; 55 Wall Street), a colonnaded lesson in the Greek orders; the **Equitable Building** (1915; 120 Broadway), whose greedy use of vertical space inspired the zoning laws governing skyscrapers; and the **Cunard Building** (1921; 25 Broadway), the beautiful domed ticket office for the grand shipping company, now a post office.

At the western end of Wall Street is the gothic spire of **Trinity Church**, once the island's tallest structure, but now dwarfed by skyscrapers. A block east is the **Federal Hall National Monument**, a Doric shrine to American constitutional history and the place where Washington became the country's first President.

Across the street is the **New York Stock Exchange**, though its grand frontage and public entrance are around the corner on Broad Street. The visitors' centre here is excellent for educating the clueless in the workings of financial trading, and lets you look out over the trading floor in action. It's all computerised these days, so except for crashes and panics, none too exciting as a spectator sport (for the buy! buy! buy! action you've seen in the movies, you want the far more frenzied **Commodities Exchange**; *see below* **World Trade Center**).

The **Federal Reserve Bank**, a block north on Liberty Street, is the world's largest gold depository (you saw Jeremy Irons clean it out in *Die Hard 3*), holding bullion for half the countries of the world. This Florentine palazzo fort is where they print money; the origin of any banknote with a big B next to its president. Take an empty canvas bag for the guided tour....

As you'd expect, the Wall Street area is fairly deserted outside of office hours. The time to see it is around midday when the suits emerge for their hurried lunches. Join them in stopping for a burger at the ultimate **McDonald's** (160 Broadway). By some quirk of individualism, it boasts liveried doormen, a special dessert menu and a Liberace-style pianist.

*The trading floor at the* **New York Stock Exchange**. *See above.*

*Play it again, Mac: Wall Street* **McDonald's**.

### Federal Reserve Bank

*33 Liberty Street, between William & Nassau Streets (720 6130).* **Open** by appointment only. **Admission** free.

The free one-hour tours through the bank must be arranged at least one week in advance; tickets are sent by post.

### Trinity Church Museum

*Broadway, at Wall Street (602 0872).* **Open** 9-11.45am, 1-3.45pm, Mon-Fri; 10am-3.45pm Sat; 1-3.45pm Sun (closed during concerts). **Admission** free.

The small museum inside features exhibits on the history of the church and its place in New York's history.

### New York Stock Exchange

*20 Broad Street, at Wall Street (656 5168 ).* **Train** 4 or 5 to Wall Street. **Open** 9.15am-4pm Mon-Fri. **Admission** free.

A gallery overlooking the trading floor, and lots of multi-media exhibits.

## World Trade Center & Battery Park City

The area to the west of Wall Street extends the city's financial district with grand developments that combine vast amounts of office space with new public plazas, restaurants and shopping areas. There are concerted efforts to inject a little cultural life into these spaces and plenty of street performers work the area in summer months, though the general atmosphere is defined by the workday schedule.

The **World Trade Center** is actually six buildings, though to most visitors it means the famous twin towers which dominate the downtown skyline (*see chapter* **Sightseeing**). Visit the observation deck – on good days you can walk outside – and spare a thought for the crazies who have climbed the walls, parachuted off the top floor or walked a tightrope between the two towers. It's the city's tallest structure and until Chicago's Sears Tower was completed also held the world height record. Building number four contains the **Commodities Exchange**, a great free floorshow.

Across the highway of West Street is **Battery Park City**, built on landfill generated by the excavations for the World Trade Center's foundations. This is partly residential, housing wealthy Wall Streeters whose high rents go to subsidise public housing elsewhere in the city. The beautiful new park here links Battery Park with the piers to the north, which are slowly being claimed for public use, allowing you to spend a pleasant afternoon strolling along the riverside from Manhattan's southern tip right up to Christopher Street, in the company of rollerbladers and cuddling couples

The **World Financial Center**, the development's centrepiece, is the ultimate expression of the city-within-a-city concept. Crowned by Cesar Pelli's four elegant post-modern office towers, it contains an upmarket retail area, a marina and a series of plazas with terraced restaurants. The stunning vaulted glass-roofed Winter Garden, with its indoor palm trees, has become a popular venue for concerts and other entertainment, most of which are free.

### World Financial Center

*West Street to the Hudson River (945 0505).* **Train** 1, 2, 3, 9, A, C or E to Chambers Street. **Admission** free.

Call for information on the busy schedule of free arts events.

### The Commodities Exchange

*9th floor, 4 World Trade Center (938 2900).* **Open** 10.30am-3pm Mon-Fri. **Admission** free.

The stock exchange can be a little undramatic in these days of computerised trading, but not the commodities exchange. This is where manic figures in colour-coded blazers scream and shout at each other as they buy and sell gold, pork bellies and orange juice.

### Lower Manhattan Cultural Council

*(432 0900).*

Information on all sorts of cultural events happening in and around this part of lower Manhattan.

## Lower East Side

The Lower East Side tells the story of New York's immigrants: the cycle of one generation making good and moving to the suburbs, leaving space for the next wave of hopefuls. It is busy and densely populated, a patchwork of strong ethnic identities; great for dining and exploration. Today, outside Chinatown and Little Italy (which, strictly speaking, are part of this area), Lower East Side residents are largely Asian or Hispanic – Puerto Rican and Dominican – though the area is more famous for its earlier settlers, most notably as a Jewish stronghold, full of people from eastern Europe.

It was here that mass tenement housing was built to accommodate the nineteenth-century influx. The original insanitary, overcrowded buildings forced the introduction of building codes. To appreciate the conditions in which the mass of immigrants lived, take a look at the reconstructions at the **Tenement Museum**.

Between 1870 and 1920 hundreds of synagogues and religious schools were established here, Yiddish newspapers were published and

*Check out the street stalls of* **Chinatown** *for imported goods of all kinds. See page 91.*

associations for social reform and cultural studies flourished. Now only 10-15 per cent of the population is Jewish. **Congregation Anshe Slonim** (172 Norfolk Street), the city's oldest synagogue, is now condominiums, and the landmark **Eldridge Street Synagogue** finds it increasingly hard to round up the ten adult males required to conduct a service.

Instead, the area today is characterised by its large Hispanic population. *Bodegas* or corner groceries abound, with their brightly coloured awnings, and there are many restaurants serving Puerto Rican dishes of rice and beans with fried plantain (*platanos*), pork chops and chicken. In the summer the streets here ring with the sounds of salsa and merengue as the residents hang out drinking beer and playing dominoes.

But in turn these people are being nudged by what could be described as the latest immigrants: the growing population of young artists, musicians and other rebels, attracted by the area's high drama and low rents. **Ludlow Street** is the main drag for these folk – an East Village extension with an increasing number of interesting shops, small clubs and hip bars, including the intriguing **Max Fish** (176 Ludlow) with its changing displays of artwork (*see chapter* **Cafés & Bars**).

Some remnants of the neighbourhood's Jewish traditions remain. **Ratner's**, at 38 Delancey Street, is a kosher dairy restaurant that has become a New York institution. The shabby **Sammy's Famous Roumanian Jewish Steakhouse** (157 Christie Street) is for those with strong stomachs. Hearty servings of East European food come complete with a jug of chicken fat on the side – but it's one of the most famous of the Lower East Side eateries. On a lighter note, **Katz's**, on the corner of Ludlow and Houston Streets, sells some of the best pastrami in New York, and the orgasms are pretty good, too, if Meg Ryan's performance in *When Harry Met Sally* is anything to go by – the scene was filmed in Katz's. For all, *see chapter* **Restaurants**.

### Israel Israelowitz Tours

*(718 951 7072).*
Phone for details of guided tours of the Lower East Side and boat tours of Jewish New York. Also lecture programmes.

### Schapiro's Winery

*126 Rivington Street, (674 4404).* **Tours** on the hour 11am-4pm Sun. **Admission** $1.
Shapiro's has been making kosher wine since 1899. The wine tours include tastings.

### Tenement Museum

*97 Orchard Street, between Delancey & Broome Streets (431 0233).* **Train** F, J, M, or Z to Essex/Delancey Street. **Open** 11am-5pm Tue-Sun. **Admission** $3; $2 under-17s. **Tours** $7; $6 students, senior citizens.
In addition to sobering re-creations of pre-1879 tenement conditions, the museum has an interesting programme of walks, exhibitions and performances about the Lower East Side.

### First Shearith Israel Graveyard

*55-57 St James Place, between Oliver & James Streets.* **Train** B or D to Grand Street.
The burial ground of the oldest Jewish community in the United States – Spanish and Portuguese Jews who escaped the Inquisition. The earliest gravestones are dated 1683.

### Eldridge Street Synagogue

*12-14 Eldridge Street (219 0888).* **Train** F to East Broadway. **Open** 11am-4pm Tue, Wed, Sun.
A beautifully decorated, and now restored, building, the pride of the Jewish congregation which once filled it.

## Chinatown

Chinatown spills out beyond Canal Street and the Bowery, but is centred around Mott Street. The New York version is far removed from the sanitised ones in San Francisco or London. More than 150,000 Chinese live and work here in a few score city blocks, and the feeling is of a very self-sufficient community. The busy streets get even wilder during the Chinese New Year festivities in January or February, and around July 4th when it is the city's source of (illegal) fireworks.

Food is everywhere. The markets on **Canal Street** sell some of the best fish, fruit and vegetables in the city. There are countless restaurants – Mott Street, from Worth right up to Kenmare Street, is lined with Cantonese and Szechuan places – and you can buy wonderful snacks from street stalls, such as bags of little sweet egg pancakes. Canal Street is also famous as a source of cheap imported trinkets and counterfeit designer items. From fake Rolexes to the cheapest 'brand-name' running shoes, it's a bargain hunters' paradise.

The statue of Confucius marks **Confucius Plaza**, near the approaches of the Manhattan Bridge. On Bayard Street is the **Wall of Democracy**, where political writings are posted discussing events in Beijing. Through the open doors of the **Eastern States Buddhist Temple of America** is the glitter of hundreds of buddhas and the smell of incense.

A noisier place altogether is the **Chinatown Fair**, at 8 Mott Street, which is really nothing more than an amusement arcade. However, doors at the back lead to the **Chinese Museum**, a place of such mystery that it is virtually impossible to gain entry – 'only groups of eight', they say – but it is supposed to contain the dragon used in the New Year festival.

### Eastern States Buddhist Temple of America

*64B Mott Street, between Canal & Bayard Streets (966 6229).* **Train** 4, 5, 6, N or to Canal Street. **Open** 9am-7pm daily.

## Little Italy

In common with the other parts of the Lower East Side, Little Italy is a vivid pocket of ethnicity, with the sights and sounds of the mother country turned up full. It's getting smaller, though, as the neighbourhood is eaten away by the growth of Chinatown and by an Italian exodus to the suburbs. Really all that's left of the Italian community which lived here since the mid-nineteenth century are the cafés and restaurants on Mulberry, between Canal and East Houston, and short sections of cross streets. There is, however, a strong ethnic pride, and limo-loads of Italian families parade in from Queens and Brooklyn to show their love for the old neighbourhood, an expression magnified during the Feast of San Genarro each September.

The restaurants here are mostly pricey and ostentatious grill and pasta houses. **Umberto's Clam House**, at 129 Mulberry Street, is worth noting, because it was the scene of a famous gangland killing in 1972, and it stays open until 6am (*see chapter* **Eating & Drinking**). Even if you choose to eat elsewhere, make your after-dinner destination one of the smaller cafés lining the streets serving rich desserts and coffee.

As you'd expect, there are great food stores (good strong cheeses, excellent wines, spicy meats, freshly made pasta and so on), and the iconic **Forzano Italian Imports**, at 128 Mulberry, the best place in New York for papal souvenirs, espresso machines, ghastly Italian pop music and football memorabilia (*see chapter* **Shopping**).

Two buildings of note here are **Old St Patrick's Cathedral** (1863; 264 Mulberry Street), which was once the premier Catholic church of New York but was demoted when the Fifth Avenue cathedral was consecrated, and the **Police Building** (1909, 240 Centre Street). Once the headquarters for the city's police, this has now been converted into co-operative apartments.

## SoHo

SoHo is designer New York, in all senses of the word. Walk around its cobbled streets, among the elegant cast iron architecture, the boutiques, art galleries and bistros, and you'll find yourself sharing the sidewalks with the beautiful people of young, monied, fashionable NYC. The chic bars and eateries are full of these trend-setters, while the shop windows display the work of the latest arrivals in the world of art and fashion.

SoHo ('South of Houston Street') was earmarked for developmental destruction during the 1960s, but the area was saved by the many artists who

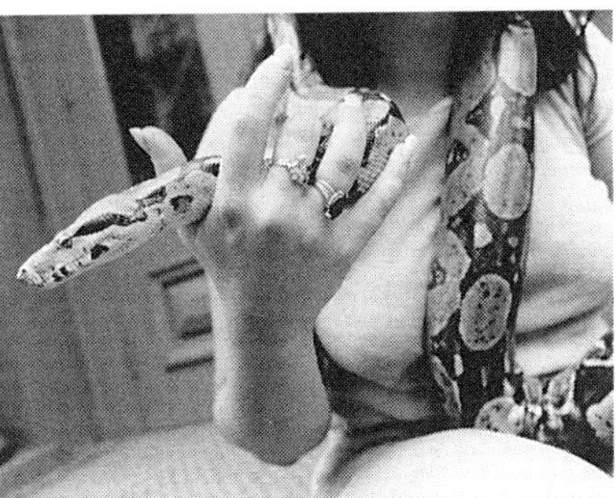

*Designer dressing, SoHo style.*

Street sculpture in arty **SoHo**. See page 91.

inhabited its (then) low-rent ex-industrial spaces. They protested against the demolition of these beautiful buildings, whose cast-iron frames prefigured the technology of the skyscraper (*see chapter* **Architecture**). As loft-living became fashionable and the buildings were renovated for residential use, the landlords were quick to sniff gentrification's increased profits.

Surprisingly plenty of sweatshops remain here, especially down towards Canal Street, carrying on the manufacturing for which these buildings were originally made. Increasingly, however, they house such businesses as graphics studios, magazines and record labels.

West Broadway is the main thoroughfare, lined with pricey shops and art galleries – the famous **Leo Castelli** is at 420 Broadway has recently upped its artiness. The **Guggenheim Museum** has opened a branch here (575 Broadway at Prince Street), exhibiting both temporary collections and selections from the museum's permanent collection. In addition Broadway has a collection of other galleries specialising in lesser-known artists. The **New Museum of Contemporary Art**, at 583 Broadway, is the young cousin of MoMA, while the **Alternative Museum** at 594 and the **Museum of African Art** next door are both worth a look.

### NYC Fire Museum

*278 Spring Street (691 1303).* **Train** C or E to Spring Street. **Open** 10am-4pm Tue-Sun. **Admission** $4 adults; $2 students; $1 under-12s.

A small but beautiful museum, with a collection of gleaming antique fire-fighting machines dating back to the 1700s. *Disabled: access.*

## TriBeCa

TriBeCa (for 'Triangle Below Canal Street') illustrates very nicely the process of gentrification in lower Manhattan. It's very much like SoHo was about 15 to 20 years ago, with some parts deserted and abandoned – the cobbles dusty and untrodden and the cast iron architecture chipped and unpainted – and other pockets throbbing with arriviste energy. In particular this is the place for new restaurants, with the occasional bar and club also working hard to establish itself.

The buildings here are generally larger than in SoHo, and especially towards the river, mostly warehouses. However, there is some fine smaller-scale cast iron architecture along White Street and the parallel thoroughfares (*see chapter* **Architecture**), and Harrison Street is home to a row of well-preserved Federal style townhouses.

As in SoHo, art is the new industry here, and there are several galleries representing the more experimental (ie hit or miss) side of things. Some notable ones are **Franklin Furnace** (112 Franklin Street) and **Artists Space** (223 West Broadway). The view from the balcony of **The Clocktower**, the gallery of the Institute for Art and Urban Resources in the tower-rooms of the old **New York Life Insurance Building** (108 Leonard Street at Broadway), is as inspiring as the art inside is experimental.

One famous TriBeCa tenant is Robert de Niro, whose **TriBeCa Film Center** at 325 Greenwich Street, the old Martinson Coffee Building, houses screening rooms and production offices and is home base to several prominent New York and visiting film makers. They dine, of course, at de Niro's **TriBeCa Grill** on the ground floor.

## Greenwich Village

Greenwich Village (call it 'the Village') has been the scene of some serious hanging out throughout its history. Stretching from 14th Street down to Houston Street and from Broadway west to the river, these leafy streets with their townhouses, theatres, coffee houses and tiny bars and clubs have witnessed and inspired Bohemian lifestyles for almost a century.

*Leafy* **Greenwich Village.**

It's a place for idle wandering; for people-watching from street-side cafés, for candle-lit dining in secret restaurants, or for hopping between bars and cabaret venues, smoothing the night away. The place is overcrowded in summer, and has lost some of its charm as the retail centre of lower Broadway has spread west, but much of what attracted New York's creative types is here still.

The jazz generation lives on in smoky clubs like **The Blue Note** and **The Village Vanguard**. Sip a fresh roast in honour of the Beats – Kerouac, Ginsberg and their ilk – as you sit in the coffee shops they frequented – Jack Kerouac's favourite was **Le Figaro Café** on the corner of MacDougal and Bleecker (*see chapter* **Cafés & Bars**).

The hippies, who tuned out in **Washington Square**, are still there in spirit, and often in person, as the square hums with pot dealers, musicians and street artists. Chess hustlers and students from the surrounding **New York University** join in, along with today's new generation of hangers out: the hip-hop kids who drive down in their booming jeeps and the Generation Y skaters/ravers who clatter around the fountain and the base of the arch (a miniature Arc de Triomphe built in 1892 in honour of George Washington).

The Village first became fashionable in the 1830s, when elegant townhouses were built around Washington Square. Literary figures including Henry James, Mark Twain and Edith Wharton lived on or near the square, and Herman Melville wrote *Moby Dick* in a house at the northern reaches of the Village. In 1870 this growing artistic community founded the **Salmagundi Club**, America's oldest artists' club, which is still extant, just above Washingon Square on Fifth Avenue.

The area continued to attract writers, and through prohibition and beyond people like John Steinbeck and John Dos Passos passed the time at **Chumley's**, a speakeasy, still unmarked at 86 Bedford Street. The **Provincetown Playhouse**, at 133 MacDougal, is where Eugene O'Neill got some big breaks. And the **Cedar Tavern** on University Place was where the leading figures of abstract expressionism discussed how best to throw paint. Jackson Pollock, Franz Kline and Larry Rivers drunk there back in the 1950s. Eighth Street, now a long procession of punky boutiques, shoe stores, piercing parlours and cheap jewellery vendors, was the closest New York got to San Francisco's Haight Street. Jimi Hendrix's **Electric Lady Sound Studios** is still here at No. 52.

In the triangle formed by West 10th Street, Sixth Avenue and Greenwich Avenue you'll see the **Jefferson Market Courthouse,** a neo-gothic Victorian pile once voted America's fifth most beautiful building. It's now a library. Across the street is **Balducci's**, one of the finest food stores in the city, and down Sixth Avenue at 4th Street you stumble on the outdoor basketball courts where some of the hottest free sports action can be witnessed (*see chapter* **Sports & Fitness**).

The western reaches of the Village (people call the area beyond Seventh Avenue 'the West Village') are quaint tree-lined streets of historic houses. This is also a famously gay area, centred on **Christopher Street**, the scene of the 1969 Stonewall riots marking the birth of the gay liberation movement. There are as many same-sex couples strolling along Christopher as straight ones, and plenty of shops, bars and restaurants that are out and proud (*see chapter* **Gay New York**).

### Salmagundi Club

*47 Fifth Avenue, near 12th Street (255 7740).* **Open** for exhibitions only; phone for details. **Admission** free.
Now the home of a series of artistic and historical societies, the club's fine nineteenth-century interior is worth a look .

## East Village

The East Village is far scruffier than its western counterpart, housing today's young bohemians, rather than the grown-up variety. East of Broadway between 14th and Houston Streets, and until recently considered part of the Lower East Side, it's where you find an amiable population of punks, hippies, homeboys and homeless (and an irritating number of unproductive trustafarians). This motley crew co-exists with older residents surviving from various waves of immigration, and provides the area with cheap but interesting clothes stores (check for quality before committing any cash), record shops, bargain meals, grungey bars and punky clubs.

**St Mark's Place** (another name for East 8th Street), with bars squeezed into tiny basements and restaurants overflowing onto the sidewalks, is the centre of all this. It's packed until the early hours with crowds browsing its cheap boutiques, comic shops, bargain record stores and bookshops. The more interesting places are off to the east, and you'll find some great little shops and cafés along Avenue A and on about 6th to 10th Streets.

**Astor Place**, with its revolving cube sculpture, is where in 1859 Peter Cooper built **Cooper Union**, the city's first free educational institute, which has a long tradition of influential political debate. This marked the boundary between the ghettos to the east and some of the city's most fashionable homes, such as **Colonnade Row**, on Lafayette Street. Facing these was the distinguished Astor Public Library, now Joseph Papp's **Public Theater**, a haven for first-run American plays and home of the New York Shakespeare Festival. Papp rescued the library from demolition and had it declared a landmark.

East of Lafayette on the Bowery is the famous **CBGB's** club ('Country, Blue-Grass, Blues'), the

*Life is lived outdoors in* **Washington Square.** *See page 94.*

birthplace of American punk, still packing in guitar bands new and used. Many other local bars and clubs successfully apply the formula of cheap beer and loud music, including **The Continental**, **Brownies** and **Under Acme**.

East 7th Street is a Ukrainian stronghold, centred on the Byzantine-looking **St George's Ukrainian Catholic Church**, built in 1977 but looking at least a century older. Further along the street is **McSorley's Old Ale House**, the oldest drinking house in the city (or so it claims) and still serving just one kind of beer, a frothy brew which it makes in the basement.

On East 6th Street, between First and Second Avenues, is '**Little India**' (one of several in New York): there are about two dozen Indian restaurants side by side, the long-running rumour being that they all share a single kitchen. East 3rd Street between First and Second Avenues has more than its share of fat men on Harleys: the headquarters of the New York chapter of Hell's Angels is here.

Towards the East River are Avenues A to D, an area sometimes known as **Alphabet City** (owing to the fact that its streets are lettered rather than numbered). Its largely Hispanic population is slowly being nudged eastward by the influx of young counterculture arrivals. The neighbourhood is famous for its heroin trade and, beyond Avenue B, can be dangerous at night. It's not without its attractions, however: the **Gas Station** (Avenue B and 2nd Street), an open-air sculpture garden, is worth a look, as is the **Nuyorican Poets' Café** (*see chapter* **Cabaret**), a focus for the recent resurgence of espresso-drinking beatniks. It's famous for its 'slams', in which performance poets battle like rappers. **Tompkins Square Park** (7th to 10th Streets, between Avenues A and B), has long been a focus for political dissent and rioting. The latest uprising was in 1991, after the controversial decision to evict the park's squatters and renovate it to suit the taste of the area's increasingly affluent residents.

North of Tompkins Square, around First Avenue and 11th Street, are remnants of earlier residents: good Italian cheese shops, Polish restaurants, discount fabric shops, empty theatres and two great Italian patisseries. Visit **De Roberti's** (176 First Avenue) for delicious cakes and **Veniero's** (342 East 11th Street) for wonderful mini-pastries and butter biscuits.

### St Mark's-in-the Bowery

*131 East 10th Street at Second Avenue (674 6377).*
**Train** L to 1st Avenue. **Open** 10am-6pm Mon-Fri.
St Mark's was built in 1799 on the site of a 1660 church on Peter Stuyvesant's farm. Stuyvesant, one of New York's first and most powerful governors, is buried here, along with most of his descendants. The church is now home to several arts groups and was the church in *The Group* where the wedding and funeral took place. Phone for details of the performances here.

# Midtown

***By day office workers fill the streets, by night actors tread the boards of Broadway.***

Midtown, 14th to 59th Streets, is the city's engine room, powered by the hundreds of thousands of commuters who pour in each day. Most hotels are here and so are most of the 'tourist' tourists. By day it's a solid business district, with clothes manufacturing around Seventh Avenue and offices everywhere else. It's also where you'll find the department stores and upscale retailers of Fifth Avenue and the Rockefeller Center. By night the area is all about big entertainment, with the neon of Times Square advertising all the Broadway shows, and restaurants of all kinds clamouring for the pre- and post-theatre crowds.

## Flatiron District

As diagonal Broadway meanders its way along Manhattan's length, it inspires a public square wherever it intersects with an avenue. Two such places, Union Square at 14th Street, and Madison Square at 23rd, used to mark the limits of a ritzy nineteenth-century shopping district known as Ladies' Mile. Extending along Broadway and west to Fifth Avenue, this was a collection of huge retail palaces attracting the 'carriage trade' of wealthy ladies buying the latest fashions and household goods from all over the world. The ground levels of most of these buildings have changed completely, making way for today's shops and restaurants, but the rest of their proud cast iron facades still stand. The Fifth Avenue section has been rejuvenated over the past few years, and is where designers like Matsuda, Paul Smith and Armani showcase their wares.

The **Flatiron Building** – originally named the Fuller Building after its first owners – is famous for its triangular ground-plan and as the world's first steel-framed skyscraper (*see chapter* **Architecture**). It stands at the south of Madison Square, giving its name to the surrounding streets, an area also known as the photo district for its preponderance of studios, photo labs and wandering models.

**Madison Square** itself is rich in history. It was the site of PT Barnum's Hippodrome and the original Madison Square Garden, the scene of prize fights, society duels and lavish entertainment intertwined with celebrity scandal. Today, these are gone, leaving a scruffy park surrounded by imposing buildings such as the **Metropolitan Life Insurance Company** (1893; Madison Avenue at 23rd Street), the **New York Life Insurance Company** (1928; Madison Avenue at 26th Street) and the **Appellate Court** (1900; Madison Avenue at 25th Street).

**Union Square** is named not after the Union of the civil war but simply for the union of Broadway and Bowery Lane (now Fourth Avenue). It's raised to accommodate the subway beneath, and has a reputation as a political hotspot, a favourite location for rabble-rousing oratory. These days it's also home to a regular farmers' market on Wednesdays and Saturdays. The square is a popular rendezvous point, with chic hangout **Coffee Shop** on its western edge and the bargain bonanza of 14th Street's downmarket retail centre extending west, offering cheap clothes and bargain electronics (*see chapter* **Shopping**).

### Union Square

*junction of Broadway, 14th Street, and Park & Fourth Avenues.* **Train** 4, 5, 6, L, N or R to Union Square.

## Gramercy Park

You need a key to enter **Gramercy Park**, something possessed only by those who live in the beautiful townhouses which surround it (or who stay at the **Gramercy Park Hotel**). Anyone, however, can enjoy the tranquillity of the surrounding district, squeezed in between Third and Park Avenues. It was developed in the 1830s, copying the concept of a London square. **The Players**, at No. 16, housed actor Edwin Booth, brother of Lincoln's assassin, John Wilkes Booth, and the foremost actor of his day. Booth had it remodelled as a club for the theatrical profession (it also had Churchill and Mark Twain as members). No. 15 is the **National Arts Club**, whose members have often donated impressive works in lieu of their subscriptions. The resulting collection is on view several times a year.

**Irving Place**, leading south from the park to 14th Street, is named after Washington Irving, who didn't actually live here (his nephew did). It does

*The secluded* **Gramercy Park.**

have a literary past, though: **Pete's Tavern**, which claims to be the oldest bar in town, was where the New York wit O Henry wrote *The Gift of the Magi.*

West of Gramercy Park is a small museum of **Theodore Roosevelt's Birthplace**. To the east is the **Police Academy Museum**, where you can see hundreds of guns, including Al Capone's, and exhibitions describing gruesome murders and other famous cases. The low, fortress-like building of the **69th Regiment Armory** (Lexington Avenue at 25th Street), now used by the New York National Guard, was where the sensational Armory Show was held in 1913. This introduced modern art – in the form of Cubism, Fauvism, the precocious Marcel Duchamp and other outrages – to the New World.

### The National Arts Club

*15 Gramercy Park (475 3424).* **Train** 6 to 23rd Street.

### Theodore Roosevelt Birthplace

*28 East 20th Street, between Broadway & Park Avenue South (260 1616).* **Train** 6 to 23rd Street. **Open** 9am-5pm Wed-Sun. **Admission** $2 adults; free under-17s, senior citizens. **No credit cards**.

The popular president's birthplace was demolished in 1916, but it has now been fully reconstructed as his boyhood home. The museum includes period rooms and a trophy room.

### Police Academy Museum

*235 East 20th Street, between Second & Third Avenues (477 9753).* **Train** 6 to 23rd Street. **Open** 9am-2pm Mon-Fri. **Admission** free. Phone for appointment. *Disabled: access.*

## Chelsea

Chelsea is the region between 14th and about 30th Streets, west of about Sixth Avenue. Its population is mostly young professionals, and given New York's homocentric creative life, this makes Chelsea an increasingly gay place to be. You'll find all the trappings of an urban residential neighbourhood on the upswing: good diners, (mostly) dull shops and a generous sprinkling of bars and fine restaurants. Its western warehouse district has a grouping of the city's dance clubs, and is now slowly being developed for residential use, with pioneer galleries like the **Dia Center for the Arts** at the very end of 22nd Street dragging the arts crowd westwards.

**Cushman Row** (1840; 406-18 West 20th Street) in the **Chelsea Historic District** gives a good idea of Chelsea's appearance when first developed in the mid-1800s: a grandeur that was destroyed 30 years later when the noisy elevated railways came to steal the sunlight and dominate the area. Just north is the **General Theological Seminary**, its garden a wonderful retreat, and over on Tenth Avenue, the flashing lights of the **Empire Diner** attract pre- and post-clubbers to its chromed 1929 art deco beauty (*see chapter* **Restaurants**).

Sixth Avenue around 27th Street can seem like a tropical forest at times, as the pavements are

*Making a clean sweep in Chelsea's* **Flower District**.

filled to overflowing with the palm leaves, decorative grasses and colourful blooms of Chelsea's **Flower District**. The garment industry has a presence hereabouts as well, spilling down from its centre a little further north.

The swank **Barneys**, one of New York's livelier department stores, is here on Seventh Avenue. Round the corner on 23rd Street is the famous **Chelsea Hotel**, where lots of famous people checked in, several of them – like Sid Vicious's girlfriend Nancy Spungeon – only to check out again (permanently). It's definitely worth a peek, with plenty of weird artwork and ghoulish guests. On Eighth Avenue you'll find the **Joyce**, a stunning renovated art moderne cinema that's a mecca for dance lovers, and the wonderful **Bessie Schonberg Theater**, where mime and poetry play. Way out towards the river is **The Kitchen**, the experimental arts centre with a particular bent for video (*see chapters* **Dance, Film** *and* **Theatre**).

When you reach the Hudson River, you'll see the piers; derelict fingers raking out into the water. These were originally the terminals for the world's grand ocean liners (this was where the *Titanic* was headed when she sank). Most are in some state of disrepair, though a recent development has transformed the four between 17th and 23rd Streets into a dramatic new sports centre and TV studio complex, **Chelsea Piers** (*see chapter* **Sports**).

### Chelsea Historic District

*Between Ninth & Tenth Avenues and 20th & 21st Streets.* **Train** A, C or E to 14th Street.

### General Theological Seminary

*175 Ninth Avenue, between 20th and 21st Streets (243 5150).* **Open** noon-3pm Mon-Fri; 11am-4pm Sat. **Admission** free.

You can walk through the grounds of the seminary during opening hours and there's a guided tour in summer (call for details).

## Herald Square & Garment District

Seventh Avenue around 34th Street has a second name: Fashion Avenue, and the streets here, gridlocked permanently by delivery trucks, have the slowest traffic in the city. The surrounding area is the **Garment District**, where midtown office blocks mingle with the buzzing activity of a huge manufacturing industry. Shabby clothing and fabric stores line the streets (especially 38th and 39th), and there are intriguing shops selling only lace, or buttons, or Lycra swimsuits. Most are wholesale only, but some will sell to the public.

**Macy's** will most definitely sell things to you, though since the parent company filed for bankruptcy protection its sales and bargains haven't been as dramatic as tourist legend might have it. A lot of what's on offer here is cheaper somewhere else, though it will impress as the biggest department store in the world. **A&S Plaza** (*see chapter* **Shopping**) across the street is a phenomenally ugly building resembling a neon and chrome jelly mould. However, this is good old American mall shopping at its best, and most of the big chains have an outlet here. This retail wonderland is **Herald Square**, named after a long-gone newspaper. The lower part is known as **Greeley Square** after the owner of the *Herald*'s rival, *The Tribune*, a paper in which Karl Marx wrote a regular column. *Life* magazine was based round the corner in 31st Street, and its cherubic mascot can still be seen over the entrance of what is now the **Herald Square Hotel**.

The famous sports and entertainment arena of **Madison Square Garden** is a block to the west, a giant doughnut of a building (*see chapter* **Sports**). It's on the site of the old **Pennsylvania Station**, McKim, Mead and White's architectural masterpiece, which was destroyed by insane 1960s planners, an act which brought about the creation of the Landmarks Commission. The rail terminal is now underground, its name shortened to **Penn Station**, as if in shame. Thankfully, the **General Post Office** (1913), designed by the same prolific firm, still stands, an enormous colonnade occupying two city blocks.

### Herald Square

*Junction of 34th Street, Broadway & Sixth Avenue.* **Train** B, D, F, N, Q or R to 34th Street.

## Broadway & Times Square

The night is lit not by the moon and stars but by acres of moving neon. A monstrous television peers down, broadcasting its soundless message to the scurrying masses, making the place feel like a giant's brashly illuminated living room. Waves of people flood the streets as the blockbuster theatres disgorge their audiences. 'The centre of the world' is how it likes to describe itself, and there are few places that represent the collected power and noisy optimism of New York quite as well as **Times Square**.

It's really just an elongated intersection, but Broadway is here, the road and the idea – for this is the **theatre district**. It's home to 30 or so grand stages used for dramatic productions and probably an equal number more which are now either peep shows, cinemas, nightclubs or just empty. The streets west of Seventh Avenue are where you'll find the area's eateries. West 46th Street here is known as **Restaurant Row** for an almost unbroken string of them.

The cinematic lowlife of **42nd Street**, from Sixth Avenue west, is increasingly neutralised. The sex industry is still here in force, but the video supermarkets and live peep shows share space with subsidised arts projects, and Disney has

*Buses gridlocked at the* **Port Authority Bus Terminal**.

announced plans for a hotel complex – Mickey's squeaky-clean influence should go a long (if perhaps regrettable) way towards sanitising the place.

As you'd expect, the offices here are full of entertainment companies: recording studios, theatrical management, record labels, screening rooms and so on. The **Brill Building**, 1619 Broadway, at 49th Street, has the richest history, having long been the headquarters of music publishers and arrangers. It's known as **Tin Pan Alley** (though the original Tin Pan Alley was West 28th Street). From here emerged the work of such names as Cole Porter, George Gershwin, Rodgers and Hart, Lieber and Stoller, and Phil Spector.

Close by is the **Hearst Magazine Building** at 959 Eighth Avenue, immortalised by inference as the newspaper headquarters of Orson Welles' *Citizen Kane* (Kane was, of course, based on print mogul William Randolph Hearst).

The great landmark on Broadway just south of Central Park is **Carnegie Hall**. Next door on 57th Street is **The Russian Tea Room,** the super-expensive caviar-and-samovar joint beloved of visiting celebrities. Less expensive, but just as authentically New York, is the **Carnegie Deli**, the city's most famous sandwich stop.

Moving west from Times Square, past the curious steel spiral of the Port Authority Bus Terminal's aerial bus park on Eighth Avenue and the knotted entrance to the Lincoln Tunnel to New Jersey, is an area known as **Hell's Kitchen**. Formerly an impoverished Irish neighbourhood, it's now been given the more real-estate-friendly name of Chelsea-Clinton and attracts the forces of gentrification. There's also a little Cuban district, around Tenth Avenue and the mid-40s.

The main attraction here is the vast **Jacob K Javits Convention Center** on Twelfth Avenue between 34th and 38th Streets: an enormous four-block structure which hosts conventions and trade shows. Finally, there are the Hudson River piers. The **Circle Line** terminal is on Pier 83, level with 42nd Street, and at the end of 46th Street you'll find the aircraft carrier **Intrepid** and the **Air Sea Space Museum** it contains.

### Actors Studio

*432 West 44th Street, between Ninth & Tenth Avenues (757 0870).* **Train** A, C or E to 42nd Street. **Open** 9am-5pm Mon-Fri. **Admission** by appointment only.
Stars of the future perform at Lee Strasberg's famous acting workshops. Obtain tickets from the International Theatre Institute (254 4141).

### Backstage on Broadway Tours

*228 West 47th Street, between Broadway & Eighth Avenues (575 8065).* **Train** B, D, F or Q to Rockefeller Center. **Tickets** $8 adults; $7 children, students. **No credit cards**.
Actors, directors and stage managers take large groups (made up of 25 or more people and you usually have to assemble your own) behind the scenes of a Broadway theatre. Reservations essential.

### Steinway Hall

*109 West 57th Street, between Sixth & Seventh Avenues (246 1100).* **Train** N or R to 57th Street. **Open** 9am-6pm Mon-Wed, Fri; 9am-7.30pm Thur; 9am-5pm Sat; noon-5pm Sun. **Admission** free.
The showrooms of the famous piano company are fascinating, and there's a recital salon.

## The Glorious Fifth

There is a certain spot on Fifth Avenue where you can look south and see the Flatiron Building, and then turn to the north and still see the trees of Central Park's bottom corner. This majestic thoroughfare is New York's main street; the route of its many parades and marches. With its gentle slope, it strolls through a region of chic department stores and past some of the city's most famous buildings and public spaces.

The **Empire State Building** is at 34th Street. Though it's visible over much of the city, only on this cross-street can you see its height from top to bottom. At 39th Street, **Lord & Taylor** is the first of the Avenue's remaining grand department stores; and a block north, impassive stone lions guard the steps of the **New York Public Library**. This beautiful Beaux Arts composition provides an astonishing escape from the noise and traffic outside. Behind the library is **Bryant Park**, once the site of New York's own Crystal Palace (1853-58), now an elegant formal lawn filled with lunching office workers and a busy schedule of free entertainment.

At 43rd Street there is the **Seth Thomas street clock** for you to set your watch. On the first block of West 44th Street is the famous **Algonquin Hotel**, where scathing wit Dorothy Parker held court at Alexander Woollcott's Round Table. The **Iroquois** and the upstart **Royalton** hotels are also here. 47th Street is known as **Diamond Row**. It is here that the city's diamond trade is conducted, and in front of glittering window displays you'll see the many orthodox Jewish traders, precious gems in their pockets, doing business in the street.

Walk from Fifth Avenue into **Rockefeller Center** (48th-51st Streets) and you will understand the masterful use of public space for which this complex of buildings is so lavishly praised. You are drawn down the Channel Gardens and gradually the mass of the GE Building rises over you. At its apex is the famous Rainbow Room restaurant and bar; gathered round it are the lower blocks of the International Building and its companions. Over on the Sixth Avenue side is **Radio City Music Hall**, built as the world's largest cinema, and the stark towers of the much later Rockefeller Center Part II.

Across the street from Rockefeller's sweeping lines is **St Patrick's Cathedral** (1878), a beautiful Gothic Revival structure and the largest Catholic Cathedral in the US.

In the 1920s 52nd Street was 'Swing Street', a row of speakeasies and jazz clubs. All that remains is the 21 Club (at No. 21), now a power lunching spot. This street also contains the **Museum of Television and Radio**. The **Museum of Modern Art** is on 53rd Street, as is the **American Craft Museum.**

The blocks of Fifth Avenue between Rockefeller Center and Central Park contain expensive retail palaces selling everything from Rolex watches to gourmet chocolate. Here, in the stretch between **Saks Fifth Avenue** (50th Street) and **Bergdorf Goodman** (58th Street), the rents are the highest in the world, and you'll find such names as Cartier, Chanel, Gucci and Tiffany's. Recently, however, some upstart neighbours have been joining them, among them the big themed outlets of the Warner Brothers Studio Store and Coca Cola Fifth Avenue. Levi's, Nike and Disney are on the way.

*The lovely* **St Patrick's Cathedral**.

The pinnacle of this malling transformation has to be **Trump Tower**, Donald's soaring chrome spire with its pink marble interior. Like an episode of *Lifestyles of the Rich and Famous*, the theme here is tasteless expenditure.

Fifth Avenue is crowned by **Grand Army Plaza**, at 59th Street. A statue of General Sherman presides over a public space with the sleek chateau of the Plaza Hotel to the west and the General Motors building with the famous FAO Schwartz toy store at ground level.

### Grand Army Plaza

*Junction of Fifth Avenue & 59th Street.* **Train** N or R to Fifth Avenue.

## Midtown East

Sometimes on New Year's Eve you can waltz in the great hall of **Grand Central Station** just as the enchanted commuters did in *The Fisher King*. This beautiful Beaux Arts terminal, with the memories of muscular steam trains and lace-curtained carriages locked into its vaulted stone passageways, is surely the city's most spectacular point of arrival. It stands at the junction of 42nd Street and Park Avenue, the latter rising on a cast iron bridge to literally run through the station building.

Rising behind it, the **Met Life** (formerly Pan Am) Building was once the world's largest office block. Its most celebrated tenants are the peregrine falcons that nest on the roof, living on a diet of

# The painted city

Rattling old carriages, decorated from top to bottom with billboard-sized names and teams of crazy cartoon characters: up to the mid-1980s, that's what the city's subway system looked like, and though the graffiti is long gone it remains a powerful image of New York.

Today the trains are brushed aluminium. Paint slides right off, so the graffiti you'll see is restricted to 'tags', writer's names scratched into the window glass. 'Pieces', the grand colourful designs that took many hours to complete, were wiped out by Mayor Koch's famous 'War on Graffiti' in the mid-1980s.

To see good New York graf, you generally have to venture out into the boroughs. It's common in poorer neighbourhoods to see store signs done by graffiti artists, as well as memorials to local youngsters, usually on the spot where they bit their bullet. In the Bronx, where it all began, artists have turned their attention to the concrete walls alongside commuter train lines.

As well as the many downtown parking lots, two particular Manhattan sites are worth checking out. The Graffiti Hall of Fame is at 106th Street between Park and Madison Avenues. It's actually just a schoolyard, but here you'll see the large-scale work of 'old-school' writers and may even bump into someone completing a piece. Another location is the small playground at Amsterdam Avenue and 98th Street, which is the home turf of veteran old-schoolers the Rock Steady Crew (they re-christened it 'Rock Steady Park'), many of whom are still active writers.

Also look out for graffiti on the sides of moving vehicles. Spon has risen to fame by using garbage trucks as his canvases, and the quality of pieces on delivery trucks is rising. There are even a few commissioned ones out there.

Many of the more famous 1980s writers have turned their attentions to gallery work, and many now also make clothes, getting their tag on hundreds of T-shirts. Newer, artsy forms of graffiti appearing downtown include lines of painted footsteps on sidewalks, as well as sprayed outlines of tools and household objects. And though the authorities have now caught him, you can still see thousands of resourceful examples of his tag, REVS and COST, either painted or, more often, stuck to street furniture in the form of small photocopied messages.

If you want to explore the scene further visit Crib, 210 East 6th Street, between Second and Third Avenues (260 9237), an East Village boutique which also sells graf-zines, fat caps and videos, or SoHo Down and Under, 300 West Broadway at Canal Street (343 2557), which sells even more of these things and is the downtown centre for graffiti culture.

*The cathedral-like interior of* **Grand Central Station**.

falcons that nest on the roof, living on a diet of pigeons which they kill in mid-air.

On the other side of the Met Life tower is the **Helmsley Building**. Built by Warren and Whetmore, the architects responsible for Grand Central, its glittering gold detail presents a fitting punctuation to the vista south down Park Avenue.

On Park itself, amid the solid blocks of mansion-sized apartments, there's the Waldorf-Astoria Hotel (No. 301); the sensation-causing glass Lever House (No.390); and the bronze and glass Seagram Building (No. 375). On Madison is the IBM Building (at 56th Street), with one of the finest atrium lobbies. Across the street is the Sony (formerly the AT&T) Building, with its distinctive Chippendale crown. Inside are Sony's new Public Arcade and Wonder Technology Lab, with hands-on displays of silicon stuff.

42nd Street going east is full of architectural interest. Worth a look is the spectacular hall of the Bowery Savings Bank (at No. 110); the art deco power and detail of the Chanin Building (No. 122); the sparkling chromed Chrysler Building (at Lexington Avenue); and the Daily News Building (No. 220), immortalised in the *Superman* films and still containing the giant globe in its lobby.

The street ends with **Tudor City**, a pioneering 1925 residential development that looks like a sort of high-rise Hampton Court. North of here is an area known as **Turtle Bay**, though you won't see too many turtles in the East River today. This is dominated by the **United Nations**, and its famous glass-walled secretariat building. Though you don't need your passport, you are leaving US soil when you enter the UN complex – this is an international zone. Optimistic peacemongering sculptures are dotted around, and the **Peace Gardens** along the East River bloom with delicate avenues of rosebeds.

South of 42nd Street is a neighbourhood known as **Murray Hill**, still a fashionable address, but with only a few streets retaining the prettiness that made it so. Townhouses of the rich and powerful were clustered here around Park and Madison Avenues. **Sniffen Court**, at 150-158 East 36th Street, is an unspoilt row of carriage houses, within spitting distance of the ceaseless traffic of the Queens-Midtown Tunnel. Near here (19 East 32nd Street) was where **Andy Warhol's Factory** enjoyed most of its 15 minutes of fame.

The **Pierpont Morgan Library** is the reason most visitors come here, two elegant buildings linked by a glass cloister, housing the collections of manuscripts, books and prints owned by the famous banker.

**Grand Central Station**

*42nd Street at Park Avenue.* **Train** 4, 5, 6 or 7 to Grand Central

# Uptown

***If you're rich and brainy you live on the west; if you're rich and artsy – or just plain rich – you live on the east. If you're poor and homeless you live in Central Park.***

At the end of the 1700s there wasn't much except farmland to be found this far north. Central Park is what made Uptown desirable, turning country estates into Fifth Avenue mansions and seducing New York society into leaving the crowded streets downtown. The park's glorious green space, which is bigger than Monaco, will always dominate Manhattan life between 59th and 110th Streets. The neighbourhoods on either side are counterpoints: the east rich and respectable, full of 'establishment' fashion and museums; the west more intellectual, revolving around the academia of Columbia University to the north and the music and performance of Lincoln Center to the south.

## The Upper East Side

The Upper East Side is all about money. The greed and gold of New York high society resides in the mansions of Fifth and Park Avenues; the old maids and young trust funders spend their spare change in Madison Avenue's plate-glassed boutiques; and rich businessmen use their tax write-offs to fund the area's cultural institutions (which their families probably founded): the museums and societies of Museum Mile and beyond.

Once Frederick Law Olmstead and Calvert Vaux had wrenched the wondrous Central Park (*see chapter* **Sightseeing**) out of pestilential swampland, fashionable New York felt ready to move north. In the mid 1800s the super-rich had built mansions along Fifth Avenue. By the beginning of this century, the merely rich warmed to the – at first outrageous – idea of living in apartment buildings, provided they could be near the park. Many grand examples of these were built along Park Avenue and the streets joining it to Fifth. Among them sprang up the blossoms of many a tycoon's philanthropic gesture – the many art collections, museums and cultural institutes which are the reason why most visitors come to the area.

**Museum Mile** is actually a promotional organisation rather than a geographical description, but since most of the museums along Fifth Avenue are members, it is an apt name. **The Metropolitan Museum of Art**, set in Central Park, is the grandest of them all. Walking north from the steps of the Met, you reach the stunning spiral design of Frank Lloyd Wright's **Guggenheim Museum** at 88th Street; the **National Academy of Design** at 89th; the **Cooper-Hewitt Museum** – set in Andrew Carnegie's mansion – at 91st; the **Jewish Museum** at 92nd; and the **International Center of Photography** at 94.

The toy-town brick fortress façade at 94th and Madison is what's left of the old **Squadron A Armory**. Just off Fifth Avenue at 97th Street are the onion domes and rich ornamentation of the **Russian Orthodox Cathedral of St Nicholas** and a little further north are **El Museo del Barrio** and **Museum of the City of New York**, at 104th and 105th Streets respectively.

There's another clump of museums near the south-east corner of Central Park. On Madison Avenue at 75th Street, the **Whitney Museum of American Art** occupies a brutal, looming cube by Marcel Breuer. The **Frick Collection**, an art-filled mansion, faces the park at 70th Street. A few blocks south is the **Society of Illustrators**.

As well as these museums, the wealth concentrated here has also been used to found societies promoting interest in the language and culture of foreign lands. Rockefeller's **Asia Society** is on Park Ave and 70th Street. Nearby are the **China Institute in America** and the **Americas Society**, dedicated to the nations of South and Central America. On Fifth Avenue there is the **Ukrainian Institute**, the **German Cultural Center** (at 83rd Street) and the **YIVO Institute for Jewish Research** (at 86th).

**Madison Avenue** used to be known as the home of the advertising industry. Now its reputation is more for ultra-expensive shops (Saatchi & Saatchi is now happily ensconced in SoHo). Don't try shopping here unless you have some serious loot. This is the place to buy established designer labels – Yves Saint Laurent, Givenchy, Missoni, Geoffrey Beenes. Rather than facing the cut and thrust of the avenue, you could buy everything at **Bloomingdale's**, that frantic, glitzy supermarket of high fashion. There are also many commercial galleries hereabouts, including the Knoedler Gallery and Hirschl & Adler Modern. This is where established artists such as Robert Rauschenberg and Frank Stella prefer to show, rather than down in the SoHo circus.

**Lincoln Center** – *the cultural heart of Uptown.*

At 66th Street and Park Avenue is the **7th Regiment Armory**, whose interiors were designed and furnished by Louis Comfort Tiffany, assisted by a young Stanford White. It now houses the Winter Antiques show, among other events.

From Lexington to the East River, things become less grand. The **Abigail Adams Smith Museum**, at 421 East 61st Street near First Avenue, is a lovely old coach house dating from 1799, operated as a museum by the Colonial Dames of America. It was part of a farm owned by the daughter and son-in-law of John Adams, the second American president.

Kim Novak, Montgomery Clift, Tallulah Bankhead and Eleanor Roosevelt all lived a little bit further west in the tree-lined streets of three- and four-storey brownstones known as the **Treadwell Farm Historic District**, 61st and 62nd Streets, between Second and Third Avenues.

The central building of **Rockefeller University** – from 64th to 68th Streets, on a bluff overlooking FDR Drive – is listed as a national historic landmark. The Founders' Hall dates from 1903, the year the university was established as a medical research centre. With the guard's permission, you may walk around the campus. Look out for the President's House and the domed Caspary Auditorium. Medical institutions, including the **New York Hospital/Cornell Medical Center**, into which the city's oldest hospital is incorporated, dominate the next few blocks of York Avenue.

### Society of Illustrators

*128 East 63rd Street, between Lexington & Park Avenues (838 2560).* **Open** 10am-8pm Tue; 10am-5pm Wed-Fri; noon-4pm Sat. Closed August. **Admission** free.
Exhibitions featuring illustration are held regularly.

### Ukrainian Institute

*2 East 79th Street, at Fifth Avenue (288 8660).* **Open** by appointment. **Admission** voluntary donation.
The institute's turreted building has been designated a national landmark. Inside, Ukrainian costumes and art are on display.

### Seventh Regiment Armory

*643 Park Avenue, at 66th Street (452 3067).* **Train** 6 to 68th Street. **Open** Mon-Fri by appointment.
*Disabled: access.*

### Abigail Adams Smith Museum

*421 East 61st Street, between First Avenue and York Avenue (838 6878).* **Train** 4, 5 or 6 to 59th Street; N or R to Lexington Avenue. **Open** *June-July* noon-4pm Mon-Fri; *Sept-May* noon-4pm Mon-Fri; 1-5pm Sun. **Admission** $3 adults; $2 students, senior citizens. **No credit cards**.
Named after the daughter of John Adams, the house, built in 1795, is often called Smith's Folly in reference to her husband, William Smith, George Washington's aide-de-camp. It's furnished in late eighteenth- and early nineteenth-century style and is surrounded by a small, formal garden.

## Yorkville

The east and north-east parts of the Upper East Side are residential neighbourhoods inhabited by the young and professional (yes, yuppies). There are endless retaurants and bars here (including the super-swank **Elaine's**), as well as gourmet food stores and, on streets like 86th, all the shops you could need.

Most of this area is known historically as **Yorkville**, extending from the 70s to 96th Street, east of Lexington Avenue. Once a pretty little hamlet on the banks of the river, Yorkville was predominantly a German stronghold. In the last decades of the nineteenth century, East 86th Street became the Hauptstrasse, filled with German restaurants, beer gardens and pastry, grocery, butcher's and clothing shops. When World War II broke out, tensions naturally developed. Nazis and anti-Nazis clashed in the streets and a Nazi-American newspaper was published here.

The legacies include **Rigo Hungarian Pastry** (on East 77th), where the strudel is sensational, **Csarda**, with its Hungarian goulash (on Second Avenue), and the **Paprikas Weiss** spice shop further up the street.

The famous comedy club Catch a Rising Star, where Robin Williams started out, has now closed, but you can still have a good laugh at the **Comic Strip**, on Second Avenue near East 81st Street (*see chapter* **Cabaret**). This is where Eddie Murphy kicked off his career.

On East End Avenue at 86th Street is the **Henderson Place Historic District**, where 24 two-storey Queen Anne row (or terrace) houses – prettily decorated with turrets, double stoops and slate roofs – commissioned by fur dealer John C Henderson, still stand. Over the street is **Gracie Mansion**, New York's official mayoral residence and the only remaining Federal-style mansion in Manhattan still used as a home. The mansion is the focal point of the **Carl Schurz Park**, named in honour of the German immigrant, senator and newspaper editor. The park is remarkable for its tranquillity and offers spectacular views over the East River. Its long promenade, the John H Finley Walk, is one of the most beautiful in the city (especially in the early morning or at dusk).

*The* **Metropolitan Museum of Art**.

### Gracie Mansion

*in Carl Schurz Park, East 88th Street & East End Avenue (570 4751).* **Train** 4, 5 or 6 to 86th Street. **Open** Wed for guided tours; phone for details. **Admission** suggested contribution $3; $ senior citizens.

This house became the official mayoral residence in 1942. The tour takes you through the mayor's living room, a guest suite and smaller bedrooms. One of the best things about it are the views down the river from this strategic site, where Washington built a battery during the war.

## Roosevelt Island

The red cable cars ('trams') that cross the East River from Manhattan to Roosevelt Island, the submarine-shaped island off the Upper East Side, offer some of the very best views of Manhattan (embark at Second Avenue and 60th Street). It was once called Welfare Island and housed a lunatic asylum, a smallpox hospital, prisons and workhouses. It is now a largely residential community of 8000 people, and accessible by road from Queens.

The Indians called it Minnahanonck, or 'island place', then sold it to the Dutch, who made a vast creative leap and named it Hog's Island. The Dutch farmed it, as did Englishman Robert Blackwell, who moved here in 1686. His old clapboard farmhouse is in Blackwell Park, adjacent to Main Street (there's only one street – with several restaurants).

A new pier faces Manhattan, and there are numerous picturesque picnic spots. The recently opened **Octagon Park** includes tennis courts, hanging gardens and an ecological park. The riverfront promenades afford fabulous views of the skyline and East River, but the tram remains the biggest attraction: you've seen it in a host of films including, most recently, *City Slickers*. Wander down the **Meditation Steps** for river views or take one of the riverside walks around the island. The latest addition to the island's attractions is the **Sculpture Center**, sited at Motorgate, the island's unusual transportation complex. Here large outdoor work is displayed, many of the pieces inspired by features of the island.

On the southern tip are the weathered neo-Gothic ruins of **Smallpox Hospital** and the burned-out remains of **City Hospital**. The **Octagon Tower** is the remaining central core of the former New

*The* **Guggenheim Museum** *– as much a work of art itself as any of the pieces it houses.*

York City Lunatic Asylum. Charles Dickens was a visitor and was disturbed by its 'lounging, listless, madhouse air'. In an early feat of investigative journalism, reporter Nellie Bly feigned insanity and had herself committed to the asylum for 10 days in 1887, and then wrote a shocking exposé of the conditions in the 'human rat trap'. The decaying buildings tend to crop up in rock videos.

**Roosevelt Island Operating Corporation**
*591 Main Street (832 4540).* **Open** 9am-5pm Mon-Fri. Call for details of events, free maps and brochures on the island.

## Upper West Side

The Upper West Side is a fairly affluent residential area, rich in cinemas, bars and restaurants, as well as bookstores and reclusive celebrities. Its reputation is serious, intellectual and politically liberal. European immigrants were attracted here in the late nineteenth century by the building boom sparked off by Central Park, as well as by Columbia University's new site to the north.

Because Americans can't deal with roundabouts, **Columbus Circle**, with its 700-ton statue of **Columbus**, is one of the most confused traffic junctions imaginable. The curved white marble slab on stilts here is New York City's **Department of Cultural Affairs**, location of the **New York Convention and Visitors Bureau**. West of the circle is The **New York Coliseum**. Apart from a few one-off events, it has been out of business since the Javits Convention Center was built in 1986. On 68th Street you can see one of the 12 movies showing at Sony's new Lincoln Square theatre – with a huge 3D Imax screen as well, it's blockbuster heaven.

It's not unusual to see men and women striding around here in evening dress. They've been to the **Lincoln Center**, the heart of classical music in the city: a complex of concert halls and auditoriims. The different buildings are linked by sweeping public plazas and populated by sensitive musical types.

From the Lincoln Center Plaza you can see a small-scale replica of the **Statue of Liberty** on top of a building on West 64th Street. Round the corner, at 2 Lincoln Square, is the small but fascinating **Museum of American Folk Art**.

It took longer for the west side to become fashionable than it did for Fifth Avenue, but once the park was built, Central Park West soon filled up with luxury apartment blocks. Once well-off New Yorkers had re-adjusted themselves to living in 'French flats', as they called them, apartment living became almost desirable.

The art deco building at 55 Central Park West is best remembered for its role in *Ghostbusters*. On 72nd Street is the **Dakota**, most famous these days as the building outside which John Lennon was murdered. It's one of New York's first great apartment buildings, and the one that accelerated the drift to the west. Sceptical New Yorkers commented that it was so far away from the centre of town that it might as well be in Dakota. The developers defiantly took up the name and ordered decorative details straight out of the Wild West. Yoko Ono and other famous residents can be seen popping in and out. The massive twin-towered

*Catch a ride on* **Central Park***'s carousel.*

**San Remo** block at 74th Street dates from 1930 and is such prime real estate that even Madonna couldn't get an apartment here.

The **New York Historical Society**, the oldest museum in the country, is at 76th Street. Across the street, the **American Museum of Natural History** attracts visitors with its stuffed and mounted creatures, dinosaur skeletons, ethnological collections and the associated **Hayden Planetarium**.

The avenues between Central Park West and Broadway – **Columbus** and **Amsterdam** – have long been gentrified and are full of restaurants, speciality shops, gourmet food outlets and fashion stores, such as **Betsey Johnson**. The neighbourhood underwent a renaissance when the Lincoln Center was built, although a good few of the old inhabitants and shops remain.

On Broadway, the **72nd Street subway** is worth seeing for its original art nouveau entrance. It's on **Sherman Square**, named after the general. The opposite triangle, at the intersection of 73rd and Broadway, is **Verdi Square**; a fitting name since – along with Arturo Toscanini and Igor Stravinsky – Enrico Caruso lived in the **Ansonia Hotel** across the street and kept the other inhabitants entertained/awake with renditions of his favourite arias. The Ansonia, a vast Beaux Arts apartment building with exquisite detailing, was also the location for *Single White Female*. Bette Midler got her break at the Continental Baths, a gay spa and cabaret that occupied the bottom few floors in the 1970s. This was also where star DJs Frankie Knuckles and Larry Levan first honed their skills.

The **Beacon Theater** on Broadway here was once a fabulous old movie palace. It's now a top-ticket concert venue with classy black music shows. The phenomenal interior is a designated landmark. A few blocks north are the **Children's Museum of Manhattan**, the famous **Zabar's**, supplier of delicious delicacies, notably caviare, and some of Manhattan's best bookstores.

Just off Broadway, a little way down the north side of 94th Street, is a quaint English-type mews called **Pomander Walk**. Nearby is the **Claremont Riding Academy** where you can hire horses to ride in Central Park (*see chapter* **Sport & Fitness**). Back on Broadway, the old movie theatre-turned-performance centre **Symphony Space** (*see chapter* **Music: Classical & Opera**) features eclectic musical programmes, including the famous Wall-to-Wall concerts.

**Riverside Park** lies between Riverside Drive and the banks of the Hudson from 72nd to 145th Streets. Once as fashionable an address as Fifth Avenue and similarly lined with opulent private houses, Riverside Drive was largely rebuilt in the 1930s with luxury apartment blocks. The park is a welcome stretch of undulating riverbank. You may see luxury yachts berthed at the little **79th Street Boat Basin**, along with a few houseboats. Further north, at 89th Street, the **Soldiers and Sailors Monument** is a memorial to the Civil War dead.

### Soldiers' & Sailors' Monument

*Riverside Drive, at West 89th Street.* **Train** 1 or 9 to 86th Street.

The 1902 monument was designed by French sculptor Paul DuBoy and architects Charles and Arthur Stoughton.

### New York Historical Society

*2 West 77th Street, between Fifth & Sixth Avenues (873 3400).* **Train** B or C to 81st Street. **Open** noon-5pm Wed-Sun. **Admission** $3 adults; $1 senior citizens, under-12s. **No credit cards**.

The Society's library has an important architectural collection, including the archives of McKim, Mead & White, and Cass Gilbert. A magnificent collection of Tiffany lamps is on display, but visits to the library are by appointment only. *Disabled: access.*

# Northern Manhattan

***Harlem isn't just jazz and soul food. Beautiful architecture, intriguing museums and the largest cathedral in the world are also found in the area north of Central Park.***

## Harlem

Harlem's reputation as a no-go area has been somewhat overstated. Certainly some parts are extremely depressed, and if you're white you should be prepared to stand out in the crowd, but a daytime visit to the main attractions should be wholly unproblematic.

Harlem is, in spirit, the Blackest place there is. Its elegant stone buildings reverberate with the history of Black America's struggle for equality. The names of great liberators, teachers and orators christen its institutions and fill its street signs, and there are constant reminders of proud Afrocentric culture, from the Francophone Africans selling their trinkets to the Jeeps booming out the latest hip-hop street politics.

When the subways arrived at the turn of the century, Harlem, previously composed of country estates, was developed for middle-class New Yorkers. When they failed to fill the rows of grandiose townhouses, the speculators reluctantly rented them out to African Americans. The area's population doubled during the 1920s and 1930s, a growth which brought the cultural explosion of the Harlem Renaissance, when it became a decadent bohemian republic and its poets, writers, artists and musicians ushered in the Jazz Age.

Nowadays Harlem's soundtrack is the rap and reggae of the younger generation and the salsa and merengue of the Cubans and Dominicans who have moved into the older black community, adding to the Hispanic populations of **Spanish Harlem**, or *El Barrio* ('the neighbourhood'). This

is the section east of Fifth Avenue above 100th Street. Browse among the colourful fruits and vegetables, spices and meats at **La Marqueta** on Park Avenue, 110th-116th Streets. **El Museo del Barrio**, Spanish Harlem's community museum, is on Fifth Avenue at 104th Street, which houses cultural artefacts of Hispanic New York.

At 116th Street and Lenox Avenue is **Masjid Malcolm Shabazz**, the silver-domed mosque of Malcolm X's ministry. Opposite this is the market where the street vendors who once lined 125th Street now ply their trade in T-shirts, tapes and 'African' souvenirs. Just north of here the **Lenox Lounge** is the still-existing bar where Malcolm X's early career as a hustler began. Further up Lenox is **Sylvia's**, the most famous of Harlem's soulfood restaurants, and even further, at 138th Street, is the **Abyssinian Baptist Church**, containing a small museum dedicated to Adam Clayton Powell Jr, the first black man to be elected to Congress (in 1941) and Harlem's representative until 1970. Just below 125th Street, on Fifth Avenue, **Marcus Garvey Park** (previously Mt Morris Park) is Harlem's only patch of green, the centre of a historic district of elegant brownstones. Some of the more beautiful are open to the public several times a year (call Mt Morris Park Community Association on 369 4241 for details).

The **Studio Museum of Harlem** has changing exhibitions about the area and its people, while the **Schomberg Center for Research in Black Culture** is the largest research collection for African-American culture (*see chapter* **Museums** for both).

125th Street is Harlem's main drag and the **Apollo Theater** is its focus. In the 1920s, during Prohibition, it was one of the places – along with the Cotton Club, Connie's and Small's Paradise – where you could listen to names like Josephine Baker, Lena Horne and Duke Ellington while sampling the bootleg liquor. Now it's used for television recordings and live entertainment along the hip-hop and R'n'B spectrum (*see chapter* **Music: Rock, Blues & Jazz**).

The area between 125th and 155th Streets west of St Nicholas Avenue is known as **Hamilton Heights**, after Alexander Hamilton, who had a farm here at Hamilton Grange (Convent Avenue at 142nd Street). This is the gentrified part of Harlem, where you'll find City College, the northern outpost of City University. It's also the location of Audubon Terrace, a double Beaux Arts row containing a group of museums: the Hispanic Society of America, the American Numismatic Society and the American Academy of Arts and Letters (*see chapter* **Museums**).

**Harlem** *'s grandiose architecture.*

### Transport

**Train** 2, 3, A, B, C or D to 125th Street.

### Harlem Spirituals

*1697 Broadway, at 53rd Street, Suite 203 (757 0425).* **Train** B, D or E to Seventh Avenue. **Open** 9am-6pm Mon-Sat. **Credit** AmEx, MC, V.

A wide range of tours are organised, including morning gospel tours, lunchtime historical tours and evening soul food and jazz tours. Prices range from $30 to $70.

## Morningside Heights

The area sandwiched between Morningside Park and the Hudson River from 110th to 125th Streets is **Morningside Heights**, a region dominated by **Columbia University**. One of the oldest universities in the USA, Columbia was chartered in 1754 as King's College (the name changed after Independence). Thanks to its large student presence, the surrounding area has an academic feel, with plenty of bookshops and cafés along Broadway and quiet leafy streets towards the west overlooking Riverside Park.

The neighbourhood has two immense houses of worship, the **Cathedral of St John the Divine** and the Baptist **Riverside Church**, speedily built with Rockefeller money and containing the world's largest carillon. You can ride to the top of the 21-storey steel-framed tower for views out across the Hudson and also of **Grant's Tomb** in Riverside Park (at 122nd Street), honouring victorious Civil War general Ulysses S Grant.

The hammering and chiselling at St John's Cathedral will continue well into the next century. Construction began in 1892 in Romanesque style, was stopped for a re-design in Gothic Revival in 1911 and wasn't restarted until 1941. There was another lapse to campaign for funds, but the last decade has seen work begin again in earnest. When the towers and great crossing are completed, this will be the world's largest cathedral. Services, concerts and tours take place inside and it's the location for funerals of the rich and famous.

### Columbia University

*Between Broadway & Amsterdam Avenue, 114th-120th Streets (854 1754).* **Train** 1 or 9 to 116th Street.

### Riverside Church

*Riverside Drive, at 122nd Street (222 5900).* **Train** 1 or 9 to 116th Street. **Open** 9am-4pm daily.

### Cathedral of St John the Divine

*Amsterdam Avenue, at 110th Street (662 2133).* **Train** 1 or 9 to 110th Street. **Open** 7am-5pm daily.

### General Grant National Memorial

*Riverside Drive & West 122nd Street (666 1640).* **Train** 1 or 9 to 125th Street. **Open** 9am-5pm daily. **Free.**

The classical temple that is more commonly known as Grant's Tomb dominates the upper reaches of Riverside Park. The architect of the Union victory, General Ulysses S Grant, was elected President in 1868 and remained an immensely popular national hero, despite being a particularly inept president. He is buried here with his wife.

## Washington Heights

The area from 155th Street to the northern tip of Manhattan is called Washington Heights. Here the island shrinks in width and the parks on either side culminate in the wilderness and forest of **Inwood Hill Park**, where, in 1626, a Dutchman called Peter Minuit 'bought' Manhattan Island from the Indians for a handful of beads. **High Bridge** (Amsterdam Avenue at 177th Street) gives an idea of how old New York got its water supply. This aqueduct carried water across the Harlem River from the Croton Reservoir in Westchester County to Manhattan. The central piers were replaced in the 1920s to allow large ships to pass below.

The main building of **Yeshiva University** (186th Street at Amsterdam Avenue) is one of the strangest in New York, a Byzantine orange-brick structure decorated with turrets and minarets. Equally unlikely is **The Cloisters** at the north end of Fort Tryon Park – a newly constructed monastery incorporating several original medieval cloisters purloined from Europe, whose tree-filled landscaped grounds might have been custom-designed for romantic picnics. It might sound naff but is in fact restrained and graceful. The project, financed by the Rockefellers, is the medieval outpost of the Metropolitan Museum, and contains illuminated manuscripts and priceless tapestries (*see chapter* **Museums**).

The neighbourhood also has two significant historic sites. **Dyckman House**, built in 1748, is the oldest surviving home in Manhattan, and something of a lonely sight on busy Broadway (at 204th Street), and **Morris-Jumel Mansion** (Edgecumb Avenue at 160th Street) was where George Washington planned some of his battles, and later where Governor Morris, one of the signatories of the Declaration of Independence, lived (*see chapter* **Architecture**).

### The Cloisters

*Fort Tryon Park (923 3700).* **Train** A to 190th Street. **Open** 9.30am-5.15pm Tue-Sun with seasonal variations. **Admission** $7 suggested donation; $3.50 senior citizens, students; free accompanied under-12s (includes same-day admission to the Metropolitan Museum).

# Homes away from homes

Amid the dreary project housing and tenements, most Puerto Rican immigrants dream of their beautiful island home. Some, however, are not content to dream; they have reproduced a bit of 'The Island' in the heart of the urban jungle.

Often the focal point of Puerto Rican village life is the *bohio*, a communal hang-out built and adorned with recycled materials and found objects. Food and drink is sold, and people hang out and sing, dance and revel into the early hours.

*Casitas* (literally 'little houses') are New York's equivalent of the *bohio*. They have popped up on plots of vacant land all over the city, creating a slice of island life among the high-rises. Serving as everything from an ongoing party to a place where old men play dominoes, the jerry-built *casitas* are a vital part of community life and identity.

A related phenomenon is the barrio's communal gardens. A vacant lot is taken over by the community, with tiny plots – often no bigger than a bath-tub – apportioned to individuals, who grow flowers or vegetables. The gardens are often adorned with devotional scenes recreated from found objects (Joseph and Mary might be clothing mannequins, with baby Jesus a partly-dismembered plastic doll), while the surrounding walls bear murals celebrating Puerto Rican culture.

*Casitas* and communal gardens are tucked away in various parts of the Lower East Side and East Harlem, as well as in the outer boroughs. If you're going to the Museo del Barrio, there are two casitas on your way from the 6 train subway station: one on a vacant lot on 103rd Street between Park and Lexington Avenues; the other around the corner on Lexington between 103rd and 104th Streets. For a look at some communal gardens try Avenue B between Houston and 6th Streets, or, for the (considerably) more adventurous, the one on 126th Street between First and Second Avenues.

# The Outer Boroughs

***You should get out more. There's plenty of New York outside Manhattan. Go visit the other four boroughs.***

If you're surprised at how compact New York is, that's because you probably haven't stepped off Manhattan yet. The city actually comprises five boroughs, each with its own character and all containing world-class museums, parks, restaurants and other attractions. Of course, Manhattan is the centre of it all, but if you want to see where the majority of New Yorkers live, find time to visit Brooklyn, Queens,the Bronx and Staten Island.

## Brooklyn

Brooklyn is no suburb. The grand spaces of its civic centre, the scale of its public buildings and the beauty of its private houses all hint at a proud and independent history. In the language of hip-hop it is a whole world: 'the Planet'. It has been part of New York for less than a hundred years.

In the middle of the nineteenth century, Brooklyn was a rich and powerful city, the third largest in the United States (today it would still be the fourth largest). In 1861 Walt Whitman declared its destiny was 'to be among the most famed and choice of the half dozen cities of the world'. To join it to New York they had to build a bridge of unimaginable length.

More even than Manhattan, Brooklyn is a collection of vitally distinct ethnic neighbourhoods. There is Jamaican Flatbush, African-American Bedford-Stuyvesant, Jewish Crown Heights, Polish Greenpoint, Italian Bensonhurst and newly trendy Williamsburg with its tripartite population of Hispanics, Hasidim and art-rebel loft-loungers. This patchwork of communities has long made for a vivid cultural life. More famous Americans come from Brooklyn than anywhere else.

*Ethnically diverse Brooklyn has several Jewish communities.*

The **Civic Center**, a reminder of Brooklyn's earlier status, is dominated by the City Hall, now Borough Hall (1851; 209 Joralemon Street at Fulton Street), and the massive General Post Office (271-301 Fulton Street).

From here it's a short walk to **Brooklyn Heights**, with its well-preserved streets of Federal-style and Greek Revival brownstones. Middagh, Cranberry, Willow, Orange, Pineapple, Pierrepont and Montague are some of the prettiest streets. Pierrepont Street is also home to the **Brooklyn Historical Society** museum and library and takes you to the Promenade overlooking the river for some breath-stopping views of lower Manhattan. Also in the Heights is the imposing **Plymouth Church of the Pilgrims**, on Orange Street, founded by the famous abolitionist Henry Ward Beecher, who is remembered with a statue there.

Stroll through Cadman Plaza Park and you will reach the **Brooklyn Bridge** (*see chapter* **Sightseeing**). This much-loved 1883 construction astounded both cities, supplanted most of the 17 ferry companies that traversed the East River and made inevitable the marriage of Brooklyn with New York. Its anchorage space now houses the occasional rave.

The **Brooklyn Museum** was designed to be the largest in the world. Though only a fifth of it was built, it is still imposing and enormous, housing 1.5 million artefacts, including one of the best Egyptian collections anywhere. Another museum worth visiting is the **New York Transit Museum**, which tells the intriguing story of New York's subways. Also nearby is the **Brooklyn Children's Museum** (*see chapter* **Children**).

*Previous page: Brooklyn's* **Promenade** *gives heart-stopping views of Manhattan.*

The grand old opera house that is the **Brooklyn Academy of Music** is a further symbol of Brooklyn's independence. It puts on a fine range of musical and theatrical productions.

The surrounding neighbourhood of **Fort Greene** is Brooklyn's bohemian centre, with an increasingly multi-ethnic population of successful creative types. This is where Spike Lee calls home, and his moviebilia store, **Spike's Joint**, is here (*see chapter* **Shopping**), as is **Junior's**, the world's best place for dessert (*see chapter* **Restaurants**).

At the **Concord Baptist Church of Christ** you can experience some old-time religion alongside the largest black congregation in the US. Let the fabulous gospel music prove that the devil doesn't have all the best tunes.

Like Manhattan, Brooklyn has a heart of green. Built by the same architects, **Prospect Park** is smaller than Central Park, but much calmer and more rural. On weekends it fills with families having barbecues and picnics, as well as active types who use its sports fields and closed road loop. On the eastern side the largely Caribbean community of Flatbush gathers: listen out for booming reggae and huge drumming circles. The park's many attractions include a new children's zoo, opened in

1993, a bandshell with a busy summer programme of jazz, hip-hop, soul, gospel, classical and opera concerts and the restored Dutch-colonial style **Lefferts Homestead**, one of the city's first buildings, which now houses a children's museum and a visitors' centre.

At the park's main entrance is **Grand Army Plaza** with the **Brooklyn Public Library** to one side and the **Soldiers' and Sailors' Memorial Arch** in the centre. Designed, like the park itself, by Olmstead and Vaux, the architects of Central Park, it commemorates Brooklyn's dead from the Civil War. The plaza is also the site of New York's only monument to John F Kennedy.

Next door to the park and behind the museum is the peaceful **Brooklyn Botanic Garden**, famous for its Japanese cherry trees and the biggest bonsai collection in the US. Visit at the weekend and you're sure to see little Catholic girls being photographed in their communion dresses and the occasional freshly wedded couple enjoying their reception among the blossoms.

**Park Slope**, the area west of the park, is another enclave of superbly elegant architecture: untouched nineteenth-century brownstone townhouses. This was the scene of Washington's 1776 retreat during the Revolutionary War.

Further afield, the rusted wonder of **Coney Island** (*see chapter* **Sightseeing**) is Brooklyn's answer to Blackpool. The beach itself is pretty dirty, but the amusement parks, boardwalk and piers which span its length are great fun. Walk along to the **Aquarium** (*see chapter* **Children**), where the collection of Beluga whales, sharks and other sea dwellers has recently been augmented by a huge (60,000sq ft) recreation of the Pacific coastline. Neighbouring **Brighton Beach** is the place to buy caviare, vodka and smoked sausages. More East European than American, it's known as 'Little Odessa' in recognition of its takeover by Russian immigrants.

### Brooklyn Historical Society

*128 Pierrepont Street, Brooklyn (1-718 624 0890).* **Train** 2 or 3 to Clark Street. **Open** noon-5pm Tue-Sat. **Admission** $2.50 adults; $1 seniors, under-12s.
Exhibits describing the borough and its history, with a research library and a programme of walking tours.

### Prospect Park

*Flatbush Avenue at Grand Army Plaza, Brooklyn (1-718 965 8999 events hotline/1 718 965 6505 Leffert's Homestead/718 399 7333 zoo).* **Train** 2 or 3 to Grand Army Plaza.

### Brooklyn Botanical Garden

*1000 Washington Avenue, Brooklyn (1-718 622 4433).* **Train** 2 or 3 to Eastern Parkway. **Open** 8am-6pm Tue-Fri; 10am-5pm Sat, Sun (with seasonal variations). **Admission** donations.
Travel between jungle and desert in the extensive conservatories here. There's also a beautiful rose garden, an outdoor café, a perfume garden for the blind and an area set aside for meditation.

### Concord Baptist Church of Christ

*833 Marcy Avenue, near Fulton Street (1-718 622 1818).* **Train** A or C to Nostrand Avenue.
Call for times of concerts and services.

## Queens

A visit to Queens is like a world tour using some kind of alternative geography. Here's Bombay, Athens, Columbia; there's Ecuador, Korea, Argentina; down the road is Kilkenny, Manila, Milan. Without a single city centre by which to define its growth, Queens, originally a handful of towns, has evolved as a patchwork of foreign cities: an urban suburbia. It is New York's new Lower East Side; today's destination for the multiple thousands of immigrants (a third of Queens residents are foreign-born) that still flood here from everywhere that isn't the US of A.

Queens County was named after Queen Catherine, Charles II's wife. It joined New York as a borough in 1898, the same year as Brooklyn and Staten Island, and as communications improved – the Queensboro Bridge ('the 59th Street Bridge') was built in in 1909 and the first train tunnels were cut under the East River in 1910 – it began to function as a residential satellite of Manhattan. Phenomenal building throughout the 1950s and 1960s merged the separate towns in a continuous sprawl, buffered only by several formal parks, highways and enormous cemeteries. Chances are that you started your visit here: **LaGuardia** and **JFK** airports are both in Queens. Should you return here you'll find many attractions in the towns of Astoria, Long Island City, Jamaica, Flushing and Forest Hills.

**Long Island City**, closest to Manhattan, is home to **PS1**, the Institute for Contemporary Art, housed in an old city school. A non-profit studio space attracting starving artists from around the world, it has open workshops, multi-media galleries, several large permanent works and controversial, censor-taunting exhibitions. Renovations are likely to keep the Institute closed until the end of 1996. Nearby, at the riverside, the **Socrates Sculpture Garden** presents a selection of large-scale sculpture by well- and lesser-known artists in a striking location, with occasional performances of music and video. A few doors down the road is the **Noguchi Museum** in Isamu Noguchi's wonderful self-designed sculpture studios, where over 300 of his works are on show in 12 galleries (*see chapter* **Museums**).

Mainly Greek Astoria is home to the **American Museum of the Moving Image**, which occupies one of the buildings of the Kaufmann-Astoria movie studios. These were opened in 1917, and WC Fields, Rudolph Valentino, Gloria Swanson and the Marx Brothers all made films here. The museum shows a well-curated programme of

*Get a new perspective on the world at the* **Unisphere**, *Queens.*

movies and a constantly changing series of pop exhibitions documenting film and television.

Further east are **Flushing** and **Flushing Meadows-Corona Park**, a huge park that contains **Shea Stadium**, home to the New York Mets baseball team, and the **USTA National Tennis Center**, where the US Open championships are played every August. The 1939 and the 1964 World's Fairs were held in Corona Park, leaving some incredible half-derelict structures and the huge stainless steel **Unisphere** globe in their wake. Outside the curved concrete structure of the **New York Hall of Science** are cast-off pieces of space rockets to marvel at. Have a look also at the ghostly amphitheatre overlooking the boating lake. A left-over 1939 World Fair pavilion is the home of the **Queens Museum**, where the main attraction is a 1:12,000 scale model of New York City made for the 1964 fair. **Corona Park** itself is the scene of weekend picnics and some hotly contested soccer matches between teams of European- and South American-born locals. You can rent bikes in the summer and there are plenty of good restaurants and coffee shops around.

Queens also has several noteworthy historical buildings. East of Flushing Meadows is the **Friends' Meeting House** (1694), built by religious protester John Bowne and still used as a Quaker meeting place, making it the oldest house of worship in the USA in continuous use. Next door is **Kingsland House**, a mid-eighteenth-century farmhouse which is also the headquarters of the **Queens Historical Society**. You can also visit John Bowne's own house, which dates back to 1661 (*see chapter* **Architecture**).

On the edge of Queens is the **Queens County Farm Museum**, where a farm dating back to 1772 is managed as it was back then. In the south of the borough, near JFK Airport, are the tidal wetlands of **Jamaica Bay Wildlife Refuge**, home to a large population of birds, plants and animals. Water-fowl flock here during the autumn migratory season. Bring your binoculars and spot both birds and planes.

### Queens Council on the Arts

*7901 Park Lane South, Woodhaven, Queens, NY 11421 (1-718 647 3377/718 291 ARTS information menu).* **Open** 9am-4.30pm Mon-Fri.

Provides exhaustive details of all cultural events in the borough, updated daily.

### Institute for Contemporary Art (PS1)

*46-01 21st Street, Long Island City, Queens (1-718 784 2084).* **Train** E or F to 23rd Street/Ely Avenue. **Open** noon-6pm Wed-Sun. **Admission** $2 suggested donation.

Closed for renovation until the end of 1996.

### Socrates Sculpture Park

*Broadway, at Vernon Boulevard, Long Island City, Queens (1-718 956 1819).* **Train** N to Broadway. **Open** 10am-sunset daily. **Admission** free.

The setting, a vacant post-industrial lot by the river, is inspiring and appropriate. Some of the pieces crammed in, like the 'Sound Observatory', are engagingly interactive.

### Friends' Meeting House

*137-16 Nothern Boulevard, between Main & Union Streets, Flushing, Queens (1-718 358 9636).* **Train** 7 to Main Street. **Open** by appointment only. **Admission** voluntary donation.

### Kingsland House/Queens Historical Society

*Weeping Beech Park, 143-35 37th Avenue, at Parson's Boulevard, Flushing, Queens (1-718 939 0647).* **Train** 7 to Main Street. **Open** 2.30-4.30pm Tue, Sat, Sun. **Admission** $2 adults; $1 under-16s, senior citizens.

Built in 1785 by a wealthy Quaker, the house was moved to a site beside Bowne House. It is now the home of the Queens Historical Society, which uses it for local history exhibitions. Staff can give you further information about the borough's historical sites.

### Queens County Farm Museum

*73-50 Little Neck Parkway in Floral Park, Queens (1-718 347 3276).* **Train** E or F to Kew Gardens, then 46 bus to Little Neck Parkway. **Open** 9am-5pm daily (farmhouse and museum galleries noon-5pm Sat, Sun). **Admission** voluntary donation.

### Jamaica Bay Wildlife Refuge

*Cross Bay Boulevard, at Broad Channel, Queens (1-718 318 4340).* **Train** A to Broad Channel. **Open** 8.30am-5pm daily. **Admission** free.

Part of a local network of important ecological sites, administered through the National Parks Service. Guided walks, lectures and all sorts of nature-centred activities.

## The Bronx

The southern section of the Bronx is a depressing lesson in American apartheid, a forbidden zone where economic polarisation, running along clear racial lines, has left a whole community for dead. With run-down public housing looming from the smouldering rubble of what look like bomb sites, this urban hell is enough to frighten away even the hardiest visitor. However, this notorious corner is but an isolated part of the borough. The subway lines fly over the battle grounds, allowing you a safe glimpse, and take you to the friendly territory of the northern parts.

The Bronx is so named because it once belonged to the family of Dutchman Jonas Bronck, who built his farm here in 1636. It is, therefore, "the Broncks'". As the rich folk of Manhattan were moving into baronial apartment blocks alongside Central Park and up Fifth Avenue, a similar process took place here, as **Grand Concourse**, a continuation of Madison Avenue, was built up in the 1920s with very grand art deco apartment buildings. This is the Bronx's main thoroughfare, well worth seeing for its sense of decaying architectural optimism.

Just west of Grand Concourse at 161st Street is the famous **Yankee Stadium**, home of New York's great baseball team. Halfway up Grand Concourse, just south of Fordham Road, is the rotunda of the **Hall of Fame of Great Americans**, a wonderful early twentieth-century institution honouring scholars, politicians and others worthy of the accolade 'great' (*see chapter* **Museums**). Several blocks north is the small clapboard house where Edgar Allan Poe lived out the last sad years of his life. Fordham Road itself leads past **Fordham University**, a Jesuit institution that was founded in 1841.

Watching a game of cricket in Van Cortlandt Park will do a lot to dispel the stereotyped impressions which the Bronx has so often to fight. Amid this vast expanse of green is **Van Cortlandt Mansion**, a fine example of pre-revolutionary Georgian architecture, open to the public since 1897 (*see chapter* **Architecture**).

In the far north of the borough, in ritzy Beverly Hills-like Riverdale, is **Wave Hill**, a small, idyllic park overlooking the Hudson River. Originally a Victorian country estate where exotic plants were cultivated, it has been home to such tenants as William Thackeray, Theodore Roosevelt, Arturo Toscanini and Mark Twain.

The reason most visitors come to the Bronx is the **Bronx Zoo** on the banks of the Bronx River. It's the largest urban zoo in the US and rare for the space and freedom given to its animals, which are kept, as far as possible, in their natural habitats (*see chapter* **Sightseeing**). Across from the zoo's main gate in **Bronx Park**, you'll find the **New York Botanical Gardens**, a comprehensive botanical collection on the scale of Kew Gardens in London (*see chapter* **Children**). The area near the zoo is **Belmont**, Little Italy in the Bronx, and a far more expansive neighbourhood of restaurants, food markets and coffee shops than its tiny counterpart in Manhattan.

Much further to the north east, facing Long Island Sound, is **Pelham Bay Park**, a large-scale park with all sorts of diversions, including the man-made shoreline of Orchard Beach (the city's favourite dumping ground for dead bodies). Inside the park is **Bartow Pell Mansion**, a Federal manor sitting among romantic formal gardens.

Perhaps the most uncharacteristic part of the Bronx is **City Island** in Long Island Sound. The island, settled in 1685 and only a mile and a half long by half a mile wide, was originally a prosperous ship-building centre, with a busy fishing industry. In the days when New York was getting started, this tiny piece of real estate was a serious competitor for Manhattan's prestige. Nowadays it offers New Yorkers a doorstep slice of New England-style maritime recreation, with marinas, seafood restaurants and nautical bars.

And finally, though you may be forgiven for not wanting to go there, the wasteland of the **South Bronx** was the birthplace of one of the late twentieth century's most influential musical innovations – hip-hop. It was here, in parks and social clubs, that DJs like Kool Herc and Afrika Bambaata (who still presides over the Universal Zulu Nation) were the first to experiment with the boom-boom-bap of cut-up records and rhyming

*The Staten Island ferry gives great (and cheap) views of Lady Liberty.*

accompaniment. Today, even West Coast rappers like Ice Cube pay homage to the 'Boogie-Down' Bronx before they start their shows.

### Wave Hill

*675 West 52nd Street, at Independence Avenue, Bronx (1-718 549 2055).* **Train** Metro North from Grand Central to Riverdale. **Open** 9am-5.30pm Tue, Thur-Sun; 9.30am-dusk Wed (with seasonal variations). **Admission** $4 adults; $2 senior citizens, students.

Wave Hill, with its formal European gardens, is now the venue for concerts, educational programmes and exhibitions, including a permanent sculpture garden featuring works by Henry Moore, Alexander Calder and Willem de Kooning.

### Bronx County Historical Society Museum

*Valentine-Varion House, 3266 Bainbridge Avenue, between Van Cortlandt Avenue & 208th Street, Bronx (1-718 881 8900).* **Train** D to 205th Street. **Open** by appointment Mon-Fri; 10am-4pm Sat; 1-5pm Sun. **Admission** $2.

The 1758 fieldstone farmhouse is a fine example of the pre-Revolutionary Federal style which was popular in the colony.

### Edgar Allan Poe Cottage

*Grand Concourse, at East Kingsbridge Road, Bronx (1-718 881 8900).* **Train** *4, C or D to Kingsbridge Road.* **Open** 10am-4pm Sat; 1-5pm Sun. **Admission** $2. Group tours by appointment.

Poe's cottage, in Fordham village (now part of the Bronx), has been moved across the street since he lived here and turned into a charming museum dedicated to his life.

### Pelham Bay Park

*(1-718 430 1890).* **Train** 6 to Pelham Bay Park.

### Bartow-Pell Mansion

*895 Shore Road, Pelham Bay Park, Bronx (1-718 885 1461).* **Train** 6 to Pelham Bay Park, then one-mile walk or take a cab. **Open** noon-4pm Wed, Sat, Sun. **Admission** $2.50 adults; $1.25 seniors; free under-12s.

The International Garden Club has administered this 1836 mansion since 1914; the grounds include formal gardens, a fountain and a nineteenth-century carriage house and stable.

### City Island

**Train** 6 to Pelham Bay Park, then BX21 bus to City Island.

Call the City Island Chamber of Commerce (1-718 670 3600) for information about events and activities.

### North Wind Undersea Institute

*610 City Island Avenue (1-718 885 0701).* **Train** 6 to Pelham Bay Park, then BX21 bus to City Island. **Open** 10am-5pm Mon-Fri. **Admission** $3; $2 children. **No credit cards.**

A charming old maritime folk museum, with whalebones, old diving gear and a 100-year-old tugboat.

### Universal Zulu Nation

*(1-718 533 1013).*

Now a truly international organisation, Afrika Bambaata's Zulu Nation works as the guardian of early hip-hop culture, arranging annual DJ competitions and the occasional concert event.

## Staten Island

Staten Island hates New York. The Islanders consistently vote to detach their community from the city, arguing that it takes their taxes to pay for its own problems and in return all it gives them is its garbage (the famous landfill at Fresh Kills is one of the world's largest man-made structures). Driving through its tree-lined suburban hills, admiring its open spaces and expansive parks, you can see why the generally well-to-do inhabitants are so keen on keeping themselves separate from the pressing inner-city concerns of the rest of NYC.

Thanks to its strategic location, Staten Island is one of the longest-settled places in America. Giovanni Da Verrazano, whose name graces the bridge connecting the island to Brooklyn (at 4260ft/1311m the world's second-longest suspension bridge, after the Humber Bridge), christened it *Staaten* (States) *Eylandt* in 1524.

In 1687 the Duke of York sponsored a sailing competition with Staten Island as the prize. The Manhattan representatives won the race and since that day it has been governed from New York.

You reach this tranquil island, of course, by the famous ferry. The ride from Battery Park in Lower Manhattan is a wonderful bargain at 50¢ a round trip (*see chapter* **Downtown**). You pass close to the **Statue of Liberty** before sailing into St George, the island's main town.

On the waterfront facing Bayonne in New Jersey is **Snug Harbor Cultural Center**. Originally a maritime hospital and home for retired sailors, it comprises 28 buildings – grand examples of various periods of American architecture – in an 80-acre park. Sailors lived here until 1960, and the city took over the site in 1976, converting it into a cultural centre with exhibitions and arts events.

Near the lighthouse at the island's tallest point is the **Jacques Marchais Center of Tibetan Art**, a collection of art and cultural treasures from the Far East, whose emphasis is on all aspects of Tibetan prayer, meditation and healing. Its Buddhist temple is one of New York's more tranquil places (*see chapter* **Museums**).

Visit **Richmondtown Restoration**, a spacious collection of 29 restored historic buildings dating back to the seventeenth century, and it feels like you're in upstate New York. Many of the buildings have been moved on site from elsewhere on the island, and there's a courthouse, general store, baker's and butcher's, as well as private homes. Actors and craftspeople in appropriate eighteenth-century clothing lurk with intent (*see chapter* **Sightseeing**).

During the Revolutionary War, **Billop House** (now **Conference House**) was where an unsuccessful peace conference took place between the Americans, led by Benjamin Franklin and John Adams, and England's Lord Howe. The building has been turned into a museum. Combine your visit here with a trip to nearby Tottenville Beach.

For details of cultural events and travel directions on Staten Island, contact the Staten Island Chamber of Commerce, 130 Bay Street, Staten Island, NY 10301 (1-718 727 1900).

### Snug Harbor Cultural Center

*1000 Richmond Terrace (1-718 448 2500).* **Transport** Staten Island ferry, then Snug Harbor trolley or S40 bus. **Open** 8am-5pm daily. **Tours** 2pm Sat, Sun. **Admission** $2 voluntary donation.

Exhibitions of painting, sculpture and photography are held in the Newhouse Center; the Staten Island Botanical Garden is here, with tropical plants, orchids and a butterfly house; opera, chamber groups and jazz musicians play in the Veterans' Memorial Hall; the Art Lab offers art classes; and there's a children's museum.

*Disabled: access.*

### Conference House (Billop House)

*7455 Hylan Boulevard, Tottenville, Staten Island (1-718 984 2086).* **Transport** Staten Island ferry, then 103 bus to Hylan Boulevard & Craig Avenue. **Open** *Mar-Dec* 1-4pm Wed-Sun. **Admission** $2 adults; $1 children, senior citizens. **No credit cards**.

John Adams, one of the US delegates, recalled that for the attempted peace conference at Billop House, Lord Howe had 'prepared a large handsome room… made [it] not only wholesome but romantically elegant'. The house is the earliest – circa 1680 – manor house in New York City, and has been restored to its eighteenth-century magnificence.

## Steam & the sidewalks

You've seen it in a hundred movies: a dramatic Manhattan street scene where strange vapours escape from manholes and billow around busy pedestrians and speeding yellow cabs. It's not a special effect. In fact, few things are more quintessentially New York than steam creeping upwards from the sidewalk.

Thomas Edison's company Consolidated Edison (Con Ed), the world's first electrical utility and still the name on New Yorkers' electricity bills, built the system in the 1890s. Even now it sells steam to more than 2000 customers, mostly to heat large office blocks and apartment buildings. The company generates 10,400,000 pounds of steam per hour during winter, which hisses through a system of underground pipes at 500°F. Many of the original pipes are still in use and inevitable wear and tear means the steam occasionally bursts its way into the street. To preserve visibility and avoid injury the miasmic vapours are funnelled away from ground-level breaks by those striped Cat in the Hat-style plastic chimneys.

The New York steam system is the largest on the planet, and while it might seem like yet another example of New York lurching towards the Third World, since most of the steam is a by-product of Con Ed's electricity generation, it's more ecologically sound than most heating methods.

# Eating & Drinking

# Restaurants, Bars & Cafés Area Index

## Outer Boroughs

CONTEMPORARY AMERICAN: River Café (p126). DINERS: Juniors (p130). SEAFOOD: Gage and Toller (p131). STEAKHOUSES: Peter Luger (p133). EASTERN EUROPEAN: Primorski (p134). MIDDLE EASTERN: Moustache (p139). SOUTH-EAST ASIAN: Planet Thailand (p142). ITALIAN: Cucina (p141).

## Northern Manhattan

SOUTHERN/SOUL FOOD: Sylvia's (p131). BARS: Lenox Lounge (p145).

## Upper East Side

CELEBRATED CHEFS: Aureole (p123); Le Cirque (p124); Daniel (p124); Sign of the Dove (p124). LANDMARKS: The Rainbow Room (p125). CHEAP EATS: Lexington Candy Shop (p129). CONTEMPORARY AMERICAN: Arcadia (p126); Arizona 206 (p126); Park Avenue Café (p126); Twins (p127). CALIFORNIAN: Mulholland Drive Café (p130). SEAFOOD: Wilkinson's Seafood Café (p132). CHINESE: Fu's (p133); Pig Heaven (p134). ITALIAN: Elaine's (p141); John's Pizzeria (p141); Primavera (p141). LATE OPENING: H&H Bagel (p140).

## Upper West Side

LANDMARK RESTAURANTS: Café des Artistes (p125); Tavern on the Green (p126). FOREVER CHIC: Café Luxembourg (p127). DINERS: EJ's Luncheonette (p130). SOUTHERN/SOULFOOD: Café con Leche (p131). ITALIAN: Carmine's (p140); Perretti Italian Café (p141). BARS: Westside Brewery (p147). CAFES: Café La Fortuna (p147); Café Mozart (p148); Hungarian Pastry Shop (p148).

## Midtown East

CELEBRATED CHEFS: An American Place (p123); Gramercy Tavern (p124); Lutèce (p124). LANDMARKS: Four Seasons (p125); The Oyster Bar (p125). CHEAP EATS: English Harbor Fish and Chips (p129). CONTEMPORARY AMERICAN: Monkey Bar (p126). DELIS: Sarge's (p130). STEAKHOUSES: Smith and Wollensky (p133). CHINESE: Chin Chin (p133); Zen Palate (p134). EASTERN EUROPEAN: Christine's (p134). FRENCH: La Grenouille (p137); Lespinasse (p134). INDIAN: Chutney Mary (p139); Dawat (p139). ITALIAN: Il Nido (p141). JAPANESE: Hatsuhana (p141). MEXICAN: Rosa Mexicano (p142). SOUTH AMERICAN/ CARIBBEAN: Tropica (p142). SOUTH-EAST ASIAN: Vong (p142). SPANISH: Bolo (p142). THEME RESTAURANTS: Fashion Café (p143). BARS: Bar 119 (p144); Old Town Bar (p146); Pete's Tavern (p146); PJ Clarke's (p146); Rainbow Promenade (p146); Monkey Bar (p145). CAFES: Henry Bendel's Salon de Thé (p148).

## Midtown West

CELEBRATED CHEFS: Le Bernadin (p124). LANDMARKS: The 21 Club (p125); Russian Tea Room (p126). CONTEMPORARY AMERICAN: 44 (p126). CHEAP EATS: Mee Noodle Shop (p129); Café Elsie (p129). CAJUN: Cajun (p130). DELIS: Carnegie Delicatessen (p130). DINERS: Empire Diner (p130); Market Diner (p131). SOUTHERN/SEAFOOD: Lola (p131). STEAKHOUSES: Frank's Restaurant (p133); Landmark Tavern (p133). CHINESE: Zen Palate (p134). EASTERN EUROPEAN: Russian Samovar (p134). FRENCH: La Luncheonette (p134); Gascogne (p135). MEXICAN: Zarela (p142); Zuni (p142). SOUTH AMERICAN/ CARIBBEAN: Cabane Carioca (p142). SOUTH-EAST ASIAN: New York Kom Tang Soot Bul House (p142). MIDDLE EASTERN: Periyali (p137). LATE OPENING: Lox Around the Clock (p140). THEME RESTAURANTS: Hard Rock Café (p143); Harley-Davidson Café (p143); Jekyll and Hyde Club (p143); Planet Hollywood (p143). BARS: The Broadway Lounge (p145); Oak Room/Blue Bar at the Algonquin (p146); Merchants (p145); Royalton (p146); The Whiskey (p147); Zip City (p147). CAFES: Big Cup Café (p147); Newsbar Inc (p148); Rumpelmayer's (p148).

## Downtown

CELEBRATED CHEFS: Bouley (p124); Chanterelle (p124); Gotham Bar & Grill (p124); Union Square Café (p124). CONTEMPORARY AMERICAN: American Renaissance (p126); NoHo Star (p126); TriBeCa Grill (p126); Zoë (p127). FOREVER CHIC: Bell Caffè (p127); Bowery Bar (p127); Coffee Shop (p128); Restaurant Florent (p128); Lucky Strike (p128); Marion's (p128); Odeon (p128); Café Tabac (p127); Time Café (p128). CHEAP EATS: Elvie's Turo-Turo (p129); Kelley and Ping (p129); Boca Chica (p129); Stingy Lulus (p129); Benny's Burritos (p129); Two Boots (p129). CAJUN Baby Jake's (p129). DELIS: 2nd Avenue Delicatessen (p130); Katz's (p130). DINERS: Jones Diner (p130); Cup 'n' Saucer (p130); Landmark Diner (p130); Aggie's (p130); Lucky Dog (p130). SOUTHERN/SOULFOOD: Acme Bar and Grill (p131); SEAFOOD: Pisces (p131); Cucina di Pesce (p131); Le Pescadou (p131). CHINESE: Bingo (p133); Canton (p133); HSF (p133); Lan Hong Kok Seafood House (p133); House of Vegetarian (p133); Lucky Chengs (p133); 20 Mott Street (p134). EASTERN EUROPEAN: Christine's (p134); Sammy's (p134). FRENCH: Alison on Dominic (p134); Bistro Jules (p134); Les Deux Gamins (p134); Felix (p134); Montrachet (p137); Provence (p137); Raoul's (p137). INDIAN: Mitali East (p139); Panna II (p139). ITALIAN: Angelo's (p139); Arturo's (p139); Barocco (p139); Il Cantorini (p140); Cascabel (p140); John's Pizzeria (p141); Il Mulino (p141); Three of Cups (p141); Umberto's Clam House (p141). JAPANESE: Avenue A Sushi (p141); Honimura An (p141); Japonica (p141); Nobu (p141). JEWISH: Ratner's (p142). MEXICAN: El Teddy's (p142). SOUTH-EAST ASIAN: Indochine (p142). SOUTH AMERICAN/ CARIBBEAN Caribe (p142). SPANISH: El Faro (p143). VEGETARIAN: B&H Dairy & Vegetarian Restaurant (p143). LATE OPENING: Around the Clock Café & Gallery (p140); Kiev (p140); Odessa (p140); Yaffa Café (p140). BARS: Babyland (p144); Bowery Bar (p127, 144); Buddha Bar (p145); Chumley's (p145); Fanelli (p145); Fez (p145); Max Fish (p145); McSorley's Ale House (p145); Milano's (p145); Nation (p145); No-Tell Motel (p145); North Star Pub (p145); NW3 (p146); Puffy's Tavern (p146); Sapphire (p146); Sophie's (p146); Temple Bar (p147); Tenth Street Lounge (p147); Three of Cups (p147); Vazac's Horseshoe Bar (p147); White Horse (p147); CAFES: @ Café (p147); 9 (p147); Café Borgia (p147); Caffè Reggio (p148); De Roberti's (p148); Espresso Bar The Original (p148); Le Figaro Café (p148); Life Café (p148); Tea & Sympathy (p148); Veniero's (p148).

# Restaurants

***New York's eating establishments are the stuff of legend – and with good reason.***

Even if you ate in a different restaurant every day of your life you would die long before visiting all the eating establishments New York has to offer. An unprecedented number of new places have appeared on the scene in the last couple of years, with openings outnumbering closings by almost three to one. Considering the wealth of culinary talent here and the pervasive influence of so many distinct cuisines it would be hard to deny that New York's dining scene is unparalleled.

Once you've seen the size of a typical New York apartment, you understand why. Most natives rarely cook even the most meagre meal, preferring to take advantage of the vast range of food available, usually only steps away, at all hours of day and night. They prefer to eat out, take out or have something delivered.

And it certainly needn't be expensive. In fact, in recent years the average price of a meal has fallen to where it was more than a decade ago. Some of the city's established venues have scaled down their menus and in many cases dropped their prices, and the number of small places offering good budget cooking is rising rapidly.

The city plays host to all national and most regional cuisines and breeds bizarre culinary cross-pollinations, such as Chino-Latino, kosher-Italian, or Bengali-TexMex. In the upper price ranges French and New American food continue to dominate Manhattan menus, though variety is the key to satisfying jaded palates and chefs are increasingly open to truly global influences.

Though the madness of the 1980s is long gone, New York restaurants do sometimes suffer from the ravages of trendiness. They open, are reviewed and become popular, then decline and close, sometimes all in the space of a few months. Those that are established poach each others' staff and strive to stay ahead of each successive food craze.

It can be as hard as it ever was to get a table in a place that is 'hot', but by the same token it's a good idea to phone ahead and check if the place that was hot last week is still in business. Some places take reservations but many prefer to operate on a first-come, first-served basis and you may have to wait in the bar. You should book ahead, where possible, at all the restaurants listed in our **Celebrated Chefs**, **Landmark Restaurants** and **Contemporary American** sections and many of those in **Forever Chic**.

New Yorkers rely on the handy pocket guide *Zagat New York City Restaurant Survey* ($10.95) for a comprehensive overview of the better places and avidly peruse the food columns of *Time Out New York*, *New York Times* and *New York*, whose listings are more up to date than any annual guide to such a frenetic and constantly changing scene can hope to be.

During the first weeks of July the city holds a Restaurant Week, when some of New York's finest establishments offer a prix fixe lunch, which in 1996 will be $19.96. It's a great way to sample the talents of chefs who are otherwise unaffordable. Needless to say, you should reserve well in advance: the obvious choices like Four Seasons, Le Cirque and Bouley are sold out pretty promptly. Check the press for details.

Few New York restaurants add a service charge to your bill, but it is the custom to double the 8.25 per cent local sales tax (the last item on your bill, above the total) as a tip. Always check your bill as it may well be wrong. Many small places accept cash only and some credit cards – AmEx, Visa and Mastercard – are more welcome than others. Almost no restaurants take personal cheques, although they may accept travellers' cheques with ID. It's best to ask before you sit down.

As with every other financial transaction in the Big Apple, restaurant customers complain immediately and vociferously if they feel that they're not getting a fair deal. Don't be afraid of offending your waiter by moaning, but never withhold a tip.

## Celebrated Chefs

### An American Place

*2 Park Avenue, at East 32nd Street (684 2122).* **Train** 6 to 33rd Street. **Lunch** 11.45am-3pm Mon-Fri. **Dinner** 5.30-9.30pm Mon-Sat. **Average** *lunch* $30; *dinner* $45-$50. **Credit** AmEx, DC, MC, V.

In his spacious Park Avenue premises, chef and proprietor Larry Forgione has built an elegant yet affordable dining experience, dedicated to the patriotic premise that neither produce, wine nor inspiration need to come from anywhere except America. The menu includes a quotation from 'friend and mentor' James Beard, the late guru of Yankee gastronomy. An inventive and frequently changing menu, strong on game and served in large pioneer portions.

*Disabled: access, toilets. Smoking at bar.*

### Aureole

*34 East 61st Street, between Madison & Park Avenues (319 1660).* **Train** N or R to Lexington Avenue; 4, 5 or 6

to 59th Street. **Lunch** noon-2.30pm Mon-Fri. **Dinner** 6-10.30pm Mon-Thur; 6-11pm Fri, Sat. **Average** *lunch* $30; *set dinner* $59. **Credit** AmEx, DC, MC, V.
On two floors of an East Side town house decorated with delicate plaster reliefs is Charles Palmer's exceptional and romantic restaurant. With fine service and an ever-surprising menu, a dinner at Aureole is always smooth and sedate. Palmer's famous appetiser of sea scallop sandwiches in crisp potato crusts is a truly sensuous experience. The garden is an exquisite place to dine in summer.
*Garden. Smoking at bar.*

### Le Bernadin

*155 West 51st Street, between Sixth & Seventh Avenues (489 1515).* **Train** B, D, F or Q to Rockefeller Center. **Lunch** noon-2.15pm Mon-Fri. **Dinner** 6-10.15pm Mon-Thur; 5.30-11pm Fri, Sat. **Average** $70. **Credit** AmEx, DC, Discover MC, V.
This renowned restaurant, owned by Gilbert and Maguy Le Coze, has soared into new realms of excellence under its new chef Eric Ripert, formerly of Bouley. Ripert takes seafood into another dimension, using food so fresh you'd swear you'd just netted it yourself. His colleague François Payard has worked equal wonders on the phenomenal desserts.
*Disabled: access, toilets.*

### Bouley

*165 Duane Street, between Greenwich & Hudson Streets (608 3852).* **Train** 1 or 9 to Chambers Street. **Lunch** 11.30am-3pm, **dinner** 5.30-11pm, Mon-Sat. **Average** *lunch* $75; *dinner* $125. **Credit** AmEx, DC, Discover, MC, V.
Bouley is a truly excellent – if occasionally crowded – Provençal country restaurant relocated in TriBeCa. The decor recalls some secluded chateau, and the voluminous menu is full of astonishing French surprises. Specials include seared black sea bass with spicy truffle vinaigrette, and a legendary chocolate soufflé. An impeccable experience which you will no doubt be sharing with a few famous faces.

### Chanterelle

*2 Harrison Street, near Hudson Street (966 6960).* **Train** 1 or 9 to Canal Street. **Lunch** noon-2.30pm, **dinner** 6-10.30pm, Tue-Sat. **Average** *lunch* $60 (précis menu $33); *dinner* $100 (précis menu $89). **Credit** AmEx, DC, Discover, MC, V.
Karen and David Waltuck's large and tasteful space in TriBeCa's landmark Mercantile Exchange Building is still a New York favourite. The casual atmosphere belies the seriousness with which food is treated. The cheeseboard remains the best in the city and the grilled seafood sausage is still the starter to go for. The menu changes every few weeks.
*Disabled: access, toilets. Pavement tables for drinks only.*

### Le Cirque

*Mayfair Baglioni Hotel, 58 East 65th Street, near Madison Avenue (794 9292).* **Train** 6 to 68th Street. **Lunch** noon-3pm, **dinner** 5.45-10.30pm, Mon-Sat. **Average** *lunch* $35; *dinner* $70. **Credit** AmEx, DC, Discover, MC, V.
If you said this was the very best restaurant in New York no-one would argue. Chef Sylvain Portay, assisted by the largest brigade of cooks in the city, produces a wide-ranging French/Italian menu which is awesome in length and equalled by a world-class wine list. His style is distinct and very different from his predecessor, Daniel Boulud (see below **Daniel**). This quintessential New York power-dining arena is orchestrated by Sirio Maccioni, the consummate patron.
*Disabled: access.*

### Daniel

*20 East 76th Street, between Fifth & Madison Avenues (288 0033).* **Train** 6 to 77th Street. **Lunch** noon-2.30pm Tue-Fri. **Dinner** 5.45-11.30pm Mon-Thur; 6-11pm Fri, Sat. **Average** $70. **Credit** AmEx, CB, DC, Discover, MC, V.
Having worked his magic at Le Cirque (see above), it's hardly surprising that Burgundian virtuoso chef Daniel Boulud's own restaurant should have entered the upper strata of New York dining the minute it opened in June 1993. It's impossible to get in unless you book some two months in advance. The food is exciting and colourful and, well, expensive.
*Disabled: access, toilets. Smoking at bar.*

### Gotham Bar and Grill

*12 East 12th Street, between Fifth Avenue & University Place (620 4020).* **Train** 4, 5, 6, L, N or R to Union Square. **Lunch** noon-2pm Mon-Fri. **Dinner** 6-10.30pm Mon-Thur; 6-11.15pm Fri, Sat; 5.30-9.45pm Sun. **Average** $65. **Credit** AmEx, DC, MC, V.
Served amongst post-modern columns in a spacious ex-warehouse, Alfred Portale's architecturally presented New American dishes are vividly flavoured, the desserts and seafood particularly bearing witness to his exceptional talents. The restaurant has captured the hearts and stomachs of Village movers and shakers now the quality of the food has caught up with the quantity of the hype that surrounded its opening. The prix fixe lunch ($19.96) is excellent value.
*Disabled: access. Smoking at bar.*

### Gramercy Tavern

*42 East 20th Street, between Broadway & Park Avenue South (477 0777).* **Train** 6 to 23rd Street. **Lunch** noon-2.15pm daily. **Dinner** 5.30-10pm Mon-Thur; 5.30-11pm Fri, Sat; 5-9.30pm Sun. **Average** *lunch* $32; *dinner* 3-course set menu $52. **Credit** AmEx, DC, MC, V.
Danny Meyer, previously of Union Square Café, runs the room; ex-Mondrian chef Tom Colicchio of Mondrian rules the kitchen, delighting patrons with healthy robust country fare at this hot new spot. Don't miss the white bean and roasted garlic soup.
*Disabled: access, toilets.*

### Lutèce

*249 East 50th Street, between Second & Third Avenues (752 2225).* **Train** 6 to 51st Street; E or F to Lexington Avenue. **Lunch** noon-2pm Tue-Fri. **Dinner** 6-10pm Mon-Sat. Closed August. **Average** *lunch* $38; *dinner* $60. **Credit** AmEx, DC, MC, V.
Chef/patron André Soltner's perennially comfortable and lovingly cared for Alsacian restaurant, with its pint-sized zinc bar (pleasantly supervised by Madame Soltner), has long had an important place in New York's culinary history. The repertoire of classic dishes on the printed menu is pretty good, but the real action is in the specials and the list of dishes still 'under development'. Ask M. Soltner for a rundown.
*Smoking at bar.*

### Sign Of The Dove

*1110 Third Avenue, at 65th Street (861 8080).* **Train** 6 to 68th Street. **Brunch** 11.30am-2.30pm Sat, Sun. **Lunch** noon-2.30pm Tue-Fri. **Dinner** 6-11.30pm Mon-Fri, Sun; 5.30-11.30pm Sat. **Average** $50. **Credit** AmEx, DC, Discover, MC, V.
The flagship of the Santo restaurant empire is romantic and accessible. The dress code has been relaxed, you can buy food at the bar and there's a cheaper prix fixe menu ($45-$55) if the carte looks too daunting. Chef Andrew D'Amico is highly regarded, blending Provençal staples with influences from slightly further afield. An elegant scene.
*Disabled: access, toilets. Pavement tables. Smoking at bar.*

### Union Square Café

*21 East 16th Street, between Union Square & Fifth Avenue (243 4020).* **Train** 4, 5, 6, L, N or R to 14th Street/Union Square. **Lunch** noon-2.15pm Mon-Fri; noon-2.30pm Sat. **Dinner** 6-10.15pm Mon-Thur; 6-11.15pm Fri, Sat. **Average** *lunch* $30; *dinner* $50. **Credit** AmEx, DC, MC, V.

*The all-night, all bright* ***Empire Diner****, its deco decor intact. See page 130.*

One of the city's consistently hot spots is Danny Meyers' casual three-star restaurant, which serves classic American cuisine with a blend of Italian influences to a comely crowd of musicians, models and moguls. Union Square is as well known for its eccentric staff and the provocative artwork it displays on the walls as it is for chef Michael Romano's beautifully executed menu.
*Disabled: access.*

## Landmark Restaurants

### The 21 Club

*21 West 52nd Street, between Fifth & Sixth Avenues (582 7200).* **Train** B, D, F or Q to Rockefeller Center. **Lunch** noon-3pm Mon-Sat (Mon-Fri in summer). **Dinner** 5.30-10.30pm Mon-Thur; 5.30-11.30pm Fri, Sat. **Average** $70. **Credit** AmEx, DC, Discover, MC, V.
Toy cars hang from the ceiling in the bar while the rustle of serious money animates the restaurant (not in fact a club) which Gordon 'lunch is for wimps' Gekko (aka Michael Douglas) was keen to be seen at in the film *Wall Street*. This centrally located speakeasy-leftover specialises in American food and is expensive. Chef Michael Lomonaco, who trained under Daniel Boulud at Le Cirque (*see above*), has managed to revitalise the menu without scaring off some of the more ancient regulars.
*Disabled: access, toilets. Smoking in lounge.*

### Cafe des Artistes

*1 West 67th Street, at Central Park West (877 3500).* **Train** 1 or 9 to 66th Street. **Brunch** noon-3pm Sat; 10am-3pm Sun. **Lunch** noon-3pm Mon-Fri. **Dinner** 5.30pm-midnight Mon-Sat; 5pm-midnight Sun. **Average** $55 (set lunch $19.50, set dinner $35). **Credit** AmEx, DC, Discover, MC, V.
The chattering classes of the Upper West Side populate this romantic Viennese palace in the early evening, as they prepare for the symphonies of Lincoln Center by downing cocktails, admiring the opulent murals and devouring bold American-style French food and great desserts in large portions. The set lunch is a bargain.
*Disabled: access.*

### Four Seasons

*99 East 52nd Street, between Park & Lexington Avenues (754 9494).* **Train** 6 to 51st Street; E or F to Lexington Avenue. **Lunch** noon-2pm Mon-Fri. **Dinner** 5-9.30pm Mon-Fri; 5-11pm Sat. **Average** $80-$100. **Credit** AmEx, DC, Discover, JCB, MC, V.
The two timeless and palatial dining rooms here are the lavish Pool Room, with a pool in the corner, and the Grill Room, aka the Bar Room, famous for its square bar. The latter is where the tycoons have their tables permanently reserved to do business over 'spa cuisine' – sophisticated American food prepared with a healthy touch by chefs Christian Albin and Stefano Battistini. Come here to see the ultimate in power dining, and don't forget to save room for the notorious cakes.
*Smoking at bar.*

### The Oyster Bar

*Grand Central Station, lower level, at East 42nd Street (490 6650).* **Train** 4, 5, 6 or 7 to Grand Central. **Open** 11.30am-9.30pm Mon-Fri. **Average** $30. **Credit** AmEx, Discover, DC, JCB, MC, V.
A meal in the Oyster Bar conjures the grand old days of romantic rail travel, but the modern noise of Grand Central is often unconducive to relaxed dining, and unfortunately the restaurant is not as special as it once was. However, the range of shellfish here is unassailable and the cavernous tiled dining room an astonishing venue. Avoid the lunchtime rush, and settle into an afternoon snack of bluepoint oysters or New England clam chowder.
*Disabled: access, toilets. Smoking in saloon room.*

### Rainbow Room

*GE Building, Rockefeller Center, 30 Rockefeller Place, between Fifth & Sixth Avenues (632 5000).* **Train** B, D, F or Q to Rockefeller Center. **Dinner** 5.30-11.30pm Tue-Sat. **Average** $100. **Credit** AmEx, DC, MC, V.
With an ambience derived from Fred and Ginger movies, the 65th-floor art deco Rainbow Room offers wraparound views of the city and has a giant chandelier poised above a revolving dancefloor. The food, from Andrew Wilkinson, is in keeping with the atmosphere, and comprises classic dishes with

an emphasis on seafood and roasts. Polish up those dancing pumps and savour the nostalgia.
*Disabled: access, toilets. Smoking in bar.*

### Russian Tea Room

*150 West 57th Street, between Sixth & Seventh Avenues (265 0947).* **Train** N or R to 57th Street. **Open** 11.30am-11.30pm daily. **Average** $60. **Credit** AmEx, DC, Discover, JCB, MC, V.
In amongst the samovars and caviar it's as if those nasty Bolsheviks never happened. The liveried waiters aren't always the friendliest in the world, and the food is much better at somewhere less famous, but the visiting movie moguls and their starlets don't mind. This eating institution will be closed for most of 1996 while new owner Warner Leroy expands and streamlines it, adding two floors of banqueting rooms, one with a stained glass ceiling. He's leaving the famous ground floor – and hopefully, the celebrity-friendly ambience – untouched, and the reopened Tea Room should be a far more efficient place to eat. If you want the atmosphere without the pain in your wallet, come for afternoon tea.
*Disabled: access.*

### Tavern on the Green

*Central Park West, at 67th Street (873 3200).* **Train** 1 or 9 to 66th Street. **Brunch** 10am-3.30pm Sat, Sun. **Lunch** noon-3.30pm Mon,Tue, Thur, Fri; 11.30am-3.30pm Wed. **Dinner** 5.30-11pm Mon-Thur; 5-11.30pm Fri, Sat; 5.30-10pm Sun. **Average** $45. **Credit** AmEx, DC, Discover, JCB, MC, V.
Festooned with lights, and with horse-drawn traps waiting to take you home, this is probably the prettiest place in the world. The food, from chef Marc Poidevin, is variable, but excellent when you consider that 1500 meals are served a day. The prix fixe early dinner is a bargain ($24.93).
*Disabled: access, toilets. Smoking in cocktail bar.*

## Contemporary American

### 44

*Royalton Hotel, 44 West 44th Street, between Fifth & Sixth Avenues (944 8844).* **Train** B, D or F Q to 42nd Street. **Breakfast** 7am-11am Mon-Fri; 7am-1.30pm Sat, Sun. **Lunch** 11.45am-3pm daily. **Dinner** 5.45-10.45pm Mon-Thur, Sun; 5.45-11.45pm Fri, Sat. **Average** $40. **Credit** AmEx, MC, V.
With innovative food and an equally innovative Philippe Starck interior, this is a favourite of the publishing and fashion crowds. The food and the waiters look fabulous, but the service can be breathtakingly inefficient. It might be a poseurs' paradise, but beware of furniture that has ripped many a leather jacket. We highly recommend the lobster omelette for breakfast.
*Smoking.*

### American Renaissance

*260 West Broadway, between Sixth & Seventh Avenues (343 0049).* **Train** 1 or 9 to Franklin Street. **Dinner** 5.30-11pm Mon-Sat. **Average** $40. **Credit** AmEx, DC, MC, V.
In this new TriBeCa haunt, Erik Blauberg serves up fantasy creations such as grouper with basil and pomegranate juice – and how about a dessert of a tomato served with fruit, nuts and ice cream in a caramel sauce?
*Smoking in bar.*

### Arcadia

*21 East 62nd Street, at Fifth Avenue (223 2900).* **Train** 4, 5 or 6 to 59th Street; N or R to Lexington Avenue. **Lunch** noon-2.30pm Mon-Fri. **Dinner** served 6-10pm Mon-Sat. **Average** $60. **Credit** AmEx, DC, MC, V.
Anne Rosenzweig has been called one of the very best young American chefs. She has ridden the wave of media acclaim with aplomb and continues to serve food that is inventive and homey: chimney-smoked lobster is a speciality; grilled leeks and corn cakes are staples. The serenity of the murals almost compensates for the lack of elbow room.
*Disabled: access. Pavement tables.*

### Arizona 206

*206 East 60th Street, between Second & Third Avenues (838 0440).* **Train** 4, 5 or 6 to 59th Street; N or R to Lexington Avenue. **Lunch** noon-3pm Mon-Sat. **Dinner** 5.30-11pm Mon-Thur; 5.30-11.30pm Fri; 5.30-10.30pm Sun. **Average** *lunch* $30; *dinner* $45. **Credit** AmEx, DC, MC, V.
At this slice of Santa Fe across the street from Bloomingdale's, David Wolzog has cooked his way into the list of top young American chefs. The style is Southwestern, which they call 'high plains haute cuisine', otherwise known as designer Tex-Mex or haute jalapeños.
*Disabled: access. Pavement tables. Smoking in lounge.*

### Monkey Bar

*Hotel Elysée, 60 East 54th Street, between Park & Madison Avenues (838 2600).* **Train** 6 to 51st Street. **Lunch** noon-2pm Mon-Fri. **Dinner** 5.30-10.45pm Mon-Thur, Sun; 5.30pm-1.15am Fri, Sat. **Average** $50. **Credit** AmEx, DC, Discover, JCB, MC, V.
An all-star team drawn from some of New York's most successful restaurants runs this re-opened landmark room in one of the city's more charming hotels. The New American food is faultless though the atmosphere is a little overcharged with after-work midtowners.
*Disabled: access, toilets. Smoking at bar.*

### NoHo Star

*330 Lafayette Street, at Bleecker Street (925 0070).* **Train** 6 to Bleecker Street. **Breakfast** 8-11.30am, **lunch** 11.30am-4.30pm, **dinner** 4.30pm-midnight Mon-Fri. **Average** $22. **Credit** AmEx, DC, Discover, MC, V.
This downtown eaterie works wonders with traditional American food, twisting sandwiches, grills and salads into fresh and healthy favourites, with Asian specials served after 6pm. The NoHo Star burger is one of the best in town.

### Park Avenue Café

*100 East 63rd, on Park Avenue (644 1900).* **Train** 4, 5 or 6 to 59th Street; N or R to Lexington Ave. **Brunch** 11.45am-2.30pm Sun. **Lunch** 11.30am-2.30pm Mon-Fri. **Dinner** 5.30-10.30pm Mon-Thur; 5.30-11.30pm Fri, Sat. **Average** $65. **Credit** AmEx, DC, Discover, JCB, MC, V.
A rather ambitious hotspot. The decor is informal but polished and makes the perfect backdrop for Manhattan's socialites. The food is exciting and wittily presented with chef David Burke at the controls. The trademark swordfish chop is outstanding. Pastry chef Dan Budd excels with a baked alaska that features a blown-sugar penguin paddling in a caramelised banana kayak.

### The River Café

*1 Water Street, at the end of Old Fulton Street, Brooklyn (1-718 522 5200).* **Train** A or C to Brooklyn Bridge. **Brunch** 11.30am-2.30pm Sun. **Lunch** noon-2.30pm Mon-Fri. **Dinner** 6-11pm Mon-Thur; 7-11.30pm Fri, Sat. **Set dinner** $65. **Credit** AmEx, DC, MC, V.
Sitting on a barge under the Brooklyn Bridge, looking over the East River into the sparkling towers of Lower Manhattan – there are few New York dining experiences to match that of the River Café. The food is exceptional, the atmosphere unbearably romantic.
*Disabled: access. Smoking at bar.*

### TriBeCa Grill

*375 Greenwich Street, at Franklin Street (941 3900).* **Train** 1 or 9 to Franklin Street. **Brunch** 11.30am-2.45pm Sun. **Lunch** noon-2.45pm Mon-Fri. **Dinner** 5-10.45pm Mon-Thur; 5.30-11.15pm Fri, Sat; 5-9.15pm Sun. **Average** $45. **Credit** AmEx, DC, Discover, MC, V.

**Twins** – *the only place where you can stay sober and still see double.*

The food is good but expensive and the atmosphere is a little cold in this restaurant owned by Robert de Niro and his mates. It's the perfect place to eyeball the film moguls, though, and the desserts are fantastic.
*Disabled: access, toilets. Patio tables. Smoking area.*

### Twins

*1712 Second Avenue, at 89th Street (987 1111).* **Train** 4, 5 or 6 to 86th Street. **Brunch** 11am-3pm Sun. **Dinner** 5pm-midnight Tue, Fri, Sat; 6pm-midnight Mon, Wed, Thur, Sun. **Average** $25-$35. **Credit** AmEx, DC, MC, V.
Above-average food served up by – yup, you guessed it – twins. Everyone from the waiters to the bus boys are two of a kind, identical twins, who bring you 'American eclectic' cuisine, which translates as everything from seafood to fondue. Lots of fun.

### Zoë

*90 Prince Street, at Mercer Street (966 6722).* **Train** 6 to Spring Street; N or R to Prince Street. **Brunch** noon-3pm Sat, Sun. **Lunch** noon-3pm Tue-Sat; 11.30-3pm Sun. **Dinner** 6-10.30pm Tue-Thur; 6-11pm Fri; 5.30-11.30pm Sat; 5.30-10pm Sun. **Average** $40. **Credit** AmEx, MC, V.
A loud, cheerful place, with a west-coast attitude and plenty of experimentation in the kitchen. This means healthy grills and roasts served with marvellous sauces, as well as plenty of vegetarian options and Chinese-style stir-fries.
*Disabled: access, toilets.*

## Forever Chic

### Bell Caffè

*310 Spring Street, between Hudson & Greenwich Streets (334 BELL).* **Train** 1 or 9 to Houston Street; C or E to Spring Street. **Open** noon-4am Tue-Sun. **Average** $18. **Credit** AmEx, MC, V.
Bell Caffè welcomes the young, cool and bohemian, enticed by its international ambience and the quality and variety of its food. The cuisine could be described as 'international peasant' – simple, healthy and cheap with an emphasis on vegetarian dishes and good pizzas, soups and salads. There's a busy schedule of music live and DJ-steered. Great sidewalk drinking in the summer.
*Disabled: access. Garden. Pavement tables. Smoking area.*

### Bowery Bar

*40 East 4th Street, at the Bowery (475 2220).* **Train** 6 to Bleecker Street. **Open** 11.30am-4am daily. **Average** $35. **Credit** AmEx, DC, MC, V.
New York's current epicentre of vacant human beauty is juxtaposed against the perennial poverty of the Bowery. Its food is dull to the point of irrelevance, but its scene is tragically and self-consciously hip. One magazine published a list of unsuccessful gambits for obtaining entry (eg 'but my models are already inside'), and some crusty East Villagers staged an energetic graffiti-led boycott campaign. (*See chapter* **Bars & Cafés**.)
*Disabled: access, toilets. Garden. Smoking at bar and some tables.*

### Café Luxembourg

*200 West 70th Street,between Amsterdam & West End (873 7411).* **Train** 1, 2, 3 or 9 to 72nd Street. **Open** noon-3pm, 5.30-12.30am, Mon-Sat; 5.30-11.30pm Sun. **Brunch** 11am-3pm Sat, Sun. **Average** $40. **Credit** AmEx, DC, MC, V.
Whether you love it or hate it, there's no arguing that this uptown hotspot has remained popular for over ten years and still draws a high-profile media crowd. The food is consistently good and the service sometimes borders on the dramatic. Booking is recommended.
*Disabled: access, toilets.*

### Café Tabac

*232 East 9th Street, between Second & Third Avenues (674 7072).* **Train** 6 to Astor Place. **Open** 5pm-1am daily. **Average** $32. **Credit** AmEx, MC, V.
The Café Tabac just used to be chic; now it verges on the overbearingly trendy. The main people-watching scene is in

*Staff at* **John's Pizzeria** *make the best pizza in town – just watch 'em.* *See page 141.*

the bar area, or you can fight your way to the upstairs dining area. The food is fine, the service terrible.
*Disabled: access to ground floor. Smoking in lounge.*

## Coffee Shop

*29 Union Square West, at 16th Street (243 7969).* **Train** 4, 5, 6, L, N or R to Union Square. **Open** 7am-6am Mon-Fri; 9am-6am Sat; 10am-6am Sun. **Average** $15. **Credit** AmEx.
If you're beautiful enough they'll seat you out on the sidewalk for passers-by to admire. The Coffee Shop is owned by ex-models and boasts some of the most attractive (and pompous) waiting staff in the city. The bar is always busy and the place has somehow managed to stay trendy far longer than its allotted 15 minutes. The food is American bistro with a hint of Brazil; the truly chic tend to be found at the back, in the World Room.
*Disabled: access. Pavement tables. Smoking at bar.*

## Lucky Strike

*59 Grand Street, between Wooster & Broadway (941 0479).* **Train** A, C or E to Canal Street. **Open** noon-4am daily. **Average** $22. **Credit** AmEx, DC, MC, V.
Keith McNally's moderately priced French bistro is still fairly hip even after all these years. It offers good, basic food (especially the mashed potatoes and french fries) and has been patronised by everybody from Giorgio Armani to Madonna. You get good tunes and models for waitstaff. A DJ sets up at the end of the bar most nights after 11pm.
*Smoking at bar.*

## Marion's

*Continental Restaurant and Lounge, 354 Bowery, between 4th & Great Jones Streets (475 7621).* **Train** 6 to Astor Place. **Dinner** 6pm-11pm Mon-Thur, Sun; 6pm-midnight Fri, Sat. **Average** $28. **No credit cards.**
Model Marion Nagy opened the doors of this delightfully kitsch diner in the 1950s and abruptly locked up shop one night after a hugely successful party. The restaurant was reopened a few years ago with the original decor and furnishings still in place. The food is okay, but it's the atmosphere that's excellent, and the bar is good.
*Disabled: access, toilets. Smoking at bar.*

## Odeon

*145 West Broadway, between Thomas & Duane Streets (233 0507).* **Train** 1, 2, 3, 9, A or C to Chambers Street. **Lunch** noon-3pm Mon-Fri; noon-3.30pm Sun. **Dinner** 6pm-2am Mon-Thur, Sun; 6pm-3am Fri, Sat. **Average** *lunch* $15-$20; *dinner* $25. **Credit** AmEx, DC, MC, V.
A trendy TriBeCa hang-out and the cornerstone of the McNally brothers' restaurant empire. The salvaged art deco looks good, and so do the beautiful people in the bar. The Odeon is chic and reliable.
*Disabled: access. Pavement tables. Smoking at bar.*

## Restaurant Florent

*69 Gansevoort Street, between Greenwich & Washington Streets (989 5779).* **Train** A, C, E or L to 14th Street/Eighth Avenue. **Open** noon-midnight daily. Closed 5am-9am weekdays. **Average** $30. **No credit cards.**
Florent, in the meat-packing district (close to the west-side club zone) is an American breakfast diner crossed with a French bistro and is populated with all manner of fabulous nightcrawlers. To make things easy, there are five colour-coded menus, each for a different time of the day. Breakfast American style is served from 2am to 11am; a lunch menu of omelettes and sandwiches comes out between 11am and 3.30pm; high tea is 3.30pm to 6pm; French-style dinner from 6pm to midnight and supper from midnight until 2am.

## Time Café

*380 Lafayette Street, between Great Jones & 4th Streets (533 7000).* **Train** 6 to Bleecker Street. **Brunch** 10.30am-4pm Sat, Sun. **Lunch** noon-4pm Mon-Fri. **Dinner** 6pm-midnight Mon-Thur, Sun; 6pm-1am Fri, Sat. **Average** $15-$20. **Credit** AmEx, MC, V.
Offering a wide variety of health-conscious yet delicious entrées, Time is a downtown favourite, populated by a funky crowd of European tourists, celebutantes and rap music moguls (Russell Simmons treats it as an extension of his apartment). Favourites are the smoked salmon sashimi and the spinach salad with fresh avocado in a miso dressing. The pizzas here are delicious and feed two people.
*Disabled: access, toilets. Pavement tables.*

## Cheap Eats

Chinatown is a great source of cheap food. The trick is to seek out the busiest places with the fewest European faces. And every neighbourhood has a pizza joint or two. Regular (basic) slices cost around $1.50 plus an extra 50¢ for each topping. There are also delis on almost every corner that will fix you a fat sandwich for $3-$5. Some of the bigger ones have self-serve hot and cold buffets. The going rate for these is around $4 per pound regardless of what it is you heap into your take-out container. Besides these staples, there are a host of places where you can eat extremely cheaply. Here are some of our recommendations.

### Elvie's Turo-Turo

*214 First Avenue, between 12th & 13th Streets (473 7785).* **Train** L to First Avenue. **Open** 11am-9pm Mon-Sat; 11am-8pm Sun. **Average** $7. **No credit cards.**
A Filipino buffet-style dining room that bustles with hungry diners after huge platefuls of Elvira Samora Cinco's specials. Lots of stews, grills and fries served with mounds of rice or noodles on plastic foam plates. A New York delight.

### English Harbor Fish and Chips

*246 East 14th Street, between Second & Third Avenues (777 5420).* **Train** 4, 5, 6, L, N or R to Union Square. **Open** 11am-10pm Mon-Sat; 2-8pm Sun. **Average** $5. **Credit** Discover, MC, V.
Imagine calling mushy peas a 'novelty'. Well, they're here at least, along with battered fish and steak and kidney pies. Confused Americans can even sample the delights of a battered sausage.
*Disabled: access. Pavement tables.*
**Branch**: 768 Ninth Avenue (664 7966).

### Lexington Candy Shop

*1226 Lexington Avenue, near 83rd Street (288 0057).* **Train** 4, 5 or 6 to 86th Street. **Open** 7am-7pm Mon-Sat; 9am-5pm Sun. **Average** $8. **No credit cards.**
It's cash only at this kitsch, family-run luncheonette and candy shop that has delighted New Yorkers for 66 years. There's an old-fashioned soda fountain, wooden phone booths and vintage counter seats. Order the grilled cheese, which is served on paper plates with a slice of pickle; wash it down with the home-made lemonade ($3.20).
*Disabled: access.*

### Mee Noodle Shop

*795 Ninth Avenue, at 53rd Street (765 2929).* **Train** C or E to 50th Street. **Open** 11.30am-11.30pm Mon-Thur, Sun; 11.30am-midnight Fri, Sat. **Average** $7.50. **Credit** AmEx.
There are at least three Chinese noodle shops named 'Mee' dotted around town. None of them is connected, but all are excellent. This, however, is the one most worth searching out. Huge portions of steaming hot food, ranging across the entire Chinese culinary spectrum (from Hunan to Szechuan to Lower East Side) for around $5, are served quick as a flash by charming waitresses. Try the seafood with Peking sauce over 'noodle on sizzling platters'.
*Disabled: access.*

### Kelley and Ping

*127 Greene Street, between Houston & Prince Streets (228 1212).* **Train** B, D, F or Q to Broadway/Lafayette. **Lunch** 11.30am5pm, **dinner** 6-11pm daily. **Average** *lunch* $5-$10; *dinner* $15-$20. **Credit** AmEx, MC, V.
This no-nonsense (though classy) noodle shop is dressed up like some Singapore trading post, which makes sense since part of it is a grocery. Great Asian food with the emphasis on Thailand and a quality far above the price. Weekday lunches are a self-serve cafeteria affair.

### Boca Chica

*13 First Avenue, at 1st Street (473 0108).* **Train** F to Second Avenue. **Brunch** noon-4.30pm Sun. **Dinner** 5.30-11.30pm daily. **Average** *brunch* $8-$10; *dinner* $15. **Credit** AmEx, DC, Discover, MC, V.
At the bottom end of the East Village is this Latin American corner bistro with great music (live at weekends) and healthy, colourful oceanside food with intriguing Brazilian flavour combinations.
*Disabled: access.*

### Stingy Lulus

*129 St Marks Place (8th Street), at Avenue A (674 3545).* **Train** L to First Avenue. **Open** noon-5am Mon-Fri; 10am-6am Sat, Sun. **Average** $15. **No credit cards.**
The service is far from attentive, but the staff are just testing to see if you really love them. Great American diner food with a few sophisticated twists, with a young, clubby clientele and a darling 1950s electric pastel astroglide interior.
*Smoking area.*

### Benny's Burritos

*113 Greenwich Avenue, at Jane Street (727 3560).* **Train** 1, 2, 3, 9 to or L to 14th Street/Seventh Avenue. **Open** 11.30am-midnight Mon-Thur, Sun; 11am-1am Fri-Sat. **Average** $10. **No credit cards.**
Your Benny's burrito is a whopping tortilla parcel of Mexican goodies, more than most mortals can lift, let alone eat at one sitting. Fresh flavoursome ingredients.
*Disabled: access. Pavement tables.*
**Branch**: 93 Avenue A (254 2054); 2160 Broadway (362 2500).

### Cafe Elsie

*358 West 47th Street, between Eighth & Ninth Avenues (765 7653).* **Train** C or E to 50th Street. **Open** noon-midnight Mon-Thur; noon-2am Fri; 11am-2am Sat, Sun. **Average** $10-$15. **No credit cards.**
This sweet little bastion of excellent home cooking is a saving grace if you're trapped between the fast-food touristland and swank pre-theatre restaurants around Times Square. There's even a summer garden. The weekend brunch (11am-4pm) includes free vodka and champagne; at other times bring your own bottle.
*Disabled: access. Patio. Smoking.*

### Two Boots

*37 Avenue A, between East 2nd & East 3rd Streets (505 2276).* **Train** F to Second Avenue. **Open** noon-midnight daily. **Average** $15. **Credit** AmEx.
The boots in question are the geographical ones of Italy and Louisiana. Hey presto: Cajun pizza! A wacky, yet strangely appropriate idea which epitomises Lower East Side culinary chutzpah in the nicest possible way. The great jukebox will keep you entertained while you wait at the bar.
*Disabled: access, toilets.*

## American

### Cajun

#### Baby Jakes

*14 First Avenue, between 1st & 2nd Streets (254 2229).* **Train** F to Second Avenue. **Brunch** 11am-4pm Sat, Sun. **Lunch** 11am-5pm Mon-Fri. **Dinner** 6-11.30pm Mon-Thur, Sun; 6pm-4am Fri, Sat. **Average** $12. **Credit** AmEx.
Fresh New Orleans food like crab cakes, po' boys and muffaletta, alongside excellent gumbo and spicy salads. The crowd is fun, the bar decorated with zippy paperback covers.
*Disabled: access, bathrooms. Smoking.*

### Cajun

*129 Eighth Avenue, at West 16th Street (691 6174).* **Train** A, C, E or L to 14th Street/Eighth Avenue. **Lunch** noon-3pm Mon-Fri; noon-4pm Sun. **Dinner** 5-11pm Mon-Thur; 5.30pm-1am Fri, Sat. **Average** *lunch* $10; *dinner* $20. **Credit** AmEx, DC, Discover, MC, V.

One of Manhattan's first, cheapest and most enduring exponents of blackened redfish, fried oysters and jambalaya, Cajun was here before the craze began and can still be relied on for hearty food and live Dixieland jazz.

*Smoking area.*

## Californian

### Mulholland Drive Café

*1059 Third Avenue, at 62nd Street (319 7740).* **Train** 4, 5 or 6 to 59th Street; N or R to Lexington Avenue. **Lunch** noon-4pm Mon-Sat. **Dinner** 6-11pm Mon-Thur, Sun; 6pm-midnight Fri, Sat. **Average** $20. **Credit** AmEx, DC, MC, V.

This is owned by heartthrob Patrick Swayze, and is renowned as a pick-up joint at night and a good healthy Californian brunching station during the day.

*Disabled: access, toilets.*

## Delicatessens

Almost all the old delis are kosher. You'll find them wherever there are mouths to be fed.

### Carnegie Delicatessen

*854 Seventh Avenue, off 55th Street (757 2245).* **Train** N or R to 57th Street. **Open** 6.30am-4am daily. **Average** $25. **No credit cards.**

Here's where to come for some of the best (and priciest) New York deli food. Famed as the setting of Woody Allen's *Broadway Danny Rose*, the Carnegie Delicatessen is also a landmark in its own right.

*Disabled: access.*

### 2nd Avenue Delicatessen

*156 Second Avenue, at 10th Street (677 0606).* **Train** 6 to Astor Place; L to Third Avenue. **Open** 7am-midnight Mon-Thur, Sun; 7am-2am Fri, Sat. **Average** $12.50. **Credit** AmEx.

The second-best deli in the city, run in traditional style by the Lebewohl family, offers chicken soup like your (Jewish) mother used to make, as well as kasha, kugel and wonderful apple strudel.

*Disabled: access, bathrooms.*

### Katz's

*205 East Houston Street, at Ludlow Street (254 2246).* **Train** F to Second Avenue. **Open** 8am-10pm Mon, Tue, Sun; 8am-11pm Wed, Thur; 8am-midnight Fri, Sat. **Average** $10. **Credit** ($20 minimum) AmEx, Discover, MC, V.

'Send a salami to your boy in the army' read the signs hanging from the ceiling. Visit the all-American Katz's for the likes of kosher pastrami, corned beef, franks, garlic salami and bologna. This is where Harry watched Sally fake an orgasm. The owner claims she wasn't faking, his food really is that good.

*Disabled: access.*

### Sarge's

*548 Third Avenue, between East 36th & East 37th Streets (679 0442).* **Train** 6 to 33rd Street. **Open** 24 hours daily. **Average** $12. **Credit** AmEx, MC, V.

Sarge's is a decent midtown deli selling excellent Nova Scotia salmon, lox, sturgeon and sable around the clock. Try the reasonable buffet platters, which could feed a small army.

*Disabled access. Smoking.*

## Diners

You're never far from a diner in New York. If you want a real greasy spoon type, then try Jones Diner (Lafayette at Great Jones Street), Cup 'n' Saucer (Canal and Eldridge Streets) or the Landmark Diner (Grand and Center Streets). None of them has a phone and, while we can't vouch for the food, the prices are probably the best in town. The following is a selection of some of our favourites.

### Aggie's

*146 West Houston Street, at McDougal Street (673 8994).* **Train** 1 or 9 to Houston Street. **Breakfast/lunch** 7.30am-5pm, **dinner** 6-10pm, Mon-Fri. **Brunch** 10am-4pm, 6-10pm Sat; 10am-4pm Sun. **Average** $20. **No credit cards.**

Aggie's is a down-home luncheonette with a pure and simple philosophy: wholesome, satisfying and fresh country cooking, with the heartiest breakfast around SoHo.

*Disabled: access, toilets.*

### EJ's Luncheonette

*447 Amsterdam Avenue, at 81st Street (873 3444).* **Train** 1 or 9 to 79th Street. **Open** 8am-11pm Mon-Thur; 8am-midnight Fri; 9am-midnight Sat; 9am-10.30pm Sun. **Average** $12. **No credit cards.**

This cartoon retro diner serves up plates loaded with stacks of buckwheat or buttermilk pancakes and syrup, thick-cut French toast and hearty omelettes with various fillings. Post-breakfast specials include chicken chilli, sweet potato and turkey hash and rice pudding.

*Disabled: access.*

**Branch**: 1271 Third Ave (472 0600).

### Empire Diner

*210 Tenth Avenue, at West 22nd Street (243 2736).* **Train** C or E to 23rd Street. **Open** 24 hours daily. Closed 4am-8am Tue. **Average** $15. **Credit** ($15 minimum) AmEx, DC, Discover, MC, V.

The flashing lights set the mood for the club you're about to visit, or recall the one you've just left. The perfectly preserved art deco Empire Diner is a 24-hour institution on the far West Side. Great soups and sandwiches and a full range of diner food: hamburgers, pasta and steaks, done with a twist (try the apple pie). There are tables outside in good weather and it's open around the clock.

### Juniors

*36 Flatbush Avenue, at DeKalb Street, Brooklyn (1-718 852 5257).* **Train** D, M, N, Q or R to DeKalb Avenue. **Open** 6.30am-12.30am Mon-Wed, Sun; 6.30am-1am Thur; 6.30am-2am Fri, Sat. **Average** $10-$15. **Credit** AmEx, DC, MC, V.

In the heart of downtown Brooklyn is this oasis of milk and sugar, home to the most fattening desserts in town and (they have a certificate to prove it) the world's best strawberry shortcake. There's a full range of diner food too, but most people just head straight to the ice-cream/milkshake/cheesecake counter and drool.

*Disabled: access, toilets. Smoking.*

### Lucky Dog

*167 First Avenue, between 10th & 11th Streets (260 4220).* **Train** L to First Avenue. **Open** 11am-11pm Mon-Thur; 11am-1am Fri; 10am-1am Sat; 10am-11pm Sun. **Average** $15. **Credit** AmEx, DC, MC, V.

A swish new diner decked out along traditional lines. In addition to above-average burgers and breakfasts, there are great healthy sandwiches and salads and a wide range of coffees and ice-cream desserts. You can ask for seconds on the blue-plate specials.

*Disabled: access.*

### Market Diner

*572 Eleventh Avenue, at 43rd Street (695 0415).* **Train** A, C or E to 42nd Street. **Open** 24 hours daily. **Average** $10-$15. **Credit** AmEx, DC, Discover, MC, V.
This is an original, not one of those retro copies hoisted in from the back of a truck. Filled with cabbies, clubbers and off-duty ladies of the night, it offers formica futurism and a menu unchanged since it was built in the 1950s.

### Whitecastle

26 locations in New York City (1-718 899 8404 for information). **Open** 24 hours daily. **Average** $3. **No credit cards**.
Who needs Mickey D's when you can have Whitecastle's notorious bullet burgers ('buy 'em by the bag'). They're square, they're steam-broiled and you can chomp them like M&Ms. As immortalised by the Beastie Boys and worshipped by hard-core junk-food fiends across the US.

## Southern & Soul Food

### Acme Bar and Grill

*9 Great Jones Street, between Broadway & Lafayette Street (420 1934).* **Train** 6 to Bleecker Street; B, D, F or Q to Broadway/Lafayette. **Open** 11.30am-midnight Mon-Fri; 11.30am-1am Sat; 11.30am-11pm Sun. **Average** *lunch* $12; *dinner* $20. **Credit** DC, Discover, MC, V.
Catfish and beer blend easily in this Dixie den of spicy Southern fare. Bands play in the cellar.
*Disabled: access to restaurant, toilets. Smoking at bar.*

### Café Con Leche

*424 Amsterdam Avenue , between 80th & 81st Streets (595 7000).* **Train** 1 or 9 to 79th Street. **Open** 7am-midnight daily. **Lunch** noon-2pm. **Dinner** 4.30pm-midnight. **Average** $15. **Credit** AmEx, MC, V.
Heavily populated by hungry locals, this simple and authentic Cuban/Creole restaurant is well worth a visit.

### Lola

*30 West 22nd Street, between Fifth & Sixth Avenues (675 6700).* **Train** F, N or R to 23rd Street. **Lunch** noon-3pm Mon-Fri. **Gospel brunch** *Sept-June* 1pm, 3pm Sun; *July, Aug* 12.30pm, 2pm Sun. **Average** $50. **Credit** AmEx, MC, V.
A mountainous order of crunchy onion rings with your drinks will sustain you past the menu's so-called 'small plates', so go straight on to the fried chicken or tasty West Indian shrimp sausage and chicken curry. Lola's is best known for live Motown-style performances and fabulous Sunday Gospel brunches.
*Disabled: access. Smoking.*

### Sylvia's

*328 Lenox Avenue, at 126th Street (996 0660).* **Train** 2 or 3 to 125th Street. **Open** 7.30am-10.30pm Mon-Sat; 1-7pm Sun. **Average** $20. **Credit** AmEx.
The busiest, most famous, and actually the best of Harlem's soul food restaurants. South Carolinan Sylvia Woods serves up ribs, chicken, collared greens and corn bread, together with creamy macaroni cheese and astonishing sweet potato pie for dessert.
*Disabled: access, toilets. Smoking.*

## Seafood

### Pisces

*95 Avenue A, at 6th Street (260 6660).* **Train** L to First Avenue. **Brunch** noon-4pm Sat, Sun. **Dinner** 5.30-11.30pm Mon-Thur, Sun; 5.30-1.30am Fri, Sat. **Average** $25. **Credit** AmEx, DC, Discover, MC, V.
If you want delicious seafood in a relaxed, hip setting, Pisces is the place. The grilled vegetables or the steamed mussels

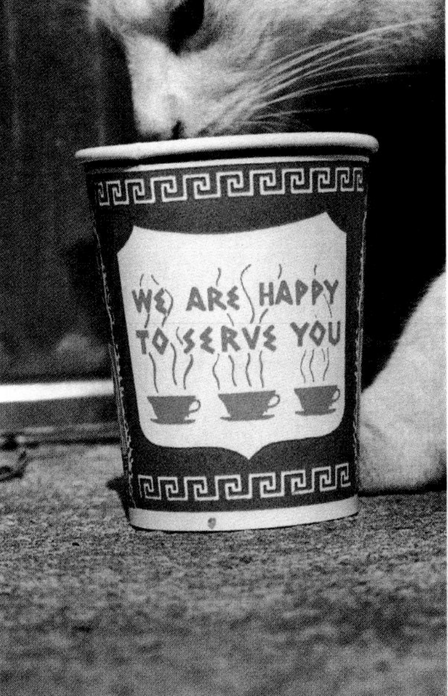


*New York's trademark coffee cup.*

make great starters; the main courses change daily. Be sure to leave room for the feverish treat of a Pisces dessert. A well-planned and affordable wine list.
*Disabled: access, toilets. Pavement tables. Smoking at bar.*

### Cucina di Pesce

*87 East 4th Street, between Second & Third Avenues (260 6800).* **Train** 6 to Astor Place; F to Second Avenue. **Open** 4pm-midnight Mon-Thur, Sun; 4pm-1am Fri, Sat. **Average** $15. **No credit cards.**
A popular and chic East Village Italian joint, attracting a smart crowd with mountainous dishes of seafood pasta.
*Disabled: access. Garden. Smoking.*

### Gage and Tollner

*372 Fulton Street, at Jay Street, Brooklyn (1-718 875 5181).* **Train** A, C or F to Jay Street. **Brunch** noon-4pm Sun. **Lunch** 11.30am-3pm Mon-Fri. **Dinner** 5-10.30pm Mon-Fri; 4-11pm Sat; 5-9pm Sun. **Average** $30. **Credit** AmEx, MC, V.
Gage and Tollner opened in 1919 and has been a seafood landmark since then. It received a jolt in 1988 when Edna Lewis arrived as chef, along with her spicy southern traditions. The treats are the crab gumbo, the salmon and the rhubarb pie.

### Le Pescadou

*18 King Street, at Sixth Avenue (924 3434).* **Train** 1 or 9 to Houston Street. **Lunch** noon-3pm Mon-Fri. **Dinner** 6-11pm Mon-Thur; 6-11.30pm Fri, Sat. **Average** $20. **Credit** AmEx, DC, MC, V.
A Provençal bistro using flavoured oils to create unique fish dishes, with a great oyster selection and an emphasis on simplicity. Particularly recommended for its excellent desserts and the jazz brunches on Sundays.
*Pavement tables. Smoking.*

ODEON

### Wilkinson's Seafood Cafe

*1573 York Avenue, between 83rd & 84th Streets (535 5454).* **Train** 4, 5 or 6 to 86th Street. **Open** 6-10.30pm Mon-Sat; 6-9pm Sun. **Average** $50. **Credit** AmEx, DC, MC, V.
A formal but friendly restaurant and bar serving perfectly prepared fish. Its warm chocolate dessert is hands down the best in the city. Very Upper East Side.
*Reservations advisable.*

## Steakhouses

### Frank's Restaurant

*885 Tenth Avenue, at 15th Street (243 1349).* **Train** A, C, E or L to 14th Street/Eighth Avenue. **Open** 10.30am-4pm, 5-11pm, Mon-Thur; 10am-3.30pm, 5-11pm, Fri, Sat. **Average** $35-$40. **Credit** AmEx, DC, Discover, MC, V.
With a woolly-looking bull overlooking the entrance, this is a wonderful slice of Americana in the Meat Market District. Frank's remains faithful to its steak and pasta formula, despite the addition of a 70-seater dining room upstairs. There never was a real Frank, but the plain cooking here has always been honest and the wine list is a good deal.
*Disabled: access, toilets.*

### Landmark Tavern

*626 Eleventh Avenue, at 46th Street (757 8595).* **Train** A, C or E to 42nd Street. **Open** 11.45am-11.30pm daily. **Average** $30. **Credit** AmEx, DC, Discover, MC, V.
This is one of the city's oldest taverns (established 1868) and serves melt-in-your-mouth steaks. The upstairs rooms are gorgeous, decorated with gilt-framed period portraits. The kitchen closes early if traffic is slow, so call and check. The area is a bit dodgy late at night.
*Disabled: access, toilets. Smoking.*

### Peter Luger

*178 Broadway, Williamsburg, Brooklyn (1-718 387 7400).* **Train** J, M or Z to Marcy Avenue. **Open** 11.45am-10pm Mon-Thur; 11.45am-11pm Fri, Sat; 1-10pm Sun. **Average** $50. **No credit cards.**
This landmark restaurant is a throwback to the old days of a neighbourhood that Sergio Leone made famous in *Once Upon A Time In America*. Its half-timbered country tavern atmosphere is at odds with the run-down Hispanic locale it now finds itself in, but the steaks are still the best in town.
*Disabled: access, toilets.*

### Smith and Wollensky

*201 East 49th Street, at Third Avenue (753 1530).* **Train** 6 to 51st Street; E or F to Lexington Avenue. **Open** 11.45am-11.30pm Mon-Fri; 5-11.30pm Sat, Sun. **Average** *grill* $40; *dining area* $55. **Credit** AmEx, DC, MC, V.
A sensational wine list and an idealised vision of what a steakhouse should be: sober décor and rowdy customers. Prosperous sports fans shout things like 'What about those Mets?' as they tuck into steak and chips or grilled lobster, with the option of a rare bottle from the back of the cellar.
*Disabled: access. Pavement tables. Smoking at bar.*

## Chinese

### Bingo

*104 Mott Street, at Hester Street (941 7228).* **Train** B or D to Grand Street. **Open** 11.30am-2.30am Mon-Thur; 11.30am-4am Fri-Sun. **Buffet** $18.95 per person. **Credit** AmEx.
A cauldron of soup sits boiling on your table, a vast self-serve indoor market of meat, fish, shellfish and vegetables provides you with limitless raw ingredients to throw in. And while you're busily self-stuffing, smiling waiters deliver spontaneous specials from the kitchen.
*Disabled: access.*

### Canton

*45 Division Street, between the Bowery & Market Street (226 4441).* **Train** B or D to Grand Street. **Open** noon-9.30pm Wed, Thur, Sun; noon-10.30pm Fri, Sat. **Average** $25. **No credit cards.**
By common consent, it's best to let owner Eileen Leang steer you to the day's specials. Cantonese fare, strong on seafood, pricier than the surrounding places, but well worth it.
*Disabled: access.*

### Chin Chin

*216 East 49th Street, between Second & Third Avenues (888 4555).* **Train** E or F to Lexington Avenue. **Lunch** noon-3pm Mon-Fri. **Dinner** 3-11.45pm Mon-Fri; 5-11.45pm Sat, Sun. **Average** $25. **Credit** AmEx, DC, Discover, MC, V.
One of the best Chinese restaurants in town, with gourmet-quality food and a great wine list. The cuisine is light and healthy and not tied to any particular region.
*Disabled: access.*

### Fu's

*972 Second Avenue, between East 51st & East 52rd Streets (517 9670).* **Train** E or F to Lexington Avenue; 6 to 51st Street. **Open** noon-midnight daily. **Average** $30. **Credit** AmEx, DC, MC, V.
Fu's has the reputation as the swankiest Chinese restaurant in town. Specialities, such as Grand Marnier shrimp, Peking duck and orange beef, feature regularly on a menu which mixes the regions and includes a selection of dishes for those on special diets.
*Smoking at bar.*

### HSF

*46 the Bowery, below Canal Street (374 1319).* **Train** 6, J, M, N, R or Z to Canal Street. **Open** 7.30am-midnight daily. **Average** $18. **Credit** AmEx, Discover, MC, V.
The massive original HSF in Chinatown is still the cheapest and one of the best places for lunchtime dim sum, as the largely Chinese clientele will attest. Dumplings, shredded duck or chicken, squid, shrimp and pastries are served in the chattering, clattering atmosphere of boomtime Hong Kong.
*Disabled: access.*

### Lan Hong Kok Seafood House

*31 Division Street, between the Bowery & East Broadway (431 9063).* **Train** B or D to Grand Street. **Open** 7.30am-10pm daily. **Average** $10. **No credit cards.**
Cheap and cheerful, with some of the best dim-sum in town. No frills and not much English spoken, but great food nonetheless.

### House of Vegetarian

*68 Mott Street, below Canal Street (226 6572).* **Train** J, M, N, R, Z or 6 to Canal Street. **Open** 11am-11pm daily. **Average** $9-15. **No credit cards.**
The sign says 'all vegetables served here', which means that the roast duck appetiser is really wheat gluten in a clever disguise. If psuedo-meat scares you there are plenty of more conventional veggie dishes.

### Lucky Chengs

*24 First Avenue, between 1st & 2nd Streets (473 0516).* **Train** F to Second Avenue. **Open** 5pm-midnight Mon-Thur, Sun; 5pm-1am Fri, Sat (dinner served from 6pm). **Average** $20-$30. **Credit** AmEx, DC, Discover, MC, V.
Excellent Chinese-based food from the Pee Wee's Playhouse region of the country, in a building that once housed one of the city's most notorious gay bathhouses. The waitresses are

all Asian transvestites with a propensity for singing Happy Birthday at the end of absolutely everyone's meal.
*Smoking at bar.*

### Pig Heaven

*1540 Second Avenue, at 80th Street (PIG 4333).* **Train** 6 to 77th Street. **Open** 11.30am-11.30pm Mon-Thur, Sun; 11.30am-12.30am Fri, Sat. **Average** $25. **Credit** AmEx, DC, Discover, MC, V.
The emphasis, as you might have guessed, is on pork, cooked in all manner of mouthwatering ways, including the speciality, Cantonese suckling pig. There are plenty of non-porcine attractions too, at David Keh's uptown eaterie.

### 20 Mott Street

*20 Mott Street, between Pell Street & the Bowery (964 0380).* **Train** 6, J, M, N, R or Z to Canal Street. **Open** 8am-1am daily. **Average** $13. **Credit** AmEx, CB, Discover, MC, V.
A three-storey Cantonese chow-house with excellent dim sum, a long menu and an inscrutable list of daily specials, make 20 Mott Street many people's idea of the quintessential New York Chinese. Bring your own wine.
*Disabled: access.*

### Zen Palate

*34 Union Square East, at East 16th Street Street (614 9291).* **Train** 4, 5, 6, L, N or R to Union Square. **Open** 11am-11pm Mon-Sat; noon-10.30pm Sun. **Average** $15-$25. **Credit** AmEx, MC, V.
A splendid vegetarian restaurant drawing inspiration from China, Japan and all points between. The 'fake' meat is so good you can take even the most unrepentant carnivore.
**Branch**: 663 Ninth Avenue (582 1669).

## Eastern European

### Christine's

*344 Lexington Avenue, between 39th & 40th Streets (953 1920).* **Train** 4, 5, 6 or 7 to Grand Central. **Open** 11am-9pm daily. **Average** $15. **Credit** AmEx, DC, MC, V.
These honest-to-goodness Polish restaurants become increasingly posh as they progress uptown. Both offer excellent potato pirogis, borscht and challah French toast.
*Disabled: access.*

### Primorski

*282 Brighton Beach Avenue, between 2nd & 3rd Streets, Brooklyn (1-718 891 3111).* **Train** D or Q to Brighton Beach. **Open** 11am-11pm daily. **Average** $25. **No credit cards**.
One of dozens of exuberant Russian nightclub/restaurants operated by recent Jewish emigrés from the Soviet Union. A visit here will make the trip on the Trans-Siberian Express out to Brighton Beach an experience which you will always remember, possibly as a lesson on the evils of drink.
*Disabled: access, toilets.*

### Russian Samovar

*256 West 52nd Street (757 0168).* **Train** 1 or 9 to 50th Street. **Lunch** noon-3pm Tue-Sat. **Dinner** 5pm-1am daily. **Average** $30. **Credit** AmEx, MC, V.
You may not recognise them, but this is where Russia's beautiful people go when they are in town. Baryshnikov and Joseph Brodsky took shares in the late 1980s. Famous customers include Norman Mailer and Gregory Hines.
*Smoking at bar and some tables.*

### Sammy's Famous Roumanian Jewish Restaurant

*157 Chrystie Street, between Delancey & Rivington Streets (673 0330).* **Train** F, J, M or Z to Essex Street; F to Delancey Street. **Open** 4-10pm Mon-Fri, Sun; 4pm-midnight Sat. **Credit** AmEx, DC, MC, V.
This is only for those with strong stomachs – the food's heavy and comes complete with a jug of chicken fat – but it is one of the most famous of the Lower East Side eateries.

## French

### Alison On Dominick

*38 Dominick Street, between Varick & Hudson Streets (727 1188).* **Train** C or E to Spring Street. **Lunch** noon-2.15pm Mon-Fri. **Dinner** 5.30-10.15pm Mon-Thur; 5.30-11pm Fri, Sat; 5.30-9.30pm Sun. **Average** $50. **Credit** AmEx, DC, MC, V.
Alison Price, together with her chef Thomas Valenti, has made this French country restaurant one of the more romantic hideaways in the city, with light – almost healthy – versions of south-western French cuisine and a quiet, jazz-tinged atmosphere.
*Disabled: access.*

### Bistro Jules

*65 St Mark's Place, between First & Second Avenues (477 5560).* **Train** 6 to Astor Place. **Lunch** noon-5.30pm, **dinner** 5.30pm-1am Mon-Thur, Sun; 5.30pm-2am Fri, Sat. **Average** $20. **Credit** AmEx.
This beautiful East Village bistro is set down from the sidewalk behind a rustic little terrace. There's terrific traditional food, jazz on Fridays and a guillotine on Bastille Day.
*Pavement tables. Smoking.*

### Les Deux Gamins

*170 Waverly Place, at Sheridan Square (807 7047).* **Train** 1 or 9 to Christopher Street. **Open** 8am-midnight Mon-Sat; 10am-midnight Sun. **Average** $25. **Credit** AmEx.
Watch the village go by as you soak up an atmosphere that's very Parisian, and bistro food that's almost as authentic.
*Disabled: access. Pavement tables. Smoking.*

### L'Espinasse

*St Regis Hotel, 2 East 55th Street, between Fifth & Madison Avenues (339 6719).* **Train** 4, 5 or 6 to 59th Street. **Breakfast** 7-11am daily. **Lunch** noon-1.30pm Mon-Sat. **Dinner** 6-10pm daily. **Average** $55. **Credit** AmEx, DC, Discover, MC, V.
Exquisite food: French with strong influences from the Far East, in a palatial old-world hotel dining room. Try parsley risotto with truffles and mushroom fricasee, or lamb chops dusted with curry powder and served with eggplant tart and carrot juice sauce.
*Disabled: access, toilets.*

### La Luncheonette

*130 Tenth Avenue, at 18th Street (675 0342).* **Train** A, C, E or L to Eighth Avenue/14th Street. **Brunch** 11.30am-3.30pm Sun. **Lunch** noon-3pm Mon-Fri. **Dinner** 6-11.30pm daily. **Average** $25. **Credit** DC, MC, V.
No-nonsense home cooking as it would be done en France: sheeps' brains, couscous and rich warming stews.
*Smoking room.*

### Felix

*340 West Broadway, at Grand Street (431 0021).* **Train** A, C or E to Canal Street. **Lunch** noon-4pm, **dinner** 6-11.30pm, daily. **Average** $36. **Credit** AmEx.
A solid SoHo bistro with an accent and an attitude. It's particularly fun in summer when the tables spill on to the

*Transvestite waitresses at* **Lucky Chengs**. *See page 133.*

XXIV
LUCKY CHENG'S
Restaurants

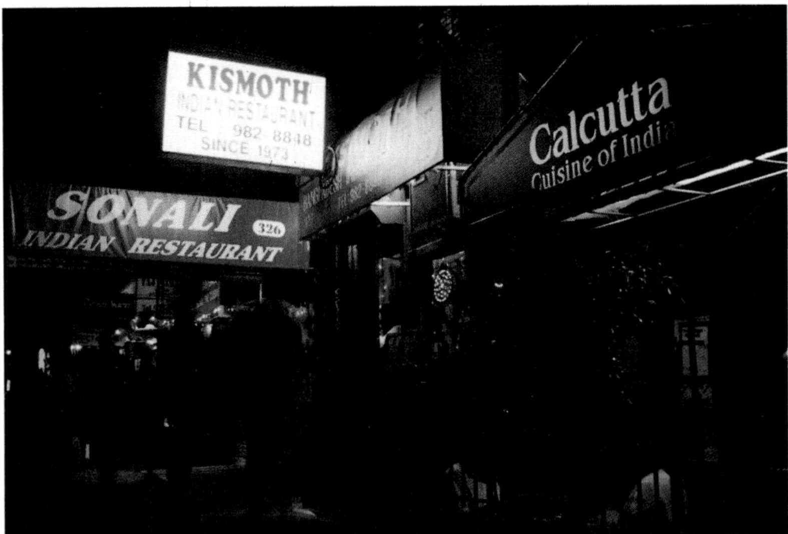


*Indian restaurants line up on 6th Street. See page 139.*

sidewalk and you can watch the comings and goings at Lucky Strike (*above*) and the ever-changing restaurants over the street. Delicious food is prepared by Eric Thiercelin.
*Disabled: access.*

### Gascogne

*158 Eighth Avenue, at 18th Street (675 6564).* **Train** 1 or 9 to 18th Street; C or E to 23rd Street. **Open** 6-10.30pm Mon-Thur; 8-11pm Fri, Sat. **Average** $35. **Credit** AmEx, DC, MC, V.
A restaurant for all seasons and one of our favourites. It is cosy and candlelit in winter, and in summer you can dine in the garden under the stars. Chef/owner Pascal Condomime is one of New York's most talented and his cassoulet is the talk of the town. Faithful to his Gascon roots, he specialises in birds of all kinds, and he can – and does – tell you a thing or two about Armagnac. His wife Carol's personal touch also helps things along. A real family-run restaurant.
*Garden.*

### La Grenouille

*3 East 52nd Street, between Fifth & Madison Avenues (752 1495).* **Train** 6 to 51st Street; E or F to Lexington Avenue. **Lunch** noon-2.30pm, **dinner** 6-11.15pm, Tue-Sat. **Set lunch** $42. **Set dinner** $75. **Credit** AmEx, DC, MC, V.
This is a timeless and eternally romantic restaurant, bedecked in flowers. The menu is classic ancien cuisine at pretty steep prices, and the guest list regularly includes Ines de la Fressange, Arnold Scaasi and Elizabeth Tilberis. There are of course frogs' legs, alongside pike quenelles, amazing choucroute with foie gras and dessert soufflés.
*Disabled: access, toilets.*

### Montrachet

*239 West Broadway, between White & Walker Streets (219 2777).* **Train** 1, 9 to Franklin Street; A, C or E to Canal Street. **Lunch** noon-3pm Fri. **Dinner** 6-10pm Mon-Thur; 6-11pm Fri, Sat. **Average** $40. **Credit** AmEx.
Montrachet – a sophisticated, loft-like TriBeCa eating space – has an exciting wine list and offers modern cuisine with a light Provençal tang. The vegetable terrine, red snapper with roast pepper, pigeon salad and roast kidneys are all excellent, and the prices are reasonable considering the standard of the cooking.

### Provence

*38 MacDougal Street, at Prince Street (475 7500).*
**Train** C or E to Spring Street. **Lunch** noon-3pm daily. **Dinner** 6-11.30pm Mon-Sat; 5.30-11pm Sun. **Average** $45. **Credit** AmEx.
A cheerful, laid-back SoHo bistro that serves up hearty country-style fare in a relaxed atmosphere. Recommended.
*Disabled: access. Garden. Smoking.*

### Raoul's

*180 Prince Street, between Sullivan & Thompson Streets (966 3518).* **Train** C or E to Spring Street. **Open** 5.30-11.30pm Mon-Thur, Sun; 5.30pm-2am Fri, Sat. **Average** $40. **Credit** AmEx, MC, V.
A classic SoHo bistro that fortunately has no connection with the Paul Bartel movie. It's usually crammed to its tin roof with downtown types, and the prices are a little high for the unambitious, but the country cooking is hard to fault. The Brasserie is larger and has live music on Fridays.
**Branch**: Raoul's Brasserie, 225 Varick Street (929 1630).
*Disabled: access. Garden. Smoking.*

## Greek/Middle Eastern

### Periyali

*35 West 20th Street, between Fifth & Sixth Avenues (463 7890).* **Train** N or R to 23rd Street. **Lunch** noon-3pm Mon-Fri. **Dinner** 5.30-11pm Mon-Sat. **Average** $55. **Credit** AmEx, MC, V, DC.
The best Greek food is in Astoria, Queens, but if you need a fix in Manhattan, this is a good one to try. It's a traditional coal-grill place offering the likes of moussaka, taramasalata and mushrooms à la Grecque, but each dish is intelligently

interpreted and subtly spiced. The innovative vegetarian appetisers and plain meat grills are also estimable.

### Moustache

*405 Atlantic Avenue, at Bond Street, Brooklyn (1-718 852 5555).* **Train** A, C or G to Hoyt/Schermerhorn Streets. **Open** 11am-11pm daily. **Average** $10-$15. **No credit cards.**

Atlantic Avenue is a strongly Arabic neighbourhood, and Moustache is the best of its restaurants. Top houmous and pitzas (pitta bread pizzas), as well as great baba gannoush. *Smoking.*

## Indian

There are many excellent, cheap-to-reasonable Indian restaurants along 6th Street, between First and Second Avenues, and on Lexington Avenue in the low 20s. Many of the smaller ones do not have liquor licenses, so you can take in your own beer or wine. The food is not as spicy as British palates might expect.

## Still smoking

After seeing New York workers huddled together in the midwinter cold, grasping at cigarettes outside their non-smoking office buildings, even the most nicotine-stained addicts have been known to find inspiration to quit. New York's smokers are treated like diseased cattle, the target of some of the strictest anti-smoking laws on the planet. And with new legislation effectively banning smoking from restaurants, your home will soon be the only place needing an ashtray.

The rule is that for a restaurant to permit smoking it must have either less than 35 seats or a specially constructed, separately ventilated smoking area. Many allow smoking at their outside tables, or at the bar (allowed if it's more than six feet away from the tables), and so a new custom is emerging of going to the bar between courses.

One place that positively encourages smoking is Orbit, a cosy women-owned bar and restaurant in the West Village which takes a militant stand on the issue (*see chapter* **Women**). For other suggestions take a look at *Lighten up New York: The Smoker's Guide to Dining* (1995) by Michael Leo, 1800 restaurants reviewed with the smoker in mind, also on the Internet (www.lighten-up.com).

As well as in most eating establishments, smoking is now outlawed in taxis, buses and the subway, in banks, hotel lobbies, public toilets, cinemas, sports arenas and other public buildings. Buy some gum.

### Chutney Mary

*40 East 20th Street, between Broadway & Park Avenue (473 8181).* **Train** N or R to 23rd Street. **Lunch** 11.30am-3pm Mon-Fri. **Dinner** 5.30-11.30pm daily. **Average** $20-$25. **Credit** AmEx, DC, Discover, MC, V.

A great name, excellent north Indian cuisine with organic ingredients, wide-ranging veggie dishes and a 40-foot waterfall in the centre of the room. What more could you need? *Disabled: access to ground floor. Smoking at bar.*

### Dawat

*210 East 58th Street, between Second & Third Avenues (355 7555).* **Train** 4, 5 or 6 to 59th Street; N or R to Lexington Avenue. **Lunch** noon-2.45pm Mon-Sat. **Dinner** 5.30-10.45pm Mon-Thur; 5.30-11.30pm Fri, Sat. **Average** *lunch* $15-$20; *dinner* $25-$30. **Credit** AmEx, DC, MC, V.

With a diverse menu written by Madhur Jaffrey, Dawat has been an immediate and runaway success, claiming the title as the most sophisticated and probably the best Indian restaurant in New York. It has a great value set lunch. *Disabled: access, toilets. Smoking section.*

### Mitali East

*334 East 6th Street, between First & Second Avenues (533 2508).* **Train** N or R to 8th Street; 6 to Astor Place. **Open** noon-midnight daily. **Average** $25. **Credit** AmEx, MC, V.

There's often a queue outside downtown favourites Mitali East and West (see branch below). The food is consistently good and there's often live music.
*Disabled: access, toilets. Pavement tables. Smoking.*
**Branch**: Mitali West, 296 Bleecker Street (989 1367).

### Panna II

*93 First Avenue, at 6th Street (598 4610).* **Train** F to Second Avenue. **Open** noon-midnight daily. **Average** $15. **No credit cards.**

Try this for good simple southern Indian food and rich, fruity curries. There are two restaurants around the corner from each other. Their coconut soup and shrimp puri are wonders.
**Branch**: Panna, 330 East 6th Street (475 9274).

## Italian

### Angelo's

*146 Mulberry Street, between Grand & Hester Streets (966 1277).* **Train** B or D to Grand Street. **Open** noon-11.30pm Tue-Thur, Sun; noon-12.30am Fri; noon-1am Sat. **Average** $30. **Credit** AmEx, DC, MC, V.

Little Italy's restaurants often let showy glitz overtake the quality of the food served. One which doesn't – and is consequently one of the best in the area – is Angelo's, serving good hearty portions of Southern Italian fare, characterised by tomato sauces, olives and chillis.
*Pavement tables.*

### Arturo's

*106 West Houston Street, at Thompson Street (677 3820).* **Train** 1 or 9 to Houston Street. **Open** 4pm-1am Mon-Thur; 4pm-2am Fri, Sat; 3pm-midnight Sun. **Average** $15. **Credit** AmEx, MC, V.

Deep inside Arturo's you could swear you were in some cosy country hideaway. Live jazz heats up this Village pizzeria, along with a coal-burning pizza oven. Sizzling pizza pies, renowned for their crisp, crusty consistency and zesty sauce, dominate the menu. There's also a full supporting cast of other Italian dishes.
*Disabled: access. Pavement tables.*

### Barocco

*301 Church Street, at Walker Street (431 1445).* **Train** 1, 9, A, C or E to Canal Street. **Lunch** served noon-3pm

# At this time of night?

The New York rules of supply and demand mean that late-night hunger will connect fairly effortlessly with late-night food. Sandwiches, bagels and other deli items are available in legions of corner groceries throughout the city, including the hundreds of Korean-owned stores that are open around the clock. Most of these will have fridge filled with juices, soft drinks, yoghurts, ice creams and beer as well as salad bars, hot food and coffee.

There's no shortage of late-opening diners, generally offering vast menus of sandwiches, cooked breakfasts, grilled food and Italian/ Greek/Jewish/etc style specials. They range from tolerable upwards. Many accept major credit cards. In addition, a large number of New York restaurants remain open very late. Look particularly in the sections **Forever Chic**, **Diners** and **Cheap Eats**.

### Around the Clock Café & Gallery

*8 Stuyvesant Street, off corner of 9th Street & Third Avenue (598 0402).* **Train** 6 to Astor Place. **Open** 24 hours daily. **Average** $10. **Credit** AmEx, DC, Discover, MC, V.

Just a stone's throw from St Mark's Place, this is the handiest place to satisfy those East Village munchies. Breakfast is served 24 hours a day, but alongside eggs, pancakes and french toast you can have omelettes, burgers, pasta, fish and Mexican food. Excellent brunch specials.

*Smoking at bar.*

### H&H Bagel

*1551 Second Avenue, between 80th & 81st Streets (734 7441).* **Train** 6 to 77th Street. **Open** 24 hours daily. **Credit** AmEx, DC, Discover, MC, V.

This is one of the city's most famous; it wholesales to a range of outlets. You'll find 13 different types of bagel, a large selection of smoked salmon and other speciality fish, sodas and juices, Häagen Dazs ice cream and deli sandwiches – and all at any time of day or night. Order your bagels with a 'schmear' (part butter, part cream cheese). This is where cabbies and cops go, so you know it's good.

*Disabled: access.*

### Kiev

*Second Avenue, at 7th Street (674 4040).* **Train** 6 to Astor Place. **Open** 24 hours daily. **Average** $8. **No credit cards**.

A pleasant, if impersonal, 24-hour coffee-shop, Kiev is especially popular for breakfast (french toast is made with challah bread). Also on the menu is solid Ukrainian soul food – borscht, pierogi and mushroom barley soup.

*Disabled: access.*

### Lox Around the Clock

*676 Sixth Avenue, at 21st Street (691 3535).* **Train** F, N or R to 23rd Street. **Open** 11am-1am Mon-Wed; 11am-4am Thur; 11am-5am Fri; 8am-5am Sat; 8am-1am Sun. **Average** $12. **Credit** AmEx, DC, MC, V.

Jewish, Middle Eastern and American dishes are served here, with lox (smoked salmon) the speciality. The interior is trashy and unusual, the clientele loud and loose and the atmosphere fun. There are tables outside in good weather.

*Disabled: access, toilets.*

### Odessa

*119 Avenue A, at 7th Street (473 8916).* **Train** F to Second Avenue. **Open** 24 hours Mon, Wed-Sun; 7am-midnight Tue. **Average** $8.50. **No credit cards**.

The last refuge of a scoundrel. Or at least where most of the East Village ends up sooner or later. Big burgers, great Polish/Ukranian food and low, low prices. Full of cops, cabbies and people who've spent nearly all their money on clubs and drugs.

### Yaffa Café

*97 St Mark's Place, between First Avenue & Avenue A (674 9302/677 9001).* **Train** 6 to Astor Place; L to First Avenue. **Open** 24 hours daily. **Average** $10. **Credit** AmEx (minimum $15).

'Open always' proclaims the mural outside. This is a long thin basement with a sunny patio out back, serving a range of grills and salads with an emphasis on health. There's plenty of brown rice and a Middle Eastern feel to the food. The servings aren't always big enough.

*Garden.*

Mon-Fri. **Dinner** served 6.30-11pm Mon-Thur, Sun; 6.30pm-midnight Fri, Sat. **Average** $45. **Credit** AmEx, DC, Discover, MC, V.

A still trendy TriBeCa Tuscan trattoria that effortlessly achieves a warm and welcoming ambience despite crackling with the static of fashionability. On the menu are excellent own-make breads and pastas, very good roasts, grilled fish, fettunta and ricotta cheesecake.

*Smoking at bar.*

### Il Cantinori

*32 East 10th Street, between University Place & Broadway (673 6044).* **Train** N or R to 8th Street. **Lunch** noon-2.30pm Mon-Fri. **Dinner** 6pm-11.30pm Mon-Thur, Sun; 6pm-midnight Fri, Sat. **Average** $45. **Credit** AmEx, DC, MC, V.

A Tuscan farmhouse transported to Greenwich Village. The photocopied menu is revised every day and features fish flown in from the Mediterranean, as well as roast quail, excellent spaghetti and possibly the best osso buco in town.

*Disabled: access. Smoking. Terrace.*

### Carmine's

*2450 Broadway, between 90th & 91st Streets (362 2200).* **Train** 1 or 9 to 86th Street. **Open** 5-11pm Mon-Thur; 5pm-midnight Fri, Sat; 3-11pm Sun. **Average** $30. **Credit** AmEx.

The service is good and unobtrusive, the atmosphere soothing, and the solid family-style cooking is served in huge portions. The tiramisu alone would feed four.

*Disabled: access. Smoking at bar.*

### Cascabel

*218 Lafayette Street, at Spring Street (431 7300).* **Train** 6 to Spring Street. **Dinner** 6-11pm Mon-Sat; 5.30-10pm Sun. **Average** $40. **Credit** AmEx, DC, Discover, MC, V.

Exquisite Italian rustic cuisine from Tom Valenti, formerly the chef of Alison On Dominick (*see under* **French**), served to warm you up for some of the world's finest desserts. The restaurant has a very genteel atmosphere, made slightly more SoHo by the rotating art collection on the walls.
*Disabled: access, toilets.*

### Cucina

*256 Fifth Avenue, between Carroll Street & Garfield Place, Brooklyn (1-718 230 0711).* **Train** M, N or R to Union Street. **Dinner** 5.30-10.30pm Mon-Fri; 5.30-11pm Sat; 5.30-10pm Sun. **Average** $30. **Credit** AmEx, MC, V.
A northern Italian restaurant which draws people out to Brooklyn with food that is as good as the best in Manhattan. Excellent pastas, dazzling antipasti, a strong wine list; the only difference is it's cheaper.
*Disabled: access, toilets.*

### Elaine's

*1703 Second Avenue, between 88th & 89th Streets (534 8103).* **Train** 4, 5 or 6 to 86th Street. **Open** 6pm-2am daily. **Average** $35. **Credit** AmEx, Discover, MC, V.
The food isn't really so great, but the celeb count is fabulous. Everyone wants to come here, so reservations are essential
*Disabled: access, toilets. Smoking.*

### John's Pizzeria

*278 Bleecker Street, between Sixth & Seventh Avenues (243 1680).* **Train** A, B, C, D, E, F or Q to West 4th Street; 1 or 9 to Christopher Street/Sheridan Square. **Open** 11.30am-11.30pm Mon-Thur, Sun; 11.30am-12.30am Fri, Sat. **Average** $12. **No credit cards.**
John's brick-baked Italian pies are crisp and delightful. With strong sauce and fresh toppings, they're the best in town.
*Disabled: access, toilets.*
**Branch**: 408 East 64th Street (935 2895).

### Il Mulino

*86 West 3rd Street, between Thompson & Sullivan Streets (673 3783).* **Train** A, B, C, D, E, F or Q to West 4th Street. **Lunch** noon-2.30pm, **dinner** 5-11.30pm, Mon-Sat. **Average** $55. **Credit** AmEx.
An archetypal bare-brick, low-lit Village restaurant rated by many as serving the best Italian food in the city. It's always crowded and the reservations system often breaks down, but it's worth waiting for the wonderful fried zucchini, boconccini and the fabulous pasta specials.

### Il Nido

*251 East 53rd Street, between Second & Third Avenues (753 8450).* **Train** E or F to Lexington Avenue. **Lunch** noon-2.30pm, **dinner** 5.30-11pm Mon-Sat. **Average** $50. **Credit** AmEx, DC, Discover, MC, V.
Trustworthy favourites cooked with grace and zest. The special raviolis are wondrous.
*Disabled: access, toilets. Smoking at bar.*

### Perretti Italian Café

*270 Columbus Avenue, at 72nd Street (362 3939).* **Train** 1, 2, 3 or 9 to 72nd Street. **Open** noon-11.30 Mon-Thur, Sun; noon-1am Fri, Sat. **Average** $20. **Credit** AmEx, DC, MC, V.
A homely Italian offering zippy Tuscan food to an increasingly trendy crowd. It has a wood-burning oven from which wonders of fish, chicken and citrus emerge.
*Disabled: access. Terrace.*

### Primavera

*1578 First Avenue, at East 82nd Street (861 8608).* **Train** 4, 5 or 6 to 86th Street. **Open** 5.30pm-midnight daily. **Average** $60. **Credit** AmEx, DC, MC, V.
An excellent, upmarket trattoria, Primavera caused a minor revolution when it opened, years ago, by introducing New Yorkers to properly al dente pasta. Under the firm hand of Nicola Civetta it continues to enjoy a reputation as the premier North Italian restaurant in the city.
*Disabled: access.*

### Three of Cups

*83 First Avenue, at 5th Street (388 0059).* **Train** F to Second Avenue. **Dinner** 6pm-2am Mon-Sat; 6pm-1am Sun. **Average** $20. **Credit** AmEx, MC, V.
Excellent but affordable Italian food in a space full of dark gothic furniture. It specialises in pizzas from a wood-burning oven and excellent antipasti. Don't miss the best bread in town and be sure to check out the 'lounge' located downstairs for its voodoo-inspired vibe (*see also* **Bars & Cafés**).
*Smoking area. Pavement tables.*

### Umberto's Clam House

*129 Mulberry Street, at Hester Street (431 7545).* **Train** 6, J, M, N, R or Z to Canal Street. **Open** 11am-4am Mon-Thur, Sun; 11am-6am Fri, Sat. **Average** $25. **Credit** AmEx.
More famous as the site of mafia boss Joey Gallo's gruesome 1972 execution than as a particularly exciting eaterie, though the clams are spicy and delicious and it the fish and chips decent. Until recently the bullet-hole still graced the window, but it looks like they finally got the glaziers in.
*Pavement tables.*

## Japanese

### Avenue A Sushi

*103 Avenue A, between 6th & 7th Streets (982 8109).* **Train** 6 to Astor Place. **Dinner** 6pm-1am Mon-Thur, Sun; 6pm-2am Fri, Sat. **Average** $20-$30. **Credit** AmEx, MC, V.
Some of the best Japanese food in the city, with a broad menu and plenty of special dishes served up in techno-cartoon surroundings of computer animation, Japanese TV commercials and a resident DJ.
*Smoking area.*

### Hatsuhana

*17 East 48th Street, between Fifth & Madison Avenues (355 3345).* **Train** 6 to 51st Street; E or F to Lexington Avenue. **Lunch** 11.45am-2.45pm Mon-Fri. **Dinner** 5.30-10pm Mon-Sat. **Average** $50. **Credit** AmEx, DC, MC, V.
Among those who know, and who spend, Hatsuhana has the edge. Perfect sushi, and an extensive list of bizarre Japanese delicacies unavailable elsewhere in the city.

### Honmura An

*170 Mercer Street, between Prince & Houston Streets (334 5253).* **Train** N or R to Prince Street. **Lunch** noon-2.30pm Wed-Sat. **Dinner** 6-10pm Tue-Thur; 6-10.30pm Fri, Sat; 6-9.30pm Sun. **Average** $40. **Credit** AmEx, DC, MC, V.
If sushi's not your thing, try this stylish traditional Japanese noodle parlour, with its atmosphere of quiet contemplation.

### Japonica

*100 University Place, at 12th Street (243 7752).* **Train** 4, 5, 6, L, N or R to 14th Street/Union Square. **Open** noon-11pm Mon-Sat; noon-10.30pm Sun. **Average** $25. **Credit** AmEx.
Wonderfully decorated, this crowded space draws a mixed crowd who come for the fresh and inexpensive sushi. There's always a queue but tables turn quickly.
*Disabled: access.*

### Nobu

*105 Hudson Street, at Franklin Street (219 0500).* **Train** 1 or 9 to Franklin Street. **Lunch** 11.45am-2.15pm Mon-Fri. **Dinner** 5.45-10.15pm Mon-Sat. **Average** $75. **Credit** AmEx, DC, Discover, MC, V.

This flashy new TriBeCa restaurant is the work of LA's Nobu Matsuhisa. In an awe-inspiring space, the menu is simply miraculous, providing jet-setting trendies with the ultimate in designer Japanese food.
*Disabled: access.*

## Jewish

### Ratner's

*138 Delancey Street, between Norfolk & Suffolk Streets (677 5588).* **Train** F, J, M or Z to Delancey. **Open** 6am-11pm Mon-Thur, Sun; 6am-3pm Fri; 7pm-1am Sat. **Average** $20. **Credit** AmEx, Discover, MC, V.
One of the few reminders that this neighbourhood was once one of the world's largest Jewish communities. Pricey considering its surroundings, but Ratner's is an institution.
*Disabled: access.*

## Mexican

### Rosa Mexicano

*1063 First Avenue, at East 58th Street (753 7407).* **Train** 4, 5 or 6 to 59th Street; N or R to Lexington Avenue. **Dinner** 5pm-midnight daily. **Average** $35. **Credit** AmEx, DC, MC, V.
Still rated as one of the best and most authentic Mexican restaurants around town, with a famous guacamole and trademark pomegranate margaritas. Ace chillis rellenos.
*Smoking at bar.*

### El Teddy's

*219 West Broadway, between White & Franklin Streets (941 7070).* **Train** 1, 9, A, C or E to Canal Street. **Lunch** noon-3pm daily. **Dinner** 6pm-12.30am Mon-Wed, Sun; 6pm-2.30am Thur-Sat. **Average** $25. **Credit** AmEx, DC, MC, V.
A trendy, new-wave Mexican restaurant with a chic pedigree, serving a mix of traditional and progressive dishes. Don't miss the jicama (savoury pear) salad, or poblane e rogada (roast chilli pepper with a creamy sauce).
*Disabled: access, toilets. Smoking.*

### Zarela

*953 Second Avenue, at 51st Street (644 6740).* **Train** E or F to Lexington Avenue. **Lunch** noon-3pm Mon-Fri. **Dinner** 5-11pm Mon-Thur; 5-11.30pm Fri, Sat; 5-10pm Sun. **Average** $25. **Credit** AmEx, DC.
Forget the sticky gloop that often passes for Mexican food, and experience the excellent menu at Zarela Martinez's festive establishment. Live music.
*Disabled: access. Smoking.*

### Zuni

*598 Ninth Avenue, at 43rd Street (765 7626).* **Train** A, C or E to 42nd Street. **Open** noon-midnight daily. **Average** $15-$20. **Credit** AmEx, DC, MC, V.
Cutesy and kitsch, Zuni is decorated with delightfully trippy Mexicana. Great simple food at bargain prices, most of which can be rendered vegetarian-friendly.
*Disabled: access.*

## South American/Caribbean

### Cabane Carioca

*123 West 45th Street, between Sixth & Seventh Avenues (581 8088).* **Train** 1, 2, 3, 7, 9, N or R to Times Square. **Open** noon-11pm Mon-Thur, Sun; noon-midnight Fri, Sat. **Average** $20. **Credit** AmEx, DC, MC, V.
The best Brazilian restaurant in the city is to be found down an almost vertical staircase festooned with gaudy murals. Feijoada, the national dish of black bean stew is the obvious choice, but codfish and grilled chicken are also up to scratch.
*Disabled: access to ground floor.*

### Caribe

*117 Perry Street, at Greenwich Street (255 9191).* **Train** A, C, E or L to 14th Street/Eighth Avenue. **Open** 11am-12.30am daily. **Average** $15-$25. **Credit** MC, V.
A great little Caribbean restaurant, full of tropical greenery. Have a daquiri and then try the excellent jerk chicken.

### Tropica

*200 Park Avenue, in the Met Life Building (867 6767).* **Train** 4, 5, 6 or 7 to Grand Central. **Lunch** 11.45am-3pm Mon-Fri; **dinner** 5-10pm Mon-Fri. **Average** *lunch* $35 **dinner** $40. **Credit** AmEx, DC, MC, V.
Good spicy Caribbean food, with the emphasis on seafood, and with a few Japanese influences creeping in. The setting is exotic and leafy, the clientele very much business based.
*Disabled: access, toilets. Smoking at bar after 3.30pm.*

## South-east Asian

Several Vietnamese and Thai places are clustered on and around Baxter Street in Chinatown, and 32nd Street west of Fifth Avenue is where you'll find many Korean restaurants.

### Indochine

*430 Lafayette Street, between Astor Place & East 4th Street (505 5111).* **Train** 6 to Astor Place; N or R to 8th Street. **Open** 6pm-midnight Mon-Thur; 6pm-12.30am Fri, Sat. **Average** $40. **Credit** AmEx, DC, MC, V.
A perennially trendy place opposite the Public Theater, where beautiful people gather among the palm leaves to sample the exquisite Vietnamese/Thai/Cambodian menu.
*Smoking at bar and some tables.*

### New York Kom Tang Soot Bul House

*32 West 32nd Street, between Broadway & Fifth Avenue (947 8482).* **Train** 6 to 33rd Street. **Open** 24 hours daily. **Average** $15. **Credit** AmEx, MC, V.
All the joys of a traditional Korean barbecue or hibachi, as well as a full menu of other enticing dishes.

### Planet Thailand

*184 Bedford Avenue, at North 7th Street, Williamsburg, Brooklyn (1-718 599 5758).* **Train** L to Bedford Avenue. **Open** 11.30am-11pm Mon-Sat; 1-11pm Sun. **Average** $10. **No credit cards.**
This is as good a reason as any for visiting the artists' republic of Williamsburg. As well as being beautifully fresh and more than delicious, the food is far spicier than the mild-tempered flavours you usually get in New York.

### Vong

*200 East 54th Street, at Third Avenue (486 9592).* **Train** E or F to Lexington Avenue. **Lunch** noon-2.30pm Mon-Fri. **Dinner** 6-11pm Mon-Fri; 5.30-11.30pm Sat; 5.30-10pm Sun. **Average** $40-$45. **Credit** AmEx, MC, V.
Possibly the best Thai food in town, served in a dreamily designed gold-leafed temple. The chef, one Jean-Georges Vongerichten, after whom the place is named, works magic on even the most traditional dishes.
*Disabled: access. Smoking.*

## Spanish

### Bolo

*23 East 22nd Street, between Broadway & Park Avenue (228 2200).* **Train** N or R to 23rd Street. **Lunch** noon-

# Theme park dining

Gather some memorabilia, house it in a burger bar, convince people that they haven't really eaten there unless they buy a $25 T-shirt to prove it, and sit back and watch the queues.

Theme restaurants are huge business, not least in New York, where there are always busloads of wide-eyed tourists from Idaho willing to be herded from their hotel to *Cats* or *Les Mis* and thence to Planet Hollywood or Hard Rock Café down the street. Here they'll eat a marginally overpriced meal, buy a marginally overpriced baseball cap and look at all sorts of marginally exciting things once owned by famous people.

Of course the latest to make the news was **Fashion Café**. When the rumours went out that Naomi, Claudia and Elle 'The Body ' MacPherson (lately joined by the self-confessed sell-out Christy Turlington) were to open a restaurant, the in-folk assumed it would be a seductive downtown affair with an exclusive air and a permanent table for Russell Simmons. Then they announced that it would be in the tourist ground zero of Rockefeller Plaza, and all became clear.

In fact Fashion Café, 51 Rockefeller Plaza, at 51st Street (765 3131) actually succeeds in making the others look classy. **Planet Hollywood**, 140 West 57th Street, between Sixth and Seventh Avenues (333 7827) and **Hard Rock Café**, 221 West 57th Street, between Broadway and Seventh Avenues (459 9320), at least manage a little spectacle. The supermodels' place is just a badly decorated bar and grill with some dull popstar clothes on the walls.

Better but lesser-known New York theme restaurants include the **Harley-Davidson Café**, 1370 Sixth Avenue at 56th Street (245 6000), and the **Jekyll and Hyde Club**, 1409 Sixth Avenue at 57th Street (541 9505), where you eat your meal amid animatronic sphinxes, skeletons and other Victorian frighteners. And themed eateries continue to proliferate, mass-marketing their way into the hearts of the unadventurous. There are many more being developed, including an all-American sports extravaganza in Times Square.

*The Sphinx speaks at* **Jekyll and Hyde**.

2.30pm Mon-Fri. **Dinner** 5.30-11pm Sun, Mon; 5.30pm-midnight Tue-Sat. **Average** *lunch* $20-$25 *dinner* $30-35. **Credit** AmEx, DC, Discover, MC, V.
The wide-awake decor immediately alerts you to the presence of vivid Spanish cuisine. But chef Bobby Flay ignores tradition so the paella is with duck, and the salad is octopus and chick pea. Intriguing and excellent.
*Disabled: access.*

### El Faro

*823 Greenwich Street, at Horatio Street (929 8210).*
**Train** A, C or L to 14th Street/Eighth Avenue. **Lunch** 11am-3pm, **dinner** 3pm-midnight, daily. **Average** *lunch* $20; *dinner* $25-$30. **Credit** AmEx, DC, Discover, MC, V.
Elbow-to-elbow cosiness and traditional mouthwatering Spanish cuisine that's guaranteed to fill you up. Share a paella or sample the house speciality of seafood in green sauce.

## Vegetarian

Almost all New York restaurants, including many of those listed in this chapter, can provide a decent variety of vegetarian dishes. For a more in-depth look, consult *Vegetarian Dining in New York City* by Arthur S Brown and Barbara Holmes.

### B&H Dairy and Vegetarian Restaurant

*127 Second Avenue, at St Mark's Place (505 8065).*
**Train** 6 to Astor Place. **Open** 7am-10pm daily.
**Average** $3-$5. **No credit cards**.
B&H looks just like a standard ham'n'eggs American diner, but serves an astonishing range of hearty vegetarian soups, juices, great home-made challa bread and veggie burgers. The antidote to prissy, self-righteous vegetarian dining.

# Bars & Cafés

***New York dispenses from an endless drinks list of everything from elegant cocktails sipped in romantic hotels to pitchers of Bud served in dim and dirty dive bars. Stay for another.***

Weak though the beer may be (New York laws prohibit brews over 5 per cent alcohol), it flows until 4am. A city statute dating back to the 1920s forces bars to close at this hour to 'air out' their premises. The law lets them open back up again at 8am, however. Most restaurants have bars and will serve drinks with no obligation to eat a meal. Most bar staff can concoct a decent cocktail and, if you stay for a couple, may eventually offer you one on the house. But steady as you go: spirits measures are very generous, equivalent to about a treble in UK terms. You must be 21 to drink here legally, and because the city has discovered that it can make money fining bars which serve under-agers, the very un-New York practice of 'carding' (asking for photographic proof of age) is suddenly rampant. And don't think grey hair will excuse you: people in their mid-30s have been turned away for not carrying ID – flattering, maybe, but more than a little inconvenient. Smoking is still allowed in most places, though sometimes only at the bar. Finally, don't forget to tip the bartender with either the change or a dollar per round.

## Bars

### Babyland

*81 Avenue A, at 5th Street (598 4099).* **Train** F to Second Avenue. **Open** 4pm-4am Mon-Fri; 8pm-4am Sat, Sun. **No credit cards.**

One of the latest in the line of East Village fun-decor bars, the theme being babies and all their associated implements. Variable drinks, but a large busy joint with a chatty, flirtatious clientele.

*Disabled: access, toilets.*

### Bar 119

*119 East 15th Street, off Union Square (777 6158).* **Train** 4, 5, 6, L, N or R to Union Square. **Open** noon-4am daily. **No credit cards.**

The rock 'n' roll rebels that populate this loud, dark, very American bar are a breed of after-work office drone, but they're all posing as extras from a nasty road movie. Grab a brew while waiting to see a band at Irving Plaza next door.

*Disabled: access, toilets.*

### Bowery Bar

*358 Bowery, at 4th Street (475 2220).* **Train** 6 to Bleecker Street. **Open** 11.30am-4am daily. **Credit** AmEx, DC, MC, V.

The epicentre of self-conscious trendiness. Current fave of

*Harlem's battered but beautiful* **Lenox Lounge**. *See page 145.*

the S&M (standing and modelling) set, and therefore full of very beautiful, very dull people and their fans. The scenes on the door can be desperate. It's actually a restaurant, but models don't eat.
*Disabled: access. Smoking in garden only.*

### Broadway Lounge

*Marriott Marquis Hotel, 1535 Broadway, between 45th & 46th Streets (398 1900).* **Train** 1, 2, 3, 7, 9, N, R or S to Times Square. **Open** 5pm-12.30am Mon-Thur, Sun; 5pm-1.15am Fri, Sat. **Credit** AmEx, CB, DC, Discover, MC, V.
The perfect way to view the hustle of Times Square – from the comfort of a sound-proof revolving bar, eight floors above the crowds. Everyone gets a window seat over Broadway at this large, very modern drinking place. The clientele is largely tourists, but the view alone really makes it worth a visit. A bar menu of appetisers is served.
*Disabled: access, toilets.*

### Buddha Bar

*150 Varick Street, at Vandam Street (255 4433).* **Train** 1 or 9 to Houston Street. **Open** 10pm-4am daily. **No credit cards.**
Dressed in delicate far-eastern fabrics, with plenty of contemplative buddhas to infuse a mood of moderation, Buddha Bar is a temple to relaxed, sociable imbibing. Except when the weekend comes and the crowds of pretty people descend. Tuesdays are backgammon nights, Sunday is women only.

### Chumley's

*86 Bedford Street, between Barrow & Grove Streets (675 4449).* **Train** E to West 4th Street. **Open** 5pm-midnight Mon-Fri; 5pm-2am Sat, Sun. **No credit cards.**
Chumley's is still a bit coy about its existence; although it hasn't been a speakeasy for decades, there's still no sign over the door. Come in, though – it's a great pubby little bar and restaurant and something of a literary landmark.

### Fanelli

*94 Prince Street, at Mercer Street (226 9412).* **Train** 6 to Bleecker Street; B, D or F to Broadway/Lafayette; N or R to Prince Street. **Open** 10am-2am Mon-Thur, Sun; 11am-3am Sat, Sun. **No credit cards.**
The oldest and one of the best bars in Soho. It has a great wooden bar, wonderful barmen, tiled floors, framed pictures of boxers on the walls and local beers. It's decidedly unpretentious and a favourite with gallery owners. Goodish food is served at lunchtime, should you require it, but most stick to straight shots of Jack.

### Fez

*at Time Café, 380 Lafayette Street, at Great Jones Street (533 7000).* **Train** 6 to Astor Place. **Open** 6pm-2am Mon-Thur, Sun; 6pm-4am Fri, Sat. **Credit** AmEx, MC, V.
Time Café next door is a sleek chrome eaterie, but Fez is a Moroccan-themed beatnik hideaway with huge sofas to flop in and massive decorative tables to perch your drinks on. There's a busy performance schedule of jazz and poetry which happens in the smoky underground level. Good bar food, too.

### Lenox Lounge

*288 Lenox Avenue (Malcolm X Boulevard), between 124th & 125th Streets (722 9566).* **Train** 2 or 3 to 125th Street. **Open** noon-4am daily. **No credit cards.**
From its battered but beautiful chrome and neon frontage via the blues and soul on the jukebox to the once-sharp suits of the customers inside, this neighbourhood favourite has all the faded glory which Harlem does so well. Famous as Malcolm X's hangout during his hustling years.
*Disabled: access, toilets.*

### Max Fish

*178 Ludlow Street, between Houston & Stanton Streets (529 3959).* **Train** F to Second Avenue. **Open** 5.30pm-4am daily. **No credit cards.**
A collection of young artists, w… insomniacs populates this bar/ga… table, a busy jukebox, conversatio… and plenty of compulsively gregari… splendid drinking den.
*Disabled: access, toilets.*

### McSorley's Old Ale House

*15 East 7th Street, between Second & Third A…es (473 9148).* **Train** 6 to Astor Place; N or R to 8th Street. **Open** 11am-1am Mon-Sat; 1pm-1am Sun. **No credit cards.**
Possibly the oldest pub in Manhattan, McSorley's is usually brimful of college jocks involved in fraternity initiation rituals, but has played host in the past to Abe Lincoln, the Roosevelts and John Kennedy. There's sawdust on the floor, just as there was in 1854, and the McSorley's creamy ale, by mug or by pitcher, is as good as it ever was.

### Merchants

*112 Seventh Avenue, at 17th Street (366 7267).* **Train** 1 or 9 to 18th Street. **Open** 11.30am-4am daily. **Credit** AmEx, DC, MC, V.
Over the street from Barney's is this classy Chelsea hangout with splendid food (don't miss the desserts) and a smart, bubbly clientele.
*Disabled: access. Pavement tables.*

### Milano's

*51 East Houston Street (226 8632).* **Train** B, D, F or Q to Broadway/Lafayette. **Open** 8am-4am Mon-Sat; noon-4pm Sun. **No credit cards.**
This long and extremely narrow drinking hole is a favourite with late-night drinkers. Huge cheap measures, strange and interesting people, delightfully seedy. In short: dive-bar.

### Monkey Bar

*Hotel Elysée, 60 East 54th Street, between Madison & Park Avenues (838 2600).* **Train** E or F to Lexington Avenue. **Open** noon-2pm Mon-Fri; 6pm-2am daily. **Credit** AmEx, DC, MC, V.
This bar was an institution throughout the 1950s, with that era's stars conducting all manner of illicit liaisons here. It's been refurbished to its former glory, and in amongst the original murals of jungle and monkeys, you'll find a very civilised recreation of the golden age of the cocktail.

### Nation

*50 Avenue A, between 4th & 5th Streets (473 6239).* **Train** F to Second Avenue. **Open** 7am-6pm, 8pm-4am, daily. **No credit cards.**
The rust and blue colour scheme at Nation is complemented by a smoochy acid jazz soundtrack and wraparound mirrors for scanning your prey among the busloads of upmarket East Villagers it attracts.

### No-Tell Motel

*167 Avenue A, between 10th & 11th Streets (475 2172).* **Train** L to First Avenue. **Open** 6pm-4am Mon-Wed, Sat, Sun; 5pm-4am Thur. **No credit cards.**
This sometimes quiet bar on the upper reaches of Avenue A is crammed with top-quality kitsch, including murals of 1950s pornography and a sign that reads 'women should come with instructions'. At the back there are several tiny rooms for illicit liaisons. This is the place to take someone else's squeeze.
*Disabled: access.*

### North Star Pub

*93 South Street, corner of Fulton Street (509 6757).* **Train** A or C to Broadway/Nassau; 2, 3, 4, 5, J, M or Z to Fulton Street. **Open** 11.30am-midnight daily. **Credit** AmEx, CB, DC, MC, V.

**Sophie's** – *the quintessential NY dive bar*

This is one of the few New York bar-restaurants that comes close to being anything like a true (ie very ordinary) British pub. Dozens of UK beers are sold, and there's HP sauce on the tables.
*Disabled: access, toilets.*

### NW3

*242 East 10th Street, between First & Second Avenues (260 0891).* **Train** L to First Avenue. **Open** 8pm-4am daily. **Credit** AmEx, MC, V.
The bouncer is famous for his appalling Dick Van Dyke fake cockney accent, a warning of the chronic Anglophilia within. Artistically lit powder-blue satin billows from the walls and funk and rare groove fills your ears. But tweak your British vowels and you'll meet endless young pretties.
*Disabled: access.*

### Oak Room/Blue Bar at the Algonquin Hotel

*59 West 44th Street, off Fifth Avenue (840 6800).* **Train** 4, 5, 6 or 7 to Grand Central. **Open** 11.30am-1am daily. **Credit** AmEx, CB, DC, Discover, MC, V.
The home of the legendary Round Table wears its heritage well. The Oak Room bar in the lobby has the sedate atmosphere of a gentlemen's club, while the adjoining, dimly lit Blue Room is the place to raise a glass of vodkatini to Dorothy Parker.
*Disabled: access, toilets. Booking advised.*

### Old Town Bar

*45 East 18th Street, near Broadway (529 6732).* **Train** 4, 5, 6, N, R or L to Union Square. **Open** 11.30am-midnight Mon-Fri; noon-midnight Sat; 3-10pm Sun. **Credit** AmEx, MC, V.
A grand old New York wood-panelled and mirrored bar that is now over 100 years old. An urban crowd of regulars stops by for good pub food, stiff drinks and witty conversation.
*Disabled: access, toilets.*

### Pete's Tavern

*129 East 18th Street, off Irving Place (473 7676).* **Train** 4, 5, 6, L, N or R to Union Square. **Open** 11.30am-11.30pm Mon-Thur, Sun; noon-12.30am Fri, Sat. **Credit** AmEx, DC, Discover, MC, V.
A busy bar, with good plain food, Pete's is a historic watering hole. They say O'Henry wrote *The Gift of the Magi* here.
*Disabled: access. Pavement tables.*

### PJ Clarke's

*915 Third Avenue, at East 55th Street (355 8857).* **Train** 6 to 51st Street; E or F to Lexington Avenue. **Open** 10am-4am daily. **Credit** AmEx, DC, MC, V.
A classic mahogany and cut-glass saloon which survived Prohibition and became famous as a location for *The Lost Weekend*. Ol' Blue Eyes is still on the jukebox and decent eats are served in the back. An assorted crowd of besuited account execs and bejeaned piss artists congregate in the bar after work to swig New Amsterdam beer from the bottle and debate economic theory.
*Disabled: access.*

### Puffy's Tavern

*81 Hudson Street, at Harrison Street (766 9159).* **Train** 1, 2, 3, 9, A or C to Chambers Street. **Open** noon-4am Mon-Fri; 3pm-4am Sat, Sun. **No credit cards.**
An artsy, but not fartsy, TriBeCa bar where friendly folks from all over gang up with old pals to reminisce, play darts and down pitchers of beer in casual surroundings.
*Disabled: access, toilets.*

### Rainbow Promenade

*GE Building (65th floor), Rockefeller Plaza, 30 Rockefeller Plaza, Sixth Avenue, at 50th Street (632 5000).* **Train** B, D, F or Q to 47-50th Street. **Open** 4pm-1am Tue-Fri; 4pm-2am Sat; noon-11.30pm Sun; 4-11.30pm Mon. **Credit** AmEx, MC, V.
Sipping cocktails on the 65th floor while the city glitters below you is one of the most impossibly romantic experiences available. Pricey, at around ten bucks a fancy drink, but worth it for the timeless class of the place. Jackets required, no jeans.
*Disabled: access with assistance, toilets. Booking advised.*

### Royalton

*44 West 44th Street, between Fifth & Sixth Avenues (869 4400).* **Train** B, D, F or Q to 42nd Street. **Open** 11.30am-1am Mon-Thur, Sun; 11.30am-2am Fri, Sat. **Credit** AmEx, DC, MC, V.
The Royalton offers a post-modern update of the elegant New York world of cocktails and romance. Whether you're waiting for dinner in the excellent restaurant or watching the lifts for emerging superstars, a drink or two here will allow your inner sophistication to kick in. The bar specialises in flavoured vodkas and vintage port. Don't miss out on Philippe Starck's interplanetary bathrooms, which, after a martini or two, can be completely defeating (*see chapter* **Accommodation**).
*Disabled: access, toilets.*

### Sapphire

*249 Eldridge Street, off Houston Street (777 5153).* **Train** C or E to Spring Street. **Open** 7pm-2.30am Mon, Tue; 7pm-4am Wed-Sun. **No credit cards**.
Sapphire is where SoHo trendies come face to face with young ex-pat UK ravers. There's a different DJ every night and on Fridays especially the place can take off. A relaxed, unpretentious scene where fresh-off-the-boat Brits club together for warmth.
*Disabled: access.*

### Sophie's

*East 5th Street, between Avenues A & B (no phone).* **Train** F to Second Avenue. **Open** 11am-4am daily. **No**

**credit cards**.
One of the quintessential New York dive bars. Two-dollar draught beers, a competitive pool table and a killer jukebox are what entices them in.

### Temple Bar
*332 Lafayette Street, between Bleecker & Houston Streets (925 4242).* **Train** 6 to Bleecker Street. **Open** 5pm-1am Mon-Thur; 7pm-2am Fri, Sat. **Credit** AmEx, DC, MC, V.
The bartenders are hand-crafted from fine aristocratic stock, and the decor is equally opulent, lending an other-worldly air to a long dark night of expensive drinking.
*Disabled: access, toilets.*

### Tenth Street Lounge
*212 East 10th Street, between First & Second Avenues (473 5252).* **Train** L to First Avenue. **Open** 5pm-3am Mon-Sat; 4pm-2am Sun. **Credit** AmEx.
It feels like a private drinking club, and people often walk past without noticing it, but inside, in its atmosphere of pampered minimalism, you sink into the padded leather sofas, and have your drinks regularly serviced by unobtainably beautiful waitresses.
*Disabled: access, toilets.*

### Three of Cups
*83 First Avenue at 5th Street (388 0059).* **Train** F to Second Avenue. **Open** 8pm-4am daily. **No credit cards**.
The restaurant above is excellent, but the bar has a separate entrance, is lit exclusively by big fat candles and is a cosy cave-like retreat, soundtracked by decent rock music.

### Vazac's Horseshoe Bar
*108 Avenue B, at 7th Street (473 8840).* **Train** L to First Avenue. **Open** noon-4am daily. **Credit** AmEx.
If it looks familiar that's because it's been in countless movies; cast, no doubt, for its unchanged spit-and-sawdust post-prohibition ambience. The drink of choice is a pitcher of cheap beer, the crowd a bizarre mix of everybody, and the activity on most people's minds involves the opposite sex.
*Disabled: access, toilets.*

### Westside Brewery
*340 Amsterdam Avenue, at 76th Street (721 2161).* **Train** B or C to 72nd Street. **Open** noon-2 or 3am daily. **Credit** AmEx, MC, V.
Beer is brewed on site. Try the Snakebite or the ever-popular Lemon Wheat. The $4 pints lure hordes of twenty-somethings.

### The Whiskey
*235 West 46th Street, lobby of Paramount Hotel (819 0404).* **Train** 1, 2 or 3 to 42nd Street. **Open** 4pm-4am daily. **Credit** AmEx, DC, Discover, JCB, MC, V.
Designed by Philippe Starck, this trendy nightspot attracts the bold and the beautiful, not least the bands and models who check in at the Paramount next door.
*Disabled: access, toilets.*

### White Horse
*567 Hudson Street, at 11th Street (243 9260).* **Train** A, C, E or L to 14th Street/Eighth Avenue. **Open** 11am-2am Mon-Thur, Sun; 11am-4am Fri, Sat. **No credit cards**.
A very pubbable pub, with beer in pints and plenty of large tables and involved conversation to match its literary history. Awful food, but ask to see where Dylan Thomas fell after he took the whiskey record (26).
*Disabled: access (bar only), toilets. Pavement tables.*

### Zip City
*3 West 18th Street, between Fifth & Sixth Avenues (366 6333).* **Train** 4, 5, 6, L, N or R to Union Square. **Open** 11.30am-2am Mon-Fri; noon-2am Sat, Sun. **Credit** AmEx, DC, Discover, MC, V.
In contrast to the dark and smoky ambience of most beery venues, Zip City manages to combine on-site brewing with a decor of Conran-style blondeness. The imbibers are Young, Urban and Professional; the tap beers (there are only three) light, medium or dark. They taste like upmarket home brew, with a delightful citrus hint and a reassuring cloudiness. Classy bottled beers (no Budweiser riff-raff) are also kept.
*Disabled: access, toilets.*

## Cafés

In the last couple of years New York has suddenly rediscovered espresso. Seemingly hundreds of coffee bars have sprung up, all catering to the wandering masses who need to sit down and collect their thoughts with a cup of black magic before re-embarking on their missions. A lot of them are chains – the McDonald's of the dark roast – and there are so many that in a year's time half of them will have undoubtedly gone bust.

However, smaller places (we've indicated which) offer a chance to smoke – hard to find in New York these days – and all have a wide range of gourmet bean brews, along with sandwiches and pastries to fill that gap, and it's all a sign that New York café society is alive and well. There's even a magazine, *Cups* ($2, free in cafés), covering the 'scene'.

### @ Café
*12 St Mark's Place, between Second & Third Avenues (979 5439).* **Train** 6 to Astor Place. **Open** 11.30am-midnight Sun-Thur; 11.30-2am Fri, Sat. **Credit** AmEx, DC, MC, V.
A great name for a cybercafé. @, largely due to its location on the anarcho-crusty strip of St Mark's, is one of the best of several Internet-educating joints that have sprung up recently. $5 gets you an hour on the Net, surrounded by helpful users, good food and great coffee.
*Pavement tables. Smoking at bar.*

### 9
*110 St Mark's Place, between First Avenue & Avenue A (982 7129).* **Train** L to First Avenue. **Open** 10am-1am Mon-Thur; 10am-2am Fri, Sat; 10am-midnight Sun. **Brunch served** 10am-4pm daily. **Credit** AmEx, MC, V.
A colourful San Francisco style café, with painted chairs and great eggs benedict, as well as coffee and cakes. Perfect for brunch.
*Disabled: access.*

### Big Cup
*228 Eighth Avenue, between 21st & 22nd Streets (206 0059).* **Train** C or E to 23rd Street. **Open** 7am-2am Sun-Thur; 7am-3am Fri, Sat. **No credit cards**.
A breezy place with a clubby, mixed crowd and lots of themed nights (bingo, fortune telling...) to add to the fun.
*Disabled: access, toilets.*

### Café Borgia
*185 Bleecker Street, at MacDougal Street (473 2290).* **Train** A, B, C, D, E, F or Q to West 4 Street. **Open** 10am-2am Mon-Thur; 10am-4am Fri, Sat. **No credit cards**.
This café in the heart of the Village is where Bob Dylan began his rise to fame. The furniture is eclectic and dark, faded murals adorn the walls. The mudcake pudding is special but prices are steep.

### Café La Fortuna
*69 West 71st Street, between Central Park West & Columbus Avenue (724 5846).* **Train** 1, 2, 3, B or C to

**The Original Espresso Bar** – *cake heaven.*

72nd Street. **Open** 12.30pm-12.30am Tue-Thur; noon-1am Fri-Sun. **No credit cards**.
Opera lovers and lovers flock to this wonderful little shop with it's small back garden. The brick walls are covered with opera memorabilia and the soundtrack is Callas and Pavarotti. Try tiramisu cake, cassata Siciliana cake and the pies and biscotti. This was one of John Lennon's hangouts.
*Disabled: access, toilets. Garden.*

### Café Mozart

*154 West 70th Street, between Columbus & Broadway (595 9797).* **Train** 1, 2, 3 or 9 to 72nd Street. **Open** 11am-3am daily. **Credit** AmEx, DC, Discover, MC, V.
This large German/Austrian flavoured coffee shop serves big bowls of caffè latte. The cakes are excellent, there is live piano music at night and it's a great place to loiter while reading magazines or playing chess.
*Smoking.*

### Caffé Reggio

*119 MacDougal Street, between West 3rd & Bleecker Streets (475 9557).* **Train** A, B, C, D, E, F or Q to West 4th Street. **Open** 9.30am-2am Mon-Thur, Sun; 9.30am-3am Fri, Sat. **No credit cards**.
One of the favourite people-watching spots in Greenwich Village, Reggio has great espresso and luscious cakes.
*Disabled: access. Smoking area. Pavement tables.*

### De Roberti's

*176 First Avenue, at East 11th Street (674 7137).* **Train** L to 1st Avenue. **Open** 9.30am-11pm Mon-Thur, Sun; 9.30am-midnight Fri, Sat. **Credit** MC, V.
A remnant of earlier residents, De Roberti's is one of two great Italian patisseries in the area. Veniero's, listed below, is the other.
*Pavement tables in summer.*

### Espresso Bar The Original

*82 Christopher Street, at Seventh Avenue (627 3870).* **Train** 1 or 9 to Christopher Street. **Open** 7am-midnight Mon-Thur; 7am-2am Fri; 8am-2am Sat; 8am-midnight Sun. **Credit** AmEx, DC, Discover, MC, V.
Just off Sheridan Square, this great new coffee shop draws in a mainly gay crowd the with great music, incredible cakes and a vast range of bean-based beverages.
*Disabled: access, toilets. Garden. Smoking.*

### Le Figaro Café

*184 Bleecker Street, at MacDougal Street (677 1100).* **Train** A, B, C, D, E, F or Q to West 4th Street. **Open** 11am-2am Mon-Thur; 10am-4am Fri, Sat; 10am-2am Sun. **No credit cards**.
It's just an old-fashioned café now the Beatniks have grown grey. Musicians pass the hat round at weekends; try to sit outside in the summer.
*Disabled: access, toilets. Pavement tables in summer.*

### Henri Bendel's Salon de Thé

*712 Fifth Avenue, corner 56th Street (247 1100).* **Train** 4, 5 or 6 to 59th Street. **Open** 11am-6pm Mon-Sat; noon-5pm Sun. **High tea served** 2-5pm daily. **Credit** AmEx, DC, Discover, MC, V.
Located on the mezzanine inside Bendel's, the Salon is decorated with colourful teapot displays and other fancy details. Take a high tea of finger sandwiches, scones, muffins and pastries (plus tea or coffee) for $14.
*Disabled: access, toilets.*

### Hungarian Pastry Shop

*1030 Amsterdam Avenue, at 111th Street (866 4230).* **Train** 1, 9, B or C to 110th Street. **Open** 9am-11.30pm Mon-Sat; 9am-10.30pm Sun. **No credit cards**.
The cakes are stale, the service is detached, but you'll find the bohemian select of Columbia University here agonising over their creative writing assignments. Stay all day amid the cramped tables of crammers.

### Life Café

*343 East 10th Street, at Avenue B (477 8791).* **Train** 6 to Astor Place. **Café open** noon-midnight Mon-Thur, Sun; 11am-2am Fri, Sat. **Bar open** 11am-2am Mon-Sat; 11am-midnight Sun. **Credit** CB, DC, Discover, MC, V.
This popular East Village café looks out on to Tompkins Square Park, and inside is a haven for healthy eaters. Salads, light meat dishes, pasta – even seaweed – are on the menu. The hot chocolate served in winter is memorable.
*Disabled: access. Smoking at bar.*

### Newsbar Inc

*2 West 19th Street (255 3996).* **Train** 1 or 9 to 18th Street. **Open** 7.30am-8pm Mon-Fri; 8am-8pm Sat, Sun. **Credit** MC, V.
This is industrial chic New York-style, designed by Wayne Turett. One entire interior wall is devoted to racks of magazines from around the world. Quiche and small sarnies are served at this rest-stop for shoppers from Fifth Avenue.
*Pavement tables.*

### Rumpelmayer's

*at the St Moritz Hotel, 50 Central Park South (755 5800).* **Train** B or Q to 57th Street. **Open** 7am-midnight daily. **Credit** AmEx, DC, MC, V.
This is an old-fashioned New York ice cream parlour, a place to try a real knickerbocker glory or egg cream after a stroll in the park.
*Disabled: access, toilets. Pavement tables.*

### Tea and Sympathy

*108 Greenwich Avenue, at 13th Street (807 8329).* **Train** 1, 2, 3, 9 or L to 14th Street/Sixth Avenue. **Open** 11.30am-10.30pm Mon-Fri; 10am-10.30pm Sat, Sun. **No credit cards**.
Flop down in this oasis of English home cooking and enjoy authentic beans on toast followed by treacle pudding and custard. Wash it down with a selection from more than two dozen kinds of proper tea (none of those waterproof American teabags). A sweet and lovely place where chatting is the thing and British stars pop in for a dose of reality. Ask owner Nicky about T-Rex....
*Pavement tables. Smoking.*

### Veniero's

*342 East 11th Street, at First Avenue (674 7264).* **Open** 8am-midnight Mon-Thur, Sun; 8am-1am Fri, Sat. **Credit** AmEx, MC, V.
A busy, bright and colourful café and bakery. Walk all the way around the huge display case to the eat-in area. Order a selection of mini-pastries with cappuccino (iced with whipped cream in the summer), then take a number, queue up and order some butter cookies to take away.
*Pavement tables in summer.*

# Shopping & Services

# Shopping

***New York is the world capital of accumulation therapy, so even if you hadn't planned it, you'd better put on your shopping shoes and distribute some dollars.***

When it comes to American pastimes, shopping is right up there with football and television. And whether you're after treasures or bargains, if you can't buy it in New York City, they don't make it any more. Don't be overwhelmed by the frenzied consumer culture here. Ignore the fact that most stores look as if their owners are preparing to flee the country: permanent closing-down sales and bazaar-like floor plans are the norm (except, of course, for the swank environs of upper Fifth Avenue and the SoHo designer stores). Some of the best shopping is to be done in places that look quite dreadful.

Be warned that it is common to find identical merchandise a few blocks away at double or half the price you have just paid. As with anything in New York, you will always do better if you know exactly what you want and have a good idea of its market value. Rest assured, however – even if you pay top dollar for something, you'd still have paid more in Europe.

The post-Christmas reductions now seem to occur earlier in December, and Presidents' Day in mid February is a good day for big sales, but there are sales on somewhere all the time, notably in the department stores. *New York* magazine has a weekly Sales & Bargains column; also check the ads in the *New York Times*.

Designers' sample sales are good sources of low-priced clothes: for information about what's on where, either pick up a copy of *The S&B Report* (available from 108 East 38th Street, suite 2000, NY 10016, 683 7612); or call the Bargain Hotline (540 0123); telephone calls are charged at $1.95 for the first minute, then at about 75¢ a minute. These are also sources for details of appliance, furniture

*The famously huge* ***Macy's****, which occupies an entire city block.* *See page 153.*

and other sales, as well as clothes. *Time Out New York*'s Check Out section lists the best of all the sales every week.

Most shops are open late, some very late indeed. Some Downtown stores in Greenwich Village and SoHo may not open until noon to compensate, however. Many open on Sunday. The 8.25 per cent city sales tax is added on at the time of purchase; it is almost never included in the price-tag. At some of the larger and more tourist-oriented places you can avoid paying this if you are having your purchase mailed or shipped outside New York State.

## Shopping Areas

### World Financial Center

Four enormous new skyscrapers built on reclaimed land and crammed with restaurants and shops are the core of Battery Park City, at the southern tip of Manhattan. In the central courtyard is the very successful Winter Garden, which is full of high palm trees and flanked by a wide variety of shops and cafés.

### SoHo

As an artists' neighbourhood turned very fashionable, SoHo is good for bookstores, art shops, antique clothes, furniture and new designers, as well as flagship stores for such designers as Comme des Garçons. Lower Broadway below Houston, bordering on SoHo, is becoming more popular for shops and art galleries, while the area further north, around Astor Place, has become enticingly tacky and touristy.

### Canal Street

Canal Street is where you get fake Rolexes and Chanel bags, as well as the best DJ mix tapes, from market stalls selling counterfeit designer wares, electronics, sports shoes cheap jeans and miscellaneous tat.

### Lower East Side

This is bargain-hunting territory. Many of the shops close early on Fridays and all day Saturdays for the Jewish Sabbath. Go during the week for serious shopping, but take a look at the mad scramble on Sundays. It's well worth trying to bargain, and cash is always preferred. Shops – particularly on the Orchard Street strip from Houston to Delancey Streets – are stuffed to the rafters with handbags, clothes, shoes, luggage, hats and cut-price garments. It's good for jeans, sneakers and leather aviator jackets. Try Cohen's Optical for discount spectacles. Also here is Ludlow Street, a blossoming strip of shops and bars full of fresh fashion talent.

### Greenwich Village

The winding streets make for pleasant wandering, though they get very busy at weekends. The Village is good for bookstores, records, casual and antique clothing and speciality food shops. Many shops don't open till 11am or noon and stay open well into the evening.

### East Village

The shops have extended into Alphabet City, and between Avenue A and Broadway, especially on St Marks Place, you'll find punky/clubby gear, second-hand clothing, books, boots and records. Many showcase shops for young new designers are here. Often the goods – lots of zany, original designs – are made on the premises; keep an eye on the quality and fit. Many shops are closed on Mondays, and almost all open and close late.

### Fifth Avenue

The lower area, 14th-23rd Streets, previously something of a shopping desert, is the latest chunk of Manhattan to be developed and has seen a number of new stores opening (and closing) in the past few years. Broadway here is famous for its antique stores and designer furniture galleries. The upper stretch, from 39th-59th Streets, is the domain of the grand department stores. Visit some of the famous Fifth Avenue stores just to see how you'd shop if you had more money than sense. Have some fun trying on all the things you'll never be able to afford.

### Madison Avenue

Madison Avenue and its environs is the place for Perry/Blahnik heels and fur coats, very expensive top designers – Ralph Lauren, St Laurent, etc – beauty salons, pet salons, Belgian chocolates and some great (but expensive) speciality shops. It's great for window shopping and celebrity spotting, especially at weekends.

### Columbus Avenue

Gentrification has run rife in the last few years, and now Columbus Avenue and, most recently, Amsterdam Avenue are littered with *gelati* stores, David's Cookies and T-shirts galore, as well as antiques, expensive designer stores and fashionable restaurants.

### Harlem

If you venture up to 125th Street, this is sneaker heaven, and the shops between Lenox and Eighth Avenues will have the very latest styles at prices lower than most of the downtown stores. This is also where to come for the cheapest hip-hop flavoured clothing

## Department Stores

### Barneys

*106 Seventh Avenue, between West 17th & West 18th Streets (593 7800).* **Train** 1, 2, 3 or 9 to 14th Street; L to Sixth Avenue. **Open** 10am-9pm Mon-Thur; 10am-8pm Fri; 10am-7pm Sat; noon-6pm Sun. **Credit** AmEx, MC, V.

If you have to choose one store to visit, make it this one. Barneys embodies modern New York style. All the top designers are represented and there's a good selection of lesser-known labels. It also stocks choice home furnishings, unusual children's clothes and a good range of Filofax essentials. The windows, particularly in December, are some of the best in town. There's an airy atrium and an elegant café on the lower floor; even the toilets are special. The $100 million flagship branch on Madison Avenue opened its doors in September 1993 and will now go head to head with Bergdorfs, Saks, Bloomingdales and other Uptown establishments in a war that *Vanity Fair* referred to as the retail equivalent of Bosnia-Herzegovina. Take a look and see how things turned out in the Upper East Side trenches.

*Free alterations.*

**Branch**: 660 Madison Avenue, at 61st Street (826 8900).

### Bergdorf Goodman

*754 Fifth Avenue, at 58th Street (753 7300).* **Train** E or F to 53rd Street. **Open** 10am-6pm Mon-Wed, Fri, Sat; 10am-8pm Thur. **Credit** AmEx, JCB, MC, V.

Bergdorf's knows style. It is one of the best of the department stores for clothes and accessory shopping, being neither too big nor too cavernous. As well as selling all the major American and European designers, Bergdorf's has a number of exclusive lines. Clothes are expensive and high quality but it has very good and famous sales and is an excellent store for celebrity spotting. The Frederic Fekkai salon on the seventh floor has a three-month wait if you want to see the man himself (everyone who is anyone, does; *see chapter* **Services**). The men's store is across the street.

### Bloomingdales

*1000 Third Avenue, at East 59th Street (355 5900).* **Train** 4, 5, 6, N or R to 59th Street. **Open** 10am-8pm Mon-Fri; 10am-7pm Sat; 11am-7pm Sun. **Credit** AmEx, MC, V.

A gigantic and still glamorous department store that has everything you could want to buy, if you can bear to search for it. However, it all tends to be a bit of a scrum, especially at weekends. The ground floor is good for handbags, scarves, hosiery and the latest jewellery, and the basement food department is famous for its array of comestibles. The big designer names are all here, as well as a good selection of cheaper clothes. There are some bright and cheerful gifts on the upper floors.

### Henri Bendel

*714 Fifth Avenue, at 56th Street (247 1100).* **Train** 4, 5, 6, N or R to 59th Street/Lexington Avenue. **Open** 10am-7pm Mon-Wed, Fri, Sat; 10am-8pm Thur; noon to 6pm Sun. **Credit** AmEx, DC, Discover, JCB, MC, V.

Bendel is, strictly speaking, not a department store and its lavish quarters more closely resemble a plush town house. An elegant winding staircase, created by artist Marie-Paulle Pelle, sweeps up through the many storeys. Designer James Mansour kept Bendel's original boutiques and has added several eye-grabbing extras. Prices are comparable with those in other upmarket stores, but somehow things look more desirable here. New additions include a Susan Bennis/Warren Edwards Shoe Salon on the fourth floor and a Claude Montana boutique on the first.

### Lord & Taylor

*424 Fifth Avenue, between 38th & 39th Streets (391 3344).* **Train** B, D, F or Q to 42nd Street. **Open** 10am-

*The determinedly tasteful* **Saks Fifth Avenue**. *See page 153.*

7pm Mon, Tue; 10am-8.30pmWed-Fri; 9am-7pm Sat; 11am-6pm Sun. **Credit** AmEx, Discover, MC, V.
Lord & Taylor's is a conservative, smart (in a conservative kind of way), rather old-fashioned store. American designers are well represented, and the furniture and shoe departments are traditionally its strengths. Service is decent and there are often good sales. It was here that the Fifth Avenue tradition of dramatic Christmas window displays began.

### Macy's

*Herald Square, 151 West 34th Street, between Broadway & Seventh Avenue (695 4400/736 5151 customer service).* **Train** B, D, F, N, Q or R to 34th Street. **Open** 10am-8.30pm Mon, Thur, Fri; 9.45am-7pm Tue, Wed, Sat; 11am-6pm Sun (hours change seasonally; open later around Christmas). **Credit** AmEx, MC, V.
It still calls itself the biggest department store in the world, and occupies an entire city block. Since the parent company went into bankruptcy protection in 1991, the excesses of its famous sales have been considerably reduced, and most things are cheaper somewhere else. But you'll find everything from designer labels to cheap colourful casuals, plus a pet shop, a fish market, a Metropolitan Museum gift shop and a bar. Watch out for the aggressive perfume sprayers and resign yourself to getting hopelessly lost. The store has its own concierge service (560 3827) to help you maximise your shopping potential.

### Saks Fifth Avenue

*611 Fifth Avenue, between 49th & 50th Streets (753 4000).* **Train** B, D, F or Q to Rockefeller Center; E or F to 53rd Street. **Open** 10am-6.30pm Mon-Wed, Fri, Sat; 10am-8pm Thur; noon-6pm Sun. **Credit** AmEx, CB, DC, Discover, JCB, MC, V.
Saks is not interested in fashion for fashion's sake but in good taste. The classic department store has all the big names, an excellent men's department, fine household linens, a newly expanded kids' section and good service, but no restaurant and no furnishings. Floors are laid out in a circle so it's less confusing than some other stores. The ground floor is packed with accessories and there's a stylish beauty area, where personal consultations and makeovers are available. Upstairs, you'll find a well-chosen selection of fashion in the Tower section, next to the escalator on upper levels.

### Takashimaya

*693 Fifth Avenue, between 54th & 55th Streets (350 0100).* **Train** E or F to 53rd Street. **Open** 10am-6pm Mon-Wed, Fri, Sat; 10am-8pm Thur. **Credit** AmEx, DC, Discover, JCB, MC, V.
The first New York branch of this Japanese department store opened in April 1993 and has been giving Bergdorfs a run for its money. The five-storey cross-cultural forum provides an eclectic mix of Eastern and Western aesthetics and the sales staff are discreet. The first two floors offer 4500sq ft of art gallery space and a men's and women's signature collection; the top floor is dedicated to designer accessories.

## Beauty Shops

Most drugstores in New York stock a range of good, cheap make-up and general beauty products (*see below* **Pharmacists**). Department stores are a good source of the major names, but you will probably pay more than you would at some of the discount stores. *See also below* **Green.**

### Aveda

*509 Madison Avenue, between 52nd & 53rd Streets (832 2416).* **Train** 6 to 51st Street. **Open** 10am-7pm Mon-Fri; 10am-6pm Sat. **Credit** AmEx, MC, V.
A small but potent boutique filled with an exclusive line of hair- and skincare products, make-up, massage oils and cleansers, all made from flower and plant extracts and free of animal by-products. A tranquil place.
**Branches**: 233 Spring Street (807 1492); 456 West Broadway (473 0280).

### Blochs Pharmacy

*Third Avenue, at 74th Street (288 2224).* **Train** 6 to 77th Street. **Open** 9am-9pm Mon-Fri; 9am-7pm Sat. **Credit** AmEx, DC, MC, V.
One of the best stores for hair accessories, with hundreds of headbands, combs, brushes, hats and other accoutrements. There's also a well-stocked cosmetics counter with Chanel, Lancôme and Clarins. And you can get prescription drugs.

### Boyd's Chemists

*655 Madison Avenue, between 60th & 61st Streets (838 6558).* **Train** 4, 5, 6, N or R to 59th Street. **Open** 8.30am-7.30pm Mon-Fri; 9.30am-7pm Sat; noon-6pm Sun. **Credit** AmEx, DC, Discover, JCB, MC, V.
This 50-year-old pharmacy, boutique and salon stocks the largest selection of hair accessories and eyeshadow ever assembled under one roof. It also offers facials, makeovers, manicures and so on. Boyd's has its own cosmetics line, Renoir, which includes all the hot matte shades from the 1960s that are so hard to find. Cher loves them; so do Lauren Bacall, Meryl Streep and Julie Andrews.

### MAC

*14 Christopher Street, between Sixth & Seventh Avenues (243 4150).* **Train** 1 or 9 to Christopher Street. **Open** noon-7pm Mon-Sat; 1-6pm Sun. **Credit** AmEx, MC, V.
Make-up Art Cosmetics, a Canadian company, is committed to cruelty-free products famed for its creamy lipsticks and otherwise unobtainable colours. The Queen of New York, drag star Lady Bunny, used to give consultations here.

### National Wholesale Liquidators

*632 Broadway, between Bleecker & Houston Streets (979 2400).* **Train** B, D, F or Q to Broadway/Lafayette. **Open** 9am-8.30pm Mon-Sat; 11am-7pm Sun. **Credit** AmEx, DC, Discover, JCB, MC, V.
A palace of crazy reductions on all manner of things including a vast selection of big brand-name cosmetics. The stock here is never the same on any two visits, so if you find something you want, buy lots of it.

## Books

New York is not short of bookshops. Most stores will mail books overseas for you (if the books are shipped out of state, you don't pay the sales tax, which usually works out about the same as mailing charges). The chain, **Barnes & Noble**, has expanded considerably in the past few years and its new 'complete and unabridged' stores offer massive discounts on recent hardbacks and bestsellers. It's uncertain what effect this will have on the smaller landmark stores like Endicott, which continue to provide meticulous service.

## General

### Barnes & Noble

*105 Fifth Avenue, at 18th Street (675 5500).* **Train** 4, 5, 6, L, N or R to Union Square. **Open** 9.30am-7.45pm Mon-Fri; 9.30am-6.15pm Sat; 11am-5.45pm Sun. **Credit** AmEx, DC, Discover, MC, V.
The world's largest bookstore and the flagship of this bustling chain is a good source of recent hardbacks and dis-

count prices. The record, tape and CD department has one of the largest classical music selections in the city, as well as videos, and there are also children's books and toys and an enormous number of used paperbacks, including many play scripts. The sales annex across the street at 107 Fifth Avenue (691 3370) has a sizeable selection of remaindered, used and out-of-print titles. Of B&Ns many branches, the new megastore at 2289 Broadway (at 82nd Street) carries over 1500 magazines and newspapers and features a children's theatre, reading area, gift-wrapping service and other attractions.

### Books & Co

*939 Madison Avenue, at East 75th Street (737 1450).* **Train** 6 to 77th Street. **Open** 10am-7pm Mon-Fri; 10am-6pm Sat; noon-6pm Sun. **Credit** AmEx, MC, V.
This excellent art and literature bookshop next to the Whitney Museum carries some small press and hard-to-get titles, and holds readings and book launches.

### Doubleday Bookshop

*724 Fifth Avenue, at 57th Street (397 0550).* **Train** 4, 5, 6, N or R to 59th Street/Lexington Avenue. **Open** 9am-11pm Mon-Sat; noon-7pm Sun. **Credit** AmEx, Discover, MC, V.
A large shop with a great selection of hardbacks and paperbacks, Doubleday stocks contemporary fiction and the classics. From the glass lift that takes you from the basement to the second floor you get a good view of the whole store.

### Gotham Book Mart

*41 West 47th Street, near Sixth Avenue (719 4448).* **Train** B, D, F or Q to Rockefeller Center. **Open** 9.30am-6.30pm Mon-Fri; 9.30am-m6pm Sat. **Credit** AmEx, MC, V.
'Wise Men Fish Here' is Gotham's motto – and well they might for the fine selection of out-of-print titles, first editions and rare books. Started by Frances Steloff in the 1920s, Gotham was one of the leaders in the fight against censorship, stocking banned books by James Joyce, DH Lawrence and Henry Miller when most others wouldn't. Upstairs is a gallery showing work on literary themes.

### Gryphon Book Shop

*2246 Broadway, between 80th & 81st Streets (362 0706).* **Train** 1 or 9 to 79th Street. **Open** 10am-midnight daily. **Credit** ($20 minimum) MC, V.
Gryphon specialises in poetry and fiction, and also stocks rock 'n' roll records. A good source for second-hand and rare books on theatre, film, music and drama.

### St Mark's Bookshop

*31 Third Avenue, between Eighth & Ninth Avenues (260 7853).* **Train** 6 to Astor Place. **Open** 10am-midnight Mon-Sat; 11am-midnight Sun. **Credit** AmEx, Discover, MC, V.
This late-night East Village literary and political bookstore stocks works on cultural criticism and feminism, and university and small press publications. Newspapers and over 800 periodicals are available, and it's the place to find the most obscure underground newspapers, magazines and imports.

### Strand Book Store

*828 Broadway, at East 12th Street (473 1489).* **Train** 4, 5, 6, L, N or R to 14th Street/Union Square. **Open** 9.30am-9.30pm Mon-Sat; 11am-9.30pm Sun. **Credit** AmEx, DC, Discover, JCB, MC, V.
As recently as the 1950s there were 40 or 50 antiquarian booksellers on Broadway between Astor Place and 14th Street. The Strand is the only one left and is reputedly the largest second-hand bookstore in the US: over two million books on all subjects. Most books are sold at half published price or less; this is a great source of review copies and remainders: a browser's paradise.

## Specialist

### A Photographers Place

*133 Mercer Street, between Prince & Spring Streets(431 9358).* **Train** C or E to Spring Street; N or R to Prince Street. **Open** 11am-8pm Mon-Sat; noon-6pm Sun. **Credit** AmEx, Discover, MC, V.
Books on all subjects by the world's best photographers.

### Biography

*400 Bleecker Street, at West 11th Street (807 8655).* **Train** A, C, E to 14th Street; L to Eighth Avenue. **Open** noon-8pm Mon-Thur; noon-10pm Fri. **Credit** AmEx, MC, V.
Proof, if proof were needed, that biography is of wide interest: this whole store is devoted to it. New titles only.

### The Complete Traveler Bookstore

*199 Madison Avenue, at East 35th Street (685 9007).* **Train** 6 to 33rd Street. **Open** 9am-7pm Mon-Fri; 10am-6pm Sat; noon-5pm Sun. **Credit** AmEx, CB, DC, Discover, JCB, MC, V.
Travel books and maps of all descriptions cover not just New York City and the US, but the world.

### Drama Bookshop

*723 Seventh Avenue, at West 48th Street (944 0595).* **Train** C or E to 50th Street. **Open** 9.30am-7pm Mon, Tue, Thur, Fri; 9.30am-8pm Wed; 10.30am-5.30pm Sat; noon-5pm Sun. **Credit** AmEx, MC, V.
In the middle of the Theatre District: play scripts, biographies, everything for the actor and theatre-goer.

### Forbidden Planet

*821 Broadway, corner of East 12th Street (473 1576).* **Train** 4, 5, 6, L, N or R to 14th Street. **Open** 10am-8.30pm daily. **Credit** AmEx, Discover, MC, V.
If you're a devotee of science fiction and fantasy, you won't be able to resist Forbidden Planet's vast selection of comics – vintage and new titles from around the world. It also has stacks of classic sci-fi fiction, as well as fantasy, horror and thriller books and magazines. There's a pricey toy section.

### Mysterious Book Shop

*129 West 56th Street, between Sixth & Seventh Avenues (765 0900).* **Train** B, D or E to Seventh Avenue; N or R to 57th Street. **Open** 11am-7pm Mon-Sat. **Credit** AmEx, DC, MC, V.
Over 20,000 new and second-hand mystery and murder titles. There's a free rare book locator service.

### New York Bound

*Associated Press Building, lobby of 50 Rockefeller Plaza (245 8503).* **Train** B, D, F or Q to Rockefeller Center. **Open** 10am-6pm Mon-Fri; noon-4pm Sat. **Credit** AmEx, MC, V.
This is a gem: nothing but books on New York, both current and out-of-print titles. You can pick up a 1930s restaurant guide, a novel from 1885, children's titles or photographic essays. The owners are extremely knowledgeable and passionate about their subject.

### Village Comics

*163 Bleecker Street, at Macdougal Street (777 2770).* **Train** A, B, C, D, E, F or Q to West 4th Street. **Open** 9.30am-8.30pm Mon-Wed; 10am-9.30pm Thur-Sat; 11.30am-7.30pm Sun. **Credit** AmEx, Discover, MC, V.
Comics are big business: shop here for complete sets,

*Budget basics at* **Canal Jeans***, page 160.*

CANAL
JEAN CO.
NEW YORK
OPEN 7 DAYS

# Mall fever

New Yorkers are extremely fortunate to have genuine streets and buildings to do their shopping in. Most Americans have to go to the mall. If you'd like to give yourself over to the mind-numbing social control of mall shopping, the Manhattan Mall (Broadway at 34th Street) is a good place to start. Not only is it one of the world's ugliest buildings (a jelly mould made of pinball machine parts?), but it contains branches of nearly every major US retail chain. After that, the malliest parts of New York include the warren of stores underneath the World Trade Center, the slightly more upmarket shops in the World Financial Center and the South Street Seaport, and of course, the pink marble 'opulence' of the outlets in Trump Tower.

To experience the real thing in all its glory, you really have to head to New Jersey. Secaucus and Paramus, only 30 minutes away, are two towns wholly devoted to shopping. At the former you'll find scores of budget-priced factory outlets for many big-name firms, Calvin Klein, Liz Claiborne and B Dalton among them, while the latter is mall heaven, with seven of the things – each of them containing 25-30 stores – sitting along the roadside. Call New Jersey Transit (629 8767) for information about its special shopping excursions by bus.

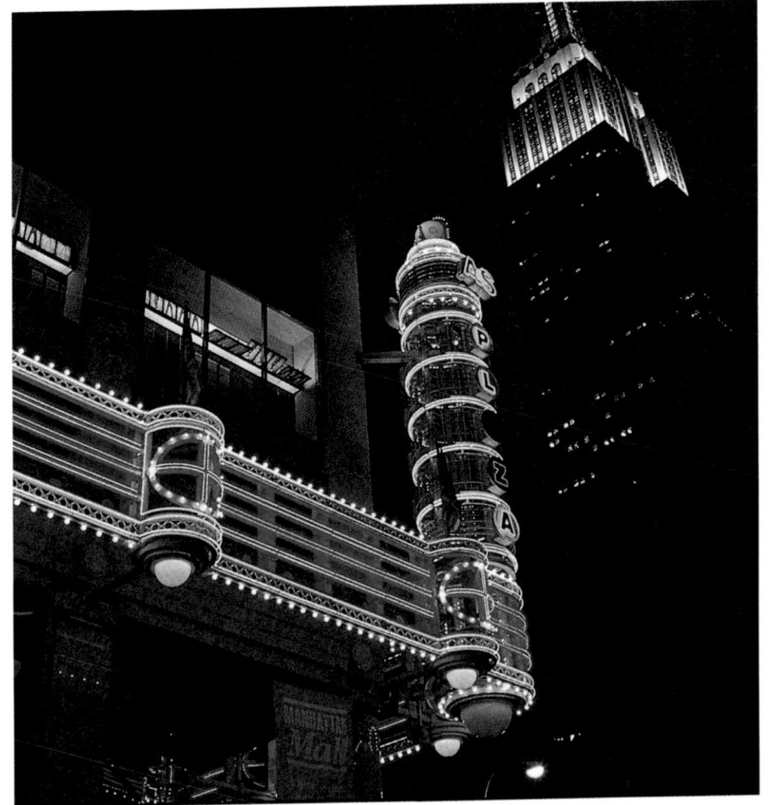

*The shopping experience from hell: the* **Manhattan Mall**.

missing back-numbers of *Marvel* or underground comics and new issues. There's a free mail order service. The Science Fiction Shop is run by the same company; it has premises here, and at 940 Third Avenue, at 56th Street (759 6255).

## Cameras & Electronics

14th Street and the Midtown electronics area offer some great bargains. Rapid turnover allows shopkeepers to price items such as Walkmans, CD players and computers at low, low prices. You should know exactly what you want before venturing inside any of these stores: if you look lost staff will certainly give you the hard sell. If buying a major item, check newspaper ads (the Science section in Tuesday's *New York Times* is good) for price guidelines. If you are really brave, you can get small things like Walkmans even cheaper in the many questionable establishments along Canal Street. However, one reason to go to a more reputable place is to get reliable advice about compatibility – you need to make sure that the item will work in the country in which you want to use it. As well as checking its voltage requirements, be aware that NTSC (the US standard) TVs, VCRs, camcorders – and videotapes – will not work in Australia or Britain. Phones and faxes are also iffy.

### 47th St Photo

*115 West 45th Street, near Sixth Avenue (398 1530).* **Train** B, D, F or Q to Rockefeller Center. **Open** 9am-7pm Mon-Wed; 9am-8pm Thur; 9.30am-3pm Fri; 10am-5pm Sun. **Credit** AmEx, Discover, MC, V.
Bargains are listed daily in big ads published in the *New York Times*. Savings on cameras, all electronic equipment, computers and software can be huge, but you should be prepared to fight and bargain.

### J&R Music World

*33 Park Row, near Centre Street (732 8600).* **Train** 4, 5 or 6 to City Hall; J or M to Chambers Street. **Open** 9am-6.30pm Mon-Sat; 11am-6pm Sun. **Credit** AmEx, Discover, JCB, MC, V.
Everything for home entertainment is here at discount prices: CD players, hi-fis, Walkmans and tapes. See the weekly ads in the *Village Voice*.

### Nobody Beats the Wiz

*726 Broadway, at 7th Street (677 4111).* **Train** N or R to 8th Street. **Open** 10am-10pm Mon-Sat; 10am-7pm Sun. **Credit** AmEx, Discover, MC, V.
We tried to beat them, but of course you can't. With Wiz's claim to match or beat any advertised price on electronic equipment, even the illegal importers on Canal Street have a hard time keeping up. See the ads in the *Voice* and load up on gear and gadgets at prices unbelievable to foreign eyes. It's not only a pricing statement, it's also their name.
**Branches** are too numerous to list: call for your nearest.

### Willoughby's

*136 West 32nd Street, between Sixth & Seventh Avenues (564 1600).* **Train** B, D, F, N, R or Q to 34th Street. **Open** 8.30am-8pm Mon-Fri; 10am-7pm Sat, Sun. **Credit** AmEx, DC, Discover, MC, V.
Willoughby's claims to be the world's largest camera and audio store – and it does seem to stock everything. Know what you are looking for, expect long queues, slow service and heavy security. This area contains many camera stores for easy price comparisons.

## Fashion

## The Designers

### Agnès B

*116 Prince Street, between Wooster & Greene Streets (925 4649).* **Train** N or R to Prince Street. **Open** 11am-7pm Mon-Sat; noon-6pm Sun. **Credit** AmEx, MC, V.
Specialises in simple designs for women, men and children – though the men's lines are available only at the new flagship branch at 79 Green Street (between Broome and Spring Streets). Kiss your savings goodbye if you find yourself actually trying an Agnès B garment on. The fit may well be close to perfect.
**Branches**: 1063 Madison Avenue (570 9333); 79 Green Street (431 4339).

### Anna Sui

*113 Greene Street, between Spring & Prince Streets (941 8406).* **Train** C or E to Spring Street. **Open** noon-7pm Mon-Sat; noon-6pm Sun. **Credit** AmEx, MC, V.
Sui is the quintessential downtown designer, selling young, innovative and reasonably priced clothing to models, movie stars and the generally trendy from her lilac- and black-decorated boudoir.

### Betsey Johnson

*130 Thompson Street, between Prince & Houston Streets (420 0169).* **Train** N or R to Prince Street. **Open** 11am-7pm Mon-Sat; noon-7pm Sun. **Credit** AmEx, MC, V.
Flamboyant, bright and sexy designs just keep on coming from Betsey Johnson, pouring out of stores resplendent with pink neon and fluorescent lighting. Some of the collections are so bright you feel as if you need to wear shades for more than just poseur points.
**Branches**: 248 Columbus Avenue (362 3364); 251 East 60th Street (319 7699); 1060 Madison Avenue (734 1257).

### Calvin Klein

*654 Madison Avenue, at 60th Street (292 9000).* **Train** 4, 5 or 6 to 59th Street. **Open** 10am-6pm Mon-Wed, Fri, Sat; 10am-8pm Thur. **Credit** AmEx, Discover, MC, V.
This flagship store opened in 1995 and sells anything and everything Calvin Klein, from the couture lines to footwear and housewares. Plus of course the ultimate in underwear to peep out from your jeans.

### Comme des Garçons

*116 Wooster Street, between Spring & Prince Streets (219 0660).* **Train** N or R to Prince Street; C, E or K to Spring Street. **Open** 11am-7pm Mon-Sat; noon-6.30pm Sun. **Credit** AmEx, DC, MC, V.
This huge, minimalist flagship store is devoted to Rei Kawakubo's architecturally constructed, quintessentially Japanese designs for men and women, with clothes exhibited like the artworks in the surrounding SoHo galleries.

### Emporio Armani

*110 Fifth Avenue, at 16th Street (727 3240).* **Train** 4, 5, 6, L, N or R to 14th Street. **Open** 11am-7pm Mon-Wed, Fri; 11am-7.30pm Thur; 1-6pm Sun. **Credit** AmEx, DC, JCB, MC, V.
Gorgeous but casual suits and separates for men and women from Giorgio Armani's diffusion line (a little disappointing close up) are showcased in a renovated Stanford White building. Cheaper but not cheap.

### Givenchy

*954 Madison Avenue, at 75th Street (772 1040).* **Train** 6 to 77th Street. **Open** 10am-6pm Mon-Sat. **Credit** AmEx, DC, MC, V.
Discreetly elegant French fashion, from the designer who dressed Audrey Hepburn.

### Issey Miyake

*992 Madison Avenue, at 77th & 78th Streets (439 7822).* **Train** 6 to 77th Street. **Open** 10am-6pm Mon-Fri; 11am-6pm Sat. **Credit** AmEx, MC, V.
This minimalist store houses Issey Miyake's women's and men's collections and accessories. His work is timeless but now features some interesting fabric innovations.

### Missoni

*836 Madison Avenue, at 69th Street (517 9339).* **Train** 6 to 68th Street. **Open** 10am-6pm Mon-Sat. **Credit** AmEx, MC, V.
Italian polychromatic fine knits made of wildly beautiful fabric, but the designs sometimes don't quite match up.

### Omo Norma Kamali

*11 West 56th Street, between Fifth & Sixth Avenues (957 9797).* **Train** B or Q to 57th Street. **Open** 10.30am-6.30pm Mon-Fri; 11am-6pm Sat. **Credit** AmEx, MC, V.
Classic-cut clothes with a slightly offbeat touch. Suits and dresses are shapely, and may have an oddly pleated skirt, a strangely shaped collar or an unusual cut-out. Relatively inexpensive knits are sold alongside great daywear, provocative swimsuits and some spectacular evening designs.

### Paul Smith

*108 Fifth Avenue, between 15th & 16th Streets (627 9770).* **Train** L, N, R, 4, 5 or 6 to 14th Street. **Open** 11am-7pm Mon-Wed, Fri, Sat; 11am-8pm Thur; noon-6pm Sun. **Credit** AmEx, Discover, MC, V.
The relaxed English gentleman look. His clothes are exemplary in their combination of wit, style and quality. Accessories too.

### Polo/Ralph Lauren

*867 Madison Avenue, at 72nd Street (606 2100).* **Train** 6 to 68th Street. **Open** 10am-6pm Mon-Wed, Fri, Sat; 10am-8pm Thur. **Credit** AmEx, DC, Discover, JCB, MC, V.
Ralph Lauren spent $14 million turning the old Rhinelander mansion into an Ivy League superstore: oriental rugs, English paintings, riding whips, leather chairs, old mahogany and fresh flowers. The homeboys, skaters and other young blades who've adopted Ralphie's togs for a season or two head straight to Polo Sport across the street at number 888 (434 8000).

### Romeo Gigli & Spazio

*21 East 69th Street (744 9121).* **Train** 6 to 68th Street. **Open** 10.30am-6.30pm Mon-Sat. **Credit** AmEx, MC, V.
This three-story former townhouse is worth visiting for the interior alone: Fornacetti screens and Murano light fittings. And then of course there's Romeo Gigli.

### Stüssy Store

*104 Prince Street, between Mercer & Greene Streets (274 8855).* **Train** N or R to Prince Street. **Open** noon-7pm Mon-Sat; noon-6pm Sun. **Credit** AmEx, DC, MC, V.
All the fine hats, T-shirts and other skatesome/surfey west-coast gear that Mr Stüssy is famous for.

### Yohji Yamamoto

*103 Grand Street, near Broadway (966 9066).* **Train** 6, J, M, N or R to Canal Street. **Open** 11am-7pm Mon-Sat. **Credit** AmEx, DC, MC, V.
The designer's flagship store is a huge, lofty space filled with well-cut designs.

### Yves Saint Laurent

*855-59 Madison Avenue, between East 70th & East 71st Streets (988 3821).* **Train** 6 to 68th Street. **Open** 10am-6pm Mon-Sat. **Credit** AmEx, DC, MC, V.
Saint Laurent is tired chic, but his clothes are still sought-after and expensive.

## The Stores

### 555 Soul/Strictly For Da Ladies

*151 Ludlow Street, between Stanton & Rivington Streets (995 9252).* **Train** F, J, M or Z to Essex/Delancey Street. **Open** noon-7pm Mon-Sat. **Credit** AmEx, D, MC, V.
Camella Ehlke's soulful triple-five designs deck out the more hip on the hip-hop continuum, as well as classy jazz-steppers and clubbers.

### APC

*131 Mercer Street, between Prince & Spring Streets (966 9685).* **Train** N or R to Prince Street. **Open** 11am-7pm Mon-Sat; noon-6pm Sun. **Credit** AmEx, MC, V.
France's answer to the Gap. Basic essentials in muted colours and minimal styling. A stunning store designed by Julian Schnabel.

### Brooks Bros

*346 Madison Avenue, at East 44th Street (682 8800).* **Train** 4, 5, 6 or 7 to Grand Central. **Open** 8.30am-7pm Mon, Thur; 8.30am-6pm Tue, Wed, Fri, Sat. **Credit** AmEx, DC, JCB, MC, V.
The classic men's store, now owned by Marks & Spencer, is still *the* place for high-quality preppy clothing – button-down shirts, madras jackets, chinos and wonderful striped dressing gowns.
**Branch**: 1 Liberty Plaza (267 2400).

### Canal Jeans

*504 Broadway, between Spring & Broome Streets (226 1130).* **Train** N or R to Prince Street; 6 to Spring Street. **Open** 10am-8pm Mon-Thur, Sun; 10.30am-9pm Fri, Sat; 11am-9pm Sun. **Credit** AmEx, DC, MC, V.
Browse among a vast acreage of jeans, T-shirts and other basics, plus new and vintage clothing and accessories, socks, T-shirts, bags and fun jewellery. Canal's prices are hard to beat on most things.

### Charivari 57

*18 West 57th Street (333 4040).* **Train** E or F to Fifth Avenue. **Open** 10.30am-7pm Mon-Wed, Fri; 10.30am-8pm Thur; 10.30am-6.30pm Sat; 12.30-6pm Sun. **Credit** AmEx, MC, V.
The good, stylish working clothes for men and women are carefully selected from a variety of designers: Gaultier, Ghost, Yamamoto.... Pricey.

### The Cockpit

*595 Broadway, between Prince & Houston Streets (925 5455).* **Train** N or R to Prince Street. **Open** 11am-7pm Mon-Sat; 12.30-6pm Sun. **Credit** AmEx, DC, Discover, MC, V.
You want to look like Cary Grant in *Only Angels Have Wings*? Then visit the Cockpit and invest in the historically correct flying jackets, trousers, boots and helmets. You'll have to go elsewhere for the aeroplane, though.

### Crib

*210 East 6th Street, between Second & Third Avenues (260 9237).* **Train** L to First Avenue. **Open** 1-9pm Mon-Fri, Sun; noon-9pm Sat. **Credit** AmEx, MC, V.
East Village guerrilla shopping at its finest, with vintage gear alongside new streetwear, accessories and graffiti magazines.

### Exploding Sky

*511 East 5th Street, between Avenues A & B* (674 7520). **Train** F to Second Avenue. **Open** 1-8pm Sun-Thur; 1pm-midnight Fri, Sat. **Credit** AmEx, D, MC, V.
Americana reconsidered as East Village workwear escaped from a psychotic Midwestern gas attendant's wardrobe. Lots of T-shirts and shirts with nasty slogans.

*Dress to express at* **Patricia Field**.

## IF

*474 West Broadway, near Houston Street (533 8660).* **Train** 1 or 9 to Houston Street. **Open** noon-7.30pm Mon-Sat; noon-7pm Sun. **Credit** AmEx, DC, Discover, MC, V.

The more avant-garde French and Japanese designers are IF favourites. Great for Martin Margiela, and with a large men's section including Gaultier, plus bags, belts, sunglasses and a shoe selection which includes Robert Clergerie.

## Liquid Sky

*241 Lafayette Street, at Prince Street (343 0532).* **Train** 6 to Spring Street. **Open** 1-8pm Mon-Sat; 2-7pm Sun. **Credit** AmEx, D, MC, V.

Your essential first stop for NYC rave togs at their best, from fresh originals to cavernous baggies and dopey hats and backpacks.

## Made In Detroit

*335 East 9th Street, between First & Second Avenues (995 2592).* **Train** L to First Avenue. **Open** noon-7.30pm Mon-Wed; noon-8pm Thur-Sat; 1-7.30pm Sun. **Credit** AmEx, MC, V.

Fast leather and chic mekanik stylings for the boys and girls of the factory floor. Motorcycle mania meets techno town.

## Mary Adams The Dress

*159 Ludlow Street, at Stanton Street (473 0237).* **Train** F to Second Avenue. **Open** 1-6pm Thur-Sun and by appointment. **No credit cards**.

For frocks' sake. Mary Adams makes beautifully girly new versions of the old-fashioned party dress, favouring silks, satins, velvets and cottons.

## New Republic

*93 Spring Street, between Mercer & Broadway (219 3005).* **Train** E or C to Spring Street; N or R to Prince Street. **Open** noon-7pm Mon-Sat; noon-6pm Sun. **Credit** AmEx, MC, V.

Beautifully made men's and women's clothing and accessories, made with a modern retro 1930s-60s feel.

## New York Leather Company

*33 Christopher Street, near Waverly Place (243 2710).* **Train** A, C, D, E, F or Q to West 4th Street. **Open** 11am-7.30pm Mon-Thur; noon-8.30pm Fri, Sat; 1-5.30pm Sun. **Credit** AmEx, Discover, JCB, MC, V.

Well cut, reasonably priced leather skirts, jackets, trousers, belts and bags in bright and traditional colours can be found here. The zip-up lambskin jackets and bomber jackets with mouton collars are great.

## The Original Levi Store

*750 Lexington Avenue, at 59th Street (826 5957).* **Train** 4, 5 or 6 to 59th Street. **Open** 10am-8pm Mon-Sat; noon-6pm Sun. **Credit** AmEx, Discover, MC, V.

This enormous store houses every piece of real Levi's ever designed. Customers are limited to buying six pairs of jeans at one time. Giant video screens with the latest videos decorate the walls.

## Patricia Field

*10 East 8th Street, near Fifth Avenue (254 1699).* **Train** N or R to 8th Street. **Open** noon-8pm Mon-Sat; 1-7pm Sun. **Credit** AmEx, MC, V.

Field is the New York Vivienne Westwood, brilliant at working club and street fashion. Her store, with its ambisexual staff, has an eclectic mix of original jewellery, on-the-edge club gear and East Village design. There's always something new, the clothing is gorgeous and durable, and the wigs are the best in town.

## Phat Farm

*129 Prince Street, between West Broadway & Wooster (533 7428).* **Train** C or E to Spring Street. **Open** 11am-7pm Mon-Wed; 11.30am-8pm Thur-Sat; noon-6pm Sun. **Credit** AmEx, MC, V.

Russell Simmons' classy and conservative take on hip-hop couture. Phunky-phresh oversized and baggy clothing.

## Studio XTC

*88 Christopher Street, at Seventh Avenue (366 5089).* **Train** 1 or 9 to Christopher Street. **Open** noon-9pm Mon-Fri; noon-midnight Sun. **Credit** MC, V.

An absolutuely fag-ulous treasure trove of all kinds of fetishistic fantasy wear for boys and their boys.

### Trash & Vaudeville

*4 St Mark's Place, between Second & Third Avenues (982 3590).* **Train** 6 to Astor Place. **Open** noon-8pm Mon-Fri; 11.30am-9pm Sat; 1-7.30pm Sun. **Credit** AmEx, MC, V.
This original punk store has two floors of fashion, accessories and shoes: stretchy tube-dresses, leathers, snakeskin boots, collar tips and jewellery.

### Untitled

*26 West 8th Street, near Macdougal Street (505 9725).* **Train** A, B, C, D, E, F or Q to West 4th Street. **Open** 11.30am-8.30pm Mon-Sat; noon-8pm Sun. **Credit** AmEx, DC, Discover, MC, V.
Best NYC locale for Vivienne Westwood: a den of lace, leather, velvet, chiffon and other pricey materials, often festooned with studs. Also a good range of new designers.

### Urban Outfitters

*628 Broadway, between Houston & Bleecker Streets (475 0009).* **Train** B, D, F or Q to Broadway Lafayette. **Open** 10am-10pm Mon-Sat; noon-8pm Sun. **Credit** AmEx, MC, V.
Clothes for urban survival. Basics include jeans and T-shirts for men and women, but this is also a good source for trendy and inexpensive clothing. Labels include Girbaud, Anthopologie, Free People and Esprit. It also stocks vintage 'urban renewal' clothing, gifts and postcards.
**Branches**: 374 Sixth Avenue (677 9350); 127 East 59th Street (688 1200).

### X-Large

*151 Avenue A, between 9th and 10th Streets (477 0012).* **Train** L to First Avenue. **Open** 1-8pm Sun-Fri; noon-8pm Sat. **Credit** AmEx, D, JCB, MC, V.
Famed as the Beastie Boys' store, X-Large keeps you up to date on what goodies Fuct, X-Girl and other west-coast potheads are designing. Also good as a graffiti connection.

## Discount Fashion

### Century 21 Department Store

*22 Cortlandt Street, off Broadway (227 9092).* **Train** 1, 9, N or R to Cortlandt Street. **Open** 7.45am-7pm Mon-Fri; 10am-7pm Sat. **Credit** AmEx, Discover, MC, V.
Some discerning shoppers report finding clothes by Romeo Gigli and Donna Karan here, but you have to visit every 10 days or so to get these kinds of bargains. Rack upon rack is heavy with discounted designer and name-brand fashions. Housewares and appliances are also offered at good discounts, plus underwear, accessories, cosmetics and fragrances, and women's shoes. Good service but no fitting rooms. Regulars use the nearby MacDonald's restroom to make sure their purchase fits.

### Daffy's

*111 Fifth Avenue, at 18th Street (529 4477).* **Train** 4, 5, 6, L, N or R to 14th Street/Union Square. **Open** 10am-9pm Mon-Sat; 11am-6pm Sun. **Credit** MC, Discover, V.
An out-of-town favourite for years, Daffy's has now opened in Manhattan. There are three floors of current mainstream fashions: silk blouses, leather jackets and bags, Calvin Klein and French lingerie, and affordable men's suits and shirts. Prices are much lower than retail stores and there are often remarkable bargains. The kids' clothes are fabulous.
**Branch**: 335 Madison Avenue (557 4422).

### Dollarbills

*99 East 42nd Street, between Lexington & Vanderbilt Avenues (867 0212).* **Train** 4, 5, 6, 7 or S to Grand Central. **Open** 10am-7pm Mon-Fri; 10am-6pm Sat. **Credit** AmEx, DC, MC, V.
Two floors of designer heaven – Versace, Montana, Byblos, Gigli and many more labels for men and women. Also discounted accessories and underwear, belts and ties.

### Loehmann's

*60-66 99th Street, Rego Park, Queens (1-718 271 4000).* **Train** G or R to 63rd Drive/Rego Park. **Open** 10am-6pm Mon, Tue; 10am-9pm Wed-Fri; 10am-7pm Sat; noon-5pm Sun. **Credit** MC, Discover, V.
It's a trek to this famous discount heaven, but well worth it for very low prices, with just enough of the designer label left on garments. Enormous turnover of stock.

### TJ Maxx

*620 Sixth Avenue, at 18th Street (229 0875).* **Train** F or L to 14th Street/Sixth Avenue. **Open** 9.30am-9pm Mon-Sat; 10am-6pm Sun. **Credit** AmEx, DC, MC, V.
This new discount designer clothes store, with its brightly-lit Woolworths-style appearance, is less of an obvious treasure trove than Century 21 (*see above*), but if you're prepared to sift through a rather high rubbish-to-glourious-discoveries ratio, you will undoubtedly find some fabulous purchases. Also household goods, luggage, shoes, etc. And at $4.99 a pair, Maxx's price for Calvin Klein underwear is the cheapest in town.

### Syms

*42 Trinity near Rector Street (797 1199).* **Train** R to Rector Street. **Open** 9am-6.30pm Mon-Wed; 9am-8pm Thur, Fri; 10am-6.30pm Sat; noon-5.30pm Sun. **Credit** AmEx, Discover, MC, V.
Syms is seven storeys of designer discount fashions for men, women and children, with labels still intact. Also shoes and luggage.

## Vintage & Second-hand Clothes

The pyramid scheme of second-hand clothes means the less you have to browse, the more you have to pay. Though we've included them, the stores along lower Broadway ask vastly inflated prices for anything except the most mundane items and unless you have money to burn should really be avoided. The alternatives, too numerous and fast-changing to list, are the many small stores between Avenue A and Second Avenue and about 6th-10th Streets. These (and the now-famous Domsey's) are where real bargains are to be found.

### Alice Underground

*481 Broadway, at Broome Street (431 9067).* **Train** B, D, F or Q to Broadway/Lafayette. **Open** 11am-7.30pm daily. **Credit** AmEx, MC, V.
A good selection of 1940s-60s gear in all sorts of fabrics and in varied condition. Prices are the high side of reasonable.
**Branch**: *380 Columbus Avenue (724 6682).*

### Allan & Suzi

*416 Amsterdam Avenue, at 80th Street (724 7445).* **Train** 1 or 9 to 79th Street. **Open** noon-7pm Mon, Tue; noon-8pm Wed-Fri; noon-7pm Sat; 1-6pm Sun. **Credit** AmEx, JCB, MC, V.
Models drop off their once-worn Alaia, Mugler and Gaultiers here. There is an awesome platform shoe collection. Great store, not cheap.

### Andy's Chee-Pees

*691 Broadway, between East 4th & East 5th Streets (420 5980).* **Train** B, D, F or Q to Broadway/Lafayette. **Open** 11am-9pm Mon-Sat. **Credit** AmEx, MC, V.
Pricey, but good for jeans and shirts.
**Branch**: 16 West 8th Street (460 8488).

**Guv'nors**, *where ex-pat Brits come for their Marmite fix. See page 164.*

### Antique Boutique

*712-14 Broadway, at Washington Place (460 8830).* **Train** 6 to Astor Place; N or R to 8th Street. **Open** 11am-10pm Mon-Sat; noon-8pm Sun. **Credit** AmEx, DC, Discover, JCB, MC, V.

One of the largest shops for vintage gear, Antique Boutique has everything from clothing and hats to jewellery and kitchenware. Not as cheap as it should be.

**Branch**: 227 East 59th Street (752 1680).

### Cheap Jack's

*841 Broadway, between West 13th & West 14th Streets (777 9564).* **Train** 4, 5, 6, L, N or R train to 14th Street/Union Square. **Open** 11am-8pm Mon-Sat; noon-7pm Sun. **Credit** AmEx, MC, V.

A great vintage selection but extortionate prices for anything nice. With army surplus gear that runs into the high hundreds, cheap is the last thing it is.

### Domsey's Warehouse

*431 Kent Avenue, Williamsburg, Brooklyn (1-718 384 6000).* **Train** J, M or Z to Marcy Avenue. **Open** 8am-5.30pm Mon-Fri; 8am-6.30pm Sat; 11am-5.30 Sun. **No credit cards**.

It seems almost a crime to alert more people to the presence of this fabulous source of second-hand clothes. Already the downtown stores are wise to its huge selection of jeans, jackets, military and industrial wear, ballgowns, shoes, hats and pretty much everything else. Especially notable are the Hawaiian shirts at around $5, the sports gear bearing high-school team names (baseball jackets are about $6) and the unreal prices on cowboy boots. It's great for all sorts of Americana, but come midweek for those amazing finds. The front part of the store sells new things, with a market-stall feel to the selection. Out back you can buy unsorted clothes by the pound. Fight it out with the old ladies for a bargain.

### Harriet Love

*126 Prince Street, between Wooster & Greene Streets (966 2280).* **Train** C or E to Spring Street. **Open** 11.30am-7pm Tue-Sun. **Credit** AmEx, MC, V.

One of the first people to sell high fashion 1930s and 40s and clothing. Antique clothes, jewellery and handbags are mixed with new but retro clothing. A nostalgia trip.

### Screaming Mimi

*382 Lafayette Street at 4th Street (677 6464)* **Train** 6 to Astor Place; N or R to 8th Street. **Open** 11am-8pm Mon-Fri; noon-8pm Sat; 1-7pm Sun. **Credit** AmEx, DC, Discover, MC, V.

The prices are more reasonable and the selection more carefully chosen than the Broadway stores around the block. Vintage trainers, all manner of vintage clothes with a few student designers thrown in. Great window displays.

### Transfer

*220 East 60th Street (355 4230).* **Train** 4, 5, 6, R or N to Lexington & 59th Street. **Open** 12.30-7.30pm Mon-Sat. **Credit** AmEx.

Well-connected Manhattanites Roberto Mitrotti and Linda Stein have collected celebrity cast-offs from Ivana Trump, Christie Brinkley, Sting's wife Trudie Styler and a host of others. This is now the best place to buy designer clothes by everyone from Azzedine Alaia to Zang Toi.

## Food

### Balducci's

*424 Sixth Avenue, at 9th Street (673 2600).* **Train** A, B, C, D, E, F or Q to West 4th Street. **Open** 7am-8.30pm daily. **Credit** AmEx, MC, V.

Over three generations, the Balducci family's grocery store has grown into a gourmet emporium that can provide every luxurious foodstuff imaginable, from exotic fruits and freshly picked funghi to edible flowers and properly-hung game birds. Balducci's also sells own-brand pasta and sauces, preserves and salamis.

### Dean & DeLuca

*560 Broadway, at Prince Street (431 1691).* **Train** N or R to Prince Street. **Open** 8am-8pm Mon-Sat; 9am-7pm Sun. **Credit** AmEx, MC, V.

**FAO Schwartz**: *fun for all – and we mean all – the family.* *See page 166.*

Dean & DeLuca is consolidating its position as *the* designer deli. Uninitiated foreigners will be amazed by the range and quality of the stock. The cheese counter is legendary, but this is the place to come for every kind of gourmet delicacy from raspberry vinegar to pâté de foie gras. There are D&D branches at the Guggenheim Museum, Rockefeller Center and Angelika Film Centre.

### The Erotic Baker

*Telephone orders only (721 3217).* **Open** 10am-6pm Tue-Fri. **Credit** AmEx, MC, V.
They get through a lot of flesh-toned icing sugar here. Need we say more?

### Gracie's Marketplace

*1237 Third Avenue, at 71st Street (737 0600).* **Train** 4, 5 or 6 to 68th Street. **Open** 7am-8.30pm Mon-Sat; 8am-7pm Sun. **Credit** AmEx, DC, MC, V.
A schism in the Balducci family (*see above*) caused Grace and her contingent to split off and move to the Upper East Side, where she has established an admirable food store with a similarly overpowering selection of all sorts of fabulous foods. The best bet for one-stop gourmet shopping in the neighbourhood. Very expensive, though.

### Greenmarket

*City-sponsored open-air farmer's markets (information 788 7900, 9am-5pm).*
There are more than 20 open-air markets, sponsored by the City authorities, in various locations and on different days. The most famous is the one in Union Square, which attracts small producers of organic cheeses, honey, vegetables, herbs and flowers. The farmers sell from the back of their flat-bed trucks and go home when they've sold out, which can be early.

### Guss Pickles

*35 Essex Street, between Grand & Hester Streets (254 4477).* **Train** F to East Broadway. **Open** 9am-6pm Mon-Thur, Sun; 9am-2pm Fri. **Credit** MC, V.
Once upon a time there was a notorious rivalry between two pickle merchants, Guss and Hollander, but eventually the thing was settled and Guss put his name over the door of the old Hollander store and became the undisputed Pickle King, selling them sour or half-sour and in several sizes. Also excellent sauerkraut, pickled peppers and watermelon rinds.

### Guv'nors

*443 East 6th Street (614 3260).* **Train** 6 to Astor Place. **Open** noon-8pm Mon-Sat; noon-7pm Sun. **No credit cards.**
A little slice of the UK in NYC, full of Marmite, Weetabix and other essential Brit delicacies. Not as wide a selection as the more established Myers of Keswick, but a younger management who can tell you where all the partying Anglos are to be found.

### Kam Man Food Products

*200 Canal Street, at Mott Street (571 0330).* **Train** J, M, N, R or Z to Canal Street. **Open** 9am-9pm daily. **Credit** MC, V.
A selection of fresh and preserved Chinese, Thai and other oriental foods, as well as utensils and kitchenware.

### Li-Lac

*120 Christopher Street (242 7374).* **Train** 1 or 9 to Christopher Street. **Open** noon-8pm Tue-Sat; noon-6pm Sun. **Credit** AmEx, Discover, MC, V.
Handmade chocolates par excellence.

### Lung Fong Bakery

*41 Mott Street, at Pell Street (233 7447).* **Train** J, M, N, R or Z to Canal Street. **Open** 7.30am-9pm daily. **No credit cards**.
Fortune cookies are but one of the delicious breads and biscuits on sale here.

### Meyer & Thompson Fish Co

*146 Beekman Street (233 5427).* **Open** *fishmongers* 3-11am Mon-Fri; *art gallery* noon-6pm Fri-Sun (other times by appointment). **Admission** *art gallery* free. **Credit** *art gallery only* AmEx.
In the afternoons the fish shop, famous for its smoked cod, turns into a gallery displaying paintings by Naima Rauam.

### Myers of Keswick

*634 Hudson Street, between Horatio & Jane Streets (691 4194).* **Train** A, C E or L to Eighth Avenue/14th Street. **Open** 10am-7pm Mon-Fri; 10am-6pm Sat; noon-5pm Sun. Closed Sun July, Aug. **Credit** AmEx.
Can't live without Heinz beans, treacle sponge or rice pudding? Hungry for Bovril, Bird's custard or Ribena? You don't have to be if you head for Myers of Keswick, popularly known as the English Shop, a little corner of *Coronation Street* in the Big Apple. You might even bump into that ex-pat Scotch egg devotee, Keith Richards.

### Paprikas Weiss

*1572 Second Avenue, between 81st & 82nd Streets (288 6117).* **Train** 6 to 77th Street. **Open** 9am-7pm Mon-Fri; 9am-6pm Sat; 11am-5pm Sun. **Credit** AmEx, MC, V.
All the different sorts of paprika (peppers) are available, along with other spices and prepared dishes.

### Raffeto's Corporation

*144 West Houston Street, at MacDougal Street (777 1261).* **Train** A, B, C, D, E, F or Q to West 4th Street. **Open** 9am-6.30pm Tue-Fri; 8am-6pm Sat. **No credit cards**.
In business since 1906, Raffeto's is the source of much of the designer pasta that is sold in gourmet shops all over town, but the shop on West Houston serves special raviolis, tortellini, fettucine, gnocchi and manicotti in any quantity to anyone who calls in, with no minimum order.

### Rigo Hungarian Pastry

*318 East 78th Street, between First & Second Avenues (988 0052).* **Train** 6 to 77th Street. **Open** 8am-4pm Mon; 8am-6pm Tue-Sat; 9am-4pm Sun. **No credit cards**.
The tortes and strudel are impossible to resist.

### Yonah Schimmel

*137 East Houston Street, between First & Second Avenues (477 2858).* **Train** F to Second Avenue; 6 to Bleecker Street. **Open** 8am-6pm daily. **No credit cards**.
You don't have to be Jewish to enjoy a nice knish, and the good name of Schimmel is synonymous with the best in the city. The Schimmel knish has a very thin crust of flaky pastry containing one of a variety of non-meat fillings, which include spinach and kasha as well as the best seller, potato.

### Zabar's

*2245 Broadway, at 80th Street (787 2000).* **Train** 1 or 9 to 79th Street. **Open** 8am-7.30pm Mon-Fri; 8am-8pm Sat; 9am-6pm Sun. **Credit** AmEx, MC, V.
By common consent the best food store in the city and, naturally therefore, the world, Zabar's is not only an excellent delicatessen but a great grocer and a first-class fish shop. The variety and quality of the coffee and cookies, cheeses and croissants is breathtaking; to sniff the air is to understand why, to many, Zabar's is Heaven. And don't miss the kitchen department upstairs. The pots, pans and appliances are surprisingly affordable. Expect to stand in line: you won't begrudge the wait.

### A Zito & Sons Bakery

*259 Bleecker Street, at Seventh Avenue (929 6139).* **Train** A, B, C, D, E, F or Q to West 4th Street. **Open** 6am-6pm Mon-Sat; 6am-2pm Sun. **No credit cards**.
The customers of this Bleecker Street bakery have included Frank Sinatra, who stopped by for a Sicilian loaf, and Bob Dylan, whose preference is for wholewheat. Tony Zito makes the best Italian bread in the Village, so if you're planning a picnic this is the place to begin.

## Gifts

For more children's clothes, books, toys and equipment, *see chapter* **Children**.

### Alphabets

*115 Avenue A (475 7250).* **Train** L to First Avenue. **Open** noon-10pm Mon-Thur; noon-midnight Fri, Sat; noon-8pm Sun. **Credit** AmEx, MC, V.
Hilarious postcards, wrapping paper and all manner of little jokey gifts are here, as well as a range of very fine T-shirts and alternative souvenirs of New York.
**Branch**: 47 Greenwich Avenue (229 2966).

### Back From Guatemala

*306 East 6th Street, between First & Second Avenues (260 7010).* **Train** 6 to Astor Place. **Open** noon-10.45pm Mon-Thur; noon-midnight Fri-Sat; 2-10pm Sun. **Credit** AmEx, Discover, MC, V.
And not just from Guatemala, either: this shop imports exotic clothing, jewellery and artefacts from over 30 countries, including Peruvian sweaters, wool scarves from Bolivia, batik shirts and trousers from Indonesia and pâpier-maché skulls from Mexico.

### Eclectiques

*55 Wooster Street, at Broome (966 0650).* **Train** C or E to Spring Street. **Open** 1-5.30pm daily.
A peculiar mix of old Vuitton luggage, Lalique and other beautiful, covetable objects.

### Forzano Italian Imports

*128 Mulberry Street, near Hester Street (925 2525).* **Train** J, M, R, Z or 6 to Canal Street. **Open** 10am-10pm Mon-Thur, Sun; 10am-midnight Fri, Sat. **Credit** AmEx, MC, V.
Apart from the unmissable souvenirs of Italy's 1982 World Cup win, there is a good sampling of Italian popular music and espresso machines.

### Hammacher Schlemmer

*147 East 57th Street, between Third & Lexington Avenues (421 9000).* **Train** 4, 5 or 6 to 59th Street; E or F to Lexington Avenue. **Open** 10am-6pm Mon-Sat. **Credit** AmEx, CB, DC, Discover, MC, V.
Six floors of executive toys for home, car, sports and leisure, each one supposedly the best of its kind. The perfect place to shop for the man, woman or child who has everything – or possibly to feel sorry for them.

### Little Rickie

*49 First Avenue, at East 3rd Street (505 6467).* **Train** F to Second Avenue. **Open** 11am-8pm Mon-Sat; noon-7pm Sun. **Credit** AmEx, DC, MC, V.
A bizarre collection of ludicrous eye-popping, mirth-making toys, cards and trinkets gathered from around the world. Visit the photo booth and have your face added to the window display.

### Love Saves the Day

*119 Second Avenue, at East 7th Street (228 3802).* **Train** 6 to Astor Place. **Open** noon-8pm Mon-Thur; 11am-11pm Fri-Sun. **Credit** AmEx, MC, V.

More kitschy toys and tacky novelties than you can shake a fat Elvis doll at. There are Elvis lamps with pink shades, Elvis statuettes, ant farms, lurid machine-made tapestries of Madonna, Pee-Wee Herman decals, glow-in-the-dark crucifixes and Mexican day-of-the-dead statues.

### FAO Schwartz

*767 Fifth Avenue, at 58th Street (644 9400).* **Train** 4, 5 or 6 to 59th Street; E or F to Lexington Avenue. **Open** 10am-6pm Mon-Wed, Fri, Sat; 10am-8pm Thur; noon-6pm Sun. **Credit** AmEx, DC, MC, V.

The famous toy store has been supplying New York kids with toys and games since 1862 and stocks more stuffed animals than you could imagine in your worst nightmares, as well as kites, dolls, games, miniature cars, toy soldiers, bath toys, and so on. This is the closest you can come to Disneyland in New York.

### Serendipity

*225 East 60th Street, between Second & Third Avenues (838 3531).* **Train** 4, 5, 6, N or R to 59th Street/Lexington Avenue. **Open** 11.30am-12.30am Mon-Thur; 11.30am-1am Fri; 11.30am-2am Sat; 11.30am-midnight Sun. **Credit** AmEx, DC, MC, V.

Serendipity has been in business for over 35 years as a restaurant and general store selling clothing and gifts. The restaurant is famous for its frozen hot chocolate.

### Warner Bros Studio Store

*1 East 57th Street, at Fifth Avenue (754 0300).* **Train** 4, 5, 6 to 59th Street. **Open** 10am-8pm Mon-Sat; 11am-6pm Sun. **Credit** AmEx, D, JCB, MC, V.

The swish outlet for anything and everything that has a Warner Bros character slapped on it. Great baseball hats and T-shirts and a few surprises.

## Green

### Body Shop

*773 Lexington Avenue, near East 61st Street (755 7851).* **Train** 4, 5 or 6 to 59th Street; N or R to Lexington Avenue. **Open** 10am-7pm Tue, Wed, Fri, Sat; 10am-8pm Mon, Thur; noon-6pm Sun. **Credit** AmEx, Discover, MC, V.

Body Shop junkies can relax; it's crossed the pond, too. For the uninitiated (where have you been?) Body Shop sells natural beauty products in no-nonsense, bio-degradable plastic bottles – at slightly higher prices here than in the UK.

**Branches**: 2159 Broadway (721 2947); 485 Madison Avenue (832 0812).

### Felissimo

*10 West 56th Street, at Fifth Avenue (956 4438).* **Train** N, R, B or Q to 57th Street. **Open** 10am-6pm Mon-Wed, Fri, Sat; 10am-8pm Thur. **Credit** AmEx, JCB, MC, V.

This five-story townhouse (behind Henri Bendel) houses a new Japanese-owned, eco-hip speciality store. It stocks an alluring selection of covetable items for the heart and home that includes jewellery, furnishings, clothing and collectibles. Service is unobtrusive and assistance is available in nine languages.

### Terra Verde

*120 Wooster Street, between Prince & Spring Streets (925 4533).* **Train** R to Prince Street. **Open** 11am-7pm Mon-Sat; noon-6pm Sun. **Credit** AmEx, MC, V.

Manhattan's first eco-market, combining art and activism. Architect William McDonough renovated the SoHo space using non-toxic building materials and formaldehyde-free paint. Get your chemical-free linens, natural soaps and solar radios here.

## Hats

### Amy Downs Hats

*103 Stanton Street, at Ludlow Street (598 4189).* **Train** F to Second Avenue. **Open** 1-6pm Wed-Sun. **No credit cards**.

Big, weird looking hats of all shapes and fabrics. Amy has gone it alone after some years of partnership at Mary Adams The Dress (*see above* **Fashion**).

### JJ Hat Center Inc

*310 Fifth Avenue, at 32nd Street (239 4368).* **Train** B, D, F, N Q or R to 34th Street. **Open** 8.45am-5.45pm Mon-Sat. **Credit** AmEx, DC, Discover, MC, V.

If you hanker after a stetson, there's a very large choice here, as well as caps, panamas, homburgs, collapsible top hats, and westerns, among others.

### Lola Millinery

*2 East 17th Street (366 5708).* **Train** 4, 5, 6, L, N or R to 14th Street. **Open** 11am-7pm Mon-Fri; 11am-6pm Sat. **Credit** AmEx, MC, V.

Probably the best-known hat designer in the city. Her designs feature classical and modern shapes with whimsical detail, suberbly made. Hats can be bought off the rack, customised or made to order.

## Home Furnishings

### Archetype Gallery

*115 Mercer Street, between Prince & Spring Streets (334 0100).* **Train** N or R to Prince Street; C or E to Spring Street. **Open** 10am-6pm Wed-Fri; noon-6pm Sat, Sun. **Credit** AmEx, MC, V.

Very unusual and unexpected new age furniture and objects by talented designers, well presented in a loft space.

### Bed, Bath and Beyond

*620 Sixth Avenue, at 18th Street (255 3550).***Train** F or L to Sixth Avenue/14th Street. **Open** 9.30am-9pm Mon-Fri; 9.30am-8pm Sat; 10am-6pm Sun. **Credit** AmEx, Discover, MC, V.

Just like the name says: everything you'll need for your house, with particular emphasis on the sheets and towels which go in those two rooms. Inexpensive and generally of good quality.

### Bennison Fabrics

*76 Greene Street, between Spring & Broome Streets (941 1212).* **Train** C or E to Spring Street. **Open** 10am-6pm Mon-Fri. **No credit cards**.

This is a favourite downtown store, with a classic but innovative range of fabrics that are silkscreened in England. Prices are steep but the fabrics – usually 70 per cent linen, 30 per cent cotton – end up in some of the best-dressed homes in town.

### Crate And Barrel

*650 Madison Avenue, at 59th Street (308 0011).* **Train** 4, 5 or 6 to 59th Street. **Open** 10am-8pm Mon-Fri; 10am-7pm Sat; noon-6pm Sun. **Credit** AmEx, Discover, MC, V.

Crate and Barrel combines mid-range antique furniture and objets with the very best and latest in household goods.

### Just Bulbs

*936 Broadway at 22nd Street (228 7820).* **Train** N or R to 23rd Street. **Open** 9am-6pm Mon-Fri. **Credit** AmEx, Discover, MC, V.

Light bulbs designed to make food look tastier, bulbs with star filaments or just a row of flamingos on a string. Thomas Edison would flip.

### Pottery Barn

*117 East 59th Street, between Lexington & Park Avenues (753 5424).* **Train** 4, 5 or 6 to 59th Street; N or R to Lexington Avenue. **Open** 10.30am-7pm Mon-Wed, Fri; 10am-8pm Thur; 10am-7pm Sat; noon-6pm Sun. **Credit** AmEx, MC, V.
A 1980s version of Habitat, Pottery Barn mixes the functional – plain ceramics, glassware and furniture – with something a little more fashion-conscious. Thus, you find Parthenon bookends, tortoiseshell glass bowls, bronze candlesticks, rattan chairs, serape blankets and books on marbling under the one roof.

### Williams-Sonoma

*20 East 60th Street, near Madison Avenue (980 5155).* **Train** 4, 5 or 6 to 59th Street; N or R to Lexington Avenue. **Open** 10am-7pm Mon-Fri; 10am-6pm Sat; noon-5pm Sun. **Credit** AmEx, MC, V.
A branch of a famous San Francisco kitchen store, Williams-Sonoma stocks all the best kinds of kitchen equipment: KitchenAid food mixers, Gaggia ice-cream machines, professional slicers, great copper and stainless steel pots, grills, fine glassware, maple salad-bowls, Sabatier knives....

### Williams-Sonoma Outlet

*231 10th Avenue, at 23rd Street (206 8118).* **Train** C or E to 23rd Street. **Open** 11am-6pm Mon-Fri; 10am-5pm Sat, Sun. **Credit** AmEx, MC, V.
An outlet store for both Williams-Sonoma and Pottery Barn, full of end-of-line and sale items. There's always a good selection of crockery, glass, frames, linen, rugs, towels and more.

## Jewellery

### Cartier

*653 Fifth Avenue, at 52nd Street (753 0111).* **Train** 6 to 51st Street. **Open** 10am-5.30pm Mon-Sat. Closed Sat July, Aug. **Credit** AmEx, DC, JCB, MC, V.
Cartier bought its Italianate building – one of few survivors of Fifth Avenue's previous life as a classy residential street – for two strands of Oriental pearls. All the usual Cartier items – jewellery, silver, porcelain – are sold within.

### David Webb

*445 Park Avenue, at 57th Street (421 3030).* **Train** 4, 5 or 6 to 59th Street; N or R to Lexington Avenue. **Open** 10am-5.15pm Mon-Thur; 10am-5pm Fri, Sat. **Credit** AmEx, DC, Discover, JCB, MC, V.
David Webb is best known for distinctive, and much imitated, gem-studded 18-carat gold jewellery. The pieces are expansive, often figurative; the quality impeccable and the prices appropriately high.

### Ilias Lalaounis

*733 Madison Avenue, at 64th Street (439 9400).* **Train** 4, 5, 6, N or R to 59th Street. **Open** 10am-5.30pm Mon-Sat. **Credit** AmEx, DC, Discover, JCB, MC, V.
This Greek jewellery designer's work is inspired by his native country's ancient symbols, American Indian and Arab designs. Expensive.

### Manny Winick & Son

*19 West 47th Street, near Fifth Avenue (302 9555).* **Train** B, D, F or Q to 47th Street/Rockefeller Center. **Open** 10am-5pm Mon-Fri; 10am-4.30pm Sat. **Credit** AmEx, Discover, MC, V.
Fine jewellery in precious metals and stones are sold alongside more sculptural contemporary pieces.

### Robert Lee Morris

*409 West Broadway, between Spring & Prince Streets (431 9405).* **Train** R to Prince Street; C or E to Spring Street. **Open** 11am-6pm Mon-Fri; noon-7pm Sat; noon-6pm Sun. **Credit** AmEx, MC, V.
Robert Lee Morris is the foremost contemporary designer making strong, striking pieces.

### Ted Muehling

*47 Greene Street, between Broome & Grand Streets (755 8000).* **Train** N or R to Prince Street. **Open** 11am-6pm Tue-Fri, Sat. **Credit** AmEx, MC, V.
Ted Muehling creates beautiful organic shapes in the studio behind the store, which sells the work of other artists, too.

### Tiffany & Co

*727 Fifth Avenue, between 56th & 57th Streets (431 3825).* **Train** 4, 5 or 6 to 59th Street; N or R to Lexington Avenue. **Open** 10am-6pm Mon-Wed, Fri, Sat.; 10am-7pm Thur. **Credit** AmEx, DC, JCB, MC, V.
Tiffany's heyday was around the turn of the century, when Louis Comfort Tiffany was designing his famous lamps and sensational art nouveau jewellery. Today, the big star is Paloma Picasso, who designs big pieces at bigger prices. Three storeys are stacked with precious jewels, silver accessories, chic watches and porcelain. Take all your credit cards.

## Leather Goods & Luggage

### Il Bisonte

*72 Thompson Street, between Spring & Broome Streets (966 8773).* **Train** C or E to Spring Street. **Open** noon-6.30pm Tue-Sat; noon-6pm Sun, Mon. **Credit** AmEx, MC, V.
Good tough basics with style: bags, belts and saddlebags, from this famous Florentine company.

### The Bag House

*797 Broadway, at 11th Street (260 0940).* **Train** 4, 5, 6, L, N or R to Union Square. **Open** 11am-6.45pm Mon-Sat; 1-5.45pm Sun. **Credit** AmEx, MC, V.
All manner of bags from the tiniest tote to something you could carry a small family in.

### Louis Vuitton

*49 East 57th Street, between Park & Madison Avenues (371 6111).* **Train** 4, 5 or 6 to 59th Street; N or R to Lexington Avenue. **Open** 10am-5.30pm Mon-Fri; 10am-5pm Sat. **Credit** AmEx, DC, Discover, JCB, MC, V.
The luggage and handbags are expensive, but beautiful.

### The $5 Bag store

*145 Avenue A, between 9th and 10th Streets (no phone).* **Train** L to First Avenue. **Open** 1-8pm Sun-Fri; noon-8pm Sat. **No credit cards.**
There really are bags for five dollars, plus quality big-name seconds which just need a lock or a strap fixing.

## Lingerie

### Allure Lingerie

*1324 Lexington Avenue, at 88th Street (860 7871).* **Train** 4, 5 or 6 to 86th Street. **Open** 11am-7pm Mon-Fri, 11am-6pm Sat. **Credit** AmEx, MC, V.
All manner of everything silky, lacy and/or supporting.
**Branch**: 1316 First Avenue (439 9561).

### AW Kaufman

*73 Orchard Street, near Grand Street (226 1629).* **Train** B, D or Q to Grand Street; F to Delancey. **Open** 10.30am-5pm Mon-Thur, Sun; 10am-2pm Fri. **Credit** AmEx, MC, V.
The tiny shop is packed to the ceiling with designer lingerie and sleepwear at discount prices. To get to see anything you must be a serious shopper.

## Liquor Stores

Most supermarkets and corner delis sell beer and aren't too fussed about ID – but may ask for proof that you are over 21. To buy wine and spirits in New York you need a liquor store. And, just to confuse you, most liquor stores don't sell beer.

### Astor Wines & Spirits

*12 Astor Place, at Lafayette Street (674 7500).* **Train** 6 to Astor Place; N or R to 8th Street. **Open** 9am-9pm Mon-Sat. **Credit** AmEx, MC, V.
A bright, modern wine supermarket that would serve as the perfect blueprint, were it not for a law preventing liquor stores from branching out. There's a wide range of wines and spirits but, of course, no beers.

### Maxwell Wine & Spirits

*1657 First Avenue, at 86th Street (289 9595).* **Train** 4, 5 or 6 to 86th Street. **Open** 9am-11pm Mon-Wed; 9am-midnight Thur-Sat. **Credit** MC, V.
Maxwell stocks popularly priced French, Italian and Californian wines, as well as vodka, gin and the usual run of rums, Scotch and bourbons.

### Park Avenue Liquor Shop

*292 Madison Avenue, between East 40th & East 41st Street (685 2442).* **Train** 4, 5, 6 or 7 to Grand Central. **Open** 8am-7pm Mon-Fri; 8am-5pm Sat. Closed Sat from July 4th to Labor Day. **Credit** AmEx, MC, V.
An unparalleled range of over 400 Californian wines is complemented by an excellent selection of spirits and fine European bottles. Buy by the case to qualify for a 16 per cent discount.

### Schumer's Wine & Liquor

*59 East 54th Street, between Park & Madison Avenues (355 0940).* **Train** 6, E or F to 51st Street/Lexington Avenue. **Open** 9am-midnight Mon-Sat. **Credit** AmEx, DC, MC, V.
Schumer's has a large selection of French, Californian and Italian wines as well as Champagnes and spirits, including Cognacs, Armagnacs and single-malt Scotches. It will deliver, too.

### Sherry-Lehmann Inc

*679 Madison Avenue, at East 61st Street (838 7500).* **Train** 4, 5 or 6 to 59th Street; N or R to Lexington Avenue. **Open** 9am-7pm Mon-Sat. Closed 5.30pm Sat during summer. **Credit** AmEx, MC, V.
Perhaps the most famous of New York's 1200 liquor stores, Sherry-Lehmann has a vast selection of scotches, brandies and ports, as well as a superb range of French, American and Italian wines.

## Mail Order

Shopping from the comfort of your hotel room or apartment sure beats fighting the crowds in the mean streets of midtown Manhattan. You can buy just about anything in America simply by picking up your phone – a power drill, contact lenses, a personal computer, or a string of pearls.

And it's not plain lazy. Some of America's smartest shoppers use this method. The prices and tax breaks make the trip to the store seem like a real waste of time. Today, 60 per cent of American adults have used catalogues to make purchases, and they've been doing so pretty much since the telephone was invented. Most services are open 24 hours and deliver within 48 hours, so it's efficient too. All you need is a phone and a credit card.

Most of the prominent stores, such as Tiffany's, Saks and Barnes & Noble, produce catalogues, while some of the major catalogues – Victoria's Secret and Sharper Image, for example – now have stores. If you know the name of your favourite store, try the toll free directory (1-800 555 1212) and see if it has a listing. Chances are it will. In the meantime, here are some to be going on with:

### Austads

*(1-800 759 4653).*
Essential for golfers, Austad's novelty items are dead funny.

### Bloomingdale's by Mail

*(1-800 777 0000).*
Some of the best this grand department store has to offer is available from the catalogue. The emphasis in on apparel.

### LL Bean

*(1-800 221 4221).*
One of the top ten catalogue companies, Bean sells country clothing (denim, khaki etc) and home accessories.

### Lillian Vernon

*(1-800 285 5555).*
Great gifts and nifty little items.

### Mac Warehouse

*(1-800 255 6227).*
One of the most affordable and effective ways of laying your hands on just about any software you could need for your Apple Macintosh.

'Genuine' market bargains. See page 170.

1-800-927-2222
THIS

### Nature's Bounty

*(1-800 645 5412).*
A hypochondriac's dream – page after page of every dietary supplement you could possibly ingest.

### Orvis

*(1-800 815 5900).*
An established and reliable source of sporting goods and clothing.

### Pottery Barn

*(1-800 922 5507).*
Cheap and fashionable home furnishings with a vaguely ethnic or country flavour.

### Sharper Image

*(1-800 344 5555).*
Innovative and eccentric lifestyle items like golf gifts, unusual wine openers and miniature binoculars. The emphasis is on quality of design.

### US Cavalry

*(1-800 777 7732).*
An astonishing collection of SAS-type survivalist gear, from camouflage toilet paper to books on how to kill people more effectively.

### Victoria's Secret

*(1-800 888 8200).*
This British catalogue sells cheap and mostly tame lingerie as well as great swimsuits and some casual clothing.

### Williams-Sonoma

*(1-800 541 1262).*
An excellent source of cutlery, crockery and kitchen basics.

## Markets

Weekend fleamarkets are great fun, for bizarre objets and unique gifts, not to mention records, books and clothes. There are a good handful, both indoor and outdoor, clustered around 25th Street on Sixth Avenue. The other favourite is on Broadway at Grand Street. They all run between 9am and 5pm.

In addition, illegal street vendors can be found all over the city, selling just about anything from fake Rolexes to (no lies) used dentures. First Avenue below St Mark's Place is a good spot, as is Avenue A here.

The following is a list of established (and legitimate) markets and antique stores dealing in everything from cabbages to items fit for kings.

### Annex Antiques Fair & Flea Market

*Sixth Avenue, at 25th Street (243 5343).* **Train** F to 23rd Street. **Open** 9am-5pm Sat, Sun.
One of the biggest fleamarkets in Manhattan, this has an incredible selection of bric-à-brac, clothing and jewellery on offer, as well as large quantities of antique furniture and paintings. Prices are remarkably reasonable.

### Antique Flea & Farmers' Market

*PS 183, East 67th Street, between First & York Avenues (737 8888).* **Train** 6 to 68th Street. **Open** 6am-6pm Sat.
Richard Nixon used to frequent this market. Powerful attractions for serious collectors include the antique lace, fine silverware, embroideries and tapestries. Fresh farm products – eggs, fish and vegetables – are also available.

*One of Sixth Avenue's many fleamarkets.*

### Greenwich Village Flea Market

*PS 41, Greenwich Street, at Charles Street (752 8475).*
**Train** 1 or 9 to Christopher Street/Sheridan Square.
**Open** noon-7pm Sat.
Of course, Greenwich Village must have a flea market. It's small – only about 65 to 70 stalls – with quite a good range of bric-à-brac, ranging from 1930s corsets to deco silverware.

### IS 44 Flea Market

*Columbus Avenue, between West 76th & West 77th Streets (316 1088).* **Train** B or C to 72nd Street. **Open** 10am-6pm Sun.
Said to be one of Andy Warhol's favourite hunting grounds. It's wonderful for ferreting out antiques, jewellery and second-hand clothes from 300-plus stalls, indoor and outdoor.

### SoHo Antique Fair and Collectibles Market

*Grand Street, at Broadway (682 2000).* **Train** 4, 5, 6, N or R to Canal Street. **Open** 9am-5pm Mon-Sat. **No credit cards.**
This market opened in 1992 and has been fabulously successful. It's small but has some amazing bargains. Some of the best dealers from the Annex (*see above*) are now here.

## Musical Instruments

### Manny's Music

*156 West 48th Street, between Sixth & Seventh Avenues (819 0576).* **Train** B, D, F or Q to Rockefeller Center. **Open** 10am-6pm Mon-Sat. **Credit** AmEx, DC, Discover, JCB, MC, V.
Manny's stocks a wide range of musical instruments and equipment at standard prices. Sam Ash (*below*) has more floorspace, but Manny's is the original. Everyone from Fats Waller to John Lennon was a customer and they have the photos to prove it.

### Sam Ash

*155, 159, 160 & 163 West 48th Street, between Sixth & Seventh Avenues (719 2625 guitars/719 5109 DJ & studio equipment/719 2661 percussion/719 4974 other instruments).* **Train** B, D, F or Q to Rockefeller Center. **Open** 10am-6pm Mon-Sat. **Credit** AmEx, Discover, JCB, MC, V.
A whole street of stores, each proffering a different set of instruments. They also deal in all types of professional studio equipment, MIDI, lighting, computers and DJ equipment. If it's not here you can't get it.

## Opticians

### Alain Mikli Optique

*880 Madison Avenue, at 71st Street (472 6085).* **Train** 6 to 68th Street. **Open** 9.30am-6.30pm Mon-Wed, Fri; 9.30am-7pm Thur; 10.30am-6.30pm Sat. **Credit** AmEx, Discover, MC, V.
French frames and eyeglasses for the bold and beautiful.

### My Optics

*42 St Mark's Place, at Second Avenue (533 1577).*
**Train** 6 to Astor Place. **Open** 11am-7pm Mon-Fri; 11am-6pm Sat; noon-5pm Sun. **Credit** AmEx, Discover, MC, V.
A full optician's service, and frames by Matsuda, Oliver Peoples, LA Eyeworks and Paul Smith.
**Branches**: 82 Christopher Street (741 9550); 96 Seventh Avenue (633 6014); 247 Third Avenue (475 8890); 431 Amsterdam Avenue (875 1234).

## Pharmacists

### Caswell-Massey

*518 Lexington Avenue, at East 48th Street (755 2254).* **Train** 6 to 51st Street. **Open** 9am-7pm Mon-Fri; 10am-6pm Sat. **Credit** AmEx, Discover, JCB, MC, V.
America's oldest chemist was established way back in 1752, but still supplies the types of product that are much appreciated: soaps made of almond cream, seaweed, lettuce or coconut oil; extracts of roses; fragrant oils; cucumber creams; huge sponges and loofahs.

### Duane Reade Drug Stores

*Empire State Building, 350 Fifth Avenue (714 2417).* **Train** 1, 9, N or R to 42nd Street. **Open** 7.30am-8pm Mon-Fri. **Credit** AmEx, Discover, MC, V.
This chain of stores offers good discounts on cosmetics, vitamins, soaps, shampoos and other essentials. There are branches everywhere.

### Kaufman Pharmacy

*Beverly Hotel, 557 Lexington Avenue, at 50th Street (755 2266).* **Train** E, F or 6 to 51st Street/Lexington Avenue. **Open** 24 hours daily. **Credit** AmEx, MC, V.
New York's only all-night full-service pharmacy. You can take prescriptions here.

### Plaza Pharmacy

*251 East 86th Street, at Second Avenue (427 6940).* **Train** 4, 5 or 6 to 86th Street. **Open** 8am-11pm Mon-Fri; 10am-11pm Sat, Sun. **Credit** AmEx, MC, V.
Prescriptions filled till late.

## Records, Tapes & CDs

## The Big Ones

### HMV

*1280 Lexington Avenue, at 86th Street (348 0800).* **Open** 9am-10pm Mon-Thur, Sun; 9am-11pm Fri, Sat. **Train** 4, 5 or 6 to 86th Street. **Credit** AmEx, Discover, MC, V.
This is the biggest record store in North America, with a jaw-dropping selection of vinyl, cassettes, CDs and videos (US videos won't play on UK VCRs).
**Branches**: 2081 Broadway (721 5900); 57 West 34th Street.

### Tower Records

*692 Broadway, at 4th Street (505 1500).* **Train** N or R to 8th Street. **Open** 9am-midnight daily. **Credit** AmEx, Discover, MC, V.
All the current sounds on CD and tape. Visit the clearance store round the block on Lafayette for knockdown stuff in all formats, including cheap vinyl of all kinds, especially classical. Tower Books opposite has a great selection of magazines, including imports.
**Branches**:1961 Broadway (799 2500).

## Dance

### 8-Ball Records

*105 East 9th Street, between Third & Fourth Avenues (473 6343).* **Train** 6 to Astor Place. **Open** noon-9pm Mon-Sat. **Credit** AmEx, MC, V.
Since the label owns the store, this is where you'll get those 8-Ball faves first. It's also a great house resource, with a broad range of imports and a fruitful bargain bin.

### Dance Tracks

*91 East 3rd St, at First Ave, (260 8729).* **Train** F to Second Avenue. **Open** noon-9pmMon-Thur; noon-10pm Fri; noon-8pm Sat, 1-6.30pm Sun. **Credit** AmEx, MC, V.
Hot off the plane with those Euro imports (which are nearly as cheap to buy here as back there), and with fast-flowing racks of domestic house, dangerously enticing bins of Loft/Paradise Garage classics and private decks to listen on, Dance Tracks is a must.

### Disc-O-Rama

*186 West 4th Street, between Sixth & Seventh Avenues (206 8417).* **Train** 1 or 9 to Christopher Street. **Open** 11am-11.30pm Mon-Fri; 10.30am-12.30am Sat; 11.30am-8pm Sun. **Credit** AmEx, D, MC, V.
Upstairs, the CDs and tapes are all at bargain prices; downstairs, the vinyl is a joy to behold: all the latest dance stuff, decent imports and tons of house and disco classics to thumb through.

### Fat Beats

*323 East 9th Street, between First & Second Avenues (673 3883).* **Train** 6 to Astor Place. **Open** 1-8pm Sun-Wed; 1-10pm Thur-Sat. **Credit** AmEx, MC, V.
This is hip-hop central, a small store with a large selection of the latest in hip-hop acid jazz and reggae. The big bonus is the second-hand stock including loads of breaks and old-school classics.

### Sonic Groove Records

*41 Carmine Street (675 5284).* **Train** 1 or 9 to Houston Street. **Open** 1-8pm Mon-Thur; 1-10pm Fri, Sat. **Credit** AmEx, MC, V.
Frankie Bones' famous Brooklyn import store is now in Manhattan, and here you'll find American and European techno, acid and hardcore.

### Temple Records

*241 Lafayette Street, at Prince Street (343 0532).* **Train** 6 to Spring Street. **Open** 1-8pm Mon-Sat; 2-7pm Sun. **Credit** AmEx, Discover, MC, V.
Underneath the fractal garments and zippy space wear of Liquid Sky (*see above* **Fashion: The Stores**) sits this haven for US and imported techno, trance and jungle. Best place to find a rave to go to.

### Vinylmania Records

*60 Carmine Street, near Bleecker Street (924 7223).* **Train** 1 or 9 to Houston Street. **Open** 11am-9pm Mon-Fri; 11am-7pm Sat, Sun. **Credit** AmEx.
The emphasis is on house, but there are strong selections of reggae, hip-hop, and disco/funk classics.

## Specialist

### Bleecker Bob's Golden Oldies

*118 West 3rd Street, between Sixth Avenue & MacDougal Street (475 9677).* **Train** A, B, C, D, E, F or Q to West 4th Street. **Open** noon-1am Mon-Thur, Sun; noon-3am Fri, Sat. **Credit** AmEx, MC, V.
Imports, independents, deleted records, tapes and CDs and all sorts of rarities are sold here. It's the place to go when you really can't find what you want anywhere else.

### Colony Record & Tape Center

*1619 Broadway, at 49th Street (265 2050).* **Train** N or R to 49th Street. **Open** 9.30am-midnight daily. **Credit** AmEx, Discover, DC, JCB, MC, V.
Colony specialises in soundtracks, show music and jazz, of which it has a large selection, and has sheet music and movie scripts, too – but it is expensive.

### Gryphon Record Shop

*251 West 72nd Street, between Broadway & West End Avenue (874 1588).* **Train** 1, 2, 3 or 9 to 72nd Street. **Open** 11am-7pm Mon-Sat; noon-6pm Sun. **Credit** MC, V.
A solidly classical store, with a sprinkling of jazz and show music. Vinyl only.

### Jazz Record Center

*236 West 26th Street, between Seventh & Eighth Avenues, eighth floor (675 4480).* **Train** A, C, E or L to 14th Street. **Open** 10am-6pm Mon-Fri. **Credit** AmEx, MC, V.

The best jazz store in the city, selling both current and out-of-print records. You can have your purchases shipped anywhere in the world.

### Midnight Records

*263 West 23rd Street, between Seventh & Eighth Avenues (675 2768).* **Train** C or E to 23rd Street. **Open** *June-Aug* noon-6pm Mon-Fri; *Sept-May* 10am-6pm Tue-Sat. **Credit** ($30 minimum) AmEx, MC, V.

A great place for rarities and hard-to-find rock records. The 1960s and 70s are the years it does best.

### Pier Platters

*56 Newark Street, Hoboken, New Jersey (1-201 795 4785).* **Train** PATH to Hoboken. **Open** 11am-9pm Mon-Sat; noon-8pm Sun. **Credit** AmEx, MC, V.

It's worth the trip across state lines to New Jersey to check out this phenomenal alternative rock scene resource. A huge collection of independents, imports and rarities.

### Record Mart

*Times Square subway station, near the N & R platform (840 0580).* **Train** 1, 2, 3, 9, N, R, S to 42nd Street. **Open** 9am-9pm Mon-Thur; 9am-11pm Fri; 10am-11pm Sat; noon-8pm Sun. **Credit** MC, V.

The largest selection of Caribbean and Latin American music in the city, much of it still on vinyl.

## Shoes

West 8th Street has a large number of shoe shops full of sneakers and boots and many designer seconds. For shoe repairs, *see chapter* **Services**.

### Anbar Shoes

*60 Reade Street, between Church Street & Broadway (227 0253).* **Train** 1, 2, 3 or 9 to Chambers Street. **Open** 8.30am-6pm Mon-Fri; 11am-6pm Sat. **Credit** AmEx, Discover, MC, V.

You can save up to 70 per cent on Jourdan, Ferragamo and other high-price footwear in this two-floor emporium.

### The Athlete's Foot

*390 Fifth Avenue, at 36th Street (947 6972).* **Train** 6 to 33rd Street. **Open** 10am-8pm Mon-Sat; noon-7pm Sun. **Credit** AmEx, Discover, MC, V.

Best of all the sneaker-led chainstores, with the widest selections and the newest models, plus minimal amounts of casual sports gear. Branches all over town.

### John Fluevog

*104 Prince Street, between Mercer & Greene Streets (431 4484).* **Train** N or R to Prince Street. **Open** 11am-7pm Tue, Wed, Sat, Sun; 11am-7.30pm Mon, Fri; 11am-8pm Thur. **Credit** AmEx, JCB, MC, V.

Unique, stylish, often outrageous and definitely unmissable.

### Lace Up

*110 Orchard Street, at Delancey Street (475 8040).* **Train** J, M or Z to Essex Street; F to Delancey. **Open** 9.30am-5.30pm Mon-Wed, Fri; 9.30am-6pm Thur, Sun. **Credit** AmEx, MC, V.

Top-range designer shoes at discount prices.

### McCreedy & Schreiber

*37 West 46th Street, between Fifth & Sixth Avenues (719 1552).* **Train** 1, 2, 3, 7, N or R to Times Square. **Open** 9am-7pm Mon-Sat. **Credit** AmEx, DC, Discover, MC, V.

This well-known quality men's shoe shop is good for all traditional American styles: Bass Weejuns, Sperry Topsiders, Frye boots and the famous Lucchese boots in everything from goatskin to crocodile.

**Branch**: 213 East 59th Street (759 9241).

### Manolo Blahnik

*15 West 55th Street, between Fifth & Sixth Avenues (582 3007).* **Train** B, D, F or Q to Rockefeller Center. **Open** 10.30am-6pm Mon-Fri; 10.30am-5.30pm Sat. **Credit** AmEx, Discover, MC, V.

From the high priest of style, timeless shoes in innovative designs and maximum taste. His clients include the world's wealthiest, most beautiful women.

### St Marks Leather Company

*83 Christopher Street, at Seventh Avenue (533 8330).* **Train** 6 to Astor Place; N or R to 8th Street. **Open** noon-8pm Mon-Wed; noon-9pm Thur-Sat; noon-8pm Sun. **Credit** AmEx ($50 minimum), DC, Discover, MC, V.

Footwear is by Justin and Nocona, Stewart boots, Western accessories and 'policeman's' shoes. Discounts on all boots and shoes.

**Branch**: 419 Park Avenue South (532 3340).

### Martinez Valero

*1029 Third Avenue, at East 61st Street (753 1822).* **Train** 4, 5 or 6 to 59th Street; B, N or R to Lexington Avenue. **Open** 10am-8pm Mon-Fri; 10am-7pm Sat; noon-6pm Sun. **Credit** AmEx, DC, MC, V.

These beautiful Spanish shoes are made of various coloured suedes and leathers used together. Styles range from elegant but practical flats to sleek heels. The men's shoes are just as well made, although not so vibrant.

### Timberland

*709 Madison Avenue, on the corner of 63rd Street (754 0434).* **Train** 4, 5 or 6 to 59th Street; N or R to Lexington Avenue. **Open** 10am-6.30pm Mon-Fri; 10am-6pm Sat; noon-5.00pm Sun. **Credit** AmEx, MC, V.

The complete American line of Timberland shoes and boots for men and women is sold (there are more styles in Europe, but these are a bit cheaper). The ruggedly elegant apparel is also available.

### Tootsi Plohound

*413 West Broadway, between Prince & Spring Streets (925 8931).* **Train** N or R to Prince Street. **Open** 11.30am-7.30pm Mon-Fri; 11am-8pm Sat; noon-7pm Sun. **Credit** AmEx, DC, MC, V.

One of the best places for shoes, Tootsi carries a good range of stylish imports, especially flats and lace-ups, at tolerable prices. Note, too, the wide and witty selection of socks for women.

**Branch**: 137 Fifth Avenue (460 8650).

### V.I.M.

*686 Broadway, between 3rd & 4th Streets (677 8364).* **Train** B, D, F, Q or 6 to Bleecker Street/Broadway Lafayette. **Open** 10am-8pm Mon-Sat; 11am-7pm Sun. **Credit** AmEx, MC, V.

They treat sneakers (trainers) like hit singles, with a 'latest release' display. This is one of the largest selections of athletic footwear in the city, complete with an overhead monorail delivery system.

**Branches**: 15 West 34th Street (736 4989); 16 West 14th Street (255 2262).

### JM Weston

*42 East 57th Street, between Madison & Park Avenues (308 5655).* **Train** 4, 5, 6, N or R to 59th Street. **Open** 10am-6pm Mon-Fri; 11am-5pm Sat. **Credit** AmEx, MC, V.

JM Weston shoes appeal to such diverse men as Woody Allen, Yves Saint Laurent and the king of Morocco. The

*American football, Grecian style, at* **Modell's.** *See page 177.*

beautiful, handmade shoes are available in 34 styles: 'Weston's don't fit you; you fit them', said Robert Deslauriers, the man who established the Manhattan store. (There's a JM Weston in Paris and the tannery is in Limousin, France.) Popular styles include the moccasin ($375), the Demi-Chasse, a double-soled shoe with an inner metal toeplate ($465) and the Monkstrap ($420 in calfskin). The shop also carries women's shoes – and they're also expensive.

## Speciality Shops

### Arthur Brown & Bros

*2 West 46th Street, between Fifth & Sixth Avenues (575 5555).* **Train** B, D, F or Q to Rockefeller Center. **Open** 9am-6.30pm Mon-Fri, 10am-6pm Sat. **Credit** AmEx, DC, Discover, MC, V.

Pens of the world unite at Arthur Brown's, which has one of the largest selections anywhere including such brands as Mont Blanc, Cartier, Dupont, Porsche and Schaeffer.

### Big City Kite Company

*1210 Lexington Avenue, at 82nd Street (472 2623).* **Train** 4, 5 or 6 to 86th Street. **Open** 11am-6.30pm Mon-Wed, Fri, Sat; 11am-7.30pm Thur; noon-5pm Sun. **Credit** AmEx, Discover, MC, V.

Go fly a kite – there are over 150 to chose from here, with all kinds of visual and acrobatic properties. Lessons and kits are available, too.

### Bird Jungle

*401 Bleecker Street, at West 11th Street (242 1757).* **Train** 1, 2, 3, 9 or L to 14th Street. **Open** 12.30-6.30pm Mon-Fri; 11am-6.30pm Sat; 11am-5.30pm Sun. **Credit** AmEx, MC, V.

Parakeets, toucans and more mundane feathered friends fly around the shop windows. Wear a hat.

### Collectors' Stadium

*214 Sullivan Street, between Bleecker & West 3rd Streets (353 1531).* **Train** A, B, C, D, E, F or Q to West 4th Street. **Open** 11am-7pm daily. **Credit** AmEx, MC, V.

This is where you may be able to find that elusive card to complete your 1938 set of Yankees baseball cards – or just ponder this US obsession.

### Condomania

*351 Bleecker Street, at 10th Street (691 9442).* **Train** 1 or 9 to Christopher Street. **Open** 11am-10.45pm Sun-Thur; 11am-11.45pm Fri, Sat. **Credit** AmEx, DC, Discover, JCB, MC, V.

Condoms in all shapes, sizes, flavours and colours. The biggest selection anywhere.

### Evolution

*120 Spring Street, between Greene & Mercer Streets (343 1114).* **Train** C or E to Spring Street. **Open** 11am-7pm daily. **Credit** AmEx, Discover, JCB, MC, V.

*Big Brother is watching you, at* **Quark Spy Center**. *See page 177.*

If you are into natural history and would like to take some home, this is the store for you. Insects in plexiglass, giraffe skulls, sea shells and wild boar tusks are among the items for sale in this relatively politically correct store – the animals died of natural causes or were culled.

### Game Show

*1240 Lexington Avenue, at 83rd Street (472 8011).* **Train** 4, 5 or 6 to 86th Street. **Open** 11am-6pm Mon-Wed, Fri, Sat; 11am-7pm Thur. **Credit** AmEx, MC, V.
Every board game imaginable, and plenty that you'll be quite surprised/intrigued/offended to discover.

### Goldberg's Marine Distributors

*12 West 37th Street, between Fifth & Sixth Avenues (594 6065).* **Train** B, D, F or Q to 34th Street. **Open** 9am-6pm Mon-Sat; 10am-5pm Sun. **Credit** AmEx, Discover, MC, V.
'Where thousands of boaters save millions of dollars,' is Goldberg's intriguing slogan. Certainly thousands of boaters do buy their marine supplies, fishing gear, nautical fashion and deck shoes here.

### Hunting World

*16 East 53rd Street, between Madison & Fifth Avenues (755 3400).* **Train** 6 to 51st Street. **Open** 10am-5pm Mon-Sat; 11am-6pm Sun. **Credit** AmEx, DC, JCB, MC, V.
Practical items for active people (Nicholas Cage and Frank Sinatra among them): T-shirts, hiking boots, golf bags, fishing gear, hats, bags and umbrellas. Comfortable, stylish gear, including the Hunt Club jacket, which hasn't had a redesign in 30 years.

### Karen's for People and Pets

*1195 Lexington Avenue, between 81st & 82nd Streets (628 2312).* **Train** 4, 5 or 6 to 86th Street. **Open** 8am-6pm Mon-Fri; 9am-6pm Sat. **Credit** AmEx, MC, V.
Karen designs and manufactures witty clothing, accessories and even fitted sheets for the dog, cat or canary in your life. A good source of pet-related presents.

### H Kauffman & Sons Saddlery & Co

*419 Park Avenue South, at 29th Street (684 6060).* **Train** 6 to 28th Street. **Open** 10am-6.30pm Mon-Wed, Fri, Sat; 9.30am-7pm Thur; noon-5pm Sun. Closed Sun July, Aug. **Credit** AmEx, DC, MC, V.
Riding equipment is mostly Western, although some English is stocked.

### Metropolitan Opera Shop

*835 Madison Avenue, between 69th & 70th Streets (734 8406).* **Train** 6 to 68th Street. **Open** 10am-6pm Mon-Sat. **Credit** AmEx, Discover, MC, V.
This Upper East Side outlet of the Metropolitan Opera sells CDs, cassettes and laser discs of every opera imaginable. There is also a wealth of opera memorabilia.

### Paramount Vending

*587 Tenth Avenue, near 42nd Street (279 1095).* **Train** 1, 9, N or R to 42nd Street. **Open** 10am-6pm Mon-Fri. **Credit** AmEx, Discover, MC, V.
An excellent source of used jukeboxes, pinball machines and bowling machines.

### Pearl Paint Co

*308 Canal Street, between Church Street & Broadway (431 7932).* **Train** 6, A, C, E, J, N, M, R or Z to Canal Street. **Open** 9am-6pm Mon-Wed, Fri, Sat; 9am-7pm Thur; 9am-5.30pm Sun. **Credit** AmEx, Discover, MC, V.
Pearl Paint is as big as a supermarket, and has everything you could possibly need to be artistic.

### Pearl River Chinese Products Emporium Inc

*277 Canal Street, corner of Broadway (431 4770).* **Train** 6, B, D, J, M, N, R or Z to Canal Street. **Open** 10am-7.30pm daily. **Credit** AmEx, MC, V.
In this downtown emporium you can find Chinese clothing, T-shirts, sweaters, children's pyjamas, cotton sheets, tablecloths, napkins, slip-on shoes, pots, woks, teapots, groceries, bonsai, medicinal herbs and traditional stationery.

### Pop Shop

*292 Lafayette Street, near Prince Street (219 2784).* **Train** N or R to Prince Street; B, D, F, Q or 6 to Broadway/Lafayette Street. **Open** noon-7pm Tue-Sat; noon-6pm Sun. **Credit** AmEx, MC, V.
All the posters, badges, bath pillows, inflatable babies, groovy fridge magnets and T-shirts were designed by the late artist Keith Haring.

### Poster America Gallery

*138 West 18th Street, between Sixth & Seventh Avenues (206 0499).* **Train** 1 or 9 to 18th Street. **Open** 11am-6pm Tue-Sat. **Credit** AmEx, MC, V.
The gallery has extensive stocks of original advertising posters from 1880 onwards from both sides of the Atlantic.

### Quark Spy Center

*537 Third Avenue, at 35th Street (889 1808).* **Train** 6 to 33rd Street. **Open** 10am-6.30pm Mon-Fri; 11am-4pm Sat. **Credit** AmEx, MC, V.
Want to catch your flatmate raiding the fridge? Let Quark design a custom-made surveillance system. It can also supply you with body armour, night vision systems and more bugs and bug detectors than James Bond would ever need.

### Rand McNally Map & Travel Center

*150 East 52nd Street, between Lexington & Third Avenues (758 7488).* **Train** 6 to 51st Street; E or F to Lexington Avenue. **Open** 9am-6pm Mon-Fri; 11am-5pm Sat. **Credit** AmEx, Discover, JCB, MC, V.
Rand McNally stocks maps, atlases and globes published by rival publishers as well as their own products.

### Spike's Joint

*1 South Elliott Place, Brooklyn (1-718 802 1000).* **Train** D, M, N, Q or R to DeKalb Avenue. **Open** 10am-7pm Mon-Sat; noon-6pm Sun. **Credit** AmEx, MC, V.
A gang of funky memorabilia from Mr Lee's movies, plus an exclusive line of jeans and jackets with the *40 Acres & a Mule* label. Spike's office is next to the store and he lives round the corner.

### Stack's Coin Company

*123 West 57th Street, between Sixth & Seventh Avenues (582 2580).* **Train** B, N, Q or R to 57th Street. **Open** 10am-5pm Mon-Fri. **No credit cards.**
The largest and longest-established coin dealer in the USA, dealing in rare and ancient coins from all over the world.

### Star Magic

*745 Broadway, near East 8th Street (228 7770).* **Train** 6 to Astor Place; R to 8th Street. **Open** 10am-10pm Mon-Sat; 11am-9pm Sun. **Credit** AmEx, MC, V.
If you're into inner or outer space, here's the space-age boutique with holograms, fine optics, maps and globes, prisms, pyramids, crystals and jewellery.
**Branches**: 275 Amsterdam Avenue (769 2020); 1256 Lexington Avenue (988 0300).

### Supreme

*274 Lafayette Street, at Prince Street (966 7799).* **Open** 11.30am-7pm Mon-Thur; 11.30am-7.30pm Fri, Sat; noon-6pm Sun. **Credit** AmEx, MC, V.
The skaters' skateboard store. The latest decks, trucks and wheels, and the fashions to go with them.

### Urban Archaeology Co.

*285 Lafayette Street, between Prince & Houston Streets (431 6969).* **Train** 6 to Spring Street. **Open** 11am-6pm Mon-Sat. **Credit** AmEx, MC, V.
This is the largest of the many stores along lower Lafayette Street specialising in the discarded everyday items of the past. The other stores concentrate on kitschy 1960s and 70s furniture and advertising objets, but here you'll find architectural and household items, from a bookshelf to a pair of 20ft-high wrought-iron gates complete with stone pillars.

### Vera Wang Bridal House

*991 Madison Avenue, at 76th Street (628 3400).* **Train** 6 to 77th Street. **Open** by appointment only. **Credit** AmEx, MC, V.
Some of the world's most famous designer's bridal creations, plus custom work at awesome prices.

### Village Chess Shop

*230 Thompson Street, between Bleecker & West 3rd Streets (475 8130).* **Train** A, B, C, D, E, F or Q to West 4th Street. **Open** noon-midnight daily. **Credit** AmEx, MC, V.
As well as checking out New York's best source of chess sets and accessories, you can stop and have a game here. David Lee Roth and Yoko Ono are among the celebrities who have dropped in to play. Private lessons are available for about $25 per hour.

## Sports

### Blades Downtown

*659 Broadway, between Bleecker & Bond Streets (477 7350).* **Train** B, D, F or Q to Broadway/Lafayette. **Open** 11am-9pm Mon-Sat; noon-7pm Sun. **Credit** AmEx, MC, V.
As the name might suggest, this is where to come for those rollerblades, as well as a wide range of skateboard and snowboard equipment and clothing. It has several branches around the city.

### Gerry Cosby

*3 Pennsylvania Plaza, inside Madison Square Garden (563 6464).* **Train** 1, 2, 3 or 9 to 34th Street. **Open** 9.30am-6.30pm Mon-Fri; 9.30am-6pm Sat; noon-5pm Sun. **Credit** AmEx, Discover, MC, V.
Huge selection of official team-wear and other sporting necessaries.

### Herman's World of Sports

*39 West 34th Street, between Fifth & Sixth Avenues (279 8900).* **Train** B, D, F, N, Q or R to 34th Street. **Open** 9am-7pm Mon-Fri; 9.30am-6.30pm Sat; 11am-6pm Sun. **Credit** AmEx, Discover, MC, V.
Herman's has it all: tennis gear, running and walking shoes, football equipment, rollerblades and helmets, bowling balls, swimsuits, jogging suits, weights, athletic bags, leotards and exercise equipment. There are branches all over Manhattan – call for details of the one nearest you.

### Modell's

*51 East 42nd Street, at Madison Avenue (661 4242).* **Train** 4, 5, 6 or 7 to Grand Central. **Open** 8am-8pm Mon-Fri; 9am-6pm Sat; 11am-6pm Sun. **Credit** AmEx, D, MC. V.
A comprehensive range of sporting equipment and clothing is sold at Modell's, and if you're after a major purchase it's worth checking here last as its often the cheapest.
**Branches**: 901 Sixth Avenue (594 1830); 200 Broadway (964 4007); 280 Broadway (962 6200); 243 West 42nd Street (575 8111).

### Paragon Sporting Goods Company

*867 Broadway, near East 18th Street (255 8036).* **Train** 4, 5, 6, L, N or R to 14th Street/Union Square. **Open** 10am-8pm Mon-Fri; 10am-6.30pm Sat; 11am-8pm Sun. **Credit** AmEx, Discover, MC, V.
A full line of sports equipment and sportswear is available at this old-fashioned store. There's a good range of swimwear, surfwear, tennis rackets, climbing gear and shoes.

# Services

***Need to buy a love potion, have your dog photographed or hire a Ferrari? Then New York is at your service.***

In New York, everything is available, almost all the time, and in a choice of attractive colours. In these pages you'll find the kinds of services you just might need during a stay here, from the essential to the ridiculous. For anything that isn't listed here, or for alternlocal atives to our recommendations, try to get hold of a copy of the *Yellow Pages/ Business to Business Yellow Pages* (call 890 1550 if you have trouble finding one). For business services, *see chapter* **Business**; for police, fire, ambulance and other emergency services *see chapter* **Survival**. Transport services can be found in *chapter* **Getting Around** and babysitters are listed in *chapter* **Children**.

Many of the large department stores offer special services, from delivery, packing and shipping, to valuations and fashion consultations.

## Acupuncturists

### Metro Acupuncture Center

*420 Lexington Avenue, room 308, between 43rd & 44th Streets (286 9170).* **Train** 4, 5, 6 or 7 to Grand Central. **Open** 10am-6pm Mon-Fri; 11am-5pm Sat. **No credit cards**.

Lin Shen Chou, the director, is an ex-president of the American Acupuncture Association and has 30 years experience. Treatments start from $40 or $60 with insurance.

## Alarm Calls

### Wake Up Service

*(233 3300).* **Open** 24 hours daily. **Fee** $5.50 one call; discounts for regular use. **Credit** AmEx, MC, V.

With this service you speak to a real person, not a machine: so you must know exactly what you want because they can get impatient.

## Auto Services

### Car Wash

#### Carzapoppin'

*610 Broadway, at Houston Street (673 5115).* **Open** 24 hours daily. **No credit cards**.

It's $4.50 for the exterior of your car to have a full shampoo and set at Carzapoppin'. Interior cleaning costs extra.

### 24-hour Gas Stations

#### Downtown

*Amoco, 610 Broadway, at Houston Street (473 5924).* **Credit** AmEx, DC, Discover, JCB, MC, V. No repairs.

#### Midtown

*Gulf, FDR Drive & 23rd Street (686 4784).* **Credit** AmEx, Discover, Gulf, MC, V. Some repairs.

#### Uptown

*Shell, Amsterdam Avenue & 181st Street (928 3100).* **Credit** AmEx, Discover, MC, V. Repairs.

## Bartenders

### JC Taylor Maid Service

*136 East 57th Street, at Lexington Avenue (838 7171).* **Train** 4, 5 or 6 to 59th Street; N or R to Lexington Avenue. **Open** 8am-6pm Mon-Fri. **No credit cards**.

Waitresses, waiters, butlers, chefs, bartenders and gourmet cooks are available to cater for private or corporate functions whatever their size.

## Celebrity Service

Do you need to fax Arnold Schwarzenegger? You can't remember Nancy Reagan's birthday? Celebrity Service can help you out. Membership is from around $250 a month or $2500 a year. In exchange you will receive contact numbers for up to five celebrities a day, a daily four-page Celebrity Bulletin and access to a service that has fame at its fingertips. Call 245 1460.

## Chess Tuition

Take a lesson with grand master **Lev Alburt**. A private one-hour session is $70. Call 794 8706 for an appointment. Games can also be had at Marshall Chess Club (23 West 10th Street, 477 3716), where membership is normally from about $240 a year but visitors are welcome for a free game or two. You can also get a game on Seventh Avenue north of Times Square, or wager on a speed game in Washington Square. *See also* **Village Chess Shop** in *chapter* **Shopping: Speciality Stores**.

## Clothes Hire

### Animal Outfits for People

*2255 Broadway, at 81st Street (877 5085).* **Train** 1 or 9 to 79th Street. **Open** by appointment only, noon-6pm Mon-Fri. **No credit cards**.

Bears and rabbits are just two of the animal costumes available for hire here. If you can't find the beast you want, have an outfit made to measure.

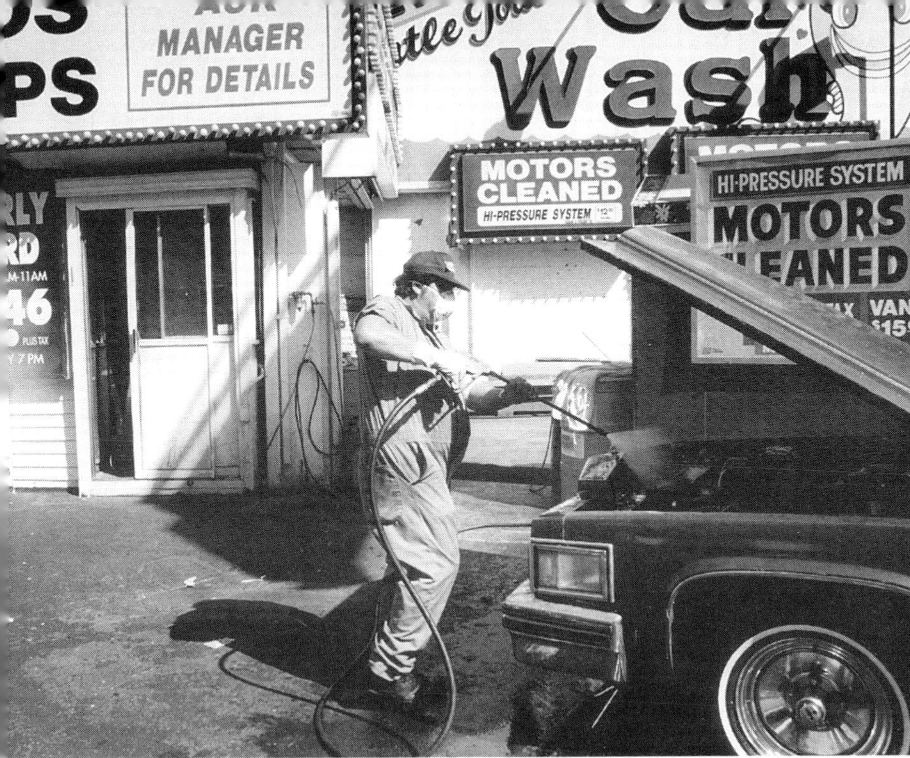


*Treat your car to a makeover at* **Carzapoppin'**. *See page 178.*

### Just Once

*292 Fifth Avenue, at 89th Street (987 0960).* **Train** 6 to 28th Street. **Open** 10.30am-6.30pm Mon-Fri; 11am-3pm Sat. **Credit** AmEx, MC, V.

This is primarily a bridal gown service, offering custom-tailored gowns for sale or hire. In addition a selection of European and American designer dresses are stocked for rental (short or long term): at the moment they're mostly cocktail frocks and formal wear, but the range may well be extended in the future.

### Zeller Tuxedos

*201 East 56th Street, at Third Avenue, second floor (355 0707).* **Train** 4, 5, or 6 to 59th Street; N or R to Lexington Avenue. **Open** 9am-8pm Mon-Fri; 10am-5pm Sat. **Credit** AmEx, MC, V.

Travellers not wishing to tote their tuxes around with them can take their pick from a large selection here, bearing labels such as Armani, Ungaro and Valentino. Hire charges are calculated on a daily basis.

## Cross-dressing

### Miss Vera's Finishing School For Boys Who Want to Be Girls

*(242 6449).*

We couldn't resist this one. Private classes run to around $375 and are taught by Veronica Vera and her 'dean of cosmetology', Paulette Powell. Day sessions are around $1000 and a weekend on the town with Vera and the girls can cost anything from $2000. Phone advice for over-18s is available at premium rates on 1-900 884. Consult the back pages of the *Village Voice* for similar services.

## Detectives & Bodyguards

### Check-a-Mate

*(toll-free 1-800 734-2660).*

This investigation service digs up the dirt on your spouse before or after the ceremony ($75 per hour; five-hour minimum). It can also get to the bottom of most mysteries. Armed and unarmed, male and female, the detectives have access to a full array of surveillance and forensic techniques. *See also below* **Elopements**.

### Tytell Typewriter Co

*116 Fulton Street, NY 10038 (233 5333).* **Open** by appointment only. **No credit cards**.

This family-run document research business has been around since the last war and helps companies, individuals and the NYPD to determine the origin of type-written notes. Handwriting analysis is also available.

## Domestic Staff

### Douglas Robert Maid Service

*200 Park Avenue South, at 17th Street (777 8455).* **Train** 4, 5, 6, L, N or R to 14th Street/Union Square. **Open** 8.30am-5pm Mon-Fri. **No credit cards**.

Staff cost $12 to $15 per hour.

### Maids Etc

*500 Park Avenue, at 59th Street (223 4455).* **Train** 4, 5 or 6 to 59th Street; N or R to Lexington Avenue. **Open** 7am-5pm daily; 24-hour answerphone. **No credit cards**.

Any kind of help, from a butler to someone who helps tidy up after a wild party. Rates from $12.50 per hour.

## Dry Cleaners

### One Hour Martinizing

*232 Ninth Avenue, near 24th Street (255 7317).* **Train** C or E to 23rd Street. **Open** 7am-7pm Mon-Fri; 8am-5pm Sat. **Credit** AmEx, DC, MC, V.

As you might guess, you can get your dry-cleaning done in an hour here, but stains such as inkspots and grease may take a day to dissolve.

### Midnight Express Cleaners

*(921 0111/1-800 999 8985).* **Open** 8am-10pm Mon-Fri; 9am-3pm Sat. **Credit** AmEx, MC, V.

Call Midnight Express and it can pick up your smellies anywhere below 96th Street within 10 to 15 minutes. It costs $7.25 for a man's suit to be cleaned, including pick-up and delivery. There are various minimum charges, depending on your location. If you're in a hotel you may have to play sneaky to avoid upsetting the concierge.

### Sutton Cleaners

*1060 First Avenue, between East 57th & East 58th Streets (755 1617).* **Train** 4, 5 or 6 to 59th Street; N or R to Lexington Avenue. **Open** 7am-6.30pm Mon-Fri; 8am-4pm Sat. Closed Sat July, Aug. **No credit cards.**

Sutton Cleaners deals with emergency one-hour jobs and tackles stains in a day or two; as well as offering a normal, non-urgent service. Same-day alterations on garments brought in before 10am. Collection and delivery is free up to 10 blocks from the store.

## Elopements

### Marcy Blum

*(688 3057).*

An international wedding consultancy that will arrange every last detail for people who want a romantic experience without the traditional complications.

## Florists

For Interflora deliveries worldwide, call City Floral on 410 0303/1-800 248 4692.

### Renny

*159 East 64th Street, between Third & Lexington Avenues (288 7000).* **Train** 6 to 68th Street. **Open** 9am-5pm Mon-Fri; 9am-3pm Sat. **Credit** AmEx, DC, MC, V.

'Exquisite flowers for the discriminating,' the slogan goes. Customers include David Letterman, Calvin Klein and a myriad party-givers. Renny also arranges over-the-top parties.

### Very Special Flowers

*204 West 10th Street, between Bleecker & West 4th Street (206 7236).* **Train** A, C, E, F or Q to West 4th Street. **Open** 10am-5pm Mon, 10am-7pm Tue-Fri; 11am-5pm Sat. **Credit** AmEx, MC, V.

And very special they are, indeed. Dried flower arrangements, exotic bonsai, miniature topiary and extravagant bouquets are the specialities.

## Furniture

### Churchill Furniture Rental

*6 East 32nd Street, between Fifth & Madison Avenues (686 0444).* **Train** B, D, F, N or R to 34th Street. **Open** 9am-6pm Mon-Thur; 9am-5pm Fri; 11am-5pm Sun. **Credit** AmEx, MC, V.

Residential furniture can be rented from Churchill for any length of time – from a day to five years.

### Furniture Medics

*(1-800 408 SERV).* **Open** 24 hours.

If you smash your hosts' Chippendale and need it fixed before their return, furniture medics will dispatch one of several local craftsmen to save your day. A consultation is never more than $55.

## Gift Deliveries

### Baskets by Wire

*(724 6900/1-718 746 1200).* **Telephone orders** 8am-7pm Mon-Sat; 9am-1pm Sun. **Credit** AmEx, DC, Discovery, MC, V.

Fruit, gourmet food, flowers and mylar or helium balloon bouquets are delivered nationwide.

### Select-a-Gram

*207 West 80th Street, near Broadway (1-800 292 1562).* **Train** 1, 9, A, B, C or D to Columbus Circle. **Office open** 9am-5pm Mon-Sat. **Telephone orders** 9am-6pm Mon-Sat. **Credit** AmEx, DC, MC, V.

Create your own gift basket with anything from Champagne to caviar to jelly beans, T-shirts and stuffed animals. Nationwide delivery.

## Hairdressers

You should always tip – unless you're disgusted with the result – about $3. And whoever washes your hair gets a dollar.

### Astor Place Hair Designers

*2 Astor Place, near Broadway (475 9854).* **Train** 6 to Astor Place; N or R to 8th Street. **Open** 8am-8pm Mon-Sat; 9am-6pm Sun. **No credit cards.**

A real New York experience, and a cheap place to get your hair cut. An army of barbers do anything from neat trims to interesting shaved designs, all to a loud rock or hip-hop accompaniment. No appointments are taken; you just take a number and wait with the crowd outside. Sunday mornings are quiet. Cuts from $10.

### Frederic Fekkai

*Bergdorf Goodman, 754 Fifth Avenue, at 58th Street (753 9500).* **Train** E or F to Fifth Avenue. **Open** 9am-6pm Mon-Wed, Fri, Sat; 9am-8pm Thur; 9am-6pm Sat. **Credit** AmEx, MC, V.

The hottest hairdresser in town, who for upwards of $90 will do wonders. He is responsible for Hilary Rodham Clinton's short do but that is apparently more a benchmark of his power than talent. Demi Moore, Barbra Streisand, David Geffen, Calvin Klein and Tina Brown are others to have been given the Fekkai chop. His minions cost considerably less. Also manicures, pedicures and massage.

### Heads & Tales Haircutting

*22 St Mark's Place, between Second & Third Avenues (677 9126).* **Train** 6 to Astor Place. **Open** 11.30am-midnight Tue-Fri; 11.30am-7pm Sat. **No credit cards.**

Heads & Tales provides a basic hairdressing service – wash, cut, styling and blow-drying. Just walk in: no appointment is necessary.

### Vidal Sassoon

*767 Fifth Avenue, at 58th Street, below FAO Schwarz (535 9200).* **Train** N or R to Fifth Avenue. **Open** 10am-6pm Mon; 9am-5pm Tue, Wed; 10am-7pm Thur; 9am-6pm Fri; 8.30am-5pm Sat. **Credit** AmEx, MC, V.

If you trust a Sassoon-in-training you can get your hair coloured, permed or trimmed for a bargain $14-$18. Show up Mon-Fri for a five-minute consultation.

## Interiors Shopping

### Design Find

*(1-516 365 4321).* **Open** by appointment only.
Interior designer Lauren Rosenberg-Moffit claims to know Manhattan like the back of her hand and will escort you on a memorable shopping tour of the city's showrooms, antique markets and back-alley stores, bringing you discounts of up to 20 per cent. Her fee varies according to your needs.

## Language Instruction

### Berlitz

*40 West 51st Street, between Fifth & Sixth Avenues (765 1000).* **Open** 7.30am-9.45pm daily by arrangement. **Train** B, D, F or Q to Rockefeller Center. **Credit** MC, V.
Learn any spoken language, either in private or group lessons.

## Laundry

Most neighbourhoods have coin-operated laundries, but busy New Yorkers usually cough up the few extra bucks to have theirs washed, dried and folded at one of the many neighbourhood services. But if you happen to have your dirty laundry on the Upper West Side we recommend **Ecomat** (362 2300) on 72nd Street between Broadway and Columbus Avenue. It's one of the city's only laundries to use natural, ecologically sound detergents. You can have your dirties collected and delivered in a natural gas fuelled van.

## Limousines & Luxury Cars

### Class Act Limousine

*631 West 130th Street, between 12th Avenue and Broadway (491 5300).* **Open** 24 hours daily. **Rates** from $40 per hour plus 20 per cent service charge for the driver. **Credit** AmEx, DC.
Standard features in Class Act's Lincoln, Cadillac, Jaguar and Mercedes limousines include a bar and a colour TV with a video and choice of 200 films.

### Roarin' Roadsters

*(1-201-569 4793).*
So you'd like to behave like a millionaire and whizz around Manhattan in a Ferrari, Porsche or Corvette? This New Jersey-based firm delivers the wheels of your choice for a fee. A top-of-the-range Ferrari will set you back around $350 a day with a two-day minimum.

*Go wild with a new style at* **Astor Place Hair Designers**. *See page 180.*

## Magazines & Newspapers

There are newsstands throughout the city. The ones below are open 24 hours daily. Unless one is listed, they have no phones.

### Downtown

*Delancey Street, at Essex Street.* **Train** F, J, M or Z to Essex/Delancey Street.
*Gem Spa, 131 Second Avenue, at St Mark's Place (529 1146).* **Train** 6 to Astor Place.
*Sheridan Square.* **Train** 1 or 9 to Christopher Street.
*Sixth Avenue, at 8th Street.* **Train** A, B, C, D, E, F or Q to West 4th Street.

### Midtown

*Broadway, at 50th Street.* **Train** 1, C or E to 50th Street.
*162 East 23rd Street, between Madison & Park Avenue.* **Train** 6 to 23rd Street.
*Eighth Avenue, at 42nd Street.* **Train** A, C or E to 42nd Street.
*Grand Hyatt, East 42nd Street, at Park Avenue.* **Train** 4, 5, 6 or 7 to Grand Central.

### Uptown

*First Avenue, at 63rd Street.* **Train** 4, 5, 6, N or R to 59th Street/Lexington Avenue.
*Broadway, at 72nd Street.* **Train** 1, 2, 3 or 9 to 72nd Street.
*Leighton's Newsstand, Columbus Avenue, at 81st Street.* **Train** B or C to 81st Street.
*Sajjadzheer Newsstand, Amsterdam Avenue, at 79th Street.* **Train** B or C to 81st Street.

## Magic

### Magickal Childe

*35 West 19th Street, between Fifth & Sixth Avenues (242 7182).* **Train** 1 or 9 to 18th Street; N or R to 23rd Street. **Open** 11am-8pm Mon-Sat; noon-6pm Sun. **Credit** AmEx, MC, V.
Customised love potions are mixed to order at this shop, which stocks everything from satanic T-shirts and goat's foot letter openers to occult herbs, oils and extracts. This is a must if you are after eye of newt or batwings by the pound. Rumour has it white magic is practised in darkened back rooms. Info on lectures and workshops also available. *See also chapter* **Shopping**.

## Nails

New York has more nail salons per capita than most other major cities. Because of this, manicures and pedicures come cheap (around $15-$20). Most of the nail stores are owned and operated by Chinese, Taiwanese or Korean women, who do a swift trade. You don't need an appointment, simply drop in and be pampered. Most salons do acrylic nails, too, but 'silk-wrap' is best.

## Music Lessons

### Drummers Collective

*541 Sixth Avenue, between 14th & 15th Streets (741 0091).* **Train** F or L to 14th Street/6th Avenue. **Open** 10am-10pm Mon-Thur; 10am-9pm Fri; 10am-6pm Sat; 11am-3pm Sun. **Credit** MC, V.
Classes and workshops for drummers of all abilities.

### Katie Agresta Vocal Studios

*119 West 88th Street, between Columbus & Amsterdam Avenues (724 1083).* **Train** 1, 2, 3, 9, B or C to 72nd Street. **Open** 11am-9pm Mon-Fri. **Credit** AmEx, MC, V.
Singing lessons cost $75 for each 30-minute session. Pupils include Annie Lennox and Cyndi Lauper.

## Pets

### Animal Medical Center

*510 East 62nd Street, near York Avenue (838 8100).* **Train** 4, 5, or 6 to 59th Street; N or R to Lexington Avenue. **Open** 24 hours daily. **Credit** AmEx, MC, V.
A useful 24-hour vet on the Upper East Side.

### Animal Travel Agency

*1926 Deer Park Avenue, Deer Park, NY (1-516 667 8924).* **Open** 8.30am-5pm Mon-Fri.
The agency's pet travel agent is an expert on airline travel regulations, so you can be sure your pet will arrive safely and comfortably. Basic shipping charges, including the collection fee, start at $250.

### Petography

*25 Central Park West (245 0914).*
Flattering portraits of your nearest and dearest by skilled photographers.

### Pet Care Network

*1645 First Avenue, at 86 Street (717 0053; home number, please call at a reasonable hour).* **Train** 4, 5 or 6 to Grand Central. **Credit** MC, V.
PCN provides an alternative to kennels. Fully insured pet sitters look after one animal at a time in the pet's own apartments. Care includes brushing, feeding, walking, medication and playtime. For a dog weighing under 40lbs the fee is $30 per day.

## Opticians

*See also chapter* **Shopping**.

### Cohen's Optical

*117 Orchard Street, at Delancey Street (674 1986).* **Train** F to Delancey Street; J to Essex Street. **Open** 9am-6pm daily. **Credit** AmEx, DC, MC, V.
The main branch of a large Manhattan firm. Thousands of frames in stock (many designer) and most prescriptions (glasses and contact lenses) can be dealt with in one hour. There's always an optician on duty.

## Picture Framers

### Acanthus and Reed

*401 East 76th Street, between First & York Avenues (628 9290).* **Train** 6 to 77th Street. **Open** 10am-6pm Mon-Fri. **Credit** AmEx, MC, V.
A tiny but elegant shop. Fees are high, but the work is lovingly done. Call first and explain what you want if you want it done quickly.

## Photographic

### Passport

#### Showbran Photo

*1347 Broadway, at 36th Street (947 9151).* **Train** B, D, F, Q, N or R to 34th Street. **Open** 7am-6pm Mon-Fri. **Credit** AmEx, Discover, MC, V.

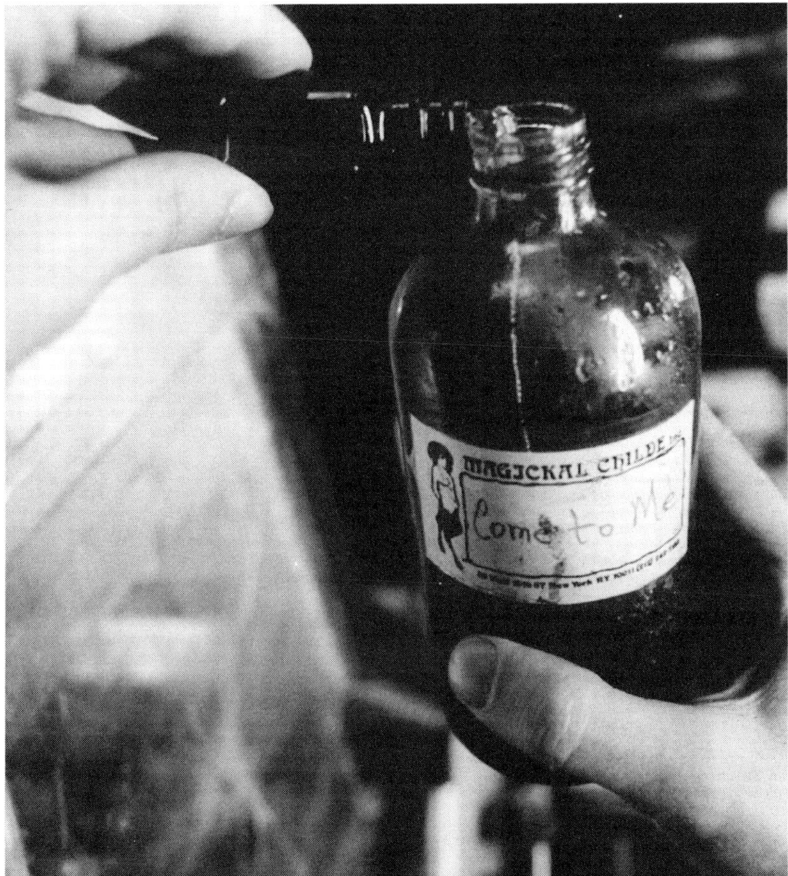


*Love for sale at* **Magickal Childe**, *in the form of personalised potions.* *See page 182.*

Passport and visa photos are taken and developed while you wait. Showbran also offers other developing and printing services and photocopying.
**Branches**: 512 Seventh Avenue (575 9580); the lobby of the Empire State Building, 33rd Street and Fifth Avenue entrances (868 5888).

## Photoshoots & Paparazzi

They say it can't buy love, but money will buy you your personal photographer who can organise a portrait session, fashion shoot or simply trail you around the city documenting your journey – guaranteed to make you feel like a celebrity. Rates vary according to the specifics of the job. Start by trying one of these. The first two are agencies for several photographers, the last for those to whom money is no object:
**Fred Marcus** (873 5588)
**Edge** (343 2260)
**Nana Goldin** (674 5396)
**Annie Leibovitz Studio** (807 0220).

## Photo Processing

Look for photo processing services in hundreds of pharmacies and most department stores. You get better results from places that develop on the premises and the best results from professional places, most numerous in the photo district (14th-23rd Streets between Broadway and Sixth Ave).

### Baboo Color Labs

*37 West 20th, between Fifth & Sixth Avenues (807 1574).* **Train** F to 23rd Street. **Open** 8am-midnight Mon-Fri; 10am-6pm Sat, Sun. **Credit** AmEx, MC, V.
This professional lab does fast, efficient work on colour and black and white prints and slides. It isn't too outrageously expensive if you just want to give your snaps a better chance of being beautiful.
**Branches**: 153 West 27th Street (229 2929); 104 Greene Street (925 8850).

### Harvey's One Hour Photo

*698 Third Avenue, between 43rd & 44th Streets (682 5045).* **Train** 4, 5, 6 or 7 to Grand Central. **Open** 8am-6pm Mon-Fri. **Credit** AmEx, MC, V.
Colour films can be developed in 60 minutes; slides and black and white need an overnight stay.

### K&L Custom PhotoGraphics

*222 East 44th Street, between Second & Third Avenues (661 5600).* **Train** 4, 5, 6 or 7 to Grand Central. **Open** 8am-8pm Mon-Fri. **Credit** AmEx, MC, V.
Slides take three hours, prints (colour and black and white) need a full day.

## Relaxation Therapy

### Let's Face It

*568 Broadway, at Prince Street, suite 604A (219 8970).* **Train** N or R to Prince Street. **Open** by appointment only. **Credit** AmEx, MC, V.
This young and talented team of beauty therapists, led by the gorgeous Marcia, do wonderful facials, pedicures, manicures, massage, waxing and general primping and preening. Facials are a bargain at $65 and include a very thorough cleansing. The place is a firm favourite with beauty writers from Condé Nast magazines like *Allure* and *GQ*.

### Madison Towers Health Center

*222 East 38th Street, between Madison & Park Avenues (685 6978).* **Train** 6 to 33rd Street. **Open** 11am-11pm Mon-Sat. **Credit** AmEx, DC, MC, V.
One of the best places in the city for shiatsu massage – clean and very relaxing. A $60 session includes eastern steam, sauna, hot and cold tubs and one-hour massage.

### Nymph

*112 Mercer Street, between Prince & Spring Streets (219 9833).* **Train** N or R to Prince Street; 6 to Spring Street. **Open** 11am-7pm Tue-Fri; 10am-4pm Sat. **No credit cards.**
The name is an acronym for New York Master Practitioners of Hair. And they mean business. Recline in the splendour of this spacious second-floor SoHo loft while having your scalp massaged with fragrant oils for a heavenly half hour ($35). It also offers cutting (from $45), colouring and perming.

### Russian and Turkish Baths

*268 East 10th Street, between First Avenue & Avenue A (473 8806).* **Train** 6 to Astor Place. **Open** 7.30am-10pm daily; women only Wed; men only Thur, Sun. **Credit** AmEx, Discover, MC, V.
This place has been around forever and is incredibly popular. Facilities include Russian steam room, Turkish steam room, redwood sauna, Jacuzzi, ice-cold pool, Swedish shower, health bar and lounge with cable TV. Entry is around $19, massages start at $26. 'Platza', a revitalising ritual that has you beating yourself with scented branches, costs $26.

### Synchro-Energize

*594 Broadway, at Houston Street (941 1184).* **Train** 6, B, D, F or Q to Broadway-Lafayette; 6 to Bleecker. **Open** daily by appointment only. **Credit** AmEx, Discovery, MC, V.
Hand over $20 ($12 students, seniors) and your brain and within 45 minutes you will feel as good as you would after a tranquil three-day vacation. 'Light and sound are used to alter your brain waves, taking you from a frenzied state of betawave activity to a relaxed, meditative theta state', they say. And that's not all. They also promise to 'stimulate all higher functions of brain activities'. Wow.

## Repairs

### Cameras & Camcorders

#### B&S Camera Repair

*110 West 30th Street, between Sixth & Seventh Avenues (563 1651).* **Train** N or R to 28th Street. **Open** 9am-6.30pm Mon-Fri; 11am-4pm Sat. **Credit** AmEx, MC, V.
All kinds of camera and camcorder problems can be solved here, with an eye to speed if necessary.

### Computers

#### Emergency Computer Repairs

*309 West 57th Street, between Eighth & Ninth Avenues (586 9319/1-800 586 9319).* **Train** N or R to 57th Street. **Open** noon-midnight daily. **Credit** AmEx, Discover, MC, V.
Specialists in Apples, IBMs and all related and their peripherals. Staff can recover your lost data and soothe you through all manner of computer disasters. On-site repairs.

### Handbags & Leather

#### Art Bag

*735 Madison Avenue, near East 64th Street (744 2720).* **Train** 6 to 68th Street. **Open** 9am-5.45pm Mon-Fri; 9am-5.30pm Sat. **Credit** AmEx, MC, V.
Art Bag are experts in handbag repair and it shows in the prices. It also makes reasonably priced copies of expensive designer bags.

#### R&S Cleaners

*176 Second Avenue, near 11th Street (674 6651).* **Train** 4, 5, 6, L, N or R to 14th Street/Union Square. **Open** *Sept-July* 7.30am-6.30pm Mon-Fri, 7.30am-5pm Sat; *Aug* 7.30am-6.30pm Mon-Fri; 7.30am-noon Sat. **No credit cards.**
Specialists in cleaning, repairing and tailoring leather jackets; prices start at $30 and cleaning generally takes three to five business days (24-hour service available).

### Tailors

#### Mr Tony Inc

*120 West 37th Street, between Broadway & Seventh Avenue (594 0930).* **Train** B, D, F, N or R to 34th Street. **Open** 8.30am-6.15pm Mon-Fri; 9am-4pm Sat. Closed Sat during summer. **Credit** AmEx, MC, V.
Major damage to clothes takes around a week to repair, minor repairs can be done in one to two days.

#### Raymond's Tailor Shop

*306 Mott Street, between Houston & Bleecker Streets (226 0747).* **Train** 6 to Bleecker Street; B, D or F to Broadway-Lafayette. **Open** 7.30am-7.30pm Mon-Fri; 9am-6.30pm Sat. **No credit cards.**
Raymond's can do alterations and repairs to 'anything that can be worn on the body'. There's an emergency service; delivery and collection is free over much of Manhattan.

### Shoes

#### B Nelson Shoe Inc

*Lower arcade, McGraw-Hill Building, 1221 Sixth Avenue, near 49th Street (869 3552).* **Train** N or R to 49th Street; 1 or 9 to 50th Street. **Open** 7.30am-5pm Mon-Fri. **Credit** AmEx, MC, V.
You can get your sneakers re-soled at Nelson, but these expert cobblers welcome any type of shoe or sole. Most dyeing and refinishing jobs are finished within 24 hours. Heel and sole replacements, lifts and half-soles usually take less than an hour.

### European Shoecrafters

*(677 0009).*
All leather repairs, from shoes to jackets, with the ease of both a pick-up and delivery service.

## Umbrellas

### Uncle Sam Umbrella Shop

*161 West 57th Street, between Sixth & Seventh Avenues (582 1976).* **Train** B, N, Q or R to 57th Street. **Open** 9.30am-6.15pm Mon-Fri; 10am-5pm Sat. **Credit** AmEx, MC, V.
Umbrellas, parasols and canes are re-covered and repaired at Uncle Sam's.

## Watches

### Falt Watch Company

*Grand Central Terminal, 42nd Street at Park Avenue, third floor (697 6380).* **Train** 4, 5, 6 or 7 to Grand Central **Open** 10am-5pm. **No credit cards.**
Staff will repair just about any watch.

## Tattoos & Piercing

Tattooing is only legal in New York by private arrangement – you can't go in off the street. There are always advertisements on the back page of *The Village Voice*. Piercing is completely unregulated so be careful.

### Gauntlet

*144 Fifth Avenue, at 19th Street (229 0180).* **Train** N or R to 23rd Street. **Open** 2.30-7.30pm Mon-Sat; 1-6pm Sun. **Credit** AmEx, MC, V.
A place with unrivalled experience, Gauntlet is the place to go if you aren't satisfied with the holes you were born with. A Prince Albert is only $35, though navels, nipples and noses remain the most popular perforations.

### Temptu

*26 West 17th Street, between Fifth & Sixth Avenues, fifth floor (675 4000).* **Train** 4, 5, 6, N, R or L to Union Square; F to 14th Street. **Open** 9am-5pm Mon-Fri. **Credit** AmEx, MC, V.
For those who can't take the needle, this is the home of the temporary tattoo. It has every design imaginable in paint-on, water-based and rubbing alcohol formats. Prices start at $1.25 a sheet. Temptu gave Robert DeNiro those nasty tats for *Cape Fear*.

## Television & VCR Rental

### Columbus TV & Video Center

*552 Columbus Avenue, at 86th Street (496 2626).* **Train** 1, 9, B or C to 86th Street. **Open** 9am-8pm Mon-Sat. **Credit** AmEx, Discover, MC, V.
VCRs and TVs of all types are available for hire.

## Video Sales & Rental

Current ID (such as a passport) plus a credit card (and sometimes proof of address) are needed if you want to rent a video from any of the following outlets. Note that US videos are NTSC format and don't work in UK or Australian VCR machines, which run on PAL.

### Kim's Video

*37 St Mark's Place, near Second Avenue (505 0311).* **Train** 6 to Astor Place **Open** 8am-midnight Mon-Sat; noon-midnight Sun. **Credit** ($20 minimum) AmEx, MC, V.
If Kim's doesn't have it, no-one else will. It carries over 7000 titles and specialises in cult, classic and foreign films, costing $3 ($3.50 for new releases) a night to rent. VCR accessories and repairs are on offer, too.
**Branches**: 99 Avenue A (529 3410); 144 Bleecker Street (260 1010); 350 Bleecker Street (675 8996).

### Tower Video

*2107 Broadway, at 74th Street (496 2500).* **Train** 1, 2, 3 or 9 to 72nd Street. **Open** 9am-midnight daily. **Credit** AmEx, MC, V.
Tower sells and rents out every type of video – culture, exercise, theatrical, special interest, music, the lot. Most tapes cost $2.99 a day to hire.
**Branches** 1535 Third Avenue (369 2500); 383 Lafayette Street (505 1166).

## Visas

### Visa Express Inc

*421 Seventh Avenue, at 33rd Street (629 4541).* **Train** A, C or E to 34th Street. **Open** 10.30am-6pm Mon-Fri. **Credit** MC, V.
Visas for all countries can be obtained here, for individual and business use, for $40. No extensions to tourist visas.

## Fun & fortune

It shouldn't surprise you that New Yorkers pay huge sums to be told that there is light at the end of the tunnel. There's hardly a street in the city without astrologists, Tarot readers, palmists or psychics.

### Frank Andrews

*(226 2194).* **Open** call before 10am for appointments.
This psychic, palmist and tarot reader is highly regarded in New York and while he won't reveal names of his living clients, he admits to having worked with John Lennon and Perry Ellis. The charge is $150 per session.

### Mary T Browne

*(242 6080).* **Open** by appointment only.
An astrologer/spiritualist/psychic who has an impressive client list that includes actors, writers, directors and Wall Street types. She's often booked weeks in advance. From $150 per hour.

### Yolanna

*245 East 58th Street, at Second Avenue (308 0836).* **Open** by appointment only.
Yolanna charges around $200 a session for her psychic services. Donna Karan, Barbra Streisand and other luminaries are said to rely on her judgement.

### Shala Mattingly

*(307 1049).* **Open** by appointment only.
Shala's speciality is past-life regression therapy; she also practises forensic hypnosis. Rates vary according to your needs; private consultations and parties considered.

# Museums & Galleries

# Art Galleries

***Whether you're a high-rolling collector or just an art-loving spectator, you'll find what you're looking for on New York's gallery trail.***

Like so many things in New York, the art world is all about geography. The uptown and midtown galleries exist in a patrician world of calculated investment and multi-million dollar status games; while the locus for edgy, experimental work is decidedly downtown. However, even downtown has changed in recent years, and most commercial galleries there deal increasingly in established names and critic-friendly newcomers, leaving it to the co-operative and non-profit galleries to take the real risks. SoHo, once home to only the most avant garde pioneers, now represents a broader than ever spectrum of the market, including galleries as staid as any you'll find on Madison Avenue (in fact several uptown galleries now have space in SoHo).

The true outlands are now in places like TriBeCa and Chelsea, where a handful of pioneer galleries are taking advantage of the development of property out by the river; and in Williamsburg, Brooklyn, where an artists' community has grown up over the last few years, creating co-operatives and grass-roots galleries and declaring a rebellious independence from the Manhattan scene.

Though things are improving, most artists and galleries are still working their way out of recession. After the crazed spending of the 1980s when prices reached unsustainable highs, the ensuing crash filtered down throughout the art world. And though the feeling is that the darkest days are over, the scene is changed forever. Everything seems a little more flat, as people play it safe and follow the pack. No longer is this the place to become an overnight sensation as the result of some overwealthy patron adopting your work – though there is still a constant stream of hopeful artists arriving here dreaming that dream.

To keep up with the art world, New Yorkers devour the reviews in the *New York Times* and *Time Out New York*, and such specialist magazines as *Artnews* ($6), *Art in America* ($4.95), *Modern Painters* ($9), and the distinctively square-shaped *Artforum International* ($7). These are available on many newsstands and in galleries and museums. For an overview of the economics of the art market, try the monthly *Art & Antiques* ($3.95). You'll find profiles of top artists and collectors, articles on what's up for auction, what to invest in and which styles and items are selling best, as well as listings of current New York exhibitions. The *Art Now Gallery Guide* is invaluable, as it lists all the exhibitions throughout the city each month, and even has helpful gallery maps. It can be purchased for $1.50 in museum bookstores, or you can try asking for a complimentary copy at a gallery.

For those buying a work of art, payment will usually be by cheque, cash or travellers' cheque: very few places accept credit cards. Don't worry about shipping: galleries are used to dealing with that side of things.

This chapter is primarily concerned with commercial galleries: if you want to find out about New York's major public collections, *see chapter* **Museums**. All opening hours given for galleries are for winter schedules, unless otherwise stated. Summer schedules (June-August) are highly erratic, with galleries open during the week often closed on Saturdays. Phone before visiting.

## Upper East Side

Many of the galleries on the Upper East Side sell masterworks at prices that are beyond most people's budgets, and sometimes even beyond the imagination. However, you can look for free, and many of the works that you'll see here are treasures that could swiftly vanish into somebody's private collection. Many of the galleries in this area, like those on 57th Street, deal in newer talent and some offer prints and multiples.

### ACA Galleries

*41 East 57th Street, at Madison Avenue (644 8300).* **Train** 4, 5 or 6 to 59th Street; N or R to Lexington Avenue. **Open** *Sept-June* 10am-5.30pm Tue-Sat; *July, Aug* 10am-5.30pm Tue-Fri.

ACA is an excellent place to see work by major nineteenth- and twentieth-century American artists, such as Georgia O'Keeffe, Milton Avery and Reginald Marsh.

### Cohen Gallery

*1018 Madison Avenue, at 79th Street, 4th floor (628 0303).* **Train** 6 to 77th Street. **Open** 10am-6pm Mon-Fri; 10am-5.30pm Sat. Closed Aug.

This is a new but already well-respected venue, and its shows have received a lot of critical attention. Recent exhibitions have featured work by young English conceptualists Damien Hirst and Matt Collishaw, among others.

### Gagosian

*980 Madison Avenue, at 76th Street (744 2313).* **Train** 6 to 77th Street. **Open** *winter* 10am-6pm Tue-Sat; *summer* 10am-6pm Mon-Fri.

American Girl in Florence *by Ruth Orkin,*
*available at the* **Witkin Gallery**. *See page 197*

Larry Gagosian is one of the more colourful figures to have emerged on the New York scene over the past few years. He's been hugely successful in secondary-market sales but shows new work as well. Some exhibitions are brilliantly curated (former top critic Robert Pincus-Witten works for the gallery). Also be sure to check out the downtown Gagosian (*listed under* **SoHo**) and 65 Thompson Street (a collaborative effort with Leo Castelli).

### Hirschl & Adler Galleries

*21 East 70th Street, at Madison Avenue (535 8810).* **Train** 6 to 68th Street. **Open** *Sept-May* 9.30am-5.30pm Tue-Fri; 9.30am-4.45pm Sat; *June-Aug* 9.30am-4.45pm Mon-Fri.

A wide variety of eighteenth-, nineteenth- and twentieth-century American and European paintings, plus American prints and contemporary work, including sculpture.

### M Knoedler & Co Inc

*19 East 70th Street, between Madison & Fifth Avenues (794 0550).* **Train** 6 to 68th Street. **Open** *Sept-May* 9.30am-5.30pm Tue-Fri; 10am-5.30pm Sat; *June-Aug* 9.30am-5pm Mon-Fri.

Knoedler shows famous abstract expressionists and other greats, such as Jules Olitski, Frank Stella, Nancy Graves, Robert Rauschenberg, Howard Hodgkin, Robert Motherwell, Richard Diebenkorn, John Walker and David Smith.

### Michael Werner

*21 East 67th Street, between Madison& Fifth Avenues (988 1623).* **Train** 6 to 68th Street. **Open** *Sept-May* 10am-6pm Mon-Sat; *June-Aug* 10am-6pm Mon-Fri.

Werner opened his Manhattan gallery during the 1980s as an international addition to his successful operation in Germany. It is a small but elegant space with finely curated exhibitions of work by such European art stars as Marcel Broodthaers, Sigmar Polke, Per Kirkeby and AR Penck.

### Terry Dintenfass

*20 East 79th Street, at Fifth Avenue (581 2268).* **Train** 6 to 77th Street. **Open** *Sept-May* 10am-5.30pm Tue Sat; call for summer hours.

Terry Dintenfass has recently moved his gallery from 57th Street to this much larger space, which is occupied in association with the Salander O'Reilly Gallery (879 6606). Dintenfass's artists remain the same; a broad selection of twentieth-century folk such as Robert Andrew Parker, Antonio Frasconi and Elizabeth Frink.

## 57th Street

The home of Carnegie Hall, the Russian Tea Room, exclusive boutiques and numerous art galleries, 57th Street is an old-style slice of elegant, moneyed New York – ostentatious and expensive but fun to explore. Most of the galleries here are established names, and therefore more staid than their SoHo counterparts. Lately, though, there has been greater commerce between the two areas, as some uptown galleries also have spaces downtown. Note that galleries here are rarely on ground level; you will need to know exact addresses to find them.

### André Emmerich

*41 East 57th Street, between Madison & Fifth Avenues (752 0124).* **Train** 4, 5 or 6 to Lexington Avenue. **Open** *Sept-May* 10am-5.30pm Tue-Sat; *June-Aug* 10am-5pm Mon-Fri.

André Emmerich's interest is divided between important modern painting, particularly from the colour-field school, and antiquities from major civilisations. Various works by David Hockney are on show (including his prints, stage sets, paintings and photographs) as well as pieces by Anthony Caro, Sam Francis and Morris Louis, Hans Hoffmann and Beverly Pepper among others.

### Blum-Helman

*20 West 57th Street, between Fifth & Sixth Avenues (245 2888).* **Train** B, N or R to 57th Street. **Open** 10am-6pm Tue-Sat. Closed Aug.

This enormous space is ideal for viewing the large-scale painting and sculpture that's shown here, including work by Ellsworth Kelly, Richard Diebenkorn, Richard Serra and Richard Tuttle.

### Marian Goodman Gallery

*24 West 57th Street, between Fifth & Sixth Avenues (977 7160).* **Train** B, N or R to 57th Street. **Open** *Sept-May* 10am-6pm Mon-Sat; *July-Aug* 10am-6pm Mon-Fri.

Marian Goodman typically presents striking installations of critically acclaimed work by American and European painters, sculptors and conceptualists. Her impressive roster of gallery artists includes such names as Art & Language, Anselm Kiefer, Christian Boltanski, Jeff Wall, Rebecca Horn and Maria Nordman.

### Marlborough

*40 West 57th Street, between Fifth & Sixth Avenues (541 4900).* **Train** B, N or R to 57th Street. **Open** *Sept-May* 10am-5.30pm Mon-Sat; *June-Aug* 10am-5.30pm Mon-Fri.

Go to the Marlborough to see work by Larry Rivers, Red Grooms, Rufino Tamayo, Bill Jacklin, Francis Bacon, Stephen Conroy, RB Kitaj, Kurt Schwitters and more. The connected gallery, Marlborough Graphics, is also strong.

### PaceWildenstein

*32 East 57th Street, between Park & Madison Avenues (421 3292).* **Train** 4, 5 or 6 to 59th Street; N or R to Lexington Avenue. **Open** *Sept-May* 9.30am-6pm Tue-Fri; 10am-6pm Sat. *June-Aug* 10am-6pm Mon-Thur; 10am-4pm Fri.

A real heavyweight, offering work by Picasso, Louise Nevelson, Mark Rothko, Jim Dine, Lucas Samaras, Alexander Calder and Julian Schnabel. Pace Prints and Primitive, at the same address, publishes prints from Old Masters to big-name contemporaries, and has a fine collection of African art.

### Robert Miller

*41 East 57th Street, at Madison Avenue (980 5454).* **Train** 4, 5 or 6 to 59th Street; N or R to Lexington Avenue. **Open** *Sept-May* 10am-6pm Tue-Sat; *June-Aug* 10am-6pm Mon-Fri.

Robert Miller shows work by Lee Krasner, Louise Fishman, Louise Bourgeois, Jedd Garet and Jean-Michel Basquiat, as well as the late Robert Mapplethorpe's controversial photography. It's also worth having a look through the beautiful catalogues produced here.

### Sidney Janis Gallery

*110 West 57th Street, between Sixth & Seventh Avenues (586 0110).* **Train** B, N or R to 57th Street. **Open** 10am-5.30 pm Tue-Sat. Closed July, Aug.

This blue-chip gallery is almost an institution. It shows both twentieth-century masters (including Braque, Picasso, Klee, Giacometti and Mondrian) and current American favourites such as Duane Michaels and George Segal. Photographer Annie Leibowitz, best known for her celebrity portraits, also exhibits here.

### Tatistcheff and Company

*50 West 57th Street, between Fifth & Sixth Avenues, 8th floor (664 0907).* **Train** B, N or R to 57th Street. **Open** *Sept-May* 10am-6pm Tue-Sat; *June-Aug* 10am-6pm Mon-Fri. Closed last two weeks of Aug.

Fans of quality representational painting in the spirit of Balthus or André Derain should come here. Artists on the roster include Lincoln Perry and Harold Reddicliff.

*From the semi-permanent collection at the* **New Museum of Contemporary Art***: works by James Albertson and Allan McCollum.* *See page 197.*

## Downtown & SoHo

SoHo's roots are bohemian, with ties to the East Village scene of previous years, whose artists and gallery owners made the place what it is today. If you're looking to discover new talent, a trawl round SoHo's smaller galleries is your best bet. Make sure you check out the summer group shows for the freshest names. Recently many of the establishment galleries have staked claims in SoHo, and serious collectors now shop both up- and downtown. The genuine penniless bohemians, meanwhile, have shipped out to suburbs such as Williamsburg (*see box page 194*).

### Broadway

#### Cavin-Morris Gallery

*560 Broadway,at Prince Street, suite 205 (226 3768).* **Train** 6 to Spring Street; N or R to Prince Street. **Open** 10am-6pm Tue-Sat. Closed Aug.
Formerly in TriBeCa, Cavin-Morris caters to those with an enthusiasm for 'Outsider Art' (often by self-taught artists) or work in that spirit. Gallery shows demonstrate a very particular sensibility. Often ethnic pieces are also available, and a recent exhibition featured Latin American art. A visit here will almost always reveal something wonderful, or at the very least surprising.

#### Curt Marcus Gallery

*578 Broadway, between Houston & Prince Street (226 3200).* **Train** 6 to Bleecker Street; B, D or F to Broadway/Lafayette; N or R to Prince Street. **Open** *Sept-May* 10am-6pm Tue-Sat; *June-Aug* 11am-6pm Tue-Fri.
This is a place for the peculiar but appealing, from Richard Pettibone's Shakerish objects to cryptic, precisely rendered paintings by Mark Innerst and Mark Tansey. Also shown here is the mysterious and resonant photography of Barbara Ess, made with a pin-hole camera, as well as compelling work by Bruce Conner and other gallery artists.

#### Lennon, Weinberg

*560 Broadway, between Houston & Prince Streets (941 0012).* **Train** 6 to Bleecker Street; B, D or F to Broadway/Lafayette; N or R to Prince Street. **Open** 10am-6pm Tue-Sat. Closed Aug and summer Sats.
American post-war and contemporary artists are represented, including Chuck Connelly, Raoul Hague, Catherine Murphy and HC Westerman.

#### Max Protetch Gallery

*560 Broadway , at Prince Street (966 5454).* **Train** 6 to Spring Street; N or R to Prince Street. **Open** *Sept-May* 10am-6pm Tue-Sat; *June, July* 10am-6pm Mon-Fri; by appointment only Aug.
As well as showing contemporary painting, sculpture, and ceramics, Max Protetch Gallery is one of the few places that finds space for architectural drawings and models by contemporary architects. Also featured here is the work of Siah Armajani, a sculptor of Iranian descent, who is particularly strong in site-specific pieces.

#### PPOW

*532 Broadway, at Spring Street, 3rd floor (941 8642).* **Train** 6 to Spring Street; N or R to Prince Street. **Open** *Sept-May* 10am-6pm Tue-Sat; *June-Aug* 10am-5pm Mon-Thur; 10am-3pm Fri.
A strong presence among the newer galleries, concentrating on narrative painting and photography. Roger Ackling, Will Mentor, Margaret Curtis and David Wojnarowicz are among PPOW's future stars.

### Grand Street

#### CRG Art

*93 Grand Street, between Mercer & Greene Streets (966 4360).* **Train** N or R to Canal Street. **Open** *Sept-May* 11am-6pm Tue-Sat; *June, July* 11am-5pm Tue-Fri; by appointment only Aug.
The name comes from the partnership of Carla Chammas, Richard Desroche and Glenn McMillan, whose newish downtown premises represent such chance-takers as Seton Smith, Mona Hatoum and Sam Reveles.

#### Paul Kasmin

*74 Grand Street, between Wooster & Greene Streets (219 3219).* **Train** A, C, E, N or R to Canal Street. **Open** *Sept-May* 10am-6pm Tue-Fri; 11am-6pm Sat; *June, July* 10am-6pm Mon-Fri. Closed Aug.
In amongst well-chosen group shows of gallery artists are names like Alesandro Twombly. Kasmin's intimate exhibitions emphasise collections of drawings, vintage photography and an occasional display of African works.

### Greene Street

#### Barbara Gladstone

*99 Greene Street, between Prince & Spring Streets (431 3334).* **Train** C or E to Spring Street; N or R to Prince Street. **Open** *Sept-May* 10am-6pm Tue-Sat; *June, July* 10am-6pm Mon-Fri. Closed Aug.
Gladstone shows high-quality painting, sculpture and photography by established artists including Jenny Holzer, Richard Prince, Rosemarie Trockel, Anish Kapoor, Matt Mullican and Vito Acconci. Emphasis is on American, English and German conceptual work.

#### Jack Tilton

*49 Greene Street , between Broome & Grand Streets (941 1775).* **Train** 6, C or E to Spring Street. **Open** *Sept-June* 10am-6pm Tue-Sat; *July* 10am-6pm Tue-Fri. Closed Aug.
Tilton's often provocative shows seem much more at home since the gallery moved here from its original uptown location. Lyle Ashton-Harris, Fabrice Hybert and Fred Tomaselli are some of the artists represented.

#### John Weber

*142 Greene Street, between Houston & Prince Streets, 3rd floor (966 6115).* **Train** B, D, F or Q to Broadway/Lafayette; N or R to Prince Street. **Open** *Sept-May* 10am-6pm Tue-Sat. Call for summer hours.
Weber shows strong conceptual and minimal work, with emphasis on sculpture. Artists include Sol LeWitt, Hans Haacke, Daniel Buren, Alice Aycock, Hamish Fulton and Allan McCollum. Work by less familiar talent is on display in the small 'project room'.

#### Metro Pictures

*150 Greene Street, between Houston & Prince Streets (925 8335).* **Train** B, D, F or Q to Broadway/Lafayette; N or R to Prince Street. **Open** *Sept-May* 10am-6pm Tue-Sat; *June, July* 10am-6pm Tue-Fri. Closed Aug.
Metro places the emphasis on very hip conceptual work – mostly installations and photography – with a keen critical edge. The work is often by younger artists and includes Cindy Sherman's unnerving cibachromes, Louise Lawler's cool photographic critiques, Mike Kelley's conflations of viciousness and pathos; Fred Wilson's meditations on the West's plundering of African culture and Martin Kippenberger's German 'bad boy' art.

#### Postmasters

*80 Greene Street, at Spring Street, 2nd floor (941 5711).* **Train** 6, C or E to Spring Street. **Open** *Sept-July* 11am-6pm Tue-Sat; by appointment only Aug.

*But is it art?* **The Marlborough Gallery** *certainly thinks so.* *See page 190.*

# Williamsburg

Now that SoHo is an establishment force in the art market, and rents for Manhattan loft-space are beyond the reach of all but the lucky few, the active machine of artistic creation has packed up its paints and clay and moved to various places off the island, in particular the post-industrial neighbourhood of Williamsburg in northern Brooklyn.

The southern part of Williamsburg is divided between the vibrant sights and sounds of a large Hispanic neighbourhood and the quiet, ordered environs of one of the world's largest communities of Hasidic Jews. However, north of here is a Polish/Italian working-class area which originally served the East River docks and is now being overrun by a class of arty young imports. There is still a lot of manufacturing here, but increasingly the old factory buildings are being occupied by artists' lofts and studios; while local bars and restaurants have emerged or evolved (centred around the Bedford Avenue station on the L line of the subway) to serve the new population's bohemian pretensions.

There are several galleries here (*see below*), though few have regular hours. Call for details, or pick up a copy of *Waterfront Week*, the neighbourhood's newsletter, available free in local bars and stores. There are also occasional summer festivals during which there are open studios and haphazard street activities.

In Williamsburg, as in SoHo in the 1980s, art is a state of mind, and in addition to many productive artists, there are plenty of wasters with no visible means of support, ambling their way from one existential conversation to the next. Join them for a moccachino in **L Café** (pictured below), 189 Bedford Avenue at North 7th Street (1-718 388 6792), for a pint of Brooklyn lager in the beautifully preserved **Teddy's**, 96 Berry Street at North 8th Street (1-718 384 9787), or for pierogis and apple sauce at neighbourhood standby **Kasia's**, 146 Bedford Avenue at North 9th Street (1-718 387 8780), with its excellent Polish diner food.

And while in the 'burg, you might want to visit the used clothes heaven of **Domseys** (*see chapter* **Shopping**), or the famous steakhouse **Peter Luger's** (*see chapter* **Restaurants**). Adventurous visitors might also want to stroll down to the derelict East River shoreline for some stunning views of midtown Manhattan.

**Art Moving**

*301 Bedford Avenue, at South 1st Street (1-718 782 4206).*

**Four Walls**

*138 Bayard Street, at Graham Avenue (1-718 388 3169).*

**Source**

*173 North 3rd Street, between Bedford Street & Metropolitan Avenue (1-718 384 9371).*

**Pierogi 2000**

*167 North 9th Street, between Bedford & Briggs Streets (1-718 599 2144).*

**Momenta**

*72 Berry Street, between North 9th & 10th Streets (1-718 218 8058).*

Drawings, photographs, videos, paintings and sculpture, all with strong conceptual leanings, are presented at this intriguing and very international gallery.

### Roger Meriens

*76 Greene Street, between Spring & Broome Streets, 2nd floor (334 9099).* **Train** 6, C or E to Spring Street. **Open** *Sept-May* 11am-6pm Wed-Sat. Call for summer hours.
Another new cutting-edge gallery. Chris Wilder, Skip Arnold, Sarah Seager and Erwin Wurm are among Merien's emerging artists.

### Sperone Westwater

*142 Greene Street, between Houston & Prince Streets (431 3685).* **Train** B, D, F or Q to Broadway/Lafayette; N or R to Prince Street. **Open** *Sept-May* 10am-6pm Tue-Sat; *June-July* 10am-6pm Mon-Fri; *Aug* by appointment only.
A stronghold of painting, and one of the best places to see work by the Italians – neo-Expressionist and otherwise – including Francesco Clemente, Sandro Chia, Mario Merz and Mimmo Paladino. You'll also find On Kawara's calendars and Wolfgang Laib's beeswax installations here.

## Mercer Street

### Holly Solomon Gallery

*172 Mercer Street, at Houston Street (941 5777).* **Train** B, D, F or Q to Broadway/Lafayette; N or R to Prince Street. **Open** *Sept-May* 10am-6pm Tue-Sat; *June-Aug* 10am-6pm Tue-Fri.
Solomon's dramatic space shouldn't be missed. She shows distinctive work by a quirky selection of artists including Nicholas Africano, Nam June Paik, Melissa Miller, Kim McConnel and Frank Majore.

## Prince Street

### Andrea Rosen Gallery

*130 Prince Street, between Wooster Street & West Broadway, 3rd floor (941 0203).* **Train** C or E to Spring Street. **Open** *Sept-May* 10am-6pm Tue-Sat; *June, July* 10am-6pm Mon-Fri; *Aug* by appointment only.
This small gallery is a great place to scout for new talent, such as Rita Ackermann's endearing but unsettling waifs. Inevitably work can be uneven but the flip side is that it is rewardingly fresh. Rosen often shows work by younger, relatively unknown artists – and prices are reasonable; she also exhibits the more familiar conceptualist Felix Gonzales-Torres. The emphasis is on experimental work. Try to check out summer group shows.

### Luhring Augustine

*130 Prince Street, between Wooster & West Broadway, 2nd floor (219 9600).* **Train** C or E to Spring Street. **Open** *Sept-May* 10am-6pm Tue-Sat; *June-Aug* 10am-6pm Mon-Fri.
Luhring Augustine's gracious gallery features work from his impressive stable of artists, which includes the Germans Albert Oehlen and Günther Förg, Britain's Rachel Whiteread and the Americans Jack Pierson, Christopher Wool, Larry Clark and Paul McCarthy.

## West Broadway

### Charles Cowles

*420 West Broadway, between Prince & Spring Streets (925 3500).* **Train** C or E to Spring Street. **Open** *Sept-June* 10am-6pm Tue-Sat; *July* 10am-5pm Mon-Fri; *Aug* by appointment only.
This gallery shows modern and contemporary paintings, sculpture and installations, including figurative sculpture by Manuel Neri and swamp paintings by David Bates.

### Leo Castelli

*420 West Broadway, between Spring & Prince Streets (431 5160).* **Train** C or E to Spring Street. **Open** *Sept-June* 10am-6pm Tue-Sat; *July, Aug* 11am-5pm Tue-Fri.
As one of the most revered personalities in New York's art world, Leo Castelli's decisions are followed with interest by collectors and dealers throughout the world, and as he reaches his 90th year, much thought is given to the shake-up that will occur after his passing. The work shown here can be expensive – Castelli is known for representing such seminal figures as Jasper Johns, Claes Oldenberg and James Rosenquist. But he also shows younger, or less familiar, artists such as Mike and Doug Starn and Sophie Calle. There is another gallery, as well as a graphics branch, at 578 Broadway (431 6279).

### Mary Boone Gallery

*417 West Broadway, between Spring & Prince Streets (431 1818).* **Train** C or E to Spring Street. **Open** *Sept-June* 10am-6pm Tue-Sat; *July, Aug* by appointment only.
One of the most powerful figures to emerge in the New York art world during the last decade, Mary Boone deserves credit for bringing to attention the work of such quintessentially 1980s painters as David Salle, Julian Schnabel and Eric Fischl. Her gallery is still a bastion of the conspicuous glamour of a few years back and Boone's current list includes such stellar names as Barbara Kruger, Sean Scully, Philip Taaffe and the late Moira Dryer.

### Sonnabend Gallery

*420 West Broadway, between Spring & Prince Streets (966 6160).* **Train** C or E to Spring Street. **Open** *Sept-May* 10am-6pm Tue-Sat; *June, July* 11am-5pm Tue-Fri. Closed Aug.
Make sure you visit this elegant venue for strong work from artists such as Haim Steinbach, Ashley Bickerton, Gilbert & George, Hiroshi Sugimoto, Jeff Koons and Anne and Patrick Poirier. Openings here are events not to be missed, with many art-world stars passing through.

## Wooster Street

### American Fine Arts

*22 Wooster Street, at Grand Street (941 0401).* **Train** A, C or E to Canal Street. **Open** *Sept-May* 10am-6pm Tue-Sat; *June-Aug* 11am-6pm Mon-Fri.
Colin de Land began his gallery business in the East Village but moved his unique space to the southern fringe of SoHo a few years ago. His shows retain a refreshingly ad hoc feeling which at times belies the consistently strong quality of the work he shows. A number of his artists are now achieving international reputations, in particular Jessica Stockholder, Jessica Diamond, Mark Dion and Peter Fend. De Land also shows work by European artists such as Christian Phillip Müller and Cosima von Bonin.

### Basilco Fine Arts

*26 Wooster Street, at Grand Street (966 1831).* **Train** A, C or E to Canal Street. **Open** *Sept-June* 11am-6pm Tue-Sat; *July* 11am-6pm Tue-Fri. Closed Aug.
After he left Sonnabend, Stefano Basilico has set up in a number of spaces, but this is the first with any kind of permanence. Dedicated to the youthful vigour of the city's emerging artists, it's a place to look for the next handful of contenders.

### Gagosian

*136 Wooster Street, between Houston & Prince Streets (228 2828).* **Train** C or E to Spring Street; N or R to Prince Street. **Open** *Sept-May* 10am-6pm Tue-Sat; *June, July* 10am-6pm Mon-Fri; *Aug* by appointment only.
A branch of Larry Gagosian's blue-chip uptown gallery, this dazzling space provides a perfect setting for the imposing,

at times mammoth, pieces it houses – by such names as Howard Hodgkin, Walter de Maria, Mark di Suvero, Richard Serra and Andy Warhol.

### Paula Cooper

*155 Wooster Street, between Houston & Prince Streets (674 0766).* **Train** C or E to Spring Street; N or R to Prince Street. **Open** *Sept-May* 10am-6pm Tue-Sat; *June-Aug* 9.30am-5.30pm Mon-Fri.
Cooper was one of the first dealers to stake out space in SoHo during the 1960s. Her artists tend to be established figures such as Carl Andre, Jonathan Borofsky, Joel Shapiro, Elizabeth Murray, Robert Wilson and Jennifer Bartlett.

### Tony Shafrazi Gallery

*119 Wooster Street, between Prince& Spring Streets (274 9300).* **Train** C or E to Spring Street; N or R to Prince Street. **Open** *Sept-May* 10am-6pm Tue-Sat; *June, July* 10am-6pm Mon-Fri; *Aug* by appointment only.
As a young man Tony Shafrazi earned notoriety by splashing paint on Picasso's *Guernica*. He has since become a paragon of respectability, handling the estate of Keith Haring and showing work by Jean-Michel Basquiat, Dennis Hopper, Kenny Scharf, Ford Beckmann and Donald Baechler.

# Downtown Beyond SoHo

## Chelsea

### Annina Nosei Gallery

*530 West 22nd Street, between Tenth & Eleventh Avenues (741 8695).* **Train** A, C or E to 23rd Street. **Open** 10am-6pm Wed-Sun.
Nosei shows work from all over the globe, but is especially committed to contemporary work by Latin American artists, including Mexican Julio Galán and Chileno Arturo Duclos.

### Matthew Marks

*522 West 22nd Street, between Tenth & Eleventh Avenues (243 1650).* **Train** C or E to 23rd Street. **Open** *Sept-May* noon-6pm Thur-Sun. Call for summer hours.
This fabulous new space is an outpost of the parent gallery on Madison Avenue, and has shown work by Nan Goldin and Ellsworth Kelly. You can expect more of Marks' artists to be brought downtown; they include Cy Twombly, Lucien Freud and Willem de Kooning.

### Pat Hearn

*530 West 22nd Street, between Tenth & Eleventh Avenues (727 7366).* **Train** C or E to 23rd Street. **Open** *Sept-May* 11am-6pm Wed-Sun. Call for summer hours.
Gallery guide Hearn started in the East Village, moved to SoHo in the 1980s and is now helping spearhead the claim-staking in Chelsea. Through all this she has retained her optimistic spirit. Her artists include conceptualists Gretchen Faust, Julia Scher and Thom Merrick as well as painters.

### Morris Healy Gallery

*530 West 22nd, between Tenth & Eleventh Avenues (243 3753).* **Train** C or E to 23rd Street. **Open** *Sept-May* 11am-6pm Wed-Sun; *June, July* 1-7pm Tue-Fri; *Aug* by appointment only.
Another great Chelsea gallery emerges as Paul Morris makes the move westwards. Joseph Stashkevetch's drawings and James Makin's sculptures provided one of the more memorable opening shows.

## Lower East Side

### Alleged Gallery

*172 Ludlow Street, between Houston and Stanton Streets (533 9322).* **Train** F to Second Avenue. **Open** 8pm-midnight Thur-Sat.
A streetwise gallery showing the work of skaters, graffiti artists and other such counter-cultural consumerist commentators. Always fun, often incisive.

## West SoHo & TriBeCa

### AC Project Room

*15 Renwick Street, near Spring & Hudson Streets, 2nd floor (219 8275).* **Train** A or C to Spring Street. **Open** 10am-6pm Tue-Sat. Closed July, Aug.
A consistently innovative space where there's a rebellious urban feel to many of the shows.

### Apex Art

*291 Church Street, at Walker Street (431 5270).* **Train** 1 or 9 to Franklin Street. **Open** 11am-5pm Wed-Sat.
An interesting gallery, where the impulse comes from the curators, not artists, allowing this erudite and well-connected bunch to experiment with cleverly themed joint shows.

### Gavin Brown's Enterprise

*558 Broome Street, at Varick Street (431 1512).* **Train** C or E to Spring Street. **Open** 11am-6pm Wed-Sat. Closed Aug.
Transplanted Londoner Gavin Brown champions young hopefuls in an admirably anti-establishment gallery.

# Non-Profit Spaces

Some of the most interesting and innovative contemporary art can be seen at the lively non-profit spaces in TriBeCa and SoHo, where the emphasis is on art rather than commerce.

### Alternative Museum

*594 Broadway, near Prince Street, suite 402 (966 4444).* **Train** 6 to Spring Street; N or R to Prince Street. **Open** 11am-6pm Tue-Sat. Closed mid Aug-mid Sept.
The Alternative Museum has a reputation for exhibitions with humanitarian and socio-political concerns, especially from artists who are well beyond the mainstream.

### Artists Space

*38 Greene Street, between Grand & Broome Streets (226 3970).* **Train** A, C or E to Canal Street. **Open** *Sept-June* 10am-6pm Tue-Sat; *July* call for hours. Closed Aug.
Laurie Anderson, Jonathan Borofsky, Cindy Sherman, Robert Longo and David Salle all had exhibitions here early in their careers. The emphasis is on innovative work in all forms, so expect performance art, installations and video art.

### The Clocktower

*108 Leonard Street, at Broadway (233 1096).* **Train** 6, J, M, N, R or Z to Canal Street. **Open** noon-6pm Wed-Sun.
Run by the Institute for Art and Urban Resources, the Clocktower is primarily a subsidised studio space. Though not always open to the public, the gallery (located in the clocktower McKim, Mead, & White added to the New York Life Insurance Building) stages provocative exhibitions.

### Dia Center For The Arts

*548 West 22nd Street, between Tenth & Eleventh Avenues (989 5912).* **Train** C or E to 23rd Street. **Open** noon-6pm Thur-Sun. Closed July, Aug.
Dia's concerns lie with extended exhibitions, especially installations, by major contemporaries. As well as continuing to exhibit Walter De Maria's *The New York Earth Room* at 141 Wooster Street and his *Broken Kilometer* at 393 West Broadway (both open noon-6pm Wed-Sat), the well-financed foundation has started showing Dan Graham's *Rooftop Urban Park Project* at its new Chelsea location. It also has an exhibition site on the Internet: http://www.diacenter.org/

### The Drawing Center

*35 Wooster Street, between Broome & Grand Streets (219 2166).* **Train** N or R to Prince Street. **Open** 10am-6pm Tue, Thur, Fri; 10am-8pm Wed; 11am-6pm Sat. Closed Aug.

The Drawing Center is devoted to showing works on paper. As well as mounting important historical exhibitions, it promotes work by emerging talent in its 'Selections' exhibitions, and features architectural drawings by the likes of Le Corbusier and Philip Johnson and work by composers such as John Cage. Artists are encouraged to submit slides.

### Exit Art: The First World

*548 Broadway, between Prince & Spring Streets, 2nd floor (966 7745).* **Train** B, D, F or Q to Broadway/Lafayette. **Open** 10am-6pm Tue-Thur; 10am-8pm Fri; 11am-6pm Sat. Closed mid July-mid Sept.

Expect the best in multimedia cross-pollinations and culture clashes at this vibrant alternative space. Also a charming tapas bar and shop that sells artists' work.

### Franklin Furnace

*112 Franklin Street, between West Broadway & Church Street (925 4671).* **Train** A, C or E to Canal Street. Call for opening hours.

Work on the theme of time and its passing is the focus of this gallery, so performance art figures heavily, as do politically motivated pieces and exhibitions of published artwork – including books, periodicals, postcards and pamphlets.

### El Museo del Barrio

*1230 Fifth Avenue, between 104 & 105th Streets (831 7272).* **Train** 6 to 103rd Street. **Open** *June-Sept* 11am-5pm Wed, Fri-Sun; noon-7pm Thur; *Oct-May* 11am-5pm Wed-Sun. **Admission** suggested donation $4 adults; $2 seniors, students; free under-12s. **Credit** AmEx, MC, V.

Nearly a quarter of New York City's population is Latino and El Museo, with a permanent collection of nearly 8000 objects, is one of the foremost Latin American cultural institutions in the United States. Exhibitions vary from contemporary to traditional art and events include film festivals and concerts.

### New Museum of Contemporary Art

*583 Broadway, between Houston & Prince Streets (219 1355).* **Train** 6 to Spring or Bleecker Streets; B, D, F or Q to Broadway/Lafayette; N or R to Prince Street. **Open** noon-6pm Wed-Fri, Sun; noon-8pm Sat. **Admission** $4 adults; $3 students, senior citizens, artists; free under-12s; free to all 6-8pm Sat. **Credit** AmEx, DC, Discover, MC, V.

The New Museum is a major venue for experimental work, focussing on recent pieces by living artists. Window displays always draw a crowd. Even during a two-month renovation in 1995, one man set-dressed wearing a monkey suit complete with furry tail.

### Sculpture Center

*167 East 69th Street, between Third & Lexington Avenues (879 3500).* **Train** 6 to 68th Street. **Open** 11am-5pm Tue-Sat. Closed July, Aug.

One of the best places to see contemporary work by emerging and mid-career sculptors. The Sculpture Center also runs an ongoing project in Roosevelt Island (*see chapter* **Uptown**).

### Thread Waxing Space

*476 Broadway, between Grand & Broome Streets, 2nd floor (966 9520).* **Train** 6 to Spring Street. **Open** 10am-6pm Tue-Sat. Closed Aug.

A true contemporary multimedia space, which hosts video, performance, poetry, lectures and visual arts exhibitions and even the occasional musical evening with a live band or DJ.

### White Columns

*154 Christopher Street, between Greenwich & Washington Streets, 2nd floor (924 4212).* **Train** 1 or 9 to Christopher Street. **Open** *Sept-June* 12pm-6pm Wed-Sun. Closed July, Aug.

Gallery director Bill Arning has launched the careers of a number of important artists from his lively alternative space, once in TriBeCa and the oldest in the city. New talent is given space in the gallery's 'white room', and shows are often guest-curated by up-and-coming critics.

## Photography

For an overview of photography exhibitions, buy the bi-monthly directory *Photography in New York International* ($2.95). *See also chapter* **Museums**.

### Janet Borden

*560 Broadway, between Prince & Spring Streets (431 0166).* **Train** 6 to Spring Street; N or R to Prince Street. **Open** *Sept-May* 10am-5pm Tue-Sat; *June, July* 10am-5pm Tue-Fri. Closed Aug.

Artists include Larry Sultan, Tina Barney and Lewis Baltz.

### Laurence Miller Gallery

*138 Spring Street, between Wooster & Greene Streets (226 1220).* **Train** 6 to Spring Street. **Open** *Sept-June* 10am-6pm Tue-Fri; 11am-6pm Sat; *July, Aug* 10am-6pm Tue-Fri.

Laurence Miller shows interesting contemporary work. Recent shows have included work by Cartier-Bresson and Helen Levitt. Gallery artists include David Levinthal.

### Pace MacGill Gallery

*32 East 57th Street, between Park & Madison Avenues (759 7999).* **Train** 4, 5 or 6 to 59th Street; N or R to Lexington Avenue. **Open** *Sept-May* 9.30am-5.30pm Tue-Fri; 10am-6pm Sat; *June-Aug* 9.30am-5.30pm Mon-Fri.

Look out for such well-known names as Weegee, Elliot Erwitt, Joel-Peter Witkin and Walker Evans.

### SoHo Photo Gallery

*15 White Street, between West Broadway & Sixth Avenue (226 8571).* **Train** 1 or 9 to Franklin Street. **Open** *Sept-May* 6-8pm Tue; 1-6pm Fri-Sun. Call for summer hours.

A long-standing co-operative photo gallery, with a constant stream of new names and exciting work.

### Staley-Wise Gallery

*560 Broadway, near Prince Street (966 6223).* **Train** R to Prince Street; B, D or F to Broadway/Lafayette. **Open** *Sept-June* 11am-5pm Tue-Sat; *July* 11am-5pm Tue-Fri; *Aug* by appointment only.

Strong themed group shows, such as the acclaimed 'Music: 1930-1990', which featured portraits by masters including Horst and Arnold Newman and fashion virtuosi like Herb Ritts. You can also see exhibits by contemporary photographers, such as Sheila Metzner and Helmut Newton.

### Witkin Gallery

*415 West Broadway, at Spring Street (925 5510).* **Train** C or E to Spring Street. **Open** *Sept-May* 11am-6pm Tue-Sat. Call for summer hours.

Witkin shows major photographers, from contemporary works by Fay Godwin, Ruth Orkin and Willy Ronis, to classic prints by Robert Doisneau and Edward Weston.

### Zabriskie Gallery

*41 East 57th Street, at Madison Avenue (307 7430).* **Train** E or F to 53rd Street; N or R to Fifth Avenue. **Open** *Sept-May* 10am-5.30pm Tue-Sat; *June-Aug* 10am-5.30pm Tue-Fri.

Zabriskie specialises in photography, showing works by Brassai, Steiglitz, Atget, William Klein and Scott Richter, but also deals in modern painting and sculpture.

# Museums

***From high art to cultural kitsch, New York's museums are true treasurehouses of art and artefacts.***

New York's museums are superb. More than 60 establishments cover everything from art, antiquities and hands-on science to Ukrainian folk costumes and doll collections. The buildings themselves are equally impressive and eclectic. Nearly everyone falters when they see the spiral **Guggenheim** for the first time, while many double-check house numbers on approaching the three-storey **Black Fashion Museum** among a row of Harlem brownstones.

Too many people gorge themselves by trying to see too many museums in one day or, worse still, all the collections at a major museum such as the **Metropolitan Museum of Art** or the **American Museum of Natural History**. Slow down and relax. Don't rush a museum but limit yourself to sybjects that are personal favourites. Think about breaking up your visit by having coffee or lunch – some of the museums have excellent cafés or restaurants (*see box*). At least this way, you will leave happy and contented rather than irritable and footsore.

Most overseas visitors find the admission prices something of a shock. Europeans especially will baulk at the high cost, which arises because most New York museums are funded privately rather than by government money. This explains why an institution like the **New York Historical Society** – the city's oldest museum – had to close for two years (it has now reopened). However, several places, including the **Guggenheim** and the **Museum of Modern Art**, have one night a week when admission is free or by voluntary donation. (*see box*).

Many of New York's famous, more established museums – such as the **Frick Collection**, the **Pierpont Morgan Library** and the relatively young **Guggenheim** – started out as private collections. **The Cloisters**, at the north tip of Manhattan in Fort Tryon, was John D Rockefeller's gift. It's a reconstructed Gothic monastery housing the Met's medieval collection. Somehow it works beautifully. When the sun's warm and the sky's a deep blue, take a picnic and admire the red tiled roof and inhale the delicate scents from the garden.

Everyone will make a beeline for whatever interests them most but don't miss the audio tour at the extremely moving **Ellis Island Immigration Museum**. If you enjoy that, take a tour at the **Lower East Side Tenement Museum**. Both places give visitors a firm understanding of the multi-cultural 'melting pot' together with an insight into why New Yorkers are driven, ambitious and 'in your face'. The **Liberty Science Center**, with its hands-on exhibits and rooftop terrace overlooking Manhattan and the Statue of Liberty, is an unexpected pleasure. If you go there at weekends when the ferry service is operating it doubles as a sightseeing trip.

The prize for most neglected museum has to go to the **Brooklyn Museum**. Its size and grandeur come as rather a shock as you emerge from the subway station but there's an even greater surprise inside: the excellent exhibits. Yet although it's the second largest and most important museum in New York, it rarely draws much in the way of crowds – even though its Egyptian collection is on a par with the Met's.

It might be traditional to save museums for a rainy day, but since most are air conditioned they also offer a glorious respite from summer heat.

Most of New York's museums are closed on New

*The* **American Museum of Natural History**.

*Venture off Manhattan to visit the world-class* **Brooklyn Museum**.

Year's Day, Washington's Birthday, Memorial Day, Independence Day, Labor Day, Columbus Day, Thanksgiving and Christmas Day. Some change their opening hours in summer.

## Major Museums

### American Museum of Natural History

*Central Park West, at 79th Street (769 5000/769 5100 for recorded information).* **Train** B or C to 86th Street. **Open** 10am-5.45pm Mon-Thur, Sun; 10am-8.45pm Fri, Sat. **Admission** suggested donation $7 adults; $4 under-18s; $5 senior citizens. **Credit** AmEx, MC, V (gift shop only).

The fun begins immediately as a towering Barosaur, rearing high on hind legs, protects its young from an attacking Allosaurus in the main rotunda. It's an impressive welcome from the largest museum of its kind in the world, and signals its most recent achievement: the reopening of the fourth-floor dinosaur halls after a four-year, $12-million renovation. The resulting gallery banishes memories of the dark dusty halls, whose low ceilings have been removed to reveal the original vaults and panoramic views of Central Park. The new exhibits, designed by the firm responsible for much of the excellent Ellis Island Immigration Museum, have been a great success, with several specimens being remodelled in the light of recent discoveries. The Tyrannosaurus Rex, for instance, was once believed to walk upright, Godzilla-style: now it stalks, head down, with tail parallel to the ground and is altogether more menacing. The rest of the museum is equally impressive – especially the realistic dioramas of stuffed animals on the ground floor. There's a particularly good Native American section and a stunning collection of meteorites, semi-precious stones and gems, including the obscenely large Star of India blue sapphire. There's also an Imax theatre showing nature programmes and innovative temporary exhibitions, such as the recent CD-ROM audio guide around the museum's permanent collection.

*Disabled: access, toilets.*

### Brooklyn Museum

*200 Eastern Parkway, at Washington Avenue, Brooklyn (1-718 638 5000).* **Train** 2 or 3 to Eastern Parkway. **Open** 10am-5pm Wed-Sun. **Admission** suggested donation $4 adults; $2 students; $1.50 senior citizens; free accompanied under-12s. **No credit cards**.

Woefully neglected, the Brooklyn Museum contains world-class collections that rival and occasionally surpass the Met's. It suffers purely because of its off-Manhattan location, despite being the second-largest museum in the state of New York and a superb nineteenth-century Beaux Arts building. The African art and pre-Columbian textile galleries are particularly good; the Native American collection is outstanding and works from the ancient Middle East are extensive. The Egyptian galleries, however, are exceptional: the Rubin Gallery's gold and silver gilded Ibis coffin, for instance, is sublime. Two floors up, the Rodin sculpture court is surrounded by paintings from French contemporaries such as Monet, Dégas and Redon. There's an art reference library on the second floor and, on the third, the renowned Wilbour Library of Egyptology. Both are open to the public by appointment only. Because there are no crowds, all the treasures can be viewed peacefully, and you're virtually guaranteed a seat in the musum café.

*Disabled: access, toilets.*

### The Cloisters

*Fort Tyron Park (923 3700).* **Train** A to 190th Street. **Open** *March-October* 9.30am-5.15pm Tue-Sun; *Nov-Feb* 9.30am-4.45pm. **Admission** suggested donation $7 adults; $3.50 senior citizens, students (includes admission to the Metropolitan Museum of Art on the same day); free accompanied under-12s. **No credit cards**.

Few people venture this far north in Manhattan, which is a shame because the Cloisters houses the Met's medieval art collections in an unexpectedly rural setting. This tranquil twentieth-century museum was constructed, as its name suggests, with monastic cloisters and Gothic chapel, in authentic Middle Ages style. The result is a convincing red-tiled Romanesque museum on a hill overlooking the Hudson

*The peaceful* **Cloisters**. *See page 199*

River, providing an oasis from the high-rises further south. Don't miss the famed Unicorn tapestries or the Annunciation Triptych by Robert Campin. There are also flower and herb gardens with more than 250 species of plants grown in the Middle Ages.
*Disabled: access, toilets.*

### Cooper-Hewitt National Design Museum

*2 East 91st Street, at Fifth Avenue (860 6868).* **Train** 4, 5 or 6 to 86th Street. **Open** 10am-9pm Tue; 10am-5pm Wed-Sat; noon-5pm Sun. **Admission** $3 adults; $1.50 students, senior citizens; free under-12s; free to all 5-9pm Tue. **No credit cards**.

The National Design Museum was closed for renovation as this guide went to press. It's due to reopen in September 1996 and is well worth a visit for both its content and architecture – the turn-of-the-century building belonged to Andrew Carnegie, then one of the wealthiest men in America. Architects responded to his request for 'the most modest, plainest, and the most roomy house in New York' by designing a 64-room mansion in the style of an English Georgian country house. His exhortations for simplicity were all but ignored, to judge by the amount of carved wood panelling everywhere. Look out for the carved bagpipes in the ceiling of the music room, now the museum shop (Carnegie was born in Scotland). This is the only museum in the United States devoted exclusively to historical and contemporary design and its changing exhibitions are always interesting.
*Disabled: access, toilets, sign language interpretation available for programmes on request with two weeks' notice (860 6977).*

### Frick Collection

*1 East 70th Street, at Fifth Avenue (288 0700).* **Train** 6 to 68th Street. **Open** 10am-6pm Tue-Sat; 1-6pm Sun. **Admission** $5 adults; $3 students, senior citizens, under-16s. No children under 10; under-16s must be accompanied by an adult. **No credit cards**.

This private, predominantly Renaissance collection, housed in an opulent residence once owned by industrialist Henry Clay Frick, makes a serene, elegant museum. American architect Thomas Hastings designed the 1914 building in eighteenth-century European style. As each room is furnished, it's more like a stately home than a museum. The paintings, sculptures and furniture on display are consistently world class, among them works by Gainsborough, Rembrandt, Renoir, Vermeer and Whistler. There are also some fine pieces by French cabinet maker Jean-Henri Riesener. The indoor garden court is particularly lovely (it was once an open carriage drive) and there's even a lily pond in the lawn. A delightfully cultural way to step back in time.
*Disabled: access, toilets.*

### Solomon R Guggenheim Museum

*1071 Fifth Avenue, at 88th Street (423 3500).* **Train** 4, 5 or 6 to 86th Street. **Open** 10am-6pm Mon-Wed, Sun; 10am-8pm Fri, Sat. **Admission** $7 adults; $4 students, senior citizens; free accompanied under-12s. Voluntary donation Friday 6-8pm. A combined 7-day pass for both Guggenheim museums costs $10 adults; $6 students, senior citizens. **Credit** AmEx, MC, V.

The museum itself is a work of modern art. Designed by Frank Lloyd Wright and completed six months after his death in 1959, the spiral Guggenheim is the youngest building to be designated a New York City landmark. As well as works by Picasso, Van Gogh, Dégas and Manet, the museum contains Peggy Guggenheim's cubist, surrealist and abstract expressionist works of art and the Panza di Biumo collection of American minimalist and conceptual art from the 1960s and 70s. The photography collection began after a donation of more than 200 works by the Robert Mapplethorpe Foundation in 1992, when the museum re-opened after its two-year renovation. The new ten-story tower, based on an early Wright design, increased the gallery space and includes a sculpture gallery with great views over Central Park. The combined ticket, including entrance to the SoHo museum, is particularly good value. Even if you don't want to see the collection you should visit just to admire the marvellously coiled white building incongruously situated among turn-of-the-century mansions on Fifth Avenue. *See chapter* **Architecture**.
*Disabled: access, toilets.*

### Guggenheim Museum, SoHo

*575 Broadway, at Prince Street (423 3500).* **Train** 6 to Spring Street; N or R to Prince Street. **Open** 11am-6pm Wed-Fri, Sun; 11am-8pm Sat. **Admission** $5 adults; $3 students, senior citizens; free accompanied under-12s. $1 reduction on all entries within one hour of closing time. **Credit** AmEx, MC, V.

The SoHo Guggenheim, housed in a nineteenth-century building, opened in 1992 to showcase selections from the Fifth Avenue museum's permanent collection as well as a number of temporary exhibitions. There's a good museum store and the attractive Time for T salon and restaurant.
*Disabled: access, toilets.*

### Metropolitan Museum of Art

*Fifth Avenue, at 82nd Street (535 7710).* **Train** 4, 5 or 6 to 86th Street. **Open** 9.30am-5.15pm Tue-Thur, Sun; 9.30am-8.45pm Fri, Sat. **Admission** suggested donation $7 adults; $3.50 students, senior citizens; free accompanied under-12s. **No credit cards**.

It would take several days to cover the Met's one and a half million square feet of exhibition space, so try to be selective or the sheer size may overwhelm you. Egyptology fans should head for the tomb of Perinebi and then peruse the finest collection outside Cairo. There's also an excellent Islamic art collection and more than 3000 European paintings, including major works by Rembrandt, Raphael and Vermeer. In 1994 the museum opened its first permanent galleries on the arts of South and Southeast Asia and recently reopened the English Decorative Arts collections and the

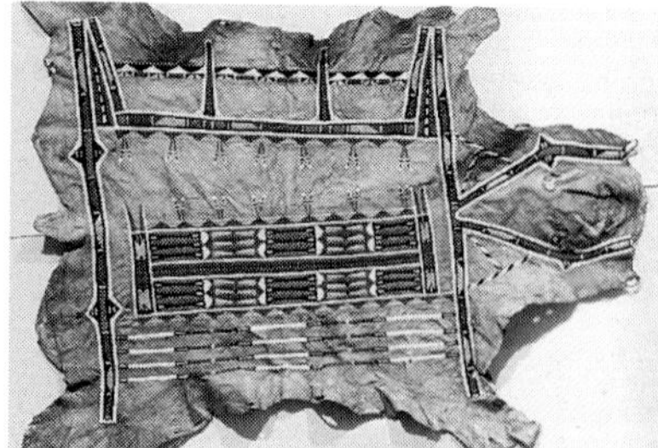

*From the* **Museum of the American Indian**.

*The much-loved sculpture garden at the* **Museum of Modern Art**.

Tiepolo Gallery after renovations. It's now the turn of the Greek and Roman halls for a face-lift, but they should be open again by summer 1996. The most recent addition, a gallery devoted to the decorative arts of the Northern Renaissance, opened in June 1995. During the summer head for the roof garden for a breather and enjoy the view over Central Park's treetops.
*Disabled: access, toilets. No strollers (prams).*

### Museum of the American Indian

*George Gustav Heye Centre, US Custom House, 1 Bowling Green, near Battery Park (668 6624).* **Train** 1 or 9 to South Ferry. **Open** 10am-5pm daily. **Admission** free.

In October 1994 the museum relocated from the top of Manhattan, north of Harlem, to its very tip – just around the corner from Battery Park and the Ellis Island ferry. Its galleries, resource centre and two workshop rooms now occupy two floors in the grandiose US Custom House. Exhibitions are thoughtfully explained, usually by Native Americans. Particularly interesting is one called All Roads Are Good, which explains the personal choices of storytellers, weavers, anthropologists and tribal leaders. Only 500 of the collection's million objects are on display: another reason, apart from the building's lofty proportions, which makes the museum seem surprisingly small and incomplete. There are plans for a Cultural Resources Center in Maryland by 1997 before the museum moves buildings – and cities – permanently in 2001, when it will take pride of place alongside other Smithsonian Institutions in Washington's National Mall.
*Disabled: access.*

### Museum of Modern Art

*11 West 53rd Street, between Fifth & Sixth Avenues (708 9400/708 9480 recorded information).* **Train** E or F to Fifth Avenue/53rd Street. **Open** 11am-6pm Mon-Wed, Sat, Sun; noon-8.30pm Thur, Fri. **Admission** $8 adults; $5 students, senior citizens; free accompanied under-16s. Voluntary donation 5.30-8.30pm Thur, Fri. **No credit cards**.

The Museum of Modern Art, or MoMA, holds a comprehensive and cutting-edge collection of twentieth-century art, encompassing paintings, design, photography, film and sculpture. Its first director, Alfred Barr, who dedicated the museum to encouraging people to understand contemporary visual art in a broad range of forms, helped stretch the boundaries of what is meant by art. The permanent collection is particularly strong in works by Matisse, Picasso and Miro, while the film and video department contains more than 13,000 films and four million film stills. The Abby Aldrich Rockefeller Sculpture Garden is lovely, overlooked by the elegant Italian Sette restaurant upstairs. There are free gallery talks at 1pm and 3pm daily (except Wednesday) and on Thursday and Friday evenings at 6pm and 7pm. A sculpture touch-tour is available to visually impaired visitors by advance appointment.
*Disabled: access, toilets.*

### Pierpont Morgan Library

*29 East 36th Street, between Park & Madison Avenues (685 0008).* **Train** 6 to 33rd Street. **Open** 10.30am-5pm Tue-Fri; 10.30am-6pm Sat; noon-6pm Sun. **Admission** $5 adults; $3 students, senior citizens; $1 children. **No credit cards**.

This charming Italianate museum was once the home of financier JP Morgan. The collection, mostly gathered during Morgan's trips to Europe, includes Rembrandts, original Mahler manuscripts and the gorgeous silver, copper and cloisonné twelfth-century Stavelot triptych. The subty colourful marble rotunda, whith its carved sixteenth-century Italian ceiling, separates the three-tiered library from the rich red study. There's a modern conservatory attached to the museum containing a soothing courtyard café. Enquire about guided tours to get the most out of the numerous treasures.
*Disabled: access, toilets.*

### Whitney Museum of American Art

*945 Madison Avenue, at East 75th Street (570 3600).* **Train** 6 to 77th Street. **Open** 11am-6pm Wed, Fri-Sun; 1-8pm Thur. **Admission** $8 adults; $6 senior citizens, students; free under-12s; free to all 6-8pm Thur. **No credit cards**.

Some may think this great grey granite cube unprepossessing but it is an entirely appropriate setting for the similarly uncompromising modern American art that it houses. Founded by the sculptor Gertrude Vanderbilt Whitney in 1930, it counts among its 10,000 works pieces by Edward Hopper, Georgia O'Keeffe, Jackson Pollock, Willem de Kooning, Alexander Calder, Lee Krasner, Mark Rothko, Jasper Johns, Robert Rauschenberg and Andy Warhol. Themed exhibitions change every three or four months and a biennial of contemporary American art is held in every odd-numbered year.

*Disabled: access, toilets.*

### Whitney Museum of American Art at Philip Morris

*120 Park Avenue, at East 42nd Street (878 2550).* **Train** 4, 5, 6, 7 or S to Grand Central Station. **Open** *gallery* 11am-6pm Mon-Fri; 11am-7.30pm Thur; *sculpture court* 7.30am-9.30pm Mon-Sat; 11am-7pm Sun. **Admission** free.

Exhibitions change so call for details.

*Wheelchair access.*

## Art & Design

### American Academy & Institute of Arts & Letters

*Audubon Terrace, Broadway, between 156th & 155th Streets (368 5900).* **Train** 1 to 157th Street. **Open** during exhibitions only 1-4 pm Tue-Sun. **Admission** free.

This organisation honours a fixed 250 American writers, composers, painters, sculptors and architects. Edith Wharton, Mark Twain and Henry James were once members and today's list includes Terrence McNally, Kurt Vonnegut and Alison Lurie. It's not strictly a museum but there are annual exhibitions open to the public and a magnificent library of original manuscripts and first editions open to researchers by appointment only.

*Disabled: access, toilets.*

### American Craft Museum

*40 West 53rd Street, between Fifth & Sixth Avenues (956 3535).* **Train** B, D or F to Rockefeller Center. **Open** 10am-8pm Tue; 10am-5pm Wed-Sun. **Admission** $5 adults; $2.50 students, senior citizens, under-12s. **No credit cards**.

The country's leading art museum for twentieth-century crafts in clay, fibre, glass, metal and wood. There are temporary shows on the four bright and spacious floors and one or two exhibitions from the permanent collection each year concentrating on a specific medium. The shop, though small, sells some unusually stylish jewellery and ceramics.

*Disabled: access, toilets.*

### Forbes Magazine Galleries

*62 Fifth Avenue, at West 12th Street (206 5548).* **Train** 4, 5, 6, N, R or L to Union Square. **Open** 10am-4pm Tue-Sat. **Admission** free; under 16s must be with an adult.

A wonderful private collection of treasures belonging to the late magazine publisher Malcolm Forbes. Toy boats and soldiers aside, galleries display historic presidential letters and – the highlight of the museum – superbly intricate pieces by the famed Russian jeweller and goldsmith Peter Carl Fabergé. The selection of more than 300 *objets de luxe* includes diamond-encrusted bonbonnières; gold and nephrite carriage clocks decorated with emeralds and pearls; and, of course, the trademark Fabergé eggs. Twelve Imperial Easter eggs are on show, made for the last two czars of Russia.

*Disabled: access.*

### International Center of Photograpy (ICP)

*1130 Fifth Avenue, at 94th Street (860 1778).* **Train** 6 to 96th Street. **Open** 11am-8pm Tue; 11am-6pm Wed-Fri; 11am-6pm Sat, Sun. **Admission** $4 adults; $2.50 students; $1 under-12s, senior citizens. **No credit cards**.

The collection began in the 1960s as the International Fund for Concerned Photography, containing work by Robert Capa, Werner Bischof, David Seymour and Dan Weiner, who were all killed on assignment. Their photographs were preserved and exhibited by Cornell Capa, brother of Robert, who went on to found the ICP in 1974. Given this heritage, it's no surprose that exhibitions are particularly strong on photo-journalism and documentary. Photographic images, Cornell said, 'are both works of art and moments in history; they sharpen human awareness and awaken conscience'. There's an extensive book shop, space for video installations and a small screening room.

*Disabled: access, toilets.*

### ICP Midtown

*1133 Sixth Avenue, at 43rd Street (768 4680).* **Train** 1, 2, 3, 7, 9, N, R or S to Times Square/42nd Street. **Open** 11am-8pm Tue; 11am-6pm Wed-Sun. **Admission** $4 adults; $2.50 students, senior citizens; $1 under-12s. **No credit cards**.

The smaller Midtown ICP has two floors of gallery space and a museum shop. Exhibitions change throughout the year.

*Disabled: access to lower gallery only; toilets.*

### Museum of American Folk Art

*2 Lincoln Square, Columbus Avenue & 66th Street (977 7298).* **Train** 1 or 9 to 66th Street. **Open** 11.30am-7.30pm Tue-Sun. **Admission** suggested donation $3. **No credit cards**.

A surprisingly small museum – considering its grand location opposite the Lincoln Center – but the exhibits are exquisite. Decorative, practical and ceremonial folk art encompasses pottery, trade signs, delicately stitched log cabin quilts and even wind toys. The craftsmanship is often breathtaking. There are occasional lectures, demonstrations and performances, and a museum shop next door.

*Disabled: access, toilets.*

### National Academy of Design

*1083 Fifth Avenue, at 89th Street (369 4880).* **Train** 4, 5 or 6 to 86th Street. **Open** noon-5pm Wed, Thur, Sat, Sun; noon-8pm Fri. **Admission** $3.50 adults; $2 senior citizens, students; free under-5s; free to all 5-8pm Fri. **No credit cards**.

The Academy comprises the School of Fine Arts and a museum containing the world's foremost collections of nineteenth- and twentieth-century American art. The arts of design are painting, sculpture, architecture and engraving with the permanent collection represented by artists and architects such as Mary Cassatt, John Singer Sargent and Frank Lloyd Wright. Temporary exhibitions in this elegant Fifth Avenue townhouse are always impressive.

### Isamu Noguchi Garden Museum

*32-37 Vernon Boulevard, at 33rd Road, Long Island City, Queens (1-718 204 7088 recorded information).* **Transport** N train to Astoria Broadway or shuttle bus from Asia Society, 725 Park Avenue, at West 70th Street, every hour on the half hour from 11.30am-3.30pm ($5). **Open** April-Nov 11am-6pm Wed, Sat, Sun. **Admission** suggested donation $4 adults; students, $2 senior citizens. **No credit cards**.

Sculptor Isamu Noguchi designed stage sets for the late Martha Graham and George Balanchine as well as sculpture

parks and immense pieces of great simplicity. Noguchi's studios are now a showcase for his work, with 12 small galleries and a sculpture garden. There's a guided tour at 2pm (call 1-718 721 1932) and films are shown throughout the day.
*Disabled: partial access.*

### Queens Museum of Art

*New York City Building, Flushing Meadows Corona Park, Queens (1-718 592 9700).* **Train** 7 tran to Willets Point/Shea Stadium. **Open** 10am-5pm Wed-Fri; noon-5pm Sat, Sun. **Admission** suggested donation $3 adults; $1.50 children, students, senior citizens. **No credit cards.**
The wide boardwalk from the subway station, away from the Mets' Shea Stadium and past the US Open tennis stadium, introduces visitors to the scale of what was once the site of the 1964-5 World Fair. The museum, in the park itself, is next to the towering steel globe of the Unisphere. It reopened recently after a three-year, $15 million renovation and, as well as its art collections, offers a fascinating insight into the visionary 1960s World Fair. There's a sleek 'Futurama' model car from General Motors and posters showing Billy Graham promoting his pavilion's 'Man in the Fifth Dimension' film, whose showings had counsellors on stand-by in case anyone wanted to accept Christ afterwards. For many people, the highlight is a permanent miniature model of New York City. It's fun to try and find where you're staying – binoculars are on hire for $1. Dusk falls every 15 minutes, revealing tiny illuminated buildings and a fluorescent Central Park. The model is constantly updated – 60,000 changes at the last count. *See chapter* **New York by Neighbourhood: The Outer Boroughs.**
*Disabled: access, toilets.*

### Nicholas Roerich Museum

*319 West 107th Street, at Riverside (864 7752).* **Train** 1 to 110th Street. **Open** 2-5pm Tue-Sun. **Admission** free.
Russian-born Roerich was a philosopher, artist, architect, explorer, pacifist and scenery painter who collaborated with Nijinsky, Stravinsky and Diaghilev. The Roerich Peace Pact of 1935, an international agreement on the protection of cultural treasures, earned him a Nobel Peace Prize nomination and the support of Einstein, HG Wells and George Bernard Shaw. Roerich's wife bought this charming townhouse specifically as a museum to house her late husband's possessions. Paintings are mostly from from his Tibetan travels and display his interest in mysticism. It's a fascinating place but Roerich's intriguing life story tends to overshadow the museum.

### Studio Museum in Harlem

*144 West 125th Street, between Seventh & Lenox Avenues (864 4500).* **Train** 2 or 3 to 125th Street. **Open** 10am-5pm Wed, Thur, Fri; 1-6pm Sat, Sun. **Admission** $5 adults; $3 students, senior citizens; $1 under-12s. **No credit cards.**
The Studio Museum started out as rented loft space in 1967. Within 20 years it had expanded onto two floors of a 60,000sq ft building – a gift from a New York bank – and became the first accredited Black fine arts museum in the country. Today it shows changing exhibitions by African-American, African and Caribbean artists and continues its prestigious artists-in-residence programme.
*Disabled: access, toilets.*

### Urban Center

*457 Madison Avenue, between 50th & 51st Streets (935 3960/439 1049 tour information).* **Train** 6 to 51st Street; E or F to Fifth Avenue/53rd Street. **Open** 11am-5pm Mon-Wed, Fri, Sat. **Admission** voluntary donation.
The Municipal Art Society founded this centre for the urban design arts in 1980. It functions as a gallery, bookshop, lecture forum and campaign office, with exhibitions leaning towards architecture, public art and community-based projects. The Center also acts as headquarters for the Architectural League and the Parks Council, but its greatest attraction must be its location: inside the historic Villard Houses opposite St Patrick's cathedral.
*Disabled: access, toilets.*

## Arts & Culture

### African

### Museum for African Art

*593 Broadway, between Houston & Prince Streets (966 1313).* **Train** 6 to Spring or Bleecker Street; N or R to Prince Street; B, D, Q or F train to Broadway/Lafayette. **Open** 10.30am-5.30pm Tue-Fri; noon-6pm Sat, Sun. **Admission** $4 adults; $2 under-12s, students, senior citizens; free under-2s. **Credit** (over $10 only) MC, V.
This tranquil museum was designed by Maya Lin – creator of the stunningly simple Vietnam Veterans' Memorial in Washington DC. Exhibits change about twice a year and the quality of works shown is high. There's a particularly good bookshop with a children's section.
*Disabed: access, toilets.*

## Unmissable art

*Annunciation* by Alessandro Botticelli (late fifteenth century). **MoMA**
*I and the Village* by Marc Chagall (1911). **MoMA**
*The Epiphany* by Giotto (1320) Metropolitan
*Purification of the Temple* by El Greco (1600). **Frick**
*Early Sunday Morning* by Edward Hopper (1930). **Whitney**
*Three Flags* by Jasper Johns (1958). **Whitney**
*Black Lines* by Wassily Kandinsky (1913). **Guggenheim**
*Dance* (1909) by Henri Matisse MoMA
*Broadway Boogie-Woogie* Piet Mondrian (1942-3). **MoMA**
*The Ducal Palace at Venice* Claude Monet (1908). **Brooklyn**
*The White Calico Flower* by Georgia O'Keeffe (1931). **Whitney**
*Gertrude Stein* by Pablo Picasso (1906) **Metropolitan**
*Les Demoiselles d'Avignon* by Pablo Picasso (1907). **MoMA**
*Aristotle With a Bust of Homer* by Rembrandt (1653). **Metropolitan**
*The Sleeping Gypsy* by Henri Rousseau (1897). **MoMA**
*The Crucifixion/Last Judgement* diptich by Jan Van Eyck. **Metropolitan**
*Starry Night* by Vincent Van Gogh (1899). **MoMA**
*Young Woman With a Water Jug* by Johannes Vermeer (1660s). **Metropolitan**
*Mistress & Maid* by Johannes Vermeer (1665-70). **Frick**

## Asian

### Asia Society

*725 Park Avenue, at East 70th Street (288 6400).* **Train** 6 to 68th Street. **Open** 11am-6pm Tue, Wed, Fri, Sat; 11am-8pm Thur; noon-5pm Sun. **Admission** $3 adults; $1 students, senior citizens; free accompanied under-12s; free to all 6-8pm Thur. **No credit cards.**
The substantial eight-storey headquarters of the Asia Society reflects its importance in promoting Asia-American relations. The Society's activities include sponsoring study missions, conferences and public programmes in both continents. Galleries show major art exhibitions from public and private collections, including the permanent Mr and Mrs John D Rockefeller III collection of Asian art. Asian musicians and performers often play here so it's well worth picking up a programme.
*Disabled: access, toilets.*

### China Institute in America

*125 East 65th Street, between Lexington & Park Avenues (744 8181).* **Train** 6 to 68th Street. **Open** 10am to 5pm Mon-Sat; 1-5pm Sun. **Admission** suggested donation $5 adults; $3 students, senior citizens; free children. **Credit** AmEx, MC, V.
With only two small gallery rooms, the China Institute is rather overshadowed by the Asia Society, but its exhibitions are impressive and range from Chinese women artists and bronze vessels to selections from the Beijing Palace Museum. The Society is particularly strong on lectures and courses, on such subjects as cooking, calligraphy, Tang poetry and Confucianism.

### Japan Society

*333 East 47th Street, near First Avenue (832 1155).* **Train** 6 to 51st Street; E or F to 53rd Street. **Open** 11am-5pm Tue-Sun during exhibitions only. **Admission** suggested donation $3. **No credit cards.**
The Japan Society promotes a number of cultural exchange programmes, special events and studies, with exhibitions taking place three or four times a year. The gallery shows both traditional and contemporary Japanese art from decorative art from the Meiji period to Buddhist prints and the use of umbrellas in Japanese art. The Society's film centre is a major showcase for Japanese cinema in the United States and there's a library and language centre in the new lower lobby wing. The Gallery is only open if an exhibition is showing, so call beforehand.
*Disabled: access, toilets.*

### Tibetan Museum

*338 Lighthouse Avenue, off Richmond Road, Staten Island (1-718 987 3478 recorded information).* **Transport** ferry to Staten Island, then 78 bus. **Open** *April-Nov* 1-5pm Wed-Sun; *Dec-March* by appointment only. **Admission** $3 adults; $2.50 , students, senior citizens; $1 children. **No credit cards.**
This mock Tibetan temple stands on the highest hilltop on the eastern seaboard. It contains a fascinating Buddhist altar and the largest collection of Tibetan art in the West, including religious objects, bronzes and paintings. There's a comprehensive (English language) library containing books on Buddhism, Tibet and Asian art. The landscaped gardens house a zoo of stone animals, with birdhouses and wishing well, and offer good views.

# Eating in museums

Museums often let visitors down when it comes to providing decent affordable food but the following institutions have got the balance right so that stopping for a coffee, a sandwich or a full-blown meal is a genuine pleasure.

### Guggenheim Museum: Dean & DeLuca

*1701 Fifth Avenue, at 89th Street (423 3655).* **Train** 4, 5 or 6 to 86th Street. **Meals served** 8am-7pm Mon-Wed, Sun; 8am-9pm Fri, Sat. **Credit** AmEx, MC, V.
The café, in a space adapted from a Frank Lloyd Wright design, appeared after the museum's renovation a few years ago. Choices range from desserts to full meals. You don't need to buy a ticket for the museum to eat here.

### Museum of Modern Art: Sette

*11 West 53rd Street, between Fifth Avenue & Avenue of the Americas (708 9710).* **Train** E or F to Fifth Avenue/53rd Street. **Lunch served** noon-5pm daily. **Dinner served** 5-10pm Mon, Tue, Thur-Sat. **Credit** AmEx, DC, Discover, MC, V.
An elegant Italian restaurant overlooking the museum's gorgeous sculpture garden.

### Pierpont Morgan Library: Museum Café

*29 East 36th Street, at Madison Avenue (685 0008).* **Train** 6 to 33rd Street. **Meals served** 11am-4pm Tue-Fri; 11am-5pm Sat; noon-5pm Sun. **Credit** AmEX, MC, V.
This is the place for light lunch or afternoon tea. Its marble floors, potted plants and high glass roof produce the effect of a spacious conservatory.

### Jewish Museum: Café Weissman

*1109 Fifth Avenue, at 92nd Street (423 3200).* **Train** 6 to 96th Street. **Meals served** 11am-5.45pm Mon, Wed, Thur, Sun; 11am-7.30pm Tue. **No credit cards.**
Although in a basement, this kosher cafe (pictured below) is light and colourful thanks to its stained glass window art. Delicious food; enormous lox sandwiches.

## European

### Hispanic Society of America

*Audubon Terrace, 613 Broadway, between 155 & 156th Streets (926 2234).* **Train** 1 to 157th Street. **Open** 10am-4.30pm Tue-Sat; 1-4pm Sun. **Admission** free.

Two limestone lions flank the entrance to this majestic building in Hamilton Heights, the gentrified area of Harlem. Outside, an equestrian statue of El Cid, Spain's medieval hero, stands on the Beaux Arts terrace between the Society's two buildings. Inside, there's an ornate Spanish Renaissance court and an upper gallery lined with paintings by El Greco, Goya and Velaquez. The collection ranges from a Roman statue of Diana to Moresque ceramic tiles but is dominated by religious artefacts – including a number of sixteenth-century tombs from the monastery of San Francisco in Cuellar, Spain. The library reading room is open 1-4.30pm Tue-Fri; 10-4.30pm Sat.

### Ukrainian Museum

*203 Second Avenue, between East 12th & 13th Streets (228 0110).* **Train** 4, 5, 6, L, N or R to Union Square. **Open** 1-5pm Wed-Sun. **Admission** $1 adults; 50¢ children, students, senior citizens. **No credit cards**.

The Ukrainian National Women's League of America provided most of the folk art collection here. It's a small, rather sorry-looking museum on two tiny floors, showing woven and embroidered textiles plus assorted crafts and objects from the nineteenth and early twentieth centuries. Fund-raising is underway for a relocation project and cultural centre.

*Disabled: access.*

## Fashion

### Black Fashion Museum

*155 West 126th Street, between Lenox Avenue & Adam Clayton Powell Jr Boulevard (666 1320/996 4470).* **Train** 2 or 3 to 125th Street. **Open** by appointment only. **Admission** suggested donation $3 adults; $2 children, students, senior citizens. **No credit cards**.

This three-storey brownstone in Harlem shows the talents of Black designers and relates the history of the Black American in fashion. One room is devoted to Ann Lowe, the seamstress who made ballgowns for American's aristocracy and designed Jackie O's wedding dress. It's a small collection, heavy on sequins and glamour – such as the 18-carat gold embroidered bustier by Jay Smith – but lovingly explained by volunteer staff. Hopefully some of the ancient mannequins will disappear during its planned renovation.

### The Museum at FIT

*Seventh Avenue, at West 27th Street (760 7970).* **Train** 1 or 9 to 28th Street. **Open** noon-8pm Tue-Fri; 10am-5pm Sat. **Admission** free.

The Museum at the Fashion Institute of Technology has the world's largest collection of costumes and textiles yet it contains only two public galleries. Exhibitions are tailored towards the 25 courses at the FIT and have covered everything from sportswear, Balenciaga and East Village fashions to a history of lingerie.

*Disabled: access, toilets.*

## Historical

### The Statue of Liberty & Ellis Island Museum

*ferry from Battery Park to Liberty Island and then on to Ellis Island (363 3200/269 5755 ferry information).* **Train** (to Battery Park) 4 or 5 to Bowling Green. **Ferries** every half hour 9.15am-4.30pm daily. **Fare** $7 adults; $5 senior citizens, $3 children 3-17, including admission. **Ticket sales** Castle Clinton, Battery Park. **Open** 8.30am-4.30pm daily. **No credit cards**.

This is one of the most exciting experiences for a first-time visitor to New York. Admire the breathtaking city skyline as the ferry leaves Manhattan and then move up front during the approach to the Statue of Liberty. There are elevators to the podium but if you want to stand inside the crown be prepared for a 22-storey climb – and, especially in peak hours during summer, a two- or three-hour wait. There's an interesting museum about the statue's history contained in the pedestal itself but, whatever you do, don't miss the Immigration Museum on Ellis Island, where the tour boat takes you on the way back to Manhattan. More than 12 million people passed through this immigrant station and the exhibitions are an evocative and moving tribute to anyone who ever packed their bags and headed for America with dreams of a better life. The audio tour, available in five languages, is highly recommended ($3.50 adults, $3 senior citizens, $2.50 under-17s). Look out for a photograph of Fiorello LaGuardia, one of Ellis Island's interpreters, who went on to become one of New York's most popular majors and now lends his name to one of the city's airports.

*Disabled: access to Ellis Island and the podium of the Statue of Liberty only.*

### Brooklyn Historical Society

*128 Pierrepont Street, near Clinton Street, Brooklyn (1-718 624 0890).* **Train** 2, 3, 4, 5 to Borough Hall; N or R to Court Street. **Open** noon-5pm Tue-Sat. **Admission** $2.50 adults; $1 children, senior citizens. **No credit cards**.

What have Woody Allen, Mae West, Isaac Asimov, Mel Brooks and Walt Whitman got in common? Answer: they were all – along with Al Capone, Barry Manilow and Gypsy Rose Lee – born in Brooklyn. Consequently they merit tributes in this tiny museum dedicated to Brooklyn's former glories. There are displays on its firefighters, the Navy Yard and local baseball team the Brooklyn Dodgers, which won the World Series in 1955 before being sold, en masse, to Los Angeles two years later. That just about sums it up really, although there is an educational centre and library ($5 research fee). It's a fine historic building, featuring the first use of terracotta ornamentation in the States, but strictly for people with a particular interest.

*Disabled: access, toilets.*

### Fraunces Tavern Museum

*second & third floors, 54 Pearl Street, corner of Broad Street (425 1778).* **Train** 1 or 9 to South Ferry. **Open** 10am-4.45pm Mon-Fri; noon-4pm Sat. **Admission** $2.50 adults; $1 children, students, senior citizens; free under-6s. **No credit cards**.

This tavern used to be George Washington's drinking hole and was a prominent meeting place for anti-British groups before the Revolution. The eighteenth-century building (which has been partly reconstructed) is an unexpectedly quaint site on the fringes of the financial district and displays most of its artefacts in period room settings. The changing exhibitions are often interesting.

### Hall of Fame for Great Americans

*West 181st Street (Hall of Fame Terrace) & University Avenue, Bronx (1-718 220 6003).* **Train** 4 to Burnside Avenue. **Open** 10am-5pm daily. **Admission** free.

The Hall of Fame is a covered walkway lined with bronze busts of pre-eminent Americans, with sections such as scientists, authors, soldiers and statesmen. As the last two suggest, the tributees are mostly male, such as the Wright Brothers, Thomas Mann and Franklin D Roosevelt. If this was in Central Park it would be a popular attraction – but it's not. Instead you have to take a long subway ride and then walk through the Bronx for 20 minutes, so it hardly seems worth it. The neglected Hall is at the back of the Bronx Community College and is built on the highest natural summit of New York City.

*Disabled: access.*

*A poignant look into the past at the* **Lower East Side Tenement Museum**. *See page 207.*

### Museum of the City of New York

*1220 Fifth Avenue, at 103rd Street (534 1672).* **Train** 6 to 103rd Street. **Open** 10am-5pm Wed-Sat, 1-5pm Sun. **Admission** suggested donation $5 adults; $3 students, senior citizens, under-13s; $8 families. **No credit cards.**

This is one of those charming little village museums brimming with photos, mementos and curious objects – except for the fact that the village whose life it records is the metropolis of New York. A vast archive of objects, prints and photographs tells the story of the city, with displays about its people and examples of the artefacts that it has produced along the way. As well as 300,000 photos and prints and 2000 paintings and sculptures there's an uparallelled collection of Broadway memorablilia, and impressive historical collections of clothing, costurmes and decorative household objects. Much of this vast treasure trove is displayed only selectively, in themed exhibitions. The museum is at its informative best when a visit is combined with one of the lectures or walking tours.

*Disabled: access, toilets.*

### New York Historical Society

*2 West 77th Street, between Central Park West & Columbus Avenue (873 3400).* **Train** B or C to 81st Street. **Open** noon-5pm Wed-Sun. **Admission** suggested donation $3 adults; $1 children, senior citizens. **No credit cards.**

The Society has now reopened after being closed for several years due to lack of funding. It was one of the first cultural educational institutions in the United States and New York's oldest museum, founded in 1804. Exhibitions are constantly changing – there's even a section on the real Pocahontas following the Disney film – while the permanent collection ranges from Tiffany lamps and lithographs to Gouverneur Morris's wooden leg and a lock of George Washington's hair.

*Disabled: access, toilets.*

### Old Merchant's House

*29 East 4th Street, between Lafayette & the Bowery (777 1089).* **Train** 6 to Astor Place. **Open** 1-4pm Mon-Thur, Sun. **Admission** $3 adults; $2 students, senior citizens; free accompanied under-12s. **No credit cards.**

Seabury Tredwell was the merchant in question. He made his fortune selling hardware and bought this elegant Greek Revival house three years after it was built in 1832. The house has been virtually untouched since the 1860s; decoration is spare (bar the lavish canopied four-poster beds) and ornamentation tasteful. Guided tours are conducted on Sundays; call for details.

### South Street Seaport Museum

*12 Fulton Street, at Front Street (669 9400).* **Train** 2,3, 4 or 5 to Fulton Street; A or C to Broadway Nassau. **Open** *Sept-May* 10am-5pm daily; *June-Sept* 10am-6pm daily. **Admission** $6 adults; $5 senior citizens; $4 students; $3 under-13s. **Credit** AmEx, MC, V.

The museum spreads out over 11 blocks alongside the harbour as a collection of galleries, historic ships, nineteenth-century buildings and a visitor centre. The staff (mostly volunteers) are exceptionally friendly and it's fun to wander around the streets, popping in to see an exhibition on tattooing before climbing on board the four-masted 1911 *Peking*. The Seaport itself is pretty touristy but it's still a charming place to spend an afternoon and there are plenty of cafés to choose from near the Fulton Market building.

## Jewish

### The Jewish Museum

*1109 Fifth Avenue, at 92nd Street (423 3230).* **Train** 6 to 96th Street. **Open** 11am-5.45pm Mon-Thur, Sun. **Admission** $7 adults; $5 students, senior citizens; free under-12s; free to all 5-8pm Tue. **No credit cards.**

The Jewish Museum is a fascinating collection of art, artefacts and media installations housed in the 1908 Warburg Mansion. The permanent exhibition tracks the Jewish cultural experience through exhibits ranging from a Statue of Liberty Hanukkah lamp and filigree silver circumcision set to a sixteenth-century mosaic wall from a Persian synagogue and an interactive Talmud. This eclectic collection – the largest of its kind in America – is also historic: most of it was rescued from European synagogues before World War II. The museum reopened after renovation in 1993 with double the gallery space and the addition of the tranquil Weissman Café.

*Disabled: access, toilets (423 3271 for information).*

### Yeshiva University Museum

*2520 Amsterdam Avenue, near West 185th Street (960 5390).* **Train** 1 to 181st Street. **Open** 10.30am-5pm Tue-Thur; noon-6pm Sun. Closed Aug. **Admission** $3 adults; $1.50 senior citizens, under-14s. **No credit cards.**

The Yeshiva University Museum usually holds one major exhibition a year and a number of changing shows, mainly on Jewish themes.

*Disabled: access.*

## Media

### American Museum of the Moving Image

*35th Avenue at 36th Street, Astoria, Queens (1-718 784 0077).* **Train** G or R to Steinway Street. **Open** noon-4pm Tue-Fri; noon-6pm Sat, Sun. **Admission** $5 adults; $4 senior citizens; $2.50 children. **No credit cards.**

This is the only museum in the US devoted to film, TV, video and digital media, but in the past it has failed to impress – perhaps things will improve after major renovations are completed in February 1996. At time of going to press, only one gallery was accessible to the public: Computer Space. The title refers to the world's first video game, the brainchild of Nolan Bushnell, who later went on to found Atari. Other games on show include the nostalgia-inducing Pac-Man and Space Invaders. Film programmes remain strong.

*Disabled: access, toilets.*

### Museum of TV & Radio

*25 West 52nd Street, between Fifth & Sixth Avenues (621 6600).* **Train** E or F to Fifth Avenue & 53rd Street; N or R to 49th Street; 1 or 9 to 50th Street; B, D, F or Q to Rockefeller Center. **Open** noon-6pm Tue, Wed, Sat, Sun; noon-8pm Thur; noon-9pm Fri. **Admission** $6 adults; $4 students, senior citizens; $3 under-13s. **No credit cards.**

A living, working archive of over 60,000 radio and TV programmes. Just head to the fourth-floor library and use the computerised system to access a favourite *Star Trek* or *I Love Lucy* episode. Minutes later, the assigned console downstairs plays up to four of your choices within two hours. The radio listening room works the same way. Cinemas provide major screenings and there are numerous galleries and changing exhibits. A must for TV and radio addicts.

*Disabled: access, toilets.*

## Military

### Sea, Air & Space Museum

*USS Intrepid, Pier 86, West 46th Street & 12th Avenue, at the Hudson River (245 2533/245 0072 recorded information).* **Train** A, C, E or K to 42nd Street. **Open** *Memorial Day-Labor Day* 10am-5pm Mon-Sat; 10am -6pm Sun; *Labor Day-Memorial Day* 10am-5pm Mon-Wed, Sun. Last admissions one hour before closing. **Admission** $10 adults; $7.50 senior citizens, children 12-17; $5 children 6-11; free first child under 6; $1 each additional child under 6. **Credit** AmEx, MC, V.

The museum is sited on the World War II aircraft carrier *Intrepid*, whose decks are strewn with space capsules and various aircraft. Audio-visual shows and hands-on exhibits will appeal to children.

*Disabled: access, toilets.*

## Neighbourhood

### Lower East Side Tenement Museum

*90 Orchard Street, at Broome Street (431 0233).* **Train** F to Delancey Street; B, D or Q to Grand; J, M or Z to Delancey & Essex. **Open** 11am-5pm Tue-Sun. **Admission** $7 adults; $6 students, senior citizens, children. All prices include tour. **Credit** AmEx, V, MC.

A fascinating look at the history of immigration via a guided tour in a nineteenth-century tenement. The building, in the heart of what was once Little Germany, contains two reconstructed apartments belonging to a German Jewish dressmaker and a Catholic Sicilian family. The highly recommended tours are at 1pm, 2pm and 3pm Tue-Fri and every 45 minutes at the weekend. The museum has a gallery, shop and video room and offers local heritage walking tours.

## Science & Technology

### Hayden Planetarium

*West 81st Street, between Central Park West & Columbus Avenue (769 5920 recorded information).* **Train** B, C or K to 81st Street. **Open** 10am-5.45pm Mon-Thur, Sun; 10am-8.45pm Fri, Sat. **Admission** $10 adults, $7 senior citizens, students; $5.50 under-12s. **No credit cards.**

The ever-popular planetarium will always appeal to star gazers and those with fond memories of Diane Keaton and Woody Allen in *Manhattan*. Programmes are extensive – with far better current material than most planetariums – and the laser technology is equally impressive. There are several galleries next to the Guggenheim Space Theater where you can wander around the enormous Ahnighito

meteorite that was found in the wastelands of Greenland. Call to check laser and planetarium show times.
*Disabled: access, toilets.*

### Liberty Science Center

*Liberty State Park, 251 Phillip Street, Jersey City, New Jersey (1-201 200 1000 recorded information).* **Transport** PATH train to Grove Street, then connecting park bus; weekend ferry service (call 800 533 3779). **Open** 9.30am-5.30pm Tue-Sun. **Admission** *exhibition halls only* $9 adults, $8 students, senior citizens; $6 children; *halls & Omnimax cinema* $13 adults; $11 students, senior citizens; $9 children. **Credit** AmEx, Discover, MC, V.
The spanking new Liberty Science Center (it opened in 1993) is an excellent museum with innovative exhibitions and America's largest and most spectacular Imax cinema. It also has an observation tower providing excellent views of Manhattan and an unusual sideways look at the Statue of Liberty. The Center's emphasis is on hands-on science so it's elbows out to try and get a look in among the over-excited kids. Even non-science addicts will enjoy this museum and it makes a great day out if travelling by ferry at the weekend.
*Disabled: access, toilets.*

### New York Hall of Science

*47-01 111th Street, Flushing Meadows Corona Park (1-718 699 0005).* **Train** 7 to 111th Street. **Open** 10am-5pm Wed-Sun. **Admission** $4.50 adults; $3 children, senior citizens; free to all 2-5pm Wed, Thur. **Credit** AmEx, MC, V.
The Hall of Science features the largest collection of hands-on science exhibits in New York City, though it has probably suffered from the opening of the Liberty Science Center. It's usually filled with groups of schoolchildren and is aimed at a much younger, lower level of understanding than the Liberty. The museum successfully demystifies science, as a result of the influence of its visionary physicist director, and plans are underway on a ten-year $80 million renovation and expansion project which promises laboratories, an observatory, auditorium and planetarium.
*Disabled: access, toilets.*

## Transport

### Fire Museum

*278 Spring Street, at Varick (691 1303).* **Train** 1 or 9 to Houston Street. **Open** 10am-4pm Tue-Sun; 10am-9pm Thur. **Admission** $4 adult; $2 students, senior citizens; $1 under-12s. **Credit** AmEx, MC, V.
A bright and cheerful three-storey museum strictly for enthusiasts only. There are two tours a day for groups of up to 30.
*Disabled: access, toilets.*

### New York Transit Museum

*Corner of Boerum Place & Schermerhorn Street, Brooklyn (1-718 243 3060).* **Train** 2, 3, 4 or 5 to Borough Hall; M, N, or R to Court Street; G to Hoyt/Schermerhorn. **Open** 10am-4pm Tue, Thur, Fri; 10am-6pm Wed; noon-5pm Sat, Sun. **Admission** $3 adults; $1.50 children, senior citizens. **No credit cards.**
Don't look for a building – the Transit Museum is housed underground in an old 1930s subway station. Its entrance, down a flight of stairs, is beneath the Board of Education building, opposite the black and white striped New York City Transit Authority Building. Vintage carriage trains with wicker seats and canvas hand straps line up alongside a selection of antique turnstiles (not looking much different from those in use today) and plenty of adverts – including one explaining how spitting 'is a violation of the sanitary code'. So there! The museum, naturally, is popular with children but it's a fun place for adults too.
*Disabled: access.*

## And The Rest...

### Abigail Adams Smith Museum

*421 East 61st Street, at First Avenue (838 6878).* **Train** 4, 5, 6, N or R to 59th Street. **Open** noon-4pm Mon-Fri; 1-5pm Sun. **Admission** $3 adults; $2 students, senior citizens; free under-13s. **No credit cards.**
An eighteenth-century coach house once belonging to the daughter of John Adams, the second American president.

### American Numismatic Society

*Audubon Terrace, Broadway, between 155th & 156th Streets (234 3130).* **Train** 1 to 157th Street. **Open** 9am-4.30pm Tue-Sat; 1-4pm Sun. **Admission** free.
A collection covering 26 centuries. For coin enthusiasts only.

### Garibaldi Meucci Museum

*420 Tomkins Avenue, Staten Island (1-718 442 1608).* **Transport** Train 1 or 9 to South Ferry, then Staten Island Ferry and bus S52. **Open** 1-5pm Tue-Sun. **Admission** suggested donation $3.
The 1840s Gothic revival home of Italian inventor Antonio Meucci and former refuge of Italian patriot Garibaldi.

## Libraries

## New York Public Library

The multi-tentacled New York Public Library comprises four major research libraries and 82 local and specialist branches, making it the largest and most comprehensive library system in the world. The library grew out of the combined collections of John Jacob Astor, Samuel Jones Tilden and James Lenox at the end of the nineteenth century. Today it holds a total of 50 million items, including nearly 18 million books, with around a million items added to the collection each year. Unless you are interested in a specific subject, you are most likely to visit the system's flagship building, officially called the Center for Humanities (*see below*). Originally founded in 1895, the Library recently celebrated its centennial and the newest branch, the Science, Industry and Business Library, is scheduled to open in summer 1996.

### Center for the Humanities

*Fifth Avenue, at 42nd Street (869 8089 recorded information).* **Train** 7 to Fifth Avenue; B, D or F to 42nd Street. **Open** 10am-6pm Mon-Thur; noon-6pm Fri, Sat. **Admission** free.
This landmark 1911 Beaux Arts building on Fifth Avenue, flanked by lions and limestone columns, is what most people mistakenly call the New York Public Library. The famous lions are crowned with holly at Christmas and during summer people sit on the steps or sip iced drinks at the outdoor tables beneath the arches. There are free guided tours of the building at 11am and 2pm, which include the beautiful public reading room, the first Gutenburg Bible brought to America and a hand-written copy of Washington's Farewell Address. The Bill Blass Public Catalog room was recently restored and renovated and now contains computers networked to the information highway where visitors can surf the Internet or World Wide Web. Special exhibitions are frequent.
*Disabled: access, toilets.*

### Donnell Library Center

*20 West 53rd Street, between Fifth & Sixth Avenues (621 0618).* **Train** B, D or F to Rockefeller Center. **Open**

*One of the hair-raising exhibits at the* **Liberty Science Center**. *See page 208.*

12.30-5.30pm Mon, Wed, Fri, Sat; 9.30am-8pm Tue, Thur. **Admission** free.
This branch of the NYPL has an extensive collection of records, films and videotapes with appropriate screening facilities. The Donnell also specialises in foreign language books – over 80 languages – and there's a children's section of more than 100,000 books, films, records and cassettes.
*Disabled: access, toilets.*

### Library and Museum of the Performing Arts

*Lincoln Center, 111 Amsterdam Avenue, at West 65th Street (870 1630).* **Train** 1 or 9 to 66th Street. **Open** noon-8pm Mon, Thur; noon-6pm Tue, Wed, Fri, Sat. **Admission** free.
Outstanding research and circulating collections on music, drama, theatre and dance.

### Science, Industry and Business Library

*Madison Avenue, between 34th & 35th Streets (930 0747).* **Train** 6 to 53rd Street. **Admission** free.
When the most recent branch of the New York Public library opens in May 96, at a cost of $100 million, it will become the nation's largest public information centre devoted to science and business. It is located in the former B Altman building and will contain a number of electronic resources.
*Disabled: access, toilets.*

### Schomburg Center for Research in Black Culture

*515 Malcolm X Boulevard, at 135th Street (491 2200).* **Train** 2 or 3 to 135th Street. **Open** noon-8pm Mon-Wed; 10am-6pm Fri, Sat. **Admission** free.
A collection relating to Black and African culture founded by the Puerto Rican Arthur Schomburg in 1926. It includes photographs, maps, paintings, exhibitions and artefacts.
*Disabled: access, toilets.*

## Other Libraries

Most of the following libraries are associated with the appropriate museums in the previous section. They are generally used by students or those with a specialist interest.

### American Craft Council Library

*6th Floor, 72 Spring Street, at Lafayette & Crosby (274 0630).* **Train** 6 to Spring Street. **Open** *Sept-June* 1-5pm Mon-Fri; *July-Aug* 1-5pm Mon-Thur; 9.30am-1.30pm Fri. **Admission** $5 non-members. **No credit cards**.

### American Museum of Natural History

*Central Park West, at West 79th Street, 4th floor (769 5400).* **Train** B or C to 81st Street. **Open** 11am-4pm Tue-Fri. **Admission** as for museum.
*Disabled: access.*

### American Numismatic Society Library

*Audubon Terrace, Broadway, between 155th & 156th Streets (234 3130).* **Train** 1 to 157th Street. **Open** 9am-4.30pm Tue-Sat. **Admission** free.

### Cooper-Hewitt Museum Library

*2 East 91st Street, at Fifth Avenue (860 6883).* **Train** 4, 5 or 6 to 86th Street. **Open** by appointment 9.30am-5pm Mon-Fri. **Admission** free.
Decorative arts and design.

### General Society Library of Mechanics and Tradesmen (Mechanics Library)

*20 West 44th Street, between Fifth & Sixth Avenues (921 1767).* **Train** 1, 2, 3, 7, 9, N or R to Times Square/42nd Street. **Open** to members only 9am-6pm Mon-Thur; 9am-5pm Fri. **Membership** $35 per year. **No credit cards**.

### Horticultural Society of New York

*128 West 58th Street, between Sixth & Seventh Avenues (757 0915).* **Train** 1, 9, A, B, C or D to Columbus Circle. **Open** 10am-6pm Mon-Fri. **Admission** free if not checking books out. **Membership** $35 basic; $75 full.
As well as books and periodicals, the library contains nursery and seed catalogues. Only members can take books out.
*Disabled: access, toilets.*

### Information Exchange of the Municipal Art Society

*Urban Center, 57 Madison Avenue, between East 50th & 51st Streets (935 3960).* **Train** 6 to 61st Street. **Open** by appointment only 10am-1pm Mon-Fri. **Admission** free.
A New York oriented archive with clippings, periodicals, books and photographs dealing with city, harbour and water environments from infrastructure and housing to the latest building proposals.
*Disabled: access, toilets.*

### International Center of Photography

*1130 Fifth Avenue, at 94th Street (860 1778).* **Train** 6 to 96th Street. **Open** summer 10am-1pm, 1.30-5pm Tue, Thur; 11am-1pm, 1.30-7pm Wed. Check hours at other times of year. **Admission** as for museum.
*Disabled: access, toilets.*

### Metropolitan Museum of Art: Uris Library and Resource Center.

*Fifth Avenue, entrance at 81st Street (570 3788).* **Train** 4, 5 or 6 to 86th Street. **Open** 10am-4.30pm Mon-Thur, Sun; 10am-8.30pm Fri, Sat. **Admission** free.
A general art reference library.
*Disabled: access, toilets.*

### Thomas J Watson Library

*Metropolitan Museum of Art, Fifth Avenue, main museum entrance on 82nd Street (879 5500).* **Train** 4, 5 or 6 to 86th Street. **Open** 10am-4.40pm Tue-Fri. Closed in August. **Admission** free.
The Watson is the largest art and archeological library in the West and is reserved for bona fide researchers only, so take along your credentials.
*Disabled: access, toilets.*

### Municipal Reference and Research Center

*31 Chambers Street, at Center Street, room 112 (788 8593).* **Train** 1, 2, 3 or 9 to Chambers Street. **Open** 10am-4pm Mon-Fri. **Admission** free.
An archive of New York City government agency publications from parking ordinances, reports and planning laws to the city charter. It's run by the city's Department of Records & Information Services.
*Disabled: access, toilets.*

### Museum of American Folk Art Library

*61 West 62nd Street, at Broadway (977 7170).* **Train** 1 or 9 to 66th Street. **Open** by appointment only. **Admission** free.
*Disabled: access, toilets.*

### New York Academy of Medicine Library

*1216 Fifth Avenue, at 103rd Street (876 8200).* **Train** 6 to 103rd Street. **Open** 9am-5pm Mon-Fri. **Admission** free.

### New York Genealogical and Biographical Society

*122 East 58th Street, between Park & Lexington Avenues (755 8532).* **Train** 6 to 59th Street. **Open** 9.30am-5pm Tue-Sat. Closed mid-August. **Admission** suggested donation $5. **No credit cards.**
This is an invaluable resource centre for tracing family histories. The society runs regular lectures and workshops on how to organise your research.
*Disabled: access, toilets.*

### New York Society Library

*53 East 79th Street, between Madison & Park Avenues (288 6900).* **Train** 6 to 77th Street. **Open** summer 9am-5pm Mon, Wed, Fri; 9am-7pm Tue, Thur; 9am-5pm Sat. Call for winter hours. **Membership** $135 per year; $90 for students; $90 for 6 month household. **No credit cards.**
This is the city's oldest library and is a venerable institution. Non-members must use the first-floor reference library only and may request three books per day. Members have access to around a quarter of a million works of fiction, history, biography, literature and travel. It's particularly strong on chemistry and alchemy and one of its collections includes 920 volumes of fiction from 1750-1830.

## Free museums

Museum Mile covers ten institutions along Fifth Avenue on the Upper East Side. Numerous processions take place along this stretch of road and on the first Tuesday of June part of it is closed to motor vehicles and – more importantly – all the museums are open to the public free of charge. But don't worry, there are other opportunities to save some cash as some museums waive the admission fee for several hours on appointed days each week. They are:

### Asia Society

*Listed under* **Arts & Culture: Asian**. Free 6-8pm Thursdays.

### Cooper-Hewitt National Design Museum

*Listed under* **Major Museums**. Free 5-9pm Tuesdays.

### Jewish Museum

*Listed under* **Arts & Culture: Jewish**. Free after 5pm Tuesdays.

### Museum of Modern Art

*Listed under* **Major Museums**. Free 5.30-8.30pm Thursdays and Fridays.

### New York Hall of Science

*Listed under* **Arts & Culture: Science & Technology**. Free 2-5pm Wednesdays and Thursdays.

### Solomon R Guggenheim Museum

*Listed under* **Major Museums**. 'Pay as you wish' Friday 6-8pm.

### Whitney Museum of American Art

*Listed under* **Major Museums**. Free 6-8pm Thursdays.

# Arts & Entertainment

# Media

***Load up on New York newsprint, surf the NYC net and go insane trying to find something good to watch on TV.***

## Newspapers & Magazines

### Dailies

The venerable **New York Times** (60¢) is excellent for serious news with a world perspective and contains a Metro section devoted to news about the city. The *Times* lives up to its claim of publishing 'All the news that's fit to print', although the international stories are usually overpowered by Macy's ads. The Sunday Arts & Leisure and the Friday Weekend sections are a reliable source of entertainment information, while Monday's supplement covers sports, the Tuesday *Science Times* is full of ads for electronic hardware and the Wednesday extra is the place to look for apartments. The famous Sunday edition ($2) is a full five pounds of newsprint with enough sections to keep you reading well into the week.

'New York's Hometown Newspaper', The **Daily News** (50¢), dates back to the 1920s when it rose to success as scandal sheet par excellence. It remains the quintessential hard-bitten New York paper, full of murders and outrage. The competing tabloid, the **New York Post** (50¢), is the city's oldest surviving newspaper, founded in 1801 by Alexander Hamilton. It now lies in the hands of Rupert Murdoch and offers pretty much the same emphasis as the *News*. Both have large sports sections, a frighteningly insular perspective, and headline writers skilled in cultivating urban paranoia. **New York Newsday** (50¢), a tabloid originating in suburban Long Island, contains magazine-like articles in addition to its wordy news coverage and regular columns. **USA Today** (50¢) reads like a government propaganda sheet, but it does have colourful weather maps. The **Amsterdam News** (60¢) is one of the oldest Black newspapers, offering a left-of-centre Afrocentric view. New York also supports two Spanish language dailies, **El Diario** (50¢) and **Noticias del Mundo** (40¢), and daily or weekly papers in every foreign tongue you can think of.

### Weeklies

We're biased and we think that the best place to find out what's going on in town is the new weekly **Time Out New York** ($1.95). Launched in 1995 and based on the tried and trusted format of its London parent, it is well on its way to being an indispensable guide to the life of the city.

The politically correct **Village Voice** ($1.25), a legacy of the Beat Generation, serves up boundless investigative articles and studious arts reviews. Natives largely ignore the features and turn to the graffiti-like ad pages for club and concert information.

Pick up the **New Yorker** ($2.50) for a calming glimpse into the disappearing world of fine wit and elegant prose, or to see how its English editor, Tina Brown, has injected life and colour since arriving in 1992. Its arts coverage is good for previews and its illustrations are excellent. **New York** ($2.95) has a more populist approach, leading with trend-based features and a weekly splattering of New York faces and phenomena.

There are plenty of free weekly papers available. Most are neighbourhood ad-sheets aimed at local residents, but **Downtown** is good for general rock listings and **New York Press** is well worth picking up, containing excellent comic strips, witty columns and good restaurant reviews. Both can be found in downtown bars and music venues, and picked up at bank cashpoints.

Read **Homo Xtra (HX)** or **Next** (both free at gay bars and clubs) for excellent listings of New York's gay culture in all its infinite variety.

*Part of the New York press gang.*

### Monthlies

Andy Warhol's magazine, **Interview** ($2.95), is still firmly New York-based, covering the world of fashion and entertainment with maximum style over content. **Paper** ($3.50) covers the city's trend-conscious set with plenty of insider buzz on bars, clubs, downtown boutiques and the people you'll find in them. **Project X** is published bi-monthly, and is where you'll find the city's painfully outrageous club kids writing about each other. **Sound Views** (free in NYC) covers the downtown rock scene; look for it in music venues.

### Outlets

If you can't find what you need in the well-stocked newsstands around the city, there are huge selections at **Eastern News** (687 1198) at the base of the Met-Life building (above Grand Central Station), **Hudson News**, 753 Broadway at 8th Street (674 6655), and **Tower Books**, 383 Lafayette Street (228 5100), which has a large collection of fanzines and obscurities and a distinctly browser-friendly attitude, as does **Nicos**, Sixth Avenue at 11th Street (255 9175). All of these carry a full range of foreign newspapers. **Hotalings**, 142 West 42nd Street (840 1868), is a specialist foreign news store, which stocks only titles from other US cities and abroad.

# Gotham City cyberspace

If you're here with a computer don't forget to explore the cyberspace which hovers above New York. It's also worth browsing websites before you arrive. There are plenty of bulletin boards based here, in addition to the US commercial services – Compuserve (1-800 848 8199), Prodigy (1-800 PRODIGY) and the much livelier America Online (1-800 827 6364). *Internet New York* (Hayden Books, 1995) gives the full lowdown.

## Bulletin Boards

### Echo

*(989 8411; 255 3839 voice).*
This is the east coast counterpart to San Francisco's famous WELL, a bulletin board with lots of intelligent and culturally literate chat with full Internet access.

### Mindvox

*(989 4141; 989 2418 voice).*
One of the city's first virtual communities, with a broad array of discussion groups including many concerning online security and developments. Also has archives so you can see what cyberspace used to look like. Internet access available.

### New York Online

*(1-718 596 5881; 1-718 596 6000 voice).*
On this Brooklyn-based Bulletin Board you'll find *Vibe* magazine and PrideNet, among other intriguing stuff.

### Sensenet

*(595 3553).*
Elegantly presented and soon to include Internet access, Sensenet is a glorious mess of wilfully weird nonsense, with plenty of anarchistic subjects.

### SonicNet

*(431 1627/941 5912 voice).*
This is where New York's modem-driven vixen Cyberbabe conducts her regular real-time *Melrose Place* forums. More usefully, it's also where you'll find an ever-increasing amount of information about the rock and indie scene, with online interviews of folk like Sonic Youth, as well as downloadable music and loads of tickets, band and concert info.

## Internet Sites

Bear in mind that these can go out of date. Check Time Out Net (*below*) for the latest.

### http://www.cen.uiuc.edu/~jl8287/letterman.html

David Letterman's hangout in cyberspace. Loads of Top Ten lists!

### http://mosaic.echonyc.com/~voice/

The beginnings of a site from the *Village Voice* newspaper. Limited city entertainment listings.

### http://www.allianceforarts.org

The New York City Culture Guide & Calendar, a growing service offering the latest news on major cultural events.

### http://www.avsi.com

Lots of artsy New York stuff, including underground film directories and the website of trendy downtown guide, *Paper* magazine.

### http://www.echonyc.com

This is Echo's website (*see* **Bulletin Boards**). There are arts reviews, events listings and a city guide. Looks good.

### http://www.timeout.co.uk

This is the *Time Out* website, where you'll find a guide to New York, including events listings, features, free classified ads and the opportunity to post up your own comments and secrets about the city. Also includes substantial guides to Amsterdam, Berlin, London, Madrid, Paris and Prague. Good and getting better!

### http://www.whitehouse.gov

Your connection to the high and mighty of US government. Register your grievances with Bill and Al.

## Television

American TV, in all its vulgarity, is a sure source of culture shock and a visit to New York, especially if it is your first time in the States, would be woefully incomplete without at least a small dose of cathode radiation. TV here is unrelentingly advertising-led and each moment of broadcasting is constructed to instill fatal curiosity for the next, with commercial breaks coming thick and fast.

The TV day is rigidly scheduled, beginning with news and gossipy breakfast magazine programmes, leading into a lobotomised cycle of soap operas, vintage re-runs and game shows, which remains unbroken until around 3pm. Then the talk shows like *Oprah* and *Ricki Lake* take over, broadcasting peoples' not-so-private problems, with subjects in the range of 'I married my mother's lesbian lover' or 'I still love my serial killer boyfriend'. Watch real people have real arguments and thank God that your'e relatively normal.

At 5pm the showbiz chat of the pre-news warm-up begins along with local news, followed by national and international news from 6.30pm. Early evening is the domain of the highest-rated shows – syndicated quizzes such as *Jeopardy* and *Wheel of Fortune* – leaving huge audiences for prime time, when action series, sports, movies, sitcoms and fly-on-the-wall 'cop-umentaries' fight it out for ratings and the ads get even more pervasive. New episodes of shows are shown once a week, but re-runs are scheduled daily, so, for example, you can see *The Simpsons* six times a week. Finally, as things begin to wind down, out come the unsubtle plugs and overblown personalities of the various late-night chat shows.

The only broadcast alternative to this ultra-consumerist programming is the sluggish elitism of public television. These stations receive little money from the government and rely heavily on 'membership' donations garnered during embarrassing on-air funding drives.

And then there is cable, 50 or so channels of basic cable, plus 'Premium' channels offering uninterrupted movies and sports coverage. 'Pay-per-view' channels have a menu of recent films, exclusive concerts and sports events to choose from. Cable is also where you'll find the paid programming and public access channels with their complement of weirdos and soft-core porn. In all, New Yorkers can receive about 80 channels, none of which have anything on them.

For full weekly TV schedules, including both broadcast and cable television, save the Sunday *New York Times* TV section or get the indispensable *TV Guide* (99¢). Daily papers have comprehensive 24-hour listings.

## The Networks

There are four major networks which broadcast nationwide. All offer ratings-led variations on a theme. **CBS** (on channel 2 in NYC) has the best network news daily at 6.30pm and the top investigative show, *60 Minutes*, on Sundays. **NBC** (channel 4) is the home of the ailing *Saturday Night Live* and the *Tonight Show*. **ABC** (channel 7) is king of the daytime soaps and **Fox TV** (channel 5), a smaller network, is popular with younger audiences for shows like *Melrose Place*, *The Simpsons* and *X-Files*.

**WWOR** (UPN 9) offers baseball and popular re-runs (*Baywatch, Married With Children, Roseanne*); **WPIX** (channel 11) is 'New York's Movie Station'. There are also two Spanish channels, **WXTV** (channel 41) and **WNJU** (channel 47). As well as Mexican dramas and titillating gameshows, these are your best bet for soccer.

## Public TV

You'll find underfunded and comically pretentious public TV on channels 13, 21, 31 and 50. Hidden among schedules of classical music, wildlife shorts, cookery and DIY shows are classy British drama (in the *Masterpiece Theater* slot) and re-runs of *Morse*, *Poirot* and *Miss Marple* (in *Mystery*). *Fawlty Towers*, *The Young Ones* and long-forgotten episodes of *EastEnders* are shown at the weekend. Channel 21 broadcasts *ITN World News* daily at 7pm and 11.30pm.

## Cable

For music, there is **MTV**, its more conservative sibling **VH-1** and **The Box**, a 24-hour video juke-box channel. Sports fans have **ESPN**, **Sportschannel** and **MSG** (Madison Square Garden). **CNN**, **Headline News** and **NY-1** offer news all day, the last with a local bias.

**Comedy Central** is 24-hour comedy, with recent British hits like *Absolutely Fabulous*, a glut of stand-up and nightly re-runs of classic *Saturday Night Live* shows starring such young guns as John Belushi and Eddie Murphy. **E!** is 'Entertainment Television', a pop-culture mix of celebrities and movie news. This is where you'll find New York icon *Howard Stern* (*see* **Radio**) conducting hilariously intrusive interviews and such tabloid TV as *The Gossip Show* and the unmissable *Talk Soup* where you can watch daily highlights from the best of America's talk shows.

**Bravo** shows the kind of arts programmes which public TV would air if it could afford them, including *The South Bank Show* and a good ratio of quality movies. Its sister station, the **Independent Film Channel**, shows uninterrupted art-house movies, but isn't available in all areas yet. **BET** stands for Black Entertainment Television, a rap and soul-filled reminder of America's tendency to cultural separatism. The **Discovery Channel** and the **Learning Channel** offer the best of science and nature programmes, and show gruesome surgical operations, often around mealtimes. **Court TV** has since scored big ratings with hot trials like the Menendez Brothers and, of course, OJ.

The **Country Channel** (musically speaking), the **Prayer Channel**, the **Home Shopping Network** and the **Weather Channel** are all self-explanatory. Watch out also for MTV's *The Goods*, its version of credit-card couch-potato consumer heaven.

Public Access TV is on channels 16, 17, 34 and 69 (only in Manhattan), which are surefire sources of bizarre camcorder amusement. Late night Channel 35 is where you'll find *The Robin Byrd Show*, a kind of chat forum for Times Square porn stars, riddled with ads for escort services and sex lines.

Premium channels, often available for a fee in hotels, include **HBO** (Home Box Office), **Showtime**, **Cinemax**, **Movie Channel** and **Disney**, all of which show uninterrupted feature films and exclusive 'specials'.

# Radio

There are nearly 100 stations in the New York area, offering a huge range of sounds and styles. In addition to the commercial stations, each with a rigid musical palette, there are several innovative and eclectic college stations. On the AM dial you can find some intriguing talk radio, from phone-in shows that attract the city's nutcase population to fervently religious stations. There's plenty of news and sports here as well.

Radio highlights are printed weekly in the Sunday *Times* and *New York* magazine. The former has a comprehensive list of stations.

## News & Talk

**WINS 1010 AM**, **WABC 770 AM** and **WCBS 880 AM** all offer news throughout the day, coupled with traffic reports essential to commuters. Ad-free public radio stations **WNYC 93.9 FM/820 AM** and **WBAI 99.5 FM** both provide excellent news, including the *All Things Considered* current affairs slot and guest-driven talk shows, notably WNYC AM's *New York and Company*.

The AM phone-in shows will take you from one extreme to the other. **WLIB 1190 AM** provides the voice of militant Black New York, with news and talk from an Afrocentric perspective, interspersed with Caribbean music. Neo-fascist Rush Limbaugh airs his scarily popular views on WCBS.

## Classical

**WNCN** lost its frequency to a hard rock station, leaving only two classical stations, **WQXR 96.3 FM** and **WNYC 93.9 FM**. Both serve a varied diet of music and opera. The highlights are well covered in the Sunday *Times* and *New York*.

## Jazz

**WBGO 88.3 FM 'Jazz 88'** plays its records in phenomenal day-long chunks of a single artist, focusing on the birthdays and anniversaries of jazz greats. Less obsessive jazz buffs will find more variety on **WCWP 88.1 FM** and **WQCD 101.9 FM**.

## Dance & Pop

American commercial radio is rigidly formatted, which makes most pop stations extremely tedious and repetitive during daylight hours. However, in the evenings and at weekends, you'll find more interesting programmes.

**WQHT 97.1 FM 'Hot 97'** is New York's commercial hip-hop station, with *Yo! MTV Raps* hosts Dr Dre and Ed Lover cooking up a breakfast show for the homies, then rap and R'n'B throughout the day and harder hip-hop, old school and reggae mix shows in the evenings and weekends, played and introduced by such luminaries as **Red Alert**, **Funkmaster Flex**, **Afrika Bambaata**, **Pete Rock**, **Marley Marl**, **Bobby Konders** and **Flavor Flav**. The station also has some of the city's best house shows, with **Tony Humphries** very late on Fridays and **Frankie Knuckles** and **David Morales** together late on Saturdays.

**WBLS 107.5 FM** is now a Black oldies station, playing classic funk, soul and R'n'B. Grandmaster Flash has a splendid mix show early on Friday and Saturday evenings, spinning old-school hip-hop, funk and disco, and there's John Robinson's house mix after midnight Friday and Saturday, with **Hal Jackson's Sunday Classics** (blues and soul) throughout most of Sunday daytime.

**WRKS 98.7 FM 'Kiss'** changed last year to 'adult contemporary' format, which translates as unremarkable American pop. The only legacy of its more soulful days is the Sunday morning gospel show (6-9am).

**WCBS 101.1 FM** is strictly oldies, while **WMXV 105.1 FM 'Mix 105'** plays a broad mix of pop hits from the 1970s to the 1990s. **WPLJ 95.5 FM** is a top 40 station, promising 'no rap and none of the hard stuff'. This translates as languid rock ballads. **WLTW 106.7 FM 'Lite FM'** plays background music popular with elevators.

## Rock

**WBAB 102.3 FM**, **WRCN 103.9 FM** and **WXRK 92.3 FM 'K-Rock'** offer a digest of hard and classic rock. 'K Rock' also attracts the city's largest group of morning listeners with **Howard Stern**'s 7-11am weekday show (*see chapter* **New York Today**). **WNEW 102.7 FM** plays more contemporary rock and **WDRE 92.7 FM** 'alternative' (indie and gothic) sounds with a British bias. **WSOU 89.5 FM** is a college station devoted to heavy metal. A similar diet can be found on the new **WAXQ 104.3**.

## Other Music

**WWRL 1600 AM** plays gospel, **WEVD 1050 AM** showtunes, big band jazz, nostalgia and **WYNY 103.5 FM** country and western.

## College Radio

College radio is innovative and free of ads. However, smaller transmitters mean that reception is often compromised by Manhattan's high-rise geography. Try **WNYU 89.1 FM** from New York University and **WKCR 89.9 FM** from Columbia for varied programming right across the musical spectrum, including excellent dance mix shows in the evenings. Highly rated **WFMU 91.1 FM** from Upsala College puts out a fine mix of specialist shows including the eerie stream-of-consciousness monologues of **Joe Frank** (6pm Mondays) and the supertough **Wildgirl** (6pm Sat), who regularly interviews monster truck racers and only plays songs which involve motor vehicles. FMU publishes a free programme guide, full of quirky music and merchandise, available in some record stores.

# Be the audience

Tickets are available for all sorts of TV shows that are recorded in New York studios. Here are details of how to get into some of the best known; the **New York Convention & Visitors Bureau** (397 8222) can provide you with information about others. A bit of blag often improves your chances. Call to inquire about the situation on standby tickets.

### Donahue

Tapings are on Mondays to Wednesdays at 4pm and on Thursdays at 1pm and 4pm. You should send off for tickets three to five months in advance, and be 16 or older. Limited standby seats are available at 2.30pm on the day of the performance.
*Donahue Tickets, NBC, 30 Rockefeller Plaza, New York, NY 10112 (664 4444).*

### Ricki Lake Show

One of the more outrageous daytime talk shows. You must be 18 or older. Tapings are on Wednesday to Friday, at 3.30 and 5.30pm. Request tickets by postcard three to four months in advance or try for a standby one hour before taping.
*Ricki Lake Show, 401 37th Street New York NY 10016 (889 6767 ext 758).*

### The Late Show with David Letterman

The foolish uncle of late night. Tapings are on Monday to Friday at 5.30pm. You have to be 16 or older. Request tickets on a postcard six months in advance, or queue for a standby ticket at noon on the day.
*Late Show Tickets, Ed Sullivan Theatre, 1697 Broadway, New York, NY 10019 (975 5853)*

### Geraldo

The talk show most likely to incite violence in its guests. Tapings are on Tuesday to Thursday at 1pm and 4pm. You must be 18 or older. Send a letter and SAE for tickets one month in advance. Standby tickets are sometimes available 45 minutes before taping.
*Geraldo tickets, CBS television, 524 W 57th Street, New York, NY 10019 (265 8520 information; 265 1283 tickets).*

### Saturday Night Live

An institution, but one always in danger of being cancelled for its increasing failure to amuse. Broadcasts and tapings are on Saturday at 11.30pm. Tickets are distributed each August by lottery. Requests (on a postcard) must be received in August. Standby tickets are distributed at 9.15am at NBC (mezzanine level of the 49th Street side of Rockefeller Plaza). And you have to be 16 or over.
*Saturday Night Live Tickets, NBC, 30 Rockefeller Plaza, New York, NY 10112 (664 3056).*

# Cabaret

***From sophisticated uptown soirées to equally sophisticated downtown drag nights, New York life is a cabaret.***

*Joey Arias, one of the drag scene's finest, at* **Bar d'O**. *See page 217.*

Cabaret has always summed up the essence of New York romance – a scene of witty women and dapper gents hobnobbing in a haze of blue smoke. Even today, New York supports more cabaret rooms than any other city in the world.

It's great to sample the classic sophistication of the formal 'uptown' scene – the appreciative hush when the singer appears, the finely-groomed audience and the timeless elegance of the surroundings. However, it's usually an expensive evening involving dinner and a high cover charge – when the room only holds 60 or so, you pay for that intimacy. Dress is always smart, and it's sometimes compulsory to make reservations: call to check.

But there are also bars and clubs all over New York which provide entertainment of a more informal nature. There are laid-back jazz clubs, where musicians come to jam after they've finished sets somewhere else; relaxed piano bars where everyone, including drinkers, bartenders, waiters and waitresses, takes turns at the mic, singing excerpts from *My Fair Lady* amid hooting and catcalls; and Village bars, cafés and cellars where you're entertained by New York's ever-growing population of consummately professional drag queens. These evenings are considerably cheaper, often entailing only a small cover charge and that famous cabaret institution: the two-drink minimum.

The list of places below is an overview of the city's most established cabaret spots. Don't forget that in addition most New York bars and clubs – and increasingly restaurants – offer some cabaret nights in their schedule, and nearly all of the city's jazz venues operate in a cabaret format, many offering restaurant-quality dining. For additional jazz hangouts *see chapter* **Music: Rock, Blues & Jazz**. For even more cabaret places *see chapters* **Restaurants, Cafés & Bars, Clubs, Gay New York** *and* **Lesbian New York**.

## Putting on the Ritz

### Café Carlyle

*Hotel Carlyle, 781 Madison Avenue, at 76th Street (744 1600).* **Train** 6 to 77th Street. **Shows** 8.45pm, 10.45pm Tue-Sat (closed July-mid September). **Admission** $45. **Cuisine** continental. **Credit** AmEx, DC, MC, V.

The epitome of chic New York, especially when Bobby Short or Eartha Kitt do their thing. Don't dress down; this is about laying down some cash and remembering it's the Naughty Nineties. If you want to rub up against some atmosphere more cheaply, Bemelman's Bar across the hall has fine piano-playing from 9.45pm to 12.30am nightly with a $10 cover.

### The Oak Room

*Algonquin Hotel, 59 West 44th Street, between Fifth & Sixth Avenues (840 6800).* **Train** 7, B, D, F or Q to 42nd Street. **Shows** 9.30pm Tue-Thur; 9.30pm, 11.30pm Fri, Sat. **Admission** $35 cover, $10 drinks minimum. **Cuisine** continental. **Credit** AmEx, DC, Discover, MC, V.

This resonant banquette-lined room is the place to savour a wealth of performers, mostly female vocalists, including cream-of-the-crop Andrea Marcovicci and Nancy La Mott.

*Smoking at bar.*

### Rainbow and Stars

*GE Building, Rockefeller Center, 30 Rockefeller Plaza, 49th Street, between Fifth & Sixth Avenues, 6 5th floor (632 5000).* **Train** B, D, F or Q to Rockefeller Center. **Shows** 8.30pm Tue-Sat. **Admission** $40 first show, dinner compulsory; $20 second show Tue-Thur, $40 Fri, Sat. **Cuisine** American seafood. **Credit** AmEx.

Just off the famous Rainbow Room, in the GE (formerly the RCA) Building, Rainbow and Stars is drenched in elegance, giving it exactly the kind of Manhattan glamour you've seen in the movies. From the 65th floor, you get a delirious view. The singers are big names like Rosemary Clooney, who work with the theatre of the place.

### The Supper Club

*240 West 47th Street, between Broadway & Eighth Avenue (921 1940).* **Train** 1 or 9 to 50th Street; N or R to 49th Street. **Open** 5.30pm-1.30am Fri, Sat; other times for various club nights. **Admission** $15. **Cuisine** American/contintental. **Credit** AmEx, DC, Discover, MC, V.

This beautifully restored theatre is the setting for dinner and dancing to a 12-piece big band. The decor and better-than-average food attracts a glamorous crowd of pre-theatre dahlings. It's also an occasional concert venue, hosting such intimacy-requiring bands as Portishead.

*Smoking at bar.*

### Tatou

*151 East 50th Street, between Lexington & Third Avenues (753 1144).* **Train** 6 to 51st Street. **Lunch served** noon-3pm Mon-Fri. **Dinner served** 5.30-10.30pm Mon-Sat. **Open** till 4am. **Admission** $15-$20 plus $20 minimum. **Cuisine** American/Mediterranean. **Credit** AmEx, MC, V.

Owned by a former Studio 54 proprietor, Mark Fleishman, this opulently decorated supper club is swathed in heavy velvet curtains and pink brocade banquettes to look like a miniature opera house. The food's pretty good (try the $25 pre-theatre menu), but the evening hots up when the bass joins the jazz piano. On Monday nights you can catch a special programme, starting around 9.30pm, of up-and-coming New York entertainers. There's dancing to contemporary club sounds every night from 11.30pm.

*Smoking.*

## Give My Regards to Broadway

### Danny's Skylight Room

*346 West 46th Street, between Eighth & Ninth Avenues (265 8133).* **Train** A, C or E to 42nd Street. **Shows** schedule varies with different acts. **Admission** $8-$15. **Cuisine** seafood and Thai. **Credit** AmEx, DC, Discover, JCB, MC, V.

A pastel nook of the Grand Sea Palace restaurant, 'where Bangkok meets Broadway' on touristy Restaurant Row. Pop-jazz, pop and cabaret, with the accent on the smooth.

*Smoking at bar.*

### Don't Tell Mama

*343 West 46th Street, between Eighth & Ninth Avenues (757 0788).* **Train** A, C or E to 42nd Street. **Shows** schedule varies with different acts. **Piano bar** 9pm-4am daily. **Admission** $6-$15 in cabaret room; free in piano bar, two-drink minimum at tables (no food served). **Credit** AmEx, V.

Showbiz pros like to visit this Theater District venue. Rainie Cole, one of the best known singer-waitresses, works here on Tuesdays and Thursdays (*see chapter* **Gay**).

*Smoking.*

### Eighty Eights

*228 West 10th Street, between Bleecker & Hudson Streets (924 0088).* **Train** 1 or 9 to Christopher Street/Sheridan Square. **Shows** 8pm, 10.30pm Mon-Thur; 8.30pm, 11pm Fri, Sat; 3pm, 5.30pm, 8pm, 10.30pm Sun. **Admission** $10-$15 plus two-drink minimum (no food except $22.50 Sunday brunch special including show and one drink). **Piano bar** 9.30pm-4am daily. **Admission** free. **No credit cards.**

Downtown's classy high-tech venue. Singers such as Mary Rodgers and Rosalind Kind (Barbra Streisand's sister) perform upstairs, while downstairs in the piano bar owner Karen Miller tickles a cultish crowd until closing time. Sunday brunch draws a crowd too.

*Smoking in piano bar.*

### Judys'

*49 West 44th Street, between Fifth & Sixth Avenues (764 8930).* **Train** 4, 5, 6, or 7 to Grand Central. **Shows** 9pm Mon-Thur; 9pm, 11pm Fri, Sat. **Admission** $8-$15, $10 minimum **Cuisine** Italian. **Credit** AmEx, MC, V.

The cosy, mirrored cabaret room feels like a music lover's living room. There's also a separate piano bar where jazz duo Judy Kreston (just one of the many Judys for whom the place is named) and David Lahm perform on Saturday nights. Judys' is popular with tourists and theatre-goers.

*Smoking at bar.*

## Roll out the Barrel

### Bar d'O

*29 Bedford Street, at Carmine Street (627 2580).* **Train** 1 or 9 to Houston Street. **Open** 5pm-4am daily. **Admission** $3-$5. **No credit cards.**

Bar d'O is a busy little mixed/gay bar packed with a bubbly crowd who come here to catch the very best acts on the drag circuit. A regular performer here is scene stalwart Joey Arias, who is guaranteed to astound with his breathtaking recreations of Billie Holiday numbers.

### Brandy's

*235 East 84th Street, between Second & Third Avenues (650 1944).* **Train** 4, 5, or 6 to 86th Street. **Piano bar** 9.30pm-3am daily. **Admission** free, two-drink minimum. **No credit cards.**

Old, local good-time piano bar where singing bartenders meet shower singers. On weekends it draws a yuppie crowd, but after 2am evolves into a people's bar for a few hours.
*Smoking.*

### The Duplex

*61 Christopher Street, at Seventh Avenue South (255 5438).* **Train** 1 or 9 to Christopher Street/Sheridan Square. **Shows** 8pm, 10pm Mon-Thur, Sun; 8pm, 10pm, 11pm Fri, Sat. **Admission** $6-$12 plus two-drink minimum. **Piano bar** 9pm-4am daily. **Admission** free. **No credit cards.**

New York's oldest cabaret has been going for over 40 years, and sets the pace for camp good-natured fun. A relaxed blend of regulars and tourists, laughing and singing along with classy drag performances, comedians and rising stars.
*Smoking.*

## All That Jazz

Almost all the established jazz clubs work to a cabaret format. For some of the larger venues, *see chapter* **Music: Rock Blues & Jazz.**

### Arthur's Tavern

*57 Grove Street, between Bleecker Street & Seventh Avenue South (675 6879).* **Train** 1 or 9 to Christopher Street/Sheridan Square. **Shows** 9.30pm daily. **Admission** free, two-drink minimum at tables. **No credit cards.**

Funky, divey-looking joint, where the schedule includes Dixieland bands and pianists Johnny Parker and Al Bundy.
*Smoking.*

### Birdland

*2745 Broadway, at 105th Street (749 2228).* **Train** 1 or 9 to 103rd Street. **Shows** 9pm, 10.30pm, midnight. **Admission** $10 Fri, Sat; $7 Thur-Sun; $5 drinks minimum. **Credit** AmEx, DC, Discover, MC, V.

A dark and sophisticated uptown bar and restaurant with regular jazz performances that are much better than the business-as-usual size of the audience might suggest.
*Smoking at bar.*

### Fez

*beneath Time Café, 380 Lafayette Street, at Great Jones Street (533 2680).* **Train** B, D, F, Q or 6 to Bleecker Street/Broadway Lafayette. **Open** 9pm-4am. **Admission** $7-$15. **Credit** AmEx, MC, V.

Fez, with its Moroccan casbah meets the Brady Bunch stylings, is New York's Beat Generation HQ, with a well-chosen programme of folksy rock, jazz and spoken word, that makes it a kind of hip speakeasy for the 1990s. The Mingus Big Band which is made up from a list of about 20 fine jazzmen, plays every Thursday.

### Five and Ten No Exaggeration

*77 Greene Street, between Spring & Broome Streets (925 7414).* **Train** N or R to Prince Street. **Shows** 8pm Tue-Sun. **Admission** $5, $10 food or drinks minimum. **Cuisine** northern Italian/French/Mexican. **Credit** AmEx, DC, MC, V.

A warm, 1940s-style supper club where even the lamps wear beaded fringes and the jiving Swing survivors share their pink-draped stage with an old Esso gas pump. Everything in the club is for sale, including rhinestone earrings, vintage radios and Coke signs.
*Smoking at bar.*

### The Five Oaks

*49 Grove Street, at Bleecker Street (243 8885).* **Train** 1 or 9 to Christopher Street/Sheridan Square. **Shows** piano players daily from 7pm. **Admission** two-drink minimum. **Cuisine** French and Cajun. **Dinner served** 7pm-1am Fri-Sun. **Brunch served** noon-5pm Sun. **Credit** AmEx, DC, MC, V.

For the last 20 years, Swing Street survivor Marie Blake has been holding court in this elegant supper club. She plays piano and sings like a female Louis Armstrong, occasionally raising one pencilled eyebrow. The bar is an entrenched gay scene, with a very mixed audience at the tables.
*Smoking at bar.*

### Iridium

*44 West 63rd Street, at Columbus Avenue (582 2121).* **Train** 1 or 9 to 66th Street. **Shows** 8.30pm, 10.30pm Mon-Thur; 8.30pm, 10.30pm, midnight Fri, Sat. **Admission** $15, $10 minimum. **Cuisine** seafood and grills. **Credit** AmEx, DC, Discover, MC, V.

There's a restaurant upstairs, but you can eat downstairs where the music is. On the whole it's trios and quartets, with a modern jazz bias. Don't miss the jazz brunches at the weekend (11.30am-4pm) when you get unlimited free cocktails.
*Smoking at bar.*

### Michael's Pub

*211 East 55th Street, between Second & Third Avenues (758 2272).* **Train** 4, 5 or 6 to 59th Street; N or R to Lexington Avenue. **Shows** 9.15pm, 11.15pm Tue-Sat. **Admission** $15-$25. **Cuisine** continental. **Credit** AmEx, DC, MC, V.

Jazz lover Woody Allen comes here to blow his horn (clarinet) Monday nights with the New Orleans Funeral and Ragtime Orchestra. Mel Torme is a regular attraction, as is Joan Rivers, and in 1993 Mickey Rooney made his cabaret debut here. This midtown pub draws such a large well-heeled crowd that you're squashed in rather like sardines.

### Tavern on the Green

*Central Park, at West 67th Street (873 3200).* **Train** B or C to 72nd Street. **Shows** 8pm, 9.30pm Tue, Thur, Sun; 8.30pm, 10pm Fri, Sat. **Admission** $13.50 Tue-Thur; $18.50 Fri-Sun. **Cuisine** continental. **Credit** AmEx, Discover, DC, JCB, MC, V.

You can dance in the oh-so-romantic garden throughout the week, preceded most nights by jazz performances in The Chestnut Room, ranging from trad to poppy. The expensive dinner menu is the same as in the main restaurant (*see chapter* **Eating and Drinking**).
*Smoking in bar/lounge.*

## Comedy

American comedy is a vast desert of traditionalists, dotted with the occasional glinting diamond of an innovative genius. The underlying aim, therefore, of going to a comedy club, is of catching that sparky young nobody fresh out of the box. In New York, you will also catch the top names: while the very biggest will be filling Broadway theatres, smaller clubs welcome such famous folk as *Saturday Night Live* cast members, lesser sitcom regulars and comics who have made it to the cable TV showcases of HBO, VH-1 or Comedy Central.

Venues vary in size from the intimate and clubby to those with full-sized stages. What gives the event its excitement is the presence of the unexpected. The next Eddie Murphy or Bette Midler could be working out a schtick; Rosanne Barr, Jim Carrey or, who knows, Homer Simpson, could stroll in. In New York, expect the improbable.

### Boston Comedy Club

*82 West 3rd Street, between Thompson & Sullivan Streets (477 1000).* **Train** A, B, C, D, E, F or Q to West 4th Street. **Shows** 9.30pm Mon-Thur, Sun; 9.30, 11.30pm Fri; 8pm, 10pm, midnight Sat. **Admission** $5 Mon-Thur, Sun; $10 Fri, Sat; two-drink minimum. **Credit** AmEx, MC, V.

This raucous Village favourite is a late-night option where the bill can include as many as 10 different acts. The first show on Saturdays is a new talent showcase.

### Caroline's Comedy Club

*1626 Broadway, at 49th Street (757 4100).* **Train** N or R to 49th Street. **Shows** 8pm Mon-Thur, Sun; 8pm, 11pm Fri; 8pm, 10.30pm, 12.30am Sat. **Admission** $12.50-$17.50, two-drink minimum. **Credit** AmEx, DC, MC, V.

Squeezed in between the porno theatres in Times Square, Caroline's harlequinned lounge is the place for up-coming TV faces and broad-appeal comics. Billy Crystal and Jay Leno honed their craft at the original Caroline's in Chelsea.

### The Comedy Cellar

*117 MacDougal Street, between West 3rd & Bleecker Streets (254 3480).* **Train** A, B, C, D, E, F or Q to West 4th Street. **Shows** 9pm-2am Mon-Thur, Sun; 9pm, 11pm Fri; 9pm, 10.45pm, 12.30am Sat. **Admission** $5 Mon-Thur, Sun; $10 Fri, Sat; two-drink minimum. **Credit** AmEx, MC, V.

Amid the coffeehouses of MacDougal Street, this well-worn underground lair conjures the counter-cultural vibe the Village is famous for, making it one of the city's best venues, with a roster to match.

*Smoking.*

### The Comic Strip

*1568 Second Avenue, between East 81st & 82nd Streets (861 9386).* **Train** 6 to 77th Street. **Shows** 8.30pm Mon-Thur; 8.30pm, 10.30pm Fri; 8pm, 10.15pm, 12.30am Sat. **Admission** $8 Mon-Thur, Sun; $12 Fri, Sat; $9 drinks minimum. **Credit** AmEx, DC, Discover, MC, V.

With New York comedy occasionally suffering from over-dilution, this pub-like stand-up club is known for separating the wheat from the chaff. Monday is amateur night – wannabes should sign up the Friday before.

*Smoking.*

### Dangerfield's

*1118 First Avenue, between 61st & 62nd Streets (593 1650).* **Train** 4, 5 or 6 to 59th Street; N or R to Lexington Avenue. **Shows** 9pm Mon-Thur, Sun; 9pm, 11.15pm Fri; 8pm, 10.30pm, 12.30am Sat. **Admission** $12.50 Mon-Thur, Sun; $15 Fri, Sat. **Cuisine** American. **Credit** AmEx, DC, MC, V.

Opened by comedian and actor Rodney Dangerfield over 20 years ago, this glitzy lounge is now one of New York's oldest and most formidable clubs – but you won't see Rodney.

*Smoking.*

### Improvisation

*422 West 34th, between Ninth & Tenth Avenues (279 3446).* **Train** A, C or E to 34th Street. **Shows** 9pm Thur; 8.30pm, 10.30pm Fri, Sat. **Admission** $10, $9 minimum. **Credit** AmEx, DC, Discover, MC, V.

Now 25 years old, this Theater District comedy club books big names and up-and-comers, avoiding the potentially embarrassing entry-level types. As you'd expect, most of the performances are of the improvisational variety.

*Smoking at bar.*

### New York Comedy Club

*241 East 24th Street, between Second & Third Avenues (696 5233).* **Train** 6 to 23rd Street. **Shows** 9pm Mon-Thur; 7pm, 9pm, 11pm Fri; 9.30pm, midnight Sat; 8pm Sun. **Admission** $5 Mon-Thur, Sun; $10 Fri, Sat; two-drink minimum. **Credit** AmEx, D, MC, V.

A relative newcomer, with a democratic approach, a busy schedule, and a bargain price.

*Smoking.*

### Stand Up New York

*236 West 78th Street, at Broadway (595 0850).* **Train** 1 or 9 to 79th Street. **Shows** 9pm Mon-Thur, Sun; 9pm, 11.30pm Fri; 7.30pm, 9.30pm, 11.30pm Sat. **Admission** $7 Mon-Thur, Sun; $12 Fri, Sat; two-drink minimum. **Credit** AmEx, MC, V.

A clinically decorated but small and cosy place, with a growing reputation for booking the very best on the circuit. Catch the untested talent in their amateur pre-shows.

## Poetry wars

On the coffee-shop circuit, the poetry scene revolves around slams – performance-oriented competitions in which writers read to win. Call for weekly listings or check *Time Out New York* for details.

### 92 Street Y Unterberg Poetry Center

*1385 Lexington Avenue, at 92nd Street (996 1100).*

Readings every Monday, costing $8-$15. Such luminaries as Saul Bellow, Adrienne Rich and John Irving are featured.

### Academy of American Poets

*Tishman Auditorium, The New School, 66 West 12th Street, at Sixth Avenue (274 0343).*

Regular series of readings ($5).

### Biblio's

*317 Church Street, at Lispenard Street (334 6990).*

Saturday is Fat Rabbit night at Biblio's – see two featured poets and a jazz ensemble for $3.

### Limbo

*47 Avenue A, between 3rd & 4th Streets (477 5271).*

At this hopping East Village coffee shop, a Tarot reader holds forth between verses. Readings are free.

### Nuyorican Poet's Café

236 East 3rd Street, between Avenues B & C (529 9329).

The Nuyorican goes beyond slams with multimedia events, staged readings and more. But strangely, no food. Cover charge $6-$15.

### Writer's Voice

*Little Theater, West Side YMCA, 5 West 63rd Street, between Central Park West & Broadway (875 4124).*

The charge here is $3-$10, though periodic 'rooftop readings' are free.

# Clubs

***You won't be able to stop dancing once you're armed with our guide to the city's club culture.***

New York's club culture is at a crossroads. The older tradition of underground dance – unbroken since the heady days of clubs like the Saint, the Funhouse and the Paradise Garage – is being revolutionised by an influx of young ravey suburban teens, schooled on techno, who now want to dance to the hard house and garage that the city's most famous DJs are known for. These kids are breaking into the long-protected club families formed or preserved at the first Sound Factory or the Shelter, and shaking things up with their wilful ignorance of the city's dancefloor history. And though this upstart intrusion may upset older clubbers (especially since these children are so badly dressed and so full of the wrong drugs), it's a welcome democratisation that – after the lean months of 1995 – promises to re-energise New York clubland.

For those used to UK club culture, New York is a bit of a shock. The star DJ who might be paid thousands of pounds to play in Britain earns about $500 a night here in his hometown. Consequently there are fewer chances to hear the big names, but when you do, you can at least be sure that they are playing for love not money.

With the exception of the hip-hop scene you should be ready for a gay presence at most New York clubs. Few dancefloors here are either wholly gay or wholly straight (the gayest nights are listed in *chapter* **Gay**), and there's no escaping the drag queens and 'gender freaks' who lend their decorative presence to many evenings.

However, going out in New York is much less intimidating than you'd imagine. Seemingly arrogant door policies are all bluff: most people can get into most places. Very few dance clubs have a dress code (any restrictions are mentioned in the listings). Don't be surprised to see a sprinkling of suits in all but the most underground of after-hours clubs –

*Groovers at the* **Limelight** *– past its sell-by date but still packing them in. See page 225.*

most places have a much broader mix of styles and people than you might be used to.

The distinction is not always made between dancing and live music venues, so be aware that 'clubs' can mean both. Also, things change fast, and most places host umpteen different nights, so it's worth phoning in advance to avoid confusion. See the ads in the *Village Voice* or the weekly listings in *Time Out New York* for information. *Project X* and *Paper* (both monthly) are also good for club reviews, as are the gay club papers: *Homo Xtra* and *Next* magazines, both free in many clubs. Look out for flyers ('invitations'), which usually confer a discount, in record stores and clubby boutiques, where you should also find the kind of people who can dispense tip-top club advice.

Clubs here are very security conscious, and door searches are the norm. Leave your knives and guns at home and you won't be troubled. A handful of venues have juice bars only, but alcohol is on sale until 4am in most places. Drugs, if you insist, are never far away and in general are high quality. On a safety note, cabs are a good idea as clubs are mostly in lonely neighbourhoods.

Midweek clubbing is a fact of life. In fact, because of the weekend's huge suburban influx (the 'bridge and tunnel' crowd), Fridays and Saturdays, at least in the more obvious places, are not always the best nights. Whatever the day, clubbing here is a late-night affair and few people will arrive before midnight. And however late you leave, there's always somewhere else to go on to.

## The Clubs

### Aqua Booty

*(229 7777 information line).* **Open** 11pm-4am last Tuesday in the month. **Admission** $5

This is where master DJ Tony Humphries plies his trade. You can be sure of meeting a few diehard New Jersey househeads here, as well as a good mix of dancefloor darlings, but monthly just isn't often enough for it to get the momentum it deserves. Call for the current location.

### Berlin

*1 West 125th Street, at Fifth Avenue (1-718 617 4783).* **Train** 2 or 3 to 125th Street. **Open** midnight Fri-8am Sat. **Admission** $8.

In the heart of Harlem you'll find the unique phenomenon of a gay hip-hop club. House, R'n'B and disco classics are thrown into the musical mix, and there's a rather more party-minded atmosphere than the surly vibes you can get at most rap spots. It's a solidly black crowd, but there's a genuine welcome for any new faces, regardless of their complexion.

### Blue Angel

*44 Walker Street, between Church Street & Broadway (226 4977).* **Train** A, C, E, N or R to Canal Street. **Open** 7pm-2am Mon-Sat. **Admission** $10, one drink minimum.

This alcohol-free strip club has grown famous for its very 1990s post-feminist take on the genre. There's continuous striptease, private dancing and, after 11pm on Thursday and Friday, a deal of sophisticated performance art. Such excited amateurs as Drew Barrymore have indulged their exhibitionism here.

### bOb

*235 Eldridge Street, at Houston Street (777 0588).* **Train** F to Second Avenue. **Open** 8pm-4am daily. **Admission** free-$5.

More a pick-up bar than a club, but home to some excellent soul, funk and reggae, and despite the crush the crowd manages to do some dancing.

### Copacabana

*617 West 57th Street, between Eleventh & Twelfth Avenues (582 2672).* **Train** 1, 9, A, B, C or D to Columbus Circle. **Open** *June-Aug* 6pm-3am Tue; 6pm-4am Thur-Sat; *Sept-May* 6pm-3am Tue; 6pm-5am Fri; 10am-5pm Sat. **Admission** $2-$20. Women must be over 23, men over 25. **Credit** (at bar only) AmEx, MC, V.

The famous Copa is a classy club catering to a 25-plus, mainly black and Hispanic clientele. A live band plays salsa and merengue every night and a DJ fills in the gaps with hip-hop, R'n'B and Latin sounds. Swank, in a costume party kind of way, with plenty of rugged caballeros and sultry senoritas. You saw it looking its best in Martin Scorsese's *Goodfellas*. The dress code requires customers to look 'casual but nice'; no jeans, sneakers, or work boots, and gents must have a collar on their shirt.

### Den of Thieves

*145 East Houston Street, between Eldridge & Forsyth Streets (477 5005).* **Train** F to Second Avenue. **Open** 8pm-4am daily. **Admission** free. **Credit** MC, V.

With music along the soul, funk, hip-hop, reggae continuum, Den of Thieves is the best of the Lower East Side club-style bars. The crowd is a youngish mix of homies and new trendies, and the place itself is a barely constructed smoky storefront dive that looks like its owners are getting ready to leave town. Tuesday's Sweet Thang is the strongest night, with plenty of funky R'n'B and hip-hop.

### Departure Lounge

*at Collective Unconscious, 145 Ludlow Street, between Stanton & Rivington Streets (254 5277).* **Train** F to Second Avenue. **Open** 10pm-4am Fri. **Admission** $5.

At the Departure Lounge you have an equal chance of hearing every record ever made, from the most experimental to the most banal. A recent flyer reads 'flaccid jazz, drip-hop, old skool wank' and you can expect avant garde, exotica, novelty records and ambient as well as jazz, soul, rock/pop and classical. Such signature quirks as naked DJs, backwards turntables and erotic vegetable videos and a healthy dose of self-deprecating satire make this an intriguing and simultaneously fun night out. Expect the unexpected.

### Don Hills

*511 Greenwich Street, at Spring Street (219 2850).* **Train** 1 or 9 to Houston Street. **Open** 11pm-4am daily. **Admission** $10.

A great-fun club where everyone is either a genuine obnoxious young rock star, or pretending to be. Thursday's BeavHer is the latest be-seen-here place where all those brats who are famous because their parents were can be found. The music is a laughing blend of just-danceable nonsense with a 1980s bias for snogging, drinking and falling over to. Squeezebox on Fridays is a similarly decadent party with a higher gay quotient and an abundance of drag.

### Egg

*Cooler, 416 West 14th Street, between Ninth & Tenth Avenues (229 0785).* **Train** A, C, E or L to 14th Street/Eighth Avenue. **Open** 10pm-4amTue. **Admission** $8.

Slip in amongst the young suburban ravers who jumped off the breakbeat scene of NASA. This Liquid Sky production throws in a wild blend of jungle, trance, techno and other digital soundscapes.

FRIDAYS DJ HEX HECTOR • SATURDAYS DJ JUNIOR VASQUEZ
Will you watch or be watched ?
TUNNEL
TUNNEL
TUNNEL 12TH AVE & 27TH ST 695.4682

# Hip-hop

Hip-hop, as ever, has an image problem as far as clubs are concerned: a reputation for rowdiness and barely contained violence. While far from being wholly deserved, this perception severely limits the number of decent rap nights, and without friends on the scene to direct you, hip-hop clubs in New York can be notoriously elusive.

A safe bet is **Mecca**, currently on Sundays at the Tunnel. This is the city's longest running rap night, steered by DJ Funkmaster Flex, and is good for spotting the occasional famous face (and a lot of industry folk). **Nells** too is hip-hop-friendly, with Monday's **Funky Buddha** a great night where everyone seems to be in a rap video 'livin' large' (this is where Tupac met the girl who put him in jail). **Don Hills** is worth a phone call as it occasionally lays on hip-hop evenings (and industry parties, for those in the know). Then there are the small-scale (constantly changing) downtown clubs – really just bars with a dancefloor – like **Den of Thieves** and a few others on the Lower East Side. Look out for nights with Stretch Armstrong, who is the best hip-hop club DJ in town.

The alternative, which isn't recommended unless you can go with someone who knows the place, is to venture uptown to Harlem or out into Brooklyn, Queens or the Bronx, where there are still many neighbourhood clubs serving up hip-hop in its rawest and most rugged form. It's here that you'll see open mic freestyle evenings, and the occasional DJ competition.

*Look out for hip-hop one-offs at* **Don Hills**. *See page 221.*

### Expo

*124 West 43rd Street, between Sixth Avenue & Broadway (819 0377).* **Train** 1, 2, 3, 9, N or R to Times Square. **Open** 10pm-4am Fri-Sun. **Admission** $15-$20. **Credit** (at bar only) AmEx, MC, V.

The owners of this long-abandoned Times Square theatre (formerly Xenon) spent about $25 buying a few lights and decorations to convert it into the club you see today. It's a shabby flea-pit with an average sound system and the kind of mainstream-with-pretensions-to-grandeur crowd that made Club USA what it was. Cafe Con Leche, an excellent and long-running night with a Hispanic flavour for the gay, straight and undecided, is on Sundays.

### Fahrenheit 451

*(604 4970 information line).* **Open** 11pm-4am Wed. **Admission** $3.

A great addition to New York clublife, Fahrenheit 451 is where you'll hear bizarro 'space-age bachelor pad' music, along with kitsch goodies from the worlds of surf, psychedelia, stripping and easy listening. Call for location.

### Giant Step

*at the Bank, 225 East Houston Street, between Essex Street & Avenue A (505 5033/714 8001 organisers' information line).* **Train** F to Second Avenue. **Open** 9pm-4am Thur; showtime around 11pm. **Admission** $10.

New York's contributions to the global acid jazz scene – phenomenal jazz instrumentalists and the unstoppable beats of hip-hop – made Giant Step a perennial favourite. Now at the Bank, the weekly party continues to blend onstage jams with the soulful funkaphonic sounds of DJs Jazzy Nice, Smash and Chillfreez. A young, collegey crowd with a charmingly multicultural dress sense dances here.

### Green Door NYC

*Coney Island High, 15 St Mark's Place, between Second & Third Avenues (674 7959).* **Open** 11pm-4am alternate Sats. **Admission** $7.

Head here for a stiff dose of East Village punkiness, with a chugging frenzy of climactic guitar faves played by a DJ for a dancing crowd of black T-shirted rock monsters. Vinyl trews, tattoos, piercings and spiky hair earn extra points.

### Jackie 60

*at Bar Room 432, 432 West 14th Street, between 9th & 10th Avenues (366 5680).* **Train** A, C, E or L to 14th Street/Eighth Avenue. **Open** 10.30pm-4am Tue. **Admission** $10.

*Draggin' it up at the* **Roxy**. *See page 226.*

A much-loved club where the collection of regulars indulge in post-Warholian art-school silliness involving poetry, film, performance and an abundance of cross-dressing. There's a theme each week and bizarre existential conversations abound in the queue for the toilet. It's cheap and very cheerful and the vibe is admirably democratic, though the club is a little tired compared to its earlier years. Downstairs is quiet enough for conversation, while there's a broad house-based mix of music at ground level.

### King

*579 Sixth Avenue, between 16th & 17th Streets (366 5464).* **Open** 5pm-4am daily. **Admission** free-$10. **Credit** MC, V.

A compact Chelsea hangout, with a sweaty little dancefloor upstairs and a relaxed, casual chill-out bar at ground level. A preponderance of gay nights, and some great mixed occasions too. Good music, mostly solid New York house.

### Konkrete Jungle

*at Wetlands, 161 Hudson Street, at Light Street (604 4224).* **Train** 1, 9, A, C or E to Canal Street. **Open** 10pm-4am Mon. **Admission** $10.

Though the artsy, avant garde DJs jumped on it straight away, and you may well hear the odd jungle set at the local raves, the drum and bass has yet to make any serious inroads into New York clublife. Its constituency here is very young, white and suburban, and though the music here is fairly credible, the scene is a million miles away from London.

### Krystal's

*89-25 Merrick Boulevard, Jamaica, Queens (1-718 523 3662).* **Train** E, J or Z to Jamaica Center. **Open** 10pm-4am Mon, Tue, Fri, Sat. **Admission** $10-$15.

If you fancy a trip out to the boroughs, you can get a slightly more gritty taste of the city's musical life. Krystals, in the Caribbean locale of Jamaica, is where you'll hear regular hip-hop and reggae, played for a boisterous local audience. Lots of dancing space and the bonus of regular live appearances and showcases.

### Latin Quarter

*2551 Broadway, between 95th & 96th Streets (864 7600).* **Train** 1, 2, 3 or 9 to 96th Street. **Open** 9.30pm-4am Thur-Sat. **Admission** $15.

The newest Latin nightclub in the city, where there's a constant roster of big salsa orchestras, linked by DJs playing a varied slice of hip-hop, house and Latin sounds.

### Limelight

*660 Sixth Avenue, at 20th Street (807 7850).* **Train** F to 23rd Street. **Open** 10pm-4am Tue-Sun. **Admission** $12-$20.

A labyrinth of rooms, passages and balconies hidden in a gothic church. On the main floor girls in cages hover over a young, hot-blooded crowd of mainstreamers, fuelled by hard club sounds, alcohol and the quest for sex. It's brutishly unsophisticated, miserably overcrowded and often extremely unpleasant (especially the oh-so 1980s humiliation scenes at the door). However, there are four other dancefloors and the smaller rooms, especially the newly renovated chapel, offer a variety of musical styles and cliques; it's also the best place to observe the 'Club Kids' and their self-conscious costumed extremes. Occasional live bands. Tuesday is Communion (alternative, gothic and industrial); Wednesday, Disco 2000 (something for everyone); Friday, Future Shock (techno rave); Sunday, Rock & Roll Church (live rock).

### Nells

*246 West 14th Street, between Seventh & Eighth Avenues (675 1567).* **Train** A, C, E or L to Eighth Ave/14th Street. **Open** 10pm-4am daily. **Admission** $7 Mon-Wed; $10 Thur, Sun; $15 Fri, Sat. **Credit** (at bar only) AmEx, MC, V.

Nells preserves its famous civility with a busy programme of different nights and an attractive and happily multi-racial clientele with money in their pockets. The usual formula is laid-back jazz and funky soul (often with live bands) upstairs, where there's a limited dining menu, and hip-hop or house dance pressure below decks. Funky Buddha every other Monday is currently the best night but the other nights are similarly reliable.

### Palladium

*126 East 14th Street, between Third & Fourth Avenues (473 7171).* **Train** 4, 5, 6, L, N or R to Union Square. **Open** 11pm-4am Fri, Sat (plus occasional other nights for live shows). **Admission** $15-$20.

The cavernous Palladium, a vast old theatre with baroque decorations, is being redefined as the city's largest hip-hop spot after years as the club of choice for the MTV generation. Radio station Hot 97 ('where hip-hop lives') is here on Fridays and Saturdays, and Palladium also hosts smaller parties, usually industry-related, in the machinery-filled Engine Room below stairs. On Sundays, this is the venue for Bump, the city's largest gay party.

### Pyramid

*101 Avenue A, between 6th & 7th Streets (no phone).* **Train** L to First Avenue. **Open** 10pm-4am Tue-Sun. **Admission** $3 Tue; $6 Thur, Sun; $10 Fri, Sat.

A small, dark, ground-level cocoon in the heart of East Village bohemia where most nights you'll find a democratic mix of low-rent freshmen, freaks and frolickers. There haven't been any nights of note here in a while but it's a reliable old war-horse so check what's going on.

### Robots

*25 Avenue B, between 2nd & 3rd Streets (995 0968).* **Train** L to First Avenue. **Open** from10pm Mon-Sat. **Admission** $5-$10.

The legendary illegal after-hours Save The Robots was closed 'finally and forever' for about three weeks, and opened up again as this extremely good semi-legal club. Upstairs there's a fine bar scene, with an elegant East Village crowd, and downstairs is the darkest, trippiest

## Rave culture

New York rave culture is alive and well. Warehouse and outdoor parties are now regular phenomena in Manhattan, the suburbs and in surrounding cities. And they're not restricted to house and techno: hip-hop rooms are increasingly popular, as are the dubby sounds of trip-hop, and you can hear an increasing amount of jungle. For information on these, as well as the latest on the Adidas 'n' backpack kids' rapidly changing clublets, drop into Liquid Sky, 241 Lafayette Street at Prince Street (343 0532), where you'll find flyers from all the local promoters and tickets for many events. Some of the most informative hotlines include:

**Liquid Sky** (226 0657)
**Mello** (631 1023)
**Satellite Productions** (465 3299)
**Solar Luv** (629 2078).

dancefloor the city has to offer. The schedule is still fairly changeable, but consistently good, as up-and-coming DJs and promoters decide it's worth building a scene here. The door policy can be a strange, as for licensing reasons they will always insist it's a private party. Just mention the friend who invited you.

### Roxy

*515 West 18th Street, at Tenth Avenue (645 5156).* **Train** A, C, E or L to Eighth Avenue/14th Street. **Open** 8pm-2am Tue, Wed; 11pm-4am Fri, Sat. **Admission** $10 Tue; $12 Wed (skate rental $5-$10); $10 before midnight, $20 after, Fri; $20 Sat.

The evergreen Roxy will always impress first-time visitors. From the decadent decor of its velvet drapes and classical statuary to its out and out vastness, it's a surefire night out. On Saturdays a physique-minded gay crowd attend and the glam quotient is upped considerably by the muscle boys on the bar and the spectacular drag queens decorating the stages. The sound system was recently revamped and resident DJs Carlos Pertuz and Andrew Tonio pump a blend of hard but melodic New York house with an increasing amount of European techno. Visit when Danny Tenaglia plays (monthly) and you will be in on one of New York's finest nights out. Fridays' Together is when the new breed of clubbers – the suburban ravers – take over, and can be excellent if a little unsettling (these kids manage to have fun while looking completely bored). Fridays' musical policy is a broad techno-to-house continuum. Roxy started as a rollerdisco, and the skating nights (Tue, gay; Wed, mixed) are the best place to experience some vibrant nostalgia for disco-era NYC clubland. The skating standard is high and novices are best advised to oggle rather than wobble.

### Sound Factory Bar

*12 West 21st Street, between Fifth & Sixth Avenues (206 7770).* **Train** F to 23rd Street. **Open** 11pm-5am daily. **Admission** $5-$12

With a top sound system and a devoted clientele, this is the club the city's dance music industry considers home. On Wednesdays Barbara Tucker hosts Underground Network (she'll probably be around the entrance counting the money) where Louie Vega spins his famous Latin-influenced New York hard house for an energetic crowd of gay black and Puerto Rican homeboys ('banjee boys') and their female friends. There are regular live showcases here. Other nights are similarly attended (Tuesday's Gag is good, gathering regular top-name guest DJs) and legend Frankie Knuckles plays here every Friday.

### Twilo (formerly Sound Factory)

*530 West 27th Street, at Tenth Avenue.* **Train** C or E to 23rd Street/Eighth Avenue. Further details unavailable at time of press.

It's a new era for the famous club, with a hostile takeover bringing new management after its notorious closure. Those in search of Junior Vasquez should head to the Tunnel (*below*). At time of writing, plans are for a Frankie Knuckles Saturday residency, and without Junior's stubborn insecurities, other nights will probably see a parade of the world's finest DJs finally allowed to guest in this legendary room. It remains to be seen who will call this home, but there's been a lot of people staying home since the Factory floor was closed in January 1995.

### Studio 84

*3534 Broadway, at 145th Street (234 8484).* **Train** 1 or 9 to 145th Street. **Open** 9pm-4am Wed-Sun. **Admission** $10-$20.

The frenzied brass of salsa and merengue can be heard throughout the city's many Spanish-speaking neighborhoods. Indulge in some Latin flavour at this energetic Dominican dance hall. DJs and live bands every night.

### System

*76 East 13th Street, between Broadway & Fourth Avenue (388 1060).* **Train** 4, 5, L, N or R to Union Square. **Open** 10pm-4am Wed-Sat. **Admission** $20. **Credit** AmEx, MC, V.

What a tragedy. System has a phenomenal sound system created by the company who kitted out London's Ministry of Sound, and was originally going to have an equally incredible line-up of regular DJs (David Morales was 'musical director'). Instead, the owner sold out, hired a wedding DJ and put the bar prices through the roof. What could have been great club is now full of the vacant rich pretending they're in a credible night-spot.

### Tunnel

*220 Twelfth Avenue, at 27th Street (695 7292).* **Train** C or E to 23rd Street. **Open** 10pm-5am Thur; 10pm-10am Fri; 9pm-4am Sun. **Admission** $15-$20.

The Tunnel is famous for having a bar and sofas in the middle of the toilets (where else do people hang out in clubs?), and three different musical environments, with New York outrageousness (strippers of both sexes, decadent art displays, a few caged drag monsters etc) packaged for a worryingly lifeless suburban crowd. However, when the Sound Factory closed the Tunnel's Saturday night after-hours parties started doing brisk business, especially now that they've enticed the homeless Junior Vasquez here with his own purpose-built two-storey DJ booth, which is larger than most New York apartments. What Junior wants, Junior gets, such is his status, and the main room, with its previously appalling acoustics has been totally revamped, with a sound system to supposedly rival the Factory's. Thursdays and Fridays are techno-based nights with plenty of good guest DJs. Mecca, the city's longest running hip-hop night is here on Sundays with Funkmaster Flex.

### Webster Hall

*125 East 11th Street, between Third & Fourth Avenues (353 1600).* **Train** 4, 5, 6, L, N or R to Union Square. **Open** 10pm-4am Thur-Sat. **Admission** $10-$20. **Credit** (at bar only) AmEx, MC, V.

Since USA closed and the Limelight really became too horrible, this is the only out and out commercial night-club worth visiting – in a fun-night-out-with-your-mates sort of way. There are always four or five different musical zones, and though the crowd is essentially the suburban influx of 'bridge and tunnellers', there are plenty of New York freaks and rampant hetero hormones to amuse newcomers.

## You're in

If you want to try a little New York VIP treatment, let Erica and friends from Out All Night Tours take you on a whirlwind tour of downtown bars followed by a hassle-free night taking in the clubs of your choice. They'll make sure your name is on all the right guest lists and do everything they can to ensure a totally glamorous experience. Depending on where you want to go and how many are in your group, the price will range from $100 to $150.

### Out All Night Tours

*55 Morton Street, #7J, NY 10014 (255 8366). e-mail allnite1@ix.netcom.com*

# Dance

***From the grand classical companies of Lincoln Center to experimental movement pieces staged in downtown lofts, New York can't stop dancing.***

New York is the dance capital of the world. It's home to the **New York City Ballet,** one of the greatest classical ballet companies of them all, the **American Ballet Theatre**, and many of the major modern companies, including those of **Merce Cunningham**, **Martha Graham** and **Alvin Ailey**.

There are two big seasons, September to February and March to June, with variations between the different companies, and individual dance events scheduled throughout the year. The spring season brings an embarrassment of dance riches, and presents ballet connoisseurs with a particular dilemma when the New York City Ballet and American Ballet Theatre perform simultaneously at **Lincoln Center** (*see below*). When choosing between shows seems impossible, the truly devoted figure out strategies which allow them to run back and forth across the plaza between the New York State Theater and the Metropolitan Opera House, catching portions of each.

Among the other classical companies is Arthur Mitchell's **Dance Theatre of Harlem**, which began as a community youth programme in 1969 and has grown into a major company of predominantly black dancers. Its repertory ranges from Balanchinian neo-classicism to a controversial 'Creole' *Giselle*, set in the Louisiana bayous. The company has no permanent home, spending most of the year on tour, but finding somewhere to perform each spring (*see page 230*).

Eliot Feld's **Feld Ballet**, a smaller and less traditional ensemble, performs at the **Joyce Theater** (*see below* **Major Venues**). You'll most likely find the regional ballet companies – many very good and directed by former NYCB dancers – at **Brooklyn Academy of Music**, or **Brooklyn Center at Brooklyn College** when they're in town. As for the international stars it's the Met you should head to. **The Paris Opera Ballet**, the **Bolshoi**, the **Royal** and the **Kirov** all perform here.

Modern dance is just as well represented, with resident companies joined by troupes from all over the US and the world. Paul Taylor, Merce Cunningham, Trisha Brown and Lar Lubovitch still head the companies they founded – in fact, all but Taylor still perform; and the Erick Hawkins, Graham and Ailey companies are thriving under second generation directors.

Dance is divided in many minds between uptown – the establishment – and downtown – the provocative and experimental. There are numerous small venues and scores of up-and-coming artists and small groups to fill them. Add the visiting international troupes, and there is a vast world of dance beyond the large, prestigious companies.

In spite of so much activity, the New York dance world is a small one. You quickly get to recognise the regular balletomanes, moping at stage door, comparing gossip about their favourite stars and tipping each other off about productions in the pipeline. Dancers and choreographers regularly

## The Nutcracker

*The Nutcracker* was a complete failure at its Russian premiere in 1892, but it was brought to the US by the San Francisco Ballet, and Balanchine's lavish 1954 version made it a national Christmas-time tradition. Today there are hundreds of versions performed all over the country, but the NYCB's production – sweet but not cloying, and chock full of glorious dancing – is still the standard by which all others are judged. It's performed at the **State Theater** from late November to early January, and though it's a hot ticket, a trip to the box office will often turn up seats.

Mark Morris's *The Hard Nut* is a kitschy variation on the theme, with sets and costumes that are a fabulous nightmare of garish sixties style. See it at **BAM**. New York Theatre Ballet (679 0401) presents a condensed version geared to the attention spans of small children. Even the Rockettes get into the act at Radio City Music Hall (*see chapter* **Music: Rock, Blues & Jazz**), doing their precision drill thing to excerpts from Tchaikovsky's glorious score. ABT has its own *Nutcracker*, available on video, but doesn't perform it in New York during the Christmas season.

attend one another's work and you might spot Peter Martins at Martha Graham, Baryshnikov at NYCB, Darci Kistler at Mark Morris, and so on.

Most of the weekly New York listings publications carry information about dance: *Time Out New York* covers events city-wide, the *Village Voice* is good for downtown and the *Sunday New York Times* strong on the established companies. You might want to pick up a copy of *Dance Magazine* ($3.95, monthly). Phone the Theatre Development Fund's NYC/On Stage service (768 1818) for information on all theatre, dance and music events in town.

## Major Venues

### Lincoln Center

Fittingly enough, the gang fights that Jerome Robbins choreographed for *West Side Story* took place in the slums where the Lincoln Center for the Performing Arts now stands: the home of classical ballet in New York. Robbins himself can still be seen haunting the plaza, usually on his way to the New York State Theater where NYCB performs his ballets.

#### New York State Theater

*Broadway, at 63rd Street (870 5570).* **Train** 1 or 9 to 66th Street. **Tickets** $17-$78. **Credit** (telephone bookings only; $1 surcharge) AmEx, MC, V.

This is the home of the New York City Ballet, whose repertory principally comprises works by Jerome Robbins and founder George Balanchine. Now under the direction of former dancer Peter Martins, the company is renowned for its adventurous music – from Bach to Webern – and sleek and brilliant dancing. The stage is large and the sightlines excellent: there's not an obstructed view in the house and even inexpensive fourth ring seats offer a good view.

*Disabled: access, toilets.*

#### Metropolitan Opera House

*Broadway, at 64th Street (362 6000).* **Train** 1 or 9 to 66th Street. **Tickets** $21-$145. **Credit** AmEx, MC, V.

The Metropolitan Opera company dominates the Opera House during the autumn and winter, but spring belongs to dance. Baryshnikov's American Ballet Theatre, under the direction of former dancer Kevin McKenzie, regularly appears here during the spring, with a repertory that mixes and matches everything from Anthony Tudor to Twyla Tharp. Its real strength, though, is the full-length classics: *Swan Lake, Romeo and Juliet, La Bayadère*. In between, you get a range of major international companies. The acoustics are wonderful, but the theatre is vast – from the top tiers the dancers can look like scurrying ants. Sit lower down if you can afford it.

*Disabled: access, toilets.*

### Other Major Venues

#### Brooklyn Academy of Music

*30 Lafayette Avenue, Brooklyn (1-718 636 4100).* **Train** 2, 3, 4, 5, B, D or Q to Atlantic Avenue; B, N or R to Pacific Street. **Tickets** $15-$35. **Credit** AmEx, MC, V.

BAM, as it's affectionately known, showcases many modern and out-of-town companies. It's an easy trip by subway, and after performances the trains are clogged with chattering Manhattanites returning to home turf. Mark Morris has appeared here, as have Miami City Ballet and Tulsa Ballet among many others. Its annual Next Wave Festival in the autumn showcases mainstream experimental music and dance performances – a painless introduction to the avant-garde. In the winter it stages the American Ballet Festival, and in spring there's the Festival of Black Dance, with everything from tap to hip-hop.

*Disabled: access, toilets.*

#### City Center Theater

*131 West 55th Street, between Sixth & Seventh Avenues (581 7907).* **Train** B, D or E to Seventh Avenue. **Tickets** $20-$50. **Credit** AmEx, MC, V.

Before the creation of Lincoln Center changed the cultural geography of New York, this was the home of both the New York City Ballet and American Ballet Theatre. City Center is a Ballets Russes dream of a theatre, all gilt and *faux* moorish décor. Its programmes feature regular performances by the Merce Cunningham, Paul Taylor, Martha Graham and Trisha Brown companies, and the Alvin Ailey American Dance Theater. City Center has also played host to Les Grands Ballets Canadiens and Maurice Béjart's gloriously vulgar *Ballet of the Twentieth Century*.

*Disabled: access, toilets.*

#### Joyce Theater

*175 Eighth Avenue, at 19th Street (242 0800).* **Train** 1 or 9 to 18th Street; A, C or E to 23rd Street. **Tickets** $15-$30. **Credit** AmEx, DC, Discover, MC, V.

The Joyce – once a seedy repertory cinema called the Elgin – has been transformed into an intimate and inviting space that presents works from many of New York's smaller companies and plays host to a variety of out-of-town ensembles. Eliot Feld began his performing career as the Prince in Balanchine's *Nutcracker* and then graduated to Robbins' *West Side Story*; now his constantly awe-inspiring Feld Ballet is resident here, performing a repertory consisting entirely of his own works (777 7710). The Erick Hawkins Dance Company, Meredith Monk, Philadanco and the Desrosiers Dance Theater all appear at the Joyce, whose summer schedule often includes close to a dozen companies. There are no bad seats in the house, though the lack of an orchestra pit is a problem.

*Disabled: access, toilets.*

## Other Venues

#### Dance Theater Workshop

*at the Bessie Schönberg Theater, 219 West 19th Street, between Seventh & Eighth Avenues (691 6500/924 0077 box office).* **Train** 1 or 9 to 18th Street; C or E to 23rd Street. **Tickets** $12. **No credit cards**.

You won't find any pointe shoes here, but experimental dance works of every kind are performed in a space that's more intimate than comfortable. Still, it's one of the most user-friendly and best organised of the downtown venues, and well worth exploring if you want to experience the full range of New York dance.

#### Danspace Project

*at St Mark's-in-the-Bowery Church, Second Avenue & 10th Street (674 8112).* **Train** 4, 5, 6, N or R to Union Square; L to Third Avenue. **Tickets** $10-$12. **No credit cards**.

Downtown and performance pieces of every stripe in a suitably non-traditional setting.

#### Dia Center for the Arts

*548 West 22nd Street, at 11th Avenue (989 5566).* **Train** N or R to Prince Street. **Tickets** prices vary. **No credit cards**.

This is a museum and gallery space that hosts weekly dance performances by young artists on Thursday and Friday evenings (except in July and August).

*Disabled: access, toilets.*

## Florence Gould Hall

*at the Alliance Française, 55 East 59th Street, between Park & Madison Avenues (355 6160).* **Train** 4, 5 or 6 to 59th Street; N or R to Fifth Avenue. **Tickets** $10-$15. **Credit** AmEx, MC, V.

Small-scale dance performances are often staged in this intimate theatre that's also used for music recitals.

## The Kitchen

*512 West 19th Street, between Tenth & Eleventh Avenues (255 5793).* **Train** A, C, E or L to 14th Street. **Tickets** $8-$25. **Credit** AmEx, MC, V.

Best known as an avant-garde theatre space, the Kitchen's programming includes the most experimental dance events, of the kind you're unlikely to see at Lincoln Center. A downtown fixture.

*Disabled: access, toilets.*

## The Knitting Factory

*74 Leonard Street, between Broadway & Church Street (219 3006).* **Train** 1 or 9 to Franklin Street. **Tickets** $5. **Credit** ($15 minimum) AmEx, MC, V.

The Knitting Factory is better known for its funky music programming, but it also offers dance events every week. This is a place for emerging artists and experimental work: expect the unexpected.

*Disabled: access, toilets.*

## Marymount Manhattan Theater

*221 East 71st Street, between Second & Third Avenues (517 0475).* **Train** 6 to 68th Street. **Tickets** $5-$10. **No credit cards**.

Owned by the school of the same name, this theatre features contemporary dance performances, as well as theatre and opera productions.

*From 'Sounddance' at the* **Merce Cunningham Studio**. *See page 231.*

# Dance Theatre of Harlem

In the 1960s, Arthur Mitchell, a star performer in Balanchine's New York City Ballet, was unique. Not for his grace, his elevation or his strength, but for the fact that he was black. He was painfully aware that his achievements in the whiter-than-white artform of classical ballet were all the more momentous for the accidental fact of his skin colour, and spurred by Martin Luther King's assassination in 1968, resolved to create a classical company made up exclusively of black dancers.

He returned to Harlem, and gave himself less than three months to forge a company; a seemingly doomed venture, since at that time there simply were no other black dancers. The world waited for his failure.

Now, 28 years later, the **Dance Theatre of Harlem** is one of the world's finest. Its programme of exciting interpretations of classic works keeps it on the road most of the year, and when it returns to New York each spring, though it has no permanent home, the tickets are the hottest in town.

**Dance Theatre of Harlem**

*466 West 152nd Street (690 2800).* **Train** A or B to 155th Street.

### Merce Cunningham Studio

*55 Bethune Street, between Washington & West Streets, 11th Floor Studio (691 9751).* **Train** A, C or E to 14th Street; 1 or 9 to Christopher Street. **Tickets** $5-$30. **No credit cards**.

Located in the Westbeth Complex, on the edge of Greenwich Village (no matter which train you take, be prepared for a good walk), the Cunningham Studio is his company's rehearsal and school space, but is also rented out to visiting companies for performances. The rooftop studio is used as an evening performance space by young choreographers resulting in phenomenal skyline views. For more details, contact the Cunningham Dance Foundation on 255 8240.

### Movement Research

*at Judson Church, 55 Washington Square South (477 6854).* **Train** A, C or E to West 4th Street. **Tickets** free.

Judson Church, located in the heart of Greenwich Village, was the centre of avant-garde dance in the 1960s. Nowadays it presents non-mainstream dance performances by established and emerging artists from September until the end of May. Reservations are necessary.

### PS122

*150 First Avenue, at 9th Street (477 5288).* **Train** 6 to Astor Place; F to Second Avenue. **Tickets** $8. **Credit** AmEx, V, MC.

Located in the East Village, PS122 was once a Public School (hence PS) and is now a Performance Space (likewise). It's dedicated to staging new and unconventional works.

### Symphony Space

*2537 Broadway, at 95th Street (864 1414).* **Train** 1, 2, 3 or 9 to 96th Street. **Tickets** $10-$15. **Credit** AmEx, MC, V.

Located in an ungentrified part of upper Broadway, this is a centre for all the performance arts, including some experimental dance works by new choreographers.

*Disabled: access, toilets.*

### Town Hall

*123 West 43rd Street (840 2824).* **Train** 1, 2, 3, 7, 9, N or R to 42nd Street/Times Square. **Tickets** $10-$25. **No credit cards**.

An attractive house on a rather seedy side street in the theatre district (but on the wrong side of Broadway, in the direction of Sixth Avenue), the Town Hall presents a variety of music and dance events, including Dance Brazil and the American Tap Dance Orchestra. It's also the New York home of trendy guru Marianne Williams.

*Disabled: access, toilets.*

## Bargains

### Bryant Park Music & Dance Half-Price Ticket Booth

*42nd Street, at Sixth Avenue (information 382 2323).* **Train** 1, 2, 3, 7, 9, N or R to 42nd Street/Times Square. **Open** noon-2pmTue-Sun. **No credit cards**.

Natives love a deal, so why not cash in on it too? Tickets for most theatres are available on the day of performance.

### Theater Development Fund

*1501 Broadway, between 43rd & 44th Streets (221 0013).* **Train** 1, 2, 3, 7, 9, N or R to 42nd Street/Times Square. **No credit cards**.

TDF offers a book of five vouchers for $20, which can be purchased at the TDF offices by visitors who bring their passport or out-of-state driver's licence. Each voucher is good for one admission at off-off-Broadway music, theatre and dance events, at venues such as the Joyce, the Kitchen, Dance Theater Workshop and PS122. TDF also provides information by phone on all theatre, dance and music events in town with its NYC/On Stage service (768 1818).

## Dance Shopping

Both the New York City Ballet and American Ballet Theatre have gift shops, open during intervals, selling everything from autographed pointe shoes to ballet-themed T-shirts and jewellery.

### The Ballet Shop

*1887 Broadway, between 62nd & 63rd Streets (581 7990).* **Train** 1 or 9 to 66th Street. **Open** 11am-7pm Mon-Sat. **Credit** AmEx, DC, MC, V.

This small but densely packed emporium carries dance books, videotapes and memora bilia.

### Capezio Dance-Theater Shop

*1650 Broadway, at 51st Street (245 2130).* **Train** C or E to 50th Street. **Open** 9.30am-6.30pm Mon-Wed, Fri; 9.30am-7.30pm Thur; 9.30am-6pm Sat. **Credit** AmEx, MC, V.

Capezio carries a good stock of professional quality shoes, practice and performance gear.

**Branches**: 136 East 61st Street (758 8833); 2121 Broadway (799 7774); 211 West 61st Street (397 3060); 1776 Broadway (586 5140).

## Dance Schools

Most major companies have their own schools and at many of them amateurs are welcome.

## Ballet

### Alvin Ailey American Dance Company

*211 West 61st Street, 3rd floor (767 0940).* **Train** A, B, C, D, 1 or 9 to 59th Street.

### Dance Theatre of Harlem

*466 West 152nd Street (690 2800).* **Train** A or B to 155th Street.

### Martha Graham School

*316 East 63rd Street (838 5886).* **Train** 4, 5 or 6 to 59th Street; N or R to Fifth Avenue.

### Merce Cunningham Studio

*55 Bethune Street (691 9751).* **Train** A, C or E to 14th Street.

### New York City Ballet School of American Ballet

*70 Lincoln Center Plaza (877 0600).* **Train** 1 or 9 to 61st Street.

## Other Dance

### Paul Pellicoro's DanceSport

*1845 Broadway, at 60th Street (307 1111).* **Train** A, B, C, D, 1 or 9 to Columbus Circle.

The man who taught Al Pacino to dance for *Scent of a Woman*. All styles of ballroom and Latin dancing.

### Ballet Hispanico School of Dance

*167 West 89th Street, between Columbus & Amsterdam Avenues (362 6710).* **Train** 1 or 9 to 86th Street.

All styles of Latin and Spanish dance, including Flamenco.

### Fareta School of Dance and Drum

*622 Broadway, at Bleecker Street (677 6708).* **Train** B, D, F or Q to Broadway/Lafayette.

Traditional dance of many African countries, as well as Cuban, Brazilian and Haitian styles.

# Film

***You've seen New York in the movies. Now see a movie in New York.***

Most visitors will have no problem connecting New York with the movies: after all, that's undoubtedly where they first saw it. Part of the wonder of seeing the city is realising that, yes, Brooklyn's Bedford Stuyvesant looks and feels exactly as it did in *Do The Right Thing*, or that the Lower East Side hasn't changed much since it was Jake La Motta's neighbourhood in *Raging Bull*.

New York is a film-making town once again. In the late 1980s and early '90s, production companies were scared off by the incredible expense of shooting here, combined with an unhelpful attitude from the local film craft unions – in 1990 Hollywood actually boycotted New York as the result of a contract dispute with local labour – but now the unions are happy again and the city government is bending over backwards to encourage location shooting.

There are even hopeful signals that the studios may once again have a serious presence in the city, as some of the old soundstages in Astoria, Queens – where Rudolph Valentino made *Monsieur Beaucaire* and *A Sainted Devil*, and the Marx Brothers fast-talked their way through *The Cocoanuts* and *Animal Crackers* – are back in continual business. Additionally, a major development on Manhattan's westside piers incorporates a series of studio spaces for both TV and movie-making.

In fact it was here, and not in Hollywood, that film-making as an industry started. Edison's laboratories perfected the technique of synchronising sound with moving pictures in nearby New Jersey, and most of the earliest production companies were based in studios in Brooklyn, Queens and The Bronx.

Today's New York is home to many movie makers and their stars, as well as a discerning and vociferous audience. There are hundreds of screens throughout the city, from the super-commercial, 12-plex blockbuster-heaven of the new **Sony Lincoln Square** to the **Anthology Film Archives** and its experimental obscurities.

New York is often used as a test market, so you can catch first-run films here long before they open in the rest of the country, and months or years before they get distributed in the UK. So whether you are eager to see the first night of Arnie's latest megabuck shirt-rippler, or to track down a rare screening of some Kenneth Anger videotapes, this is your city.

For programme details breeze through the weekly *Time Out New York*, or find the listings sections of the *Village Voice*, *New York* or the *Times*. You could also consult the Moviephone service (*see page 237* **Film on-line**). For additional movie madness see the video rental stores listed in chapter **Services**.

## First-run Cinemas

There are scores of first-run cinemas throughout the city. New releases come and go relatively quickly, and if a film does badly it might only be showing for a couple of weeks. Tickets usually cost $8, with discounts sometimes available for seniors, these usually restricted to weekday performances starting before 5pm. Friday is the opening night for most films, and the queues then can be murderously long. If you are queuing, check whether you're in the 'ticket buyers' line' or the 'ticket holders' line'. The first showings on Saturday or Sunday (around noon or 1pm) are relatively free of crowds, even for brand new releases.

### Cineplex Odeon Worldwide

*340 West 50th Street, at Eighth Avenue (246 1583).* **Train** C or E to 50th Street. **Tickets** $2. **No credit cards.**

For the empty-of-pocket, this seven-screen theatre shows Hollywood movies recent but not new, at the bargain price of $2 a film.

### Sony Lincoln Square

*1988 Broadway, at 68th Street (336 5000).* **Train** 1 or 9 to 66th Street. **Tickets** $8 adults; $4.50 seniors, children 2-12. **Imax tickets** $9 adults; $7.50 seniors; $6 children 2-12. **Credit** AmEx, MC, V.

Across Broadway from the high culture of the Lincoln Center, Sony has constructed a cinematic entertainment centre which is almost a theme park rather than a dull old movie multiplex. There are fibreglass decorations everywhere conjuring classic movie sets, enough popcorn vendors to bloat entire armies, a gift shop selling movie memorabilia and 12 decent-sized screens of first-run blockbusters. The added attraction is the centre's huge Imax screen, which apart from being truly enormous (eight storeys high), is seen through 3D headsets. The films here are the usual show-off-the-technology stuff: majestic herds of buffalo and ultra-vivid underwater adventures, and last 35-45 minutes each.

*Disabled: access.*

### The Ziegfield

*141 West 54th Street, between Sixth & Seventh Avenues (765 7600).* **Train** B, D, F or Q to Rockefeller Center. **Tickets** $8 adults; $4.50 seniors, under 12s. **Credit** AmEx, Discover, MC, V.

A place rich in history, home once to the Ziegfield Follies, and still the grandest picture palace in town. Often the place for glitzy New York premieres, but always the biggest screen on which to see new releases.

# Celluloid suggestions

Put yourself in a New York state of mind by cramming some of these movies before you arrive: anything by Woody Allen (especially *Manhattan*); anything by Martin Scorsese (especially *Taxi Driver* and *Goodfellas*); anything by Spike Lee (especially *Do The Right Thing*); *Carlito's Way*; *Midnight Cowboy*; *Metropolis*; *Marathon Man*; *Crossing Delancey*; *Ghostbusters*; *Wall Street*; *Bonfire of the Vanities* (read the book, don't see the movie); *On The Waterfront* (OK, so it was New Jersey); *Last Exit to Brooklyn*; *Die Hard with a Vengeance*; *Saturday Night Fever*; *Sweet Smell of Success*; *Seven Year Itch*; *Breakfast at Tiffany's*; *Paris is Burning*; *42nd Street*; *King Kong* (the 1933 original); *West Side Story*; *Cruising*; *The Eyes of Laura Mars*; *Angels With Dirty Faces*; *Kids*; *The Goodbye Girl*; *Dog Day Afternoon*; *Barefoot in the Park*; *The Lost Weekend*; all the *Batmans*; the very end of *Planet of the Apes*; *Andy Warhol: Superstar*; *Naked City*; *Moonstruck*; *Wigstock: The Movie*; *Desperately Seeking Susan*; *Escape From New York*; *The Fisher King*; *Year of the Dragon*; *The Heiress*; *Smoke*....

## Revival & Art Houses

The following cinemas specialise in showing art movies or old films.

### Angelika Film Center

*Corner of Houston & Mercer Streets (995 2000/995 1081 box office).* **Train** 6 to Bleecker Street; B, D, F or Q to Broadway Lafayette; N or R to Prince Street. **Tickets** $8 adults; $4 students, senior citizens, under-12, before 5pm, Mon-Fri. **Credit** AmEx.

A six-screen cinema with very diverse programming, featuring new and foreign films, double features of old movies, retrospectives and science fiction films. There's an espresso bar to hang out in before or after the show.

*Disabled: access.*

### Angelika 57

*225 West 57th Street, at Seventh Avenue (586 1900).* **Train** B, D or E to Seventh Avenue. **Tickets** $8 adults; $4 senior citizens and students. **Credit** AmEx.

This large old 556-seater single-screen theatre was renovated in 1993; it shows an eclectic mix of films similar to its downtown sibling (*see above*).

*Disabled: access.*

### Carnegie Hall Cinema and Carnegie Screening Room

*887 Seventh Avenue, at 56th Street (265 2536).* **Train** 1, 9, A, B, C or D to Columbus Circle. **Tickets** $8 adults; $4.50 seniors before 5pm Mon-Fri. **Credit** AmEx, MC, V.

Carnegie Hall houses two cinemas, which show slightly offbeat American and European movies such as *Barcelona* and *Jeffrey*, although you won't find anything too experimental.

### Cinema Village

*22 East 12th Street, between Fifth Avenue & University Place (924 3363).* **Train** 4, 5, 6, L, N, or R to Union Square. **Tickets** $8 adults; $4 children, senior citizens before 5pm Mon-Fri. **No credit cards.**

A true revival house, Cinema Village usually changes its double bill daily, mixing Hollywood and European classics like *Breakfast at Tiffany's* and *Jules et Jim* with newer art movies and mini festivals. It has midnight horror shows at the weekends, and is the home of the annual New York Lesbian and Gay Film Festival.

### Film Forum

*209 West Houston Street, between Sixth Avenue & Varick Street (727 8110/727 8112 box office).* **Train** 1 or 9 to Houston Street. **Tickets** $7.50; $4.50 members, senior citizens before 5pm. **No credit cards.**

Now in an attractive new home, the three-screen Film Forum offers some of the best new films, documentaries and art movies, as well as long series of revivals.

*Disabled: access.*

### The Kitchen

*512 West 19th Street, between Tenth & Eleventh Avenues (255 5793).* **Train** A, C, E or L to 14th Street. **Admission** varies, phone for details. **Credit** AmEx.

New York's oldest experimental arts centre, the Kitchen presents innovative and alternative work by avant-garde video and film makers.

*Disabled: access.*

*And you thought you were going to see a movie. The humungous* **Sony Lincoln Square**.

### Lincoln Plaza Cinemas

*30 Lincoln Plaza; entrance on Broadway, between 62nd & 63rd Streets (757 2280).* **Train** 1, 9, A, B, C or D to 59th Street/Columbus Circle. **Tickets** $8 adults; $4.50 senior citizens Mon-Fri. **No credit cards**.
Commercially successful and worthy European art-house movies, such as *Café Au Lait* or *Cinema Paradiso* can be seen here, alongside biggish American independent productions like *Kids*.

### The Paris

*West 58th Street, between Fifth & Sixth Avenues (980 5656).* **Train** N or R to Fifth Avenue. **Tickets** $8 adults; $4 children, senior citizens before 5pm Mon-Fri. **Credit** AmEx, MC, V.
Situated beside Bergdorf Goodman and opposite the Plaza Hotel, the Paris has a stylish programme of European art-house movies, alongside such eminently revivable films as Buñuel's *Belle De Jour*.

### Public Theater

*425 Lafayette Street, below Astor Place (539 8500/260 2400 box office).* **Train** 6 to Astor Place. **Tickets** $7.50 adults; $6.50 senior citizens, students. **No credit cards**.
The small cinema attached to Joseph Papp's New York Shakespeare Theater shows an odd, but exciting, mix of films under its 'Films at the Public' programme.
*Disabled: access (front row only).*

### Quad Cinema

*East 13th Street, between Fifth & Sixth Avenues (255 8800/255 2243 box office).* **Train** 4, 5, 6, L, N or R to Union Square. **Tickets** $7.50 adults; $4 seniors, under 12s. **No credit cards**.
Four screens showing a broad selection of foreign films, American Independents and documentaries, with a preponderance of those dealing with sexual and political issues, and often movies you can't see anywhere else.
*Disabled: access to some screens.*

## Museums & Societies

Special film series and experimental films are often shown by museums and galleries other than the ones mentioned here. Check the press for details. *See also chapter* **Museums**.

### Anthology Film Archives

*32 Second Avenue, at Second Street (505 5181).* **Train** 6 to Bleecker Street. **Tickets** $7 adults; $5 students, senior citizens; $4 members; $1 under-14s. **Credit** AmEx.
This is one of New York's treasures and it houses the world's largest collection of written material documenting the history of independent film- and video-making. The Archives are sponsored by some of the biggest names in film and have a full programme of films, talks and lectures.

### American Museum of the Moving Image

*35th Avenue, at 36th Street, Astoria, Queens (1-718 784 0077).* **Train** R or G to Steinway Street; call 1-718 784 4777 for travel information on shuttle bus services from Manhattan. **Open** 10am-4pm Tue-Fri; noon-6pm Sat, Sun. **Museum admission** free. **Tickets** *Tue-Thur, Sun* free; *Fri, Sat* $5 adults; $4 over-65s; $2.50 students, under-18s. **Credit** AmEx, MC, V.
The first museum in the US devoted to moving pictures is to be found in the old Paramount building. Over 700 films

and videos are on show each year, covering everything from Hollywood classics and series devoted to a single actor or director, to industrial safety films. An inspired and entertaining schedule.
*Disabled: access, toilets. Educational programmes. Guided tours. Shop.*

### Film Society of Lincoln Center

*Lincoln Center, 70 Lincoln Center Plaza, Broadway & West 65th Street (875 5610).* **Train** 1 or 9 to 66th Street. **Tickets** $7.50; $4 seniors. **No credit cards.**
The Society was founded in 1969 to promote film and support film-makers. It operates the Walter Reade Theater (built 1991), equipped with state-of-the-art equipment for showcasing contemporary film and video. The programme is usually organised in long themed series, with a decisively international perspective; culminating every September in the **NY Film Festival** (*see below* **Film Festivals**).
*Disabled: access, toilets.*

### International Center of Photography

*1130 Fifth Avenue, at 94th Street (860 1777).* **Train** 6 to 96th Street. **Open** 11am-8pm Tue; 11am-6pm Wed-Sun. **Admission** $4 adults; $2.50 students, seniors. **No credit cards.**
The ICP holds regular screenings, mostly on the history and technique of photography.
*Wheelchair access.*

### Metropolitan Museum of Art

*Fifth Avenue, at 82nd Street (535 7710).* **Train** 4, 5 or 6 to 86th Street. **Open** 9.30am-5.15pm Tue-Thur, Sun; 9.30am-8.45pm Fri, Sat. **Admission** suggested donation $7 adults; $3.50 students, senior citizens; free under-12s **No credit cards.**.
The Met shows a full programme of documentary films on art, many of which relate to exhibitions on display, in the Uris Center Auditorium (near the 81st Street entrance). There are usually one or two screenings a day. In addition there are occasional themed film series, with weekend showings.
*Disabled: access, toilets (disabled services phone 879 5500). No strollers (prams) on Sundays.*

### Millenium Film Workshop

*66 East 4th Street (673 0090).* **Train** F to Second Avenue. **Tickets** $6 non-members, $4 members. **No credit cards.**
This media/arts centre holds film-making classes and workshops, and has several screenings a week of avant-garde works, sometimes introduced and discussed by the directors.

### Museum of Modern Art

*11 West 53rd Street, between Fifth & Sixth Avenues (708 9400/708 9480 recorded information).* **Train** E or F to 53rd Street/Fifth Avenue. **Open** 11am-6pm Mon, Tue, Sat, Sun; noon-8.30pm Thur, Fri. **Admission** $8 adults; $5 students, senior citizens, under-16s accompanied by an adult; voluntary donation Thur. **No credit cards.**
MoMA was one of the first institutions to recognise film as an art form. Its first director, Alfred H Barr, believed that film was 'the only great art peculiar to the twentieth century'. The museum has massive archives of films, to which accredited film students and researchers have access (appointments must be made in writing). MoMA holds about 25 screenings a week, often part of seasons based on the work of a particular director or on some other theme; entry is free with museum admission.
*Disabled: access, toilets.*

### Museum of TV & Radio

*25 West 52nd Street, between Fifth & Sixth Avenues (621 6600).* **Train** E or F to 53rd Street. **Open** noon-6pm Tue, Wed, Fri-Sun; noon-8pm Thur. **Admission** $6 adults; $4 students, senior citizens; $3 under-13s. **No credit cards.**
Television and radio works, rather than film, are archived here: there are some 30,000 programmes, which can be viewed at private consoles. There are also two small screening rooms and a 63-seat video theatre where a number of different programmes are shown daily.
*Disabled: access, toilets.*

### Naturemax Theater

*American Museum of Natural History, Central Park West at 79th Street (769 5200).* **Train** B or C to 81st Street. **Screenings** every hour on the half-hour, 10.30am-4.30pm daily. **Admission** museum admission plus $7 adults; $5 senior citizens, students; $4 children. **No credit cards.**
The screen is four storeys high and the daily programmes concentrate on the natural world. At the weekend it's usually crowded with children and parents.
*Disabled: access, toilets.*

## Locating locations

Between 100 and 150 films are shot in New York each year and if you wander around the city long enough, chances are you'll eventually bump into the bright spotlights and location trailers of a movie set. You might then watch a scene being shot, burble an embarrassed hello to one of your most idolised movie stars, or even get picked out of the crowd to be an extra.

But if you're in the know you don't have to rely on chance. The Mayor's Office runs a programme to encourage filming in the city, and if you drop in you can pick up a list of all the productions that have licences to film here, including limited details of the movie and a run-down of where it'll be shooting. Get one in person or send a stamped addressed envelope and get ready for your close-up.

### The Mayor's Office of Film, Theater and Broadcasting

*1697 Broadway, 6th floor, New York, NY 10019 (entrance on 53rd Street) (489 6710).* **Train** B, D or E to Seventh Avenue. **Open** 9am-5pm Mon-Fri.

### Whitney Museum of American Art

*945 Madison Avenue, at 75th Street (570 3676).* **Train** 6 to 77th Street. **Open** 11am-6pm Wed, Fri-Sun; 1-8pm Thur. **Admission** $8 adults; $6 students, seniors, free under-12s; free to all 6-8pm Thur. **No credit cards.**
In keeping with its brief of showing the best in contemporary American art, the Whitney has a busy and varied schedule of film and video works, and many of its exhibitions have a strong moving image component, including the famous Biennial showcase of contemporary art works; entry is free with museum admission.
*Disabled: access, toilets.*

## Foreign Language Films

Most or all of the above institutions will screen films in languages other than English, but the following are some which show only foreign films.

### Asia Society

*725 Park Avenue, at 70th Street (517 2742).* **Train** 6 to 68th Street **Open** 11am-6pm Tue-Sat; noon-5pm Sun. **Admission** $7 non-members; $5 members. **Membership** £75 a year. **Credit** AmEx, MC, V.
Shows films from India, China, many other Asian countries, as well as Asian-American films.

### French Institute

*55 East 59th Street, between Park & Madison Avenues (355 6160).* **Train** 4, 5, 6, N or R to 59th Street. **Open** 11am-7pm Tue-Fri; 11am-3pm Sat, Sun. **Admission** $7 non-members; $5.50 students, senior citizens; free members. **Membership** $60 per year. **Credit** AmEx, MC, V.
The Institute – the cultural mission of the French government – shows movies from back home, usually subtitled (never dubbed).
*Disabled: access, toilets.*

### Goethe Institute

*1014 Fifth Avenue, at 83rd Street (439 8700).* **Train** 4, 5 or 6 to 86th Street. **Tickets** prices vary.
This German language teaching institute shows regular German films in various locations round the city.

### Japan Society

*333 East 47th Street, at First Avenue (752 3015).* **Train** 4, 5, 6 or 7 to Grand Central. **Open** 10am-5pm Mon-Sat. **Tickets** $7 non-members; $5 members, students, seniors (some free films). **No credit cards.**
The Japan Society has a busy schedule of Japanese films, including two or three big series annually.
*Disabled: access, toilets.*

## Libraries

### Donnell Library Center

*20 West 53rd Street, between Fifth & Sixth Avenues (621 0618).* **Train** B, D, F or Q to Rockefeller Center. **Open** noon-6pm Mon, Wed, Fri; 9.30am-8pm Tue, Thur; 10am-5.30pm Sat. **Admission** free.
A branch of the New York Public Library, the Donnell shows and circulates films (phone to check screening times).
*Disabled: access, toilets.*

### Library and Museum of the Performing Arts

*Lincoln Center, 111 Amsterdam Avenue, at West 65th Street (870 1670).* **Train** 1 or 9 to 66th Street. **Open** noon-7.45pm Mon, Thur; noon-6pm Wed, Fri, Sat. **Admission** free.
The library has an extensive research collection of books, periodicals, clippings and posters on film, as well as a vast catalogue of film memorabilia. *See also chapter* **Museums**.

## Film Festivals

Every September and October, for more than a quarter of a century, the Lincoln Center film society has been running the prestigious **New York Film Festival**. More than 25 American and foreign films are given New York, US or world premières and the festival usually features several rarely seen classics as well as the New Directors series. Opening- and closing-night screenings are held in the grand Avery Fisher Hall. Tickets for new films by known directors are often hard to come by: booking opens several weeks in advance. The society, in collaboration with the Museum of Modern Art, is also responsible for the **New Directors, New Films** festival held in April. *See* **Film Society of the Lincoln Center** (*page 234,* **Museums & Societies**).

Cinema Village runs an annual NY **Gay and Lesbian Film Festival** each July, and there is a month-long **Black Film Festival** in August as one of the attractions of the annual Harlem Week, with a blend of militant documentaries and features involving Black music and culture. Screenings are at the Adam Clayton Powell Jr State Office Building, 163 West 125th Street (873 5040). Car-less New Yorkers have their very own 'drive-in' film festival in **Bryant Park** each year June to September. The park, on Sixth Avenue between 40th and 42nd Streets, has a series of free summer Monday night (8.30pm) screenings of classics like *Strangers On A Train* or *Casablanca* on a giant screen. *See chapter* **New York by Season**.

In addition, many of the art-house cinemas arrange their own, smaller festivals and series, often in conjunction with other institutions.

## Film on-line

New York has an excellent phone service for screening details. Simply dial 777-FILM and for the cost of a regular call you can touch-tone your way around an updated, automated system that gives the times and locations of screenings around the Tri-State area. It's often helpful if you know your area's zip code. The system is foolproof and you can even pre-book your seats using a credit card to avoid the queues. The only drawbacks are that it doesn't include all the independent theatres and you have to listen to the announcer's obnoxiously upbeat voice.

# **Music:** Classical & Opera

***New York's orchestras and opera companies are among the finest in the world. We take you on a conducted tour.***

First impressions may leave you wondering how the full-volume bustle of New York could ever find space or time for classical music, but a quick browse through the listings soon proves otherwise. In fact, New York may be the most music-dense metropolis in the western world.

The scene is concentrated around the famous stage of **Carnegie Hall** and the cultural village of **Lincoln Center**, but classical music of all cultures fills scores of other auditoria and all manner of less formal venues, from churches and schools to restaurants, parks, atriums and even subway stations. Big-name soloists and ensembles from all over the world appear here regularly, as do major US symphony orchestras.

Admittedly the city has a slight problem in moving with the times. The arts establishment is still associated with the conservative snobbery and prestige of ostentatious philanthropism, and consequently the grand old institutions tend to err on the side of stuffiness. However, plenty of more adventurous ensembles and venues exist outside their staid ranks, and you should have no problems finding something of interest.

New York now has only two classical music stations. **WQXR** (96.3 FM) relies heavily on masterworks from the heavy hitters: no surprises, bad or good. **WNYC** (93.9 FM) caters for a more adventurous listener, aiming for a diverse mix of lesser-known works by the masters and masterworks by lesser-known composers.

The city's weekly entertainment publications all carry listings of classical music, as does the *New York Times*' Sunday edition. The Theatre Development Fund (*listed under* **Bargains**) also provides information on all music events via its NYC/On Stage service (768 1818). Bear in mind that apart from outdoor events, almost all the major institutions are dormant during summer.

## Behind the scenes

It's possible to go behind the scenes at several of the city's major concert venues without having to resort to years of practising your scales. **Lincoln Center's Guided Tours** (875 5350) escort you inside all three of the centre's major halls; **Backstage at the Met** (769 7000) takes you behind the scenes of the famous opera house. **Carnegie Hall** also offers a programme of tours (903 9790), including some that combine a backstage peek with afternoon tea at the Russian Tea Room next door. Finally, you can sit in on rehearsals of the New York Philharmonic. These are usually during the Thursdays before concerts.

## Lincoln Center

*between Columbus and Amsterdam Avenues, 62nd to 65th Streets (875 5400 programmes & information).* **Train** 1 or 9 to 66th Street. **Credit** AmEx, MC, V. Tours are available; *see box* **Behind the Scenes**.

### Metropolitan Opera House

*(362 6000).* **Tickets** $43-$175.
*Disabled: access, toilets.*

### New York State Theater

*(870 5570).* **Tickets** $17-$78.
*Disabled: access, toilets.*

### Avery Fisher Hall

*(875 5030).* **Tickets** $10-$55.

### Alice Tully Hall

*(875 5050).* **Tickets** $25-$40.
*Disabled: access, toilets.*

In the 1950s, the tenements and playgrounds that were the setting for Leonard Bernstein's *West Side Story* were demolished. The land, an area at the south-west corner of Central Park, was developed

*The Met's classic production of* Turandot.

into Lincoln Center, a four-block complex of buildings and interlinked public spaces that was to be home for many of the city's most important musical institutions. The striking concrete-pillared 1960s architecture of the New York State Theater, Metropolitan Opera House and Avery Fisher Hall surrounds a black marble fountain by Philip Johnson. In addition to these three great halls, the centre is home to the drama stages of the Lincoln Center Theater building – housing the Vivian Beaumont and Mitzi E Newhouse theatres – the Guggenheim bandshell set outside in Damrosch Park and the New York Public Library of the Performing Arts (870 1630), hidden between the theatres. On the library's ground floor you can listen to recordings from the collection at private turntables; on the third floor is a wonderful archive of research materials, including programmes, cuttings, pressbooks and photographs; and the second floor houses an exhibition space.

For indoor dining at Lincoln Center, check out Café Vienna and the Panevino Ristorante in Avery Fisher Hall (874 7000) and the Grand Tier Restaurant at the Met (799 3400). However, dining elsewhere, either before or after the performance, is usually the best plan. There are plenty of places either north up Broadway or south below Columbus Circle (*see chapter* **Eating & Drinking**).

Lincoln Center is an institution that tends to rely on the tried and true. The annual 'Great Performers' series, for example (Oct-June), will bring you the likes of Jessye Norman, Seiji Ozawa, Luciano Pavarotti, Kiri Te Kanawa, Yo Yo Ma and Daniel Barenboim (preview phoneline 533 7400; includes samples). The Kronos Quartet is about as daring as it gets. But the theatres are accessible, the programming extensive and the atmosphere charged with anticipation. And there are few more pleasant places to sit on a summer evening than around that fountain.

## Metropolitan Opera House

With enormous murals painted by Marc Chagall hanging inside its five geometric arches, the Met is the grandest of the Lincoln Center buildings and an unforgettably spectacular place to see an opera. The theatre is a riot of gold and crimson, the casts are an international who's who of current stars, the productions are as lavish as they come and the audience is knowledgeable and fiercely partisan – subscriptions stay in families for generations. It's home to the Metropolitan Opera, and the place that visiting impresarios are most likely to make their New York home. Tickets are expensive, however, and unless you can afford good seats, the view won't be that great.

Everyone loves to be snide about the Met, deriding its conservative programming and lavish productions on the one hand and sniping when it produces new works like Philip Glass's *The Voyage* and John Corigliano's *Ghosts of Versailles* on the other ('trendy' is a favourite criticism). In the end, however, this is the big one, and truly unrivalled.

## New York State Theatre

Philip Johnson's 'jewel box' of chandeliers and glass is home to the New York City Opera, which has tried to upgrade its second-best reputation by being defiantly popular. This means hiring only American singers, performing many works in English, mounting classy productions of classic musicals (*South Pacific*, *The Pyjama Game*), going heavy on the old favourites (*Butterfly*, *Bohème* et al) and projecting translations on to the proscenium arch during foreign language productions. At half the price of the Met, NYCO is easy on the pocket, and the theatre itself is a gem. The upper levels are steep and the acoustics are notoriously unbalanced but there are no obstructed sightlines and few partial views.

## Avery Fisher Hall

Originally called Philharmonic Hall, this was where the New York Philharmonic, the city's finest symphonium, moved when it left Carnegie Hall. Unfortunately the acoustics were worse than unbearable and it took the largesse of electronics millionaire Avery Fisher, and the several major internal reconstructions he sponsored, to make the sound quality good enough for the building's role as Lincoln Center's major concert arena.

Its 2,700-seat auditorium is now both handsome and comfortable. It's home to the New York Philharmonic (information 875 5656), now under the direction of Kurt Masur. This is the country's oldest orchestra, founded in 1842, and one of the world's very finest. Its evangelical philosophy has given rise to a series of free open-air concerts (800,000 came to Central Park in 1982) and regular open rehearsals.

In addition the theatre hosts performances by ensembles from all over the US and the world; in a single season you could see the symphony orchestras of Boston, San Francisco, Chicago and Philadelphia, as well as the Moscow Philharmonic, Orchestre Nationale de France, State Symphony of Russia, Orchester der Beethovenhalle Bonn and Bournemouth Symphony Orchestra. The famous annual 'Mostly Mozart' series is also held here in July and August.

## Alice Tully Hall

Alice Tully Hall seats 1,000 and is an excellent house for recitals and chamber music, with beautiful acoustics. It's home to the Chamber Music Society (875 5788) and recitals by students at the Juilliard school. Lincoln Center's 'Serious Fun' performance arts series is also here.

*Students at **Juilliard** perform in their annual festival. See page 243.*

## Other Concert Halls

### Carnegie Hall

*154 West 57th Street (247 7800).* **Train** 1, 9, A, B, C or D to 59th Street/Columbus Circle; N or R to 57th Street. **Tickets** $9-$125. **Credit** AmEx, MC, V.

Tchaikovsky conducted the opening concert in 1891, and despite being slated for demolition in the 1960s, Carnegie Hall still presents a varied programme of American and international stars, as well as popular acts such as Liza Minelli and Neil Sedaka. There are actually two auditoriums, Carnegie Hall itself and the smaller Weill Recital Hall, which showcases 'the lighter side of Carnegie Hall' (and the cheaper). From the Dresden Staatskapelle to the St Petersburg Philharmonic, the heavy hitters are well represented. Other programmes feature piano recitals, choral performances, chamber music, jazz and popular events such as the recent tribute to Frank Sinatra. Tours are available; *see box* **Behind the Scenes**.

*Disabled: access, toilets.*

### Brooklyn Academy of Music

*30 Lafayette Street, Brooklyn (1-718 636 4100).* **Train** 2, 3, 4, 5, D or Q to Atlantic Avenue. **Tickets** $15-$30. **Credit** AmEx, MC, V.

Brooklyn Academy of Music – or BAM, as it's known – is a quick subway ride from midtown and offers an extensive programme of music and dance in a beautiful house that's America's oldest academy for the performing arts. The Academy is known for having a slightly more radical take on things than its Manhattan counterparts, having launched the careers of the likes of Philip Glass, and offers up an annual overview of the more established avant garde in its Next Wave Festival of theatre and music each winter. A recent collaborative project with the Metropolitan Opera will bring rarely performed works to the stage.

*Disabled: access, toilets.*

### Kaufmann Concert Hall at the 92nd Street Y

*1395 Lexington Avenue, at 92nd Street (415 5440).* **Train** 4, 5 or 6 to 86th Street. **Tickets** $10-$40. **Credit** AmEx, MC, V.

That's Y as in YMCA, but banish all thoughts of sweaty gym clothes. Kaufmann Concert Hall is an excellent professional space, and programming is extensive and imaginative. Home to the New York Chamber Symphony under Gerard Schwartz.

*Disabled: access, toilets.*

### Merkin Concert Hall

*Abraham Goodman House, 129 West 67th Street, between Broadway & Amsterdam Avenue (362 8719).* **Train** 1 or 9 to 66th Street. **Tickets** $8-$50. **Credit** AmEx, MC, V.

This unattractive theatre is shamefacedly tucked away on a side street in the shadow of Lincoln Center, but it's nevertheless worth seeking out for its adventurous programming, heavy on recitals and chamber works.

*Disabled: access, toilets.*

### Florence Gould Hall at the Alliance Française

*55 East 59th Street, between Park & Madison Avenues (355 6160).* **Train** B or Q to 57th Street; 4, 5 or 6 to 59th Street; N or R to Fifth Avenue. **Tickets** $15-$35. **Credit** AmEx, MC, V.

Recitals and chamber works are performed in a small, intimate space.

*Disabled: access, toilets.*

### Town Hall

*123 West 43rd Street, at Sixth Avenue (840 2824).* **Train** 1, 2, 3, 7, 9, B, D, N or R to 42nd Street/Times Square. **Tickets** prices vary. **No credit cards**.

A wonderful, intimate stage (the seats wrap round it) and excellent acoustics, but the programme is limited and the location – a side street near Times Square – is pretty seedy.

## Other Venues

These are some of the more notable spaces. In addition, many other museums, libraries and galleries stage music, usually chamber ensembles.

### Bargemusic

*Fulton Ferry Landing, Brooklyn (1-718 624 4061).* **Train** A to High Street. **Tickets** $15-$23. **No credit cards**.

There are two concerts a week all year round on this barge moored by the Brooklyn Naval Yard. A magical experience, with gorgeous views of the Manhattan skyline, but dress up warm in winter. There are some fine restaurants nearby.

### CAMI Hall

*165 West 57th Street, between Sixth & Seventh Avenues (397 6900).* **Train** A, B, C, D, 1 or 9 to 59th Street/Columbus Circle. *No credit cards.*

Opposite Carnegie Hall, this 200-seat recital hall is rented out for individual events, mostly by classical artists.

*Disabled: access, toilets.*

### Kosciuszko Foundation House

*15 East 65th Street, at Fifth Avenue (734 2130).* **Train** 6 to 68th Street; N or R to Fifth Avenue. **Tickets** $10-$15. **Credit** MC, V.

The foundation features music with a Polish connection. From September to June, there's a chamber music series and other events, including the Chopin Piano Competition. The venue is an old town house on the Upper East Side.

### Metropolitan Museum of Art

*Fifth Avenue & 82nd Street (570 3949).* **Train** 6 to 77th Street. **Tickets** $15-$30. **Credit** AmEx, Discover, MC, V.

Concerts here are held in the Grace Rainey Rogers Auditorium, near the haunting Egyptian galleries. This is reckoned to be the city's best chamber music venue and tickets sell out quickly.

*Disabled: access, toilets.*

### New York Public Library for the Performing Arts

*40 Lincoln Center Plaza (870 1630).* **Train** 1 or 9 to 66th Street. **Tickets** free.

There are recitals, solo performances and lectures in the Bruno Walter Auditorium.

*Disabled: access, toilets.*

### Roulette

*228 West Broadway, at Franklin Street (219 8242).* **Train** 1 or 9 to Franklin Street; A, C or E to Canal Street. **Tickets** $7. **No credit cards**.

The place to go for a range of experimental music, from classical to jazz and rock, in a TriBeCa loft. Very Downtown.

### Symphony Space

*2537 Broadway, at 95th Street (864 1414).* **Train** 1 or 9 to 96th Street. **Tickets** $10-$20. **Credit** AmEx, MC, V.

The neighbourhood is a funky and ungentrified strip of upper Broadway and Symphony Space's programming is eclectic to a fault. But the free 'Off the Wall to Wall' marathons, which mix music, dance and whatever else is on offer, are well worth being in on.

*Disabled: access, toilets.*

### Theodore Roosevelt's Birthplace

*28 East 20th Street, at Fifth Avenue (260 1616).* **Train** 6 to 23rd Street. **Admission** $1.

Free Saturday afternoon concerts are performed from late September to May in this reconstruction of Roosevelt's home.

### World Financial Center

*Bounded by Liberty, Vesey & West Streets, and the Hudson River (945 0505).* **Train** 1 or 9 to Cortland Street; 2 or 3 to Park Place.
The glassed-in Winter Garden with its palm trees springing straight from the marble floor, as featured in *Bonfire of the Vanities,* is fabulous. The free concerts (timed to fit the workday schedule and usually amplified) range from chamber music to Eno-esque music for public spaces.
*Disabled: access, toilets.*

## Schools

As well as school productions, these venues also play host to professional companies.

### Sylvia and Danny Kaye Playhouse

*Hunter College, East 68th Street, at Lexington Avenue (772 4448).* **Train** 6 to 68th Street. **Tickets** $20-$45. **Credit** MC, V.
This newly refurbished theatre offers student productions, plus an eclectic programme of professional music and dance.
*Disabled: access, toilets.*

### Brooklyn Center at Brooklyn College

*Campus Road & Hillel Place, off Nostrand Avenue, Brooklyn (1-718 951 4543).* **Train** 2 or 5 to Flatbush Avenue. **Tickets** $25-$40. **Credit** AmEx, MC, V.
BCBC's Whitman Hall is a well-kept secret, mostly because of its out-of-the-way location. Wide-ranging programming mixes dance, music and special events. Recent attractions have included the Bolshoi Symphony and the San Francisco Western Opera Theater and solo concerts by Leontyne Price and Andre Watts.
*Disabled: access, toilets.*

### Greenwich House Music School

*46 Barrow Street, between Bedford Street & Seventh Avenue South (242 4770).* **Train** 1 or 9 to Christopher Street. **Tickets** $8 adults; $4 students, seniors. Student recitals free to all. **Credit** AmEx, MC, V.
A busy and varied schedule of chamber concerts by students, faculty and visiting guests, in its Renee Wieler Concert Hall.

### Juilliard School of Music

*Paul Recital Hall, 60 Lincoln Center Plaza (769 7406).* **Train** 1 or 9 to 66th Street.
Admission is free, and the students can be frighteningly good.
*Disabled: access, toilets.*

### Manhattan School of Music

*120 Claremont Avenue, at 122nd Street (749 3300).* **Train** 1 or 9 to 125th Street. **Tickets** mostly free. **No credit cards**.
Now directed by Marta Istomen, formerly of Washington's Kennedy Center, the school offers masterclasses, recitals and off-site performances by its students.

### Mannes College of Music

*150 West 85th Street, between Columbus & Amsterdam Avenues (580 0210 ext 28).* **Train** 1 or 9 to 86th Street; B or C to 86th Street. **Tickets** free.
Most concerts are performed by Mannes students, including repertory works and some new productions.
*Disabled: access.*

### John L Tischman Auditorium

*at the New School, 66 West 12th Street, at Sixth Avenue (229 5689).* **Train** 1, 2, 3 or 9 to 14th Street. **Tickets** $5. **No credit cards**.
The New School offers a modestly priced chamber music series that runs from April to October, featuring up-and-coming young musicians as well as more established artists.

## Opera

The Metropolitan Opera and New York City Opera may be the big guys, but they're not the only ones

# The free outdoors

During the summer months, most of the city's musical institutions take a break and move out into the city's parks and open spaces. All these concerts are free, as are other open-air events in museum entrances and gardens, public plazas and the atriums of many large buildings.

### Central Park

*See chapter* **Sightseeing**.
This vast oasis takes on a magical air on summer nights when the New York Philharmonic and the Metropolitan Opera stage concerts here (some with fireworks). Bethseda Fountain is a favoured spot for classical buskers.

### Bryant Park

*Sixth Avenue, at 42nd Street (983 4142).* **Train** 1, 2, 3, 7, 9, N or R to 42nd Street/Times Square.
Directly behind the 42nd Street branch of the New York Public Library, Bryant Park is a serene, attractive and distinctly European park with a substantial free concert series.

### Lincoln Center Out of Doors

*Lincoln Plaza & Damrosch Park, Lincoln Center (875 5108).*
Call for information about the extensive and wide-ranging series of free summer performances.

### New York Botanical Garden

*200th Street & Southern Boulevard, Bronx (1-718 817 8700).* **Train** C or D to Bedford Park Boulevard.
The botanical garden schedules events whenever the weather and budget permit, and the setting alone is worth the eight-block walk from the subway.

### Washington Square Park

*West 4th Street & LaGuardia Place (431 1088).* **Train** A, B, C, D, E, F or Q to West 4th Street.
The park is in the heart of Greenwich Village. The summer concert series, with performances on Tuesdays at 8pm throughout June, July and August, features chamber orchestra and ensemble works.

### Museum of Modern Art Summergarden

*53rd Street, between Fifth & Sixth Avenues (708 9480).* **Train** E or F to 53rd Street.
Twentieth-century works are performed in the MoMA sculpture garden. You'll think you're in a Woody Allen movie. Bring your own neuroses.

in town. These companies perform a varied repertory, including the warhorses and smaller-scale works, from Puccini's *Suor Angelica* to the suite from Bizet's *Carmen*.

### Amato Opera Theatre

*319 Bowery, at 2nd Street (228 8200).* **Train** 6 to Bleecker.

### American Chamber Opera Company

*6 East 87th Street, at Fifth Avenue (781 0857).* **Train** 4, 5 or 6 to 86th Street.

### DiCapo Opera Theatre

*DiCapo Theatre, 184 East 76th Street, between Second & Third Avenues (759 7652).* **Train** 6 to 77th Street.

### Henry Street Settlement Opera Production Group

*466 Grand Street, at Pitt Street (598 0400).* **Train** F to Delancey Street.

### Magic Circle Opera Repertory Ensemble

*St Peter's Church, 54th Street & Lexington Avenue (724 2398).* **Train** F to 53rd Street; 6 to 51st Street.

### Regina Opera Company

*Regina Hall, 65th Street & 12th Avenue (718 232 3555).* **Train** B to 62nd Street; N to New Utrecht Avenue.

## Churches

New York's churches are home to a wide variety of music, both sacred and secular. The magnificent Cathedral of St John the Divine is as likely to be the setting for chanting by Tibetan monks or a performance of Beethoven's Ninth Symphony as Handel's *Messiah*. Excellent acoustics and serene surroundings make them particularly attractive places to experience live classical music, and as a bonus, some (though not all) are free or very cheap.

### The Cathedral of St John the Divine

*Amsterdam Avenue & 112th Street (662 2133).* **Train** 1 or 9 to 110th Street.
*Disabled: access.*

### Church of the Heavenly Rest

*Fifth Avenue & 90th Street (289 3400).* **Train** 4, 5 or 6 to 96th Street.
*Disabled: access, toilets.*

### Corpus Christi Church

*529 West 121st Street (666 9350).* **Train** 1 or 9 to 125th Street.

### Riverside Church

*Riverside Drive & 122nd Street (222 5900).* **Train** 1 or 9 to 125th Street.
*Disabled: access, toilets.*

### St Bartholomew's Church

*109 East 50th Street, between Park & Lexington Avenues (751 1616 ext 227).* **Train** E or F to Fifth Avenue; 6 to 51st Street.
*Disabled: access, toilets.*

### St George's Stuyvesant Square

*16th Street, east of Third Avenue (460 0940).* **Train** L, N, R, 4, 5 or 6 to 14th Street/Union Square.
*Disabled: access, toilets.*

### St Patrick's Cathedral

*Fifth Avenue, at 50th Street (753 2261).* **Train** B, D, F or Q to Rockefeller Center; 6 to 51st Street.

### St Paul's Chapel

*Broadway, at Fulton Street (602 0747).* **Train** 2, 3, 4, 5, J, M or Z to Fulton Street.
A combined programme with nearby Trinity Church.
*Disabled: access.*

### St Thomas Church Fifth Avenue

*1 West 53rd Street, at Fifth Avenue (757 7013).* **Train** B, D, F or Q to Rockefeller Center.
Some of the finest choral music in the city.
*Disabled: access, toilets.*

## Getting Tickets

Expect a booking fee of $2-$3 per ticket.

### CarnegieCharge

*(247 7800).* **Open** 11am-6pm daily. **Credit** AmEx, MC, V.
For Carnegie Hall events.

### Centercharge

*(721 6500).* **Open** 10am-8pm Mon-Sat; noon-8pm Sun. **Credit** AmEx, MC, V.
For events at Alice Tully Hall and Avery Fisher Hall at Lincoln Center. For other Lincoln Center venues call the company concerned.

### Ticketmaster

*(307 4100).* **Open** 9am-10pm Mon-Sat; 9am-9pm Sun. **Credit** AmEx, MC, V.
Sells tickets for New York City Opera and performances at BAM, as well as Broadway musicals.

## Bargains

### Bryant Park Music & Dance Half-Price Ticket Booth

*42nd Street, at Sixth Avenue (information 382 2323).* **Train** 1, 2, 3, 7, 9, N or R to 42nd Street/Times Square. **Open** noon-2pm, 3-7pm, Tue, Thur, Fri; 11am-2pm, 3-7pm, Wed, Sat; noon-6pm Sun. **No credit cards**.
Tickets for most venues (though seldom the Met) are available on the day of performance, most at half price.

### New York Philharmonic Audience Services

*Avery Fisher Hall, 132 West 65th Street (875 5030).* **Train** 1 or 9 to 66th Street. **Open** 10am-8.30pm (depending on performance schedule) Mon-Sat; noon-5.45pm Sun. **Credit** AmEx, DC, MC, V.
Half-price tickets can be purchased after 6pm – call between 10am and 4.30pm Monday to Fridayto ask about availability. The related Ticket Buyers Club allows you three orchestra tickets at considerable discounts.

### Theater Development Fund

*1501 Broadway, near 42nd Street (221 0013).* **Train** 1, 2, 3, 7, 9, N or R to 42nd Street/Times Square. **No credit cards**.
TDF offers a book of five vouchers for $20, which can be bought at the TDF offices by visitors who bring their passports or out-of-state driver's licence. Each voucher is good for one admission at an Off-Off Broadway music, theatre or dance event, at such venues as the Joyce, the Kitchen, Dance Theater Workshop and PS122. TDF also gives information over the phone on all theatre, dance and music events in town with its NYC/On Stage service (768 1818).

# **Music:** Rock, Blues & Jazz

***From hard rock and hip-hop, via delta blues and be-bop to reggae, punk and power-pop.***

It was touring musicians who christened New York 'The Big Apple', deciding that of all their destinations this was the one that brought most reward. The city is home to jazz, the birthplace of hip-hop and second only to Chicago in the quality of its blues. Add to this a thriving rock scene fuelled by hundreds of aspiring young bands and a resurgence in live funk and soul driven by the breakbeat tastes of rap and you have a city where, musically speaking, anything is possible.

For medium to large gigs, get a ticket as soon as possible: they sell out fast. In the event of an emergency, 'scalpers' (ticket touts) are generally available, but you need to have ready cash and an eye for a counterfeit to use their services. For shows in bars and clubs the emphasis is usually on sales on the door, so no advance tickets are issued. Shows often begin later than advertised – especially in clubs that make their money from the bar. Big places, on the other hand, are very prompt and you'll miss the support bands if you're too casual. If you intend to drink, take a picture ID that proves you're over 21. At concerts you are very likely to be 'carded', even if you are obviously old enough. This is done at the door, where drinkers are issued with a plastic wristband. Some places even ask for ID to claim a place on the guest list.

The city attracts a constant flow of big names, and a barrage of bright young things, all eager to put New York in the list on the back of their tour T-shirts. The East Village is teeming with aspiring guitar heroes providing the local scene with all types of rock. Live hip-hop, apart from the big shows at places like the **Palladium** (*see chapter* **Clubs**) and the **Apollo**, is underpublicised and hard to find out about, though live performances and open mic shows often crop up at club nights. Jazz tends to be expensive, and happens mostly in venues where the food and drink add plenty more to your bill. Latin music is booming in New York, its popularity spreading far beyond the Hispanic community. Many clubs host Latin nights, including the **Copacabana** and **SOBs** (*see chapter* **Clubs**).

New York's splendid parks are the setting for a huge amount of free music, starting at the end of March with the annual You Gotta Have Park celebration. Rock and pop events are held throughout the summer at Central Park Summer Stage (360 CPSS), as well as the Prospect Park Bandshell (1-718 855 7882) in Brooklyn and at South Street Seaport (669 9430). For general information on activities in the parks of all five boroughs, call the City Parks Department (360 3456).

### TICKETS

You can try getting tickets direct from the venue first to save any booking fee (or from **Irving Plaza** (*listed under* **Major Venues**), whose box office sells tickets for many of the big venues without a service charge), but for convenience's sake (box offices usually take cash only) you will be unable to avoid going through the telephone services of **Ticketmaster** (307 7171), with its high charges and virtual monopoly. Credit cards are required for telephone booking, though tickets can be purchased in person with cash from the Ticketmaster outlets in **Tower**, **HMV**, **Bloomingdales** and **Discorama** (*see chapter* **Shopping**) and the **Apollo Theatre**. There's also a Ticketmaster outlet in Bryant Park, corner of 42nd Street and Sixth Avenue.

To find out what's going on, see the ads in the *Village Voice* or the listings in *Time Out New York*. *The Aquarian* ($1.50) is good for rock information, as are *New York Press* and *Downtown* (both free, *see chapter* **Media**). Keep an eye out for flypostings and 'invitations' (flyers), too. For more live music venues, *see chapters* **Clubs**, **Cabaret**, **Gay New York** *and* **Eating & Drinking**. For where to buy music, *see chapter* **Shopping**.

## Major Venues

### Academy

*234 West 43rd Street, between Seventh & Eighth Avenues (840 9500 box office/249 8870 concert hotline).* **Train** 1, 2, 3, 7, 9, N or R to Times Square. **Admission** $10-$25. **Credit** AmEx, MC, V at Ticketmaster; cash only at box office.

The Academy has the traditional converted theatre format with standing room downstairs, seats in the dress circle and plenty of gilded swirls around the speaker stacks. It's a cosy place to see a largish group, although the overpriced and overcrowded bar is best ignored.

### Apollo Theater

*253 West 125th Street, between Malcolm X & Adam Clayton Powell Jr Boulevards (Lenox & Seventh Avenues)(749 5838).* **Train** 2, 3, A, B, C or D to 125th Street. **Admission** $5-$30. **Credit** AmEx, MC, V at Ticketmaster; cash only at box office.

There is no more atmospheric place to see a hip-hop gig, and with a steady schedule of soul and R&B stars, the 'world famous' Apollo Theater has regained its status as the mecca of black entertainment. Wednesday at 7.30pm is Amateur Night – once a launching pad for stars such as Lena Horne, Ella Fitzgerald and Michael Jackson, and now full of militant black comedians and soul singers eagerly hitting as many notes as they can before they reach the right one. Amateur Night, which is taped for NBC's *Showtime at the Apollo*, is a fun way to see the Apollo audience in all its glory, cheering and booing the good, the bad and the ugly. Tickets range from $5 to $20. An obvious police presence, especially for the rap gigs, means there's no need to worry about venturing into Harlem at night, although if you're white, you'll feel fairly conspicuous. The subway and bus stops are located close to the theatre, and there are plenty of cabs around after a show.

### Beacon Theater

*2124 Broadway, at West 74th Street (496 7070).* **Train** 1, 2, 3 or 9 to 72nd Street. **Admission** $20-$40. **Credit** AmEx, MC, V at Ticketmaster; cash only at box office.

Worth a visit just to see its astonishing decor, the all-seater Beacon Theater hosts an eclectic programme of big acts and is the stage of choice for established soul and R&B performers. Past stars have included Bob Dylan, Bryan Ferry, Ruben Blades and Millie Jackson. Comfortable, with decent sound in a beautiful setting.

### Irving Plaza

*17 Irving Place, at 15th Street (777 6800).* **Train** 4, 5, 6, L, N or R to Union Square. **Admission** $10-$25. **Credit** AmEx, MC, V at Ticketmaster; cash only at box office.

A hard-working venue, with a very busy schedule of medium-sized bands. The unusual interior – it has an all-round balcony over a large long dancefloor – ensures a good view from anywhere in the house. There are still strange oriental decorations left over from its time as an off-Broadway theatre. Billie Holiday, Miles Davis, Bob Marley and the Police have all played here; nowadays the programme is a varied mix, including comedy and country as well as rock and pop from performers from Jesus Lizard to Tricky.

### Jones Beach

*Long Island (1-516 221 1000).* **Train** LIRR from Grand Central to Freeport, then bus to the beach. **Admission** $18-$45. **Credit** AmEx, MC, V at Ticketmaster.

From July to September Jones Beach stages an eclectic programme of performances: Diana Ross, the Beach Boys, Barry White and PJ Harvey have all performed under the setting sun at this beachside amphitheatre. The quintessential Jones Beach experience however, is seeing Bon Jovi or Van Halen play to the big-haired mall-rats of Long Island's suburbs.

### Manhattan Center

*311 West 34th Street, between Eighth & Ninth Avenues (279 7740).* **Train** A, C or E to 34th Street. **Admission** $10-$20. **Credit** AmEx, MC, V at Ticketmaster.

A vast ballroom with grand balconies, high up in the old New Yorker Hotel. As well as the occasional trade show or Moonie mass-wedding, you get such old funkers as Bootsy Collins and George Clinton turning up to play here.

### Madison Square Garden

*Seventh Avenue, between 31st & 33rd Streets (465 6741).* **Train** 1, 2, 3 or 9 to 34th Street. **Admission** from $22.50. **Credit** AmEx, DC, Discover, MC, V.

Madison Square Garden is better suited to the crunch of ice hockey and the sweat of basketball than to the rhythms of music of any kind. The lights never really go down and the stage is miles away from most seats, making a concert here about as atmospheric as an evening in an airport departure lounge. It fits 20,000 rock fans into its multi-purpose environs, for shows of only the very biggest name performers.

### Meadowlands

*East Rutherford, New Jersey (1-201 935 3900).* **Bus** from Port Authority Bus Terminal (564 8484). **Admission** from $22.50. **Credit** AmEx, MC, V.

New Jersey's answer to Madison Square Garden comes complete with racetrack and football stadium. Its Byrne Arena (or the Giants Stadium next door) is the place to see state natives Bon Jovi or Bruce Springsteen.

### Paramount

*Seventh Avenue, between 31st & 33rd Streets (465 6741).* **Train** 1, 2, 3 or 9 to 34th Street. **Admission** varies. **Credit** AmEx, Discover, DC, MC, V.

Underneath Madison Square Garden is this comfortable but sanitised modern venue hosting a broad selection of big-name pop that's not yet large enough for the Garden. Good sight lines as the stage is way down below all the seats.

### Radio City Music Hall

*1260 Sixth Avenue, at 50th Street (247 4777).* **Train** B, D, F or Q to Rockefeller Center. **Admission** from $25. **Credit** AmEx, MC, V.

This art deco palace is the classiest act in town and, providing the promoter has hired a big enough sound system, one of the best places to see a band. It was built to be the world's largest movie theatre and the scale of its architecture is breathtaking. Musically, you'll find recent chart-toppers as well as major superstars such as James Brown. Spend some time looking around (don't miss the bathrooms, which are the size of squash courts). In the daytime you can have an hour-long guided tour behind the scenes for $12/$6 children (632 4041 for information).

### Roseland

*239 West 52nd Street (247 0200/249 8870 concert hotline).* **Train** B, D or E to Seventh Avenue. **Admission** from $15. **Credit** AmEx, MC, V at Ticketmaster; cash only at box office.

They still have ballroom dancing at this gracious and enormous dance palace from 2.30pm to 11pm on Thursday ($7) and Sunday ($11). Admire the tatty collection of famous hoofers' dancing shoes in the lobby and visit the huge coat-check area downstairs. There are two stages, so you could see a long thin show or a short wide one. As well as big rock shows, this is often the site of huge DJ-driven dance parties.

### Town Hall

*123 West 43 Street, between Sixth Avenue & Times Square (840 2824).* **Train** 1, 2, 3 or 9 to Times Square. **Admission** $15-$25. **Credit** AmEx, MC, V at Ticketmaster; cash only at box office.

A venerable old theatre, designed by McKim, Mead and White, that hosts some medium to large concerts by such folk as Marianne Faithful and Paul Weller.

## Rock

### Brownies

*169 Avenue A, between 10th & 11th Streets (420 8392).* **Train** L to First Avenue. **Open** 6pm-2am daily. **Admission** $6-$8. **No credit cards.**

A loud, basic bar filled with loud, basic bands. Top of the venues specialising in 'nearly-ready-for-CBGB's' groups.

*The one-and-only* **Apollo Theater**, *the hardest-working venue in showbusiness.*

NAT KING COLE WALK
APOLLO
NO PARKING
APOLLO
AMATEUR NITE EVERY WED
WITH HOST MONTERIA IVEY
Coca-Cola
JUL 29
THE FABULOUS FAKES

*Coati Mundi pops up at the* **Mercury Lounge**.

### CBGB's

*315 the Bowery, at Bleecker Street (982 4052).* **Train** 6, B, D, F or Q to Bleecker Street/Broadway-Lafayette. **Open** 7.30pm-4am Mon-Fri; 8.30pm-4am Sat, Sun. **Admission** $5-$10. **No credit cards**.

The legendary home of American punk is nearing the end of its third decade. A true spit and sawdust atmosphere and a constant barrage of great bands, new and old, ensures that rock music – from metal to indie – still rules. Great acoustics and a crystal clear sound system help sharpen up any band.

### Continental

*25 Third Avenue, at St Mark's Place (8th Street) (529 6924).* **Train** 6 to Astor Place. **Open** 4pm-2am daily. **Admission** $3-$6; free Mon-Thur. **No credit cards**.

This was once the Continental Divide, decorated with dinosaurs (the Jurassic kind, not the rock variety). Now it's just the Continental and the dinosaurs are long gone. The beermonsters and their pitchers remain, however, here for the cheap-beer, four-bands-a-night ambience. Bands are variable but always loud and the size of the crowd generally depends on how many friends the drummer has.

### Lauterbach's

*335 Prospect Avenue, between Sixth & Seventh Avenues, Brooklyn (1-718 788 9140).* **Train** R to Prospect Avenue. **Open** 5pm-3am Wed-Sun; 5pm-3am Tue. **Admission** free-$5. **No credit cards**.

This Brooklyn home of 'original rock 'n' roll' features local bands and their friends. Alice Lauterbach, now in her 60s, tends the bar and sells earplugs for $1. It's a good place to hear up-and-coming bands but it does book nearly everyone that asks to play here, so you take your chances. Cheap beer and good pool tables. Take a car service home (the fare into Manhattan is about $10-$15 plus tip) – off-peak F trains are few and far between.

### Maxwell's

*1039 Washington Street (1-201 798 4064).* **Train** PATH from 33rd, 23rd, 14th, 9th or Christopher Streets to Hoboken; bus 126 from Port Authority Bus Terminal; or cab (about $5-$7). **Open** 5pm-2am Mon-Thur, Sun; 5pm-3am Fri, Sat. **Admission** $5-$12. **Credit** AmEx, DC, MC, V.

Bands who play here will be playing somewhere bigger and more expensive in the future. Maxwell's has a good track record for booking the very best in rising stars and it's well worth the trip under the river. It has a super-casual ambience and favours good old rock 'n' roll with an alternative twist. There are occasional movie screenings, acoustic sets, and homestyle American food – french fries and burgers. And when you find yourself in Hoboken, note that it reputedly has more bars per head than anywhere in the US.

### Mercury Lounge

*217 East Houston Street, at Avenue A (260 4700).* **Train** F to Second Avenue. **Open** 6pm-4am daily. **Admission** $5-$15. **Credit** MC, V.

With a good ear for booking future indie faves like Morphine and Bikini Kill and a strange knack for attracting bands seemingly above its station, Mercury Lounge has quickly built itself a firm reputation.

### Under Acme

*9 Great Jones Street, at Lafayette Street (420 4755).* **Train** 6 to Bleecker Street. **Open** 6pm-2am Fri-Sun. **Admission** $3-$6. **No credit cards**.

The cajun restaurant upstairs (*see chapter* **Restaurants**) hides this cosy favourite where newly signed indie biggies are showcased and noisy guitar locals get busy.

## Blues

### Chicago B.L.U.E.S

*73 Eighth Avenue, at 14th Street (924 9755).* **Train** A, C, E or L to 14th Street/Eighth Avenue. **Open** 5pm-2am daily. **Admission** free-$10. **Credit** AmEx, MC, V.

After several failed incarnations in the space of a few years, this elegant but nondescript bar at the top of the West Village is now doing good business by inviting a steady stream of fine Chicago musicians to its stage.

*Washington Square, the place for impromptu hip hop.*

### Dan Lynch Blues Bar

*221 Second Avenue, at 14th Street (677 0911).* **Train** 4, 5, 6, L, N or R to Union Square. **Open** 8am-4am Mon-Sat; noon-2am Sun. **Admission** free Mon-Thur, Sun; $5 Fri, Sat. **No credit cards.**

This unpretentious neighbourhood bar plays host to first-rate blues bar bands amid a good-time atmosphere shared by old-timers and regulars. A similar experience is to be had at the spin-off bar, Dan Lynch 2, 29 St Mark's Place, between Second and Third Avenues (353 0692).

### Manny's Car Wash

*1558 Third Avenue, between 87th & 88th Streets (369 2583).* **Train** 4, 5 or 6 to 86th Street. **Open** 5pm-3am daily. **Admission** $3-$25; free Sun. **Credit** AmEx, MC, V.

Every evening, authentic Chicago-born blues blares from the tiny stage of this elongated nightspot on the city's Upper East Side. Patrons are generally locals and can be tatty, serious blues lovers or junior Wall Streeters ogling the single women (women get free admission and drinks on Monday nights). Kenny Neal jams on Sunday nights, other times you're likely to see the top musicians in the country stopping by on their way through town: Jeff Healey, Gatemouth Brown, Junior Wells, even Bruce Willis have played here. It's mostly standing room, with limited seating around the stage.

### Terra Blues

*149 Bleecker Street, at Thompson Street (777 7776).* **Train** A, B, C, D, E, F or Q to West 4th Street. **Open** 7pm-3am daily. **Admission** $5-$10. **Credit** AmEx, MC, V.

Gracing the stage at this busy Village bar are a wide range of blues-based artists, both local and imported, ranging from authentic Chicago guitar pickers to locals Milo Z and their party-time rhythms.

### Tramps

*51 West 21st Street, between Fifth & Sixth Avenues (727 7788).* **Train** F, N or R to 23rd Street. **Open** show nights only. **Admission** $5-$20. **Credit** (not for tickets) AmEx.

Tramps offers a phenomenal schedule of American roots music, whether it's blues, bluegrass, cajun or funk. Now entering its third decade, it's branching out beyond its original true blues policy and now reggae and some African sounds are heard here as well. The building is the wrong shape for a club this size, and there's an annoying column in front of the stage, so try and grab a table near the action.

## Jazz

### Blue Note

*131 West 3rd Street, between MacDougal Street & Sixth Avenue (475 8592).* **Train** A, B, C, D, E, F or Q to West 4th Street. **Shows** 9pm, 11.30pm daily; 1am Fri, Sat. **Admission** $20-$60 plus $5 drink minimum. **Credit** AmEx, MC, V.

'Jazz capital of the world' is how this famous club subtitles itself, and a list of those who have played here would impress even the most jaded of jazz buffs. Recent acts have included the Dave Brubeck Quartet, Phyllis Hyman, Ray Charles, Lionel Hampton and Max Roach. It's still top of the bops, although there are signs that newer places may be beginning to exploit its complacency. As with most of the city's established jazz venues it can be very pricey, but from Tuesday to Saturday you can pay $5 to enjoy the after-hours set of a less established musician from 12.30 to 4am, which sometimes includes the last set of the headliner. At the weekend (Saturday and Sunday from noon to 6pm), $14.50 will get you a jazz brunch, including food, music and one drink. Dinner is served nightly between 7pm and 1am and runs to around $24 a head.

# Rock sites

"Up to Lexington 'n' one, two, five/feel sick and dirty, more dead than alive," wrote Lou Reed in *I'm Waiting For The Man*, thus immortalising the corner of Lexington Avenue and 125th Street, a New York junction with not much else to recommend it.

New York's rock roots go back to the late 1950s; not to rock 'n' roll (there was virtually none in the city), but to the first flush of the folk boom. By 1961 clubs were flourishing in the bohemian atmosphere of the Village, particularly around the Bleecker and MacDougal axis, although the first, **Gerde's Folk City** (11 West 4th Street), was further east. Gerde's was followed by the **Gaslight** (116 MacDougal) and the still operating **The Bitter End**. These and a host of other coffee houses and bars became the centre of a new movement, spearheaded by the likes of Phil Ochs, Judy Collins, Fred Neil and Bob Dylan.

By 1965 the folkies were going electric and several clubs embraced amplification, notably the **Night Owl** (118 West 3rd Street) and **The Café Au Go Go** (152 Bleecker Street), which became home base for The Lovin' Spoonful and the Blues Project respectively. And in the summer of 1966 you could see an unknown Jimi Hendrix and his band (known as Jimmy James and the Blue Flames) at the **Cafe Wha?** (115 MacDougal Street).

By 1967 the real scene had shifted to the East Village, especially St Mark's Place, where an old Polish social centre, **The Dom** (23 St Mark's Place), was turned into a mixed-media venue by Andy Warhol to promote his protegés the Velvet Underground. By the end of the year the place had become the more commercial **Balloon Farm** and subsequently the **Electric Circus**. The Circus endured until the end of the decade and is now a community centre.

The real rock centre of the era was round the corner: the **Fillmore East** (105 Second Avenue) was the rock theatre par excellence where all the best-known acts played. It closed in 1971, reopened in 1980 as **The Saint**, a gay disco, and was demolished in 1995.

In 1972 The New York Dolls ushered in a new era at the **Mercer Arts Center** (Broadway at Mercer Street) with their celebration of all things glam and trash. The Mercer remained the centre of the scene until it collapsed (literally – the building fell down) in August 1973. By then punk was starting to happen, and the scene shifted to that legendary bar with the worst toilets in the world, **CBGB's**, home to the likes of Television and Patti Smith.

Outside of the downtown area, few venues have passed into legend, though exceptions include two infamous late-night (and sadly gone) hangouts: **The Scene** (301 West 46th Street), where a seriously drunk Jim Morrison once tried to proposition Hendrix while the latter was playing, only to be thwarted by Janis Joplin, and **Max's Kansas City** (213 Park Avenue South at 17th Street), where the final Lou Reed-led line-up of the Velvets were resident for part of 1970.

In addition to old venues the serious rock historian should visit the **Chelsea Hotel** (222 West 23rd between Seventh and Eighth Avenues), the site of a Warhol movie, a Lou Reed song, where Janis entertained all and sundry and where Nancy, of Sid and Nancy, checked out for the last time.

In the 1960s, the **Albert Hotel** (University Place at 9th street), was the last word in tolerance. It was the only place that accepted unmarried interracial couples and allowed the Spoonful and the Blues Project to rehearse in its roach-infested and waterlogged basement. Like the Chelsea it still exists, but it's now an apartment complex.

And finally, lest we forget, no rock visit to New York is complete without a moment of silence outside the **Dakota** (1 West 72nd Street), where Mark Chapman met John Lennon, and John Lennon met his maker (*see picture*).

### Bradleys

*70 University Place, between 10th & 11th Streets (473 9700).* **Train** 4, 5, 6, L, N or R to Union Square. **Shows** 10pm, midnight, 2am, daily. **Admission** $10-$15 plus $8 drink minimum. **Credit** AmEx, DC, Discover, JCB, MC, V.
Over 20 years old, this smoky neighbourhood club is a haven for trad jazz lovers. Considered to be one of the best in Greenwich Village, it's the place where jazz musicians go to relax after their gigs. Dinner is served 5.30pm to 2.30am.

### The Five Spot

*4 West 31st Street (631 0100).* **Train** B, D, F, N, Q or R to 34th Street. **Shows** 9pm, 11pm Mon-Thur, Sun; 9pm, 10.30pm Fri, Sat. **Admission** from $25 upwards plus $15 drink minimum. **Credit** AmEx, MC,V.
This turn-of-the-century hotel ballroom hosted the inaugural party for New York's best-loved mayor, Fiorella LaGuardia, in the 1930s. An incredible marble and gold-leaf palace, it sat empty for 14 years before being lovingly restored and reopened as a jazz venue in early 1993. The top-rate acoustics have already attracted such division-one talent as Ray Charles, Stéphane Grappelli, Shirley Horn and Ramsey Lewis, and it looks like the Five Spot could take some of the steam from the older jazz venues. Dinner is served from 6pm to 1am.

### Knitting Factory

*74 Leonard Street, at Church Street (219 3006).* **Train** A, C or E to Canal Street. **Admission** $8-$15. **Credit** AmEx, MC.
The Knitting Factory is the centre of New York's avant-garde music scene, featuring an upfront blend of experimental jazz and other music. Recommended for anyone who likes their music to go off the rails a little. Now moved from their narrow but much loved space on Houston Street to this fine location, the café and bar are open throughout the day, and the main room is the perfect size (250 seats) for the kind of acts that play. The Factory's *Alterknit Theatre* runs a varied schedule of artsy cinema, performance and spoken word.

### Sweet Basil

*88 Seventh Avenue South, between Bleecker & Grove Streets (242 1785).* **Train** 1 or 9 to Christopher Street. **Shows** 9pm, 11pm Mon-Thur; 9pm, 11pm, 12.30am Fri; 2pm, 6pm, 9pm, 11pm, 12.30am Sat; 2pm, 6pm, 9pm, 11pm Sun. **Admission** $15 plus $10 drink minimum. **Credit** AmEx, MC, V.
Past players here have included Art Blakey and Abdullah Ibrahim, but the emphasis now is on the traditional. An electrified big band belonging to trumpeter Miles Evans plays every Monday. There's a jazz brunch on Saturdays and Sundays with a $6 drink minimum.

### Village Vanguard

*178 Seventh Avenue South, at Perry Street (255 4037).* **Train** A, C or L to 14th Street/Eighth Avenue. **Open** 8.30pm-2am Mon-Wed; 8.30pm-1am Thur, Sun; 8.30pm-2.30pm Fri, Sat. **No credit cards**.
Still going strong after 30 years, this smoky basement club has seen the likes of John Coltrane and Miles Davis and, more recently, Pharoah Saunders. The Monday night regular is Vanguard, a 17-piece jazz orchestra.

## Other Venues

### AKA

*77 West Houston Street, at West Broadway (330 8133).* **Train** 1 or 9 to Houston Street/BDF to Broadway Lafayette. **Admission** $5-$10. **Open** 7pm-4am daily. **No credit cards**.
A wide-ranging list of genres – from hip-hop to salsa to poppy rock – are serviced, for a cool knowing crowd, at this reasonably well-secluded venue.

### Le Bar Bat

*311 West 57th Street, between Eighth & Ninth Avenues (307 7228).* **Train** 1, 9, A, B, C or D to Columbus Circle. **Admission** $10-$20; free before 9pm (8.30pm Sat). **Open** 5pm-4am daily **Credit** AmEx, MC, V.
A bizarre bar venue set in an old cave-like recording studio. The bands here are usually happy party-time funk and soul providers and the crowd a jolly bunch of after-workers.

### The Bitter End

*147 Bleecker Street, at Thompson Street (673 7030).* **Train** A, B, C, D, E, F or Q to West 4th Street. **Admission** $5. **Open** 7.30pm-2am daily. **No credit cards**.
A real fixture on the scene since the folksy days before Dylan went electric, though constantly in danger of closure. Line-ups are still mostly folk-based, with five or six acts a night.

### The Bottom Line

*15 West 4th Street, near Broadway (228 6300).* **Train** N or R to 8th Street. **Open** 6pm-2am on show days. **Admission** $15-$25. **No credit cards**.
Short on glamour, long on history, this institution serves as a record industry showcase for the up-and-coming, as well as the recently arrived. You can enjoy quality acts almost any night of the week in an unpretentious atmosphere, with usually two shows a night. You are expected to order drinks and it's best to get there early so you won't be served in darkness after the show starts (you'll also get the best seats).

### The Cooler

*416 West 14th Street, between Ninth & Tenth Avenues (229 0785).* **Train** A, C, E or L to 14th Street/Eighth Avenue. **Open** 8pm-4am daily. **Admission** free-$15. **Credit** AmEx, MC, V.
You kind of wish they'd turn the refrigeration machines back on, as this former meat warehouse with its metal walls can get steamy hot. Smallish bands and DJ-steered experimentation form the soundtrack in a venue that tries hard to be thought of as avant garde.

### New Music Café

*380 Canal Street, at West Broadway (941 1019).* **Train** 1 or 9 to Canal Street. **Open** 8pm-3am daily. **Admission** $5-$10. **No credit** cards.
As progressive as its busy schedule will allow, the NMC packs in (literally, it can be very cramped) all sorts of music from the mundane to the inspiring.

### SOBs

*204 Varick Street, at Houston Street (243 4940).* **Train** 1 or 9 to Houston Street. **Open** 5pm-3am Mon; 8pm-3am Tue-Sat. **Admission** $10-$20. **Credit** AmEx, DC, JCB, MC, V.
SOBs (Sounds of Brazil) is a centre for world music, with an exotic bookings policy majoring on Latin jazz and Afrocentric entertainment. Everything from north African rai to soca, salsa, Afro-pop, reggae and Haitian music can be heard here, as well as the half-forgotten stars of 1970s funk and soul. Look out for concerts staged by the Groove Academy promotion team, which is dedicated, George Clinton-style, to the preservation of funk.

### Wetlands

*161 Hudson Street, at Light Street (966 4225).* **Train** 1, 9, A, C or E to Canal Street. **Open** 5pm-4am Mon-Fri; 9pm-4am Sat; 5pm-11pm Sun. **Shows** 10pm Mon-Sat; 6pm, 10pm Sun. **Admission** free-$15. **Credit** (bar only) AmEx, MC, V.
The ecologically-minded Wetlands revives 1960s consciousness in politics and music, encouraging the hippy vibe of today's young ravers. Music here has a vaguely rootsy feel, with reggae, hip-hop and even jungle sneaking their way into a schedule of Dead-head-sympathetic sounds. There's a VW bus inside which spews out ecological leaflets, and you can snack on organic appetisers.

# Sport & Fitness

***Whether you want to watch from the sidelines or head for the thick of the action, as long as you're in New York you'll never be short of sport.***

## Spectator Sports

'How about those Mets?'

Mention sports (never 'sport') and the average New Yorker will turn into an experienced team manager and offer a barrage of educated opinion. This is a town where most people read the paper from the back to the front and where arguments over half-remembered sporting trivia are far more vociferous than any disputes about politics, sex or religion. Sport is one of life's essential nutritional requirements here.

### INFORMATION

All the daily papers carry a massive amount of sports analysis and give listings of the day's events and TV coverage. On Mondays they list the coming week's local team fixtures in Major League baseball, NBA basketball, NFL football and NHL hockey. *New York Newsday* also includes full league results for British football (under 'soccer'). *The New York Times'* excellent Sports supplements appear on Sundays and Mondays. Buy *Sports Illustrated* ($2.95) to get a feel for things (weekly). For news of special events contact the New York Convention and Visitors Bureau on 397 8222 (9am-6pm Mon-Fri; 10am-6pm Sat, Sun).

### TICKETS

Your first call for tickets should be to the team itself. You may be refered to Ticketmaster (307 7171), which sells the same tickets with a booking fee added. For many events, however – especially football and basketball – demand for tickets far outstrips supply. If you are certain that neither the team nor Ticketmaster can help, you have two options: to go to a tout or a ticket broker. If you are staying in a hotel, it's worth having a word with the concierge, as they often have wily connections for tickets.

### TOUTS

If you buy from a ticket tout, known here as 'scalpers', you won't be able to get your money back if you're tricked but, provided you're careful, it can be a fairly reliable way of buying seats. Before you part with any cash, check that the ticket has the correct details (date etc), and make sure you know where your seats will be. (Diagrams of stadium seating arrangements are printed in the front of the *Yellow Pages*.) Sometimes (but very rarely) touts will over-estimate demand and as game time nears will try to off-load their tickets at bargain prices.

### TICKET BROKERS

Ticket brokers offer much the same service as touts, although their activities are slightly more regulated. It's illegal in New York State to sell a ticket for more than its face value (plus booking fee) so these firms operate from other states by phone. They can almost guarantee tickets for 'sold out' events, and tend to deal in the better seats. Not surprisingly, this is a service you have to pay for. Good seats for the NBA basketball play-offs run close to $1000 and tickets for most Giants football games *start* at $100. Look under 'Ticket Sales' in

*Check out a pick-up basketball game.*

the *Yellow Pages* for brokers. Three of the more established are Prestige Entertainment (1-800 2 GET TIX), Ticket Window (1-800 SOLD OUT) and Union Tickets (1-800 CITY TIX).

## Baseball

Baseball is 'America's Favorite Pastime', and enthusiasm for the game runs to religious proportions, though the long '95 players' strike weakened support. Local teams are the Yankees and the Mets. The season runs from April to October; tickets for the average game are easy to get hold of.

### The Mets

*Shea Stadium, 126th Street & Roosevelt Avenue, Flushing, Queens (1-718 507 TIXX ticket information).* **Train** 7 to Shea Stadium. **Open** for information 9am-5.30pm Mon-Fri. **Admission** $6.50-$15. **Credit** AmEx, MC, V.
*Disabled: access, toilets.*

### New York Yankees

*Yankee Stadium, River Avenue & 161st Street, Bronx (1-718 293 4300 information/1-718 293 6000 ticket office).* **Train** 4, C or D to 161st Street. **Open** for information 9am-5pm Mon-Fri; 10am-3pm Sat and during games. **Admission** $11.50-$18. **Credit** AMEx, Discover, MC, V.
*Disabled: access, toilets.*

## Basketball

The season runs from October to July. Local players include the famous professionals of the Knicks and the Nets, the two NBA teams, as well as the rising stars of the region's college sides. Tickets for most NBA games, however, range from expensive to unobtainable. If you miss out, exciting basketball action can be had for free by watching the hustlers play *White Men Can't Jump*-style pick-up games on street courts. The park on Sixth Avenue at West 4th Street, where games are reckoned to be the world's toughest, is the place to be. Even the stars come out to play.

### New York Knickerbockers (Knicks)

*Madison Square Garden, Seventh Avenue at 33rd Street (465 JUMP recorded information menu).* **Train** A, C or E to 34th Street. **Open** for information 9am-6pm Mon-Fri; 10am-3pm Sat. **Admission** official prices are fairly meaningless. Ticket information is usually restricted to 'this game is sold out'.

### New Jersey Nets

*Meadowlands Arena, East Rutherford, New Jersey (1-201 935 8888 information/1-201 935 3900 tickets).* **Bus** from Port Authority Bus Terminal, $3.25 each way (564 8484 for information). **Open** for information 9am-6pm Mon-Fri; 10am-2pm Sat. **Admission** $16-$44.50. **Credit** AmEx, MC, Visa.
Tickets are usually available except for the bigger games, making this your best bet for on-court action.
*Disabled: access.*

## Boxing

*The Paramount, Madison Square Garden, Seventh Avenue at 33rd Street (465 6741 recorded information).* **Train** A, C or E to 34th Street.
The Golden Gloves Boxing Championships, a long-running New York tradition and amateur boxing's most prestigious competition, happen here every January.

## Cricket

Cricket, although considered incomprehensible by most Americans, is played by about a million people in the US. New York, with large populations of Indians, Pakistanis and West Indians, not to mention ex-pat Brits, has about 20 teams and at least two parks where the sound of leather on willow can be heard during the season, which runs from April to October.

### Walker Park

*Richmond Avenue, Staten Island.* **Transport** ferry to Staten Island, then S61 or S74 bus.
The Staten Island Cricket Club (1-718 447 5442) plays here most weekends during the season.

## Big screens & beer-nuts

The great American sports fan needs two things: a ready supply of beer (essential if you are to find baseball interesting), and a nearby audience for his great match-play insights. These elements are readily available in that favourite American institution: the sports bar.

Hundreds of New York bars provide TV sport as a drinking companion, but a few more go to extremes to take you to big-screen sporting heaven. **Mickey Mantle's**, 42 Central Park South between Fifth and Sixth Avenues (688 7777), projects the action onto ten huge screens amid a midtown post-work happy-hour atmosphere. The **Sporting Club**, 99 Hudson Street at Franklin Street (219 0900), has nine giant screens plus digital scoreboards and quiz/betting machines on the bar.

Taking the sports bar theme to its limits and beyond is **Hackers Hitters and Hoops**, 123 West 18th Street between Sixth and Seventh Avenues (929 7482), which is actually a bar with a sporting club attached, boasting two basketball courts, two baseball batting cages, a golf simulator, a mini-golf game and two giant screens.

But if you get tired of the televisual glitz of US franchise sports, there's always **McCormacks**, 365 Third Avenue, at 27th Street (683 0911), the best place if you just want to watch British football in the company of some ex-pat hooligans.

### Van Cortlandt Park

*The Bronx.* **Train** 1 or 9 to 242nd Street.
There are six or seven pitches here and the New York Cricket League (1-201 343 4544) arranges Sunday matches. *See chapter* **New York by Neighbourhood: Outer Boroughs**.

## Football

American football, a cross between chess and war, provides some of Stateside's sport's most spectacular action. The season runs from August to December and is followed by the play-offs for the Superbowl, which is played on the third Sunday in January. There are two local teams, both of which play at Giants Stadium.

### New York Giants

*(1-201 935 8222 recorded information).*

### New York Jets

*(1-516 538 6600 information/1-516 538 7200 single tickets).*
The Giants have a 20-year waiting list for season tickets so the only way to see a game is to know someone with a season ticket or pay blood money to a broker. The Jets are slightly more accessible. They have a waiting list of 13,000 but sell scattered single seats for $25 on a first-come, first-served, cash-only basis from the New York Jets office, 1000 Fulton Avenue, Hempstead NY, and via Ticketmaster.
*Disabled: access by arrangement.*

### Giants Stadium

*Meadowlands Sports Complex, East Rutherford, New Jersey (1-201 935 3900 for information on events other than Giants/Jets).* **Bus** from Port Authority Bus Terminal $3.25 each way (564 8484 for information).

## Horse Racing

There are three major race tracks near New York – Belmont, Aquaduct and the Meadowlands. If you fancy a flutter but not the trek to Long Island or Jersey, head for an Off Track Betting Shop ('OTB') and catch the action and atmosphere there instead.

### Aqueduct Racetrack

*110th Street & Rockaway Boulevard, Ozone Park, Queens (1-718 641 4700).* **Train** A to Aqueduct Racetrack. **Season** Nov-May. **Admission** clubhouse $3.50; grandstand $2. **No credit cards.**
Thoroughbred flat races are held here six days a week (Wed-Mon) during the season.
*Disabled: access.*

### Belmont Park

*Hempstead Turnpike & Plainfield Avenue, Belmont, Long Island (1-718 641 4700).* **Train** Pony Express from Penn Station to Belmont Park. **Season** May-Oct. **Admission** clubhouse $4; grandstand $2. **No credit cards.**
Thoroughbred flat racing six days a week (Wed-Mon) in season. The third leg of the Triple Crown, the Belmont Stakes, is held on the second Saturday in June.

### Meadowlands Racetrack

*East Rutherford, New Jersey (1-201 935 8500).* **Bus** from Port Authority Bus Terminal, $3.25 each way (564 8484 for information). **Season** Jan-Aug trotting; Sept-Dec thoroughbred. **Admission** clubhouse/grandstand $2. **No credit cards.**
Races six days a week (Mon-Sat) during seasons.

## Ice Hockey

A fast, skilful sport with spectacular violence never far away. Tickets are not too hard to get (with the possible exception of Rangers games, since they are one of the league's strongest teams). Tickets for all fixtures go on sale at the beginning of the season, which runs from October to April.

### New York Islanders

*Nassau Memorial Coliseum, Hempstead Turnpike, Uniondale, Long Island (1-516 794 4100 Islanders information).* **Train** Long Island Railroad (1-718 217 5477) from Grand Central to Westbury Station. **Open** 10.45am-5.45pm daily and during games. **Admission** $19-$60. **Credit** AmEx, MC, V.

### New York Rangers

*Madison Square Garden, Seventh Avenue at 33rd Street (465 MSG1/465 6486 Rangers information).* **Train** A, C or E to 34th Street. **Admission** $18-$65. **Credit** AmEx, Discover, MC, V.
*Disabled: access.*

### New Jersey Devils

*Meadowlands Arena, East Rutherford, New Jersey (1-201 935 6050 Devils information).* **Bus** from Port Authority Bus Terminal, $3.25 each way (564 8484 for information). **Open** 9am-6pm and during games. **Admission** $18-$50. **Credit** AmEx, MC, V.

## Soccer

Football, sorry, 'soccer', is very popular in New York, notably amongst the ethnic teams of the outer boroughs. You can catch matches every weekend, played in full international strip and to a very average standard, in the parks in the Polish, Italian and Latin American neighbourhoods. A higher standard of play can be seen in the A-League games of the New York Centaurs, established in the wake of America's hosting of the 1994 World Cup. In addition to the A-League there are hopeful signs that a major professional league will be established: April 1996 will see the start of Major League Soccer, with two local 'franchises' (ie teams): one to be based at Giants Stadium, and another in nearby Piskataway, New Jersey.

### New York Centaurs

*Downing Stadium, Randalls Island, off 125th Street/Triborough Bridge (355 8358).* **Bus** M35 to Randall's Island. **Tickets** $8-$15. **No credit cards.**
The semi-professional A-League in which the New York Centaurs play started in 1995 and offers football of UK Third Division/Vauxhall Conference standard. The season is May-September and matches are played on Sundays.
*Disabled: access by arrangement.*

## Tennis

### US Open

*USTA Tennis Center, Flushing, Queens (1-718 760 6200 for information and tickets).* **Train** 7 to Shea Stadium. **Dates** late August to early September. **Admission** $25-$50 day tickets. **Credit** AmEx, DC, Discover, MC, V.
Tickets go on sale at the end of May.
*Disabled: access.*

*Catch some darts (and drinking) action at* **Muffin's Pub**. *See page 257.*

**Virginia Slims Championship**
This event is staged at Madison Square Garden (*listed under* **Boxing**) in the second and third week of November. The top 16 women's singles players and top 32 doubles compete for $3.5 million in prizes. For information and tickets (day tickets are $15-$45), call 465 6500. Tickets go on sale at the end of April.

## Other Spectator Events

**WWF Wrestling** might not be exactly a sport, but it's a great spectator event. Hulk Hogan and his cartoon character friends and enemies battle it out at Madison Square Garden (465 MSG1).

**Monster Truck Racing** is worth seeing if you like the idea of giant pick-ups splashing through a field of mud and crunching their way over parked cars. Events are scheduled fairly regularly at Nassau Coliseum (1-516 794 9300) and Meadowlands Arena (1-201 935 3900).

# Active Sports

There's no excuse for staying soft and flabby during your stay here. The New York quest for fitness may not have reached Californian levels but the natives do invest a good deal of time and money in their bodies. Excellent facilities exist for most forms of physical recreation, although with some it might be your wallet that gets the most exercise.

## General Information

**Department of Parks and Recreation**
*(360 3456 24-hour recorded information).*
Information on sports activities in city parks.

**Women's Sports Foundation**
*(1-800 227 3988 information and referral service).*
**Open** 9am-5pm Mon-Fri.
Staff here are happy to answer any queries you may have about women's events, facilities and sporting history.

## Baths

**Tenth Street Baths**
*268 East 10th Street, between First Avenue & Avenue A (674 9250).* **Train** L to First Avenue. **Open** 8am-10pm daily. **Admission** $19. **Credit** AmEx, Discover, MC, V.
Traditional Russian, Turkish and Swedish baths, with a juice and salad bar, lockers, security boxes and sun deck. Massages are $26 for 30 minutes, $42 for an hour. Wednesday is women's day, Thursday and Sunday are men only and the rest of the week it's mixed.

## Boating

**Loeb Boathouse**
*Central Park, near Fifth Avenue at 74th Street (517 4723).* **Train** 6 to 77th Street. **Open** *May-Sept* 10.30am-6pm daily; *spring & autumn* 10.30am-6pm Sat, Sun. **Rates** $10 per hour plus $20 refundable deposit. **No credit cards.**
The Central Park lake stretches across almost the park's entire width. Boats can be hired on the Fifth Avenue side at the boathouse, which incorporates an Italian restaurant.

## Bowling

**Bowlmor Lanes**
*110 University Place, at 12th Street (255 8188).* **Train** 4, 5, 6, L, N or R to Union Square. **Open** 10am-1am Sun-Thur; 10am-4am Fri, Sat. **Rates** $3.25 per person per game; $1 shoe rental. **No credit cards.**
A bar, grill, pro shop and a massive 44 lanes.

**Leisure Time Recreation**
*625 Eighth Avenue, at the Port Authority Bus Terminal (268 6909).* **Train** A, C or E to 42nd Street. **Open** 10am-11pm Mon-Thur, Sun; 10am-2am Fri, Sat. **Admission** $3.50 per person per game weekdays before 5pm; $3.75 other times; $2 shoe rental. **Credit** (minimum $25) MC, V.
Let fly a few strikes down one of 30 lanes while you're waiting for your bus. Or sink some shots at the bar.

## Boxing

### Gleason's Gym

*15 Front Street, Brooklyn (1-718 797 2872).* **Train** F to York Street. **Open** 7am-8pm Mon-Fri; 9am-4pm Sat. **Admission** $2 to watch, $10 to work out. **No credit cards.**

The centre of boxing in NY for years – Mike Tyson and Riddick Bowe both call this home. It offers excellent work-out and training facilities and top-level instruction and you can watch young contenders training and sparring.

## Cycling

### AYH Five-Borough Bicycle Club

*AYH Hostel, 891 Amsterdam Avenue, NY 10025 (932 2300).*

Advice and courses on all aspects of cycling, from risking death in the busy Manhattan streets to scenic mountain biking outside the city limits. It also arranges the excellent Annual Five-Borough Bike Tour (in May).

## Cycle Hire

You can rent bikes in and around Central Park, where the 7.2 mile road loop is closed to traffic at the weekends.

### Loeb Boathouse

*Central Park, near Fifth Avenue at 74th Street (861 4137).* **Train** 6 to 68th Street. **Open** *Mar-Nov* 10am-6pm Mon-Fri; 9am-6pm Sat, Sun. **Rates** *3-speed* $8 per hour, $32 per 8-hour day; *10-speed* $10 per hour, $40 per day. **No credit cards.**

A passport or credit card is held as security.

### Metro Bicycles

*1311 Lexington Avenue, at 88th Street (427 4450).* **Train** 4, 5 or 6 to 86th Street. **Open** 9.30am-6.30pm daily. **Rates** $6 per hour, $25 per 8-hour day. **Credit** AmEx, Discover, MC,V.

Leave a driving licence or credit card as security.

## Darts

### Muffin's Pub

*699 Second Avenue, between 37th & 38th Streets (599 9349).* **Train** 4, 5, 6, 7 or S to 42nd Street. **Open** 10am-4am daily.

With ten boards, this is darts heaven. It's home to nine of the city's 70 teams and it's free ($10 deposit on the house darts). Just buy a drink and play.

## Fitness Classes

See the ads in the city's weekly papers and mags for just some of the hundreds of gyms and health clubs. Most require annual membership, but the following will allow guests to pay per day or per class. For more fitness facilities, *see below* **YMCA**.

### Crunch Fitness

*54 East 13th Street, between University Place & Broadway (475 2018).* **Train** 4, 5, 6, L, N or R to Union Square. **Open** 6.30am-10pm Mon-Thur; 8am-8pm Fri-Sun. **Rates** *one class* $15; *10 classes* $99. **Credit** AmEx, MC, V.

Crunch attracts a young, clubby clientele. The Lafayette Street branch has more free weights and the University Place branch offers the most classes.

**Branches** 404 Lafayette Street (614 0120); 162 West 83rd Street (875 1902).

### Equinox

*897 Broadway, at 19th Street (780 9300).* **Train** 4, 5, 6, L, N or R to Union Square. **Open** 5.30am-11pm Mon-Thur; 5.30am-10pm Fri; 8am-9pm Sat, Sun. **Rates** $26 per day. **Credit** AmEx, Discover, MC, V.

Its reputation is built on its aerobics classes, of which there are dozens, from steps to hip-hop. There are also plenty of free weights and cardiovascular machines. The day rate gives you access to all facilities, including classes.

**Branch** 344 Amsterdam Avenue (721 4200).

### Lotte Berk Method

*23 East 67th Street, between Fifth & Madison Avenues (288 6613).* **Train** 6 to 68th Street. **Open** 7.30am-7pm Mon-Thur; 7.30am-6.30pm Fri; 8.30am-1pm Sat; 10am-1pm Sun. **Rates** *one class* $18; *10 classes* $165. **No credit cards.**

The Lotte Berk method borrows from yoga and ballet. The emphasis is on strengthening and stretching to reshape the body. It's pretty tough – even professional dancers are recommended to start with the beginners' classes.

### Steps

*2121 Broadway, at West 74th Street (874 2410).* **Train** 1, 2, 3 or 9 to 72nd Street. **Open** 9am-8pm Mon-Fri; 9am-6pm Sat; 10am-6pm Sun. **Rates** *one class* $10.50; *10 classes* $90 (valid for 2 months). **No credit cards.**

Single classes in low-impact aerobics, exercise, stretch and body sculpting. Also ballet, jazz, tap and theatre dance from beginners to advanced level, with a very theatrical clientele.

## Golf

*See also box* **Chelsea Piers**.

### Kissena Park Golf Course

*164-15 Booth Memorial Avenue, Queens (1-718 939 4594).* **Train** 7 to Main Street, Flushing, then Q65 bus. **Open** dawn-dusk daily. **Green fees** $15.50, $8.75 after 3pm Mon-Fri; $17.50, $9.75 after 3pm Sat, Sun. **Club rental** $10 per round. **No credit cards.**

A short 'executive' course with great views of the Manhattan skyline. Pro lessons are available at $35 for 30 mins. Book six and get one free. Par 64.

### Silver Lake Park

*Victory Boulevard & Clove Road, Staten Island (1-718 447 5686).* **Transport** ferry to Staten Island, then S67 bus. **Open** dawn-dusk daily. **Green fees** $15.50; $7.25 under-16s, senior citizens Mon-Fri; $17.50 Sat, Sun; $2 booking fee. **Credit** MC, V.

The course is difficult with narrow fairways and hills to negotiate. Console yourself with nature when your golf ball ends in the woods once again – it's a very picturesque setting. Par 69.

### Van Cortlandt Golf Course

*Van Cortlandt Park, Park South & Bailey Avenue, Bronx (1-718 543 4595).* **Train** 1 or 9 to 242nd Street. **Open** 7am-dusk Mon-Fri; 6am-dusk Sat, Sun. **Green fees** $23.50 Mon-Fri; $25.50 Sat, Sun. **Club rental** from $20 per round. **Credit** MC, V.

This is the oldest course in the country, and is rich in history, being easily the most 'New York' of the city's 13 public courses. It's relatively short but challenging – narrow with lots of trees and hilly in places. Lessons are available at $35 for 30 minutes. Par 70.

### Richard Metz Golf Studio

*425 Madison Avenue, at 49th Street, 3rd Floor (759 6940).* **Train** E, F or 6 to 51st Street/Lexington Avenue.

**Open** 10am-8pm Mon-Thur; 10am-7pm Fri; 10am-5pm Sat. **Rates** *1 lesson* $60; *5 lessons* $250; *10 lessons* $350. **Credit** AmEx, DC, Discover, JCB, MC, V.
Practice your swing into a teaching net and then analyse the movement on video. Lessons last half an hour, and cater for all levels. There are three nets, putting areas and a golf shop.

## Horse Riding

### Claremont Riding Academy

*175 West 89th Street, at Amsterdam Avenue (724 5100).* **Train** 1 or 9 to 86th Street. **Open** 6.30am-10pm Mon-Fri; 6.30am-5pm Sat, Sun. **Rental** $30 per hour. **Lessons** $55 per 30 min, groups $70 per hour. **No credit cards.**
The academy teaches English-style (as opposed to Western) riding. Beginners use an indoor arena; experienced riders can also ride six miles (9.6km) of trails in Central Park.

### Jamaica Bay Riding Academy

*7000 Shore Parkway, Brooklyn (1-718 531 8949).* **Transport** by car via Belt Parkway. **Open** 9am-5pm Mon, Wed, Sat, Sun; 9am-10pm Tue, Thur. **Guided trail ride** $23. **Lessons** $45 per hour. **No credit cards.**
The trail ride, through the 300-acre Jamaica Bay Wildlife Refuge, lasts 45 minutes. English and Western riding.

## Hot-Air Ballooning

### Lift and Drift Balloon Tours

*371 Route 6, Port Jervis, NY (1-914 856 8550).* **Open** 1 May-31 October daily; hours vary. **Flights** one-hour $165 per person. **Credit** MC, V.
At about an hour's drive, this is the closest ballooning to Manhattan. Flights leave at dawn (6am) and dusk (6pm) to ensure optimum wind conditions. The morning flight includes breakfast and the evening includes champagne. You drift peacefully above tree-level, rising gently to around 2000 feet, from where you can see New York across the Orange County countryside. Great views.

## Chelsea Piers

*Piers 59-62, West 17th-23rd Streets at the Hudson River (336 6666).* **Bus** M23 to Hudson River.

As if there weren't enough going on in New York already, four of the city's huge abandoned Hudson River piers have been transformed into the most extensive public sports complex in the United States. The 1.7 million square feet of Chelsea Piers boasts an astounding list of facilities: two full-size ice rinks, two open-air roller rinks, indoor soccer pitches, baseball batting cages, basketball and sand volleyball courts, a pool, restaurants, a sun-deck, the state's largest gym, the Northeast's largest rock-climbing wall, the world's longest indoor running track and an outdoor golf driving range so large it seems impossible that it's in Manhattan.

The whole thing is built in the remains of the city's famous maritime passenger terminals – it was here that the Titanic was headed when it sank – and also houses film and TV studios, a marina and a sporting goods superstore. At time of writing it is only partially open, but plans are that all facilities will be open to the public on a day-rate basis, some of them 24 hours a day.

## Pinball & Video Games

### Broadway Arcade

*1659 Broadway, at 52nd Street (247 3725).* **Train** 1 or 9 to 50th Street. **Open** 8am-1am daily.
Headquarters of the professional and amateur pinball associations.

### Playland

*Broadway, at 42nd Street (no phone).* **Train** 1, 2, 3, 9, N, R or S to 42nd Street. **Open** 8am-2am daily.
Altogether sleazier, but always up with the latest games.

## Pool & Billiards

### Chelsea Billiards (pool)

*54 West 21st Street, between Fifth & Sixth Avenues (989 0096).* **Train** F to 23rd Street. **Open** 24 hours daily. **Admission** $8 per hour for first player, $2 for each additional player Mon-Thur, Sun; $12 per hour first player, $2 per hour each additional player Fri, Sat; 20 per cent discount students, senior citizens. **Credit** AmEx, MC, V.
A comfortable and welcoming pool parlour with full-size snooker tables, too. Hot dogs and snacks are available.

### Julian's

*138 East 14th Street, between Third & Fourth Avenues (598 9884).* **Train** 4, 5, 6, L, N or R to Union Square. **Open** 10am-2am Mon-Thur, Sun; 10am-4am Fri, Sat. **No credit cards.**
There are 12 tables in Manhattan's most atmospheric club. Rates are $8 per person for three hours.

## Racing Car Driving

### Bertil Roos School of Motor Racing

*Pocono International Raceway, Pennsylvania (1-717 646 7227/1-800 RACE NOW).* **Open** 9am-5pm Mon-Fri. **Courses** half-day $395, one-day $795, three-day $1995. **Credit** Discover, MC, V.
Drive a single-seater Formula 2000 car at speeds of up to 140mph around the raceway, two hours' drive from the city, and spot cabbies training for the Manhattan streets....

### Skip Barber Advanced Driving School

*Lime Rock Park Raceway, Connecticut, and Bridgehampton, Long Island (both locations 1-203 824 0771/1-800 221 1131).* **Open** 8.30am-8pm **Courses** advanced driving (not available in Bridgehampton) one-day $495, two-day $975; Formula Ford racing half-day $395, three-day $1995. **Credit** AmEx, MC, V.
Formula Ford cars don't have wings like the Formula 2000, but they still reach 120mph without too much trouble. The advanced driving courses, taken in a BMW 325i, include skid-pan training.

## Racquetball

Racquetball is a bit like squash. It's played in a four-sided court, but the ball is softer and the racquet is like a small version of a tennis racquet with looser strings. A high-energy game.

### Manhattan Plaza Racquet Club

*450 West 43rd Street, between Ninth & Tenth Avenues (594 0554).* **Train** A, C or E to 42nd Street. **Open** 6am-midnight daily. **Rates** $18-$26 per court per hour, plus $10 guest fee. **Credit** AmEx, MC, V.

Rates vary according to the time of day. The club also has five hard tennis courts ($28-$38 per court per hour, plus $20 guest fee).

## Rollerblading

The latest terror on New York streets is the quiet skish-skish of psychopathic rollerbladers. It's not unusual to see them on the Avenues reaching 30mph facing oncoming traffic. A slightly more sane variety can be found whirling around Central Park, either on the road loop (closed to traffic at weekends) or near the bandshell at 72nd Street. The 'coneheads', or slalomers, stroke their stuff at Central Park West and 67th Street, across from Tavern on the Green.

To give it a try yourself, visit Wollman Memorial Rink (*see below* **Skating**). If you'd prefer to be indoors, head for the Roxy (*see chapter* **Clubs**) or to the new Chelsea Piers complex (*see box*). If you don't want to be restricted to the rink, you can rent skates from the many rollerblade shops close to the park. Try Blades, 158 East 86th Street (996 1644) and 120 West 72nd Street (787 3911). Stick with the pack and follow the flow of traffic. At weekends there are plenty of people around to rescue you if you wipe out and even a volunteer force of NYRS skate patrollers (in red T-shirts with white crosses) who run free stopping clinics for beginners. You'll find them on Saturdays and Sundays from 12.30-5.30pm at the 72nd Street entrace near the Rumsey playfield.

### New York Road Skaters

*PO Box 1120, NY 10023 (534 7858).*

A non-profitmaking organisation offering group classes ($13), skating tours of the city and more.

## Running

Join the joggers in Central Park, Riverside Park or round Washington Square in the early morning or early evening. It's best, for women especially, to avoid jogging alone. And don't carry anything that's obviously valuable.

### New York Road Runners Club

*9 East 89th Street, between Fifth & Madison Avenues (860 4455).* **Train** 4, 5 or 6 to 86th Street. **Open** 10am-8pm Mon-Fri; 10am-5pm Sat; 10am-3pm Sun. **Membership** from $30. **Credit** AmEx, Discover, MC, V.

Contact the club – the world's largest running club – for information on short runs, safety, local runs, children's classes and marathons.

### The New York City Marathon

Held annually in early November, the marathon attracts over a million spectators and 25,000 runners, who follow a course through the five boroughs, ending in Manhattan. Other big events include the Empire State Building Run-Up in February, the 100-Mile Championship at Shea Stadium in June, the Governor's Island 10K Run in July and the Fifth Avenue Mile in September. For information call the New York Road Runners Club (*see above*).

*Central Park, New York's jogging mecca.*

## Sailing

### New York Sailing School

*231 Kirby Street, City Island, Bronx (1-718 885 3103/1-800 428 7245).* **Train** 6 to Pelham Bay Park, then BX29 bus. **Open** 10.30am-6pm Tue-Sun. **Credit** AmEx, Discover, MC, V.

If you have some form of sailing certificate you can rent boats and venture into Long Island Sound. Here are boats ranging from J22s right up to a 39ft Beneteau. Rentals are $80-$450 per day. Otherwise take one of the many courses. The beginners' package lasts three days, with 33 hours on the water, and costs $445 at the weekend.

### New York Harbor Boating

*The Enterprise, North Cove Yacht Harbor, World Financial Center (786 0400 24-hour recorded information).* **Train** 1, 9, A or C to Chambers Street. **Open** dawn-dusk. **Credit** MC, V.

J24 sailing boats are for rent from $90 for half a day and there are larger boats at larger prices, right up to a Beneteau 43. You need the relevant certification, although a captain can be provided for an extra fee. Harbour Boating runs an ASA-certified sailing school and offers a 'learn to sail' course for $395, or an introduction to sailing for $50 an hour.

## Skating

### Rockefeller Center Ice Rink

*1 Rockefeller Plaza, Fifth Avenue, between 49th & 50th Streets (757 5731/757 5730 recorded information).* **Train** B, D, F or Q to Rockefeller Center. **Open** *Oct-April* 9am-1pm, 1.30-5.30pm, 6-10pm, Mon-Fri; 9am-noon, 12.30-3pm, 3.30-6pm, 6.30-10pm, Sat, Sun. **Rates** $8 adults, $6.50 under-12s Mon-Thur; $9 adults, $7 under-12s, Fri-Sun. **Skate hire** $4. **No credit cards.**

The famous outdoor rink, under the giant statue of Prometheus, is perfect for atmosphere, but a little small. It's unmissable however, when the giant Christmas tree is lit.

### Wollman Memorial Rink

*Central Park, at 63rd Street (517 4800).* **Train** *4, 5, 6, N or R to 59th Street/Lexington Avenue.* **Open** *ice skating* Oct-Mar, *rollerskating and rollerblading* Apr-Sept, 10am-5pm Mon; 10am-9.30pm Tue-Thur; 10am-11pm Fri, Sat; 10am-9.30pm Sun. **Rates** $6 adults; $3 under-12s, senior citizens. **Skate hire** ice skates, rollerskates $3.25; rollerblades $6.50. **Credit** AmEx, MC, V. A credit card is needed as deposit for rollerblades.

Manhattan's largest outdoor rink, playing a wide variety of music. You can stay as long as you like.

## Skydiving

### Skydive Long Island

*East Moriches, Long Island (1-516 878 5867).* **Open** 9.30am-dusk Wed-Fri; 8am-dusk Sat, Sun. **Courses** static line $200; tandem jump $215. **Credit** MC, V.

The static line course includes 5½ hours of training culminating in a jump with an automatically releasing chute. In a tandem jump you have an instructor strapped on to you so you only need half an hour of training beforehand. Subsequent jumps are $70 each (static), $160 (tandem).

## Squash

The West Side YMCA (*listed under* **YMCA**) has some courts and offers a day rate for membership. Court use is free for members. There are few other places where you can play squash cheaply.

### City Hall Squash Club

*25 Park Place, between Church Street & Broadway (964 2677).* **Train** 2 or 3 to Park Place. **Open** 7am-9pm Mon-Thur; 7am-8pm Fri; 11am-4pm Sun. **Rates** vary; call for details. **Credit** AmEx, MC, V.

## Swimming

### Municipal Pools

*Parks Department Hotline 1-800 201 PARK*

An annual membership fee of $25, payable by money order only (available at post offices) at any of the pools, entitles you to use all New York's municipal pools, both indoor and outdoor, for free for a year. Outdoor pools are free to all, and open June-September. You need proof of your name, an address in the New York City area and a passport-size photograph to register. Some of the best city-run pools are: Asser Levy Pool, 23rd Street, at FDR Drive (447 2020); Carmine Street Recreation Center, Clarkson Street & Seventh Avenue South (242 5228); East 54th Street Pool, 348 East 54th Street, at First Avenue (397 3154); West 59th Street Pool, 59th Street, between Tenth and Eleventh Avenues (397 3159).

### Sheraton Manhattan Hotel

*790 Seventh Avenue, at 51st Street (581 3300).* **Train** B, D or E to Seventh Avenue. **Open to non-residents** 6am-9pm daily. **Admission** $20 for non-residents. **Credit** AmEx, DC, Discover, MC, V.

Pricier than the usually free municipal pools, but much less crowded. The place to come if you want to swim in peace.

## Tennis

To play on municipal courts, including those on Central, East River and Riverside Parks, you'll need a permit from the Department of Parks (360 8111). They cost $50 ($20 seniors, $10 under-18s) and are valid for the season (April-November).

### HRC Tennis

*on the East River, at Wall & South Streets (422 9300).* **Train** 2 or 3 to Wall Street. **Open** 7am-midnight daily. **Court fees** $60-$120 per hour. **Credit** AmEx, MC, V.

This is part of the New York Health & Racquet Club. There are eight green clay courts under bubbles on twin piers by the river and five tennis pros on hand to give lessons ($28 per hour plus court fees).

*Blading across the Brooklyn Bridge.*

### Midtown Tennis Club

*341 Eighth Avenue, at West 27th Street (989 8572).* **Train** 1 or 9 to 28th Street. **Open** 7am-midnight Mon-Thur; 7am-8pm Fri; 8am-8pm Sat, Sun. **Court fees** $25-$60 per hour. **Credit** AmEx, MC, V.

Eight indoor hard courts, four uncovered in the summer.

### Sutton East Tennis Club

*488 East 60th Street, at York Street (751 3452).* **Train** 4, 5, 6, N or R to 59th Street/Lexington Avenue. **Open** *Oct-April* 7am-midnight daily. **Court fees** non-members $32-$104 per hour. **No credit cards**.

The club has eight red clay courts and 11 pros (lessons are from $48, or from $410 for 10).

## YMCAs

There are Ys throughout the five boroughs, all offering a wide range of facilities. Three of the Manhattan sites offer day rates for visitors. Membership of a Y in another country may get you discounts; and if you're already paying for accommodation, the sports facilities are included.

### Harlem YMCA

*180 West 135th Street, at Seventh Avenue (281 4100).* **Train** B or C to 135th Street. **Open** 9.30am-9pm Mon-Fri; 10am-6pm Sat. **Membership** $10 per day, $60 per month, $450 per year. **Credit** MC, V.

Boasts a four-lane swimming pool, basketball court, full gym and a sauna.

### Vanderbilt YMCA

*224 East 47th Street (755 2410).* **Train** 6 to 51st Street. **Open** 6am-10pm Mon-Fri; 8am-7pm Sat, Sun. **Membership** $15 per day, $85 per month, $785 per year. **Credit** AmEx, MC, V.

Two swimming pools, a running track, a steam sauna and a gym with basketball, handball and volleyball – plus yoga and aerobic classes.

### West Side Branch YMCA

*5 West 63rd Street, between Broadway & Central Park West (787 4400).* **Train** 1, 9, A, B, C or D to Columbus Circle. **Open** 6.30am-9.30pm Mon-Fri; 8am-8pm Sat; 9am-5pm Sun. **Membership** $15 per day, $100 per month; classes free. **Credit** MC, V.

Two pools and three gyms with all the equipment you could imagine, plus an indoor track, squash courts and facilities for basketball, volleyball, handball, racquetball, boxing, aerobics and yoga. There is also a full range of classes. Day rate includes access to everything.

## Yoga

### Integral Yoga Institute

*227 West 13th Street, between Seventh & Eighth Avenues (929 0586).* **Train** A, C, E or L to 14th Street/Eighth Avenue. **Open** 10am-8.30pm Mon-Fri; 9am-5.30pm Sat. **Rates** $8 per class. **No credit cards**.

A variety of classes is offered; you don't need to book.

### Jivamukti Yoga Center

*149 Second Avenue, between 9th & 10th Streets, Second floor (353 0214).* **Train** 6 to Astor Place. **Open** 7am-9.15pm Mon-Fri; 10am-5.45pm Sat, Sun. **Classes** $6 non-members; $12, $55 for 5 members. **Membership** $150 3 months. **No credit cards**.

This is Yoga Express: high-impact East Village spritualism involving much chanting, hatha yoga and meditation. You can take open, basics, basics II or Astanga classes, all lasting one hour 45 minutes.

# Theatre

***To paraphrase the bard: All New York's a stage and we are merely waiters (till our big break).***

New York is famous for the improvised absurdism of its daily life. Luckily the city's bizarre energy is also captured on stage, and there is more professional theatre here than in the rest of the country combined. In fact, no matter what your sexual, cultural or political persuasion, your age or the language you speak, there is bound to be something that will excite you.

Theatre is divided into three main categories: Broadway, Off-Broadway and Off-Off Broadway. This is historically a matter of a theatre's audience capacity rather than its location, though Broadway theatres are all in or around Broadway and Times Square. Off-Broadway venues are mostly clustered around Greenwich Village. More importantly, however, this three-way division is a classification of the philosophies underlying a production, and therefore of the kind of show you're likely to see.

## INFORMATION

The Sunday 'Arts and Leisure' and the Friday 'Weekend' sections of the *New York Times* are reliable sources of information, as are the listings in *Time Out New York*, *New York* magazine, the *New Yorker* and the *Village Voice*.

In addition there are several interactive phone lines offering everything from plot synopses and show times to an agent ready to sell you tickets (you will need a touch-tone phone). The best is **New York City On Stage** (768 1818), a service of the Theater Development Fund, which will tell you everything you need to know about performances on Broadway, Off-Broadway and Off-Off-Broadway, as well as classical music, dance and opera events. The **Broadway Show Line** (563 2929) gives similar information, but is restricted to Broadway and Off-Broadway shows, and you must know which show you are interested in before you can use it. The Association for a Better New York's service (**765 ARTS**) is wide-ranging, detailed and less commercial: useful for smaller productions and one-off events. This service is categorised by venue rather than show names.

## BUYING TICKETS

Provided you have one of the major credit cards, buying Broadway tickets requires little more effort than picking up a telephone. Almost all Broadway and Off-Broadway shows are served by one of the city's 24-hour booking agencies. The information lines above will refer you to ticket agents, often on the same call. **Telecharge** (239 6200) and **Ticketmaster** (307 7171) carve up the bulk of the shows between them, with the smaller **Ticket Central** (279 4200) specialising in Off-Broadway and Off-Off-Broadway shows. Be aware that you will pay a service charge to the agency, but since most theatres don't take telephone bookings, you don't have a lot of choice, except to buy tickets in person from a theatre's box office. Call first to check when it's open.

The cheapest full-price tickets on Broadway are for standing room and cost about $15, but few theatres offer these and you should check at the box office. If a show is sold out, you can try for stand-by tickets just before show time, although they're not likely to be discounted. As a general rule, tickets are slightly cheaper for matinees and previews, and students or groups of 20 or more will usually get a reduction.

Another method is to look out for 'two-fers' – vouchers which allow you to buy two tickets for the price of one. These are found wherever tourist information is gathered, especially in hotel lobbies, and promote long-running Broadway shows and occasionally the larger Off-Broadway ones.

However, there is a foolproof way of buying tickets for even the most popular Broadway shows at as little as half-price (plus a $2.50 service charge). **TKTS** sells tickets at 75 or 50 per cent of their face value from its booth in Times Square. Shows with available seats are clearly posted on a display next to the ticket windows. Bring a list of what you'd like to see and you'll find many of your choices available. A trick is to go at around 7pm when most shows are soon to start and the day's queue has died down. The choice of shows won't be too much different from earlier.

### TKTS

*West 47th Street & Broadway (221 0013 recorded information).* **Train** 1, 2, 3, 7, 9, N, R or S to Times Square. **Open** 3-8pm daily for evening performances; 10am-2pm for Wed and Sat matinees. **No credit cards.**
The main TKTS is conveniently situated in the heart of the Theater District at the peculiar triangle formed by the meeting of Broadway, Seventh Avenue and 47th Street. Queues

**En Garde Arts** *on location on Wall Street.* *See page 266.*

are often long, so get there in good time, and enjoy the spectacle of Times Square while you're waiting (or wing it and arrive at the last minute – see above). TKTS booths accept cash and travellers cheques only and deal in Broadway and Off Broadway tickets.
**Branch**: mezzanine level, 2 World Trade Center (221 0013 recorded information).

## Broadway

Broadway is booming. In recent years more tickets have been sold than ever before; box office takings for newly opened shows have repeatedly broken records and, by putting big-name movie stars in leading roles, Broadway – 'The Great White Way' – is now competing directly with Hollywood for its audiences.

Theatrical Broadway is the district around Times Square between about 41st and 53rd Streets. This is where the grand theatres are clustered together, most built in the first 30 years of the century. The area is a lot less seedy than it was a few years ago: stay where there are plenty of people and you have little to worry about. Here the big shows are hard to ignore; blockbuster names like *Cats*, *Phantom*, *Les Miserables* and *Miss Saigon* declare themselves on vast billboards.

However, there is more to Broadway than the undemanding glitzy entertainment of a Cameron Mackintosh production; in recent years provocative new dramas like Tony Kushner's *Angels in America* have engaged audiences here to resounding success, as have many revived classics from the likes of Cocteau, Turgenev and Shakespeare.

Other noticeable trends are the revival of old-time musicals – *Guys and Dolls*, *42nd Street* and *Crazy For You* – and the idea of staging movies. If you're tired of *Grease*, there are plans for Broadway to catch *Saturday Night Fever*.

One company to look out for is the irrepressible **Roundabout Theatre** (869 8400), which in just over a decade has gone from near-bankrupt Off-Broadway status to a thriving Broadway success story: a critically acclaimed home of the classics, with a steady roster of the world's finest actors. From 1996 the company will produce eight plays a year in its Criterion Centre.

There are 38 theatres designated as being on Broadway. Full-price tickets cost up to $60.

### Backstage on Broadway Tours

*228 West 47th Street, New York, NY 10036 (575 8065; fax 575 8482/toll free 1-800-445-7074).* **Tickets** $8 adults; $7 students. **No credit cards**.
For a more intimate glimpse behind the curtain, Backstage on Broadway is a unique tour where you learn about New York's theatreland directly from a professional actor, stage manager or director. Your lecturer will meet you at a specific theatre. It's for groups of 25 or more – though you may be able to be added to a group – and you must book in advance, ideally a month before your visit.

## Off-Broadway

As a general rule, Off-Broadway theatres have fewer than 500 seats and are located in Greenwich Village, which was the counter-cultural centre of Manhattan in the 1950s. Because Off-Broadway is less of a slave to commercial success, it can offer

*Broadway is thriving as shows attract record numbers of punters.*

# Shakespeare for free

The New York Shakespeare Festival began in 1954 under the leadership of Joseph Papp. It was known then as the Shakespeare Workshop and based in a church basement on the the Lower East Side. In 1956, the first Free Shakespeare Summer Festival was staged at the East River Park Amphitheater. It became part of the Central Park landscape when the company's tour truck collapsed near Belvedere Lake. The Delacorte Theater was built on the site in 1962. Two years later, the Mobile Theater was developed to tour city parks and playgrounds. Seeking a year-round home for the production of new American plays, Papp saved the Astor Library from demolition, named it the Public Theater and had the building declared a landmark.

### Shakespeare in the Park

*Delacorte Theater, Central Park at West 79th Street (539 8500 for general information).* **Train** B or C to 81st Street. **Festival** Tue-Sun June-Sept.

If you're visiting New York during the summer, this is an absolute must. Shakespeare in the Park takes place in the outdoor Delacorte Theater and is well known for its boisterous, star-studded performances of the Bard's work. 1995's *The Tempest* with Patrick Stewart (Captain Jean-Luc Picard from *Star Trek: The Next Generation*) was so successful that the show ended up on Broadway. Tickets are free and are distributed at 1pm on the day of performance only, from both the Delacorte Theater and the Public Theater (*see above* **Off-Broadway**). Normally 11.30am-noon is a safe time to get there, but when the shows feature box office giants (such as Meryl Streep, Denzel Washington, Kevin Kline, Patrick Stewart) the queue starts as early as 7am. Take breakfast, lunch, dinner.... Two tickets are allotted per person.

more 'serious' stuff, some of which is easily as polished as the best Broadway offering and often superior in quality. There are considerable variations in standards among the many Off-Broadway productions, however, and the selection below is a guide to the most reliable theatres/repertory companies. Check the media for other venues. Tickets will be around $10-$30.

### Astor Place Theater

*434 Lafayette Street, at Astor Place (254 4370).* **Train** 6 to Astor Place. **Credit** AmEx, MC, V.

Astor Place is best known for off-beat productions and is expected to continue its very long run of Blue Man Group Tubes, a messy, colourful audience-participation romp (don't worry: no-one's forced to join in). Opinions vary as to whether this show is utterly asinine or truly profound, but it is without doubt enormous fun, and a harmless way to see just how crazy New York can get.

### Brooklyn Academy of Music

*30 Lafayette Avenue, off Flatbush Avenue, Brooklyn (1-718 636 4100).* **Train** 2, 3, 4, 5, D or Q to Atlantic Avenue. **Credit** AmEx, MC, V.

Brooklyn's grand old opera house – as well as the associated Carey Playhouse and Majestic Theater – stages the famous Next Wave Festival in the last three months of each year. This is a programme of musical, theatrical and dance pieces by American and international artists. What you get is the established avant garde: Stephen Berkoff, Cheek by Jowl and Robert Wilson headlined in 1995.
*Disbled: access, toilets.*

### Circle Repertory Company

*159 Bleecker Street, between Thompson & Sullivan Streets (239 6200).* **Train** A, B, C, D, E, F or Q to West 4th Street. **Credit** AmEx, DC, Discover, MC, V.

Circle Repertory Company is one of New York's premier companies and has been hailed as 'the chief provider of new American plays'. Indeed, the company produces five new American plays each season, and has introduced audiences to works such as *Talley's Folly*, *Burn This* and *Prelude to a Kiss* and playwrights including Lanford Wilson, William Hoffman and Terrence McNally. Tickets cost $35 to $45.

### The Public Theater

*425 Lafayette Street, between Astor Place & East 4th Street (539 8500).* **Train** 6 to Astor Place; N or R to 8th Street. **Credit** AmEx, DC, MC, V.

One of the most consistently interesting theatres in the city. Dedicated to the production of New American playwrights and performers, the Public also presents new explorations of Shakespeare and the classics and hosts a late-night Performance Artist Series. There are five stages here, so there's a constant circulation of short-run theatrical goodies, not to mention a real thespie hangout scene in the lobby.
*Disbled: access, toilets.*

### Lincoln Center

*150 West 65th Street, between Amsterdam & Columbus Avenues (362 7600).* **Train** 1 or 9 to 66th Street. **Credit** AmEx, DC, Discover, MC , V.

The Lincoln Center Complex houses two amphitheatre-shaped drama venues: the 1040-seat Vivien Beaumont Theater and the 290-seat Mitzi E Newhouse Theater. Both receive some government subsidies, but the bulk of their revenue is derived from earnings and corporate and foundation gifts. Expect polished productions of new and classic plays, with many a big-name actor.
*Disbled: access, toilets.*

### La Mama ETC

*74A East 4th Street, between the Bowery & Second Avenue (475 7710).* **Train** 6 to Astor Place. **Credit** AmEx, MC, V.

Well into its fourth decade, La Mama is a solid fixture of the city's dramatic life, bringing in a great many international groups as well as home-grown talent. It's a cavernous space where they do all kinds of extraordinary things with the stage: sometimes it takes up most of the theatre. Boundaries are tested here and new ground broken. Sam Shepard's *Angel City* and Harvey Fierstein's *Torchsong Trilogy* started here.
*Disbled: access.*

### Manhattan Theater Club

*City Center, 131 West 55th Street, between Sixth & Seventh Avenues (645 5590/581 1212 box office).* **Train** D or E to Seventh Avenue. **Credit** AmEx, MC, V.

Manhattan Theater Club has gathered a reputation for sending young plays off to Broadway. The club's two theatres, in the City Center, are the 299-seat Mainstage Theater, which offers four plays by both new and established playwrights each year, and the more flexible Stage II Theater, a venue for works in progress, workshops and staged readings. One of the club's highlights is its Writers in Performance series, a forum for readings, performances and lectures. Guest speakers have included Isabel Allende, Eric Bogosian and Toni Morrison.

### The Orpheum

*126 Second Avenue, at East 8th Street (477 2477).* **Train** 6 to Astor Place. **Credit** AmEx, MC, V.
This 340-seat East Village theatre has staged a wealth of riveting, contentious, thought-provoking dramas. Past productions include *Little Shop of Horrors,* David Mamet's *Oleanna* and the British bang-on-a-can dance troupe Stomp.

## Off-Off Broadway

It's here that the most innovative and daring are willing to experiment and expose, charm and shock. The technical definition of Off-Off Broadway is a show by performers who don't have to be card-carrying pros at a theatre with less than 100 seats. Pieces may combine various media, including music, dance, mime, film, video and the typically New York performance monologue, a strange combination of theatre and psychotherapy.

But Off-Off Broadway is not restricted to experimental work. At venues like **Theater for the New City**, and from companies such as the **Jean Cocteau Repertory Company**, you'll also see classical and more traditional contemporary plays.

The list that follows is by no means exhaustive. It provides a few examples of venues, some of them well off the beaten track, where the visitor is most likely to see what's on the cutting edge of the New York theatre and performance scene. Tickets will be in the $5-$15 range. As venues are often shared with the city's vibrant dance and cabaret scenes, *see also chapters* **Dance** *and* **Cabaret**.

### Bouwerie Lane Theatre

*330 the Bowery, at Bond Street (677 0060).* **Train** F to Second Avenue; 6 to Bleecker Street. **Credit** AmEx, MC, V.
Bouwerie Lane Theatre, housed in the old cast iron German Exchange Bank (built in 1876), was founded in 1973 by Eve Adamson. It's the resident theatre of the Jean Cocteau Repertory Company, and probably the New York's only theatre with a standing company devoted to producing the classics in rep. Recent works include Dostoevsky's *The Idiot, Much Ado About Nothing* and *Waiting For Godot.*

### CBGB's 313 Gallery

*313 the Bowery, at 2nd Street (677 0455).* **Train** 6 to Bleecker Street. **No credit cards.**
Next door to the famous punk venue is this multi-purpose space which is a consistently good bet for a wide range of unusual theatre and other small-scale performance.
*Disbled: access.*

### Dixon Place

*258 the Bowery, at Houston & Prince Streets (219 3088).* **Train** 6 Bleecker Street; B, D, F or 6 to Broadway/Lafayette. **Tickets** $5-$8; half-price students, senior citizens. **No credit card**s.
One of New York's hidden treasures, which is actually just someone's loft put to good use. This bohemian stronghold provides a venue for emerging artists and performances dealing with controversial issues ignored by the mainstream. Programming consists mainly of works in progress, including performance art, music, dance, plays and poetry readings. On the first Tuesday of the month there's an open stage.

### En Garde Arts

*(941 9793).*
A theatre company which uses sites of cultural history as a backdrop, presenting site-specific theatre throughout the city. It gave us Stonewall 25 on the scene of the original riots and in 1995 produced JP Morgan Saves the Nation entirely on Wall Street.

### HERE

*145 Sixth Avenue, at Dominick Street (647 0202).* **Train** C or E to Spring Street. **Tickets** $10-$15. **Credit** AmEx, MC, V.
A busy arts centre with two well-used theatres, a gallery and a great coffee lounge, HERE puts on entertaining shows by both small theatre groups and cabaret acts. In winter it is the home of the Coney Island Sideshow, a gruesome collection of latter-day circus performers.
*Disbled: access, toilets.*

### The Kitchen

*512 West 19th Street, between Tenth & Eleventh Avenues (255 5793).* **Train** A, C or E to 23rd Street. **Credit** AmEx, MC, V.
A small, experimental theatre whose season runs from September to May and presents an eclectic repertoire of video, readings, music, dance and performance art. A good place to see real edgy New York experimentation.
*Disbled: access, toilets.*

### The Performing Garage (Wooster Group)

*33 Wooster Street, between Broome & Grand Streets (966 3651).* **Train** A, C or E to Canal Street. **No credit cards.**
The Performing Garage features the works of the Wooster Group, whose members include Richard Foreman, Willem Dafoe and Spalding Gray, who developed his well-known monologues, among them *Swimming to Cambodia*, here. As well as presenting deconstructed versions of the theatre classics, the venue hosts a visiting artists series, dance performances and monthly readings.

### Performance Space 122

*150 First Avenue, at East 9th Street (477 5288).* **Train** 6 to Astor Place; N or R to 8th Street. **Credit** AmEx, MC, V.
One of New York's most exciting venues, housed in an abandoned school on the Lower East Side. It's a non-profit-making arts centre for experimental performance, with two theatres presenting dance, performance, music, film and video. Artists develop, practise and present their work here, and it has provided a platform for Whoopi Goldberg, Meredith Monk and Phillip Glass. PS122 continues to shock with such pieces as Ron Athey's self-mutilations.

### Naked Angels Theater Company

*(727 0020).*
This co-operative company of nearly 40 actors and playwrights (including Joe Mantello and Jon-Robin Baitz) stages plays on the cautious (ie entertaining) side of the cutting edge – moderately experimental theatre and performance events.

### Theater for the New City

*155 First Avenue, at 9th Street (254 1109).* **Train** L to First Avenue. **Tickets** $5-$10. **No credit cards.**
Hard-hitting political dramas are performed by the Living Theater group in one of the building's four theatres. Recent productions have included Lawrence Holder's *M,* exploring Nelson and Winnie Mandela's marriage, and Jean Claude van Italie's version of Bulgakov's *Master and Margarita.*
*Disabled: access.*

# In Focus

# Business

***How to win friends and influence people in the business capital of the world.***

Laurie Anderson once pointed out that American men have only two role models: the salesman and the cowboy. This is the first important lesson in doing business in New York. Everyone you'll deal with is one part foot-in-the-door, fast-talking encyclopaedia seller, and in equal measure a maverick, self-interested pioneer.

For the salesman part, American selling culture is deeply ingrained in the society, so even the most timid-seeming person will be able to switch on all the convincing bluster of a PT Barnum at a moment's notice. The need for cutting through the patter is learnt fast. When it comes to the cowboy, it's that fierce individualist streak which explains why everyone is so ambitious. People work hard here – very hard – but only because they want to reach the top rung and kick their boss off the ladder. Most people's dreams are of financial autonomy, and even the most deeply embedded corporate cog is only turning up at the office in the hope of one day running the whole machine.

What's more, everyone is awarded (or gives themself) a grandiose title. There may be only three people in a company, but rest assured, one is President and CEO, another is Chairman and the office boy is Vice President, Caffeine Distribution.

Corporate hospitality may be impressive here, but don't think it runs wild. Nowhere more so than in New York is the chestnut about free lunches to be heeded. And note that New Yorkers will generally avoid drinking at lunchtime.

Business language here is full of metaphors of sport and war. There are winners and losers, negotiations are the battlefield or the ballpark, and a scream of triumph is released after a deal is made (and the 'opponent' lies 'defeated'). The lesson is that there is no room for 'understandings'. If something has gone unmentioned, don't assume it will be done as you'd like. Specifically, don't be embarrassed about talking 'bottom-line' terms. No-one is ashamed to talk about money. If *you* are, they will stiff you – get it in writing. Equally, brag loud and long about what you can offer, otherwise they'll listen to someone else. As any salesperson will tell you: it's as easy as ABC: Always Be Closing.

## Information

The business world's bible, the *Wall Street Journal* (75¢), contains all the up-to-date facts and figures on US and worldwide commerce. In-depth business profiles are published in *Fortune* ($4.50) and *Forbes* ($5) magazines; *Inc* ($3) is a glossy, monthly mag which makes business seem like fun. You'll find many more business mags at newsstands.

### Dow Jones Report

*(976 4141).* **Open** 24 hours recorded information.

### New York Chamber of Commerce and Industry

*Battery Park Plaza, between State & Whitehall Streets (493 7500).* **Train** 6 to 33rd Street. **Open** 9am-5pm Mon-Fri.
The Chamber gives advice on local needs and provides market information. The NYC Partnership organises training programmes.

### NYC Department of Business Services

*110 William Street, near Fulton Street (696 2442).* **Train** 2, 3, 4, 5, J or M to Fulton Street. **Open** 9am-5pm Mon-Fri.
Free advice on starting and running a business, plus information about grants or loans the city may be able to offer.

## Stock Exchanges

### Commodities Exchange Center

*4 World Trade Center, off Liberty Street (938 2000).* **Train** 1, 9, N or R to Cortlandt Street. **Open** 10.30am-3pm Mon-Fri.
There are four exchanges here: the New York Mercantile Exchange, which trades crude oil, heating oil, unleaded gasoline, platinum and palladium; the Coffee, Sugar, and Cocoa Exchange; the New York Cotton Exchange, which trades cotton, frozen orange juice and a number of indexes; and the Commodities Exchange, which trades in precious metals. The Visitors' Gallery is on the ninth floor.

### International Monetary Market

*67 Wall Street, near William Street (363 7000).* **Train** 4 or 5 to Wall Street. **Open** 9am-5pm Mon-Fri.
This is the marketing division of IMM; the head office is in Chicago. No trading is done here but the office will help anyone from brokers to institutional users and give advice on applications for futures and options .

### New York Stock Exchange

*11 Wall Street, at Broad Street (656 3000).* **Train** 4 or 5 to Wall Street. **Open** 9.30am-4pm Mon-Fri.
The New York Stock Exchange still operates as an auction house: specialist market makers and brokers trade on the floor trying to make a megabuck. More than 10,000 institutions with $3 trillion in securities under management have access to and use the Exchange's market system. The visitors' center is at 20 Broad Street (*see chapter* **Sightseeing**).

### Taylor Rafferty

*205 Lexington Avenue, at 32nd Street (889 4350).* **Train** 6 to 33rd Street. **Open** 9am-5pm Mon-Fri.
The London Stock Exchange's New York office.

*Looks like the guy on the left got stiffed – literally.*

## Libraries

*See also chapter* **Museums**.

### Brooklyn Public Library (Business Branch)

*280 Cadman Plaza West, at Tillary Street (1-718 722 3333).* **Train** 2 or 3 to Jay Street/Borough Hall. **Open** 10am-8pm Mon; 1-8pm Tue; 1-6pm Thur; 10am-6pm Fri; 10am-5pm Sat. **Admission** free.
This library, which is separate from the NYPL (*see below*) is a great resource for all types of US business information.

### NYPL Science, Industry and Business Library

*188 Madison Avenue, at 34th Street (930 0709).* **Train** 6 to 33rd Street. **Admission** free.
This is the New York Public Library's new state-of-the-art business library. It opened in May 1996 at a cost of $100 milion, and contains a vast range of business and industry resources, many of which are accessible online either on terminals within the building or by calling in.

## Importing & Exporting

### US Customs Service (New York Region)

*6 World Trade Center, off Vesey Street (466 4547 general customs information/1-800 697 3662 recorded information).* **Train** 1, 9, N or R to Cortlandt Street. **Open** 8am-4.30pm Mon-Fri.
The source of all information on importing goods and merchandise. Staff deal with enquiries on import duty, licences and restricted goods. There's a useful magazine, *Importing into the US* ($5.50).

### US Department of Commerce

*6 World Trade Center, off Vesey Street (264 0634).* **Train** 1, 9, N or R to Cortlandt Street. **Open** 9am-5pm Mon-Fri.
Regulates and encourages exports from the US.

### Department of Economic Development (International Division)

*1515 Broadway, between West 44th & West 45th Street (827 6217).* **Train** 1, 2, 3, 7, 9, N or R to Times Square. **Open** 9am-5pm Mon-Fri.
Information on development in business, industry, tourism and exports.

### Governor's Office of Regulatory Reform

*Alfred E Smith Building, 17th floor, PO Box 7027, Albany, NY 12225 (1-518 486 3292/1-800 342 3464).* **Open** 9am-5pm Mon-Fri.
Free information on which – if any – New York State permits are necessary for starting up a particular business. Topics covered include incorporation, employment, taxes, and business standards.

## Services

### Aircraft Charter

#### Executive Fliteways

*2111 Smithtown Avenue, between Railroad & Lakeland Avenues, Ronkonkoma (1-516 588 5454/1-800 533 3363).* **Open** 24 hours daily. **Credit** AmEx, MC, V.
Operates a call-up flight service within the US and Canada; flights can be arranged in 90 minutes. Flights are all chartered, so you pay for a return journey. New York to Washington in a turbo-prop costs $2289; New York to Boston is $1928; New York to Chicago is $7063 in a Lear jet or $15,500 in a Gulfstream.

### Air Couriers

#### DHL Worldwide Express

*2 World Trade Center, off Liberty Street (1-800 225 5345).* **Train** E to World Trade Center. **Open** 8.30am-8.30pm daily. **Credit** AmEx, DC, Discover, MC, V.
Will send a courier to pick up from any address in New York

City, or you can deliver packages to its offices and drop-off points in person. No cash transactions. As well as its international services, DHL also operates a messenger service within New York.

### Federal Express

*Various locations throughout the city, call with your zip code for the nearest; or, for free pick-up at your door (777 6500/1-800 247 4747 international).* **Open** 24 hours daily. **Credit** AmEx, DC, Discover, MC, V.
An overnight letter to London costs $28.50. Next-day delivery in the US by 10.30am is $15.50; by 3pm it's $12.50. You save $2.50 off the cost of the package if you deliver it to a Federal Express office. Packages for overseas should be dropped off by 3pm, packages for destinations in the US by 10.30pm.

## Cellular Phones

### InTouch USA

*(391 8323/1-800 872 7626).* **Open** 9am-5pm Mon-Fri. **Credit** AmEx, Discover, MC, V.
The city's largest cellular communication rentals company, renting out phones by the day, week or month. It also hires out satellite pagers (with nationwide coverage), portable faxes, and walkie talkies and can deliver.

## Computers

There are hundreds of computer dealers in Manhattan. If you are considering a purchase you should buy from out of state to avoid sales tax. Many out-of-state dealers advertise in New York papers and magazines.

### Kinko's

*24 East 12th Street, between University Place & Fifth Avenue (924 0802).* **Train** 4, 6, L, N or R to Union Square. **Open** 24 hours daily. **Credit** AmEx, Discover, MC, V.
A very efficient and friendly place to use computers and copiers. It has several workstations and design stations including IBM and Apple and all the major programmes. Colour output is available. There are many branches throughout Manhattan.

### User-Friendly

*139 West 72nd Street, between Columbus & Amsterdam Avenues (580 4433).* **Train** 4, 5 or 6 to 86th Street. **Open** 9am-10pm Mon-Thur; 9am-6pm Fri; 11am-7pm Sat; noon-8pm Sun. **Credit** AmEx, MC, V.
Macs and PCs with all the big programmes, in three locations. Some have more facilities than others so check first.
**Branches**: 1477 Third Avenue (535 4100); 401 Sixth Avenue (675 2255).

### USPC

*360 West 31st Street, between Eighth & Ninth Avenues (594 2222).* **Train** A, C or E to 34th Street. **Open** 9am-5pm Mon-Fri. **Credit** AmEx, MC, V.
Rent by the day, week, month or year from a range of computers, sytems and networks from IBM, Compaq, Apple and Hewlett Packard for use on your premises. Delivery within one hour is possible.

## Desktop Publishing

### Fitch Graphics Ltd

*130 Cedar Street, near World Trade Center (619 3800).* **Train** 1, 9, N or R to Cortlandt Street. **Open** 8am-11pm Mon-Fri. **Credit** AmEx, MC, V.
A full-service desktop publishing firm, with colour laser output and all pre-press facilities. They work with both Apple Mac and IBM platforms and have a bulletin board for customers to deal with them online.
**Branch**: 25 West 45th Street (840 3091).

## Mailbox Rental

### Mail Boxes Etc USA

*1173 Second Avenue, between 61st & 62nd Streets (832 1390).* **Train** 4, 5 or 6 to 59th Street; N or R to Lexington Avenue. **Open** 9am-6pm Mon-Fri; 10am-5pm Sat. **Credit** AmEx, MC, V.
Mailbox rentals, mail forwarding, overnight delivery, packaging and shipping, as well as a phone-message service, photocopying and faxing, telexing, typing and business printing. There are nearly 30 other locations in Manhattan, many offering 24-hour access to mailboxes.

## Messenger Services

### Breakaway

*43 Walker Street, at Church Street (219 8500).* **Train** 1 or 9 to Canal Street. **Open** 7am-7pm Mon-Fri; by arrangement Sat, Sun. **Credit** AmEx, Discover, MC, V.
A highly recommended city-wide messenger service with 25 messengers who promise to pick up within 15 minutes of a request and deliver within the hour.

### Jefron Messenger Service

*141 Duane Street, between West Broadway & Church Street (964 8441).* **Train** A or C to Chambers Street. **Open** 7am-6pm Mon-Fri. **No credit cards.**
Jefron specialises in import/export documents.

## Office Rental

### Bauer Business Communications Centre

*New York Hilton, 1335 Sixth Avenue, at West 54th Street (262 1329).* **Train** B, Discover, F or Q to Rockefeller Center. **Open** 7am-5pm Mon-Fri. **Credit** AmEx, Discover, MC, V.
Rent fully equipped desk space here, with full back-up office services. Workstations have a PC, printer and a selection of useful software. Office services include word-processing, faxing, photocopying, transcription, office equipment rental and a reference library.

### World-Wide Business Centres Inc

*575 Madison Avenue, between East 56th & East 57th Streets (605 0200).* **Train** 4, 5 or 6 to 59th Street; N or R to Lexington Avenue. **Open** 9am-5.30pm Mon-Fri. **Credit** AmEx.
The company provides furnished, staffed offices, from half a day to long term, equipped with fax, computers and phones. Fax and secretarial services are available without rental of office space.

## Photocopying

### Servco

*130 Cedar Street, opposite 2 World Trade Center (285 9245).* **Train** 1, 9, N or R to Cortland Street. **Open** 8.30am-5.30pm daily. **No credit cards.**
Photocopying, offset printing, blueprints and binding services are available.
**Branches**: 9 Murray Street (285 8207); 56 West 45th Street (575 0991).

### Kinko's Copy Center

*24 East 12th Street, between Fifth Avenue & University Place (924 0802).* **Train** 4, 5, 6, L, N or R to Union Square. **Open** 24 hours daily. **Credit** AmEx, Discover, MC, V.

Copying, faxing and passport photos, plus on-site use of Apple Macs ($12 per hour, $24 for big graphics machines, charged by the minute).
**Branches**: six in Manhattan, call for your nearest.

## Postal Service

### US General Post Office

*380 West 33rd Street, at Eighth Avenue (967 858 5/330 4000 Postal Information Line).* **Train** A, C or E to Penn Station. **Open** 24 hours daily, for all services except money orders and registered mail (open 8am-6pm daily).
This is the city's main post office. Call the number to find out your nearest branch office, or call the information line to hear a vast menu of recorded postal information.

## Printing

### Dependable Printing

*Flatiron Building, 175 Fifth Avenue (533 7560).* **Train** N or R to 23rd Street. **Open** 8.30am-6pm Mon-Fri; 10am-4pm Sat. **Credit** MC, V.
Offset and colour printing, large-size Xerox copies, colour laser printing, binding, rubber stamps, typing, forms, labels, brochures, flyers, newsletters, manuscripts, fax service, transparencies and more.
**Branch**: 257 Park Avenue South (982 0353).

### Directional Printing Services

*280 Madison Avenue, between 39th & 40th Streets (213 6700).* **Train** 4, 5 or 6 to 42nd Street. **Open** 9.30am-5.30pm Mon-Fri. **No credit cards**.
Specialises in assisting international firms and offers foreign language typesetting and printing, as well as graphic design, brochures, reports, etc.

## Secretarial Service

### Dial-a-Secretary

*521 Fifth Avenue, between 43rd & 44th Streets (348 9575).* **Train** 4, 5, 6, 7 or S to Grand Central. **Open** 24 hours by appointment only. **No credit cards**.
Can deal with any typing or word-processing job at any hour of day or night. One page of single-spaced typing costs from $8.90; double-spaced is $3.95; the hourly rate starts at $35.
**Branch**: 126 East 83rd Street, between Lexington & Park Avenues (348 8982).

## Telegrams

### Western Union

*(1-800 325 6000).* **Open** 24 hours daily. **Credit** MC, V.
Use the number to arrange telegrams at any time of day or night and the service is charged to your credit card. If you want to write it in person, or don't have a credit card, the service is available in branches at various locations throughout the city; phone the number above to find the location of your nearest branch. Western Union can organise international money transfersfrom accounts in the States to other countries but not vice versa.

## Telephone Answering Service

### Messages Plus

*1317 Third Avenue, between 75th & 76th Streets (879 4144).* **Train** 6 to 77th Street. **Open** 24 hours daily. **Credit** AmEx, MC, V.
Messages Plus provides telephone answering services, with specialised (eg medical, bilingual) receptionists if required, and plenty of different ways of delivering your messages; credit card order-taking services with the option of a number, call-forwarding, database generation and pager rental. Faxes and telexes sent and delivered.

## Translation

### All Language Services

*545 Fifth Avenue, at 45th Street (986 1688/fax 986 3396).* **Train** 4, 5, 6, or 7 to Grand Central. **Open** 24 hours daily. **Credit** MC, V.
Will type or translate documents in any of 59 languages and provide interpreters.

## Writers

### Dial-A-Writer

*1501 Broadway, betweeen 43rd & 44th Streets, suite 302 (398 1934/24-hour answering service).* **Train** 1, 2, 3, 7, 9, N or R to Times Square. **Open** 9am-5pm Mon-Fri. **No credit cards**.
A referral service for professional writers, researchers, editors and publicists.

# Trade Conventions

For further information get in touch with the **New York Convention & Visitors Bureau** (397 8222). New York's two principal convention centres are:

### Jacob K Javits Convention Center

*655 West 34th Street, at Eleventh Avenue (216 2000).* **Train** 1, 2, 3, 9, A, C or E to Penn Station.

### New York Passenger Ship Terminal

*711 Twelfth Avenue, near 55th Street (246 5451).* **Train** C or E to 50th Street.

## Lobby lizards

Those with offices based outside of the city regularly come to town and set up shop in some of New York's most prestigious hotel lobbies. The *New York Times* has described them as the city's 'business homeless' but they are certainly shrewd. For the cost of ordering snacks or beverages, they conduct their meetings, sometimes back-to-back all day, in luxurious splendour. Favourites among this crowd are the **Stanhope** (995 Fifth Avenue/288 5800), the **Marriott Marquis** (1535 Broadway/398 1900) and the **Royalton** (44 West 44th Street/869 4400). Another, more informal option is the **Jonathan Morr Espresso Bar** (133 Greene Street, between Prince and Houston Streets/260 8962), a huge loft given over to a coffee bar, where you can sit for hours, receiving company or poring over reports, without being moved on like a vagrant. Food, beer and wine is served here too.

# Children

***For the big kid in all of us; or for the ones you've brought with you.***

There are plenty of opportunities for children's fun in New York; just ask the ten-year old who 'borrowed' a subway train in 1995, driving it so perfectly from station to station that no-one noticed until he was stopped by the automatic brakes when he went too fast. Luckily, there are plenty of more legal ways to keep children amused, and if you thought New York was one of the last places on earth to bring your offspring, you're in for a pleasant surprise. There is a wealth of child-centred entertainment, services and cultural and educational activities here.

Most of the sights and sounds of New York will amaze the younger visitor without any extra effort on your part. And in addition, there are theatre companies, museums, puppet shows, places for picnics, ice skating rinks, boat rides, tram rides, horse rides, zoos and more. And if you've had enough, there are armies of accomplished babysitters waiting to relieve you of your parental duties.

Friday's *New York Times* and the weekly *Time Out New York* and *New York* magazines have good listings of children's activities. Call or write to the **Alliance for the Arts** for your copy of the *Kids Culture Calendar*, which lists highlights of upcoming events: 330 West 42nd Street, Suite 1701, New York, NY 10036 (947 6340). Also read the monthly *Parentguide Magazine*, 13th floor, 419 Park Avenue South, New York, NY 10016 (213 8840). This is distributed free in libraries, playcentres and other children-intensive places and gives details of events in New York City, Long Island and New Jersey.

For more ideas, *see also chapters* **Sightseeing**, **New York by Season**, **Trips Out of Town** *and* **Sport & Fitness**.

## Entertainment

### Amusement Parks

The bigger theme parks are outside the city. *See chapter* **Trips out of Town**.

#### Astroland

*1000 Surf Avenue, at West 8th Street, Coney Island, Brooklyn (1-718 372 0275).* **Train** B, D, F or N to Stillwell Avenue/Coney Island.

The famous Coney Island amusement park is rather run down and tacky now, but a delight to children nonetheless. In the summer months you can still ride the frightening Cyclone roller coaster, watch a snake-charmer, bite into a Nathan's famous hotdog and enjoy the sun and sand.

*New York is a surprisingly child-friendly city.*

## Circuses

### Big Apple Circus

*(268 0055).* **Tickets** $10-$49. **Credit** only for Ticketmaster bookings (307 4100).

This fairly traditional circus spends its time touring various locations throughout the five boroughs of New York City, including a regular winter season (Oct-Jan) in Damrosch Park at Lincoln Center and spring dates in various city parks. Performances usually last about two hours, and are based around a theme – the Wild West one year, the monkey kingdom another, for instance.

*Disabled: access by arrangement (268 2500).*

### Ringling Brothers and Barnum & Bailey Circus

*Madison Square Garden, Seventh Avenue, between 31st & 33rd Streets (465 6741).* **Train** A, C or E to Penn Station. **Season** April. **Tickets** $8.50-$25. **Credit** AmEx, DC, Discover, MC, V.

The original American circus, this has three rings and plenty to keep you glued to your seat. It's understandably popular, so reserve seats well in advance.

### Cirque Du Soleil

*Battery Park, near World Financial Center.* **Tickets** $10-$50.

This famous and unmissable French-Canadian spectacle visits New York once a year, usually in spring. It's a mesmerising blend of traditional nineteenth-century circus (with no animals) and truly innovative contemporary performance sensibilities. The music, costumes and staging are pure fantasy; younger children might find the stylish clowns a little grotesque. Tickets are snapped up fast.

## Libraries

Many of the New York Public Library's branch libraries have special children's centres and activities such as story-telling and workshops. They are also good places to meet other parents and find out about other children's activities. Consult the library's *Events for Children* pamphlet, published monthly and available free at all branches.

### Central Children's Room

*Donnell Library, 20 West 53rd Street, between Fifth & Sixth Avenues (621 0636).* **Train** E or F to 53rd Street/Fifth Avenue. **Open** 12.30-5.30pm Mon, Wed, Fri, Sat; 9.30am-5.30pm Tue; 12.30-8.pm Thur; 1-5pm Sun. Closed Sun during Aug.

This is the best children's room, with regular story-telling, films, workshops and exhibitions.

## Museums & Exhibitions

Children of all ages will enjoy many of the museums listed in *chapter* **Museums**, especially the new dinosaur hall at the **Natural History Museum**; the **Liberty Science Center**; the **New York Hall of Science**; the **Museum of the Moving Image**; the **Seaport Museum**; and the **Sea, Air & Space Museum**, which is a fabulous collection of military and maritime junk housed on an aircraft carrier, including space capsules, a submarine and the world's fastest spy plane. Of the museums listed in *chapter* **New York by Neighbourhood**, try the **Fire Museum (Downtown)**, the **Police Academy Museum (Midtown)**, **Queens County Farm Museum** and **Staten Island Children's Museum** at Snug Harbor (both in **Outer Boroughs**). In addition the following are especially suitable for children.

### Brooklyn Children's Museum

*145 Brooklyn Avenue, at St Mark's Avenue, Brooklyn (1-718 735 4432 recorded information).* **Train** 3 to Kingston Avenue (5 blocks from St Mark's Place); B44, B45, B47 or B65 bus. **Open** *winter* 3-5pm Wed-Fri; noon-5pm Sat, Sun; *summer* noon-5pm Mon, Wed-Sun. **Admission** suggested donation $4. **No credit cards**.

Founded in 1899, this was the world's first museum designed specifically for children. You reach the exhibits via a walkway leading through a long, water-filled tunnel. In the music studio children can dance on the keys of the walk-on piano and play around with synthesizers. The Boneyard features an elephant's skeleton, along with other old bones. There's a hands-on exhibit about measurements and dimensions plus a greenhouse and special workshops. The museum, which reopens after renovations in spring 1996, can be a little difficult to get to.

*Disabled: access, toilets.*

### Children's Museum of Manhattan

*212 West 83rd Street, between Broadway & Amsterdam Avenue (721 1234).* **Train** 1 or 9 to 86th Street. **Open** 1.30-5pm Mon, Wed, Thur; 10am-5pm Fri-Sun. **Admission** $5; $2 senior citizens; free under-2s. **Credit** AmEx, Discover, MC, V.

The star exhibits include the Brainatarium, an animated multi-media presentation about the brain, with games, push-buttons and puzzles; and the World of Pooh, where Winnie the Pooh's forest is recreated. The whole purpose of the museum is allowing children to discover things for themselves, hence the fascinating hands-on exhibits, which include making cartoons and artworks, using Morse code, playing television camera operator and designing cityscapes with lights. Films, workshops and a listening library are also offered, and there is an outdoor environmental centre. There are no eating facilities, but you may leave for lunch and return on the same ticket.

### Sony Wonder Technology Lab

*550 Madison Avenue, between 55th & 56th Streets (833 8100).* **Train** 4, 5 or 6 to 51st Street. **Open** 10am-6pm Tue-Sat; noon-6pm Sun (schools groups have priority 10am-noon Tue-Fri). **Admission** free.

A treasure chamber of the latest digital toys built around six hands-on interactive workstations. There's a bit of a 'what do you want to do when you grow up' feel about the whole thing, as kids play at medical diagnosis, remix songs, design computer games or edit a music video (Billy Joel's *River of Dreams*). Best of all is the High Definition Interactive Theater, where the audience directs the action in an exciting video adventure. Next door, the retail centre is also fun; costumes and props from Sony-related movies are displayed alongside the Walkmans and VCRs. Get here early – by 2.30pm at weekends, or you might not get in.

*Disabled: access, toilets.*

## Music

### The Little Orchestra Society

*Florence Gould Hall, 55 East 59th Street, between Park & Madison Avenues (704 2100).* **Train** 4, 5 or 6 to 59th Street. **Performances** throughout the year; call to check. **Tickets** from $15. **Credit** MC, V.

Orchestral concerts for children aged three to 12, combining classical music with dance, puppetry, theatre and mime. In addition, the New York Philharmonic regularly presents programmes tailored to children's tastes here.

*Disabled: access by arrangement.*

## Puppets

### Puppet Company

*31 Union Square West, at 16th Street & Union Square, loft 2B (741 1646).* **Train** 4, 5, 6, B, D, L, N or R to 14th Street. **Shows** *Oct-April* 1pm, 3pm Sun. **Tickets** $7.50. **No credit cards.**

Both marionettes and hand puppets are used in a variety of performances, including musical variety and playlets. Performances are suitable for three- to seven-year-olds and last about 50 minutes; reservations are essential.

### Puppetworks

*338 Sixth Avenue, at 4th Street, Brooklyn (1-718 965 3391).* **Train** M, N or R to Union Street. **Shows** 12.30pm, 2.30pm Sat, Sun. **Tickets** $7 adults; $5 children 2-18. **No credit cards.**

The company, which uses marionettes exclusively, was established way back in 1938. Four different shows, such as *Aladdin, Puss in Boots* and *The Sorcerer's Apprentice*, are offered each year and are suitable for children over four.

*Disabled: access, toilets.*

### Swedish Cottage Marionette Theater

*Central Park (988 9093).* **Train** B or C to 81st Street. **Performances** 10.30am, noon Tue-Fri (for groups of 10 or more); noon, 3pm Sat. **Tickets** $5 adults; $4 children 2-12. **No credit cards.**

The company, run by New York's Department of Parks and Recreation, has been touring New York's parks and boroughs since 1938, but only opened this theatre in 1972. Performances run from December to June and include such classics as *Rumpelstiltskin* and *The Magic Flute*. *Cinderella* is scheduled for 1996. The theatre is in the middle of the park.

*Booking essential. Disabled: access.*

## Theatres

### Miss Majesty's Lollipop Playhouse

*Grove Street Playhouse, 39 Grove Street, near Seventh Avenue South (741 6436).* **Train** 1 or 9 to Christopher Street. **Performances** 1.30pm, 3pm Sat, Sun. **Tickets** $7; free under-2s. **No credit cards.**

The company's forte is comic adaptations of the classics for children between two and nine. It's very popular, so reservations are essential.

*Disabled: access, toilets.*

### Open Eye Theater

*(977 2639).* **Tickets** prices vary; discounts for children, students & senior citizens. **No credit cards.**

A touring company which stages plays for 'multi-generational audiences' ie suitable for anyone over eight. *Souvenirs of Old New York* and *A Woman Called Truth*, about the life of Sojourner Truth, are typical. Open Eye has no permanent performing address.

### Tada! Youth Ensemble

*120 West 28th Street, between Sixth & Seventh Avenues (627 1732).* **Train** 1 or 9 to 28th Street. **Performances** *Jul, Aug* noon, 2pm Mon, Wed, Fri, Sat; *Dec, Jan* 7.30pm Fri; 1pm, 3pm Sat, Sun. **Tickets** $12 adults; $6 under-16s. **No credit cards.**

Musicals performed by and for children. The cast is made up of kids aged 8 to 17, drawn from auditions of young hopefuls from city schools. The shows are usually musical comedies, specially commissioned by Tada! They are extremely well presented and very popular.

*Booking advisable. Disabled: access, toilets.*

### Thirteenth Street Repertory Company

*50 West 13th Street, between Fifth & Sixth Avenues (675 6677).* **Train** 4, 5, 6, L, N or R to Union Square. **Performances** 1pm Sat; 1pm, 3pm Sun. **Tickets** $7. **No credit cards.**

Four-year-olds and up enjoy musicals and fairytales lasting about 45 to 50 minutes.

*Booking advisable. Disabled: access, toilets.*

# Outdoor Activities

## Botanical Gardens

### Discovery Center

*Brooklyn Botanic Gardens, 1000 Washington Avenue, Brooklyn (1-718 622 4544).* **Train** 2 or 3 to Eastern Parkway/Brooklyn Museum. **Open** *winter* 8am-4.30pm Tue-Fri; 10am-4.30pm Sat, Sun; *summer* 8am-6pm Tue-Fri; 10am-6pm Sat, Sun. **Admission** free.

A great place for children to learn about plants and nature through some inventive exhibits, such as a synthetic oak tree which has doors and holes hiding creatures that live in a real tree trunk. Potting benches are at child height.

*Disabled: access, toilets.*

### New York Botanical Gardens

*Southern Boulevard, at 200th Street, Bronx (1-718 817 8705).* **Train** 4, C or D to Bedford Park, then BX26 bus. **Open** *April-Oct* 10am-6pm Tue-Sun; *Nov-March* 10am-4pm Tue-Sun. **Admission** $3 adults; $1 seniors, children 6-16; free under-6s; free to all Wed, 10am-noon Sat. **No credit cards.**

The Gardens run weekend workshops, in which children aged five to 10 can grow plants, make horticultural crafts and eat some of the garden produce.

*Disabled: access, toilets.*

## Central Park

Central Park is a wonderland for all ages, but there are plenty of places and programmes specially aimed at children. Call Arts in the Park (988 9093) for information on an extensive programme of children's arts events and activities here and in other parks throughout the city. In addition, the Urban Park Rangers (360 2774) organise guided walks and other activities. The Parks Department activities hotline (360 3456) provides a huge menu of events of all kinds in all the New York parks.

Children's focal points in the park include **Belvedere Castle**, overlooking the Belvedere Lake; and the **Dairy**, an information centre with an interactive exhibition on the history of the park. Near the Dairy are the beautiful antique carousel (90¢ a ride) and the **Heckscher Playground**, which has handball courts, horseshoes, several softball diamonds, a puppet theatre, a wading pool and a crèche. For more about Central Park, *see chapter* **Sightseeing**.

### Charles A Dana Discovery Center

*110th Street, near Fifth Avenue (860 1370).* **Train** 2 or 3 to 110th Street. **Open** *mid Feb-mid Oct* 11am-5pm Tue-Sun; *mid Oct-mid Feb* 11am-4pm Tue-Sun. **Admission** free.

Now Harlem Meer has been fully restored and stocked with fish, you can take the kids fishing here. Poles and bait are given out (accompanying adults need to show ID) to children over 5 until 90 minutes before closing time. Other activities include birdwatching and painting. Environmental workshops run from 1pm to 3pm on Saturday and Sunday.

*Disabled: access, toilets.*

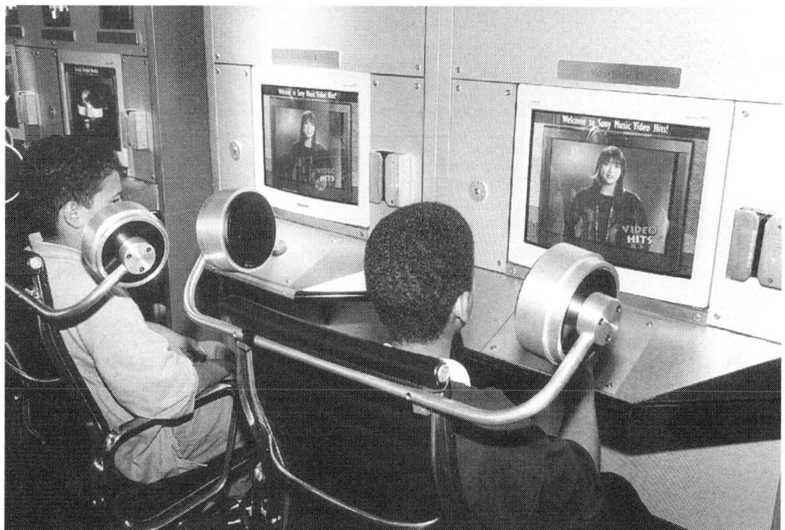


*Kids get to direct their own videos at the* **Sony Wonder Technology Lab**. *See page 273.*

### Conservatory Water

*77th Street, near Fifth Avenue.* **Train** 6 to 77th Street.
Every weekend there are model yachts racing around this ornamental pond, and when the boatmaster is around you can hire one of the remote-controlled vessels for $7 to $10 an hour and have a go at some wind-powered fun. Be warned – it's not as speedily responsive as Nintendo.

## Zoos

### New York Aquarium for Wildlife Conservation

*Surf & West 8th Street, Brooklyn (1-718 265 3405).* **Train** D to West 8th Street. **Open** 10am-5pm daily. **Admission** $6.75 adults; $3 children 2-12, senior citizens. **No credit cards.**
See the famous Beluga whale family, a re-creation of the Pacific coastline and an intriguing glimpse of the kind of things that manage to live in the East River, plus the usual dolphin show and some truly awesome sharks. It's right by the sea, a mere stroll from the action of Coney Island, making the area a good destination for a family day out.
*Disabled: access, toilets.*

### Bronx Zoo

*Corner Fordham Road & Bronx River Parkway, Bronx (1-718 367 1010 recorded information).* **Train** 2 or 5 to Bronx Park East. **Open** 10am-5pm Mon-Fri; 10am-5.30pm Sat, Sun. **Admission** $6.75 adults; $3 children 2-12, senior citizens; free under-2s; free to all Wed. **No credit cards.**
The animals live in reconstructed natural habitats, in one of the world's largest and most magnificent zoos. Inside is the Bronx Children's Zoo, with lots of domestic animals to pet plus wonderful exhibits which let the viewer see the world from the viewpoint of the animal – whether it's perching or climbing. Camel and elephant rides are organised from April to October. *See also chapter* **Sightseeing**.
*Disabled: access, toilets.*

### Central Park Wildlife Conservation Center

*Fifth Avenue, at 64th Street (861 6030).* **Train** B or Q to Lexington Avenue. **Open** *Apr-Oct* 10am-5pm Mon-Fri; 10.30am-5.30pm Sat, Sun; *Nov-Mar* 10am-4.30pm daily. **Admission** $2.50 adults; $1.25 seniors; 50¢ children 3-12.
This small but perfectly formed zoo is one of the highlights of the park. You can watch seals frolic both above and below the waterline, crocodiles snapping at monkeys swinging on branches of tropical forest and huge polar bears swimming endless underwater laps like true neurotic New Yorkers.

# Services

## Babysitting

Playgroups and other daycare options are licensed by the Bureau for Day Camps and Recreation, an office of the New York City Department of Health, 65 Worth Street between Broadway and Church Street (334 3187). The bureau publishes a booklet listing approved groups. They range from free to expensive.

### Avalon Nurse Registry & Child Service

*162 West 56th Street, near Seventh Avenue (245 0250).* **Train** B or Q to 57th Street. **Open** 8am-6pm Mon-Fri; 9am-8pm Sat, Sun. **No credit cards.**
Get yourself a full- or part-time nanny or a casual babysitter from Avalon. Live-in nursing care for newborn babies starts from $130 a day; the live-out fee is $15 an hour (eight hours minimum). Casual babysitting costs $7-$10 an hour, depending on the baby's age, plus travelling expenses.

### Baby Sitters' Guild

*60 East 42nd Street, near Madison Avenue, suite 912 (682 0227).* **Train** 4, 5, 6 or 7 to Grand Central. **Open** 9am-9pm daily. **No credit cards.**

Long- or short-term babysitters cost $10-$20 an hour and speak 16 languages between them. You can get away with as little as an hour's notice, and the service is 24 hour.

### WonderCamp Entertainment

*27 West 23rd Street, between Fifth & Sixth Avenues (243 1111).* **Train** F, N or R to 23rd Street. **Open** 10am-6.30pm Mon-Thur, Sun; 10am-8pm Fri, Sat. **Admission** $4.95 Mon-Fri; $5.49 Sat, Sun. **Credit** AmEx, MC, V.
Indoor entertainment with an American camp theme, for children aged one to ten. The snag is, an adult has to accompany them, but once inside they are kept thoroughly busy. *Bookings not accepted. Disabled: access, toilets.*

## Hairdressers

### Short Cuts

*104 West 83rd Street, between Columbus & Amsterdam Avenues (877 2277).* **Train** 1, 9, B or C to 86th Street. **Open** 10am-6pm Tue-Sat. **No credit cards.**
Take the stress out of getting your child's hair cut by taking him/her along to Short Cuts, where kids get special treatment to make them feel at ease. The average cut is $18. *Reservations advisable.*

# Shopping

## Clothes

### Gap Kids

*60 West 4th Street, at Broadway (643 8995).* **Train** B, D, F, N, Q or R to 34th Street. **Open** 10am-9pm Mon-Sat; 10am-8pm Sun. **Credit** AmEx, Discover, MC, V.
All the clean, simple, well-made clothes you'd expect from Gap, but in sizes for children of all ages. There are 11 branches throughout the city. Call for details.

### Me-Ki Kids

*149 Avenue A, between 9th & 10th Streets (995 2884).* **Train** 6 to Astor Place. **Open** 1-7pm Mon-Fri; noon-6pm Sat, Sun. **Credit** MC, V.
Seriously trendy clothes for kids. Some accessories, too.

### San Francisco Clothing

*975 Lexington Avenue, between 70th & 71st Streets (472 8740).* **Train** 6 to 68th Street. **Open** 11am-7pm Mon-Fri; 11am-6pm Sat. Closed Sat summer. **Credit** AmEx, MC, V.
This successful clothing store opened a kids section when owners Mindy and Howard Partman reproduced. The clothes are comfortable and stylish and include T-shirts, bandanna dresses, booties and more.

### Shoofly

*465 Amsterdam Avenue, near West 83rd Street (580 4390).* **Train** 1, 9, B or C to 86th Street. **Open** 11am-7pm Mon-Sat; noon-6pm Sun. **Credit** AmEx, MC, V.
Boaters, caps, fleece-lined boots, braces, gloves and shoes are to be found among the Flintstones furniture, tree trunks and animal footprints that comprise the decor.

## Toys

### The Enchanted Forest

*85 Mercer Street, between Spring & Broome Streets (925 6677).* **Train** 6 to Prince Street. **Open** 11am-7pm Mon-Sat; noon-6pm Sun. **Credit** AmEx, DC, Discover, JCB, MC, V.
A gallery of books, beasts and handmade toys in a magical forest setting.

### FAO Schwartz

*767 Fifth Avenue, at 58th Street (644 9400).* **Train** 4, 5 or 6 to 59th Street; E or F to Lexington Avenue. **Open** 10am-7pm Mon-Wed, Fri, Sat; 10am-8pm Thur; 11-6pm Sun. **Credit** AmEx, DC, Discover, JCB, MC, V.
The famous toy store has been supplying New York kids with toys and games since 1862 and stocks more stuffed animals than you could imagine in your worst nightmares, as well as kites, dolls, games, miniature cars, toy soldiers, bath toys, and so on. This is the closest you can come to Disneyland in New York.

### Penny Whistle

*1283 Madison Avenue, near East 91st Street (369 3868).* **Train** 4, 5 or 6 to 86th Street. **Open** 9am-7pm Mon-Fri; 10am-6pm Sat; 11am-7pm Sun. **Credit** AmEx, MC, V.
Children are encouraged to play and experiment with the unusual and educational toys.
**Branches**: 448 Columbus Avenue (873 9090).

### B Shackman & Co

*85 Fifth Avenue, at 16th Street (989 5162).* **Train** 4, 5, 6, B, D, L, N, Q or R to 14th Street/Union Square. **Open** 9am-5pm Mon-Fri; 10am-4pm Sat. **Credit** AmEx, MC, V.
Old-fashioned toys, miniatures, dollshouse furniture, wind-up toys and flick books make this nostalgic for adults and fascinating for kids.

### Tiny Doll House

*1146 Lexington Avenue, between 79th & 80th Streets (744 3719).* **Train** 6 to 77th Street. **Open** 11am-5.30pm Mon-Fri; 11am-4pm Sat. Closed Sat Aug. **Credit** AmEx, MC, V.
Everything in the shop is tiny: miniature furniture and furnishings for dollshouses, including chests, beds, kitchen fittings and cutlery. Adults love it.

### Toys 'R' Us

*A&S Plaza, 1293 Broadway, at 34th Street (594 8697).* **Train** B, D, F, N, Q or R to 34th Street. **Open** 9am-9pm Mon, Fri; 9am-8pm Tue, Wed, Sat; 9am-9.30pm Thur; 11am-7pm Sun. **Credit** AmEx, Discover, MC, V.
Clothing is generally cheaper than elsewhere and quite fashion-conscious. The infant and toddler department carries everything from blankets and booties to rattles, sleepwear and playwear. The toy section is just as comprehensive: if it's brightly coloured, plastic and loud, then it'll be here. There's also a sports department and a new book section.
**Branch**: 24-32 Union Square East (674 8697).

# Workshops & Classes

### Arts & Crafts Workshops

Branches of the New York Public Library regularly hold free workshops that are both informative and entertaining. Call its Office of Children's Services (340 0906).

### Dance

*See chapter* **Dance** for a list of schools offering classes.

### Modern Art Workshops

*Museum of Modern Art, 11 West 53rd Street, between Fifth & Sixth Avenues (708 9400).* **Train** B, D, F or Q to Rockefeller Center. **Tours** 10-11am Sat. **Admission** $8 adults; $5 students, senior citizens; free under-16s. **No credit cards.**
Guided family tours examining the highlights of MoMA. The entrance is at the John Noble Recreation Center, 18 West 54th Street. Highly recommended.

### 92nd Street Y

*1395 Lexington Avenue, between 91st & 92nd Streets (415 5650).* **Train** 4, 5 or 6 to 86th Street or 96th Street.
The incredibly busy 92nd Street Y runs a vast array of classes and programmes for kids, from music lessons to mini-camps. There are classes to make you a better parent, too.

# Gay New York

***You're here, you're queer, where should you go? A guide to gay New York in all its variety.***

If you're gay you'll love New York. And guess what – New York will love you back. In a survey to mark 1994's Gay Games, *New York* magazine found that a sizable majority of New Yorkers were accepting and appreciative of the cultural contributions of the city's enormous gay population. New York is proud of its fags.

The scene is still centred around the **West Village**, with Christopher Street and Sheridan Square offering a homo ground zero (marked during Dinkins' mayorship by some hideous sculptures of same-sex couples). However, this area has been so gay for so long that it verges on self-parody. The bars here are full of out-of-towners, and while some are fun, especially the many cabaret joints, many are just too commercial.

And as the West Village has grown increasingly predictable, other areas have flourished. The **East Village** is such a menagerie that gender and sexuality are never an issue, and several bars here are worth a visit. **Uptown**, too, has its gay highlights: Broadway, and Columbus Avenue between Columbus Circle and 86th Street, are affluent strips of bars and shops, full of clean-cut young things.

But the city's most vibrant gay region is now **Chelsea**. Its clubs and bars provide a busy nightlife for its ever-growing stock of guppies, extending the freedom area of the West Village north well beyond 30th Street, with boutiques, galleries and gyms springing up to take advantage of the pink population's spending power.

Throughout most of Manhattan, meeting people is no problem. Street-level eye contact is a way of life, and a visitor should find it easy to turn a glance into a conversation. For more serious old-style open-air cruising head to the **Ramble** in Central Park (near the 81st Street entrance on Central Park West) or the disused piers along the **Hudson River** (at the end of Christopher Street). This is the domain of the 'Pier Queens', where the vogueing houses and 'banjee boys' (gay homeboys in baggy hip-hop gear indistinguishable from their straight cousins) hang out rain or shine. Making friends here is just about the only way to find out about the innumerable Paris Is Burning-style vogueing balls which happen in secret locations throughout the five boroughs. Finally, don't miss out on your chance to visit the exclusively gay beaches of Fire Island, an easy day trip away from the city (*see box page 283*).

The best day to be gay and in New York is undoubtedly **Gay Pride**, held on the last Sunday in June every year, when thousands of out and proud people revel in the liberty this incredible city affords. Another key event is **Wigstock**, on Labor Day, an East Village festival of drag transposed to the aforementioned piers. For more details *See chapter* **New York by Season**.

AIDS has claimed the lives of thousands of New Yorkers, and there are many support groups for this and for the other problems touching the gay community. **The Lesbian and Gay Community Services Center** is the focus for hundreds of protest and social/cultural groups and is a great place to get your bearings. Activism is strong in New York, but so is hedonism, and the same people who man crisis hotlines by day will be pounding the dancefloor by night.

Apart from much of the activism and the larger events, the men's and women's gay scenes are fairly separate in New York, and as a reflection of that, this section is really for men only. Refer to *chapter* **Lesbian New York** for information on the NY lesbian scene.

## Accommodation

### Aaah Bed and Breakfast

*PO Box 2093, New York, NY 10108 (246 4000/fax 765 4229).* **Rates** $60-$150 in private homes; $45 singles, $85 doubles in hotel. **Credit** (for hotel and deposit only) AmEx, MC, V.

A reservation service which places guests in private homes and allows you to request a particular neighbourhood and specify gay or lesbian accommodation. It also has a bed and breakfast hotel on West 58th Street.

### Chelsea Mews Guest House

*344 West 15th Street, NY 10011, between Eighth & Ninth Avenues (255 9174).* **Train** A, C or E to 14th Street/Eighth Avenue. **Rates** *single* $75; *double* $75-$150. **No credit cards**.

Built in 1840, this guest house has accommodation for gay men and women. The rooms are comfortable and well furnished; no smoking throughout and no meals are served.

### Chelsea Pines Inn

*317 West 14th Street, NY 10014 (929 1023/fax 645 9497).* **Train** A, C, E or L to 14th Street/Eighth Avenue. **Rates** $55-$85 (doubles only). **Credit** AmEx, DC, Discover, MC, V.

A conveniently central location near the West Village and Chelsea for gay and lesbian guests. The rooms are clean and comfortable; some have private bathrooms and all have radio, television and air conditioning.

*A happy couple celebrates at Gay Pride, probably the best party in the world.*

**Colonial House Inn**
*318 West 22nd Street, between Eighth & Ninth Avenues, NY 10011 (243 9669/1-800 689 3779).* **Train** C or E to 23rd Street. **Rates** $65-$150. **No credit cards.**
A beautiful townhouse inn on a quiet street in Chelsea run by gay men for a gay and lesbian clientele. It's a great place to stay though some of the cheaper rooms are quite small. There's a lovely living room for coffee and lounging.

**Incentra Village House**
*32 Eighth Avenue, between 12th & Jane Streets, NY 10014 (206 0007).* **Train** A, C, E or L to Eighth Avenue/14th Street. **Rates** $99-$109. **Credit** AmEx, MC, V.
Two cute townhouses perfectly situated in the West Village make up this guest house run by gay men. The rooms are spacious and interestingly decorated, though not always hitting the heights of cleanliness.

## Bars

Most bars in New York offer themed nights, drinks specials and happy hours, and the gay ones are no exception. Don't be shy, remember to tip the bartender and carry plenty of business cards. Hardly any places actively bar women but some may cultivate an unwelcoming atmosphere. *See also chapters* **Bars & Cafés** *and* **Cabaret**.

### Chelsea

**Champs**
*17 West 19th Street, between Fifth & Sixth Avenues (633 1717).* **Train** N or R to 23rd Street. **Open** 4pm-4am daily. **No credit cards.**
Busy and crowded, this gay sports bar combines the big games on big screens with big guys dancing on the big bar. Jock heaven.

**Rawhide**
*212 Eighth Avenue, at West 21st Street (242 9332).* **Train** C or E to 23rd Street. **Open** 8am-4am daily. **No credit cards.**
Rope 'em and ride 'em at this friendly, dimly lit neighbourhood bar, a favourite with the denim-wearing Wild Western crowd and full of barfly regulars. If you need a top-up after a long night of clubbing, it opens early in the morning.

**The Spike**
*120 Eleventh Avenue, at West 20th Street (243 9688).* **Train** C or E to 23rd Street. **Open** 9pm-4am daily. **No credit cards.**
The Spike lives up to most visitors' preconceptions of a New York gay bar. It's a former hardcore leather venue with a few old clones hanging around that has otherwise been taken over by a new and more varied generation of cruisers and pre-clubbers. The weekend scene retains an easy-going and fairly traditional leather flavour.

**Splash**
*50 West 17th Street, between Fifth & Sixth Avenues (691 0073).* **Train** 1 or 9 to 18th Street. **Open** 3pm-4am daily. **No credit cards.**
A huge and friendly place, dressed up in the tiles and styles of a shower room. Meet hundreds of fresh-faced gay yuppies direct from the city's gyms, watch the splendidly entertaining custom-made videos or oggle the go-go boys as they take showers in cubicles above the bar. From 5pm to 9pm it's executive hour, when the music is lower and you get to drink fresh juice or sip an aromatic cappuccino.

### East Village

**The Bar**
*68 Second Avenue, at East 4th Street (674 9714).* **Train** F to Second Avenue. **Open** 4pm-4am daily. **No credit cards.**
After a decade in business, this is one of the more established gay bars in town, refreshingly beery and brimming with

pick-up potential. At night, it gets crowded with young locals. It's also known as an ACT-UP (Aids Coalition to Unleash Power) hangout, and activists abound.

### Crowbar

*339 East 10th Street, between Avenues A & B (420 0670).* **Train** 6 to Astor Place; L to First Avenue; N or R to 8th Street. **Open** 10pm-4am daily. **Admission** $3 after 11pm. **No credit cards.**
This popular East Village bar consistently wins the best gay bar accolade, thanks to its eclectic crowd and great themed parties almost every night. Hot porn videos, a dark back-room and performances, DJs and live music. Very crowded and well worth the visit. The owners are opening up a second bar in Chelsea.

### Tunnel Bar

*116 First Avenue, at East 7th Street (777 9232).* **Train** 6 to Astor Place; N or R to 8th Street; F to Second Avenue. **Open** 2pm-4am daily. **Admission** free. **No credit cards.**
A small, fun place with a mixed crowd of cruisey locals, run by gay comedian Mr Ed. Lights are low to assist in meeting and greeting, and on Tuesdays and Thursdays porno movies are shown all day. There's pool and pinball, and themed evenings like Friday's underwear night: press those Calvins.

### Wonder Bar

*505 East 6th Street, at Avenue B (777 9105).* **Train** F to Second Avenue. **Open** 8pm-4am daily. **No credit cards.**
Very East Village, with lots of kitschy decorations and a menagerie of loyal customers, including a fair few women. A tiny back room provides diversion, but the main event here is good-natured fun.

## West Village

### Hangar

*115 Christopher Street, at Hudson Street (627 2044).* **Train** 1 or 9 to Christopher Street. **Open** 3pm-4am Mon-Fri; 2pm-4am Sat; 1pm-4am Sun. **No credit cards.**
If you insist on visiting one of the bars along the gay tourist-trap Christopher Street/Sheridan Square axis, this is about the best choice. Lively music nights, weekend strippers and a clientele that includes locals as well as curious visitors.

### The Lure

*409 West 13th Street, at Ninth Avenue (741 3919).* **Train** A, C or E to 14th Street/Eighth Avenue. **Open** 8pm-4am daily. **No credit cards.**
A new addition to the scene, this lively fetish bar attracts a broad and energetic crowd. On Wednesdays it hosts Pork, a fun and sexy occasion when the raucous music and the hot bodies encourages the crowd to act like pigs. A strict dress code (leather, rubber, uniforms, no cologne...) ensures no casual hangers-on.

### Stonewall

*53 Christopher Street, at Seventh Avenue (463 0950).* **Train** 1 or 9 to Christopher Street/Sheridan Square. **Open** 4pm-4am daily. **No credit cards.**
Landmark bar, where the 1969 gay rebellion against police harassment took place. Back then the Stonewall was actually in the building next door. Ask the bartender to talk you through the story. Good pool table and a friendly crowd, but more a historical monument than an exciting bar.

### Uncle Charlie's

*56 Greenwich Avenue, between Sixth & Seventh Avenues (255 8787).* **Train** 1 or 9 to Christopher Street/Sheridan Square. **Open** 3pm-3am Mon-Thur, Sun; 3pm-4am Fri, Sat. **No credit cards.**
The Big Mac of gay bars, Uncle Charlie's attracts a wide and diverse crowd of men from all over New York. Women are

welcome. It's one of the best places to go after work and is usually busy on week nights. A good place to start.

## Midtown & Uptown

### Stella's

*266 West 47th Street, between Broadway & Eighth Avenue (575 1680).* **Train** C or E to 50th Street. **Open** noon-4am daily. **Admission** free Mon-Wed; $5 after 8pm Thur-Sun (includes one drink). **No credit cards.**
'It looks like Atlantic City' was one comment about this newly opened pick-up bar, filled to bursting with hustlers of all descriptions. It's sleazy, cruisey and it's all for sale, and there's the added bonus that Stella, the matriarchal dyke who runs the joint, will step in to adjudicate any complaints about the trade you may encounter.

### The Works

*428 Columbus Avenue, between West 80th & West 81st Streets (799 7365).* **Train** B or C to 81st Street. **Open** 2pm-4am daily. **Admission** free. **No credit cards.**
The major hangout for young gay men on the Upper West Side attracts a decidedly yuppity crowd. On Sunday afternoons there's a popular beer blast: between 6pm and 1am you pay $5 to drink all the beer you can manage. All contributions go to the Gay Men's Health Crisis.

# Clubs

Almost all the clubs in New York have gay nights; many of those listed are one-nighters rather than venues. There are also a large number of fund-raising parties and other one-off events worth looking out for. For more clubs, the majority of which are gay-friendly, as well as more information about some of the ones below, *see chapter* **Clubs**.

## Dance Clubs

### Bump!

*Sundays at the Palladium, 126 East 14th Street (473 7171).* **Train** 4, 5, 6, L, N or R to Union Square. **Open** 11pm-4am. **Admission** $12. **No credit cards.**
After Club USA (its original location) closed, Bump relocated to the cavernous hulk of the Palladium and is now the city's biggest gay night, with top DJs, plenty of PAs from the stars of music and porn, and mini-parties off in the other rooms, including the Hispanic ¡Ai Papi! upstairs and the foam-filled Engine Room down below.

### Café Con Leche

*Sundays at Expo, 124 West 43rd Street, between Sixth Avenue & Broadway (819 0377).* **Train** 1, 2, 3, 9, N or R to Times Square. **Open** 10pm-4am. **Admission** $15. **No credit cards.**

A must-see for those unfamiliar with the world of vogueing houses, banjee boys and other unique New York phenomena. Salsa and merengue on one floor for the Latinas and deep deep house for the rest of the very mixed crowd.

### Columbia Dance

*Earl Hall, Columbia University, Broadway, at 116th Street (854 1488).* **Train** 1 or 9 to 116th Street. **Open** 10pm-2am first Fri & third Sat of the month. **Admission** $5 Friday; $6 ($4 with student ID) Sat. **No credit cards.**

On the first Friday and third Saturday of every month, the prestigious Ivy League university hosts the Columbia Dance. Hang out with the thousands of graduate and undergraduate students who enjoy this ever-popular venue and maybe even help one of them with his homework.

### Edelweiss

*578 Eleventh Avenue, at 43rd Street (629 1021).* **Train** A, C or E to 42nd Street. **Open** 8.30pm-4am daily. **Admission** $15 (free before 9pm). **No credit cards.**

A long-running and fun-loving congregation of transvestites, transsexuals, drag queens, fags, dykes and their admirers.

### Gotham Rodeo

*Saturdays at 39 West 19th Street, between Fifth & Sixth Avenues, 5th floor (570 7399).* **Train** B, D, F, N, Q or R to 23rd Street. **Open** 8pm-3am. **No credit cards.**

A gay hoe-down with both kinds of music: country and western. Cowboys and bareback riders two-step the night away in this dusty old rock venue. Lessons are available from 8-9pm.

### King

*579 Sixth Avenue, between 16th & 17th Streets (366 5464).* **Open** 4pm-4am daily. **Train** F or L to 14th Street/Sixth Avenue. **Admission** free-$10. **No credit cards.**

It evolves from a bar to a club at different stages of the week, but most, if not all nights are firmly gay-oriented. There's an upstairs 'private attic' to help you attain that regal feeling. Events include cabaret, Wednesday's amateur strip contests, go-go gods and the ever-popular Milk, now here on Mondays.

### Lick-It

*Wednesdays at Limelight, 47 West 20th Street, at Sixth Avenue (807 7850).* **Train** F, N or R to 23rd Street. **Open** 10pm-4am. **Admission** $15. **No credit cards.**

On most nights there'll be a gay enclave in at least one of the Limelight's many rooms, and the club's semi-permanent collection of gender freaks and ravenous omnisexuals ensures a good (though frantic) time. Lick It! is famous for its hot-sex ambience, with go-go boys, peepshows and a young student population. Res-Erection on Fridays is another cruisey night. Use the 20th Street entrance or you might get stuck in the straight parts of the club.

### Roxy

*515 West 18th Street, between Ninth & Tenth Avenues (645 5156).* **Train** A, C, E or L to Eighth Avenue/14th Street. **Open** 8pm-2am Tue, Wed; 10pm-4am Fri, Sat. **Admission** $10 Tue; $12 Wed (skate rental $5-$10); $15 before midnight, $17 after, Fri, Sat. **No credit cards.**

After a tired year or two, the Roxy is back in business as a fine weekend favourite. The Saturday nights attract a packed and cruisey crowd of gym bunnies, amid go-go boys and drag queens. Tuesday's Rollerballs is a gay rollerdisco.

### Saint at Large

*(674 8541 information line)*

The Saint Club, with its huge aluminium domed interior, was where New York's gay men first enjoyed dancefloor freedom. It was also where they felt the initial impact of AIDS. The club closed several years ago, but the decadent clientele keeps the memory alive with a series of four huge parties each year: the Black Party, White Party (referring not to skin colour, but to the mood of the event), Hallowe'en and New Year's Eve. Massive and very New York.

### Sound Factory Bar

*12 West 21st Street, between Fifth & Sixth Avenues (206 7770).* **Train** F, N or R to 23rd Street. **Open** 11pm-5am daily. **Admission** $5-$12. **No credit cards.**

All nights are gay or very homo-friendly.

### Sugar Babies

*Mondays at The Bank, 225 East Houston Street, at Essex Street (477 8427).* **Train** F to Second Avenue. **Open** 11.30pm-4am daily. **Admission** $5. **No credit cards.**

Live drumming on the dancefloor spices Troy Parrish's fine deep house, as a young mixed crowd of East Villagers and art students gyrate in this former financial institution.

### Tunnel

*220 Twelfth Avenue, at 27th Street (695 7292).* **Train** C or E to 23rd Street. **Open** 10pm-10pm Sat; 11pm-noon Sat. **Admission** $15-$20. **No credit cards.**

The big shake-up was the arrival of Junior Vasquez, who had his own personal sound system and DJ booth built in order to steer the crowd through Tunnel Saturdays. He brought a sizeable section of the Factory family with him, though they're diluted by a motley crew of upstarts from the Tunnel's more pretentious past. *See chapter* **Clubs**.

### Twilo (formerly Sound Factory)

*530 West 27th Street, at Tenth Avenue.* **Train** C or E to 23rd Street/Eighth Avenue. Details unavailable at time of press.

It's a new era for the famous club, with a hostile takeover bringing new management after its notorious closure. It remains to be seen who will call this home, but what's certain is that it's the best venue in the city for losing yourself in dance, and that lots of Factory children have been staying home waiting for it to re-open. *See chapter* **Clubs**.

## Sex Clubs

Today's licensed and monitored safe-sex clubs are a far cry from the infamous bath-houses that preceded them, but New York has several places where dancing and drinking are truly secondary activities. For more, including specialist tastes and private, unrestricted possibilities, see *HX* magazine's 'Getting Off' section.

### East Side Club

*227 East 56th Street, between Second & Third Avenues (888 1884/753 2222 recorded information).* **Train** N or R to Lexington Avenue. **Open** 24 hours daily. **Admission** $25 a year; $10 a day. **No credit cards.**

In style at least, reminiscent of the New York steam-houses of days gone by, though the action these days is considerably tamer. However, there are showers, saunas, plenty of opportunities to make contact and private rooms for $14. Photo ID is required.

### Zone DK

*540 West 21st Street, between 10th & Eleventh Avenues (no phone).* **Train** C or E to 23rd Street. **Open** 11pm-8am Fri, Sun; 1pm-8am Sat. **Admission** $8. **No credit cards.**

DK stands for Dog Kennel, and there's one above the bar, along with a wide range of torture/restraint equipment (hire paddles from the bartender). Hot dancers, huge porn screens,

*Pointing the way to the West Village epicentre of New York's gay scene.*

good music (though no-one dances), body shavers and the focus: a well-monitored sex room. Saturdays at The Zone are straight-ish S&M occasions until 3am, after which it's gay again. No alcohol.

## Restaurants

Few New York restaurants would bat an eye at same-sex couples enjoying an intimate dinner: *see chapter* **Restaurants**. The neighbourhoods mentioned above have hundreds of great restaurants which are de-facto gay places, and many that are gay owned and operated. Here are a few of the gayest places in town.

### David's Pot Belly Stove Café

*94 Christopher Street, at Seventh Avenue (242 8036).* **Train** 1 or 9 to Christopher Street. **Open** 24 hours daily. **Average** $20-$25. **Credit** AmEx, DC, MC, V.
In the heart of Christopher Street, this old and famous gay restaurant serves solid home cooking in a romantic English country cottage atmosphere.

### Nadines

*99 Bank Street, at Greenwich Street (924 3165).* **Train** 1 or 9 to Christopher Street. **Lunch** noon-4pm Mon-Fri; 11am-4pm Sat, Sun. **Dinner** 5.30pm-midnight Mon-Thur, Sun; 5.30pm-1am Fri, Sat. **Average** $15-$20. **Credit** AmEx, DC, MC, V.
A cutesome campy retreat serving American cuisine in a bordello-style decor.

### Townhouse Restaurant

*206 East 58th Street, at Third Avenue (826 6241).* **Train** 1 or 9 to Christopher Street. **Brunch** noon-4pm Sun. **Lunch** noon-3.30pm Mon-Sat. **Dinner** 5-11pm Mon-Thur; 6-11pm Sun; 5pm-midnight Sat. **Average** $20. **Credit** AmEx, DC, MC, V.
A very elegant uptown haunt for true gentlemen and their gentlemen friends. Very gay but somehow full of old-world discretion. Decent and affordable continental food.

### Universal Grill

*44 Bedford Street, at Seventh Avenue South (989 5621).* **Train** 1 or 9 to Christopher Street. **Brunch** 11am-4pm Sat, Sun. **Lunch** 11.30am-3.30pm Mon-Fri. **Dinner** 6pm-midnight daily. **Average** $20-$25. **Credit** AmEx.
Great music, good food from the Californian healthy grill spectrum, with Eastern European influences, and more gay couples than youll see in any other eating establishment.

## Gyms

*See chapter* **Sport & Fitness** for more fitness facilities, including the YMCAs.

### American Fitness Center

*128 Eighth Avenue, at 16th Street (627 0065).* **Train** A, C, E or L to Eighth Avenue/14th Street. **Open** 6am-midnight Mon-Fri; 9am-9pm Sat, Sun. **Membership** $699 per year; $155 per month; $15 per day. **Credit** AmEx, DC, MC, V.
A recent addition to the Chelsea scene, this enormous place is barbell-bunny heaven. Vast and spotless, with 15,000sq ft of free-weight space and acres of cardiovascular machines.

### Chelsea Gym

*267 West 17th Street, at Eighth Avenue (255 1150).* **Train** A, C, E or L to 14th Street. **Open** 6am-midnight daily. **Membership** $399-$499 per year; $100 per month; $36 per week; $10 per day. **Credit** MC, V.
There are hundreds of gyms in New York, but this is one of the gayest and one of the few offering day rates. It's men-only, and there are three nautilus machines, loads of free weights and a sauna, steam room and showers.

## Information

### Publications

The *Village Voice* is more or less a gay paper in its outlook, and *Time Out New York* has excellent gay listings, but New York's true gay weeklies are *HX* (Homo Xtra), *Next*, which both include expansive listings for bars, dance clubs, sex clubs, restaurants, cultural events and group meetings, and loads of particularly funny personals; and *New York Native* and *Stonewall*, which offer more political coverage and serious articles. All these are free at gay venues and stores. National publications include *Out* ($3.95) and *The Advocate* ($3.95), both monthly. *New York Gayellow Pages* ($4.95), essential for planning a longer stay, provides a wide range of general information pertaining to the greater New York area. It's available at Oscar Wilde Memorial Bookstore.

## TV

There is an abundance of gay-related broadcasting, though as nearly all of it is on the public access cable channels there are confusing regional variations and you may not be able to watch on a hotel TV. Some of the funniest is to be found on Channel 35 (in most of Manhattan), which is where the infamous Robin Byrd hosts her *Men For Men* softcore show. Manhattan Neighbourhood Network (channels 16, 17, 34 and 69 on all Manhattan cable systems) has plenty of gay shows, ranging from drag queens enjoying their 15 minutes of fame to serious discussion programmes. *Next* and *HX* have good TV preview sections.

## Bookshops

Most New York bookshops have gay sections: *see chapter* **Shopping**.

### A Different Light

*151 West 19th Street, between Sixth & Seventh Avenues (989 4850).* **Train** 1 or 9 to Christopher Street/Sheridan Square. **Open** 10am-midnight daily. **Credit** AmEx, MC, V.
The biggest and best gay and lesbian bookstore in New York; great for browsing, and with plenty of free readings, film screenings and art openings. Useful bulletin boards with local information, and a cute café.

### Oscar Wilde Memorial Bookshop

*15 Christopher Street, between Sixth & Seventh Avenues (255 8097).* **Train** 1 or 9 to Christopher Street/ Sheridan Square. **Open** 11.30am-7.30pm daily. **Credit** AmEx, Discover, MC, V.
New York's oldest gay and lesbian bookshop, stocked to the brim, with plenty of discounts.

## Centres & Phone Lines

### Lesbian and Gay Community Services Center

*208 West 13th Street, between Seventh & Eighth Avenues (620 7310).* **Train** 1, 2, 3, F or L to 14th Street/Seventh Avenue. **Open** 9am-11pm daily.
Founded in 1983, the Center provides political, cultural, spiritual and emotional sustenance to the gay community. While it principally offers programmes and support for the city's residents, there's plenty to interest the visitor. You'll be amazed at the diversity of groups (more than 250) that meet here. It also houses the National Museum and Archive of Lesbian and Gay History.

### Gay Men's Health Crisis

*129 West 20th Street, between Sixth & Seventh Avenues (807 6664/807 6655 AIDS advice hotline 9am-8pm Mon-Fri; 9am-5pm Sat; recorded information menu at other times).* **Train** 1 or 9 to 23rd Street. **Open** 10am-6pm Mon-Fri.
This was the first organisation in the world to take up the challenge of helping people with AIDS. It has a three-fold mission: to push the government to increase services; to help those who are sick by providing services and counselling for them and their families; and to educate the public and prevent the further spread of HIV. There are 204 staff and 2200 volunteers. The support groups meet mainly in the evenings.

### Gay And Lesbian Switchboard

*(777 1800).* **Open** 24 hours daily.
A phone information service only. Callers who need legal help can be referred to lawyers, and there's information on bars, restaurants and hotels. Switchboard is especially good at giving advice to people who have just come out and to those who may be feeling suicidal. There are also apartment and job listings and details of all sorts of other gay and lesbian organisations.

### NYC Gay and Lesbian Anti-Violence Project

*647 Hudson Street, at Gansevoort Street (807 0197).* **Train** 1, 2 or 3 to 14th Street. **Open** 10am-8pm Mon-Thur; 10am-6pm Fri; switchboard open 24 hours daily.
Advice and support for the victims of anti-gay and anti-lesbian attacks. The project also provides advice on going to the police and works with the NYPD Bias Unit. Short- and long-term counselling are available.

## Fire Island

Over the years, Fire Island, a long thin strip of land off the southern coast of Long Island, has become the summer habitat of choice for New York's affluent gay men. One particular area has become synonymous with sun- and sea-worshipping queens, exclusively gay beaches, flamboyant parties and general seasonal extravagance. There are two destinations in particular to which the gay masses flock: **Cherry Grove** and **The Pines**. Most of the accommodation here is in private houses, many of which are rented out in timeshares. Make friends with the right person and you could land yourself an invite. Otherwise you might have to settle for a day trip as there is very little hostel/hotel accommodation, and what there is is fairly unpleasant. One exception to this rule is Pines Bed and Breakfast, on 1-516 597 6162.

### Getting There

By car or LIRR train from Penn Station to Sayville, then by passenger ferry. The station is about two miles from the ferry terminal and cabs are always around. There are between eight and 20 sailings a day, depending on the day and season. The ferry costs $7.50 round trip. If you're exceptionally well-heeled or in a tremendous hurry to hit the beach, there is a seaplane service which flies from 34th Street in Manhattan directly to Fire Island. The cost is around $150.
**Long Island Railroad (LIRR)** (1-718 217 5477 for schedules). **Tickets** $6-$9.
**Sayville Ferry Company** (1-516 589 0810 for schedules).
**North American Flying Service** (1-201 440 1941) for seaplane service.

# Lesbian New York

***The gay girl scene in New York is a long way behind the boys', but it's definitely catching up fast.***

*Cosying up on Christopher Street Pier, where gay women are out in force.*

All right, girlies, get out your walking, dancing, running gear, and get ready to take over the most fabulous city in the world. New York can be a tough town, especially for women, but if you use your common sense about keeping safe, and concentrate on having a good time, there should be very little to worry about. There are people running around, filling the streets till dawn, and you should be there too.

If Paris is for lovers, New York is for cruisers; the best way to see and be seen is to get out there and walk: everywhere. The lesbian scene is less integrated with the gay scene than it is in some cities, but dykes are definitely out and about in greater numbers than ever before. More and more, they can be seen in traditionally gay haunts like Christopher Street and Chelsea; these sometimes look more like 'Christine Street' and 'Chel-she'.

The Upper East Side and Brooklyn's Park Slope remain home to many hard-working yuppie lesbians; the East Village and Williamsburg in Brooklyn are fast being overrun with a new breed of arty, out loud and proud dykes. These punky radical femmes have their own parties, protests and parades, and are well represented in events organized by ACT UP and the Lesbian Avengers.

There are plenty of great bars and clubs for gals; you just have to know where and when to go. Boys still have the upper hand when it comes to dance clubs, though more and more women's spots are opening now. And plenty of twirly girls have decided: if you can't beat 'em, join 'em, so there's sure to be a female enclave stepping out on even the most hard-core buddy-boy dance floor.

It's a fantastic time for performance and theatre for women. The main women's performance space is **W.O.W Café** at 59 East 4th Street, between Second Avenue and the Bowery (460 8067), where you can see original, high-quality productions by women. Other spots to catch the hippest, freshest new performers are **PS122**, **HERE** and **Dixon Place**, which is lesbian-owned and -run. Cinemas like **Angelika**, **Cinema Village** and the **Quad** show the latest in foreign, experimental and gay and lesbian films; and Village cabarets, like **Eighty-Eights** and **The Duplex**, feature plenty of female performers, and not just show-tune-crooning fag-hags either. For details of all, *see chapters* **Theatre**, **Film** *and* **Cabaret**. *See also chapter* **Gay New York**.

## Accommodation

Some of the most affordable accommodation in Manhattan is exclusively for women. *See also chapters* **Accommodation** *and* **Gay New York**.

### Allerton Hotel for Women

*130 East 57th Street, at Lexington Avenue (753 8841).* **Train** 4, 5 or 6 to 59th Street; N or R to Lexington Avenue. **Rates** *single room* from $60. **No credit cards**.
This is an unfashionably decorated, clean, cheap and safe women-only hotel in a respectable but dull area. It's good for those on a budget or cautious students.

### Colonial House Inn

*318 West 22nd Street, at Eighth Avenue (243 9669/1-800 689 3779).* **Train** C or E to 23rd Street. **Rates** $65-$99. **No credit cards**.
A beautiful townhouse inn on a quiet street in Chelsea, run by gay men for a gay and lesbian clientele. It's a great place to stay, though some of the cheaper rooms are quite small. There's a lovely living room for coffee and lounging.

### East Village Bed and Breakfast

*Apt 6, 244 East 7th Street, at Avenue C (260 1865).* **Train** F to Second Avenue. **Rates** (bed & breakfast) *single* $50; *double* $75. **No credit cards**.
A small, friendly, women-only B&B deep in the bowels of the East Village, run by women. There are only two rooms here so early reservations are essential.

### Incentra Village House

*32 Eighth Avenue, between 12th & Jane Streets (206 0007).* **Train** A, C, E or L to Eighth Avenue/14th Street. **Rates** $99-$129. **Credit** AmEx, MC, V.
Two cute townhouses perfectly placed in the West Village make up this guest house run by gay men (gay women welcome). The rooms are spacious and interestingly decorated, though not for the cleanliness obsessed.
*Disabled: access, rooms.*

### Markle Residence for Women

*123 West 13th Street, between Sixth & Seventh Avenues (242 2400).* **Train** F or L to 14th Street/Sixth Avenue. **Rates** from $107 a week incl two meals (one month minimum); otherwise $60 per night. **Credit** MC, V.
Women-only Salvation Army accommodation in a nice Village location, the Markle has clean, comfortable rooms with telephone and private bathrooms.
*Disabled: access, rooms.*

## Going Out

### Bars

While the women's club scene has taken off recently, the number of bars for women has remained the same since the stone age, although there are a few new casual hangouts.

#### Boiler Room

*86 East 4th Street, between First & Second Avenues (505 0688).* **Train** F to Second Avenue. **Open** 4pm-4am daily. **No credit cards**.
A great new funky East Village hangout. It's mixed during the week with a major girl scene on Sundays: drag king performances, a pool table and cheap drinks every night.

#### Crazy Nanny's

*21 Seventh Avenue South, corner of Leroy Street (366 6312).* **Train** 1 or 9 to Christopher Street. **Open** 4pm-4am daily. **Credit** MC, V.
Old faithful. A loud neon disco lesbian bar, with a pool table downstairs and DJ and dancing upstairs. It's started to stage different events every night and sports a nicely diverse clientele. Straight men aren't strictly speaking allowed, but some nights the DJ will attract a mixed trendy crowd.

#### Henrietta Hudson

*438 Hudson Street, at Morton Street (243 9079).* **Train** 1 or 9 to Christopher Street. **Open** 3pm-4am Mon-Fri; 1pm-4am Sat, Sun. **Credit** AmEx, MC, V.
A watering hole for pretty girls with lots of hair, mostly from out of town. Women love it for cruising: it's laid out so you can eye up everyone at once, then make your choice and make a move. Thursday is singles night.

#### Julie's

*204 East 53rd Street, between Second & Third Avenues (688 1294).* **Train** 6, E or F to Lexington Avenue/51st Street. **Open** 5pm-at least midnight daily. **No credit cards**.
An elegant bar for professional women in search of the same, which will stay open as late as 4am if business is good. Hors d'oeuvres are served from 5-8pm.

#### Ruby Fruit

*531 Hudson Street, at Charles Street (929 3343).* **Train** 1 or 9 to Christopher Street. **Open** 3pm-2am Mon-Thur; 3pm-4am Fri, Sat; noon-2am Sun. **Credit** AmEx, DC, MC, V.
A beautiful and energetic mixed lesbian and gay bar with a varied programme of cabaret and music.

### Clubs

Great club nights are the holy grail of New York City. Something that's fabulous one week sucks the next, and so the search continues. These are the current lesbian hot spots, but don't panic if they're desolate dungeons in a few months' time: there are bound to be new nights and venues blossoming in their place. Most women-only nights and places are reasonably OK about accompanied men – especially if they are gay.

#### Café Tabac

*232 East 9th Street, between Second & Third Avenues (674 7072).* **Train** 6 to Astor Place. **Open** 5pm-1am daily. **Admission** free.
The upstairs room at Tabac remains the hot spot to meet and greet on a Sunday night. Few people eat, though there's

food available. Instead the girls table-hop or cruise the pool room. A high concentration of beauty, and plenty of celeb dykes out playing.

### Clit Club

*Fridays at Bar Room, 432 West 14th Street, between Ninth & Tenth Avenues (366 5680).* **Train** A, C, E or L to 14th Street/Eighth Avenue. **Open** 10pm-5am Fri. **Admission** $5.

The granny of girl nights is still rocking. With great DJs and bodacious go-go girls, CC is still packing them in every Friday night, offering deep house music with excursions into disco for lipstick Lolitas, motorcycle mechanics and anyone in between. Even accompanied men probably won't get in, except on Saturdays.

### Eden

*Saturdays at l'Udo 432 Lafayette Street, at 8th Street (388 0978).* **Train** N or R to 8th Street; 6 to Astor Place. **Open** 11.30pm-3am Sat. **Admission** $5.

This weekly theme party is the only place for young lovelies to be on a Saturday night. DJs, dancers and an upscale downtown crowd. Make pretty poses in the garden as well.

### Girl World

*Industria, 775 Washington Street, between Jane & West 12th Streets (366 1114/255 6915 party information).* **Train** A, C, E or L to Eighth Avenue/14th Street. **Admission** $10.

Formerly monthly, these great theme parties are now at random intervals. When they happen, they're easily the funnest girl nights in town. Themes have included Bond Girl and Spanking.

### Juicy

*at Buddha Bar, 150 Varick Street, at Vandam Street (255 4433).* **Train** 1 or 9 to Houston Street. **Open** 11pm-5am alternate Sundays. **Admission** $5 girls; $10 boys.

Girls, girls, girls!!! This hot night has professional strippers joined by enthusiastic amateurs for the girliest women's night going. It got celebrity overrun recently when Kate Moss and others decided to test the waters. Constantly changing and a really fun night to check out. Men must be accompanied by two or more girls to get in.

### Squeezebox

*Fridays at Don Hills, 511 Greenwich Street, at Spring Street (334 1390).* **Train** C or E to Spring Street. **Open** 10pm-4am Fri. **Admission** $10.

Squeezebox is New York's hippest, hottest drag/dyke rock and roll party. With great bands like Lunachicks and Tribe 8 performing, and tattooed go-go boys and girls gyrating on the bar, amid a super-mixed crowd you can count on seeing plenty of the hottest downtown dykes around.

### W.O.W. Bar

*(631 1102 information hotline).* **Open** 9.30pm-4am Fri. **Admission** $6-$10. **No credit cards**.

On Friday nights this women-only club heats up with go-go dancers, videos and the occasional themed event. The last Friday in every month is Fetish Friday, when resident dominatrix Mistress Leda does her thing. The organisers are also opening S.O.S. (Sex on Saturday). Call their hotline for details and of W.O.W's current home.

## Restaurants

There are no restaurants just for women, or even primarily for women, but here are a few of the nicer places where you can chat and chew in a woman-friendly atmosphere and be guaranteed that no-one will stare if you're on your own. *See also chapter* **Restaurants**.

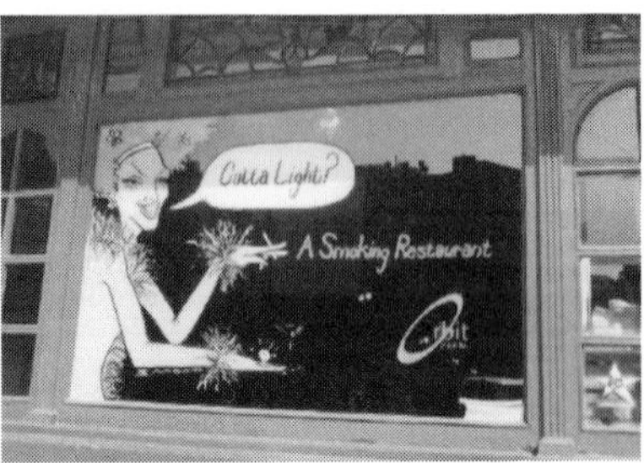


*Want a cig? Go into* **Orbit**.

### Brunch Buddies

*(1-800 2 FIND US).* **Open** 7-11pm Mon-Fri.

A food-inspired dating agency for lesbians and gay men.

### Big Cup

*228 Eighth Avenue, at 21st Street (206 0059).* **Train** C or E to 23rd Street. **Open** 7am-2am Mon-Thur, Sun; 7am-3am Fri, Sat. **No credit cards**.

A big bustling coffee joint with mis-matched chairs, magazines and a friendly, flirtatious clientele. Stay all day.

### Cowgirl Hall of Fame

*519 Hudson Street, at 10th Street (633 1133).* **Train** 1 or 9 to Christopher Street. **Lunch served** noon-4pm, **dinner served** 5-11pm, daily. **Credit** AmEx.

In name and spirit, this is a great girl place to eat, though it's not known as a particularly lesbian joint. It's a fun Tex-Mex restaurant with C&W music drifting from the jukebox and cowgirl memorabilia all over the walls. Women with kids come again and again because their high-chair and entertainment needs are amply met by the sympathetic single parent owner, Sherri, while the pre-club scene revs up on frozen margaritas at the steerhorn-decorated bar.

### Kaffeehaus

*131 Eighth Avenue, between 16th & 17th Streets (229 9702).* **Train** A, C, E or L to Eighth Avenue/14th Street. **Open** 11am-1am daily. **Brunch served** 11am-4pm Sat, Sun. **Dinner served** 6pm-midnight daily. **Credit** AmEx, DC, MC, V.

This cosy spot, owned by two fair frauleins, serves hearty fare as well as divine desserts, and – no surprise – kaffee.

### Orbit

*46 Bedford Street, at Seventh Avenue South (463 8717).* **Train** 1 or 9 to Houston Street. **Brunch served** 11am-3pm Sat, Sun. **Dinner served** 5.30-11.30pm Mon-Thur; 5.30pm-12.30am Fri, Sat. **Credit** AmEx, MC, V.

This is mainly a restaurant, but the bar at the lesbian- and gay-owned Orbit is always hopping, and it proudly sports its pro-smoking policy, with a cartoon drag queen proclaiming 'every drag counts'.

# Information

## Publications

Gloria Steinem's stalwart bi-monthly *Ms* ($5.95) is still read for its mainstream feminist features; *The Advocate* ($3.95) and *Out* ($3.95) are monthly glossies for guys and gals. Relatively new on the scene are *Girlfriends* ($4.95) and *Deneuve* ($3.95), a couple of colourful and fun monthly magazines for gay women, with profiles and features about women in the know and in the news.

For entertainment information, pick up *The Village Voice, Paper* or *Time Out New York*; or get hold of *HX* and *Next*, which are both free in gay spots weekly, and are the best sources of up-to-the-minute nightlife and entertainment information. Though they're centred around gay boys there are plenty of listings for women's events as well.

Other gay girl mags include the rather tacky *Bad Attitude* ($3.95) and the far better, quarterly *On Our Backs* ($5.95). Most of these titles should be available at the bookshops listed below.

Finally, if you have access to cable TV, be sure to tune in to Dyke TV, Tuesday 8pm, on Channel 34 (Manhattan only), an entertaining hour of girl goings-on around the country.

## Bookshops

Alternative bookshops are a key first stop for any visiting lesbian keen to lay her hands on up-to-the-minute information on bars and clubs, from sedate soirées to full-on S&M events. Browse in a relaxed atmosphere, scan the noticeboards and leave with fistfuls of club flyers. Most bookshops will have women's sections: *see also chapters* **Gay New York** *and* **Shopping**.

### A Different Light

*151 West 19th Street, between Sixth & Seventh Avenues (989 4850).* **Train** 1 or 9 to Christopher Street/Sheridan Square. **Open** 10am-midnight daily. **Credit** AmEx, MC, V.
This is the biggest and best gay and lesbian bookstore in New York; great for browsing, and with plenty of free readings, screenings and art openings scheduled. There's a cute café at the front.

### Creative Visions

*546 Hudson Street, at Perry Street (645 7573).* **Train** 1 or 9 to Christopher Street. **Open** noon-11pm daily. **Credit** AmEx, MC, V.
A new gay and lesbian bookstore/café, run by women. Rather sparse, but a comfortable atmosphere.

### Oscar Wilde Memorial Bookshop

*15 Christopher Street, between Sixth & Seventh Avenues (255 8097).* **Train** 1 or 9 to Christopher Street/Sheridan Square. **Open** 11.30am-8.30pm daily. **Credit** AmEx, Discover, MC, V.
New York's oldest gay and lesbian bookshop, filled to the brim, with plenty of discounts.

## Centres & Phone Lines

### Barnard Center for Research on Women

*101 Barnard Hall, 3009 Broadway, at 117th Street (854 2067).* **Train** 1 or 9 to 116th Street. **Open** 9.30am-5pm Mon-Fri.
An academic centre with a distinctly offputting name; this is the place to explore scholarly feminism, through a calendar of classes, lectures and film screenings. The library has an extensive archive of feminist journals and government reports.

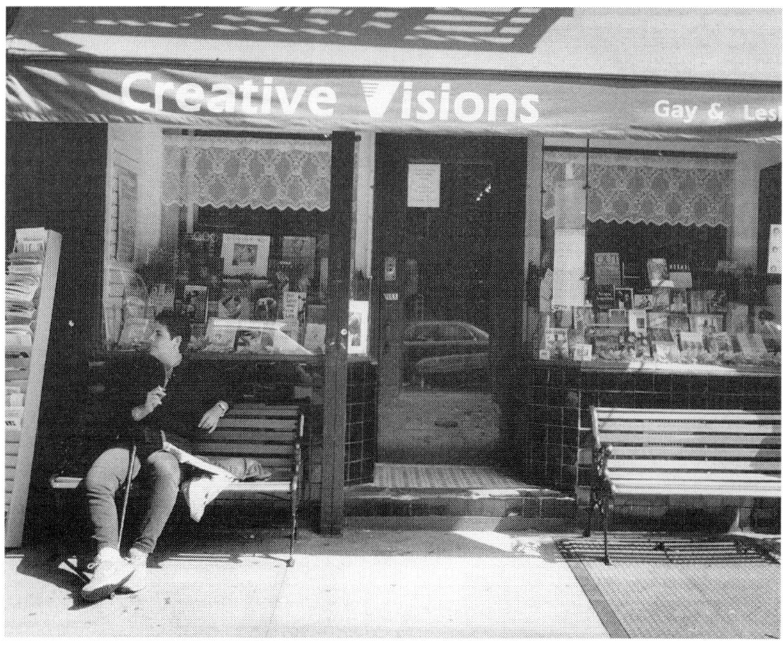


*Bookshops, such as* **Creative Visions**, *are good starting points for sussing the scene.*

### Lesbian and Gay Community Services Centre Inc

*208 West 13th Street, between Greenwich & Seventh Avenues (620 7310).* **Train** 1, 2, 3, F or L to 14th Street. **Open** 9am-11pm daily. **Membership** from $25 per year. **No credit cards.**

The epicentre for most of the lesbian (and gay) organisations in the city. Drop in and pick up its newsletter of ongoing events, meetings and dances. Check out books and videos from the Vito Russo library or just hang out and meet some New Yorkers. Events and meetings here range from women's wrestling and 'Desert Heart' dyke dances to writers' workshops and ACT-UP meetings. Straight women in search of hip clubs, support groups or political campaigning groups should also check in here.

### Lesbian Herstory Educational Foundation

*PO Box 1258, New York, NY 10116 (1-718 768 3953/fax 1-718 768 4663).* Call for an appointment.

Newly housed in the Park Slope area of Brooklyn (becoming known as 'Dyke Slope' for its large and growing lesbian population), the Herstory Archives, as they're known, were started by Joan Nestle and Deb Edel in 1974, and have reached massive proportions, now including over 10,000 books (theory, fiction, poetry, plays), 1400 periodicals and innumerable personal memorabilia. You too can donate a treasured possession (T-shirt, photo album, badge collection) and become part of Herstory.

### Lesbian Switchboard

*(741 2610).*

The switchboard operators are primed to deal with crises but are also happy to give all sorts of advice, from accommodation to clubs and restaurants.

### National Organisation for Women (NOW)

*22 West 21st Street, between Fifth & Sixth Avenues (807 0721).* **Train** 4, 5 or 6 to 14th Street. **Open** 10am-5pm Mon-Fri.

NOW is a political campaigning organisation, not a drop-in centre, but you can call in at the Manhattan branch to pick up the bi-monthly newsletter *NOW-NYC News* or the Chapter Calendar. NOW divides its energies between various support groups for women (especially those divorced or separated) and campaigning for better treatment for women in society.

## Health

AIDS is now an epidemic in New York, so you should always practise safer sex. The public healthcare system is practically non-existent and costs of private health care are exorbitant, so make sure you have comprehensive insurance coverage.

### Community Health Project

*(675 3559 10am-10pm Mon-Thur).*

CHP, based at the Lesbian and Gay Community Centre (*listed under* **Information: Centres & Phone Lines**), is the place for lesbian women to go for cheap health check ups.

### Lesbian Aids Project

*(337 3532).*

GMHC's information/counselling initiative for lesbians.

### Planned Parenthood

*Margaret Sanger Centre, 380 Second Avenue, between 21st & 22nd Streets (677 3320).* **Train** 6 to 23rd Street. **Open** 8.30am-4pm Mon-Fri.

This is the main branch of the best known, most reasonably priced network of family planning clinics in the States. Counselling and treatment is available for a full range of gynaecological needs, including abortion, treatment of STDs, HIV testing and contraception; phone for an appointment.

### Women's Health Line

*(230 1111).*

Run by NOW (*see above*), this service offers free or low-cost referrals to hospitals on Manhattan and in the four outer boroughs for all family planning needs from contraception to abortion.

## Safety

New York women are used to the brazenness with which they are stared at by the city's population of dubious male streetlife. Think of it as your way of putting beauty into their sad lives. If they get verbal or start following you, unless you are confident about your acid-tongued retorts, ignoring them is better than responding. Walking into the nearest shop is your best bet to get rid of really persistent offenders.

As for more serious safety issues, the key thing is that all New Yorkers are either totally paranoid, or relish delivering frightening war stories to visitors. Whatever you've heard, with a minimum of awareness and common sense you can reduce the chances of anything happening to you to almost zero. Take the usual big-city precautions: stay in areas where there are people, don't carry or wear anything that could catch a thief's eye and as far as possible try not to look lost or vulnerable. Look as if you know where you are going and you will probably get there safely.

Advice issued by the Crime Prevention Department of the police includes: never carry anything you'd fight for; don't carry a separate wad of 'mugger's money', simply hand over all the money you have on you (if you're found to have kept money back, you'll be in worse trouble); and, while resisting is rarely a good idea, you should never ever resist when a weapon is involved. For further safety advice, *see chapter* **Essential Information**.

### Brooklyn Women's Martial Arts

*Center for Anti-Violence Education, 421 Fifth Avenue, between 7th & 8th Streets, Brooklyn (1-718 788 1775).* **Train** F or R to Fourth Avenue/9th Street. **Open** 11am-8pm Mon-Fri. **No credit cards.**

A centre dedicated to martial arts training for women and children. Its programmes teaches defensive techniques for real-life situations, including both physical and non-physical methods of dealing with aggression or attack. Free childcare is offered, and classes are in the evenings or at weekends. Classes in karate and *tai chi* are also offered.

### Rape Hotline

*Sex Crimes Report Line of the New York Police Department (267 7273).* **Open** 24 hours daily.

Reports of sex crimes are handled by a female detective from the New York Police Department's Bureau, who will inform the appropriate precinct, send an ambulance if requested and provide counselling and medical referrals. A detective from the Sex Crimes Squad will interview the victim, and you can request to be seen in your own home.

# Students

***Pass notes on New York's educational requirements.***

New York would miss them if they weren't here, but students don't figure very largely in the life of the city. There is little of the student-only entertainment culture familiar on European campuses. One reason is that American scholars tend to be too busy working to pay for their education to have much fun – in addition to their studies, most are compelled to hold down jobs to support themselves. But a better explanation is simply that there is such a vast range of accessible entertainment possibilities throughout the city that there is no need for students here to segregate themselves.

There are few more exciting places to study than New York, and its colleges and universities attract people from all over the world. Most vocational courses here have strong links with the city's businesses and are consequently well-equipped to launch graduates into employment. Interning (working for free) at a major company is an essential part of many students' time here.

The admissions offices of most US educational institutions accept applications directly from international students and can also supply details about visas, fees, student housing (on- or off-campus) and other information. The **Institute of International Education** (IIE) has an information centre and holds a directory of US educational institutions and course catalogues, as well as information on financial aid. It's at 809 United Nations Plaza, New York, NY 10017 (883 8200). UK students can contact the **Fulbright Commission**, 62 Doughty Street, WC1N 2LS (0171 404 6994) or the US International Commission Agency at any US embassy for information on study in the US. The **Council on International Educational Exchange** (CIEE), 33 Seymour Place, London W1H 6AT (0171 706 3008) can arrange places and visas for summer courses at a clutch of Stateside colleges and smooth the bureaucracy for sandwich-course students looking for internships.

## Immigration

On entering the US as a student, you will need to show a passport, a special visa (*see below*) and proof of your plans to leave (a return airline ticket). Even if you have a student visa, you may be asked to show means of support during your stay (cash, credit cards, travellers' cheques, etc).

If you must bring prescription drugs to the US, make sure the container is clearly marked and that you bring your doctor's statement or a prescription. Of course, marijuana, cocaine and most opiate derivatives and other chemicals are not permitted and possession of them is punishable by stiff fines and/or imprisonment. Check with the **US Customs Service** in your country if you have any questions about what you can bring to the US. Customs allows you 200 cigarettes, $100 worth of gifts and all your personal belongings duty free. If you carry more than $10,000 worth of currency, you will have to fill out a report. If you lose, or need to renew your passport once in the US, contact your country's embassy (*see chapter* **Survival**).

### Visas

Non-nationals who want to study in New York (or anywhere else in the US) must apply for either an F-1 or M-1 visa. The M-1 is for vocational courses where practical training – including off-campus training or employment – may be necessary. The F-1 is for wholly academic courses. If you are enrolling in an authorized exchange visitor programme – including many summer courses and programmes such as BUNAC (*see below* **Work**) – you should apply for a J-1 visa. Wait till you're accepted on the course or programme before worrying about immigration. You will be guided through the process by an official from the school in question.

You are admitted as a student for the length of your course, plus a limited period of any associated (and approved) practical training, plus a 60-day grace period. After this you must leave the country or apply to change or extend your immigration status. Requests to extend a visa must be submitted 15 to 60 days before the initial departure date. The rules are strict and you risk deportation if you break them.

Information on these, and all other immigration matters, is available from the **US Immigration and Naturalisation Service** (INS). Its New York office is in the Jacob Javits Federal Building, 26 Federal Plaza, New York, NY 10278. The 'Ask Immigration' hotline (206 6500) is a vast menu of recorded information in English and Spanish. It is available 24 hours daily and is clear and helpful. Advisors are available on the same number from

8am to 5.30pm Mon-Fri. If you already know what forms you need, you can order them by calling 870 3676. You can visit INS between 7.30am and 3.30pm Mon-Fri.

## Work

When you apply for your student visa, you will be expected to prove your ability to support yourself financially (including the payment of school fees), without working, for at least the first nine months of your course. After the first nine months, you may be eligible to work part-time, though you must have specific permission to do so. In addition, holders of M-1 visas are allowed to work throughout their course (including the first nine months) provided the employment is approved practical training connected with the course. Provided you are not being paid, this should not affect your immigration status.

If you are a British student wanting to spend a summer vacation working in the States, contact BUNAC at 16 Bowling Green Lane, London EC1R 0BD (0171 251 3472), which can help arrange a temporary job and the requisite visa.

## Student Identification

Foreign students should get themselves an **International Student Identity** (ISIC) **Card** as proof of student status and to secure discounts. These can be bought from your local student travel agent (ask at your students' union). If you buy the $18 card in New York, you will also get basic accident insurance – a bargain. The **Council on International Educational Exchange** can supply one on the spot. It's at 205 East 42nd Street, New York, NY 10017 (661 1414) and is open from 9am-5pm Mon-Fri.

Note that a student identity card may not always be accepted as proof of age for drinking (you must be 21, *see chapter* **Bars**).

# Student Services

## Accommodation

Medium- to long-term accommodation is expensive and hard to find in Manhattan. However, if you're studying here as part of a US college or university programme, the institution will help you out. The larger colleges have many residential properties and usually provide very nice hall of residence-type accommodation for foreign students (they often lump together the non-Americans in an 'International House'). If somewhere like this is unavailable, or if you'd prefer to share an apartment, many institutions also run a flat- or roommate-finder operation.

If you'd like to live with a US family for an extended period, **World Learning** coordinates homestay programmes for international visitors. You will live in the home of the host, and get a realistic exposure to American culture (with all its joys and horrors). For details, in the UK, contact **Experiment in International Living**, Otesaga, West Malvern Road, Malvern, Worcestershire WR14 4EN (01684 562 577) at least three months in advance. In the US, write to World Learning, 419 Boylston Street, Boston, MA 02116 (1-617 247 0350). The **Institute of International Education** (IIE) publishes the Homestay Information Sheet, listing many homestay programmes. Write to the IIE at 809 United Nations Plaza, New York, NY 10017 (883 8200).

Several of the hostels listed in *chapter* **Accommodation** offer special rates for long-term residents. They include:

### De Hirsch Residence at the 92nd Street Y

*YMHA, 1395 Lexington Avenue, NY10128, at 92nd Street (415 5650/1-800 858 4692/fax 415 5578).* **Train** 4, 5 or 6 to 96th Street. **Rates** (for stays over two months) *single* from $650 per month; *shared rooms* from $525 per person per month. **Credit** AmEx, JCB, MC, V.

Although this is nominally a Hebrew organisation, people of all (or no) religion can stay. It's close to many of New York's finest museums, as well as Central Park's jogging track. For long stays you must submit an application and go through a screening process to gain admittance. Applicants will have to attend an interview, although special procedures can be arranged for foreign students. A special emphasis is placed on your interest in learning from a 'group living situation'. Indeed, there are no private baths.

**Hotel services** *Disabled: access, rooom, toilets. Health club. Laundry. TV room. Sundeck.*

**Room services** *Air-conditioning in most rooms. Maid & linen service.*

## Travel

Most agents do discount fares for under-26s; UK specialists in student deals include Council Travel, 28a Poland Street, London W1V 3DB (0171 287 3337) and 205 East 42nd Street, NY 10017 (661 1450), and STA Travel, based in the UK but with more than 100 offices worldwide. In London, contact them at 86 Old Brompton Road, London SW7 3LQ (0171 937 9971); in the US, call 1-800 777 0112.

## Medical Care

If you're enrolled in a course of study with a US college or university, you are usually eligible for treatment at the campus clinic. It may still be advisable to obtain medical insurance: ask your college authorities for advice.

If you need dental treatment, the NYU Dental Center, 345 East 24th Street, at First Avenue (998 9800) gives 25 per cent student discounts on top of its already low fees (about half of commercial rates). Your treatment will be by an about-to-graduate student, under supervision.

For futher healthcare information *see chapter* **Survival**.

# Trips Out of Town

# Trips Out of Town

***See the vast range of historic sites and majestic scenery that lie within easy reach of New York. Or just hit the beach.***

The residents of New York City only live here so they can earn enough money to leave town as often as possible. The astonishing weekend congestion at all points of exit is testimony to New Yorkers' overwhelming desire to escape. They do so to engage in those activities for which the concrete pressure cooker of Manhattan is not suitable: to connect with nature, open spaces and normal people.

### GENERAL INFORMATION

Most bookstores with travel sections have guidebooks covering the surrounding areas. Some of the larger magazine stores will carry a number of the periodicals specific to resort towns (there are lots of these, especially for the more affluent vacation communities).

The *New York Times* is always worth watching for articles on nearby attractions, and its Sunday travel section is crammed with getaway suggestions and advertising for resorts and guesthouses. Watch out too for late specials on flights to nearby cities, which are usually advertised in the midweek editions.

### GETTING AROUND

All of the places listed below include information on how to get there. *See chapter* **Essential Information** for a list of decent car hire companies. New York rates are exorbitant and you can save up to 50 per cent by renting a car from somewhere outside of the city – even if it's from the same firm. Hoboken or Jersey City in New Jersey, or Greenwich in Connecticut are good bets for this, but you should book as far in advance as you can to get the best price.

Metro North (532 4900) and the Long Island Railroad, or LIRR (1-718 217 LIRR), are the two main commuter rail systems. Both offer themed tours in the summer. Amtrak (582 6875/toll-free 1-800 USA RAIL) is the national rail service for intercity travel. Call the Port Authority Bus Terminal (564 8484) for information on all bus transport from the city.

For schedules of flights out of New York you will usually have to call a specific airline. The airports will tell you which airlines fly where but not when. **JF Kennedy Airport** is 1-718 244 4444, **LaGuardia** 1-718 476 5000 and **Newark** 1-201 961 2000.

## Life's a Beach

You can get sand between your toes for a minimum outlay ($1.25) by visiting the three beach areas accessible on the subway. These are **Coney Island** (*see chapter* **New York by Neighbourhood: Outer Boroughs**), **Rockaway Beach** (A, C, or H train to Rockaway Park Beach) and **Orchard Beach**, a little slice of Puerto Rico in the Bronx (6 train to Pelham Bay Park). These are usually noisy and crowded and often dirty (Pelham Park is the current favourite place for dumping murder victims), but for a slightly larger investment you can find yourself on some very pleasant stretches of oceanfront.

## Long Island

Escaping to the small towns and vast beaches that comprise Long Island, the long appendage that lies to the east of Manhattan Island, is relatively quick and easy. The beaches improve the further you travel from Manhattan and some, like those in the Hamptons, are among the most unspoilt in America. You can reach sea and sand by hopping on a train on the Long Island Rail Road (LIRR), which leaves from Penn Station (call 1-718 217 LIRR). In the summer, there are shuttle buses from the train stations to the various beaches.

If you want an easy beach experience, take the LIRR to **Long Beach**. The Atlantic, which is warm enough to swim in from July to September, is a few short blocks away from the station. The beach can be absolutely packed in the summer.

Next is **Jones Beach**, where some of New York's biggest summer concerts are staged.

**Robert Moses Beach** is the furthest of the three, but is to be recommended for its white sand and the boardwalks which wind through the shrubs of the endless dunes.

In the summer season between Memorial Day (late May) and Labor Day (early September), harried New Yorkers scramble over each other to get out to their beachside rental homes in the Hamptons (West, East and South), Fire Island (*see chapter* **Gay New York**), Sag Harbor, Bridgehampton, Shelter Island and Montauk.

The **Hamptons** are the perfect backdrop for the socialites, artistes and celebrities who drift from benefit bash to benefit bash throughout the sum-

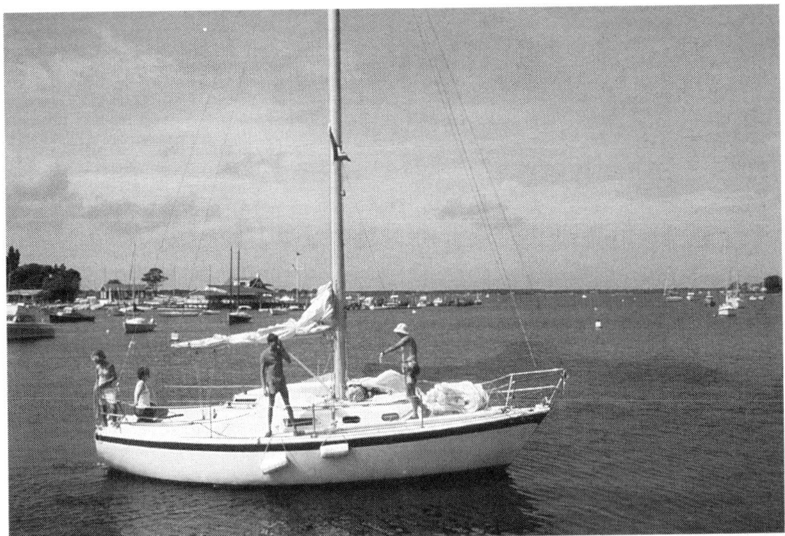

*Take a boat: it's the only way to reach* **Shelter Island**.

mer season. Their homes, wonderful as some are, can't help but be upstaged by the spectacular beaches.

**Montauk Point** is Long Island's furthest tip – remote and not too crowded. It's too far for a day trip but is full of holiday cottages and motels. These can be fairly expensive at the height of the season, but pre- and post-season deals abound.

Try Fort Pond Lodge, Second-House Road, Montauk (1-516 668 2042), a quiet, old-style motel set on a lake and minutes from the ocean ($70 a night). Rent a bike and you're all set. Although Montauk is decidedly unpretentious when compared to the Hamptons, it attracts its share of celebrities, including Mick Jagger and Keith Richards.

For more information contact:

**Southampton Chamber of Commerce**
*76 Main Street, Southampton, NY 11968 (1-516 283 0402).*

**East Hampton Chamber of Commerce**
*4 Main Street, East Hampton, NY 11937 (1-516 324 0362).*

**Montauk Chamber of Commerce**
*Box 5024, Montauk, NY 11954 (1-516 668 2428).*

## Shelter Island

The fact that this tiny island can only be reached by ferry from Long Island, combined with its lack of commercialisation, keeps it free from crowds. There are a few gift shops and an ice cream parlour but little else to distract you from sailing, cycling, fishing or just relaxing on the beach. About a third of its area, **Mashomack Preserve**, is unpopulated except for birds.

The first house was built here in 1652 and the island gained a reputation as a refuge for pirates (Captain Kidd is thought to have buried treasure here). Quakers who were driven out of Boston settled here; you can visit the **Quaker Cemetery** on the outer boundary of **Sylvester Manor**. Other historic destinations are the **Shelter Island Historical Society** museum, **Manhasset Chapel Museum** and **Haven House**.

If you have time, take the four-minute ferry ride to **Sag Harbor**. The information centre on Main Street will tell you what you can do. Try to see the **Sag Harbor Whaling Museum** (1-516 725 0770); open 10am-5pm Mon-Sat, 1-5pm Sun.

There aren't many hotels on Shelter Island, but the following are worth a try. The Chequit Inn (Shelter Island Heights; 1-516 749 0018) costs between $112.50 and $195 a night and is only open during the summer months. The Pridwin Hotel and Cottages at Crescent Beach (1-516 749 0476) is $109-$199 a night for rooms, $229 for a cottage. For more information contact:

**Shelter Island Chamber of Commerce**
*Box 598, Shelter Island, NY 11964 (1-516 749 0399).*

**Transport**

Sunrise Express Bus Service from New York City to Greenport (1-516 477 1200; $29 return) or Long Island Railroad from Penn Station to Greenport (1-718 217 LIRR); then take the ferry(75)¢.

HAIRLOOM
BEAUTY

## The Jersey Shore

A prime target for New Yorkers' scathing wit is New Jersey and everyone in it. So the Jersey shore will not be high on their list of recommended destinations. But Jersey's hundred miles of Atlantic seafront includes some splendid beaches and places worth a visit for an insight into American ocean-side culture. In general, the places closest to New York are the least worth visiting. The best beaches are often private (definitely the case in **Long Beach** and **Ocean Beach**); the public ones are usually choked with noisy crowds from northern Jersey's industrial cities. If you're a Bruce Springsteen fan you might want to make the pilgrimage to **Asbury Park**, a remarkably unpleasant stretch of coastline.

At the opposite end of the shore, **Cape May** (*see below*), on the southernmost tip of New Jersey, is the country's oldest seaside resort and has a delicate nineteenth-century feel to it. Just north is **Wildwood**, home to a monstrous boardwalk – a wooden promenade filled with fairground rides, sideshows and food stalls. **Coney Island** pales into insignificance beside this enormous fun palace. Try some saltwater taffy, or maybe frozen custard, a pork roll or an elephant ear – all local delicacies. Ride on the roller-coasters or the huge Ferris wheel, have an old-time photo taken, or just stroll along the boardwalk, watching real-life Americans at play. The beaches here are suitably enormous.

The beaches north of Wildwood, at **Avalon**, **Sea Isle City** and **Strathmere** are very pleasant and less commercialised. The town centres still have their share of amusingly awful nightspots, however, where you can watch tribal masses of twenty-somethings get ecstatic as cover bands play Billy Joel songs. The area just inland is a mass of tiny islands, bays and inlets. These connect the different beaches and provide the perfect setting for sailing, fishing, windsurfing and jet-skiing.

**Atlantic City** has little in the way of attractive coastline. What draws people here is gambling – and lots of it (*see below* **The Bright Lights**). Further up the coast, however, are some beautiful spots, such as **Island Beach**, which is a national park. The comparatively limited access here means unspoilt beaches, and the natural scenery is quite beautiful.

### New Jersey Division of Tourism

*CN 826, Trenton, New Jersey 08625 (1-609 292 2470/toll-free 1-800 JERSEY 7).*

### New Jersey Department of Parks

*501 East State Street, Trenton, New Jersey 08625 (1-609 292 2797).*

*The impeccably preserved* **Cape May**.

*Life on* **Bear Mountain**. *See page 296.*

## Cape May

Cape May in southern New Jersey, 160 miles out of New York City, is the nation's oldest seaside resort. Its 600 Victorian 'gingerbread' homes make the entire town a national landmark. The best time to go is early September, when the crowds have thinned but the water is still warm enough to swim in. Rent a bike and visit **Cape May Point**, where the Atlantic meets **Delaware Bay** and visitors sift through the sand for pieces of polished quartz known as Cape May diamonds. **Cape May Point State Park** has a lovely bird sanctuary and one of the country's oldest lighthouses, built in 1744.

Cape May was the prime vacation spot until a fire ravaged the town in 1878. US presidents and colonial luminaries were among those who came here for relaxation. Later visitors included the young Wallis Warfield, later known as the Duchess of Windsor, who came to the Columbia Hotel in 1917 to plan her coming-out party.

The **Physick Estate**, at 1048 Washington Street (1-609 884 5404), is a Victorian mansion built in 1859 which now operates as a museum of Victorian life. Tours run from spring to autumn, from 11am to 3.30pm Tue-Sun.

If you want to stay, be warned that in the summer and during October's Victorian Week most hotels have two- to four-night minimum stay. The Victorian Rose, 715 Columbia Avenue (1-609 884 2497) is a seven-room bed and breakfast and costs $70-$135 a night. The Chalfonte Hotel at 301 Howard Street (1-609 884 8409) includes breakfast and dinner in its $102-$158 room rate.

### Greater Cape May Chamber of Commerce

*PO Box 109, Cape May, NJ 08204 (1-609 884 5508).*

### Mid-Atlantic Center for the Arts

*PO Box 340, Cape May, NJ 08204 (1-609 884 5404).*

### Transport

New Jersey Transit bus from Port Authority Terminal (1-201 762 5100). By car, take the Garden State Parkway (from the Lincoln or Holland tunnel) south to the last exit.

**Santa's Workshop**. *See page 297.*

## Life's a Mountain

Nearly half the population of New York State is crammed into the five boroughs of New York City. This leaves the other 47,000 square miles relatively unpopulated. Hikers and skiers will be pleased to hear that this area includes some of the most dramatic mountain scenery in the United States.

### Bear Mountain

For a fine day-trip alternative to the beaches, Manhattan's closest wilderness is to be found at **Bear Mountain State Park**, Palisades Parkway and route 9W (1-914 786 2701). It's only an hour by bus (Short Line Buses 736 4700; $19 round-trip from Port Authority Terminal).

The bus will drop you at an appalling visitors' centre with really gross fast food and hundreds of unadventurous families picnicking in the car park, but a ten-minute walk along one of the many trails will put you right out there away from it all.

If you have a car, take yourself off to the area around **Cranberry Lake**, where there's a campsite and a trail lodge and things are organised less for the day-tripping hordes and more for the serious hiker.

### The Catskills

The **Catskills** mountain range, an offshoot of the **Appalachian Mountains**, just 90 miles from the city, is New York's nearest major forest and park area. The landscape is magnificent. There are hiking and cycling trails, trout-filled streams, whitewater rapids for canoeing, golf courses, tennis courts, campsites, ski resorts and lakes.

As well as the Catskills' natural beauty, there are other attractions. You can explore mountain caverns at **Ice Caves Mountain** in Ellenville (1-914 647 7989), tour wineries in **Ulster County** (1-914 331 8642) and go on organised canoe trips on the Delaware and other rivers running through the park. **East Durham** is the home of the **Zoom Flume Water Park** (1-518 239 6271), although this is something of a tourist trap.

A taste of local history can be found at the **Hurley Patentee Manor** (1-914 331 5414) in Hurley, the **Tulthilltown Grist Mill** (1-914 255 5695) in Gardiner and **Fort Delaware** (1-914 252 6660) in Narrowsburg.

**Kingston**, the largest town in the Catskills, is home to the **Hudson River Maritime Museum** (1-914 338 0071) and a well-stocked **Trolley Museum** (1-914 331 3399). The **Rhinebeck Aerodome** (1-914 758 8610), in Rhinebeck, has vintage World War I aeroplane displays.

There are several ski resorts in the Catskills. The most famous of these is **Hunter Mountain**, where the 46 trails are usually packed with New Yorkers during the season. The snow at **Ski Windham**, another large mountain resort, is 100 per cent machine-made (as at most of the mountains in the area) and the facilities are similar to those at Hunter.

The Catskills have a good range of accommodation. The Mohonk Mountain House Hotel (1-914 255 1000) is a lavish castle on a secluded lake where rooms cost $268-$372 a night (full board for two people). A more economical option is Jingle Bells Farms (1-914 255 6588), an intimate bed and breakfast costing $100 a night.

There are some great wineries in the area, including **Benmarl Winery** (1-914 236 4265) and **Brotherhood Winery** (1-914 496 9101).

The only thing you can't escape in this wilderness is New Yorkers: from Friday night to Sunday evening the Catskills is packed with them. At the weekends, the road between the Catskills and New York City is backed up for miles. If you possibly can, it would be wise to plan your trip to avoid the traffic jams.

For more information, contact the following:

**Delaware County Chamber of Commerce**
*97 Main Street, Delhi, NY 13753 (1-607 746 2281).*

**East Durham Information Center**
*(1-518 622 3939).*

**Greene County Promotion Department**
*Box 527, Catskill, NY 12414 (1-518 943 3223).*

**Greene County Resort Association**
*Box 332, Cairo, NY 12413.*

**National Park Service, Upper Delaware National Scenic and Recreational River**
*PO Box C, Narrowsburg, NY 12764 (1-914 252 3947).*

**Sullivan County Office of Public Information**
*(1-914 794 3000).*

**Ulster County Public Information Office**
*County Office Building, Box 1800, Kingston, NY 12401 (1-914 331 9300).*

**Ulster County Chamber of Commerce**
*7 Albany Avenue, Kingston, NY 12401 (1-914 338 5100).*

## The Adirondacks

The largest area of untouched beauty in the state is **Adirondack Park**, in the north-east. At least 40 per cent of the park is officially classified as a wilderness – the largest in the US outside Alaska. Route 87 runs north through the eastern side of the park and is the best road from the city (the journey takes about four hours). The park is suitable for all the usual outdoor activities, and, despite some nine million visitors each year, remains relatively unspoilt.

**Lake George** is a long, thin lake, dotted with tiny islands and surrounded by mountains, which runs along the south-eastern side of the park. **Glens Falls**, at the south end, is a booming tourist town. North of Lake George is **Lake Champlain**. Straddling the Vermont/New York state border and continuing north beyond the Canadian border into Quebec, it is the largest lake in Adirondack Park and a popular vacation spot. **Port Kent** and **Plattsburgh** are the two major towns on Lake Champlain. For people who enjoy feeling terrified, **Ausable Chasm** (1-518 834 7454) is a narrow (20ft/6m) gorge in Lake Champlain where you can ride the roaring rapids, *Deliverance*-style. This hair-raising excursion runs daily from mid-May until mid-October from 9am until 4pm ($12.95 adults, $7.95 under-12s, free for the under-sixes).

**Saranac Lake** (1-518 891 1990) and **Tupper Lake** (1-518 359 3328) are two gorgeous spots, with a full complement of hotels, campsites and other outdoor facilities. Robert Louis Stevenson rented a house on Saranac Lake; he called the area 'Little Switzerland' and wrote *The Master of Ballantrae* there.

The three highest mountains in the park are Whiteface, Marcy and Jo. Marcy, at 5,344 feet (1,036 metres) above sea level, is the highest in New York State. Whiteface (*information* 1-518 946 2223), replete with alpine glacier, has some of the most challenging ski slopes in the east, as well as gentler runs for the novice, and high-speed lifts.

The nearby town of **Lake Placid** (*information* 1-800 462 6236) was the scene of the 1932 and 1980 **Winter Olympics**. It has a long tradition of hospitality towards visitors and some very European architecture, with small chalet-style shops, bars, clubs, restaurants and hotels. In the summer months, golfing, boating, fishing, camping and hiking are all available.

Other big ski resorts in the Adirondacks include **Gore Mountain** (1-518 251 2411/1-518 251 2523 for recorded information on conditions) and **Big Tupper** (*information* 1-518 359 3651). These raw and beautiful peaks can be dangerous. The winds can get up to 60mph (96kph) and the temperature down to -60°F (-15°C).

**Santa's Workshop** (1-518 946 2211), Northpole NY, is the oldest theme park in the United States and a great place for kids. This alpine village, near Lake Placid, has Santa Claus, his helpers, reindeer, storybook characters, children's rides, crafts and music shows.

Besides nature, there are other things that draw people to the Adirondacks. The **Ballard Center of the Arts** in Malone, the **Hyde Collection** (1-518 792 1761) in Glens Falls, the **Adirondack**

*You could ride the raging rapids at* **Ausable Chasm**, *but then again, why bother?*

**Museum** (1-518 352 7311) at Blue Lake Mountain and North River's **Barton Mines Corporation** (1-518 251 2706), the largest garnet mine in the world, are just a few of the cultural nuggets in this massive wilderness.

For more information, contact:

### Central Adirondack Association

*Old Forge, NY 13420 (1-315 369 6660).*

### Lake Placid Chamber of Commerce and Visitor Bureau

*216 Main Street, Lake Placid, NY 12946 (1-518 523 2445).*

## Outdoor Pursuits

If you're windswept and outdoorsy you needn't leave your adventuresome pastime behind just because you're in New York. There are few activities which aren't possible in the region. Here are just some which are. For more see *chapter* **Sports.**

## Boating

Boating, canoeing and whitewater rafting are popular sports in the many rivers, waterways, lakes, sounds, bays and ocean within reach of New York. The network of canals instrumental in the industrialisation of America, though still used commercially, is a prime leisure resource, with access free to everyone. The Erie Barge Canal links east with west by joining the Atlantic Ocean and Hudson River to the St Lawrence River and the Great Lakes. The Champlain Canal connects the 110-mile (176 kilometre) Lake Champlain with the Hudson River.

### NYS Tour Boat Association

*PO Box 365, Rifton, NY 12471 (toll free 1-800 852 0095).*
Offers information on the many boating operators throughout New York State

### Port Jervis Tri-State Chamber of Commerce

*10 Sussex Street, PO Box 121, Port Jervis, NY 12771 (1-914 856 6694).*
Information on several operators which offer trips down the Delaware River, including whitewater rafting

### Batenkill Sports Quarters

*Route 313, Cambridge, NY 12816 (1-518 677 8868).*
This company offers canoe, kayak and tubing trips.

### McDonnell's Adirondack Challenges

*Box 855, Saranac Lake, NY 12983 (1-518 891 1176).*
McDonnell's arranges canoeing and kayaking, as well as hiking, fishing and camping for individuals and groups.

### Middle Earth Expeditions

*HCRO1 Box 37, Lake Placid, NY 12946 (1-518 523 9572).*
Outdoor pursuits for groups and individuals.

### Rivett's Boat Livery

*PO Box 601, Lake Trail, Old Forge Lake, Old Forge, NY 13420 (1-315 369 3123).*
Boat rentals, sales and service.

### Wild and Scenic River Tours

*Route 97, Barryville, NY 12719 (1-914 557 8783/toll-free 1-800 836 0366).*
Canoeing, kayaking and white-water rafting

## Camping

There are 500 public and privately owned campsites (or 'campgrounds', as they are called here) throughout New York State. Some are deep in the wilderness and only accessible by boat; others are relatively close to a town or city. Reservations are recommended, but not always necessary. For more information, contact:

### New York State Office of Parks, Recreation and Historic Preservation

*Empire State Plaza, Albany, NY 12238 (1-518 474 0456).*
Information on all parks and park activities within the state.

### New York State Campgrounds

*(toll-free 1-800 456 CAMP)*
Call to make campsite reservations.

## Climbing

If the indoor climbing wall at the 59th Street Recreation Center isn't scenic enough for you, the climbing club there will give you the best advice on where to head. The **Shawangunks**, or 'Gunks', in the Catskills offer some of the best climbing in the country, with sheer limestone cliffs over 300 feet high.

You need to buy a day pass ($5) from the Mohonk Preserve, 1000 Mountain Rest Road, Mohonk Lake, Newpaltz NY 12561 (1-914 255 0919). The local equipment store, Rock and Snow, at 44 Main Street, Newpaltz NY 12561 (1-914 255 1311) will be happy to give advice.

### Tents and Trails

*21 Park Place (227 1760).* **Open** 9.30am-6pm Mon-Wed, Sat; 9.30am-7pm Thur, Fri; noon-6pm Sun. **Credit** AmEx, Discover, MC, V.
Apart from the supermarket-style chain *Eastern Mountain Sports*, this is the only specialist climbing equipment store in Manhattan. Full of colourful ropes and friendly advice.

## Cycling

A choice of landscapes in the area means that there is something for cyclists of every stripe, from recreational to racing, touring to mountain biking. Drop into one of New York's many bike stores and look out for cycling mags. For information on cycling in a particular area, contact the local Chamber of Commerce.

For more information contact:

### New York State Office of Parks, Recreation and Historic Preservation

*Empire State Plaza, Albany, NY 12238 (1-518 474 0456).*

### League of American Bicyclists

*190 West Ostend Street, suite 120, Baltimore, Maryland 21230 (1-410 539 3399).*
Membership organisation offering all sorts of advice.

For snowboarding, see page 300.

## Fishing

You can fish in New York State's 70,000 miles (112,000 kilometre) of streams and rivers and 4,000 lakes and ponds. The first day of the fishing season (check dates with DEC, *see below*) is a big day in the New York social/sporting calendar. Check the newspapers the day before for stock reports.

The favourite fishing spots in New York State are Lakes Erie and Ontario (two of the Great Lakes), Chitauqua Lake, St Lawrence River, the Finger Lakes, Oneida Lake, Lake Champlain and Lake George and the Delaware, Hudson and Allegheny rivers. Burr Pond and Kent Fall State Parks, both in Connecticut, are also favoured spots for freshwater fishing, as are Caleb Smith and Connetqout River State Parks, both in Long Island.

There are plenty of coastal areas where sea fishing is permitted. The resorts on Long Island and the Jersey shore have companies which charter boats and equipment. These operators can usually also take care of licensing requirements (sea-fishing requires a different licence from inland).

For freshwater fishing you must get a fishing licence ($14 resident; $35 non-resident, for the season, 3 and 5-day passes available) if you are aged between 16 and 69. People over 65 get a discount. Licences can be purchased at most fishing tackle stores. For information on licenses for New York call 1-718 482 4987; for New Jersey, 1-609 292 2965; for Connecticut, 1-203 722 8040. To get a licence by post, or for other fishing information, write to:

### Department of Environmental Conservation (DEC)

*50 Wolf Road, Albany, NY 12233 (1-518 474 2121/1-518 457 3521).*

### Urban Angler

*118 East 25th Street, 3rd Floor, between Lexington and Park Avenues (979 7600).* **Train** 6 to 28th Street. **Open** 10am-6pm Mon-Fri; 10am-5pm Sat. **Credit** AmEx, MC, V.
The best fly-fishing store in New York. For licences, equipment and friendly information on the best places to fish in the region, both surf casting (saltwater) and freshwater, this is the place to come.

### Capitol Fishing

*218 West 23rd Street, between Seventh and Eighth Avenues (929 6132).* **Train** 1 or 9 to 23rd Street. **Open** 9am-6pm Mon-Wed, Fri; 9am-7pm Thur; 9am-5pm Sat. **Credit** AmEx, Discover, MC, V.
Both saltwater and freshwater equipment are sold here. It's also possible to hire equipment, depending on what you need.

## Hiking

Some of the most spectacular and challenging trails in the country can be found in New York State. The most famous, and popular, of these is the **Appalachian Trail**; stretching from Maine to Georgia, this 2,100 mile (3,360 kilometre) trek is tackled by four million hikers annually. For more information about hiking in the region, contact:

### Adirondack Mountain Club

*RR3 Box 3055, Lake George, New York 12845 (1-518 668 4447).*

### Appalachian Mountain Club

*New York-North Jersey Chapter, 5 Tudor City Place, East 41st Street, New York, NY 10016 (986 1430).* **Open** 8.30am-5.30pm Wed-Fri.

### Finger Lakes Trail Conference

*PO Box 18048, Rochester, NY 14618-0048 (1-716 288 7191).*

### Long Island Greenbelt Trail Conference

*23 Deer Path Road, Center Islip, New York 11722 (1-516 360 0753).*

## Horse Riding

New York has some splendid countryside for horse riding with miles of horse-trails and special facilities for riders and horses as well as parks, campgrounds and riding stables where you can hire horses. For information on these, contact the local Chamber of Commerce. Check whether or not you will be covered by the stable's insurance; some only insure experienced riders and only if you go no faster than a walk.

Forty-one of New York State's counties have county fairs, almost all with equestrian events. They are usually held during summer. For information on these, contact the NYS Department of Agriculture and Markets, Winners Circle, Capital Plaza, Albany, NY 12235 (1-518 457 0127).

The following addresses are useful for all equestrian enquiries:

### American Horse Show Association in NYS

*220 East 42nd Street, New York, NY 10014 (972 2472).*

## Skiing & Snowboarding

For information on the excellent skiing in the area, search out some of the specialist ski magazines and consult the ubiquitous *Sunday Times* Travel section. As well as the **Catskills** and **Adirondacks**, there are challenging ski resorts nearby in the **Berkshires**, 110 miles from New York City on the Massachusetts border.

Some of the larger sports stores arrange all-inclusive day-trips by bus during the season, usually to Hunter Mountain, for both skiing and snowboarding, including equipment rentals and tuition if necessary. Day trips cost around $50-60. Some of the best-organised are run by Blades, Paragon and Scandinavian.

### Blades

*659 Broadway, at Bleecker Street (477 7350).* **Train** 4, 5, 6, B, D, F, Q to Broadway Lafayette/Bleecker Streeet. **Open** 11am-9pm Mon-Fri; noon-9pm Sat; noon-7pm Sun. **Credit** AmEx, MC, V.

The emphasis is on snowboarding, and the Blades trips are usually noisy bus-fulls of young board rats, with lots of sponsorship freebies (stickers, CDs, sports drinks) given away amid the spiky teenage haircuts.

### New York Ski Club

*AYH, 891 Amsterdam Avenue, at 103rd Street (932 2300).*

Trips and advice for anyone skiing on a budget.

### Paragon Sports

*867 Broadway, at 18th Street (255 8036).* **Train** 4, 5, 6, L, N, R to Union Square. **Open** 10am-8pm Mon-Sat; 11am-6.30 Sun. **Credit** AmEx, Discover, MC, V.

Paragon's trips are slightly more adult, with a more even blend of skiers and boarders.

### Scandinavian

*40 West 57th Street, between Fifth & Sixth Avenues (757 8524).* **Train** B or Q to 57th Street. **Open** 10am-7pm Tue-Fri; 10am-6pm Sat; 11am-5pm Sun. **Credit** AmEx, Discover, MC, V.

A ski shop with a wide range of equipment, as well as information leaflets and a great deal of helpful advice. Though board rentals are available, the emphasis here is definitely on skiing.

### Snow conditions & information

**Adirondacks**: *Whiteface* 1-518 946 2223; *Lake Placid* 1-800 462 6236; *Gore Mountain 1-518 251 2411/1-518 251 2523; Big Tupper* 1-518 359 3651.
**Berkshires** *Catamount* 1-518 325 3200/1-413 528 1262).
**Catskills** *Hunter Mountain* 1-518 263 4223/toll-free 1-800 FOR SNOW. **Ski Windham** 1-518 734 4300/toll-free 1-800 729 4SNO.

## Whale Watching

### Okeanos Ocean Research Foundation

*Viking Dock, Montauk Harbor (1-516 668 5700; reservations 1-516 369 9840).* **Credit** Discover, MC, V.

You must arrive at 9.30am and be prepared for a four- to seven-hour trip. Daily whale watching trips run between July 1 and Labor Day, after which there are weekend trips and seal and bald eagle cruises.

*Another rip-roaring night out at the* **Turning Stone Casino.**

## The Bright Lights

## Gambling

Because it is largely illegal in most states, gambling is as exciting to the average American as alcohol is to a 15-year old. If you're not content with New York's various city and state lotteries, and the heavily-promoted Off Track Betting fails to turn you on, you'd better leave town. Las Vegas is a continent away but you can hop on a bus and be haemorrhaging money on the blackjack tables in **Atlantic City** or **Oneida** within a couple of hours.

### Atlantic City

*New Jersey.* **Transport** Greyhound bus (toll-free 1-800 231 2222) from Port Authority to various casinos; return bus picks you up at the Atlantic City Bus Terminal, two blocks from Boardwalk. **Fare** $23 return.

The trip to Atlantic City takes about two and a half hours. The town is famous for its faded glamour, its mafia connections and its casinos. While many New Yorkers disparage the place, anyone who's never encountered organised, excessive gambling before will find it amazing. The most famous of its 12 casinos are **Trump Plaza**, **Caesar's Palace** and Donald Trump's latest, the **Taj Mahal**. Once you're inside one casino, you can get to the others by way of the **Boardwalk**, which runs along the edge of the Atlantic Ocean, or take the Pacific Avenue bus ($1.25). Either bring your own spending money or just watch the crazed antics of the frenzied crowd.

Besides bars, restaurants and gift shops, there are floor shows and, at some casinos, concerts (the Rolling Stones played the live telecast of the Steel Wheels tour at the arena attached to Trump Plaza). The annual Miss America Pageant is held in the Atlantic City Convention Center at 2314 Pacific Avenue. Shoppers should head for Ocean One, a vast shopping mall set right on the water. Call the Atlantic City Visitors' Bureau (1-609 348 7130) for more information.

### Turning Stone Casino

*Oneida, New York (1-315 361 7711).* **By car** Take route 90 past Utica to exit 33 (about 300 miles). **Open** 24 hours daily. **Credit** AmEx, DC, MC, V.

The various Indian Nations, independent from state gambling laws, are free to make their own rules about games of chance. Since they can turn a huge profit, many fast growing gambling resorts are the result. Turning Stone, in the beautiful countryside east of the Finger Lakes, was recently opened by the Oneida Indian Nation. In terms of the number of games tables, it's the largest casino in the world. There are 16 roulette wheels, 122 blackjack tables, 20 crapshoots (dice), 10 baccarat tables and eight big six (poker) tables. It was only completed in September 1993, so little in the way of sleazy resort services have sprung up to help you fritter away your winnings. If you break the bank, head to Syracuse and book into the king size suite at the **Embassy** (toll-free 1-800 EMBASSY) for $136 a night. If you lose everything, there's a **Super 8 Motel** (1-315 363 5168) in Oneida for $51 a night.

## Theme Parks

### Action Park

*Vernon, New Jersey, on Route 94, 48 miles from Manhattan (1-201 827 2000).* **Transport** *by car* take route 80 west, to route 23 north, to route 94 north; *by bus* NJ Transit (1-201 762 5100). **Open** 10am-8pm daily June-September; 10am-8pm Sat, Sun Oct-May. **Admission** $27 adults Mon-Fri; $28 Sat, Sun; $14 after 3.30pm; $14 children under 4ft tall; free under 3s; $13 disabled, senior citizens. **Credit** AmEx, CB, DC, JCB, MC, V.

Bungee jumping, go-kart racing, the terror of the Slingshot, which propels you 14 storeys into the air, and the world's largest water park are the attractions here. The setting is beautiful – 200 acres of woods and hills – and there's a cable car ride to the top of nearby Mount Hamburg. Don't forget your swimming gear because the best rides are definitely the wet ones. You can save plenty of cash (up to $9 per person) by redeeming vouchers offered in cross-promotions with companies like Coca Cola, McDonalds, Burger King and Shoprite. Call up the Park and ask where to find the latest discount vouchers.

### Six Flags Great Adventure

*Jackson, New Jersey, on route 537, 50 miles from Manhattan (1-908 928 1821).* **Transport** *by car* take exit 7A off the New Jersey turnpike or exit 98 off the Garden State Parkway to Interstate 195, exit 16; by *bus* NJ Transit (1-201 762 5100) from Port Authority. **Open** 10am-10pm daily May-Sept (closing times may vary); 10am-8pm Sat, Sun pre- and post-season. **Admission** $31 adults; $19.95 under 14s; free under 3s; a dollar less without safari park. **Credit** AmEx, Discover, MC, V.

'Bigger than Disneyland and a whole lot closer' is the slogan with which this theme park entices Manhattanites. There's a huge drive-through safari park, a massive collection of top-of-the-range rides and the obligatory fast food and junky souvenirs. Not to be missed is the Great American Scream Machine, the world's highest/fastest roller-coaster, and the new Batman ride, a particularly scary roller-coaster which, instead of the normal carriages, has you hanging down from the track with your legs dangling in the breeze. As with Action Park, call to find out about promotional discounts.

### Playland

*Rye, New York (1-914 967 2040).* **Transport** Metro-North from Grand Central to Rye, then connecting bus ($1.15). **Open** *summer* noon-11pm Tue-Thur, Sun; noon-midnight Fri, Sat; call for details of winter hours. **Admission** free; 36 tickets $16; 24 tickets $12 (rides 'cost' 3-5 tickets). **No credit cards.**

An old-fashioned amusement and theme park set on the banks of the Long Island Sound. The 65-year-old facility is known for its new and historic amusement rides and attractions, including the Derby Racer and the Dragon Coaster, as well as the new Magic Carpet. There's a separate Kiddie Land for little children. There are also picnic grounds, a pool and, of course, the beautiful beach. You may recognise Playland from a scene in the film *Big*.

## On the History Trail

If you're keen on history or just enjoy scenery, you'll get both with a trip up the **Hudson Valley**. Beautiful summer residences of famous New Yorkers line the river (*see below*). Most are open from March until the end of the year, daily from 10am to 5pm, and closed on Tuesdays.

You can get information from Historic Hudson Valley, 150 White Plains Road, Tarrytown, NY 10591 (1-914 631 8200), which also offers boat trips from Manhattan or New Jersey up the Hudson to several of the historic houses.

Another way to see them is by car (*see chapter* **Essential Information** for a number of car rental firms). The Historic Hudson Valley office and any of the sites listed can provide you with detailed driving instructions.

Metro-North, the commuter railway that leaves Manhattan's Grand Central Station, is a fast, easy and scenic way to get to towns near these sights, with themed tours often available (call 532 4900 for fare and schedule information). Or you can take Amtrak trains from Penn Station (call 1-800 USA RAIL for information).

### Montgomery Place

*River Road, Annandale-on-the-Hudson, New York (1-914 758 5461).* **Transport** Amtrak train to Rhinecliff Station (call 1-800 USA RAIL for fare information), then call the Blue Coach cab service when you arrive (1-914 876 2900). **Admission** $6 adults; $3 children over 6. **Open** *April-Oct* 10am-5pm Mon, Wed-Sun; call for out-of-season hours. **Credit** AmEx, V.

A fabulous mansion in lush grounds about 100 miles from Manhattan. It was built in 1804 for Janet Livingston Montgomery, the widow of a Revolutionary War patriot, and is set in 434 acres along the Hudson River. There are formal gardens, woodlands, views of the Catskill Mountains and a lawn where games are played and lemonade is served. Visitors may pick their own raspberries in July and peaches in August (call 1-914 758 6338 for picking conditions).

### Phillipsburg Manor

*Upper Hills, Tarrytown, New York (1-914 631 3992).* **Transport** *by car* north on New York State Thruway (I-87), take exit 9 for Tarrytown and the sign is two miles on the left; *by train* Metro-North to Tarrytown, then 5-mile cab journey. **Admission** $7 adults; $4 children over-six. **Open** *March-Dec* 10am-5pm Mon, Wed-Sun. **Credit** AmEx, MC, V.

The Manor was once the home of Frederick Flypse (later called Flypsen, then Philipse), who came to the New World in the early 1650s as Governor Peter Stuyvesant's carpenter. Through business acumen and some shrewd marriages, Frederick managed to elevate his landholding of about 52,500 acres to the status of 'Lordship or Mannour of Philpsborough'. At the Upper Mills, which was just a small portion of his holding, Frederick constructed a dam, grist mill and Manor House, with a Dutch church adjacent to the property. A lively film explains the Manor's history up to the 1940s, when John D Rockefeller bought the property to preserve it as a historical site. It was officially declared a protected site in 1969 (even though it only covers 20 acres now). The grist mill still works and the Dutch barn is filled with animals. Guides wear period costumes. It's a charming place.

### Sunnyside

*Tarrytown, New York (1-914-591 8763).* **Transport** *by car* north on New York State Thruway (I-87), take exit 9 for Tarrytown and go one mile south on Route 9; *by train* Metro-North to Irvington, NY, then a 20-minute walk, or call 1-914 631 0031 for a cab. **Admission** $7 adults; $4 children over 6; $6 senior citizens. **Open** *March-Dec* 10am-5pm Mon, Wed-Sun. **Credit** AmEx, MC, V.

This is the delightful home of Washington Irving, author of *Rip Van Winkle* and *The Legend of Sleepy Hollow*. Sunnyside was built on the banks of the Hudson in 1835. Chatty guides in period costume lead you through the home; you can escape them by strolling though the lovely grounds. Irving is buried in Sleepy Hollow Cemetery, between Sunnyside and Phillipsburg Manor (*see above*). Ask for directions.

### Van Cortlandt Manor

*Croton-on-Hudson, New York (1-914 271 8981).* **Transport** *by car* north on New York State Thruway (I-87), take exit 9 for Tarrytown then go nine miles north; *by train* Metro-North to Croton-on-Hudson, then 10-minute walk. **Open** *March-Dec* 10am-5pm Mon, Wed-Sun. **Admission** $7 adults; $4 children over 6.

*The pastoral setting of* **Phillipsburg Manor**.

Set into a hillside overlooking the Croton and Hudson Rivers, the mansion was once home to Pierre Van Cortlandt, the state's first Lieutenant Governor, and his son Phillip, who served both as an officer under General Washington and a US Congressman. Now, there's a gift shop and picnic area in his estate.

### Cold Spring

*New York.* **Transport** Metro-North Hudson Line to Cold Spring. **Fare** $14.

Any time of the year, Cold Spring offers spectacular close-up views of the Hudson River. It's only 50 miles from Manhattan, but it seems like more. Once you arrive by train, walk through the underpass to get to Main Street, where a number of narrow-frame houses with porches and shutters sit alongside the four-storey commercial buildings. The place is tiny but has plenty of shops. For nearly a century life centred around the Cold Spring Foundry, an ironworks which opened in 1817 making gun tubes and steam engines. Head down to the water where you'll find a gazebo, the town dock and a tiny beach. You'll get a great view of the lush, green Hudson Highlands across the way. The Main Street Café (129 Main) sells fresh-baked buns for breakfast, good sandwiches and home-made fruit pies. Hudson House (2 Main), a landmark 1832 inn, serves American food; Dockside Harbor (1 North Street), which is on a grassy point by the water, has a seafood menu and a play area for children. Cold Spring is very popular with New Yorkers in the autumn.

### Museum Village

*Monroe, New York (1-914 782 8247).* **Transport** *by car* take the New York State Thruway (I-87) north to exit 16 at Harriman. Go four miles west along Route 17 to exit 129; *by bus* Shortline bus from Port Authority to Museum Village (1-800 631 8405 for fare and schedule information). **Open** 10am-5pm Wed-Fri; noon-5pm Sat, Sun, first weekend in May to first weekend in December. **Admission** $8 adults; $6 senior citizens; $5 children aged 3-15; free under 3. **Credit** MC, V.

About 55 miles outside Manhattan lies a 17-acre replica of a nineteenth-century village, dedicated to the re-creation of the lives of American Civil War troops. There are about 25 exhibition buildings, all with authentic details, some of which are staffed by guides and craft workers dressed in period costume. On Labor Day, the last weekend in August, historical re-enactors march in and recreate life circa 1864 for the annual Civil War Weekend. They sleep in Union and Confederate 'dog' tents, cook on open fires, participate in mock battles and trot around on horseback. Women in hoop skirts mourn the 'dead' and a blacksmith hammers in his shop. Children can join drill sergeants or help make craft items.

## New York State

Surrounding the cast iron and concrete grandeur of the city, New York State offers scenery of stupendous natural beauty. The best time to admire its grandeur is in the autumn, when the trees turn deep scarlet, flaming orange and soft gold. Against a backdrop of crashing waterfalls, soaring mountain peaks and seemingly endless forests, visitors can appreciate the less frenetic charms of the United States.

In addition to the regions covered below, and in the sections above, there are a number of other places that should be seen if you're driving through the state. The **Thousand Islands Region** on the St Lawrence Seaway is a favourite vacation spot for New Yorkers and Canadians. Boating and fishing are the main interests.

Glaciers carved gouges right through the middle of the state and left long bony indentations called the **Finger Lakes**. This area has become popular for any outdoor activity, for its vineyards and wineries, and for **Watkin's Glen** gorge and raceway. **Rochester** and **Syracuse** are the biggest local cities. One highlight in Rochester is the **Kodak Factory** tour and museum. **Alleghany State Park** and **Chautauqua Lake** are huge natural refuges in the very southwestern corner of the state near Jamestown. Throughout the state, wonders can be found in the most unlikely places. For instance, **Elmira**, near the southern border of New York, where Mark Twain summered and wrote much of his best work, or **Corning**, where you can go on the Corning Glass Factory Tours.

For more information on all activities in New York State contact:

### Hostelling International

*891 Amsterdam Avenue, at 103rd Street, NY 10025 (932 1860).*

The American Youth Hostels organisation is an excellent source of information on all outdoor activities state- and nationwide.

### New York State Tourist and Travel Information Center

*(1-518 474 4116/toll-free 1-800 225 5697).*

## Albany

Although overshadowed by New York City, **Albany** is the capital of the **Empire State**, and the nation's oldest chartered city (1686). The **Empire State Plaza**, overlooking the city, is where many of the state government buildings are located. The imposing **Corning Tower** is open from 9am until 4pm every day, and there are daily tours of the **State Capitol** building. The **Institute for the Performing Arts** (1-518 445 1711) has striking and unusual architecture, as evinced by its nickname: The Egg. The **Albany Institute of History and Art** (1-518 463 4478) is the elegant home of a wonderful collection of locally made silver and furniture. Other places near Albany worth a visit are **Schenectady**, **Saratoga** and **Cooperstown**.

Just 70 miles (112 kilometres) west of Albany, in Cooperstown, is the most important baseball diamond in the world. This is where Abner Doubleday invented baseball in 1839 and where you will find the **Baseball Hall of Fame** (1-607 547 7200). The Hall is filled with memorabilia from the national pastime. Next to the museum is the **Abner Doubleday Memorial Field** where Abner worked out the finer points of the game.

For more information about the Greater Albany area, contact Albany County Convention and Visitors' Bureau at 52 South Pearl Street, Albany, New York 12207 (toll-free 1-800 258 3582/1-518 434 1217).

## Niagara Falls

**Niagara Falls** may be a long way from New York City, but good things are worth travelling for and this is one of the best. No matter what is done (and plenty is) to make a buck off this natural wonder, its beauty and power remain undiminished.

The Falls, which are part of the Niagara River, separate the United States from Canada and Lake Erie from Lake Ontario. **American** and **Bridal Veil Falls** are in the United States and **Horseshoe Falls** are in Canada.

The 182 foot (55-metre) high falls span 3,175 feet (953 metres) and throw three quarters of a million gallons of water over the edge per second. A bridge out to Goat Island, which separates the two countries' waterfalls, provides an impressive view of the cascades. You can see the mist and rainbows produced by the falls and hear the loud thunder especially well from here. The Cave of the Winds is where raincoats are an absolute must. Visitors go down in the lift to the bottom of the American falls, travel a short way and can look out through the falls while standing under and behind them. The water acts as a prism when there is sufficient light, so it can be like standing in a rainbow.

Other attractions on the American side are the observation tower on Prospect Point, which provides a panoramic view of the falls, and the Maid of the Mist Boat Trips, which get close enough to the falls for all and sundry to be tossed around and thoroughly drenched. Further down the gorge are the infamous whirlpools, the Schoelkopf Geological Center, the Robert Moses Niagara Power Plant, which supplies the whole East Coast with electricity, and Old Fort Niagara. The Canadian side of the falls (accessible by bus from Buffalo) has the best views of the water, and some incredibly kitsch honeymoon hotels. The biggest attraction, apart from the water, is the Native American Center, a

*The* **Saratoga** *racing season lasts through August.*

fascinating collection of artefacts housed in a turtle-shaped building.

The area has more to offer than the falls. **Buffalo**, New York State's second largest city, is one of the most attractive newly renovated old industrial cities of America. Buffalo has a professional football and hockey team and a brand new major league baseball team and field. In addition to the attraction of high-class spectator sports, there are the Erie Canal, Lakes Erie and Ontario, and the fabulous Albright-Knox Museum of Art.

For more information contact:

**Greater Buffalo Convention and Visitors' Bureau**

*107 Delaware Avenue, Buffalo, NY 14202 (1-716 852 0511/1-800 283 3256).*

**Niagara County Convention and Visitors' Bureau**

*139 Niagara Street, Lockport 14094 (toll-free 1-800 338 7890).*

**Niagara County Tourism and Fishing Office**

*139 Niagara Street, Lockport 14094 (1-716 439 7300).*

## Saratoga

*Transport* Amtrak train (toll-free 1-800 USA TRAIN), 3½ hours, about $65 return); Greyhound bus (971 6363), 4 hours, about $50 return).

Located about 175 miles north of Manhattan, **Saratoga** gained fame for its mineral-water baths and racetrack. Its heyday was in the 1870s but it's still a deservedly popular tourist destination. Visit in August when the **Saratoga Race Track** (1-518 584 6200) – the country's oldest and loveliest – begins its season.

From June through early September the **Saratoga Performing Arts Center**, formed in 1966, attracts lovers of classical, jazz and pop music, ballet and opera. In July, the New York City Ballet takes up residence here for three weeks, followed by the Newport Jazz Festival. The New York City Opera and Philadelphia Orchestra continue the season.

The wealthy built beautiful homes here and the highest concentration is along Union Avenue, North Broadway and Caroline Street. There is also the **National Museum of Racing**, Union Avenue and Ludlow Street (1-518 584 0400), and the **National Museum of Dance**, South Broadway (1-518 584 9330).

You should also visit the mineral bath and get a massage at the **Roosevelt Mineral Baths** in Saratoga Spa State Park (1-518 584 2011). View the area, plus the Green Mountains of Vermont, from a hot air balloon, on a tour with Adirondack Balloon Flights.

While the cost of a stay at the Adelphi Hotel on Broadway (1-518 587 4688) may be steep for the average tourist ($90-$150 q night off-peak; from $125 peak season), you should at least take a look at its lobby. Built in 1877, it's the only remaining grand hotel in town. Most of the fine restaurants and bars seem to be on Broadway. For nightlife, make a reservation at Caffe Lena on Phila Street (1-518 583 0022): everybody's played here, including Bob Dylan in 1962.

For more information about Saratoga, contact:

**Saratoga County Chamber of Commerce**
*494 Broadway, Saratoga Springs, NY 12866 (1-518 584 3255/584 4471).*

**Saratoga County Promotion Department**
*County Municipal Center, Ballston Spa, NY 12020 (toll-free 1-800 526 8970).*

**Adirondack Balloon Flights**
*PO Box 65, Glens Falls, NY 12801 (1-518 793 6342).* **Open** April-November (call for details). **Price** $175 per person. **Credit** AmEx, Discover, MC, V.
A breathtaking way to see the beauty of the Adirondacks and the Lake George region, as well as the Green Mountains of Vermont. The one-hour balloon ride is especially beautiful during the autumn. Flights are scheduled around sunrise and three hours before sunset and may be cancelled because of bad weather.

**Harness Track Tour**
*(1-518 584 2110).*
Hour-long tours of Saratoga start at 10am and 11am Mon-Fri from May to early September.

**Saratoga Performing Arts Center (SPAC)**
*Saratoga Springs, NY 12866-0826 (1-518 584 9330/584 7100 credit card reservations).* **Open** *June-first week in Sept* 10am-5pm Mon-Sat; 1-5pm Sun. **Credit** AmEx, MC, V.
Tickets for the New York City Opera events cost from $13 for a seat on the lawn to $42 for an orchestra box; Newport Jazz Festival day tickets are $29 for a lawn seat bought in advance to $40 for an orchestra seat. Tickets for the New York City Ballet or the Philadelphia Orchestra cost from $13to $30.50, and you will pay up to $70 for the Ballet's gala performance at the end of the season in July. All SPAC events have facilities for the disabled.

## General Information

For more information on areas worth visiting within New York State contact:

**Allegheny State Park, Recreation and Historic Preservation Region**
*Salamanca, NY 14779 (1-716 354 9121).*

**Allegheny County Museum and Travel Information Center**
*Court Street, Belmont, NY 14813 (1-716 268 9293).*

**Central New York State Park Region**
*Jamesville, NY 13078 (1-315 492 1756).*

**Finger Lakes Association**
*309 Lake Street, Penn Yan, NY 14527 (1-315 536 7488).*

**Mark Twain Country Information Office**
*215 East Church Street, Elmira, NY 14901 (1-607 734 5137).*

**Northern Chautauqua County Chamber of Commerce**
*212 Lakeshore Drive, Dunkirk, NY 14048 (1-716 366 6200).*

**Rochester/Monroe County Convention and Visitors' Bureau**
*126 Andrew Street, Rochester, NY 14604 (1-716 546 3070).*

**Syracuse Convention and Visitors' Bureau**
*572 South Salina Street, NY 13202 (1-315 470 1800).*

**Thousand Islands State Park and Recreation Region**
*Keewaydin State Park, Alexandria Bay, NY 13607 (1-315 482 2593).*

**Thousand Islands International Council**
*Alexandria Bay, NY 13607.*

**Wine Country Tourist Association**
*Hammondsport, NY 14840.*

# City Life

New York is hardly representative of American cities. In fact most Americans think of it as another planet entirely. If you'd like to step out of Manhattan's whirling maelstrom for a few days and see the sights of a more typical urban US, three of the country's most important cities are within four or five hours' drive.

## Boston

The city of **Boston** was the birthplace of the United States as an independent nation. Its antique architecture and winding streets tell the story of the early colonists leading up to their violent rebellion against British rule. Until 1755 it was the biggest city in America, home to the country's earliest waves of immigrants, and throughout the colonial period it remained the busiest foreign port in the British Empire. This early and rapid growth in the seventeenth and eighteenth centuries has left it with a refreshingly human scale. Its preserved gentility and the noticeably low impact of the automobile make it a real contrast to New York and most American cities.

Walking the Freedom Trail, marked throughout its length by red bricks set in the street, is the easiest way to take in the city's history. Start at the Visitor Information Center on **Boston Common**, once an area of grazing land bordering the sea until nineteenth century landfill turned the estuary into the residential area of the Back Bay. Follow the trail past the gilded dome of the **State House** (1798), still the seat of Massachussetts' government and **Park Street Church**, where William Lloyd Garrison announced his campaign to abolish slavery in 1829.

King's Chapel **Burying Ground** and **Old Granary Burying Ground** are the resting places for the city's first colonists and such famous American patriots as Samuel Adams, Paul Revere and John Hancock. The **Old State House**, lovingly restored to its original 1712 condition, was where the Declaration of Independence was read on 18 July 1776. A ring of stones outside marks where five people were killed when soldiers fired on an angry crowd in the 1770 Boston Massacre.

**Old North Church** and **Copp's Hill Burial Ground** were the two places lit by signal lanterns to alert Paul Revere that the British were coming. Revere entered the history books by riding several miles at a furious pace to carry the warning to nearby Lexington and the mass of the Patriot forces. The **USS Constitution** ('Old Ironsides') is the world's oldest warship still afloat – you can take a ferry from Long Wharf to Charlestown Navy Yard to see it. If you would prefer a more rapid look at the city there are numerous trolley bus companies operating a sightseeing circuit. These allow you to step on and off at a multitude of strategic places.

Competing tourist trails include the **Harborwalk**, with a maritime theme, starting at the National Park Service Visitors' Center (*see below*); and the **Black Heritage Trail**, at the Boston African-American National Historic Site, 46 Joy Street (1-617 742 5415). The waterfront is where you'll find the excellent **New England Aquarium, Central Wharf** (1-617 973 5200), the **Children's Museum**, 300 Congress Street (1-617 426 6500), and the **Computer Museum**, same address (1-617 426 2800). The **Boston Tea Party Ship and Museum**, Street Bridge (1-617 338 1773), is based around the event which provoked the rejection of British rule: the dumping, in 1773, of a British cargo of tea into the harbour.

Boston has a thriving stand-up comedy scene, and is also home to TV's *Cheers*, or at least the Bull and Finch, 84 Beacon Street, Beacon Hill (1-617 227 9605), where the exterior shots were filmed.

The Boston Symphony Orchestra, Symphony Hall, 301 Huntingdon Avenue (1-617 266 1492), gives its famous Boston Pops concerts in May and June. Over the river in Cambridge is where you'll find the hushed lawns and studious cloisters of Ivy League academia that is **Harvard University**.

## Getting There

If you're driving take Interstate 95 through Connecticut and Rhode Island. The trip can be made in under four hours. Greyhound buses (1-800 231 2222) leave from Port Authority almost every hour and cost around $48 return. Amtrak (582 6875) runs trains nearly as frequently at $80$-90 return. If you look out for bargains, off-peak discounts and student reductions, it will cost you around the same to fly, especially if you can book as early as possible in advance. Both Delta (239 0700) and USAir (1-800 428 4322) run regular air shuttles from New York. Call 1-800 23 LOGAN for Logan Airport information.

## Accommodation

**Boston International AYH Hostel**
*12 Hemenway Street (1-617 536 9455).*
A bed in a dorm is $16 for member and non-members.

**Newbury Guest House**
*261 Newbury Street (1-617 437 7666).*
Doubles from $95, suites from $125.

**The Bostonian**
*at Sameuil Hall Marketplace (1-617 523 3600).*
Doubles from $245, suites from $335.

**Bed and Breakfast Agency of Boston**
*47 Commercial Wharf, Boston, MA, 02110 (1-617 720 3540/toll-free 1-800 248 9262/toll-free from UK 0800 895128).*

## Useful Addresses

**Visitor Information Center**
*Park Street Subway, Boston Common (1-617 536 4100).*

**Greater Boston Chamber of Commerce**
*1 Beacon Street, 4th floor, Boston, MA 02108 (1-617 227 4500).*

**Greater Boston Convention and Visitors' Bureau**
*PO Box 490 Prudential Tower, Suite 400 Boston Massachusetts 02199 (toll-free 1-800 888 5515).*

**National Park Service Visitors' Center**
*15 State Street, Boston MA 02129 (1-617 242 5642).*

# Washington DC

The seat of government and the nation's capital city was moved to Washington in the uninviting swamplands of DC – 'District of Columbia' – with the express purpose of dissuading politicians from staying there too often. The city was built throughout the nineteenth century to a plan drawn up in 1800 by Frenchman Pierre L'Enfant and the African American Benjamin Manneker. It is full of gracious avenues and imposing buildings, home not only to the various government offices but also to an abundance of national cultural institutions. Because of the lobbying system, there is also a heavy corporate presence here.

Washington is a city with a double life, however. Beyond the formal grandeur there are neighbourhoods of extreme poverty where guns and crack are the tools of the local economy. Although Washington was the first city to have a black majority (proudly christened 'Chocolate City'), as in all of urban America the wealth here is very clearly divided along racial lines. Come and see the high-powered wheels of government in action, but don't forget that Washington is also the scene of appalling violence, a place where the world's surgeons are sent to learn about bullet-wounds.

Take a free tour around the **US Capitol**, the famous white-domed home of the Senate and the House of Representatives. Other government attractions include the **US Supreme Court**, where you can oversee proceedings as the laws of the land are tossed around; and of course the **White House**, home and office to the president. The largest library in the world, the **Library of Congress**, grew from Thomas Jefferson's private reading collection and now contains 100 million books.

Monuments to various leaders and visionaries abound. The simple obelisk of the **Washington Monument**, at 555 feet the world's tallest masonry structure, lies at the centre of the large formal park known as the **Mall**. In its western corner Abraham Lincoln is immortalised by the **Lincoln Memorial**, a colonnade containing his huge bronze statue. The **Jefferson Memorial** lies among the flower trees of East Potomac Park.

Also in the Mall, don't miss the extremely moving sculptural symbolism of the **Vietnam Veterans' Memorial**. The other great monument of war, the **Iwo Jima Memorial**, the famous sculpture of World War II GIs erecting a flagpole, is on the other side of the Potomac River, to the north of **Arlington National Cemetery**, which is full of the country's top dead people.

*You don't have to don fancy dress to view the* **Liberty Bell**. *See page 309.*

If it begins with 'National', chances are you'll find it in Washington DC. The **National Museum of Natural History** is at the north of the Mall between 9th and 12th Streets (1-202 357 2747); the **National Museum of American History** is next door between 12th and 14th Streets (1-202 357 1481); and the **National Air and Space Museum**, on the south side of the Mall between 4th and 7th Streets (1-202 357 1400), is the city's most popular destination.

The **National Museum of African Art** is on the south side of the Mall at 950 Independence Avenue (1-202 357 4860); The **National Museum of American Art** is on G Street between 7th and 9th Streets (1-202 357 3111); the **National Gallery** is on the north of The Mall between 3rd and 7th Streets (1-202 737 4215).

**The National Archives**, north side of the Mall at 7th Street and Constitution Avenue (1-202 501 5400), not only house the Declaration of Independence, the Bill of Rights and the US Constitution, but also has a 1297 copy of the Magna Carta and the infamous Watergate tapes. The latest addition is the **US Holocaust Memorial Museum** (1-202 488 0400).

Other galleries include the **National Portrait Gallery**, F Street between 7th and 9th Streets (1-202 357 2920); the **Sackler Gallery**, south side of the Mall at 1050 Independence Avenue (1-202 357 2104) with its oriental collections; the **Corcoran Gallery**, 17th Street between E Street and New York Avenue (1-202 638 3211); and the **Phillips Collection**, 1600 21st Street at Q Street (1-202 387 2151) with its excellent modern work. The **National Museum of Women in the Arts** is at 1250 New York Avenue (1-202 783 5000).

Many of these galleries and museums are part of the **Smithsonian Institute**, 'the nation's attic'. The visitor centre for the institution is at the Castle, halfway down the Mall. It's the place to go for details on all the various attractions.

Don't miss the hour-long tours round the **FBI Headquarters**, Pennsylvania Avenue between 9th and 10th Streets (1-202 324 3000). Crime detection techniques are explained, and the tour ends with a blazing display of automatic gunfire.

Other insights into America's power structures can be gained at the **Bureau of Printing and Engraving**, 14th Street at C Street (1-202 622 2000), where ordinary paper rolls through some inky presses and emerges as millions of dollars. The club and bar scene is fairly unimpressive. Head to the **Kennedy Center** (1-202 467 4600) instead for more highbrow entertainment.

## Getting There

If you're driving, take Interstate 95 south through New Jersey and Pennsylvania. The trip can be made in about five hours. Greyhound buses (toll-free 1-800 231 2222) leave from Port Authority every hour, costing around $50 return. Amtrak (582 6875) runs trains nearly as frequently from $90 return.

Because of the volume of traffic between New York and DC, with off-peak discounts and student reductions it will cost you around the same to fly. Both Delta (239 0700) and USAir (1-800 428 4322) fly regular air shuttles from New York and there's a flight every half hour. In addition Continental (319 9494), TWA (290 2121) and United (1-800 241 6522) all run services between the two cities.

## Accommodation

### Washington International AYH Hostel

*1009 11th Street, NW (1-202 737 2333).*
Dorm beds $13 per night for members, $21 for non-members.

### Harrington Hotel

*436 11th Street, NW (1-202 628 8140).*
Doubles from $65.

### Hay-Adams Hotel

*1 Lafayette Square, NW (1-202 638 2260).*
Be the president's neighbour for $255 per night (double room).

### Bed & Breakfast Ltd

*PO Box 12011, Washington DC 20005 (1-202 328 3510).*
This agency will track down B&B accommodation.

## Useful Addresses

### DC Committee to Promote Washington

*1212 New York Avenue, NW, Suite 200, Washington DC 20005 (1-202 347 2875/ toll-free 1-800 422 8644).*

### Washington Convention and Visitor Association

*1212 New York Avenue, NW, Suite 600, Washington DC 20005 (1-202 789 7000).*

### Visitors' Center

*1455 Pennsylvania Avenue, NW, Washington DC 20005 (1-202 789 7038).*

# Philadelphia

When Charles II rid himself of a troublesome non-conformist, William Penn, by giving him a chunk of the New World, Pennsylvania was founded. Penn, a Quaker, created the 'holy experiment' of a colony based on tolerance.

The capital was built in 1682 on a grid system of Penn's devising which became the norm for American cities. He called his city Philadelphia, meaning 'City of Brotherly Love', and was unique in signing a treaty for peaceful co-existence with the local American Indians.

Penn's example attracted similar settlers. Catholics, Mennonites from Germany and other Quakers like himself migrated here. Freed from the shackles of discrimination, they put all their efforts into trading and commerce, and built Philadelphia into the British Empire's second largest city.

It was here that the Declaration of Independence was first read, and also where the US Constitution was drawn up. Philadelphia was the emerging nation's capital for many years during the War of Independence and remained so until the grandiose designs of Washington DC were made a reality in 1800 (*see above*).

With its traditions of tolerance, Philadelphia became a key destination in the North for many of the black people freed from slavery after the civil war, and the city provided America with its first black mayor.

Like Boston, much of the city's history is tied up in the events of the American Revolution. If you visit **Independence Hall** you can see where the Declaration of Independence was drawn up, as well as the Constitution itself. **Congress Hall** next door was the home of the nation's first government, while the **Old City Hall** was the first home of the Supreme Court.

These buildings are all in the **Independence Hall National Park**, which also includes the **Franklin Museum**, commemorating the wit and wisdom of Benjamin Franklin, the **Free Quaker Meeting House**, the **B Franklin Post Office** postal museum, and the **Philosophical Hall** which Franklin founded as a debating arena. In fact the whole city is full of places where Franklin, Jefferson, Washington etc ate, slept, worked and worshipped.

You can't miss seeing the **Liberty Bell**, the famous cracked bell which rang out for each patriot victory and was later adopted as an anti slavery symbol. It can be found in a small purpose-built museum on Market Street.

The importance of Philadelphia as a port is emphasised in the **Independence Seaport Museum**, 211 South Columbus Boulevard, at Walnut Street (1-215 925 5439). Art hotspots include the **Philadelphia Museum of Art**, Franklin Parkway at 26th Street (1-215 763 8100), not only a world-class art gallery but also a featured location in the film *Rocky*; the **Rodin Museum**, Franklin Parkway at 26th Street (1-215 763 8100); and the **Museum of American Art**, Broad Street and Cherry Street (1-215 972 7600).

Other museums worth a visit include the **Franklin Institute Science Museum**, 20th Street and Franklin Parkway (1-215 448 1208), with its truly amazing **Planetarium**, **Futures Center** and **Omniverse** movie screen. The literary **Rosenbach Museum** at 2010 Delancey Street (1-215 732 1600) keeps Joyce's manuscript for *Ulysses*.

There's also the **University Museum of Archaeology and Anthropology**, Spruce Street and 33rd Street (1-215 898 4000); the **Institute of Contemporary Art**, Sansom Street and 36th Street (1-215 898 7108); the **Academy of Natural Sciences**, 19th Street and Franklin Parkway (1-215 299 1020); and the wonderful **Mutter Museum**, 19 South 22nd Street (1-215 563 3737), which is full of strange medical exhibits and other gruesome pickle-jar type things.

While you're in Philadelphia, don't forget this is the cheese capital of the nation. Enjoy some cheese fries, grab a slice of cheesecake, and wander down to the southside of town where the Italian neighbourhood provides visitors with the best cheese steaks in town – the essential Philly dish.

The city's nightlife is centred around **South Street**, a yuppified strip of bars and restaurants. For more low-brow entertainment head to any of the music bars catering to the large and influential student population.

Be warned, this is very much a college town and the cro-magnons on the door rigorously enforce the over-21 drinking rule and won't let you in without ID – even if you look positively middle-aged.

## Getting There

It'll take you about two and a half hours by car to get to Philadelphia from New York on Interstate 95. The **Greyhound** company (toll-free 1-800 231 2222) runs buses practically every hour at a return price of $30. **Amtrak** (582 6875) trains are around $50 return.

If you want to fly, almost all the domestic airlines operate between the two cities for around $80 return. Call Philadelphia International Airport (1-215 492 3181).

## Accommodation

### Chamounix Mansion International AYH Hostel

*West Fairmount Park (1-215 878 3676).*
Dorm beds $12.50 members and non-members.

### The Village Guest House

*808 South 2nd Street (1-215 755 9770).*
Close to the main drag, the Guest House has rooms from $55, including breakfast.

### Comfort Inn

*100 North Delaware Avenue (1-215 627 7900).*
Rooms start at $69, including breakfast.

### Bed and Breakfast Center City

*1804 Pine Street, Philadelphia, PA 19103 (1-215 735 1137).*

## Useful Addresses

### Philadelphia Convention and Visitors' Bureau

*1515 Market Street, Suite 2020, Philadelphia, PA 19102 (1-215 636 3300).*

### Visitor Center

*1525 JFK Boulevard (1-215 636 1666).*

### Independence Hall National Park

*313 Walnut Street, Philadelphia, Pennsylvania 19106 (1-215 597 8974).*

# Survival

# Survival

***Essential contacts, visitor information and where to turn for help if the Big Apple turns sour.***

All 1-800 numbers can be called toll free.

## Emergencies

### Ambulances

In an emergency dial 911 for an ambulance or call the operator on 0.

To complain about slow service, non-attendance or poor treatment call the Department of Health Emergency Medical Service (1-718 416 7000).

### Fire

In an emergency dial 911.

### Police

In an emergency dial 911.

For the location of the nearest police precinct or for general information about police services call 374 5000.

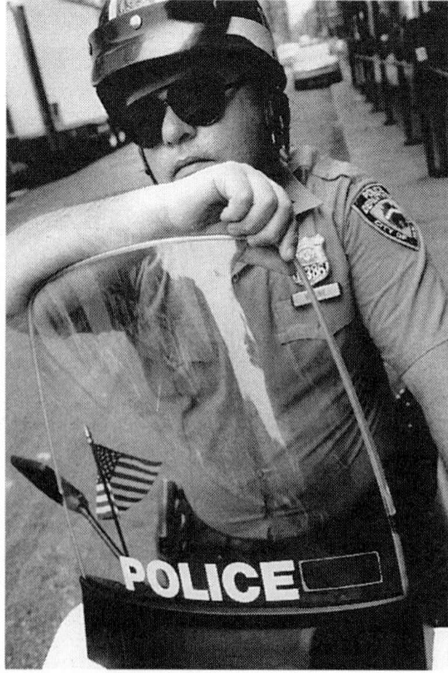


*New York's finest (see above).*

## Help Lines & Agencies

### Child Abuse

**Childhelp's National Child Abuse Hotline**

*(1-800 422 4453).* **Open** 24 hours daily.
Trained psychologists provide general crisis counselling and can help in an emergency. Callers include abused children, parents having problems with children, and runaways.

**New York Society for the Prevention of Cruelty to Children**

*(233 5500).* **Open** 9am-5pm Mon-Fri; recorded referral service in English and Spanish at other times.
Investigates reports of child abuse in Manhattan. If a situation seems dangerous to a child, they can remove the child, and must file a petition for a civil procedure in family court within three days.

**New York State Child Abuse and Maltreatment Register**

*(1-800 342 3720).* **Open** 24 hours daily.
This is the State government agency to which child abuse occurrences should be referred.

### Consumer Problems

**New York City Department of Consumer Affairs**

*(487 4444).* **Open** 9.30am-4.30pm Mon-Fri.
Report complaints on consumer-related affairs to the department.

**Better Business Bureau**

*(533 6200).* **Open** 9am-5pm Mon-Fri.
Advice on consumer-related complaints: shopping, services etc. Each call costs 95¢.

### Crime Victims

**Victim Services Agency**

*(577 7777).* **Open** 24 hours daily.
Telephone and one-to-one counselling for any victim of domestic violence, personal crime or rape, as well as practical help with court processes, compensation and legal aid.

### Domestic Violence

**Victim Services Domestic Violence Hotline**

*(1-800 621 4673).* **Open** 24 hours daily.
Trained social workers offer help, advice and shelter space to battered women. Working women pay a fee.

**New York State Domestic Violence Hotline**

*(1-800 942 6906/1-800 942 6908 Spanish).* **Open** 24 hours daily; Spanish line 9am-5pm daily.
Referrals to local programmes and, if necessary, shelter are given, as well as information on the legal options available.

## Electricity, Gas & Water

### Con Ed Emergency Line

*Gas emergency (683 8830).* **Open** 24 hours daily.
*Electrical or steam emergency (683 0862).* **Open** 24 hours daily.
Call these numbers if you smell gas or spot a steam leak, or if your electricity fails. Gas leaks are dealt with quickly. Other problems tend not to be.

### Public Service Commission Emergency Hotline

*(1-800 342 3355).* **Open** 7.30am-7.30pm Mon-Fri.
Advice on what to do if your gas or electricity is cut off because you can't pay the bill.

## Financial Help

If you do run out of cash, don't expect your embassy or consulate to lend you money – they won't, though they may be persuaded to repatriate you. Otherwise, you can have money wired to **Western Union**; call (1-800 325 6000) for the nearest office. Another service is **American Express MoneyGram**, which has 1300 locations in Manhattan alone (1-800 926 9400 for information and nearest office).

## Gambling

### Gamblers Anonymous

*445 West 45th Street, NY 10116 (265 8600).* **Open** 9am-11pm daily.
Information and meetings for compulsive gamblers.

## Legal Help

### Legal Aid Society

*(577 3300).* **Open** 9am-5pm Mon-Fri.
Free advice and referral on legal matters.

### Community Action For Legal Services

*(431 7200).* **Open** 9am-5pm Mon-Fri.
A government-funded referral service for people with any kind of legal problem.

### Marriage licences

*(669 2400).* **Open** 8.30am-4.30pm Mon-Fri.
Call this number for information on getting a licence.

## Rape

### Sex Crimes Report Line of the New York Police Department (NYPD)

*(267 7273).* **Open** 24 hours daily.
Reports of sex crimes are handled by a female detective from the NYPD's Bureau. She will inform the appropriate precinct, send an ambulance if requested and provide counselling and medical referrals. A detective from the Sex Crimes Squad will interview the victim, and you can request to be seen in your own home. Matters relating to violence against gay people, child victimisation and referrals for the family and friends of victims are also handled.

### St Lukes/Roosevelt Hospital Rape Crisis Center

*(523 4728).* **Open** 9am-5pm Mon-Fri, recorded referral message at other times.
This centre provides a trained volunteer who will accompany you through all aspects of reporting a rape and getting emergency treatment.

### Bellevue Hospital Rape Crisis Service

*(561 3755).* **Open** 9am-5pm Mon-Fri.
Immediate counselling and referral as well as emergency medical treatment, which is free to victims of rape.

### Mental Health Counselling Hotline

*(734 5876).* **Open** 24 hours daily.
Trained therapists will talk to you day or night, and will deal with all kinds of emotional problems, not just the consequences of rape.

## Runaways

### National Runaway Switchboard

*(1-800 621 4000).* **Open** 24 hours daily.
Runaways, homeless children and parents of runaways, are given guidance by trained staff, who can also refer victims of child abuse, attempted suicides, or those who have drug problems to the appropriate help agencies. Advice is given on places to stay and the hotline will send messages to parents if requested.

## Senior Citizens

### New York City Department for the Ageing

*(442 1000 information and referral; 442 3010 bilingual helpline).* **Open** 9am-5pm Mon-Fri.
Emergency help, information on crimes against the elderly, financial advice, counselling and so on are provided.

### Senior Action Line

*(669 7670).* **Open** 11am-1pm Mon-Fri.
Immediate counselling and referral service for all sorts of problems.

## Suicide

### Help Line

*(532 2400).* **Open** 24 hours daily.
Trained volunteers will talk to anyone contemplating suicide, and can also help with other personal problems and practical things like insurance. An interpretation service, offering 26 languages, operates from 9am to 9pm daily.

### The Samaritans

*(673 3000).* **Open** 24 hours daily.
People thinking of committing suicide or suffering from depression, grief, sexual anxiety or alcoholism can call this organisation for advice.

### Mental Health Counselling Hotline

*(734 5876).* **Open** 24 hours daily.
Trained therapists will talk to you day or night, and will deal with all kinds of emotional problems.

# General Information

### Bus & Subway information

*(1-718 330 1234).* **Open** 6am-9pm; recorded information menu at other times.

### New York Convention and Visitors Bureau

*2 Columbus Circle, at West 59th Street & Broadway (397 8222).* **Train** 1, 9, A, B, C or D to Columbus Circle. **Open** 9am-6pm Mon-Fri; 10am-6pm Sat, Sun, public holidays.
A barrage of leaflets on all manner of things; free, helpful advice on accommodation and entertainment; coupons for discounts; and free maps. The phone number gives you access to either a multilingual human or a huge 24-hour

*If you're really skint you can always busk it!*

menu of recorded information services. In addition to the main office there are booths at 2 World Trade Center, JFK Airport International Arrivals Building, Grand Central Station and Penn Station.

### New York telephone directories

The *Yellow* and *White Pages* have a mine of useful information at the front, including theatre seating diagrams maps as well as phone numbers. Hotels will have copies, otherwise try libraries or Nynex (the phone company) payment centres.

### Pay services

These information lines add extra weight to your phone bill. An opening message should tell you how much per minute you are paying.

### Stock Market prices

*(976 4141 recorded information).* **Open** 24 hours daily.

### Time

*(976 1616 recorded information).* **Open** 24 hours daily.

### Sports scores

*(976 1313).* **Open** 24 hours daily.

### Weather forecast

*(976 1212 recorded information).* **Open** 24 hours daily.

## Breakdowns/Car Towing

Towing prices are regulated by the city and everyone charges the same, ie the maximum.

### A Manhattan Towing

*510 Canal Street (239 4953).* **Open** 24 hours daily. **No credit cards.**

This towing company serves all five NYC boroughs. It provides road service for all minor work and battery recharging, and can open the car doors if you've lost the keys.

### Citywide Towing

*522 West 38th Street, between Tenth & Eleventh Avenues (727 7240).* **Open** 24 hours daily. **No credit cards.**

All types of repairs are done here on foreign and domestic autos. Free towing is offered if the firm gets the repair job.

## Communications

## Post Offices

### US General Post Office

*380 West 33rd Street, at Eighth Avenue (967 8585; 330 4000 Postal Information Line).* **Train** A, C or E to Penn Station. **Open** 24 hours daily, except for money orders and registered mail (open midnight-6pm daily).

This is the city's main post office. Phone to find out your nearest branch office, or call the information line to hear a vast menu of recorded postal information. There are 59 full service post offices in New York and, while queues are invariably long, stamps are available from self-service vending machines at face value. The opening times of post offices are usually 9am-5pm Mon-Fri; Saturday opening hours vary from office to office.

### Express letters

*(967 8585).*

Phone the central number for information. You need to use special envelopes and fill out a form. These can be obtained either at a post office or by organising a pick up. You are guaranteed 24-hour mail delivery to major US cities. Letters – both domestic and international – must be sent before 5pm.

## Stamps

Stamps are available at all post offices, and can also be obtained from vending machines in most drugstores (where they cost more). Airmail letters costs 60¢ for the first 0.5oz (14g) and 40¢ each additional 0.5oz to anywhere in the world. It is 32¢ to send a letter within the US, and 50¢ to send a postcard anywhere in the world.

## Telegrams

### Western Union

*(1-800 325 6000).* **Open** 24 hours daily.
Telegrams to addresses worldwide are taken over the phone, 24 hours daily, and charges added to your phone bill. Not available from payphones.

## Poste Restante

### Poste Restante

*c/o General Delivery, General Post Office, 421 Eighth Avenue, NY NY 10001.*
'General delivery' is what the Americans call poste restante. Ask people to address letters as above. You will need to show some form of identification – a passport or ID card – when picking up letters.

# Foreign Consulates

**Argentina** *(603 0400).*
**Australia** *(408 8400).*
**Austria** *(737 6400).*
**Bahamas** *(421 6420).*
**Bangladesh** *(867 3434).*
**Barbados** *(867 8435).*
**Belgium** *(586 5110).*
**Brazil** *(757 3085).*
**Myanmar** *(535 1310).*
**Canada** *(596 1700).*
**Chile** *(980 3366).*
**China (People's Republic of)** *(868 7752).*
**Colombia** *(949 9898).*
**Costa Rica** *(425 2620).*
**Cyprus** *(686 6016).*
**Czech Republic** *(535 8814).*
**Denmark** (223 4545).
**Dominican Republic** (768 2480).
**Ecuador** *(808 0170).*
**Egypt** *(759 7120).*
**El Salvador** *(889 3608).*
**Estonia** *(247 1450).*
**Finland** *(750 4400).*
**France** *(606 3688).*
**Germany** *(308 8700).*
**Ghana** *(832 1300).*
**Great Britain** *(745 0200).*
**Greece** *(988 5500).*
**Grenada** *(599 0301).*
**Guatemala** *(686 3837).*
**Guyana** *(527 3215).*
**Haiti** *(697 9767).*
**Honduras** *(269 3611).*
**Hungary** *(593 2700).*
**Iceland** *(686 4100).*
**India** *(879 7800).*
**Indonesia** *(879 0600).*
**Ireland** *(319 2555).*
**Israel** *(499 5300).*
**Italy** *(737 9100).*
**Jamaica** *(935 9000).*
**Japan** *(371 8222).*
**Kenya** *(486 1300).*
**Kuwait** *(973 4300).*
**Korea** *(752 1700).*
**Lebanon** *(744 7905).*
**Lithuania** *(354 7840).*
**Luxembourg** *(888 6664).*
**Madagascar** *(986 9491).*
**Malaysia** *(490 2722).*
**Malta** *(725 2345).*
**Mexico** *(689 0456).*
**Monaco** *(759 5227).*
**Morocco** *(758 2625).*
**Nepal** *(370 4188).*
**Netherlands** *(246 1429).*
**Nigeria** *(808 0301).*
**Norway** *(421 7333).*
**Pakistan** *(879 5800).*
**Panama** *(421 5420).*
**Paraguay** *(682 9441).*
**Peru** *(481 7410).*
**Philippines** *(764 1330).*
**Poland** *(889 8360).*
**Portugal** *(246 4580).*
**St Vincent** *(687 4490).*
**Saudi Arabia** *(752 2740).*
**South Africa** *(213 4880).*
**Russia** *(348 0926).*
**Spain** *(355 4080).*
**Sri Lanka** *(986 7040).*
**Sudan** *(573 6033).*
**Sweden** *(751 5900).*
**Switzerland** *(758 2560).*
**Thailand** *(754 1770).*
**Trinidad and Tobago** *(682 7272).*
**Turkey** *(949 0160).*
**Uruguay** *(753 8191).*
**Venezuela** *(826 1660).*

# Disabled

### Mayor's Office for People With Disabilities

*52 Chambers Street, near Broadway, Room 206 (788 2830).* **Train** 1, 2, 3, A or C to Chambers Street. **Open** 9am-5pm Mon-Fri.
The office organises services for disabled people and offers help and advice.

### Lighthouse Incorporated

*111 East 59th Street, between Park & Lexington Avenues (821 9200/1-800 334 5497).* **Train** 4, 5 or 6 to 59th Street; N or R to Lexington Avenue. **Open** 9am-5pm Mon-Fri.
In addition to running a store selling handy items for sight-impaired people, this organisation can provide help and information for the blind dealing with life – or a holiday – in New York City.

### New York Society for the Deaf

*817 Broadway, at 12th Street (777 3900).* **Train** L, N, R, 4, 5 or 6 to Union Square. **Open** 9am-5pm Mon-Thur; 9am-4pm Fri.
Contact the association for advice and information on facilities for the deaf.

# Gay & Lesbian

*See also chapters* **Gay New York** *and* **Women's New York**.

### Gay and Lesbian Switchboard

*(777 1800)*. **Open** noon-midnight daily with recorded information menu at other hours.
Help, information and chatty advice of all sorts is provided. Good for visitors.

### Gay Men's Health Service (GMHC) Hotline

*(807 6655/ttd 645 7470)*. **Open** 9am-9pm Mon-Fri, Sun; 9am-3pm Sat; recorded information menu at other times.
GMHC was the world's first organisation to meet the threat of AIDS. Its hotline gives information on all aspects of safe sex and HIV-related health services.

### Lesbian and Gay Community Services Center

*208 West 13th Street, near Eighth Avenue (620 7310)*. **Train** 1, 2 or 3 to 14th Street. **Open** 9am-11pm daily.
The home or meeting place for over 250 gay and lesbian groups of all natures. The homo nerve centre of New York.

### Lesbian Switchboard

*(741 2610)*. **Open** 6-10pm daily.
An unfunded advice service, the switchboard is staffed by volunteers. Good for general information about lesbian events in the city.

### NYC Gay and Lesbian Anti-Violence Project

*647 Hudson at Gansevoort (807 0197)*. **Train** 1, 2 or 3 to 14th Street. **Open** 10am-8pm Mon-Thur; 10am-6pm Fri; 24-hour hotline.
Advice and support for the victims of anti-gay and anti-lesbian attacks. The Anti-Violence Project also provides advice about going to the police and works with the New York Police Department Bias Unit. Short- and long-term counselling is available.

## Medical Treatment

## Emergency Rooms

You will have to pay for emergency treatment – at least $75. All major cards will be accepted. Emergency rooms are always open at:

### Cabrini Medical Centre

*227 East 19th Street, between Second & Third Avenues (995 6120)*. **Train** 4, 5, 6, L, N or R to Union Square.

### Mount Sinai Hospital

*Madison Avenue & West 100th Street (241 7171)*. **Train** 4, 5 or 6 to 96th Street.

### Roosevelt Hospital

*428 West 59th Street, off Ninth Avenue (523 4000)*. **Train** 1, 9, A, B, C or D to Columbus Circle.

### St Luke's Hospital Centre

*West 113th Street & Amsterdam Avenue (523 3335)*. **Train** 1 or 9 to 116th Street.

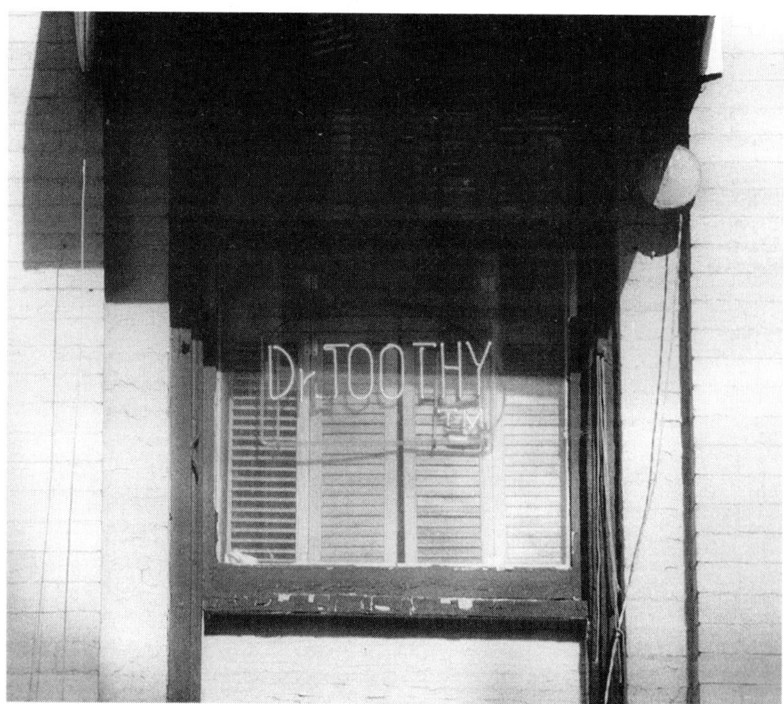


*For out-of-hours dental treatment, see* **Dentists** *page 317.*

### St Vincent's Hospital
*Seventh Avenue at 11th Street (604 7998).* **Train** 1, 2, 3, 9 or F to 14th Street; L to Sixth Avenue.

### Urgent Care Center New York Hospital
*520 East 70th Street, between York Avenue & the East River (746 0795).* **Train** 6 to 68th Street.

## Clinics

Walk-in clinics offer treatment for minor ailments. Most require immediate payment, although some will wait for your insurance company to pay out (always carry your insurance certificate with you). The basic fee is listed; if any treatment is given you'll probably be charged extra.

### Eastern Women's Center
*44 East 30th Street, between Park & Madison Avenues (686 6066).* **Train** 6 to 33rd Street. **Open** 1-4pm Mon; 1-5.30pm Tue-Fri; 1.30-3pm Sat. **Credit** AmEx, MC, V.
Pregnancy tests cost $20; counselling and gynaecological tests are also available.

### Immediate Medical Care
*2462 Flatbush Avenue, Brooklyn (1-718 252 4414).* **Open** 10am-8pm Mon-Fri; weekend hours vary. **Basic fee** $65. **Credit** AmEx, MC, V.

### Doctors Walk-in
*57 East 34th Street, between Park & Madison Avenues (683 1010).* **Train** 6 to 33rd Street. **Open** 8am-5.30pm Mon-Fri; 10am-1.30pm Sat. **Basic fee** $75. **Credit** AmEx, MC, V.
If you need X-rays or lab tests, go as early as possible and no later than 4pm Mon-Fri. No lab work is done on Saturday.

## Dentists

### Emergency Dental Associates
*(1-800 439 9299).*
24-hour dentist's.

### New York University College of Dentistry
*(998 9800).* **Open** 9am-9pm Mon-Fri. **Credit** AmEx, DC, Discover, JCB, MC, V.
If you need your teeth fixed on a budget you can become a subject for some of the final year students to learn on. They're slow but proficient and an experienced dentist is always on hand to supervise. The price is roughly half commercial rates.

## Doctors: House Calls

If you want to complain about misconduct or excessive charges call the Department of Health's Professional Medical Conduct Division (613 2650).

### Doctors on Call
*(1-718 238 2100).* **Basic fee** private address from $80-$95; hotel from $125. **Credit**: MC, V (private addresses only).
Doctors will make house calls round the clock. Expect to wait about two hours.

### Doctors' Home Referral/Home Call Service of New York Medical Society
*(1-718 745 5900/1-718 238 2100).* **Open** 24-hour referral service.

## Drugstores: Late-opening

### Kaufman's
*557 Lexington Avenue, at 50th Street (755 2266).* **Train** 6 to 51st Street. **Open** 24 hours daily. **Credit** AmEx, MC, V.
Manhattan's only round-the-clock full-service pharmacy. Delivery is free within a ten-block radius.

### Plaza Pharmacy
*251 East 86th Street, between Second & Third Avenues (427 6940).* **Train** 4, 5 or 6 to 86th Street. **Open** 8am-10pm Mon-Fri; 10am-10pm Sat, Sun. **Credit** AmEx, MC, V.
Delivery is free within five blocks.

### Windsor Pharmacy
*1419 Sixth Avenue, at 58th Street (247 1538).* **Train** B, D, N or R to 57th Street. **Open** 8am-midnight Mon-Fri; 9am-midnight Sat, Sun. **Credit** AmEx, Discover, MC, V.

# Health Advice

## Abortion/Contraception Advice

### Planned Parenthood
*Margaret Sanger Centre, 380 Second Avenue, between 21st and 22nd Streets (677 3320).* **Train** 6 to 23rd Street. **Open** 8am-4pm Tue-Sat. **Credit** AmEx, MC, V.
Counselling and treatment is available for a full range of gynaecological needs, including abortion, sexually transmitted diseases, HIV testing and contraception services; phone for an appointment.

### NYC Department of Health Bureau of Maternity Services and Family Planning
*(442 1740).* **Open** 9am-5pm Mon-Fri.
Leaflets, contraceptives and advice. Phone for appointment.

## AIDS/HIV Positive

### AIDS Resource Centre
*275 Seventh Avenue, at 25th Street (633 2500).* **Train** N, R to 28th Street. **Open** 9.30am-5.30pm Mon-Fri.
Deals with housing and emergency shelter problems for people with AIDS.

### Gay Men's Health Crisis Hotline
*(807 6655/ ttd ??645 7470).* **Open** 10am-6pm Mon-Fri.
Advice and support, including practical help, for people with, or concerned about, HIV and AIDS.

### New York City AIDS Information Hotline
*(447 8200).* **Open** 9am-8.40pm; recorded information at other times.
Advice and referral service.

## Drug/Alcohol Abuse

### Alcoholics Anonymous
*(647 1680).* **Open** 24 hours daily

### Alateen Information Centre
*(254 7230).* **Open** 24 hours daily.

### Cocaine Anonymous
*(262 2463).* **Open** 9am-midnight daily.
Recovering addicts help those who want to stop using cocaine and other mind-altering substances (including alcohol).

### Drug Abuse Information Line
*(1-800-522 5353).* **Open** 24 hours daily.
This state-run programme refers callers to recovery programmes throughout New York City and State.

**Drugs Anonymous**
*(874 0700).* **Open** 24 hour answering service.
Information on drug-recovery programmes for users of marijuana, cocaine, alcohol and other addictive substances, as well as referrals to DA meetings.

## Sexually Transmitted Diseases

**Herpes Hotline and Advice Centre**
*(213 6150).* **Open** 9am-6.45pm Mon-Thur; 9am-3pm Fri
A private medical practice offering advice and treatment.

**NYC Department of Health VD Information Hotline**
*(427 5120).* **Open** 8am-4pm Mon-Fri.
Information, and referral for treatment and counselling

# Law

**Sandback & Birnbaum Criminal Law**
(517 3200/toll-free 1-800 766 5800). **Open** 24 hours.
This is the number to have in you head when the cops read you your rights in the middle of the night.

# Left Luggage

Left-luggage lockers appear to be a thing of the past, for security reasons. However there are baggage rooms at Penn Station, Grand Central Station and the Port Authority Bus Terminal where you can leave baggage for around $2 per day.

# Lost Property

For property lost in the street contact the police. For lost credit cards, *see below* **Money**.

## Airports

**JFK**
Contact the airline on which you're travelling, or phone 1-718 244 4444 for further information.

**LaGuardia**
Contact your airline or phone 1-718 476 5115.

**Newark**
Contact your airline or phone 1-201 961 6000.

## Buses & Subways

*New York City Transit Authority, Eighth Avenue/34th Street Subway Station, near the A train platform.* **Open** 8am-noon Mon-Wed, Fri; 11am-6.45pm Thur.

## Railways

**Grand Central Station**
*(532 4900).*
For items left on Metro North or Long Island Railroad.

**Penn Station**
*(630 7389).*
For items left on Amtrak.

## Taxis

*(221 TAXI).*

# Money

*See also chapter* **Essential Information**.

## Banks

Normal banking hours are 9am-3.30pm Monday to Friday (some banks stay open later on Fridays).

## Lost Credit Cards

**American Express Travellers' Cheques**
*(1-800 221 7282).*

**American Express Card**
*(1-800 528 2121).*

**Diners Club**
*(1-800 234 6377).*

**Discover**
*(1-800 347 2683).*

**Mastercard/Access**
Contact the issuing bank.

**Visa travellers' cheques**
*(1-800 227 6811).*

**Visa**
Contact the issuing bank.

# Newspapers

All major foreign newspapers are available from:

**Eastern Newsstand**
*Pan Am Building, 200 Park Avenue, at East 45th Street (697 8445).* **Train** 4, 5, 6 or 7 to Grand Central. **Open** 5.30am-10pm Mon-Fri; 8am-5pm Sat. **Credit** AmEx, MC, V.

**Hotalings**
*142 West 42nd Street, between Sixth Avenue & Broadway (840 1868).* **Train** 1, 2, 3, 7, 9, N or R to Times Square. **Open** 7.30am-9pm Mon-Fri; 7.30am-8pm Sat, Sun. **Credit** AmEx, V.

# Religion

## Baptist

**Calvary Baptist**
*123 West 57th Street, between Sixth & Seventh Avenues (975 0170).* **Train** B, Q, N or R to 57th Street.

**Judson Memorial Baptist**
*55 Washington Square South (477 0351).* **Train** A, B, C, D, E, F or Q to West Fourth Street.

## Bretheren

**Church of Bretheren**
*27 West 115th Stree, between Fifth & Lenox Avenues (369 2620).* **Train** 2 or 3 to 116th Street.

## Buddhist

**New York Buddhist Temple**
*331 Riverside Drive (678 0305).* **Train** 1 or 9 to 103rd Street.

Services are held at 10.30am on Sunday in Japanese and at 11.30am in English.

## Episcopal

### Cathedral Church of St John the Divine

*Amsterdam Avenue, at 112th Street (316 7400).* **Train** 1 or 9 to Cathedral Parkway.

### Church of the Ascension

*Fifth Avenue, at 10th Street (254 8620).* **Train** N or R to 8th Street.

### Church of the Transfiguration

*1 East 29th Street, between Fifth & Madison Avenues (684 6770).* **Train** 4 or 5 to Lexington Avenue.

### Grace Episcopal

*802 Broadway, at East 10th Street (254 2000).* **Train** N or R to 8th Street; 6 to Astor Place.

### Holy Trinity

*316 East 88th Street, near Second Avenue (289 4100).* **Train** 4, 5 or 6 to 86th Street.

### St Bartholomew's

*109 East 50th Street, near Lexington Avenue (751 1616).* **Train** 6 to 51st Street; E or F to Lexington Avenue.

### St George's

*209 East 16th Street, between Second & Third Avenues (475 0830).* **Train** 4, 5, 6, L, N or R to Union Square.

### St James'

*865 Madison Avenue, at East 71st Street (288 4100).* **Train** 6 to 68th Street.

### St Luke's Chapel

*487 Hudson Street, near Christopher Street (924 0562).* **Train** 1 or 9 to Christopher Street.

### St Mark's-in-the-Bowery

*Second Avenue & East 10th Street (674 6377).* **Train** 6 to Astor Place.

### St Martin's Episcopal

*230 Lenox Avenue, at 122nd Street (534 4531).* **Train** 2 or 3 to 125th Street.

### St Thomas

*Fifth Avenue & 53rd Street (757 7013).* **Train** 6 to 51st Street; E or F to Lexington Avenue.

### Trinity Church

*Broadway & Wall Street (602 0800).* **Train** 1, 2, 3, 9, A or C to Chambers Street.

## Greek Orthodox

### Holy Trinity Cathedral

*319 East 74th Street, between First & Second Avenues (288 3215).* **Train** 6 to 77th Street.

## Jewish

### Central Synagogue

*652 Lexington Avenue, at 55th Street (838 5122).* **Train** 6 to 51st Street; E or F to Lexington Avenue.

### Congregation Rodeph Shalom

*7 West 83rd Street, near Central Park West (362 8800).* **Train** B or C to 81st Street.

### Fifth Avenue Synagogue

*5 East 62nd Street, near Fifth Avenue (838 2122).* **Train** 4, 5 or 6 to 59th Street; N or R to Lexington Avenue.

### Park Avenue Synagogue

*50 East 87th Street, at Madison Avenue (369 2600).* **Train** 4, 5 or 6 to 86th Street.

### Sherarith Israel Spanish and Portuguese Synagogue

*2 West 70th Street, near Central Park West (873 0300).* **Train** B or C to 72nd Street.

### Stephen Wise Free Synagogue

*30 West 68th Street, near Central Park West (877 4050).* **Train** 1 or 9 to Lincoln Center.

## Lutheran

### Holy Trinity

*Central Park West, at 65th Street (877 6815).* **Train** 1 or 9 to Lincoln Center.

### St John's Lutheran

*81 Christopher Street, near Seventh Avenue (242 5737).* **Train** 1 or 9 to Christopher Street.

## Methodist

### Christ Church

*520 Park Avenue, at 60th Street (838 3036).* **Train** 4, 5 or 6 to 59th Street; N or R to Lexington Avenue.

### John Street United Methodist

*44 John Street, near Nassau Street (269 0014).* **Train** 4 or 5 to Wall Street.

## Mormon

### Church of Latter Day Saints

*Columbus Avenue, at West 65th Street (873 1690).* **Train** 1 or 9 to Lincoln Center.

## Muslim

### Mosque of Islamic Brotherhood

*130 West 113th Street at St Nicholas Avenue (662 4100).* **Train** 2 or 3 to 116th Street. Call for information.

## Non-Denominational

### Church of the UN

*777 UN Plaza, East 44th Street & First Avenue (661 1762).* **Train** 4, 5, 6 or 7 to Grand Central.

### Riverside Church

*Riverside Drive, at 122nd Street (222 5900).* **Train** 1 or 9 to 125th Street.

## Presbyterian

### Church of the Covenant

*310 East 42nd Street, near Second Avenue (697 3185).* **Train** 4, 5, 6 or 7 to Grand Central.

**Fifth Avenue Presbyterian**
*Fifth Avenue, at 55th Street (247 0490).* **Train** 4, 5 or 6 to 59th Street; N or R to Lexington Avenue.

## Roman Catholic

**Church of Our Saviour**
*59 Park Avenue, at 38th Street (679 8166).* **Train** 4, 5, 6 or 7 to Grand Central.

**Holy Apostles**
*296 Ninth Avenue, at 28th Street (807 6799).* **Train** C or E to 23rd Street.

**Holy Trinity Chapel**
*Washington Square South (674 7236).* **Train** A, B, C, D, E, F or Q to West 4th Street.

**Immaculate Conception**
*414 East 14th Street, near First Avenue (254 0200).* **Train** L to First Avenue.

**St Ignatius Loyola**
*980 Park Avenue, at East 84th Street (288 3588).* **Train** 4, 5 or 6 to 86th Street.

**St James**
*23 Oliver Street, near Chatham Square (233 0161).* **Train** 4, 5 or 6 to Brooklyn Bridge; J or M to Chambers Street.

**St Jean Baptiste**
*184 East 76th Street, near Lexington Avenue (288 5082).* **Train** 6 to 77th Street.

**St Patrick's Cathedral**
*Fifth Avenue, at 50th Street (753 2261).* **Train** B, D, F or Q to Rockefeller Center.

**St Paul the Apostle**
*415 West 59th Street, between Ninth & Tenth Avenues (265 3209).* **Train** 1, 9, A, B, C or D to Columbus Circle.

**St Vincent Ferrer**
*Lexington Avenue & 66th Street (744 2080).* **Train** 6 to 68th Street.

## Unitarian

**All Souls Unitarian**
*1157 Lexington Avenue, at East 80th Street (535 5530).* **Train** 6 to 77th Street.

**Community Church of New York**
*40 East 35th Street, between Park & Madison Avenues (683 4988).* **Train** 6 to 33rd Street.

## Other

**Metropolitan Community Church of New York**
*446 West 36th Street (629 7440).* **Train** A, C or E to 34th Street, Penn Station.
A church of lesbian, gay, bisexual and transgendered people.

# Restrooms

Public toilets are rare in New York. You will find some at the Port Authority Bus Terminal, Penn Station and Grand Central Station. Otherwise you will always find toilet facilities in cafés and bars, department stores and the public lobbies or atriums of large buildings. Fast food outlets also have readily accessible toilets. The following can be recommended:

**Grand Hyatt Hotel**
*42nd Street, at Lexington Avenue.* **Open** 24 hours daily.

**The Waldorf-Astoria**
*50th Street & Park Avenue.* **Open** 24 hours daily.

**Barneys**
*Seventh Avenue, at West 17th Street.* **Open** 10am-9pm Mon-Thur; 10am-8pm Fri; 10am-7pm Sat.

**Citycorp Centre**
*52nd Street & Fifth Avenue.* **Open** 7am-midnight Mon-Fri; 8am-midnight Sat, Sun.

**Park Avenue Plaza**
*Park Avenue, between East 52nd & East 53rd Streets.* **Open** 8am-10pm daily.

**Trump Tower**
*725 Fifth Avenue, near 57th Street.* **Open** 8am-10pm daily.

**GE Building**
*30 Rockefeller Plaza.* **Open** 8am-7pm Mon-Fri.

# Security

## Locksmiths

The following is a selection of emergency locksmiths open 24 hours daily. All require proof of residency or car ownership plus ID.

**Champion Locksmiths**
*16 locations in Manhattan (362 7000).* **Rates** $15 call-out charge day or night plus minimum of $35 to fit a lock. **Credit** AmEx, MC, V.

**Elite Locksmiths**
*470 Third Avenue, between East 32nd & 33rd Streets (685 1472).* **Rates** $35 during the day; $75-$90 at night. **No credit cards.**

# Transport

*See also chapter* **Getting Around**.

## US Airlines

**Central Airlines Ticket Office**
*100 East 42nd Street, at Park Avenue (986 0888).*
This office issues tickets and is an information centre for Delta, Northwestern, Continental, Virgin Atlantic, American and Scandinavian airlines.
**Alaska Airlines** *(1-800 426 0333).*
**America West** *(1-800 235 9292).*
**American** *(1-800 433 7300).*
**Continental** *(319 9494 US & Mexican destinations; 1-800 231 0856 international destinations).*
**Delta** *(239 0700).*
**Kiwi International Airlines** *(1-800 538 5494).*
**Northwest** *(1-800 225 2525 domestic flights; 1-800 447 4747 international flights).*
**Tower Air** *(1-718 553 8500).*
**United** *(1-800 241 6522).*
**US Air** *(1-800 428 4322).*

## Foreign Airlines

**Aer Lingus** *(557 1110).*
**Aeroflot** *(332 1050).*
**AeroMexico** *(1-800 237 6639).*
**Air Afrique** (586 5908).
**Air Canada** *(1-800 776 3000).*
**Air France** *(247 0100).*
**Air India** *(751 6200).*
**Air Jamaica** *(1-800 523 5585).*
**Alitalia** *(582 8900).*
**Avianca** *(246 5241).*
**British Airways** *(1-800 247 9297 reservations; 1-718 397 4397 flight arrivals; 1-718 553 5500 flight departures).*
**BWIA** *(1-800-327 7401).*
**Cathay Pacific** *(1-800 233 2742).*
**China Airlines** *(399 7877).*
**Czech Airlines** *(765 6022).*
**Ecuatoriana Airlines** *(1-800 328 2367).*
**Egyptair** *(395 0900).*
**El Al** *(852 0600).*
**Finnair** *(1-800 950 5000).*
**Iberia** *(1-800 772 4642).*
**Japan Airlines** *(1-800 525 3663 reservations; 1-800 525 2355 flight information).*
**KLM** *(1-800 374 7747).*
**Korean** Air *(1-800 438 5000).*
**Kuwait** Airways *(308 5454 reservations; 1-718 656 4720 flight information).*
**Lan-Chile** *(582 3250 reservations;1-718 995 6962 flight information).*
**Lot Polish** (869 1074).
**Lufthansa** *(1-800 645 3880).*
**Nigeria** Airways *(935 2700).*
**Olympic** *(838 3600).*
**Pakistan** *(370 9158).*
**Qantas** *(1-800 227 4500).*
**Royal Air Maroc** *(974 3850).*
**Royal Jordanian** *(949 0050).*
**Sabena** (Belgian World Airlines) *(1-800 955 2000 reservations; 1-800 873 3900 flight information).*
**Saudi Arabian Airlines** *(751 7117).*
**Swissair** *(1-800 221 4750).*
**TAP Air Portugal** *(1-800 221 7370).*
**Tarom** (Romanian Air) *(687 6013).*
**Trans World Airlines** *(290 2121 domestic flights; 290 2141 international flights).*
**Varig Brazilian Airlines** *(682 3100).*
**Viasa** (Venezuelan International Airways) *(1-800 468 4272).*
**Virgin Atlantic** *(1-800 862 8621).*

## Airport Information

**JFK International Airport** *Jamaica, Queens (244 4444).*
**La Guardia Airport** *Flushing, Queens (1-718 476 5000).*

For information on travel to and from the three major airports, call 1-800 AIR RIDE, or, for more option, including public transport and relatively inexpensive limo hire; *see chapter* **Getting Around**.

# Size conversion chart for clothes

| **Women's clothes** | | | | | | | | | |
|---|---|---|---|---|---|---|---|---|---|
| British | 8 | 10 | 12 | 14 | 16 | • | • | • | • |
| American | 6 | 8 | 10 | 12 | 14 | • | • | • | • |
| French | 36 | 38 | 40 | 42 | 44 | • | • | • | • |
| Italian | 38 | 40 | 42 | 44 | 46 | • | • | • | • |
| **Women's shoes** | | | | | | | | | |
| British | 3 | 4 | 5 | 6 | 7 | 8 | 9 | • | • |
| American | 5 | 6 | 7 | 8 | 9 | 10 | 11 | • | • |
| Continental | 36 | 37 | 38 | 39 | 40 | 41 | 42 | • | • |
| **Men's suits/overcoats** | | | | | | | | | |
| British | 38 | 40 | 42 | 44 | 46 | • | • | • | • |
| American | 38 | 40 | 42 | 44 | 46 | • | • | • | • |
| Continental | 48 | 50/52 | 54 | 56 | 58/60 | • | • | • | • |
| **Men's shirts** | | | | | | | | | |
| British | 14 | 14.5 | 15 | 15.5 | 16 | 16.5 | 17 | • | • |
| American | 14 | 14.5 | 15 | 15.5 | 16 | 16.5 | 17 | • | • |
| Continental | 35 | 36/37 | 38 | 39/40 | 41 | 42/43 | 44 | • | • |
| **Men's shoes** | | | | | | | | | |
| British | 8 | 9 | 10 | 11 | 12 | • | • | • | • |
| American | 9 | 10 | 11 | 12 | 13 | • | • | • | • |
| Continental | 42 | 43 | 44 | 45 | 46 | • | • | • | • |
| **Children's shoes** | | | | | | | | | |
| British | 7 | 8 | 9 | 10 | 11 | 12 | 13 | 1 | 2 |
| American | 7.5 | 8.5 | 9.5 | 10.5 | 11.5 | 12.5 | 13.5 | 1.5 | 2.5 |
| Continental | 24 | 25.5 | 27 | 28 | 29 | 30 | 32 | 33 | 34 |

**Children's clothes**

In all countries, size descriptions vary from make to make, but are usually based on age or height.

# Further Reading

## History

**Allen, Irving Lewis**: *The City in Slang.* How New York living has spawned hundreds of new words and phrases.
**Federal Writers' Project**: *The WPA Guide To New York City.* A wonderful snapshot of 1930s New York, by the writers employed by FDR's New Deal.
**Fitch, Robert**: *The Assassination of New York.* Essay on the economic death of New York in the 1980s.
**Hood, Clifton**: *722 Miles.* History of the subway.
**Koolhaas, Rem**: *Delirious New York.* New York as terminal city. Urbanism and the culture of congestion.
**Lewis, David Levering**: *When Harlem was in Vogue.* A study of the 1920s Harlem renaissance.
**Liebling, AJ**: *Back Where I Came From.* Personal recollections from the famous *New Yorker* columnist.
**O'Connell, Shaun**: *Remarkable, Unspeakable New York.* History of New York as literary inspiration.
**Pye, Michael**: *Maximum City: The Biography of New York.* Uniquely angled and unmissably stylish history.
**Riis, Jacob**: *How The Other Half Lives.* Pioneering photo-journalist record of gruesome tenement life.
**Rosenzweig, Roy, & Elizabeth Blackman**: *The Park and its People.* A lengthy history of Central Park.
**Sante, Luc**: *Low Life.* Opium dens, brothels, tenements and suicide salons in 1840-1920s New York.
**Schwartzman, Paul, & Rob Polner**: *New York Notorious.* New York's most infamous crime scenes.
**Stern, Robert M**: *New York 1930.* A massive coffee-table slab with stunning pictures.
**Stern, Robert M**: *New York 1960.* Another.
**Still, Bayrd**: *Mirror for Gotham.* New York as seen by its inhabitants, from Dutch days to the present.

## Culture & Recollections

**Chauncey, George**: *Gay New York.* New York gay life since the 1890s.
**Cole, William (Ed)**: *Quotable New York.* Hundreds of hilarious quotes about the city.
**Donaldson, Greg**: *The Ville: Cops and Kids in Urban America.* Gripping sociology of Brownsville, Brooklyn.
**Friedman, Josh Alan**: *Tales From Times Square.* Sleaze, scum, filth and depredation in Times Square.
**Kinkead, Gwen**: *Chinatown: A Portrait of a Closed Society.*
**Toop, David**: *Rap Attack 2; African Rap to Global Hip Hop.* The best cultural history of hip-hop.
**Cooper, Martha, & Henry Chalfant**: *Subway Art.*
**Torres, Andrés**: *Between Melting Pot and Mosaic.* African Americans' and Puerto Ricans' role in the city's life from 1945 to 1995.
**Trebay, Guy**: *In The Place To Be.* Wonderfully observed essays by a leading *Village Voice* writer.
**Wyatt Sexton, Andrea** (ed): *The Brooklyn Reader.* Thirty writers celebrate America's favourite borough.

## Architecture

**Wolfe, Gerard R**: *A Guide to the Metropolis.* Historical and architectural walking tours.
**Gayle, Margaret**: *Cast Iron Architecture in New York.*
**Goldberger, Paul**: *The City Observed.* The *New York Times'* architecture critic leads you round the city.
**Klotz, Heinrich**: *New York Architecture 1970-90.* A vast and beautiful full-colour volume.
**Sabbagh, Karl**: *Skyscraper.* How a skyscraper is built.
**Willensky, Elliot, & Norval White**: *American Institute of Architects Guide to New York City.* A comprehensive directory of important buildings

## In-depth Guides

**Bell, Trudy**: *Bicycling Around New York City.*
**Berman, Eleanor**: *Away for the Weekend.* Trips within a 250 mile radius of New York.
**Brown, Arthur S, & Barbara Holmes**: *Vegetarian Dining in New York City.* Includes vegan places.
**Freudenheim, Ellen**: *Brooklyn – where to go, what to do, how to get there.*
**Leon, Ruth**: *New York's Guide to the Performing Arts.* Astonishingly detailed directory of performance venues.
**Marden, William**: *Marden's Guide to New York Booksellers.* Over 500 dealers and stores.
**Michel, John & Barbara**: *Antiquing New York.* Over 1000 antique dealers, markets and fairs listed.
**Miller, Bryan**: *NY Times Guide to Restaurants in New York City.* By the famous food critic.
**Rovere, Vicki**: *Worn Again, Hallelujah!* Guide to NYC's thrift stores and treasure troves.
**Sandvick, Victoria, & Michael Ian Bergman**: *Single in New York.*
**Steinbicker, Earl**: *Daytrips From New York.*
**Zagat**: *New York City Restaurants.* The leading, and bewildering, comprehensive guide.
*Internet New York* (Hayden Books, 1995). The lowdown on New York related websites and other Internet goodies.
*Shopping Manhattan* (Penguin US, 1992).

## Fiction

**Auster, Paul**: *New York Stories.* Walking the Manhattan grid in search of the madness behind method.
**Baldwin, James**: *Another Country.* Racism under the bohemian veneer of the 1960s.
**Barnhardt, Wilton**: *Emma Who Saved My Life.* Big ambitions set against colourful 1970s NYC.
**Ellison, Ralph**: *Invisible Man.* Coming of age, black and in 1950s New York.
**Friedman, Kinky**: *Kinky Friedman Crime Club.* Cigar-chomping cowboy 'tec wisecracks through '90s NYC.
**Janowitz, Tama**: *Slaves of New York.* Satires of 1980s NYC bohemia.
**Kramer, Larry**: *Faggots.* Hilarious gay New York.
**Miller, Henry**: *Crazy Cock.* Most of Miller's novels are set in Brooklyn; this is 1920s Greenwich Village.
**Price, Richard**: *Clockers.* Cops, kids, crack in urban Jersey City, but just as easily the South Bronx.
**Runyan, Damon**: *On Broadway.* Basis for the musical Guys And Dolls.
**Selby, Hubert Jr**: *Last Exit to Brooklyn.* Tale of 1960s Brooklyn dockland degredation.
**Smith, Betty**: *A Tree Grows in Brooklyn.* An Irish girl in 1930s Brooklyn.
**Wharton, Edith**: *Old New York.* The short novels here include *The Age Of Innocence.*
**Wolfe, Tom**: *Bonfire of the Vanities.* Rich/poor, black/white. An unmatched slice of 1980s New York.

# Index

c

**t**



**u**



**v**

# New York Guide

## Advertisers Index

Please refer to the relevant sections for addresses/telephone numbers

# Maps

# Trips Out of Town

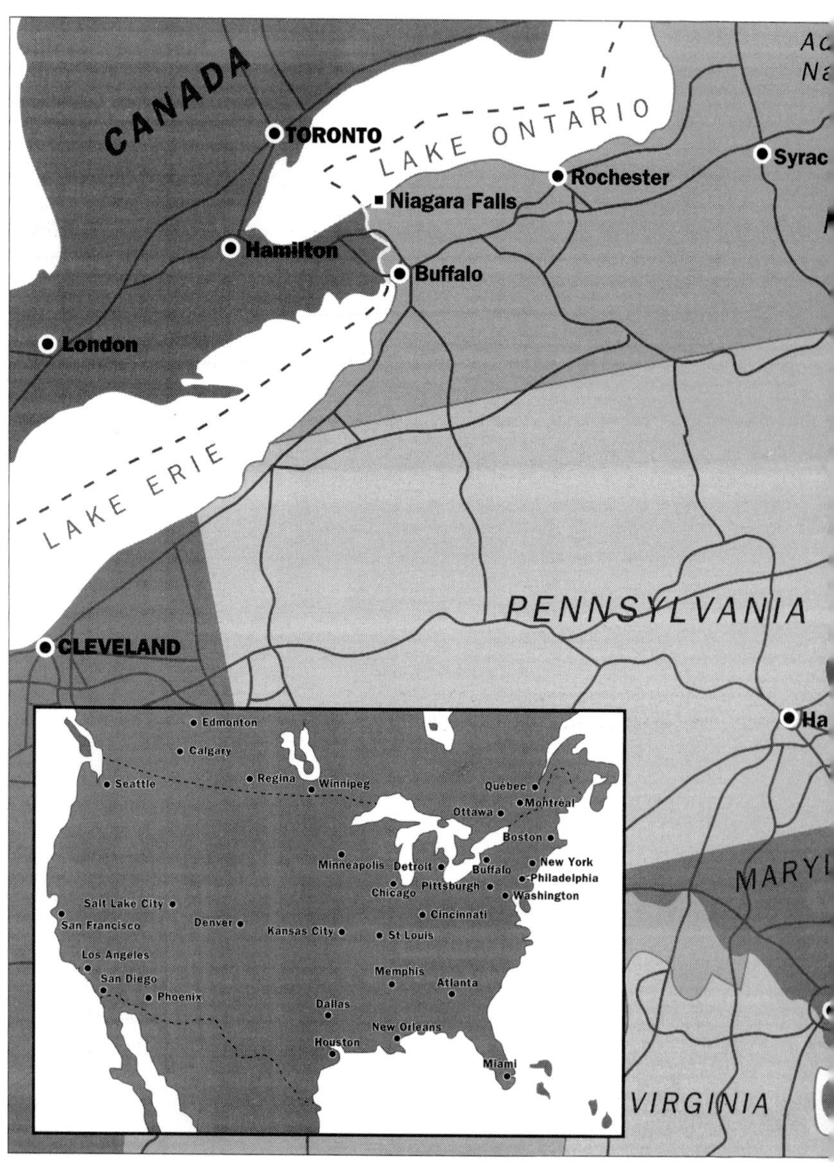

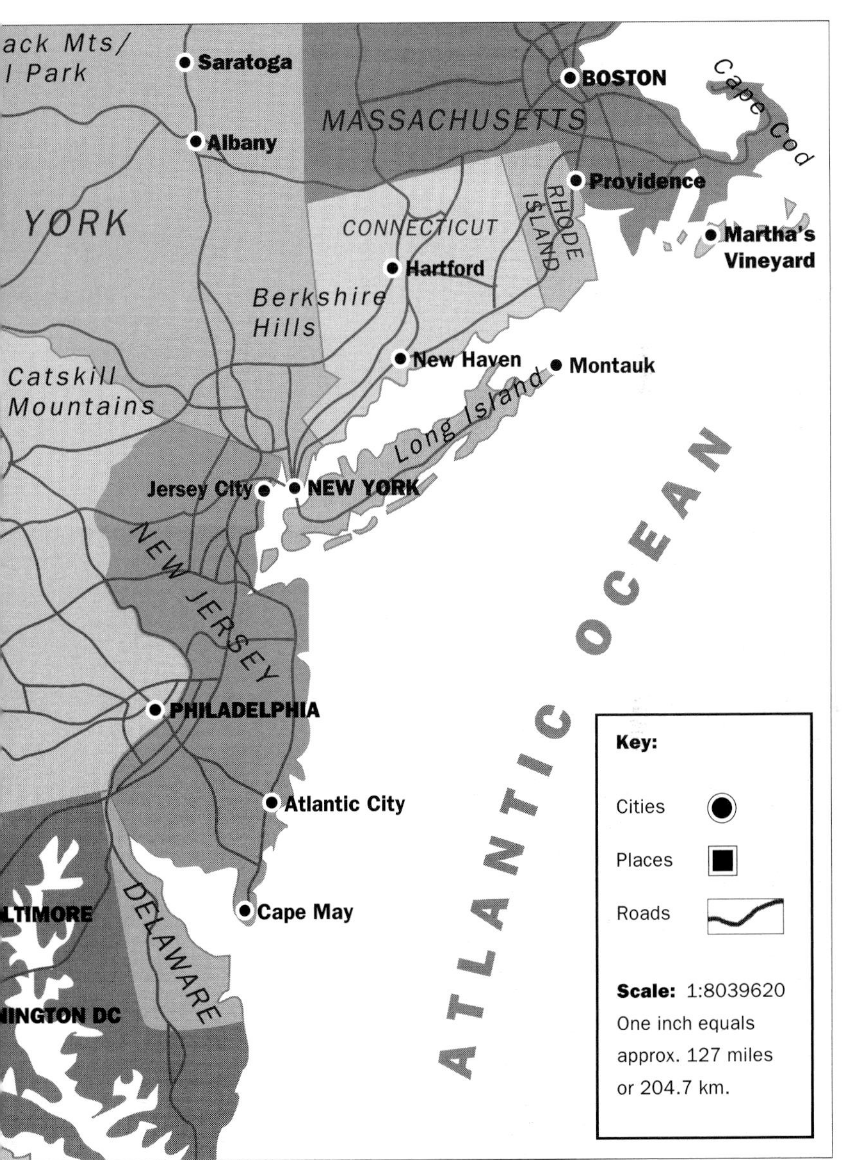
ack Mts/
l Park
Saratoga
BOSTON
Cape Cod
MASSACHUSETTS
Albany
Providence
YORK
RHODE ISLAND
CONNECTICUT
Martha's Vineyard
Hartford
Berkshire Hills
New Haven
Montauk
Catskill Mountains
Long Island
Jersey City
NEW YORK
NEW JERSEY
ATLANTIC OCEAN
PHILADELPHIA
Atlantic City
Cape May
LTIMORE
DELAWARE
INGTON DC
Key:
Cities
Places
Roads
Scale: 1:8039620
One inch equals approx. 127 miles or 204.7 km.

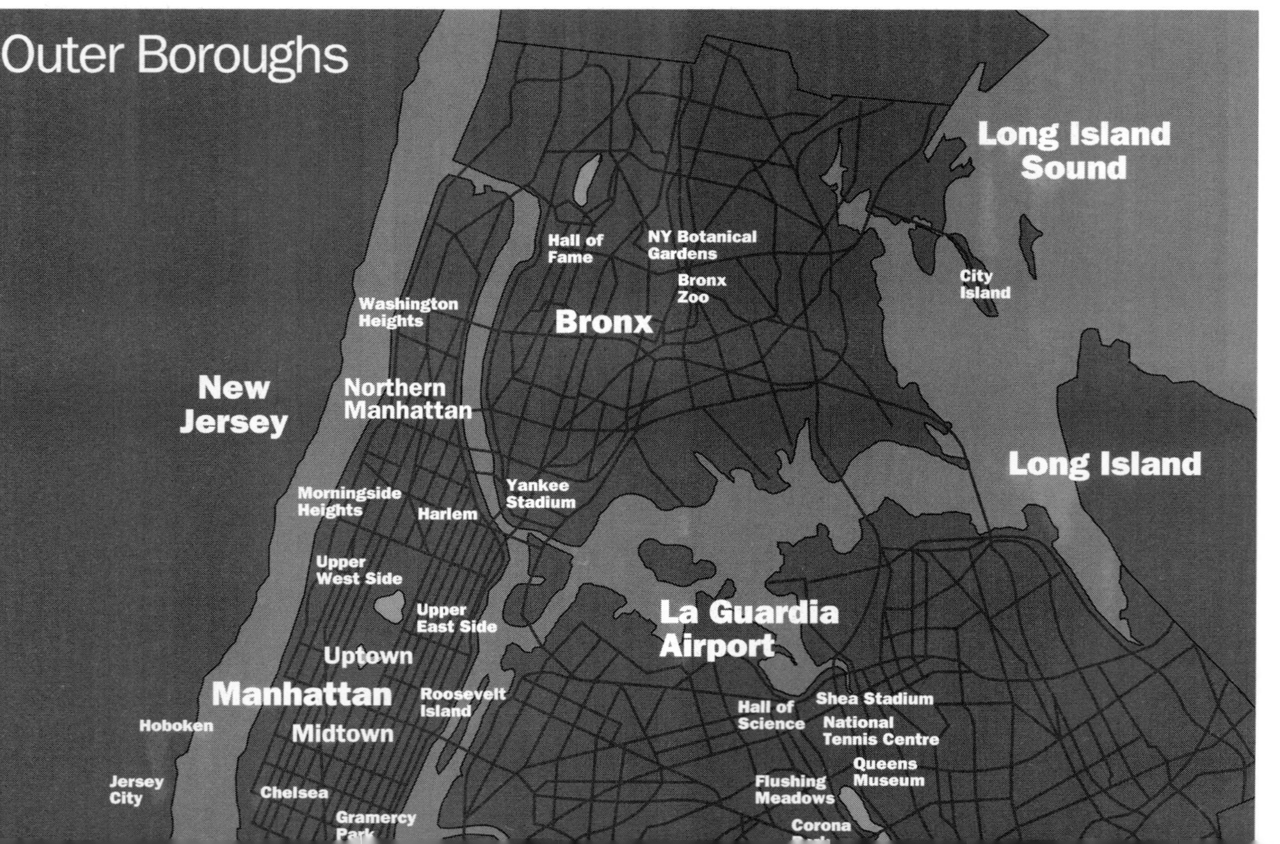

Outer Boroughs
Long Island Sound
Hall of Fame
NY Botanical Gardens
Bronx Zoo
City Island
Washington Heights
Bronx
New Jersey
Northern Manhattan
Long Island
Morningside Heights
Harlem
Yankee Stadium
Upper West Side
Upper East Side
La Guardia Airport
Uptown
Manhattan
Roosevelt Island
Hall of Science
Shea Stadium
Hoboken
Midtown
National Tennis Centre
Queens Museum
Jersey City
Chelsea
Flushing Meadows
Gramercy
Corona

Lower East Side
Ellis Island
Wall Street
Williamsburg
Liberty Island
Brooklyn Heights
Governors' Island
Brooklyn Museum
Botanic Gardens
Prospect Park
Hudson River
Brooklyn
JFK Airport
Jamaica Bay
Staten Island
Brighton Beach
NY Aquarium
Coney Island
Rockaway Beach
N
© Words&Pictures

# Street Index

***Map starts page 342.***

Mt Morris Park Avenue E23
Mt Morris Park West E23
Mulberry F5
Murray D4

N.D. Perlman Place F9
Norfolk G7
N. Moore B34
Nagle Avenue B34
Nassau E3-4
New E2-3
New H6
Ninth Avenue C9-14
North End Avenue D4

145th Street Bridge E26
Old Broadway B24
Old Slip E2
Oliver F5
Orchard G6
Overlook Terrace B32

Paladino Avenue G23
Park Avenue E11-25
Park Avenue South E10
Park Place D4
Park Row F5
Park Terrace East B35
Park Terrace West B35
Patchin Place B8
Payson Avenue B34
Pearl E2-3/F4
Peck Slip F3
Pell F5
Penn Plaza Drive C11
Perry C8
Phil. Randolph Square D22
Pike G5
Pine E3
Pinehurst Avenue B31
Pitt G7
Platt E3
Post B34
Prince E7

Queens Mid. Tunnel G12
Queensboro Bridge G15

Reade E5
Rector D3
Rector Place D3
Renwick D6
Republican Al E4
Ridge G7
Riverside Drive B16-33
Rivington F7
Rob. F. Wagner Sr. Place F4
Rockefeller Plaza D13
Roosevelt Square C23
Rutgers G5
Rutgers Slip G5
Rutherford Place F9
Ryders Al E3

S. Williams E2
Schiff Parkway G7
Seaman Avenue B34
Second Avenue F7-24
Seventh Avenue D9-14
Seventh Avenue South D7-8
Sheridan square D8
Sherman Avenue B34
Shinbone Al E7
Sickles B33
South End Avenue D3
South F2-5
Spring D6
Spruce E4
St Marks Place F8

St James Place F5
St Johns Lane D6
St Lukes Place D7
St Nicholas Avenue B27-32
St Nicholas Terrace C24
Staff A34
Stanton F7
Staple D5
State E2
Stone E2
Stuveysant F8
Stuyvesant Square F9
Suffolk G7
Sullivan D7
Sutton Place G14
Sutton Place Square G14
Sylvan Terrace C29
Szold Place H8

T. Shevchenko Place F8
Tenth Avenue C33-35
Terrace View Avenue B37
Thames D3
Thayer B33
Theatre Al E4
Third Avenue Bridge F25
Third Avenue F8-24
Thomas E5
Thompson D7
Tiemann Place B24
Times Square C12
Transverse Road D15-20
Triboro Bridge H23
Trimble Place E5
Trinity Place E3
Tudor City Place F12
Tunnel Entrace F12
Tunnel Exit F12
Twelfth Avenue A9-16

Union Square East E9
Union Square E9
Union Square West E9
University Place E8

V. Marcontonio Avenue G23
Van Corlear Place C37
Vandam D6
Vanderbilt Avenue E13
Varick D5-6
Vermilyea Avenue B34
Vestry D6
Vesey D4
Vietnam Veterans Plaza E2
View Avenue B37
Village Square D8

Wadsworth Avenue B30-32
Wadsworth Terrace B32
Walker E5
Wall E3
Wanamaker Place F8
Wards Island Bridge G20
Warren D4
Washington C6-8
Washington Square East D8
Washington Square West D8
Washington Square North D8
Washington Square South D8
Washington Bridge D31
Washington Mews D8
Washington Place E8
Water F2-5
Watts D6
Waverly Place E8
Weehawken C7
West 4th C8
West 8th D8
West 10th D7

West 11th C8
West 12th B8
West Broadway D4-7
West End Avenue B15-21
West Houston C7
West Thames D3
West Side Highway B-D2-16
West Union Intl. Plaza D23
White E5
Whitehall E2
Willet H6
William E3
Williamsburg Bridge I7
Willis Avenue Bridge G24
Wooster E6
Worth E5

York Avenue G15-21
York D6

## Parks

Battery Park E2
Beach Park D5
Bowling Green E2
Bryant Park D12
Carl Shurtz Park G18
Central Park D15-21
Chelsea Park B11
City Hall Park E4
Col. Chase Young Park E26
Columbus Park F5
Corlears Hook Park H6
Damrosch Park B15
Dewitt Clinton Park B14
East River Park I6-8
Esplanade Gardens D27
Fort Tryon Park A33
Gov. Smith Park F4
Gramercy Park E10
Harlem River Park D27
High Bridge Park C28-33
Ingwood Hill Park B35
Isham Park B35
Jackie Robinson Park C27
J. Hood Wright Park B30
James J. Walker Park D7
John Jay Park G17
Madison Square Park E10
Morningside Park C22-23
Mount Morris Park E23
N. St Marks Cem. F8
Randall's Island Park I23-4
Riverside Park B16-33
Roger Morris Park C28
Sakura Park B23
Sara Roosevelt Park F6
Seward Park B23
St Nicholas Park C24-5
Straus Park B21
Stuyvesant Square Park F9
T. Jefferson Park G22
Thomas Paine Park E5
Tompkins Square Park G8
Trinity Cemetery B27
Union Square Park E9
Washington Square Park D8

## Concert halls

Carnegie Hall D14
City Center D14
Lincoln Center B-C15
Radio City Music Hall D13
Paramount Theater C11

## Hospitals

Bellevue Hospital G10
Beth Israel Hospital F9
Beth Israel North G18
Coumbia Presbyterian B29
Harlem Hospital E25
Lenox Hill Hospital E17
Memorial Sloan Kettering F16
Metropolitan Hospital F20
Mount Sinai Hospital E20
New York Hospital Cornell Medical Center G16
New York Downtown E3-4
New York University Medical Center G11
Roosevelt Hospital B-C15
St Clair Hospital B-C13
St Luke's Hospital C22
St Vincent's Hospital D8

## Museums

American Craft Museum D14
American Museum of Natural History C17
The Asia Society E17
The Cloisters B33
Cooper-Hewitt Museum E19
The Frick Collection E16
Guggenheim Museum E19
International Center of Photography E19
Jewish Museum E19
Metropolitan Museum of Art D18
Museum of the American Indian E2
Museum of Modern Art D14
Museum of the City of New York E20
Museum of TV & Radio D14
New York Historical Society C17
Pierpont Morgan Library E12
Whitney Museum E17
Washington Heights Museums B28

## Places of interest

Circle Line Cruises A12
Citicorp Center E14
City Hall E4
Empire State Building D11
Javits Convention Center B11-12
Madison Square Garden C11
New York Public Library D12
New York Stock Exchange E3
Rockefeller Center D13
Riverside Church B23
St John the Divine C22
St Patrick's Cathedral E13-14
South Street Seaport F3
Statue of Liberty Ferry E1
T.K.T.S. D13
Trinity Church E3
Trump Tower E14
United Nations F13
Visitors & Convention Center C14
World Trade Center D3-4
World Financial Center D3-4

## Transport terminals

Ellis Island Ferry D1
George Washington Bridge Bus Terminal B30
Grand Central E12
Hoboken Ferry C4
Passenger Ship Terminal A14
Pennsylvania Station C11
Port Authority Bus Terminal C12
Roosevelt Island Tram F15
Staten Island Ferry E2

# New York Subway map

 A free copy of the map is available at any subway token booth.
Transport Authority information: *English-speakers* 718 330 1234/*non English-speakers* 718 330 4847.
In addition to the traditional subway token, a magnetic fare card, the 'Metrocard', may be used at certain subway stations.

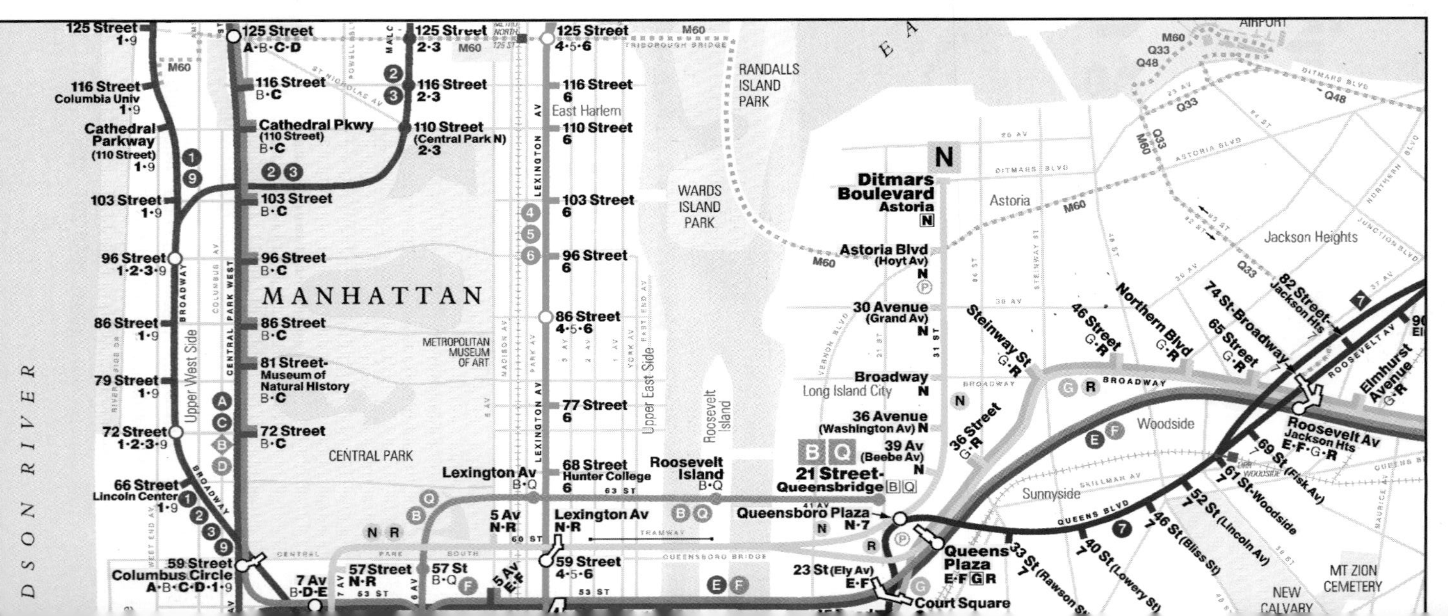

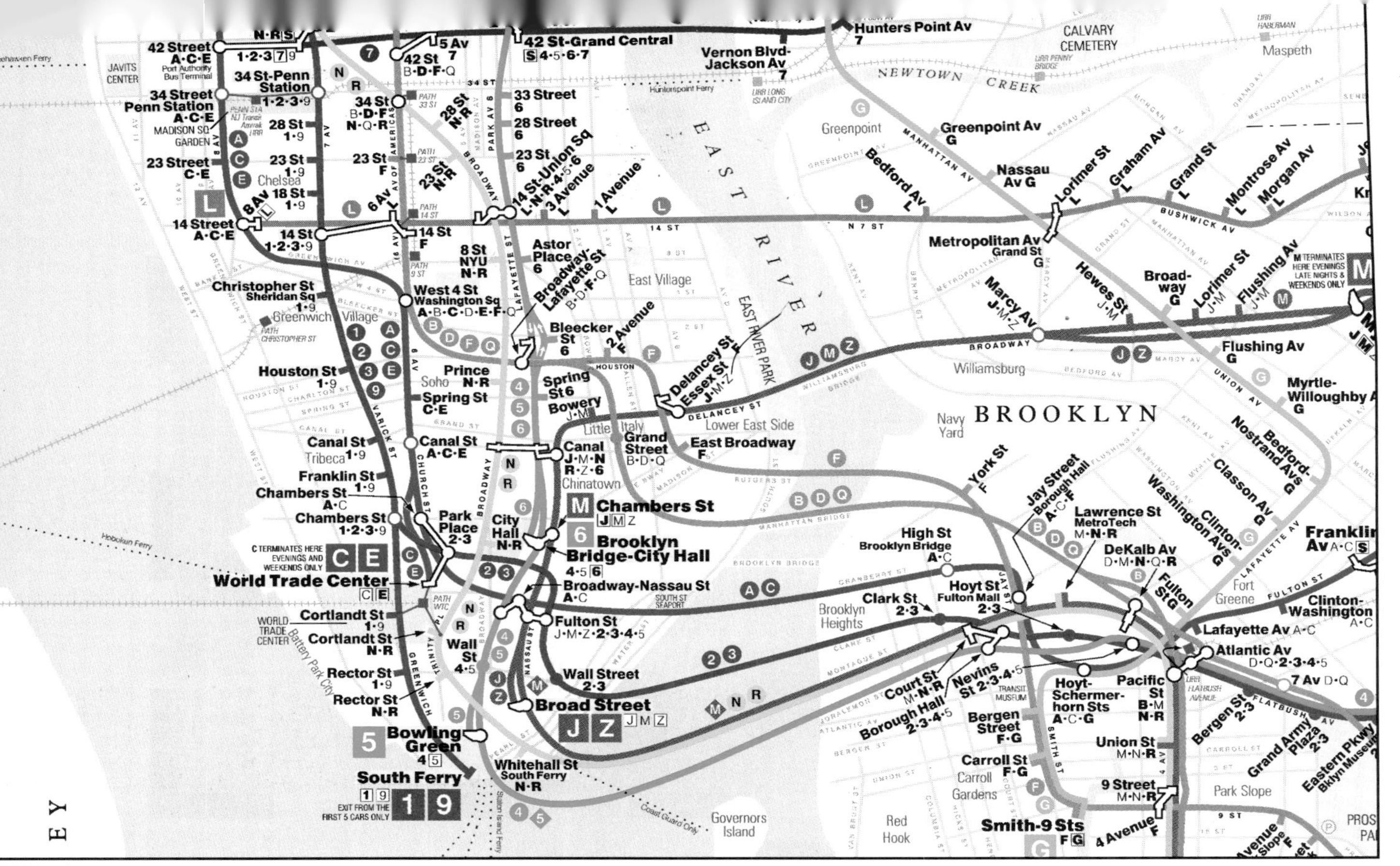

42 Street A·C·E
Port Authority Bus Terminal
34 Street Penn Station A·C·E
MADISON SQ GARDEN
34 St-Penn Station 1·2·3·9
42 St-Grand Central S 4·5·6·7
5 Av 7
42 St B·D·F·Q
34 St B·D·F N·Q·R
33 Street 6
28 Street 6
23 St 6
28 St 1·9
23 St 1·9
18 St 1·9
23 St F
23 Street C·E
14 Street A·C·E
14 St 1·2·3·9
14 St F
14 St-Union Sq L·N·R·4·5·6
3 Avenue L
1 Avenue L
Astor Place 6
8 St NYU N·R
West 4 St Washington Sq A·B·C·D·E·F·Q
Christopher St Sheridan Sq 1·9
Houston St 1·9
Spring St C·E
Prince St N·R
Bleecker St 6
Broadway Lafayette St B·D·F·Q
2 Avenue F
Spring St 6
Bowery J·M
Delancey St
Essex St J·M·Z
Grand Street B·D·Q
East Broadway F
Canal St A·C·E
Canal St 1·9
Canal St J·M·N R·Z·6
Franklin St 1·9
Chambers St A·C
Chambers St 1·2·3·9
Chambers St J M Z
Brooklyn Bridge-City Hall 4·5·6
City Hall N·R
Park Place 2·3
C TERMINATES HERE EVENINGS AND WEEKENDS ONLY
World Trade Center C E
Cortlandt St 1·9
Cortlandt St N·R
Broadway-Nassau St A·C
Fulton St J·M·Z·2·3·4·5
Wall Street 2·3
Wall St 4·5
Broad Street J M Z
Rector St 1·9
Rector St N·R
Bowling Green 4 5
Whitehall St South Ferry N·R
South Ferry 1 9
EXIT FROM THE FIRST 5 CARS ONLY
Staten Island Ferry
Governors Island
Hunters Point Av 7
Vernon Blvd-Jackson Av 7
Greenpoint Av G
Nassau Av G
Metropolitan Av Grand St G
Bedford Av L
Lorimer St L
Graham Av L
Grand St L
Montrose Av L
Morgan Av L
Marcy Av J·M·Z
Hewes St J·M
Lorimer St J·M
Flushing Av J·M
M TERMINATES HERE EVENINGS LATE NIGHTS & WEEKENDS ONLY
Flushing Av G
Broadway G
Myrtle-Willoughby Av G
Bedford-Nostrand Avs G
Classon Av G
Clinton-Washington Avs G
Fulton St G
Franklin Av A·C·S
Clinton-Washington A·C
Lafayette Av A·C
Atlantic Av D·Q·2·3·4·5
7 Av D·Q
Pacific St B·M N·R
DeKalb Av D·M·N·Q·R
Lawrence St MetroTech M·N·R
Jay Street Borough Hall A·C·F
York St F
High St Brooklyn Bridge A·C
Hoyt St Fulton Mall 2·3
Clark St 2·3
Nevins St 2·3·4·5
Hoyt-Schermerhorn Sts A·C·G
Court St M·N·R
Borough Hall 2·3·4·5
Bergen Street F·G
Carroll St F·G
Smith-9 Sts F G
Union St M·N·R
9 Street M·N·R
4 Avenue F
Bergen St 2·3
Grand Army Plaza 2·3
Eastern Pkwy Bklyn Museum
BROOKLYN
EAST RIVER
NEWTOWN CREEK
CALVARY CEMETERY
JAVITS CENTER
Maspeth
Greenpoint
Williamsburg
Navy Yard
Fort Greene
Brooklyn Heights
Carroll Gardens
Red Hook
Park Slope
Chelsea
Greenwich Village
Soho
Tribeca
Chinatown
Little Italy
Lower East Side
East Village
Battery Park City
East River Park

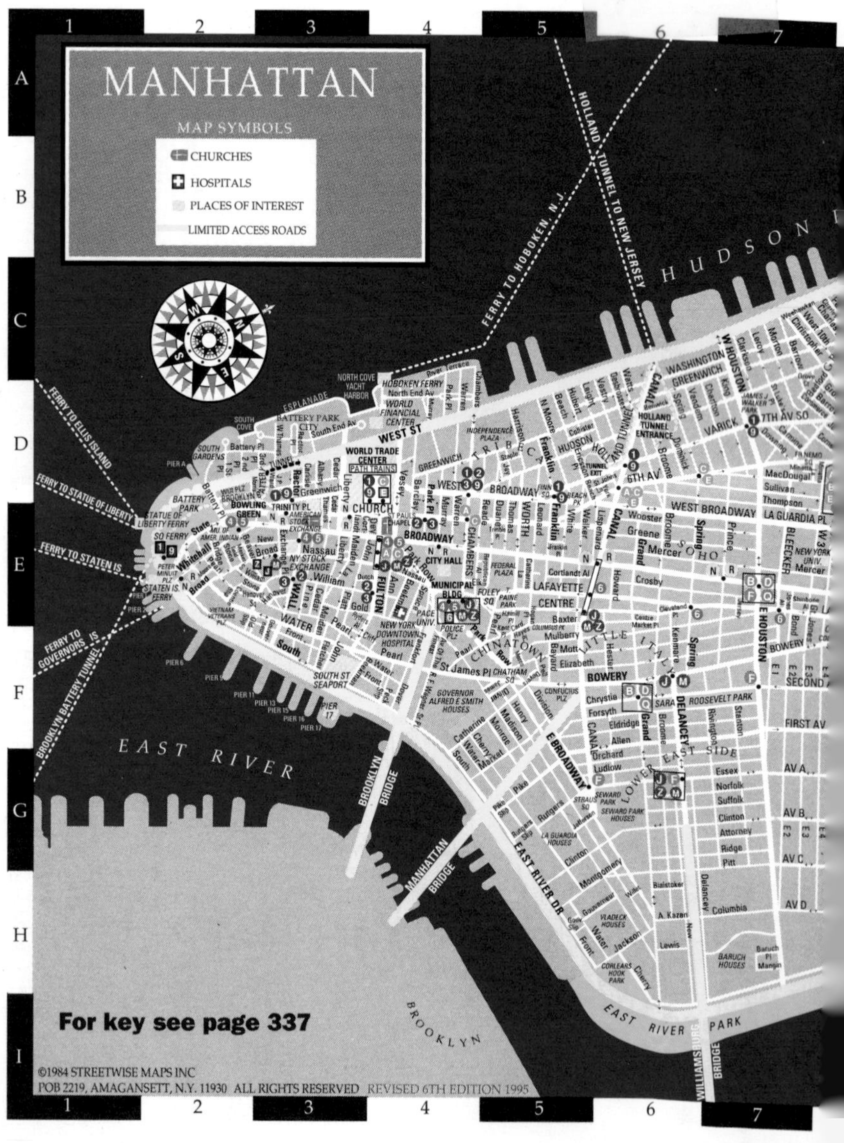
MANHATTAN
MAP SYMBOLS
CHURCHES
HOSPITALS
PLACES OF INTEREST
LIMITED ACCESS ROADS
HUDSON
EAST RIVER
BROOKLYN
HOLLAND TUNNEL TO NEW JERSEY
FERRY TO HOBOKEN, N.J.
FERRY TO ELLIS ISLAND
FERRY TO STATUE OF LIBERTY
FERRY TO STATEN IS
FERRY TO GOVERNORS IS
BROOKLYN BATTERY TUNNEL
BROOKLYN BRIDGE
MANHATTAN BRIDGE
WILLIAMSBURG BRIDGE
EAST RIVER PARK
EAST RIVER DR
WORLD TRADE CENTER
WORLD FINANCIAL CENTER
BATTERY PARK CITY
TRIBECA
SOHO
CHINATOWN
LITTLE ITALY
LOWER EAST SIDE
For key see page 337
©1984 STREETWISE MAPS INC
POB 2219, AMAGANSETT, N.Y. 11930 ALL RIGHTS RESERVED REVISED 6TH EDITION 1995

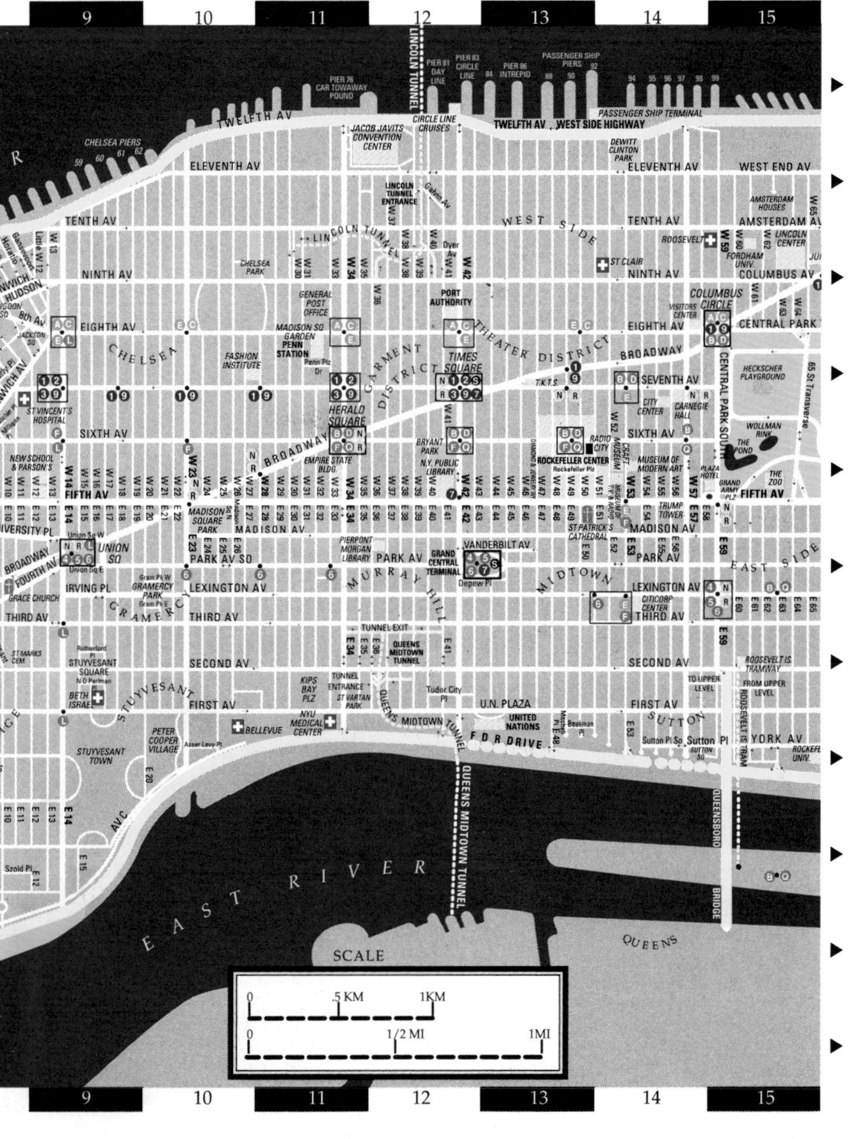

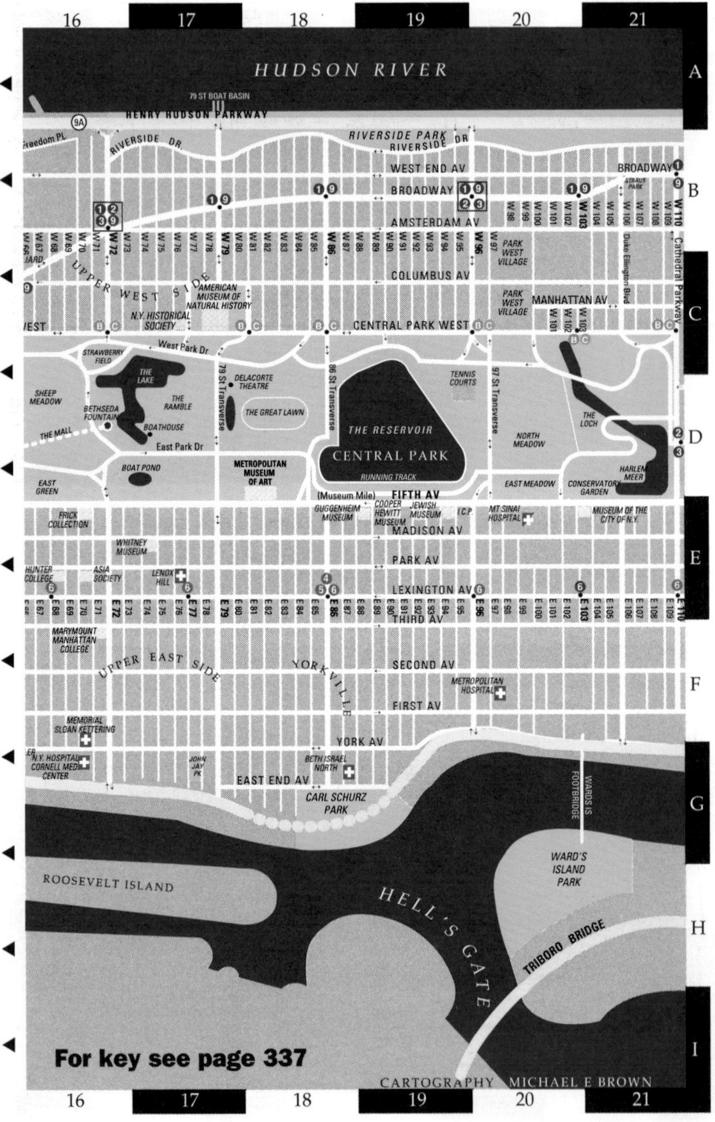
HUDSON RIVER
79 ST BOAT BASIN
HENRY HUDSON PARKWAY
RIVERSIDE DR
RIVERSIDE PARK
WEST END AV
BROADWAY
AMSTERDAM AV
COLUMBUS AV
CENTRAL PARK WEST
MANHATTAN AV
PARK WEST VILLAGE
UPPER WEST SIDE
AMERICAN MUSEUM OF NATURAL HISTORY
N.Y. HISTORICAL SOCIETY
STRAWBERRY FIELD
THE LAKE
SHEEP MEADOW
BETHSEDA FOUNTAIN
THE MALL
THE RAMBLE
BOATHOUSE
DELACORTE THEATRE
THE GREAT LAWN
THE RESERVOIR
CENTRAL PARK
RUNNING TRACK
TENNIS COURTS
NORTH MEADOW
THE LOCH
HARLEM MEER
BOAT POND
EAST GREEN
METROPOLITAN MUSEUM OF ART
EAST MEADOW
CONSERVATORY GARDEN
FIFTH AV
(Museum Mile)
FRICK COLLECTION
GUGGENHEIM MUSEUM
COOPER HEWITT MUSEUM
JEWISH MUSEUM
I.C.P.
MT SINAI HOSPITAL
MUSEUM OF THE CITY OF N.Y.
MADISON AV
WHITNEY MUSEUM
PARK AV
HUNTER COLLEGE
ASIA SOCIETY
LENOX HILL
LEXINGTON AV
THIRD AV
MARYMOUNT MANHATTAN COLLEGE
UPPER EAST SIDE
YORKVILLE
SECOND AV
METROPOLITAN HOSPITAL
FIRST AV
MEMORIAL SLOAN KETTERING
YORK AV
N.Y. HOSPITAL CORNELL MED CENTER
JOHN JAY PK
BETH ISRAEL NORTH
EAST END AV
CARL SCHURZ PARK
WARDS IS FOOTBRIDGE
WARD'S ISLAND PARK
ROOSEVELT ISLAND
HELL'S GATE
TRIBORO BRIDGE
For key see page 337
CARTOGRAPHY MICHAEL E BROWN

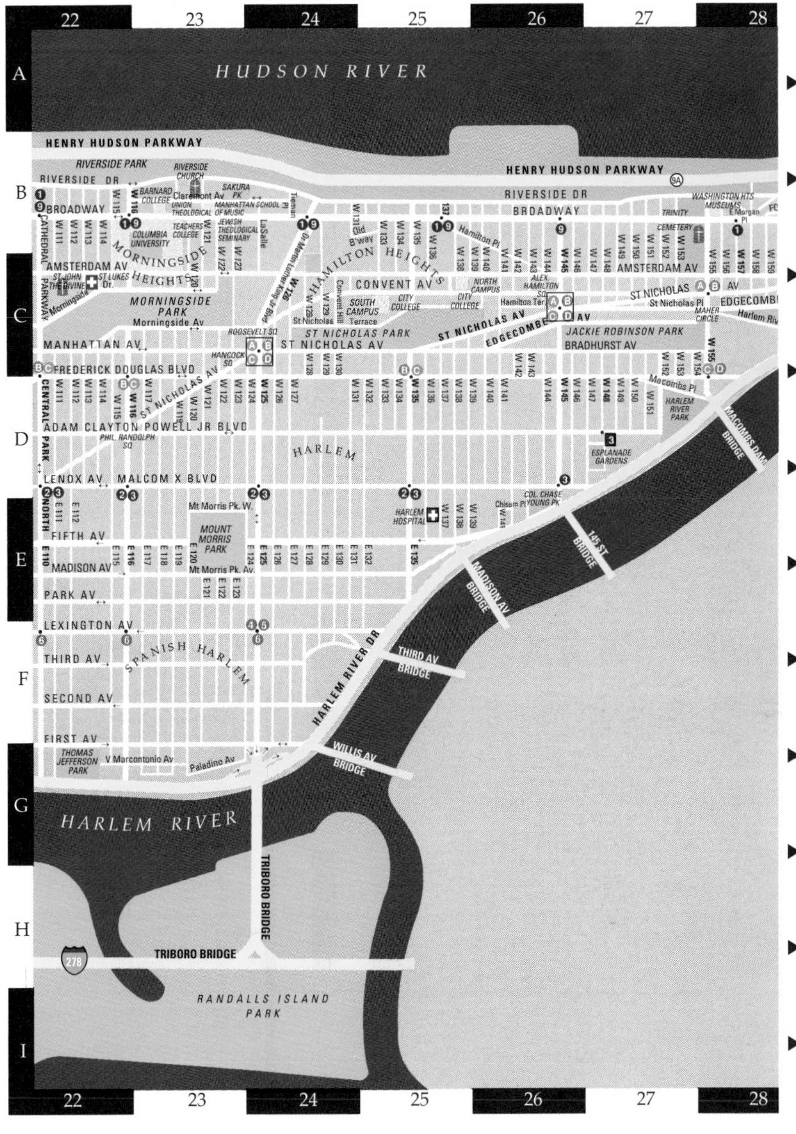
HUDSON RIVER
HENRY HUDSON PARKWAY
RIVERSIDE PARK
RIVERSIDE DR
BROADWAY
AMSTERDAM AV
MORNINGSIDE HEIGHTS
COLUMBIA UNIVERSITY
MORNINGSIDE PARK
MANHATTAN AV
FREDERICK DOUGLAS BLVD
ST NICHOLAS AV
HAMILTON HEIGHTS
CONVENT AV
ST NICHOLAS PARK
CITY COLLEGE
JACKIE ROBINSON PARK
EDGECOMBE AV
BRADHURST AV
ADAM CLAYTON POWELL JR BLVD
HARLEM
LENOX AV
MALCOM X BLVD
MOUNT MORRIS PARK
HARLEM HOSPITAL
FIFTH AV
MADISON AV
PARK AV
LEXINGTON AV
THIRD AV
SPANISH HARLEM
SECOND AV
FIRST AV
THOMAS JEFFERSON PARK
HARLEM RIVER DR
MADISON AV BRIDGE
THIRD AV BRIDGE
WILLIS AV BRIDGE
145 ST BRIDGE
MACOMBS DAM BRIDGE
HARLEM RIVER
TRIBORO BRIDGE
RANDALLS ISLAND PARK
278

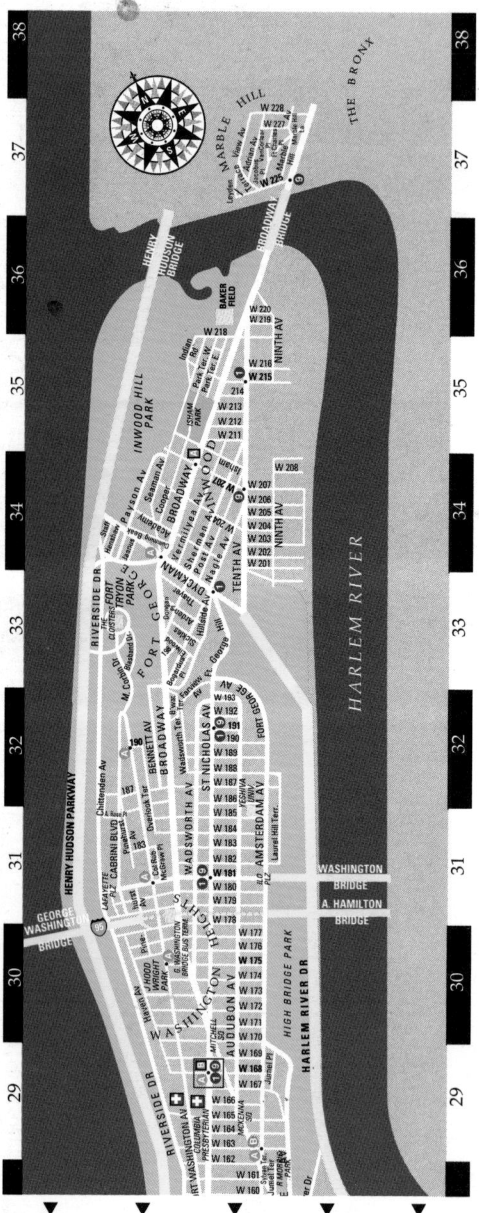


For key see page 337

MANHATTAN
SUBWAY KEY

- 1 Broadway 7th Av Local
- 2 3 Broadway 7th Av EXPRESS
- 9 Broadway 7th Av Skip Stop
- 4 5 Lexington Av EXPRESS
- 6 Lexington Av Local
- 7 42nd St Flushing Line
- A 8th Av EXPRESS
- C E 8th Av Local
- B D Q 6th Av EXPRESS
- F 6th Av Local
- R Broadway Local
- N Broadway Local
- J M Nassau St local
- Z Nassau St EXPRESS
- L 14th St Canarsie Line
- S 42nd St Shuttle

Free interchange between lines

1 • N

- • SUBWAY STOP INDICATOR
- 2 SUBWAY SIGN SYMBOL
- 1 TERMINAL STOP